From the reviews of *China: A History*:

By the same author

Into India
When Men and Mountains Meet
The Gilgit Game
Eccentric Travellers
Explorers Extraordinary
Highland Drove
The Royal Geographical Society's History of World Exploration
India Discovered
The Honourable Company
The Collins Encyclopaedia of Scotland (with Julia Keay)
Indonesia: From Sabang to Merauke
Last Post: The End of Empire in the Far East
The Great Arc
India: A History
Sowing the Wind: The Seeds of Conflict in the Middle East
Mad about the Mekong: Exploration and
Empire in South East Asia
The Spice Route: A History
The London Encyclopaedia (3rd Edn) (with Julia Keay)

CHINA

JOHN KEAY

Harper
Press

HarperPress
An imprint of HarperCollins*Publishers*
1 London Bridge Street, London SE1 9GF

Visit our authors' blog at www.fifthestate.co.uk
Love this book? www.bookarmy.com

This Harper*Press* paperback edition published 2009
10

First published in Great Britain by Harper*Press* in 2008

Copyright © John Keay 2008 and 2009

Maps and diagrams © HarperCollins*Publishers*,
designed by HL Studios, Oxfordshire

John Keay asserts the moral right to be identified as the author of this work

A catalogue record for this book is available from the British Library

ISBN 978-0-00-722178-3

Set in Minion by Palimpsest Book Production Limited, Grangemouth, Stirlingshire

Printed and bound in Great Britain by CPI Group (UK) Ltd, Croydon CR0 4YY

Mixed Sources
Product group from well-managed
forests and other controlled sources
www.fsc.org   Cert no. SW-COC-1806
© 1996 Forest Stewardship Council

FSC is a non-profit international organisation established to promote the
responsible management of the world's forests. Products carrying the FSC label
are independently certified to assure consumers that they come
from forests that are managed to meet the social, economic and
ecological needs of present and future generations.

Find out more about HarperCollins and the environment at
www.harpercollins.co.uk/green

For Julia

The Master said, 'Is it not a pleasure, having learned something, to try it out at due intervals? Is it not a joy to have like-minded friends come from afar? Is it not gentlemanly not to take offence when others fail to appreciate your abilities?'

Confucius, *The Analects,* Book I, i[1]

He who does not forget the past is master of the present.

Sima Qian, *Shiji*[2]

CONTENTS

LIST OF ILLUSTRATIONS

China, Vol 4, Physics and Physical Technology Part 2, Mechanical
Engineering, 1965, Cambridge University Press. Originally from Yü
Chhang-Hui's *Fang Hai Chi Yao*, 1842)

The Qingming scroll: 'Going on the River at the Qingming Festival' by
Zhang Zeduan (The Palace Museum, Beijing)

The walls and gateway, Nanjing (AFP/Getty Images)

Jizhou plan of the Great Wall (Collection of the National Museum of
China – C14.2142)

The Great Wall today (Adam Tall/Robert Hardin)

Qingbai porcelain bowl (Kimbell Art Museum/Corbis)

Ming blue-and-white vase (© RMN/Richard Lambert)

Xu Yang's 'Bird's-Eye View of the Capital' hanging scroll, colour on silk,
1767 (Palace Museum, Beijing. Ref. X146672)

The Mongol leader Dawaci (bpk/Ethnologisches Museum, Staatliche
Museen zu Berlin/Photo: Waltraudt Schneider-Schütz)

Engraving of cannons on camel-back (Library of Congress)

Scroll painting of the Kangxi emperor's tour of the south by Yang Jin,
c. 1644–*c.* 1726. (© RMN/© Thierry Ollivier)

The *Qing* Qianlong emperor preparing to receive Macartney, engraving
1793 after original by William Alexander (Getty Images)

Court portrait of the Qianlong emperor (The Palace Museum, Beijing.
Ref: G6465)

Packing porcelain for export (Private collection. Photo © Bonhams/
Bridgeman Art Library)

The hongs of Canton (Private collection/Roy Miles Fine Painting/
Bridgeman Art Library)

Taiping encampment at Tianjin (Harvard-Yenching Library, Harvard
University)

The execution of Boxer insurgents (Getty Images)

The empress dowager Cixi (portrait, 1905–6, by Hubert Vos)
(akg-images)

Pu-yi, 'the Last Emperor' (The Art Archive/Culver Pictures)

Chiang Kai-shek and Zhang Xueling (Getty Images)

The Shanghai bund in 1930 (Getty Images)

The Nanjing Massacre, December 1937 (Getty Images)

LIST OF MAPS AND DIAGRAMS

ACKNOWLEDGEMENTS

This book is heavily indebted to a legion of China specialists, some of whom are mentioned in the text and others in the source notes and bibliography. I know few of them personally but I hope their views have not been misrepresented. It also owes much to Ian Paten for his painstaking editing, to Caroline Hotblack who brought a rare understanding to the picture research, and to Louise McLeman for the design and HL Studios for labouring over the maps and tables. I am most grateful to all of them. A word of thanks, too, to the inventor of wheeled luggage, without which the squirreling home of trunkloads of books would have crippled me, and to the makers of that China-traveller's essential, the plastic cafetière.

Richard Johnson of HarperCollins suggested the book. He also championed it, commissioned it, and oversaw every stage of its production. This is the fifth book on which we have worked together. His support and friendship have been so invaluable that mere acknowledgment seems insulting. The same goes for Julia, to whom I am married. For three years she has lived this book as much as I have. It was she who fathomed the working of China Railways, hauled me from the path of oncoming traffic, and almost never complained. She has read every word of the text and drew the roughs for the maps and tables, often at the expense of her own work. No one could have been readier with encouragement and support. Ideally her name should be beside mine on the title page. Instead it is as near as possible, on the dedicatory page.

John Keay
May 2008

INTRODUCTION

REWRITING THE PAST

CHINA'S ECONOMIC RESURGENCE IN THE POST-MAO era has not been without its casualties. Gone are the Chairman's portraits, the mass parades of flag-waving workers and the hoe-toting brigades on their collectivised farms. Apartment blocks, tightly mustered and regimentally aligned, perform the new choreography; flyovers vault the rice paddies, cable cars abseil the most sacred of mountains, hydrofoils ruffle the lakes beloved of poets. Familiar features in the historical landscape have either disappeared or been reconfigured as visitor attractions. Iconised for a market as much domestic as foreign, they make inviting targets for another demolitionist fraternity, that of international academe. When history itself is being so spectacularly rewritten, nothing is sacred. The Great Wall, the Grand Canal, the Long March, even the Giant Panda? Myths, declare the revisionist scholars, facile conflations, figments of foreign ignorance now appropriated to gratify Chinese chauvinism.

Contrary to the tourist brochures, the Great Wall has been shown to be not 'over 2,000 years old', not '6,000 miles [9,700 kilometres] long', not 'visible from outer space' – not visible on the ground in many places – and never to have been a single continuous structure.[1] It did not keep out marauding nomads nor was that its original purpose; instead of defending and defining Chinese territory, it was probably designed to augment and project it.[2] Those sections near Beijing that may conveniently be inspected today have been substantially reconstructed for just such inspection; and the rubble and footings from which they rise are those of Ming fortifications no older than the palaces in the Forbidden City or London's Hampton Court.

Likewise the Grand Canal. Reaching from the Yangzi delta to the Yellow River (Huang He), a distance of about 1,100 kilometres (700 miles), the canal is supposed to have served as a main artery between China's productive heartland and its brain of government. Laid out in the seventh century AD, it did indeed connect the rice-surplus south to the often cereal-deficient north, so fusing the two main geographical components of China's political economy and supplying a much-needed highway for bulk transport and imperial progresses. Yet it, too, was never a single continuous

1

construction, more a series of well-engineered waterways interconnecting the various deltaic arms of the Yangzi, and elsewhere linking that river's tributaries to those of the Huai River, whose tributaries were in turn linked to the wayward Yellow River. The system was rarely operational throughout its entirety because of variable water flow, the rainy season in the north not coinciding with that in the south; colossal manpower was needed to haul the heavily laden transports and work the locks; dredging and maintenance proved prohibitively expensive; and so frequent were the necessary realignments of the system that there are now almost as many abandoned sections of Grand Canal as there are of Great Wall.[3]

More controversially, the Long March, that 1934–35 epic of heroic communist endeavour, has been disparaged as neither as long nor as heroic as supposed. It is said the battles and skirmishes en route were exaggerated, if not contrived, for propaganda purposes; and of the 80,000 troops who began the march in Jiangxi in the south-east, only 8,000 actually foot-slogged their way right round China's mountainous perimeter to Yan'an in the north-west. As for the rest, some perished but most simply dropped out long before the 9,700-kilometre (6,000-mile) march was completed. And of those who did complete it, one at least seldom marched; Mao, we are assured, was borne along on a litter.[4]

Maybe the Giant Panda, a byword for endangered icons if ever there was one, is on safer ground. In the 1960s and '70s the nearly extinct creature, together with some acrobatic ping-pong players, emerged as a notable asset in the diplomatic arsenal of the beleaguered People's Republic. Much sought after by zoos worldwide, the pandas, especially females, were freely bestowed on deserving heads of state. The presentations were described as 'friendship gestures', and experimental breeding was encouraged as if a successful issue might somehow cement the political entente. But not any more. From sparse references in classic texts such as the 'Book of Documents' (Shu-jing or Shangshu, bits of which may date from the second millennium BC) a pedigree of undoubted antiquity has been constructed for the panda and a standard name awarded to it. Now known as the Daxiongmao or 'Great Bear-Cat', its habits have been found sufficiently inoffensive to merit its promotion as a 'universal symbol of peace'; its numbers have stabilised, perhaps increased, thanks to zealous conservation; and lest anyone harbour designs on such a national paragon, no longer may Giant Pandas be expatriated. All are Chinese pandas. Foreign zoos may only lease them, the lease being for ten years, the rental fee around $2 million per annum, and any cubs born during the rental being deemed to inherit the nationality of their mother – and the same terms of contract. Like its piebald image as featured in countless brand logos, the Giant Panda has itself become a franchise.

None of this is particularly surprising or regrettable. All history is subject to revision, and the Chinese having taken a greater interest in their history – and for longer – than any other civilisation, theirs is a history that has been more often rewritten than any other. During the last century alone the history books had to be reconfigured at least four times – to create a Nationalist mythology, to accommodate the Marxist dialectic of class struggle, to conform to Maoist insistence on the dynamics of proletarian revolution, and to justify market socialism's conviction that wealth creation is compatible with authoritarian rule.

A much-publicised claim that modern China has inherited 'the longest continuous civilisation in the world' (its length being anything from 3,000 to 6,000 years, depending on the credibility of the publication) should perhaps be subjected to the same forensic scrutiny as phrases like 'the Great Wall' and 'the Giant Panda'. Though now widely deployed by the Chinese themselves, the claim sounds suspiciously like another glib foreign generalisation. Three to six thousand years of continuous civilisation could simply indicate three to six thousand years of what others have found a continuously perplexing civilisation. Certainly the nature of that civilisation needs careful definition; so do the motives of those who have championed it; and the insistence on continuity seems particularly suspect in the light of the last century's revolutionary ructions. As with the segmented Great Wall and the surviving snippets of Grand Canal, the discontinuities in China's record may deserve as much attention as the proud concept into which they have been conflated.

One continuity is obvious: Chinese scholars have been obsessed by their country's past almost since it had one. Like other societies, the ancient Chinese subscribed to the idea that their land had once hosted a primordial perfection, a prehistoric Eden, characterised in this instance by a virtuous hierarchy in which cosmic, natural and human forces operated in harmonious accord. To guide mankind to a new realisation of this idealised past, it was history, not revelation, which provided directions; and it did so by affording solutions to present dilemmas and insights into the future that were derived from written texts. Ancient compilations, such as the 'Book of Documents', thus acquired canonical status and were treated to the respect, as well as the exegetical analysis, reserved in other lands for the scriptures of divine revelation. Familiarity with the standard texts was not just a mark of scholarship but a basic indicator of Chinese identity and a measure of cultural proficiency.

It was also an essential requisite for government service. Precedent and practice, culled from the textual records, came to serve as the currency of political debate. Correctly interpreted, historical precedent could legitimise a ruler, sanction an initiative or forewarn of a disaster. It might also be manipulated so as to legitimise a usurper, sanction repression or forestall reform. Among the educated elite it sometimes served as a coded critique whereby, through reference to the past, unfavourable comment might be passed on current policies without necessarily incurring the wrath of those responsible for them. Conversely it could be officially used to confuse an issue or offload responsibility.

In 1974, by way of discrediting Lin Biao (or Lin Piao, the military man previously named as Mao's successor), the leadership of the Chinese Communist Party mounted a campaign against Confucius (Kong Qiu), the cultural colossus most closely associated with the whole textual tradition. What the fifth-century BC sage had in common with the twentieth-century revolutionary was, of course, 'reactionary' leanings. But since, in the case of Lin Biao, these were not immediately obvious to cadres acccustomed to idolising Lin as the most 'progressive' of communist leaders, it was necessary that he be paraded for censure alongside a teacher whose doctrines, in the aftermath of the Cultural Revolution, could not be mistaken for other than the rankest form of reaction. The principle, borrowed from ballistics and familiar to all China-watchers, was simply that of aiming at a far target to hit a near one. Becoming an official campaign, this 'Anti-Lin Biao–anti-Confucius' linkage duly induced a rush of hot air from Marxist study groups which deflected attention from the otherwise mysterious demise and disgrace of the unfortunate Marshal Lin.[5]

In a century as rife with revolutions (Nationalist, communist, cultural, market-socialist) as the last, the revisionists have sometimes been pushed to keep up with the pace of events; but their predicament is nothing new. The onus of constantly reviewing the historical record, of refining, reinterpreting and extending it, has weighed heavily on every Chinese rulership since time immemorial. At periods of dynastic change it could be particularly acute, but even in the golden age of Tang (AD 618–907) the management of history ranked in terms of political sensitivity on a par with the management of the economy today. Historiography was not some scholarly pastime but a vital function of government. Within the imperial bureaucracy the Director of the Historiographical Office enjoyed all the perquisites of great seniority and commanded a large and highly qualified staff that generated copious paperwork (and before that, woodwork, slivers of bamboo being the earliest form of stationery).

An analysis of official history-writing under the Tang has revealed the painstaking compilation methods employed by the Historiography Office to extend the historical record using near-contemporary sources.[6] A first stage saw material drawn from the formal Court Diaries and the Record of Administrative Affairs being supplemented by submissions from various government departments to produce the summation of official transactions known as the Daily Calendar. These Daily Calendars were then distilled into the year-on-year Veritable Records, which in turn were used to produce the reign-on-reign National Histories, which in turn formed the basis of each dynasty's Standard History.

Naturally this cumulative approach involved much repetition; and while, perhaps mercifully, only a fraction of all this material survives, that which is lost can to some extent be reconstructed from its quotation elsewhere. Given the compilation of parallel records by the empire's numerous provincial governments, given the existence in various forms of other, non-official, texts, and given a tendency to gloss and extrapolate from all these materials for the purpose of compiling encyclopedias, anthologies, biographical dictionaries and other massive compendia, it cannot be said that China's history is short on documentation.

SPADEWORK

No apology is offered, then, for adding another divot to this tumulus of erudition. The intention here is simply to make China's history more accessible, while the hope is to make it more relevant.

Those transmitted texts, official or otherwise, deal almost entirely with the activities of China's ruling elite and are available to us only in a form ready edited and packaged by that elite. More exciting fare, fresh picked from the Chinese landscape and untainted by scholarly processing, was once thought to be at a premium. When in the early twentieth century archaeological explorers from Europe stumbled upon ancient Buddhist sites sand-buried along the Silk Road in Gansu and Xinjiang provinces, an unseemly gold rush ensued to secure for the museums of Britain, France, Germany and Russia a share of what was supposedly China's last great artistic and documentary treasure trove. In fact, the Silk Road bonanza proved to be just the beginning of an archaeological explosion. Laid bare later in the twentieth century were the Anyang oracle bones, the Tarim Mummies, a whole gamut of neolithic sites, and most famously 'the terracotta army' and numerous royal tombs of the Han period (202 BC–AD 220).

China's history, long enough already, has been getting longer by the year. Existing accounts need constant updating; and new discoveries have now become so embarrassingly abundant that the resultant time lag between the dig and the publication of its report leaves works-in-progress, like this one, in danger of being outdated before they are written.

'When digging into the soil of the North China plain or northern Chekiang [Zhejiang], centres of Chinese civilisation from the earliest times onward,' remarked Erik Zurcher in the 1950s, 'it is actually difficult *not* to find anything'.[7] Zurcher was writing about the spread of Buddhism in the fourth and fifth centuries AD. Adherents of the new faith evidently had an uncanny knack of unearthing Buddhist relics in Chinese soil just when opponents were deploring the Indian, and so non-Chinese, origins of their faith. Such finds, besides supposedly authenticating Buddhism's long association with China, were considered highly auspicious. Just as the fall of an imperial dynasty was usually accompanied by a series of depressing portents – floods, drought, locusts, etc. – so the rise of a new dynasty was heralded by a rash of favourable omens, none more so than the excavation of some hoary artefact. Since antiquity itself was so highly regarded, the discovery of, say, a Bronze Age urn clearly signified Heaven's approval of whatever new dispensation laid claim to its discovery.

Something of the same thinking may have influenced Chinese archaeology in the mid-twentieth century. The Nationalist revival had its own need of historical legitimisation, and so did the Republic of China, declared in 1912, and the People's Republic, in 1949. Scholars and officials brought up on the Standard Histories of the historiographical tradition and now fired by the spirit of national reassertion knew to look for the origins of Chinese civilisation in the north of the country. Resources were duly directed there and, as noted by Zurcher, diggers in that region could hardly fail to be rewarded. To general delight, the spadework yielded ample corroboration of the authenticity and antiquity of an ancient Chinese civilisation in the northern provinces, especially the Yellow River (Huang He) basin, which corresponded to that described in the earliest texts and histories. Only incorrigible sceptics, mostly from outside China, wondered whether devoting as much archaeological attention and resources to other parts of China, such as the Yangzi basin or the south, might not yield comparable finds that would necessarily qualify this northern bias in early Chinese history.

Such doubts have since been vindicated. By the end of the twentieth century the expansion in archaeological activity compared well with the exponential growth being enjoyed by the economy. Indeed, the two were related. Funds were now available for more widespread excavation, and because so much of the Chinese landscape was being torn up anyway for construction projects, the finds came thick and fast. On the other hand, their study and conservation acquired still greater urgency. Mechanical excavators might unearth in minutes what spadework might not turn up in years, and just as quickly they might destroy it.

A typical example was provided by a 1970s hospital extension at Mawangdui on the outskirts of Changsha, capital of the southern province of Hunan. Construction of the hospital's new ward 'accidentally disturbed' an adjacent mound that archaeologists had earmarked for attention back in the 1950s.[8] The matter was reported to the provincial authorities, and when orders were issued for immediate excavation, a swarm of Mao-suited archaeologists descended on the site and duly reclaimed one of the greatest hoards of modern times. There were three immense tombs dating from the second century BC, and each contained a nest of monumental coffins, within one of which were found a well-preserved female corpse and the oldest silk paintings and maps ever to have been discovered in China. Also recovered were texts containing early versions of some of the Chinese classics and enough artefacts, apparel, insignia, lacquerware, jades, weapons and other grave goods to justify the construction of Changsha's grand new museum – and then fill it. In 1983 another mound, this time in the middle of Guangzhou (Canton), the capital of neighbouring Guangdong province, yielded magnificent tombs of similar period that prompted presentation of the site itself as an imaginative museum within walking distance of the city's main railway station. Elsewhere in Guangzhou, site clearance for the erection of a plaza has lately revealed a 2,000-year-old wooden watergate. The oldest in the world and now comfortably encased within the gleaming new plaza, it may be reached by taking the elevator down to floor B1.

Opulent finds like these located far from the supposed epicentre of ancient Chinese civilisation in the Yellow River basin call for radical revision of received ideas about what the rest of China was like before, and immediately after, the birth of Christ. But with more new discoveries being reported every week, no such bold reappraisal has yet been presented. *The Cambridge History of Ancient China*, published in 1999, frankly admitted defeat. Unable to reconcile the literary sources with these new 'material' sources – or unable to find a contributor prepared to have a go – the editors compromised by commissioning parallel chapters for the same periods, one based on textual sources and the next on archaeological sources. Sometimes they support one another, sometimes not. Early Chinese history still awaits a convincing rewrite.

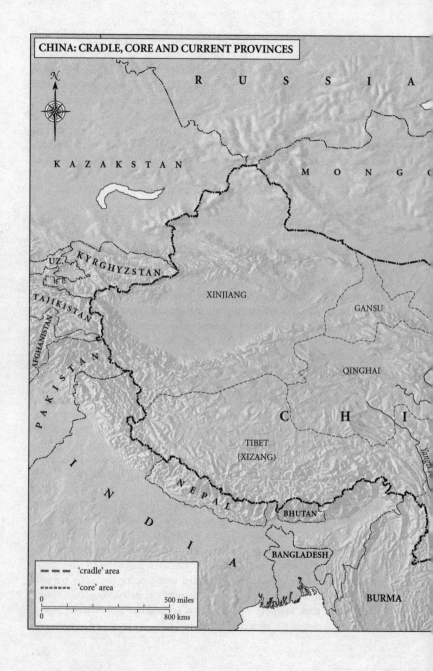

CHINA: CRADLE, CORE AND CURRENT PROVINCES

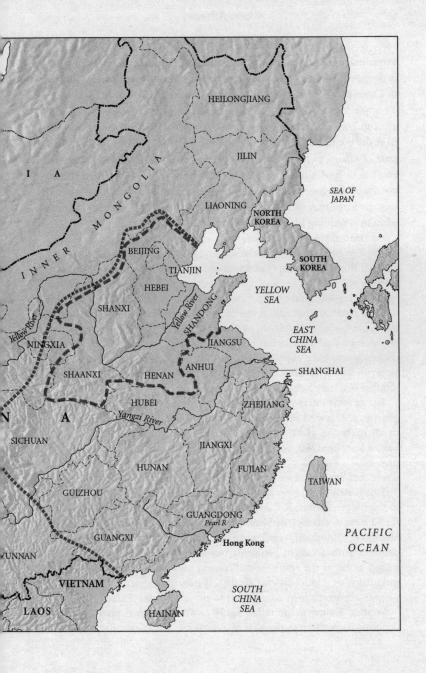

CRADLE, CORE AND BEYOND

While making but a modest contribution on this front, the present work is designed to meet the much more pressing need for an overall history of China that does not take for granted a foreknowledge of the subject or an acquaintance with the Chinese language. A glance at the existing literature in English suggests an international consensus, not to say conspiracy, to make the subject as daunting and incomprehensible as possible. This state of affairs, in part a legacy of competitive scholarship in the colonial era, will be fearlessly addressed; for China's history is long enough and its culture challenging enough without gratuitous complication. Confronting this challenge may mean taxing the reader, but not, it is earnestly hoped, without rewarding his or her effort.

As lamentable as the obfuscations are the depths of ignorance from which foreigners approach Chinese history. Most people could name half a dozen Roman emperors but few could name a single Chinese emperor. Confronted with an array of Chinese proper names in their Romanised spellings, English-speakers experience a recognition problem, like a selective form of dyslexia, that makes the names all seem the same. Unfamiliarity lies at the root of the problem, particularly in respect of Chinese geography, chronology and translation conventions. It can best be overcome by diligence and long exposure, but at the risk of irritating those already superior to such difficulties, what follows (and the accompanying tabulations) may help as an introduction.

For adminstrative purposes China is today divided into twenty-eight provinces. A few of these provinces are of quite recent provenance, and in all cases the areas they denote have undergone change. But most have a long pedigree, and it is not therefore unreasonable to employ the provincial terminology retrospectively so as to provide a geographical framework for the whole spread of Chinese history.

Fortunately the names of the provinces often contain helpful clues as to their whereabouts. *Bei*, *dong*, *nan* and *xi* are Romanised renderings of the Chinese words for 'north', 'east', 'south' and 'west', and *shan* is 'mountain'. Shandong ('Mountain-east', once spelled 'Shantung') is therefore the province with a rugged peninsula below Beijing. It originally extended inland as far as the north–south Taihang mountains; hence 'east of the mountains' or 'Mountain-east'. By the same dazzling logic, Shanxi province ('Mountain-west') is its counterpart to the west of the Taihang range.

West of Shanxi is the rather easily confused Shaanxi province (here denoting its position to the west of a district called Shaanzhou). All three provinces abut, or once abutted, the fickle Huang He (Yellow River). So too, fingering between Shandong and Shanxi, does the province of Hebei ('River-north', the river being the self-same Huang He). Naturally the province to the south of the river is therefore Henan ('River-south'), although because the river has so often switched course, a bit of Henan is now on the north bank. These five northern provinces (Henan, Hebei, Shaanxi, Shanxi and Shandong) engross the entire extent of the rich alluvial plain of the lower Yellow River basin which, according to textual tradition, was where China's earliest history was enacted. They have thus been traditionally regarded as the 'cradle' provinces of Chinese civilisation and were the focus of those mid-twentieth-century archaeologists.

South of Henan come more provincial twins. In the case of Hubei and Hunan, the *Hu-* denotes the great 'lake', or 'lakes' into which the lower Yangzi spills before meandering on to the coast. These two provinces therefore lie respectively north and south of the great lakes and so, roughly, north and south of the Yangzi itself. South again, and completing this spine of 'core' China come Guangdong and Guangxi. *Guang* means something like 'enlarged (southern) territory'. These two once 'enlarged' provinces in the extreme south thus lie respectively east (*-dong*) and west (*-xi*) of one another. Beyond them in the South China Sea, the island province of Hainan is the country's southernmost extremity.

Returning north towards the Shandong peninsula by way of the coast, the provinces of Fujian, Zhejiang and Jiangsu plus adjacent Jiangxi and Anhui are smaller, and their names are not so obviously derived from compass bearings. Some contain directional elements, but most have been formed by combining the names of two of their more important centres. Thus Fujian combines *Fu*zhou, its port-capital, with *Jian*ning, a city at Fujian's inland extremity.[9] The *-zhou* ending, incidentally, once indicated an 'island' of 'Chinese' settlement in what was otherwise a still unacculturated region; it then came to denote the district that pertained to it, and now more commonly the principal city of the region. This same *-zhou* was once rendered in English as *-chow* or *-choo*; hence nineteenth-century toponyms like 'Foochow' (Fuzhou), 'Soochow' (Suzhou), 'Hangchow' (Hangzhou), etc. More obviously, 'Beijing' (Peking, Pekin, etc.), the national metropolis within Hebei province, translates as 'north-capital', and Nanjing (Nanking), on the Yangzi in Jiangsu province, as 'south-capital' – which until 1937 it was.

All the provinces mentioned so far, plus those of Guizhou in the southwest and Sichuan, a vast region comprising most of the upper Yangzi basin, are sometimes said to constitute central, inner or 'core' China. Terms like 'central' and 'inner' are highly controversial, no distinction between centre and periphery, or inner and outer China, being either physically convincing, historically consistent or politically acceptable. It may, though, be helpful to adopt this phrasing to distinguish the seventeen productive, populous and long-integrated 'core' provinces, which have already been mentioned, from the traditionally less productive, less populous and less historically integrated provinces lying at the extremities of modern China.

Into this latter category fall the remaining eleven provinces, many of them large territories of sharp contrasts and emotive repute. Taiwan, a long island off the coast of Fujian, was once known to Europeans as Formosa. It was subsequently alienated from the mainland by Japanese occupation in the first half of the twentieth century and Nationalist occupation in the second half. About as far from Taiwan as Texas is from Florida, Yunnan in the south-west has also had a chequered relationship with the rest of the country. Straddling the climatic divide between torrid South-East Asia and arid central Asia, its forests are frequented by the odd elephant while yak grunt across its high passes. Farther north and west, the howling wastes and azure skies are those of Qinghai and Xizang, which together comprised the vast plateau region once vaguely known to non-Chinese as Tibet. Today Tibet is usually identified just with Xizang. North and west again, all that remains is Xinjiang. Largely desert though far from deserted, this is the largest of all China's provinces and the remotest. It was once known to the Chinese as 'the Western Regions' and to non-Chinese as Eastern or Chinese Turkestan. The current designation simply means 'the New Territories' (*Xin-jiang*); indigenous activists would prefer 'Uighuristan', they being largely Muslim, Turkic-speaking Uighurs.

Returning east along China's northern perimeter, elongated Gansu province and diminutive Ningxia province offer oasis-dotted access routes from the 'core' provinces into Xinjiang and Mongolia respectively. Sandwiched between the swamps of Qinghai and the sands of the Gobi, the east–west 'Gansu corridor' has become as much a cliché in Chinese history-writing as 'the Tibetan plateau'. Ningxia, with a north–south axis, is strung along the upper reaches of the Yellow River and juts into the neighbouring province of Nei Monggol, otherwise Inner Mongolia. Although Outer, or northern, Mongolia is not part of today's China, its border bisects the Gobi desert in a long east–west arc that leaves all to the south of it as a Chinese province. The sand and steppe of this Nei Monggol thus serves as a glacis to those several sections of 'long wall' that have been conflated into the Great Wall. Nei Monggol's northern perimeter is China's longest international frontier, and its southern perimeter marches with no less than eight other provinces – Gansu, Ningxia, Shaanxi, Shanxi, Hebei and the three provinces of erstwhile Manchuria.

These last, in the north-eastern appendage that used to be called Manchuria – or by the Japanese 'Manchukuo' – are all named after rivers. Heilongjiang, the most northerly province, is also the Chinese name for the Amur river; the Sino-Russian border here follows its course. Jilin province to the south derives from the Manchurian word for 'alongside (the Songhua River)'; it marches with North Korea. And Liaoning, to the south-west, is named for the Liao River; it adjoins Hebei province and extends to within 300 kilometres (185 miles) of Beijing; south across the gulf of Bohai, Liaoning faces Shandong's peninsula.

So ends the circuit of the eleven peripheral provinces, within which lie the seventeen core provinces, of which the five most northerly comprise the 'cradle' provinces. The administrative patchwork is completed by various smaller entities, such as the municipalities of Beijing and Shanghai and the special-status enclaves of Hong Kong and Macao. Numerous other autonomous entities based on ethnic minority concentrations should also be mentioned; these may be autonomous districts within the provinces, or autonomous regions comprising a whole province, such as Xizang/Tibet.

Admittedly, there are more scientific ways of deconstructing China's geography. In a continental landmass roughly the size of the United States and located within approximately the same degrees of latitude (the Tropic of Cancer, which grazes the Florida Keys, shaves southern China), much the same physical variations may be found. Extremes of climate and altitude result in wildly different average rainfalls, in soil conditions that range from swamp to sand dune and steppe, and in vegetational cover that runs from the riotous to the non-existent.

Rivers and mountains provide a better guide to settlement patterns, although the neat North American sequence of prairie, desert, mountain and coast is not to be found. Most of China's rivers run west to east, from the high and dry uplands of Qinghai and Xizang to the moister plains towards the coast. Between the Huang He (Yellow River) in the north and the Yangzi in the middle, two rivers, the Han, a major tributary of the latter, and the Huai, whose course has sometimes been borrowed by the former, observe the same eastward trend. So do rivers to the south of the Yangzi, such as those that come together in Guangxi and Guangdong to form the Pearl River estuary off which lies Hong Kong. All these rivers indulge in extravagant contortions, however. The Yangzi, once released by Xizang's (Tibet's) ramparts, zigs south towards Vietnam before zagging

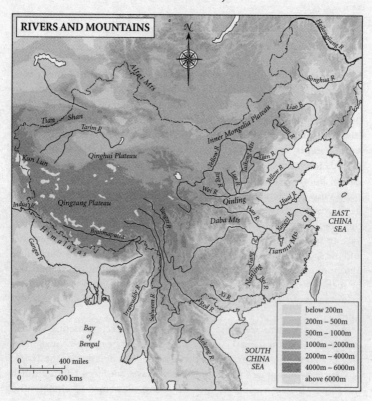

RIVERS AND MOUNTAINS

EAST
CHINA
SEA

Bay
of
Bengal

	below 200m
	200m – 500m
	500m – 1000m
	1000m – 2000m
	2000m – 4000m
	4000m – 6000m
	above 6000m

0   400 miles

0   600 kms

SOUTH
CHINA
SEA

north back to Sichuan; the Yellow River performs a near-somersault as it arcs towards Mongolia and back.

For such acrobatics, China's cavalcade of mountains is responsible. As well as the much-photographed karst stacks of the south, the Himalayan giants, the gaunt Pamirs and the shy Tian Shan, numerous less-celebrated ranges corrugate large parts of the country and offer an important corrective to the notion that all those rivers eventually compose themselves to water lush coastal plains. With a few exceptions, such as the Yangzi delta, China's coast is in fact quite rugged. So are all of its southern provinces. Conversely Sichuan, though riven by mountains of its own and located far inland above the Yangzi gorges, contains some of China's most fertile plains and is today the fourth most populous of its provinces.

THE DYNASTIC DYNAMIC

While the geography of China's history could be broken down in numerous ways, there is no such range of options in respect of its chronology. The passage of time, like the spread of space, was carefully studied in ancient China and meticulously ordered. The history of India has scarcely a single unchallenged date prior to the ninth century AD, but China's history yields dates, verifiable by eclipses, that go back to the ninth century BC; and not just year-dates but also the month, the day and sometimes even the hour may be given. Adjusting clock and calendar to synchronise with the diurnal, planetary and astral cycles was essential to cosmic harmony and so a major preoccupation of all Chinese rulers. History literally told the time; dates, in the form of reign-years, ticked away the minutes, dynasties tolled the hours. A periodisation based on the succession of dynasties has thus invariably been the preferred way of breaking down the long sweep of Chinese history.

The establishment of a dynasty, whose rulers would reign by right of birth and who would care for the tombs and reputation of their founder and his successors, was the ambition of every would-be sovereign, whether pretender, usurper or invader. Even rebellious peasant leaders often assumed imperial rank. Over the course of Chinese history the number of self-declared dynasties must exceed a hundred. But only dozens actually, partly or temporarily realised this ambition; and of these, only a few were favoured by the historians with recognition as part of China's 'legitimate' dynastic succession.

The criteria for inclusion in this august company were not consistent. Until 221 BC dynasties consisted of kings, and only thereafter of emperors. No royal dynasties and few imperial dynasties exercised uncontested sway. Even some of the 'legitimate' imperial dynasties controlled only half, or less, of what at the time was regarded as China; they might therefore coincide with another 'legitimate' dynasty in the other half of the country. Nevertheless, a single 'legitimate' dynasty at any one time was the general rule, and while far-ruling and long-lived dynasties, preferably of distinguished indigenous origin, could expect to be included in the 'legitimate' succession, local, short-lived dynasties of foreign or undistinguished origin could only hope for inclusion.

A succession of twenty or so 'legitimate' dynasties – not to mention the hundred or so individual dynasts of which they are composed – is still an indigestible mouthful; and it is made more so by some dynasties adopting the same name as that of others whose lustre they claimed to be reviving.

In the case of such clones, it is usual to add a geographical determinant (*Eastern* Zhou, *Northern* Wei, etc.) or a sequential one (*Former* Han, also known as *Western* Han, or *Later* Han, also known as *Eastern* Han).

Mercifully some dynasties acquired a semi-permanency and soldiered on for centuries, winning a reputation for administrative integration, military endeavour, political stablility, cultural distinction and personal magnificence. The five imperial dynasties that lasted longest – each for three to four centuries – constitute the great plateaux of Chinese history and are well worth memorising. Cross-reference to contemporary empires elsewhere may help. They are:

HAN   (Former and Later), 202 BC–AD 220, coeval with the Roman
          republic and early empire
TANG, 618–907, coeval with the expansion of Arab empire
SONG (Northern and Southern), 960–1279, coeval with the Crusades
MING, 1368–1644, coeval with the early Ottoman and Mughal empires
QING   (or Manchu), 1644–1912, coeval with Europe's global expansion.

Many other dynasties of note will be encountered. Ironically the one that most nearly approached the Chinese imperial boast of ruling 'All under Heaven' was not Chinese at all but Mongol. This was the Yuan dynasty (1279–1368), under one of whose emperors the Venetian Marco Polo supposedly found employ.

Some dynasties lasted only a decade or two and, achieving little, will scarcely merit mention. Others, though short-lived, changed the whole course of Chinese history. Such a dynasty was the Qin (221–206 BC). Its founder was the first to impose a fragile unity on the whole of 'core' China and the first to assume the title of *huangdi*, or 'emperor'. In fact he is known to history simply by this title – *Qin* Shi Huangdi, or the Qin 'First Emperor'. Like near-identical bookends, the Qin, the first imperial dynasty and one of the shortest, is matched at the other end of the chronological shelf by the Qing, the last imperial dynasty and one of the longest.

Had all subsequent emperors followed *Qin* Shi Huangdi's excellent example of being known by a numbered reign – First, Second, Third Emperor, etc. – much confusion would have been avoided. Unfortunately no such custom developed. Although emperors and kings of the same name often occur, they are never distinguished by a number, like Louis I–XVIII or the English Georges, only by name. Nor is there much consistency about which of an emperor's several names is the one that history has chosen to remember him by. Personal names being too personal for an emperor, the choice lay between the various auspicious titular names assumed during and after his lifetime. For some dynasties it is customary to call individual emperors by their temple names; for others it is their posthumous names which are used: and in the case of the Ming and Qing dynasties, names adopted for their various reign periods have been extended to the emperors themselves. Hence the seeming anomaly of a Qing emperor, such as the long-reigning one (1735–95) whose temple name was Gaozong, being known to history as 'the Qianlong emperor', that is 'the Qianlong *period* emperor'. Just calling him 'Emperor Qianlong' would be like calling Mao Zedong 'Chairman Great-Leap-Forward'.

For the purposes of this book, emperors will be called by whatever name has gained the widest currency. In addition, purely by way of a reminder, each will be prefaced in italics by the name of the dynasty to which he belonged. Hence '*Song* Renzong' and 'the *Qing* Qianlong emperor'.

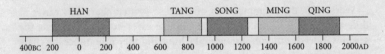

THE BIG FIVE DYNASTIES

THE TRIUMPH OF PINYIN

Sadly – indeed catastrophically for the wider understanding of China – few of these names will be familiar to readers primed on existing works in English. Until recently the Emperor *Tang* Taizong usually appeared in English translation as *T'ang* T'ai-tsung, Emperor *Song* Renzong as *Sung* Jen-tsung and the *Qing* Qianlong emperor as the *Ch'ing* Ch'ien-lung emperor. Hebei and Henan provinces were Hopei and Honan, Beijing was Peking, and the Giant Panda was not Daxiongmao but Ta-hsiung-mao. Something like 75 per cent of all Romanised renderings of Chinese characters have been changed in the last thirty years, often beyond the point of easy recognition. In the long run, the change can only be for the good, although at the present time it remains a challenge and a source of no little confusion.

Previously a system called Wade-Giles (after its two late nineteenth-century creators) governed the spelling of Chinese words in English. Wade-Giles was not straightforward, involving nearly as much diacritic punctuation – hyphens, single inverted commas – as letters. More disastrously, its use was far from universal. Another system was common in the United States, and other European languages had their own systems. To say that linguistic scholarship was failing the student of China would be an understatement. Standardisation became imperative.

But because Chinese characters are not made up of individual letters and so are not alphabetical, their rendition into scripts that use letters (alphabetical scripts) has always been fraught. While Arabic script, for instance, can be rendered letter by letter into Roman script without much attention to its sound, the letter-less Chinese script can be rendered in Roman script only by replicating its sound, that is its pronunciation, not the script itself. This raises other problems. Roman script has no way of indicating the five tones used in Chinese speech. Additionally, many Chinese words that are quite different when written in Chinese script may read as exactly the same when their sound is spelled out in English. The names of two Tang emperors, for instance, when written in Chinese involve totally different characters, but when rendered in the latest Romanised script become indistinguishable; both appear as 'Xuanzong'.

Worse still, the pronunciation of Chinese written characters varies in different parts of China. All literate Chinese can read the characters; the script is indeed common throughout China. But they pronounce the characters in accordance with their local or regional dialect (technically 'topolect' or 'regionalect'). Thus strangers on a train may happily share the same newspaper though quite unable to converse with one another. Foreigners, mostly European, who began arriving on the China coast in numbers from the late sixteenth century, found spoken Chinese a lot easier than written Chinese. A recent authority has calculated that, for an English-speaker, learning to speak Chinese is twenty per cent more difficult than learning to speak French; on the other hand, learning to read and write Chinese is five hundred per cent more difficult than learning to read and write French. Foreign scholars, armed with a quickly won understanding of spoken Chinese, proceeded to tackle the written characters by representing them in their own languages using the Chinese pronunciation with which they were now familiar. Unfortunately this pronunciation was almost exclusively that of the Guangdong and Fujian provinces to which foreign contacts were at the time largely restricted. The topolects were thus those of Cantonese (Canton = Guangzhou, capital of Guangdong) and of the Hakka and Hokkien people of Fujian. They were barely recognisable to the majority of Chinese, who, living in the Yangzi basin or the north, mostly spoke a topolect that foreigners called Mandarin.

Not unnaturally, northerners came to resent finding even their place-names being mispronounced and mistranslated.

And there was yet another complication. The foreigners in question were Portuguese, Spanish and Italian, then Dutch, English, French, American and Russian, each of whose languages rendered some vowel sounds and consonants quite differently. 'J', for instance, is pronounced one way in Spanish, another way in French and yet another in English. Any representation of Chinese speech had to take account of such inconsistency, and hence that variety of different Romanising systems, each tailored to a different European language; hence too the absurdity of what purported to be transcriptions of Chinese characters being in fact English, French, Spanish, etc., renderings of Chinese regional speech as spoken by only a provincial minority of the Chinese nation.

To standardise the rendering of Chinese characters in all alphabetical languages, and to supersede this chaos, yet another system was developed in the 1950s. This was Pinyin, the form used throughout this book. China being at the time dependent on the Soviet Union for much technical assistance, the task involved Russian scholars and originally envisaged the possibility of Pinyin using not the Roman (or Latin) script but the Cyrillic script of Russia. Only slowly, at Chinese insistence and as Sino-Soviet relations deteriorated from the late 1950s, did Pinyin settle for the Roman script; and only after strong Chinese promotion and the People's Republic of China's (PRC's) admission to the UN in 1971 did it win international recognition. But as of the 1980s Pinyin may claim to have been universally accepted and as of the 1990s most (though by no means all) works on China have used it. It is taught and displayed, albeit discreetly, along with the Chinese characters throughout China; it could conceivably one day supersede them.

It is not perfect. Pinyin's Marxist inventors seem to have projected their belief in equality of opportunity on to the letters of the keyboard. Keys such as 'q', 'x', 'y' and 'z', for which Western languages have little use, are awarded major roles. 'Z' has never been so busy, while 'r', that most useful of consonants in English, is practically redundant. More seriously, the subtleties of the Chinese characters, hinted at in Wade-Giles' scatter of diacritic punctuation marks, is largely lost; tonal marks, though available, rarely appear: the number of quite different Chinese words rendered by the same jangling word of Pinyin is increased; and on the pronunciation front, in trying to meet all national variations, Pinyin ends up by satisfying none. Officially it is said to indicate how a word should be pronounced in the 'common speech' (or Putonghua) of the people of the People's Republic. In reality Putonghua, being approximately a down-classed version of 'Mandarin', is spoken largely in the north. Elsewhere in China, Pinyin spellings may prove a poor guide to pronunciation. Even in the north the visitor would do well to study how all those 'q's, 'x's and 'z's are actually enunciated before trying them out on a Beijing bus conductor.

A MATTER OF SCALE

C. P. Fitzgerald, the pre-Pinyin author of several works on Chinese history in English, neatly sounded a final caveat, albeit one common to other traditions. China's dynastic historians, he noted, 'while indefatigable in the recording and collection of facts, arranged these compendious materials in a manner which makes direct translation of the original texts a baffling and unrewarding task'.

> Consequently Chinese history has been very little translated into any European language, and such scholarly works of this kind as exist are so packed with names of individuals and titles of office as to be wholly indigestible to the ordinary reader. Such direct translations, while invaluable to the student and the scholar, can never reach a wide public.[10]

Fitzgerald was writing in the 1950s, since when more and better translations have appeared. But his reservations about the difficulty of translation, and about its unedifying product, still hold good. Ancient Chinese texts written in early forms of the Chinese script present major problems of interpretation in themselves, and these are exacerbated by the interpolations and omissions of the writers and copyists responsible for the texts as they now survive. Such editing may sometimes have been deliberate and so can be instructive. But just as often it accidentally resulted from rough handling and the ravages of time. Damp, sunlight or termites could obliterate the ink of the characters; and since the bamboo slivers on which each column of text was written were held together only by a perishable thread, they could rather easily become unstrung and get shuffled or lost. Even the 'pages' of near-orginal texts, such as those found in the caves along the Silk Road or in the tombs of Mawangdui, were in no fit state for instant reading and presented scholars with a major problem of identification and arrangement. The modern translator has thus not only to tease some sense out of his text but also to tease out of it the accumulated errors, accretions, misattributions and random misplacements of centuries. Contested readings of quite important passages may result.

Fitzgerald's subject was the Empress Wu Zetian (AD 690–705), who, though by no means the only woman to exercise imperial authority, was the only woman ever to assume the imperial title. His book was therefore a biography, possibly the earliest in English of any pre-Qing Chinese ruler, and is still something of a novelty. Chinese histories devote considerable space to biographical material. Typically the first half of any National or Standard History is a chronological account of the reign or reigns in question and the second half a collection of short biographies of the major participants. The information given, however, is often formulaic – forebears, birth, auspicious youthful encounters, career appointments, demise, summational homily. It is not of a sort that lends itself to the subtle characterisation, brilliant insights and narrative thrust expected of the modern biographer.

Similarly the chronological chapters of these histories, while careful with the facts, unsparing of the intrigues and exemplary with the dates, are short on the chance detail, the hint of drama and the trails of causation that make for engrossing history. Relying heavily on the texts, many modern histories of China, in English as well as Chinese, necessarily share their peculiarities. 'Indefatigable in the recording and collection of facts', they too present these 'compendious materials' to sometimes 'baffling and unrewarding' effect. Important events and pronouncements follow one another in orderly succession but without much indication of their significance or the thinking behind them. The not very exciting biographies are reserved till the end of each reign; and because each reign, however brief, is often treated separately, it can be hard to detect those broader lines of policy, economic trends, social changes and external problems that span a longer period.

Also evident is a tendency to emulate the prolixity of the Standard Histories. *The Cambridge History of China*, though still incomplete at the time of writing, already extends to some sixteen hefty volumes with more required just to keep up with the march of events. Meanwhile Joseph Needham's *Science and Civilisation in China* has passed the twenty-volume mark.

Certainly, China merits the grand treatment. A vast country with an interminable pedigree, an idiosyncratic culture, a traumatic recent past and an exciting future can hardly be taken at a canter. But it should not be supposed from all the groaning shelves that China's history is therefore altogether unlike that of other nations. It is not. In China, too, empires rise and fall, personalities shine, progress is fitful, peace ephemeral, social justice elusive. The difference is one of degree, not kind, of scale, not character. Forewarned of the difficulties, the reader will find China's history just as instructive and rewarding as any other – only more so.

At 1.3 billion, the people of China currently account for about a fifth of the world's total population. Soon they may consume about a fifth of the world's natural resources. But if China's history proves anything, it is that this should cause no surprise. From such statistics as exist it would seem that even in Han/Roman times the Chinese population was vast, probably not much less than a fifth of the world's total then. Its cities were, and long remained, the most crowded, and its fields the most productive. In science, technology and industry it led the way. Were it to do so again, it would mark a reversion to a precedence among nations that demography justifies, history sanctions, and which the rest of the world might actually find comparatively benign.

In the course of time China's population has fluctuated wildly as a result of catastrophic natural disasters and appalling conflicts; but recovery has been no less dramatic. Likewise its productive and technical superiority has been much eclipsed, most obviously during the eighteenth and nine-teenth centuries, but never to the extent of deterring an inventive, industrious and always numerous people.

Elsewhere such preponderant assets might well have encouraged global ambitions. In the eighth to tenth centuries, a then predominantly Buddhist China was aware that Buddhism in India, the 'Holy Land' of its birth, was in crisis. But while a similar crisis in Christianity's 'Holy Land' was about to bring wave after wave of Crusaders from European Christendom to Palestine, not so much as a knight from Chinese 'Buddhadom' ventured into northern India. And this despite heart-rending reports of the neglect and devastation to which India's Buddhist sites were subject and despite a demonstrated capacity for successful military intervention south of the Himalayas.

Five hundred years later the Chinese, like their Spanish and Portuguese contemporaries, were in a position to mobilise the resources and develop the know-how for launching transoceanic armadas. They duly did so, reaching out to South-East Asia and across the Indian Ocean, but not with a view to amassing 'Christians and spices' like Vasco da Gama, nor to extract gold and silver, exploit the labour of others or appropriate their lands. Ultimately and perhaps quaintly, their objective was simply to promote and extend that vital cosmic harmony throughout 'All under Heaven'.

Since this implied recognition of the emperor as the 'Son of Heaven', a degree of subservience was indeed involved. It was not, however, onerous or extractive. It could be beneficial. The favourable reception that awaited Vasco da Gama when in 1498 he reached south India was attributed by one of his Portuguese companions to Indian expectations of fair treatment and ample reward from all pale-skinned seafarers, a legacy of earlier contacts with Chinese navigators. No permanent overseas representation or settlement had resulted from these contacts; rather than seek ways to make the voyages pay for themselves, the Ming emperors had discontinued them. Chinese empire would remain restricted to China and its immediate neighbours. A fifth of the world's population would advance no claim to a fifth of the world's cultivable surface area.

Admittedly, China's relations with her inner Asian neighbours were less friendly. Military excursions would reach as far afield as what are now Burma, India, Nepal, Pakistan, Afghanistan, Tajikistan, Uzbekistan, Kyrghyzstan and Kazakhstan. Like the great sea voyages, however, they resulted in little or no colonisation; and for every excursion there were usually provocative incursions, often of serious and lasting effect.

Nearer to home the Koreans, Vietnamese and Mongolians, not to mention non-Chinese peoples currently within China's borders such as those of Tibet, Xinjiang and the south, would certainly contest China's neighbourly credentials. But the hostility has usually been reciprocal. Across one of the longest and least defensible land frontiers in the world, China (as defined at any given moment) confronted formidable foes. The catalogue of nomadic and semi-nomadic peoples who menaced the settled regions of China's north and west may seem inexhaustible and included confederations of the most martial peoples in Asian history – Xiongnu, Turkic, Tibetan, Muslim, Mongol and Manchu. To this list could be added later seaborne intruders – the European powers in the nineteenth century and Japanese imperialists in the twentieth. Though no amount of provocation can excuse the recent oppression of, for instance, Tibet, it is a matter of record that the Chinese people have suffered far more militarily from outsiders, and been obliged to stomach far more culturally and economically from them, than outsiders ever have from China. If the idea of the Great Wall as a purely defensive bastion has usually found such favour, it is because it fits so well with this perception. But as what follows may suggest, when history is at its most obliging, the history-writer needs be at his most wary.

Finally, an apology. Histories like this usually award priority to the recent. The narrative slows, like a train drawing into a station, as it approaches the platform of the present. Braking hard through the nineteenth century, it crawls obligingly through the twentieth towards the buffers of the twenty-first. This book, in devoting more space to the distant past and less to the recent past, may go to the other extreme. But since no culture is so historically conscious as China's, the remote is often more relevant. To the Chinese the First Emperor (r. 221–210 BC) is a colossus, while the Last Emperor (r. 1909–11) is largely unknown. That he ended his days mulching the flower beds in a Beijing park might seem to justify this ignorance. The centuries of greatest interest to foreigners – post-1500 in the case of Europeans, post-1750 in the case of Americans – reflect their own historical perspectives, not those of the Chinese. And as you, the reader, know full well, the train of history does not in fact stop for the convenience of a book. This book's 'now' is already your 'then'. Histories themselves become history before they reach the shelves. What seemed immediate at the time of writing is already being swallowed up by the distance ahead like a tail-light disappearing down the track of futurity.

1

RITES TO WRITING

PRE C. 1050 BC

THE GREAT BEGINNING

THOUGH BY NO MEANS A GODLESS people, the ancient Chinese were reluctant to credit their gods – or God – with anything so manifestly implausible as the act of creation. In the beginning, therefore, God did not create heaven and earth; they happened. Instead of creation myths, China's history begins with inception myths and in place of a creator it has a 'happening situation'. Suggestive of a scientific reaction, part black hole, part Big Bang, this was known as the Great Beginning.

> Before Heaven and Earth had taken form all was vague and amorphous [declares the third-century BC *Huainanzi*]. Therefore it was called The Great Beginning. The Great Beginning produced emptiness, and emptiness produced the universe. The universe produced *qi* [vital force or energy], which had limits. That which was clear and light drifted up to become Heaven while that which was heavy and turbid solidified to become earth ... The combined essences of Heaven and Earth became the *yin* and *yang*.[1]

A more popular, though later, version of this genesis myth describes the primordial environment as not just amorphous but 'opaque, like the inside of an egg'; and it actually *was* an egg to the extent that, when broken, white and yolk separated. The clear white, or *yang*, ascended to become Heaven and the murky yolk, or *yin*, descended to become Earth. Interposed between the two was the egg's incubus, a spirit called Pan Gu. Pan Gu kept his feet firmly in the earth and his head in the heavens as the two drew apart. 'Heaven was exceedingly high, Earth exceedingly deep, and Pan Gu exceedingly tall,' says the *Huainanzi*.[2] Though not the creator of the universe, Pan Gu evidently served as some kind of agent in the arrangement of it.

Further evidence of agency in the ordering and supporting of the self-created cosmos came to light quite recently when a silk manuscript, stolen from a tomb near Changsha in the southern province of Hunan in 1942, passed into the possession of the Sackler Collection in Washington, DC. The manuscript features both text and drawings and is laid out diagramatically in the form of a cosmograph. This is a common device that uses a model of the cosmos and its various phases to assist the reader in divining the best time of year for a particular course of action. Dating from about 300 BC, the silk stationery of the manuscript, though carefully folded within a bamboo box, has suffered much wear and a little tear. Not all of the text is legible, and not all of what is legible is intelligible. But one section appears to contain a variation on the same cosmogony theme. In this case a whole family – husband and wife ably assisted by their four children – take on the task of sorting out the universe. First they 'put things in motion making the transformations arrive'; then, after a well-earned rest, they calculate the divisions of time, separate heaven and earth, and name the mountains ('since the mountains were out of order') and likewise the rivers and the four seas.[3]

It is still dark at the time, the sun and the moon having not yet appeared. Sorting out the mountains and rivers is only possible thanks to enlightening guidance provided by four gods, who also reveal the four seasons. The gods have to intervene again when, 'after hundreds and thousands of years', the sun and the moon are finally born. For by their light it becomes apparent that something is wrong with the Nine Continents: they are not level; mountains keep toppling over on top of them. The gods therefore devise as protection a canopy, or sky-dome, and to hold it up they erect five poles, each of a different colour. The colours – green, red, yellow, white and black – are those of the Five Phases or Five Elements, an important (if not always consistent) sequence that will recur in Chinese history and philosophy almost as often as those complementary opposites of *yin* and *yang*.

The relevant section of the Changsha silk manuscript concludes with the words: 'The God then finally made the movement of the sun and the moon'. This enigmatic statement is about as near to creationism as the Chinese texts get. But it should be noted that the spirits, gods, even God, never actually create things; they only set them in motion, support them, organise them, adjust them and name them. In Chinese tradition the origin of the universe is less relevant than its correct orientation and operation, since it is by these that time and space can be calculated and the likely outcome of any human endeavour assessed.

Less relevant still in Chinese tradition is the origin of man. In another version of the Pan Gu story, it is not Pan Gu's lanky adolescence which suggests a degree of personal agency in the creative process but his post-humous putrescence. In what might be called a decomposition myth, as Pan Gu lay dying, it is said that:

[his] breath became the wind and the clouds; his voice became the thunder; his left eye became the sun, and his right the moon; his four limbs and five torsos became the four poles and the five mountains; his blood became the rivers; his sinews became geographic features; his muscles became the soils in the field; his hair and beard became stars and planets; his skin and its hairs became grasses and trees; his teeth and bones became bronzes and jades; his essence and marrow became pearls and gemstones; his sweat became rain and lakes; and the various worms in his body, touched by the wind, became the black-haired commoners.[4]

India's mythology matches this with a dismemberment myth. Out of the corpse of a sacrificial victim the Vedic gods supposedly hacked a hierarchy of caste, with the priestly Brahmin being born of the victim's mouth, the martial *ksatriya* of his arms, the house-proud *vaisya* of his thighs, and the wretched *sudra* of his feet. The Brahminical imagination responsible for this conceit overlooked the possibility of a section of the human race being derived from an intestinal infestation. Perhaps only an elite as sublimely superior as China's could have assigned to their raven-haired countrymen an origin so abject. When in later times foreigners came to resent the arro-gance of Chinese officialdom, their grounds for complaint were as nothing compared to those of China's unregarded masses.

From both of the above examples an early insistence on social stratifi-cation – on a superior 'us' and an inferior 'them' – is inferred; and it is thought to be corroborated in China by the numerous other myths empha-sising that heaven and earth had to be physically separated. While Pan Gu could bridge the gap between them because he was so 'exceedingly tall', and while both men and gods later managed excursions back and forth, the distance eventually became too great. Only those possessed of magical powers, or able to attach such a medium to their persons or families, could hope to make the trip. Celestial intercourse, in other words, was reserved for the privileged few and this set them apart from the toiling many.

In the *Shangshu*, the fourth-century BC 'Book of Documents' that provided twentieth-century etymologists with a Chinese word for 'panda', such myths slowly begin to gel into history. Here a named 'emperor' is credited with having separated Heaven and Earth by commanding an end to all unauthorised communication between the two. The link was duly severed by a couple of gods who were in his service. There was to be, as he put it, 'no more ascending and descending'; and 'after this was done', we are told, 'order was restored and the people returned to virtue'.

The 'emperor' in question was Zhuan Xu, the second of the mythical 'Five Emperors' whom tradition places at the apex of China's great family tree of legitimate sovereigns. All of the 'Five Emperors' combined in their persons both divine and human attributes. Their majesty was awesome and their conduct so exemplary that it would inform political debate throughout the millennia to come. In fact, providing an unassailable example of virtuous and unitary rule seems to have been their prime function. Of the five, the first was the revered 'Yellow Emperor'; Zhuan Xu was second; the third and fourth were the much-cited Yao and Shun; and the last was Yu. Unlike his precursors, each of whom had deferred to a successor who was not his own son, Yu yielded to the principle of hereditary succession, named his son as his heir, and so founded China's first recognised dynasty, the Xia.[5]

The Xia were kings; the title of 'emperor' is not given them and would remain in abeyance for the next 1,400 years. They have, however, been given approximate dates (traditionally *c.* 2100 BC – *c.* 1600 BC but probably a few centuries later) and a rough location in the lower Yellow River basin, otherwise the Zhongyuan or 'Central Plain' that stretches across northern China from Shandong province to Shaanxi province. Unlike 'the Five Emperors' the Xia are not considered semi-divine; they may have actually existed. They left no documentary evidence or any material remains that can certainly be attributed to them; even China's earliest historians could find comparatively little to say about them. But archaeologists have unearthed cultures one of

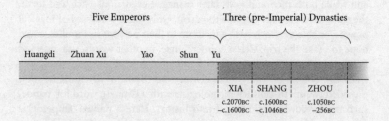

THE FIVE EMPERORS AND THE THREE (pre-Imperial) DYNASTIES

Five Emperors				Three (pre-Imperial) Dynasties		
Huangdi	Zhuan Xu	Yao	Shun	Yu		
				XIA	SHANG	ZHOU
				c.2070BC –c.1600BC	c.1600BC –c.1046BC	c.1050BC –256BC

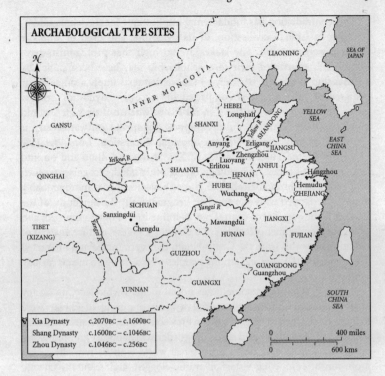

ARCHAEOLOGICAL TYPE SITES

Xia Dynasty	c.2070BC – c.1600BC
Shang Dynasty	c.1600BC – c.1046BC
Zhou Dynasty	c.1046BC – c.256BC

which could have been Xia, and there is evidence of what may be some early form of writing that could have been in use at the Xia court.

On the other hand, excavation has failed to substantiate a unitary kingdom or culture that was anything like as unique, widespread, dominant and long-lasting as that which later textual tradition awards to the Xia; and with important reservations, the same may be said of the still more illustrious Shang (r. *c.* 1750–*c.* 1040 BC) and Zhou[6] (r. *c.* 1040–256 BC), who, together with the Xia, comprise the first 'Three Dynasties'. Rather, all the material evidence now points to a plethora of localised Neolithic and Bronze Age cultures, some distinct and some less so, that arose and coexisted both within the Central Plain and far beyond it. The dawn of Chinese history is thus badly obscured by a major contradiction. The written record contained in classic texts dating from the fourth and third century BC (and generally accepted ever since) does not always coincide with the material record as excavated and analysed by the highest standards of modern scholarship in the twentieth century.

This contradiction has fundamental implications for the whole understanding of China's civilisation, of its dynamics, and even of who the Chinese were and are. The stakes are so high that protagonists have occasionally overstated their case; scholarship may have been sullied by partisanship as a result. Basically all the written texts imply a single linear pedigree of rulership; it is comprised of successive 'dynasties' centred geographically on the north's Central Plain, whence their superior and quintessentially 'Chinese' culture supposedly spread outwards; and it stretched chronologically, like an apostolic succession, from 'the Five Emperors' to 'the Three Dynasties' of Xia, Shang and Zhou and on into less contentious times. Archaeology, on the other hand, recognises no such neat pedigree. Chronologically the Three Dynasties appear more probably to have overlapped with one another; geographically the kingdoms of the Central Plain were not as central nor as influential as once supposed; and as for the developments that led to a distinct 'Chinese' culture, instead of radiating outwards from the Central Plain they germinated and interacted over a much wider area and among peoples who were by no means racially uniform.

It is as if, standing in some outer portal of the Forbidden City or any other traditional Chinese architectural complex, one group of scholars were to focus on the inward vista of solemn grey courtyards, airy halls and grand stairways all centrally aligned in receding order, while another group, looking outwards, were to gaze down on the real world with its typically urban profusion of competing vistas, all traffic-clogged, architecturally chaotic and equally intriguing. Reconciling the two seems scarcely possible, although recent moves in that direction offer some encouragement.

Archaeologists have become more mindful of the limitations of their discipline as new finds overturn confidence in their own earlier hypotheses; the survival of relics from the remotest past is acknowledged as being as arbitrary as their often accidental discovery; and such evidence as may be lacking is not taken as proof of its never having existed – or of its never one day coming to light. Meanwhile the textual scholars have been coming round to the idea that their sources may be selective and that those who compiled them long after the times they describe may have had their own agendas. For instance, 'Xia', the name of the first dynasty, is the same as that used by the people of the Central Plain in the last centuries BC (when the historiographical tradition was taking shape) to distinguish themselves from other less 'Chinese' peoples (often described as *di*, *man*, *rong* or *yi*, words that are habitually translated into English as 'barbarian'). Much later the word 'Han' would make a similar transition from dynastic name to ethnic tag and is now used as the official term for China's supposedly mono-ethnic majority. Both examples suggest that the validity of the ethnic tag derives substantially from the prominence accorded to the original dynasty. Thus talking up the Xia dynasty in the texts may have been a way of enhancing a sense of privileged identity among those who regarded themselves as inheritors of the Xia kingdom and so the 'Xia people'.

Modern scholarship is well placed to recognise such special pleading. It cannot be a coincidence that throughout the Nationalist and communist era champions of the linear textual tradition have generally been resident in China and employed there, while those who emphasise a regional and pluralist interpretation of Chinese identity have generally been foreigners, often Westerners, Japanese or Chinese residing outside China. Deconstructing China, questioning its cohesion and puncturing its presumption, has a history of its own – which of course in no way vitiates the research or invalidates the findings of its scholars.

GLINT OF BRONZE

Hangzhou, a city of 6 million, lies south-west of Shanghai and about 150 kilometres (90 miles) south of the Yangzi delta. As the capital of Zhejiang province, it hosts a provincial museum, which is located on an island in West Lake, the most celebrated of many so-named water features in China, all of them rich in cultural associations and now ringed with modern amenities. Sidestepping the ice-cream sellers and the curio stalls, visitors step ashore to be greeted in the museum's foyer by a shiny brass plaque with an English text introducing the 'Hemudu Relics'. Hemudu is the name given to a local Neolithic culture that flourished from about 5000 BC. A whole floor of the museum is devoted to it, with window-dressed tableaux of Hemudu mannequins whittling and grinding among the artfully scattered 'relics' of their Stone Age settlements. But the new plaque also has a general point to make. After outlining the achievements of the Hemudu people in house-building, the firing of fine black pottery and the carving of jade and ivory, it concludes with a bold statement: 'The excavations at Hemudu Relics have proved that the Yangzi River Valley was also the birthplace of Chinese nation as well as the Yellow River Valley [*sic*]'.

Until recently this would have been heresy. The Yangzi valley and the whole of southern China were held to be alien environments in prehistoric times, populated by non-Sinitic (non-Chinese-type) hunter-gatherers and too pestilential for settled agriculturalists. Rather were the more favoured (in ancient times) plains and valleys of the north the obvious candidates for the birthplace of China's prehistoric culture; that was where fossils of an erect hominid known as 'Peking man' had been discovered in the 1920s; it was where a Chinese form of *Homo sapiens* was supposed to have developed, and where some of the earliest crop seeds had been sown. It was also where, much later, China's recorded history would begin and whence its achievements would spread and its rulers project their authority. Not unreasonably, then, the same was taken to be true of the intervening Neolithic and Chalcolithic periods.

It was only in the early 1980s, and then not without misgivings, that a Chinese scholar first publicly questioned this accepted view. He suggested it was 'incomplete', though one might now call it downright mistaken. Examples of dozens of distinct Neolithic cultures, like the 'Hemudu Relics', have been excavated at sites ranging from Manchuria in the extreme north-east to Sichuan in the west and Guangdong and Fujian in the deep south. None is significantly more 'advanced' than the others; and many more sites undoubtedly remain to be discovered. Indeed, later references to this period as being that of 'Ten Thousand States' (or 'Chiefdoms') may not be too wide of the mark.

As usual with Neolithic peoples, pottery provides a ready means of classification and so is used to distinguish them. Burial sites can also be revealing. But graveyards and ceramic workshops presume the existence of a settled population. The first conclusion to be drawn from the new discoveries is that settlement based on growing crops and husbanding domesticated animals was a development common to many regions of China and not just the north's Central Plain. If millet was grown in the Yellow River region from perhaps 8000 BC, so was rice grown in the Yangzi region from about the same time. Silk production based on silkworm rearing, a form of animal husbandry unique to China, also has a remote provenance and is now known to have been practised in the Yangzi valley from at least the third millennium BC.

The links, if any, between these Neolithic cultures are as yet unclear. For the Indian subcontinent and for inner Asia, trails of diffusion have been proposed to fit the distribution patterns of pottery types and other distinctive artefacts; population movement in the form of migration, colonisation or conquest has often been inferred from them. But such theorising may owe something to retrospective assumptions. In both cases the incidence in later times of migrations, mostly inward in India, both inward and outward in inner Asia and Siberia, may have been projected back into prehistory. Consequently early settlement in these regions is supposedly fluid, with levels of technology uneven and population shifts frequent.

The more static model preferred in China may likewise reflect later historical orthodoxy. Neolithic cultures are grouped into regional 'spheres of interaction' rather than into peripatetic societies tracking across the face of the country; and attention is directed to those cultures and sites exhibiting the most in the way of continuity and internal development. Perhaps because so much archaeological effort was initially expended on the Yellow River basin in the north's Central Plain, the key locations in this context are indeed concentrated in the north. Here, notable for their red pottery, often with painted designs, the so-called 'Yangshao' settlements (c. 5000–3000 BC and so contemporary with Hemudu), were succeeded by larger concentrations of the black-pottery 'Longshan' culture from about 3000 BC. Some 'Longshan' sites have urban proportions. Though centred in Shandong they are scattered over a much greater area than the Yangshao settlements. They introduce a building material called *hangtu* that was produced by pounding the friable loess soil into a concrete consistency; it would remain in use for the construction of foundations and walls until replaced by concrete itself in the twentieth century. And to the delight of archaeologists the 'Longshan' people honoured their dead with lavishly furnished tombs.

The size of some 'Longshan' tombs and the wealth and nature of their grave goods betray a highly stratified society. Privileged clans (or 'lineages') evidently exalted their ancestors in order to legitimise their own position, and through the mediation of this ancestry enjoyed a monopoly on contact with the gods. In this context they lavished on their dead both exotica, such as carved ivories, and a great variety of ritual objects ranging from vessels for food and drink to musical instruments and jade objects. Many such items incorporate pictorial devices known to have been used in shamanic intercourse with the supernatural world of ancestors and gods.

It all sounds mildly familiar. 'Longshan' society, or some part of it, could well have been that over which the Xia kings ruled. Erlitou, a Longshan type-site near Luoyang on the south side of the Yellow River in Henan province, has been confidently dated to c. 1900–c. 1350 BC, which roughly synchronises with the revised dates deduced for the Xia dynasty from later textual sources. Erlitou has therefore been tentatively assigned to the Xia. Moreover the site has yielded two types of material evidence, one apparently primitive, the other highly sophisticated, that connect its culture unmistakably to that of the later (or more probably overlapping) Shang and Zhou dynasties. In fact these material finds constitute prime sources for the social, cultural and political history of the second and early first millennia BC.

The first of them is burnt bones, mostly the shoulder blades of various animals that have been subjected to fire so as to produce a cracking. The cracking was 'read', much like entrails by the Greeks, to discover supernatural responses to human predicaments. More will be said of the practice, for it led to the earliest extant form of documentation and the first certain appearance of a written script in China. The other source material encountered at Erlitou, however, is even more sensational. For here were discovered some of the earliest examples of bronze-casting, a technology that more than any other defines ancient China's culture and whose hefty products – urns, tureens, jugs – age-blackened or verdigris-tinged but otherwise deceptively pristine, still grace the galleries of the world's museums.

Robert Bagley puts it better in the *Cambridge History of Ancient China*: 'Artifacts of cast bronze are technologically and typologically the most distinctive traits of material culture in second millennium [BC] China . . . [and furnish] a revealing index of cultural development.'[7] Indeed, bronze came to occupy much the same position in ancient China as stone in the contemporary civilisation of Egypt or, later, those of Iran (Persia) and Greece. Enormous effort was devoted to producing bronze-ware, highly sophisticated ideas were expressed through it, some of the earliest inscriptions are found on it, and its durability has ensured that plentiful examples have survived. Bronze production in China, though inferior in its labour requirement to, say, the great megalithic constructions of pharaonic Egypt, was yet on a sufficiently large scale to be rated an 'industry'. Single vessels weighing close to three-quarters of a tonne have been excavated at Anyang in Henan province; elsewhere the total bronze component in one fifth-century BC tomb (at Suizhou) was found to amount to 10 tonnes. 'Nothing remotely comparable is known elsewhere in the ancient world.'[8]

Compared to quarrying and carving stone, the technology involved in casting bronze was infinitely more demanding. Earlier small-scale production in Gansu province suggests that China's metallurgical skills may have actually originated in China; certainly the abundance of suitable ores argues for an indigenous development, as do the advanced ceramic skills needed to create the moulds and achieve the high furnace temperatures for bronze-casting. The most impressive products were large vessels, often incorporating an udder-like tripod base but taking a variety of different shapes – known as *ding, gue, jia*, etc. – depending on their function as food containers, cooking pots, ale jugs, etc.

All at first replicated pottery designs but were then subjected to increasing elaboration in both shape and decoration. The ceramic moulds in which they were cast were themselves considerable achievements, with the decoration being incised on the inner side of the outer mould so that it emerged as raised on the finished product. (Engraving of the finished surface came later.) The moulds, both inner and outer, were cut into sections for the first pourings, typically three sections for the three-legged urn known as a *ding* but many more for more complex shapes. The vertical joins of the moulds ran up through the legs to the top of the vessel. Each section, including devices like spouts and handles, was cast separately but was recast as part of the whole in the final pouring. This eliminated any need for soldering or jointing while encouraging decorative designs, patterns and inlays, often with an animal motif, that were repeated within the subdivisions which resulted from the use of sectional moulds.

Ingenious as well as skilful, the technique underwent rapid development; so did the vessel shapes and the often fantastic ornamentation given them. Studying these variations, art historians have been able to chart the whole development of bronze-casting, to place surviving examples in a sequence of styles, assign rough dates to each style-type, and draw important conclusions from the distribution of the find-sites.

These find-sites are not, as once seemed likely, confined to the north's Central Plain. Although the earliest style associated with Erlitou (1900–1350 BC) is little found outside the Yellow River basin, later styles, especially those associated with the Erligang culture (*c.* 1500–1300 BC), achieved a wide distribution. Some bronze-ware may have been gifted or traded; but the discovery of foundries producing almost identical vessels as far afield as Hubei province and the Yangzi argues for some more fundamental contact. It is reasonable to assume that where such a specialised and prestigious technology was transferred, cultural beliefs and social assumptions must also have been transferred, and this in turn could imply some form of political hegemony. The bronze record thus suggests that in the fifteenth to thirteenth centuries BC 'a state' in the north's Central Plain with a highly sophisticated culture expanded its influence over a large part of the region immediately to its south and east.

Archaeologically this expansive entity is known as Erligang after the name of its type-site at Zhengzhou, a city on the Yellow River in Henan province. Focusing exclusively on such excavated sources, Bagley declares Erligang 'the first great civilisation of East Asia';[9] and most historians, latching on to its dates and location, take their cue from this and gratefully identify Erligang culture with the dynasty known in written sources as the Shang. But as with Erlitou and the Xia dynasty, so with Erligang and the Shang dynasty: the two do not quite fit. Erligang's expansion and primacy look to have been shorter-lived than Shang's. Although bronze production continued to increase, and nowhere more so than in the north, elsewhere as of about 1300 BC distinctive individual styles emerged, suggesting a resurgence of cultural and political autonomy in the Yangzi region, Sichuan and the north-east at a time when the texts would suggest that Shang reigned supreme.

Besides such tantalising glimpses of political activity, the bronze industry reveals something of the nature of Erligang, and so perhaps Shang, society. Since bronze is an alloy, deposits of copper and tin (plus some lead) had first to be located, mined and then, in the casting process, carefully combined to ensure an ore ratio suitable to the size and type of vessel desired. Abundant fuel for the furnaces was also essential; and because foundries were located within the oversight of the supposed 'capital', the transport requirement must have been considerable. Society was by now, therefore, not just hierarchically stratified but organised into productive functional groups, reasonably stable and closely controlled. Skilled artisans had to be trained and maintained, a labour force that was both servile and surplus had to be mobilised, and a ruling lineage clique with a steady demand for finished products of exceptional quality had to direct operations. Only sparingly were metals used for weapons and scarcely at all for tools or agricultural implements. Bronze-casting was the prestige monopoly of a demanding elite. The bulk of all production went to the manufacture of the vessels required for ritual purposes by this elite; and to judge by their find-sites, many of these vessels were ultimately or specifically destined to accompany deceased members of the elite to their graves.

The vast complex of tombs at Anyang, north of the Yellow River but still in Henan province, has been dated to around 1200 BC. Although Erligang's cultural reach had by then retracted, this indisputably late Shang centre betrays no signs of decline. More thoroughly explored than any other site, Anyang's necropolis and the cyclopean foundations of its adjacent city convey a compelling, if gruesome, impression of late Shang might. The largest tomb occupies an area nearly as big as a football pitch. As if from each opposing goal and touchline, four sloping subways or ramps converge on a central vertical shaft, at the base of which lies the collapsed burial chamber. This was cruciform, about 200 square metres (240 square yards) in area, 3 metres (10 feet) high and 10.5 metres (34 feet) below ground. Five sacrificial pits were found within it, and the central area had been floored with timbers to accommodate the sarcophagus. Unfortunately tomb robbers had got there long before the archaeologists. The site had been largely cleared of grave goods, and the same fate had befallen most of the other Anyang tombs. To date there is only one notable exception.

Dying just 150 years after Tutankhamun, a Shang royal consort called Fu Hao was interred at the Anyang site around 1200 BC and remained undisturbed until AD 1976. The tomb is a small one, without ramps. 'Lady Hao' – her name is found engraved on her bronzes – may have been cherished but she was too gender-handicapped to merit more than 'a lesser tomb' with a simple shaft of room-size dimensions about 7.5 metres (25 feet) deep. Her burial chamber was nevertheless richly furnished. The nested coffins, though badly decayed by seepage, had once been lacquered red and black; the walls had probably been painted and textiles draped over the coffin. Most of the surviving grave goods must have originally been inside the outer coffin. Yet the inventory for this fairly small space included 195 bronze vessels (the largest of which weighed 120 kilograms – 265 pounds), more than 271 smaller bronze items, 564 objects of carved bone and an extraordinary 755 of jade, the largest such collection ever found. 'If the [bigger] tombs were richer than this, their contents are beyond imagining,' says Bagley.[10]

Sixteen skeletons were also found in the tomb. They were distributed within, around and above the coffin. The Shang elite did not like its members to leave this world alone; relatives, retainers, guards, servants and pets accompanied them as part of the grave offering. Ritual demanded, and spectacle no doubt encouraged, human sacrifice on a grand scale. In the larger tombs the victims have been counted in their hundreds. Some skeletons are complete, others dismembered or decapitated, the cranium often having been sawn off, perhaps for bone carving. Some of the mutilated victims may have been convicts or captives taken in war. The killing of prisoners is thought to have been common practice, and the skeletons include different racial types. The quality of Shang mercy, if such a thing existed, was ever strained and made no clear distinction between friend and foe. Men (and occasionally women and children) were as conspicuously expended in the cause of ritual as were bronze and jade.

How all this extravagance was funded is unclear. No great agricultural revolution occurred at the time, no major irrigation effort is known, and no significant introduction – the ox-drawn plough once had its champions – has been generally accepted. Nor do trade or conquest seem to have been important contributory factors. The Shang apparently just used existing resources of land and labour to greater effect. 'This leads to the inevitable conclusion', writes Kwang-chih Chang of the Academia Sinica, 'that the Shang period witnessed the beginning in this part of the world of organised large-scale exploitation of one group of people by another within the same society'; it also witnessed 'the beginning of an oppressive governmental system to make such exploitation possible'.[11]

While members of the ruling clans frequented the great buildings whose pounded earth foundations testify to ambitious architecture and gracious living, the 'black-haired commoners' lived in covered pits, used crude clay utensils, and laboured in the fields with Stone Age tools of wood and flint. Malnutrition has been noted in many skeletons. Leisure must have been rare, insubordination fatal. Cultural excellence came at a price in Bronze Age China; the bright burnish of civilisation was down to the hard rub of despotic power.

FINDING FAMILY

This somewhat harsh picture of second-millennium BC China may be tempered by further research at those sites that have lately come to light in more distant parts of the country. The Qijia culture of Gansu and Qinghai provinces, for instance, besides providing examples of pre-Erlitou bronze working, was reported in 2005 to have yielded evidence of another abiding ingredient in Chinese civilisation, namely 'the oldest intact noodles yet discovered'. Dated to about 2000 BC, they were found at a site called Lajia and had been made from millet flour.[12]

More elaborate artefacts, including several enormous bronze bells, from sites in Hubei and Hunan provide early testimony of the more vibrant art and culture of the Yangzi region; but they have been eclipsed by finds from further upriver in Sichuan. There two recent discoveries made in and around Chengdu, today a megalopolis of about 12 million, have confounded art historians and left any notion of a single bronze tradition teetering on the edge of the melting pot. Sacrificial pits accidentally discovered at Sanxingdui in 1986, and the site at Jinsha uncovered during road construction in 2001, produced large quantities of animal bones and elephant tusks but not one human skeleton. More sensationally, they yielded an array of bronze busts and figures, gold masks and jades quite unlike anything discovered elsewhere in China. A bronze statue, 2.6 metres (8.5 feet) tall (including its pedestal) and dated to about 1200 BC, is of an elongated and gesticulating figure with stylised features more Aztec than Chinese. Likewise some disassembled bronze fruit trees, like gigantic table decorations complete with foliage, peach-like fruit and frugivorous birds, all of bronze, have no known counterpart.

Also uncovered at Sanxingdui were the *hangtu* (pounded earth) foundations of a large city. This method of construction has suggested some contact with either Erlitou or Erligang. On the other hand, the temptation to link Sichuan's sites, however weird and wonderful, with later kingdoms in the same region known in the texts as Shu and Ba has proved irresistible. A similar connection has been proposed between the Hubei/Hunan bronze sites and the Yangzi region's later kingdom of Chu. Inconvenient data is thus yoked to the orthodoxies of textual tradition, and unaccountable art forms accommodated within the framework of existing research.

No such accommodation, however, has yet been extended to the most controversial discovery of all. In 1978 the Chinese archaeologist Wang Binghua unearthed a large collection of graves at Hami in the deserts of eastern Xinjiang province. It was not where one would expect to find an ancient culture of any relevance to the more favoured parts of China; if Chengdu is as far from Beijing as Denver from New York, Hami might be likened to some place in remotest Idaho.

Similar graves had been noted thereabouts by European travellers earlier in the twentieth century, though without exciting their interest. The new graves were dated to about 1200 BC, but of their contents little was heard until ten years after Wang's discovery. It was then, in 1988, that Victor Mair, an American academic who was guiding a tour for the Smithsonian Institute, wandered into a new section of the provincial museum in Urumqi, the Xinjiang capital. Parting the hanging curtains that served as a door, he pushed inside and thus famously 'entered another world'.

> The room was full of mummies! Life-like mummies! These were not the wizened and eviscerated pharaohs wrappped in yards of dusty gauze that one normally pictures when mummies are mentioned. Instead they were everyday people dressed in their everyday clothes. Each one of the half dozen bodies in the room, whether man, woman or child, looked as if it had merely gone to sleep for a while and might sit up at any moment and begin to talk to whomever happened to be standing next to its glass case.[13]

Mair was transfixed; as a scholar of early Eastern linguistics and literature, he might actually have understood any rasped utterances coming
from the desiccated corpses. He gave them all names and called one after
his brother; the resemblance was uncanny. This 'Ur-David' ('the first
David'), or 'Charchan Man', lay with his head on a pillow and 'his expressive hands placed gently upon his abdomen'. His woollen shirt and trousers
were in a fetching shade of maroon 'trimmed with fine red piping'. Inside
his white thigh-length boots he wore felt socks 'as brightly coloured as a
rainbow'.

With further such imaginative licence the well-preserved female corpse
discovered at a neighbouring site became 'the Beauty of Kroran' (or 'the
Beauty of Loulan'). She had gone to her grave in tartan plaid of Celtic
weave, and when a copy of her head was re-fleshed by a plastic surgeon
for a TV documentary, she looked almost presentable. Personalising the
mummies in this way was irresistible; for to Mair they were not only 'life-
like' but decidedly Mair-like. It was a case of instant recognition, then
ardent adoption. The American had found family.

And therein, for the Chinese, lay the problem. 'The Tarim Mummies'
(Tarim being the name of the river that once drained the now waterless
Tarim basin of eastern Xinjiang) are mostly not of Mongoloid race but
of now DNA-certified Caucasoid or Europoid descent. Some had brown
hair; at least one stood 2 metres (6.5 feet) tall. They are similar to the
Cro-Magnon peoples of eastern Europe. So are their clothes and so
probably was their language. It is thought to have been 'proto-Tocharian',
an early branch of the great Indo-European language family that includes
the Celtic, Germanic, Greek and Latin tongues as well as Sanskrit and
Early Iranian.

But Mair and his disciples would not be content to stop there. Several
hundred mummies have now been discovered, their preservation being
the result of the region's extreme aridity and the high alkaline content of
the desert sands. The graves span a long period, from *c.* 2000 BC to AD
300, but the forebears of their inmates are thought most probably to have
migrated from the Altai region to the north, where there flourished around
2000 BC another Europoid culture, that of Afanasevo. Such a migration
would have consisted of several waves and must have involved contact
with Indo-European-speaking Iranian peoples as well as Altaic peoples.
Since both were acquainted with basic metallurgy and had domesticated
numerous animals, including horses and sheep, the mummy people must
themselves have acquired such knowledge and may have passed it on to
the cultures of eastern China.

According to Mair and his colleagues, therefore, the horse, the sheep, the wheel, the horse-drawn chariot, supplies of uncut jade and probably both bronze and iron technology may have reached 'core' China courtesy of these Europoid 'proto-Tocharians'. By implication, it followed that the Europeans who in the seventeenth to nineteenth centuries AD would so embarrass China with their superior technology were not the first. 'Foreign Devils on the Silk Road' had been active 4,000 years ago; and thanks to them, China's ancient civilisation need not be regarded as quite so 'of itself'. It could in fact be just as derivative, and no more indigenous, than most others.

Needless to say, scholars in China have had some difficulty with all this. Patriotic sentiment apart, national integration has also seemed to be at stake. 'Xinjiang separatists' – who would prefer to be called 'Uighur nationalists' – were reported to have readily adopted Mair's findings in order to contest Beijing's claim that their province was historically part of China and so bolster their own claim to autonomy. The mummies had become heavily politicised, and the Chinese authorities found themselves suspected of wilfully neglecting the conservation of mummy sites, obstructing research, suppressing its findings and concealing such evidence, including the mummies themselves, as was already available.

Feelings ran high, though they may now be subsiding. The Uighurs, a Turkic-speaking people who have been settled in Xinjiang since no earlier than *c.* AD 600, and who then adopted Islam, can scarcely claim to have much in common with Chalcolithic Europoids of the second and first millennia BC who spoke an Indo-European language and of whose beliefs next to nothing is known. Uighur ancestors could have intermarried with later Tocharian-speakers; equally they could have obliterated them. Moreover, the People's Republic of China is not postulated on the basis of there being a single Chinese race or a historically defined territory. The Uighurs, like the Tibetans and other minority groups, may have good reason to resent 'Han' supremacism, but history can be an unreliable ally.

Whether the mummy people played a part in the transfer of technologies and raw materials is more worthy of debate. Certainly China's main source of jade has always been in the Kun Lun mountains in southern Xinjiang. Jade objects, like those cut for the tomb of 'Lady Hao', have been geologically sourced to the Kun Lun, and any people occupying the intervening region may well have been involved in the supply of jade. Metallurgy is less certain. Though the Afanasevo people produced small copper implements, according to the latest research 'they did not know how to melt or cast metal'.[14] Judging from the artefacts so far credited to the mummy people, neither did they, although around 900 BC it would be in Xinjiang that iron would make its Chinese debut.

Horses, horsemanship and chariots are a different matter. They, like jade, were almost certainly acquired by the Chinese from their central Asian neighbours. Chariots first appear in burials, sometimes complete with horses and charioteers, at Anyang (*c.* 1240–*c.* 1040 BC) and other Shang sites. Their large many-spoked wheels have been declared the first wheels to be found in China and their horses the first draught animals found in China. There is no Chinese evidence for the earlier development of wheeled transport or of horsemanship. But the assumption that these skills were indeed acquired from outside China does not mean that they came from Xinjiang. As will be seen, China's equestrian neighbours in Mongolia are a more likely source.

IN THE ORACULAR

Until such time as sites like those in Xinjiang and Sichuan have been more extensively explored, the uncertainties outweigh the certainties and speculation has free rein. By way of contrast, the sprawling city-site located at modern Anyang in Henan has been subjected to exhaustive excavation. It lies at the heart of what was 'core' China, and at Anyang, more than anywhere else, the archaeologists could be reasonably confident of exciting finds.

Interest was first stirred, so the story goes, when in 1899 a pharmacist in Beijing was found to be supplying malaria sufferers with a medicinal powder supposedly ground from old 'dragon bones'. Dragons never having been that plentiful, the bones were in fact an assortment of flat scapulas (shoulder blades) from cattle plus numerous plastrons (ventral or under-belly shells) from turtles; but they looked old, and some had what appeared to be writing scratched on them. This discovery was made by a malaria patient whose brother happened to be a noted scholar of ancient Chinese scripts. When the latter recognised the scratched characters on the bones as similar to those found on some of the later Shang bronzes, the hunt was on.

After much prevarication and long sleuthing, the bones and shells were traced back to villagers living in the vicinity of Anyang. Stocks from there seemed inexhaustible. Amateur collectors, many of them foreigners, found a surprising number for sale in Beijing's antique stores; and since the scratched characters could be transferred to paper in the manner of brass-rubbings, scholars worldwide found ample employment in trying to decipher them. Meanwhile suppliers, instead of scraping off the squiggles that devalued good 'dragon bones', had begun scratching them on to take advantage of the curio market. 'A hundred forgeries for every genuine piece' was how the historian H. G. Creel described the situation in 1935; collections of bones, 'not one of which was genuine', were 'being bought for many hundreds of dollars'.[15]

Happily this did not deter the archaeologists. Excavations at Anyang got under way in the late 1920s, and with interruptions for wars and revolutions, continued in the 1930s, the 1950s and the 1970s. Expectations that the site would prove to be a Shang 'cult-centre' were confirmed by uncovering the monumental foundations of more than fifty large buildings and by sensational finds like those football-pitch-size tombs and the opulent grave goods of 'Lady Hao'. The Shang, whose historicity had previously been as suspect as that of the Xia, were thus handsomely authenticated; textual tradition was vindicated, and archaeology was acknowledged as the key to further validation of the supposed centrality and superiority of north China's remotest past.

As noted, these hopes have not yet been fully realised. Subsequent discoveries elsewhere in China have undercut cherished traditions as often as they have corroborated them. But at least the 'dragon bones' did not disappoint. More finds and painstaking analysis of their incised characters established that the Shang elite was indeed literate and that the Chinese script of today is unique in being the direct descendant of one used in the second millennium BC. Moreover, China's documented history is found to begin not with a collection of cryptic runes, not with some interminable Homeric epic, but much as it intended to go on – with an official and distinctly bureaucratic archive, albeit inscribed on shells and bones. Additionally the inscriptions have afforded telling insights into the complex world of Shang ritual and governance, which, by anticipating later trends, add further weight to that contentious claim about China's three to four (if not six) thousand years of continuous civilisation.

More than 100,000 fragments constituting about 7,000 scapulas and plastrons, most of them considered genuine, have now been recovered. Over a quarter came from a single location, suggesting deliberate 'safe-deposit' storage. The bones span some 3,000 years, from the late-fourth-millennium BC Longshan culture to that of the Zhou dynasty in the early first millennium BC. But it was the Shang, while based at Anyang in *c.* 1240–1040 BC, who standardised their use and valued them as instruments of record. It was also they who first introduced turtle plastrons to supplement, and increasingly replace, scapulas. Perhaps plastrons, being rarer, were better suited to a royal art like divination; perhaps turtles, being exceptionally long-lived, offered a more appropriate symbolism; or perhaps shells simply produced a more articulate cracking. Additionally it was the Shang who established the practice of pre-boring small indentations in orderly sequence down the length of the bones and shells and sometimes numbering them, each such 'bullet-point' being thus readied for the application of the crack-producing fire. And finally it was the Shang who adopted the custom of engraving alongside each cracking a written summary of the divination, including the date and the name of the diviner, and of then storing – one might almost say 'filing' – the completed 'documents'.

None of these advances should be underestimated. The skill involved in getting bones and shells to produce a tidy cracking may have been no less than that involved in interpreting the result. Recent experiments, mostly with bones, have rarely been reassuring. A Japanese scholar, while hosting an academic barbeque, tried charcoal briquets, then a red-hot poker, on a scapula pre-drilled with indentations to the standard depth. Nothing happened. 'I got rather fed up,' he says, 'and threw the whole damn thing in the whole mess of charcoal . . . Divination was not auspicious.' Later, because of the smell, he removed the smouldering bone. As he did so, it began to crack. '"Pak! pak! pak!" It was terrific. We had truly reconstructed the Archaic Chinese [character] *pak*.' *Pace* the *pak*, though, this was obviously not how the Shang did it; the barbequed facsimile was burnt to a cinder and quite incapable of being either 'read' or annotated. Shang bones, it was concluded, must have been much drier and the heat source, possibly some oleaginous hardwood, much hotter.[16]

On the reasonable assumption that today's recovered hoard of bones and shells represents only a small fraction of the original archive, another scholar has suggested that the Shang may have consulted their gods daily.[17] The solemnity of a ritual that would usually have been performed in one of the ancestral halls to the accompaniment of music, incense, offerings of food and drink, and perhaps animal sacrifice, was apparently undiminished either by frequent repetition or by the seemingly trivial nature of the information that was sometimes sought.

Since 'reading' the oracular cracks themselves is a skill quite lost to posterity, all that is known about these transactions comes from what scholars have been able to make of the inscriptions recording them. These inscriptions were added to the bones and shells after the firing and were positioned as close to the relevant cracking as possible. They were often first painted on with a fine brush, then inscribed with a knife, and the resulting incisions were sometimes filled with a pigment. Whether for future reference or display, the Shang clearly intended their records to look impressive.

In the modern quest to understand them, about 4,000 individual characters of 'Archaic Chinese' script have been isolated, and around half of these have been 'translated or identified with varying degrees of certainty'. 'There is no question that the language [as] written is Chinese', according to a leading authority.[18] Some of the characters contain a pictorial element, many anticipate later forms of the same character, and like classical Chinese they are arranged in columns to be read from top to bottom; crucially each character represents a meaning, not (as in most other scripts) the sound, alphabetically represented, of the word used to express that meaning. Finally there is sufficient evidence in the characters themselves and in their grammatical relationships to suggest that this writing had been practised for some time. Presumably it was used on more perishable materials such as bamboo, bark or textiles that have not survived. It seems, then, that the importance attached to literacy in China and the use of a recognisably Chinese script, perhaps the two most characteristic features of 'Chinese civilisation', had a long pre-Anyang (*c.* 1240–*c.* 1040 BC), and probably pre-Shang (*c.* 1750–*c.* 1040 BC), history. A few tentatively identified characters found on stone and dated to Neolithic times may yet substantiate this.

Considering the difficulties of translation, and considering the 'shorthand' form of expression necessitated by the cramped confines of a corner of bone, it is surprising how many of the inscriptions are intelligible. Perhaps the most frequently asked 'charges' (that is 'questions', but phrased as statements) merely invite reassurance from the other world: 'Tonight there will be no disasters' or 'In the next ten days [i.e. a Shang 'week'] there will be no disasters'. To these the desired 'answer' is the character meaning 'auspicious', that is 'affirmative'; the cracking has been 'read' as approving the 'charge'; no disasters tonight. Often the charge is formulated in a 'will it/won't it' form for double reassurance: 'On the next day ... [we] should not make offering to Ancestor Yi' is followed by 'On the next day ... we should make offering to Ancestor Yi'. In asking the same question twice any ambiguity in one cracked response might be clarified by the other. Sometimes multiple-choice charges are posed – Fu is to inspect the district of Lin; it should be Qin who does it; it should be Bing who does it. An 'auspicious' endorsement of any of these settles the matter.[19]

'One reason the king divined so much was precisely because he had so much to divine about,' says David Keightley.[20] Everything, from the vagaries of the weather to the likely source of the royal toothache, the best day for a successful hunt or the prospects of victory over an enemy, had to be submitted for consideration by the supernatural concourse of gods and ancestors. It was as if the king conceived of himself as the pivotal persona in a transcendental bureaucratic hierarchy; its lower, earthly, departments were comprised of clan subordinates with their own local jurisdictions and its higher, celestial, departments of those ancestors and deities with a superior and sometimes specialised knowledge whom only the king, via divination, could approach. 'The living and the dead were thus engaged in a communal, ritually structured conversation in which, just as the king's allies and officers made reports to him, so the Shang king made reports to his ancestors . . .'[21]

Though constituting a hierarchy of their own, ancestors, spirits and deities are not easy to distinguish. *Di*, the supreme deity equivalent to the king, was usually invoked indirectly and may or may not have been equated with the progenitor of the Shang lineage. But he seems to have fallen out of favour towards the end of the Anyang period and would disappear altogether under the Zhou dynasty. Other spirits responsible for the crops and the rivers were also consulted, as were once-ruling ancestors of the direct lineage plus a few Great Lords who were not royal ancestors. All these might be asked to intercede with *Di* or to act on their own. The ancestors, in particular, were expected to show loyalty to their lineage and to engage in its temporal concerns as actively as they had in life. Thus the stocking of royal tombs with food and drink in ritual bronze or ceramic vessels may not have been intended simply to provide sustenance for the deceased but also to ensure that they had the means to fulfil this intercessionary role by conducting their own ritual offerings.

Many such ancestors are named in the divinatory inscriptions. It was by identifying the names of some of them with those of kings as given in later texts that scholars were able to corroborate the Shang's historicity. But if the ancestors were usually on the side of the Shang, the supernatural concourse as a whole was far from being a rubber stamp. Royal proposals were not invariably endorsed, and *Di* especially could be a stern master. He might incite the Shang's enemies rather than connive with the Shang against them, or inflict catastrophe rather than avert it. A famous example concerned 'Lady Hao', who is identified in the inscriptions as a consort of King Wu Ding and who is presumed to be she of the extravagantly furnished tomb excavated intact at Anyang. When Lady Hao became pregnant, Wu Ding hoped for a male heir – the Shang succession was patrilinear – and duly lobbied the gods to that effect. His 'charge' that 'Lady Hao's child-bearing will be good' did not, however, bring the desired response. As 'read' by Wu Ding from the cracking, it said only that 'If it be on a *ding* day that she gives birth, there will be prolonged luck'. This was much too vague, so the king tried again. The response was still ambiguous: all now depended on the baby being born on either a *ding* day or a *geng* day, these being like, say, Thursday and Saturday in the Shang's ten-day week. The odds were still stacked against a happy outcome, and sure enough, 'After 31 days, on *jiayin* day, she gave birth and it was not good; it was a girl.'

Verificatory comments like this, added some time after the divination, are comparatively rare. Occasionally a weather forecast proved accurate – 'It really did rain' – or a hunt productive – the whole bag is listed. But the outcome of weightier matters, such as wars, is often uncertain and has to be inferred. Evidently the solemn performance of ritual consultation was more important than the efficacy or accuracy of the response. The object of the exercise was to exalt the Shang lineage, both living and dead, by demonstrating to dependants, subjects and enemies alike how long and distinguished this lineage was and how diligently the king strove to engage and mobilise it.

Such reassurance was needed in an environment that was both physically and politically hostile to the formation of a proto-state and a sophisticated culture. It has been deduced that the climate of the Yellow River basin was warmer and wetter in the second millennium BC than it is today. Average temperatures could have been as much as 2–4 degrees Celsius higher and scrub and woodland that much thicker. But the winters must still have been harsh. The usual grains were millets and perhaps wheat, rarely rice. Presumably because of the frosts, freshwater turtles were in short supply and plastrons had to be solicited from the Shang's southern neighbours; when some arrived alive, they were kept in ponds, but it does not appear that they bred. Other game was plentiful; buffalo, boar, deer and tigers are specified. But the tigers were probably of the Siberian species; and tropical trophies such as elephants and peacocks are rarely mentioned. Written sources from the succeeding Zhou period describe rivers so frozen that armies could march across the ice. Early autumn snowfalls and late spring frosts were accounted occupational hazards, critical for farmers and dynasts alike since no natural disaster was devoid of political portent.

Elsewhere in the ancient world, the famous zones of precocious literacy and urbanisation in the Nile, Tigris/Euphrates and Indus valleys were spared such conditions; there, as the weather warmed, the rising rivers obligingly irrigated the fields; when it cooled, gentle rains watered winter crops; the living was easy and the seeds of civilisation might germinate almost spontaneously. But five to ten latitudinal degrees farther north, upper China was no such incubator. Here life was precarious and survival laborious. Irrigation was almost unknown in Shang times, harvests were hit and miss, and meat, both hunted and reared, figured prominently in the dietary and sacrificial regimen. It may not be fanciful to suggest that the confidence with which the Shang used fire to melt bronze and crack bones owed something to discrimination acquired in fuel foraging and to long cold nights huddled round a glowing hearth.

The political climate was no more benign. The late Shang polity is usually described as 'a segmentary state', meaning that those under its direct rule were few while those under its outlying subordinates could be many. Subordinates and allies were usually joined to the Shang lineage by ties of kinship; they were the sons or brothers of kings, or descendants of such. They upheld Shang ritual observance and were in turn upheld by it. They revered the same divine-cum-ancestral host, followed the same mortuary customs and doubtless used the same script and calendar. Yet such shared interests did not guarantee their unflinching loyalty nor preclude their taking independent local action.

In between these centres of Shang power, numerous scattered and despised communities, probably speaking a different language, retained a full and sometimes formidable autonomy. Because of this presence, the Shang territories were neither contiguous nor easily defined. Kinship, not territory, linked the Shang domains. But from place-names and lineages mentioned in the oracular inscriptions it seems that at the end of the second millennium BC the Shang realm reached no farther than what is now northern Henan province and south-eastern Shanxi. Beyond were other 'segmentary states', some of them just as powerful with, as already noted, their own bronze-casting capacity and perhaps their own litera-ture. Small and vulnerable, both within and without, the Shang were at best 'first among equals' and by the eleventh century BC possibly not that.

More 'segmented' than 'state', then, Shang rule depended heavily on the energy of the sovereign. Judging by their divinations, the late Shang kings well appreciated this. As well as fulfilling their hectic ritual schedule, they 'went out', as the bones put it, repeatedly – to hunt, to fight, to oversee agriculture and to inspect their subordinate domains. They also removed their 'capital' (or cult centre) whenever it was thought to have become inauspicious, usually by reason of an enemy threat or some natural visit-ation. How often it moved is unclear since the site of the 'capital' was always called just 'this place' or 'Shang' (and latterly 'Yin') regardless of its location. Later texts mention seven removals, of which the Anyang site was certainly not the first but possibly the last. In fact Shang kingship has been well described as 'peripatetic'.[22]

For all the lineage boasting, for all the mortuary consumption, the technological precocity, the ritual rectitude and the despotic power, the late Shang kingdom was but a local proto-state and one among many. It may have enjoyed greater dominion prior to 1200 BC but not thereafter. In no way did it anticipate the great unitary empire of ten centuries later. Yet by 1045 BC, the currently preferred date for Shang's defeat by the Zhou, it had demonstrated many of the cultural traits that have come to be seen as typically, even peculiarly, Chinese; and it may well have been for this reason that later textual tradition selected the Shang for inclusion in that apostolic succession of dynasties.

The emphasis on kinship and lineage, on ancestor-worship, ritual observance and a calendrical system based on these, is obvious. Keightley also notes in the Shang's ritual dealings what he calls 'a characteristic this-worldliness' that would colour later Chinese philosophy and religion.[23] The ancestors and the gods had a practical part to play in human affairs; they were not so removed and transcendent as to be credited with impossible responsibilities like the creation of the world or the imposition of moral 'commandments'; they were there, in and about their tombs and temple-tablets, to be consulted, activated and used – for their example, their wisdom and their considerable influence.

Shang bronze-casting and its astounding artistic achievements provide early evidence of China's technological genius and aesthetic sophistication; but as is now clear, these skills and sensitivities were not exclusive to the Shang. Writing, on the other hand, may have been. It is remarkable enough that over three thousand years ago the Shang used a script that is recognisably Chinese today; that this script must have had a long pre-Anyang history is even more remarkable; and the use the Shang made of it is especially relevant. From the first, literacy was put to bureaucratic purpose. It was used to record official transactions and so, in effect, to produce historical documentation. Into the new era of textual record in the first millennium BC, literacy, authority and history went hand in hand.

2

SAGES AND HEROES

C. 1050 BC − *C.* 250 BC.

FOOTPRINTS OF ZHOU

THIRD AND LAST OF THE PRE-IMPERIAL 'Three Dynasties' (Xia, Shang, Zhou), the Zhou supplanted the Shang as the supreme power in the lower Yellow River basin in *c.* 1045 BC. They would still be there nearly 800 years later. In the course of this dynastic marathon some thirty-nine kings followed one another, mostly in orderly father-to-son succession. None of China's subsequent ruling lineages would last more than half as long; in fact the Zhou probably hold the world record for dynastic longevity.

Yet eight centuries – even BC ones – under a single dynasty could scarcely elapse without witnessing fundamental change. During this long haul the Zhou presided over an explosion in intellectual and artistic creativity that saw the composition of China's first classic texts and a transformation in society, government, statecraft and warfare. History finally clambers out of the dark burial chambers and the bone-filled sacrificial pits into the fitfully documented light of day. Dates cease to be approximate, territories cease to be disjointed; battle sites can be located and the fortunes of war discerned. Coinage appears; so do public works such as defensive walls and schemes for irrigation and flood control. Horizons expand. New cities are created and more land is brought under cultivation. From the

FORMER/WESTERN ZHOU KINGS, c.1045BC–770BC

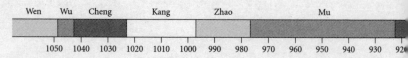

often laconic texts, there emerge recognisable personalities pursuing intelligible careers. Kinship and lineage are no longer the essential requisites for office; professional strategists and diplomats tout their services and tilt the scales of power. From the court, bureaucratic practices spread throughout the civil and military administration. Ritual undergoes what has been called a revolution. Subordinate jurisdictions emerge to parody and humble the mighty Zhou while competing aggressively with one another. State-formation proves, if anything, rather too successful.

In this catalogue of achievement nothing so became the Zhou themselves as their beginning. The early kings would be seen as epitomising ideals of just and virtuous rule, and their conduct would be the most closely studied and frequently cited of any in Chinese history. The later Zhou kings, on the other hand, would be more notable for the calibre of their contemporaries. Theirs was the age of Confucius and other sages, the birth era of Chinese philosophy, and the most fertile in terms of speculative enquiry and rational analysis. The long Zhou centuries, paralleling those of ancient Greece, combine both a heroic age and a classical age. In terms of China's civilisation, they are seminal times.

Yet they get short shrift in some history books. One substantial and respected work manages to hurdle the Zhou's eight centuries in as many pages, most of these being devoted to an explanation of the Chinese script and an excursion into world history.[1] The Zhou deserve better, although it has to be admitted that their story is poorly served by the surviving texts. 'These are but the dim footprints of ancient kings,' declared Laozi, the personification of Daoist (Taoist) teaching, during a supposed conversation with Confucius recorded in the fourth-century BC *Zhuangzi*. 'They tell us nothing of the force that guided their [i.e. the ancient kings'] steps . . . They are made by shoes but they are far from being shoes.'[2]

Nor is this forensic challenge the only problem facing the historian. Come the texts, come the Chinese penchant for naming names – then renaming ('rectifying') them while reappropriating the originals for other purposes. Non-Chinese readers will be appalled by the swarm of

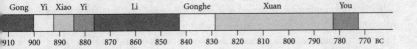

Gong	Yi	Xiao	Yi	Li	Gonghe	Xuan	You	
910	900	890	880	870	860	850	840	830	820	810	800	790	780	770 BC

same-sounding people, places and titles lying in wait for them. Like those readers wedded to the idea of China's manifest destiny as a unitary empire, they will be impatient to escape the enigmatic Zhou for their nemesis at the hands of Qin and for the triumphalism of *Qin* Shi Huangdi, 'the First Emperor'.

To be fair, Zhou rule, though long, was not often glorious. Initiative deserted all but a handful of kings; their defeats outnumbered their victories, and retraction soon overwhelmed expansion. Arguably Zhou's eight centuries comprised one of assertion followed by seven of reversion. Stripped progressively of territories, manpower, resources and relevance, they were eventually left with nothing but their legitimacy; had their kingdom been an empire, its protracted decline and fall would have rivalled that of Rome. Perhaps China needed the chaos of Zhou's last centuries to appreciate the order, and accept the sacrifices, that the Qin experiment in integration would involve. Or perhaps the Zhou centuries tell a different and more controversial story. Their combination of dynastic longevity, intellectual activity and, for the most part, low-level strife, far from demonstrating the necessity of unification, could suggest the vitality of more restricted allegiances and more local cultural traditions. Perhaps it was empire, not multi-state competition, which was the aberration.

Ironically the Zhou themselves, in justifying their initial success, provided a rationale for their eventual downfall. Their origins are disputed, but by the twelfth century BC they had established a jurisdiction in the valley of the Wei, a Yellow River tributary whose corridor of cultivation and passage (the main east–west railway nows runs alongside the Wei) fingers into the hills and deserts of Shaanxi province. It had once been, and may still have been, the western marches of the Shang domain, and it exposed the Zhou to frequent contact with a possibly proto-Tibetan frontier people called the Chiang. Zhou chiefs married Chiang brides, and it was with Chiang support that a Zhou leader, assuming the title of King Wen, challenged the Shang. On a third sortie down the Yellow River valley to the east, Wen's son and successor, King Wu, engaged the Shang host at a place called Muye. The date, by the latest calculation, was 1045 BC. The Zhou triumphed while the Shang were routed and their king committed suicide. After suppressing further resistance, King Wu of Zhou returned to his Wei valley home (near Xi'an, today another of those cities of 6 million souls) and died there within two years of his victory.

Later commentators, looking back with the benefit of hindsight – not to mention sideways for contemporary approval – had a ready explanation for this success: the Zhou had won Heaven's approval by their

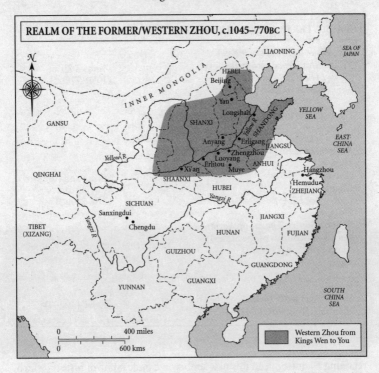

REALM OF THE FORMER/WESTERN ZHOU, c.1045–770BC

Western Zhou from Kings Wen to You

outstanding virtue while the Shang had forfeited it by their extreme degeneracy. Drunkenness, incest, cannibalism, pornographic songs and sadistic punishments enliven the catalogue of liturgical improprieties and governmental omissions later imputed to the last Shang king. Since the virtue that had once led to Shang's elevation had deserted it, so had its right to rule. Dynasties, like the seasons and the planets, conformed to a cyclical pattern. They ascended and declined at Heaven's cosmic behest. The Shang were doomed because Heaven had transferred its earthly 'mandate' to a worthier and more virtuous lineage. Defeat at Muye was therefore inevitable; indeed, the battle should have been a walkover.

This concept of 'Heaven's Mandate' or 'Heaven's Command' (*tian ming*) may, though, have been news to the Shang. As revealed in the oracle bones, Shang's supreme deity had been the stern and awesome *Di*; 'Heaven' as an impersonal and infallible authority receives scarcely a mention in the bone inscriptions. It seems, then, to have been the Zhou who, while for a time

CLASSIC TEXTS AND THEIR PROVENANCE	
Shanghsu (Book of Documents) *Yi Zhoushu (Zhou documents)* *Yijing (The Classic of Changes)* *Shijing (Book of Odes [Songs])*	Western Zhou (1050–770BC)
Chunqiu (Spring and Autumn Annals: Zuozhuan) *Zhanguoce* *Lunyu (Confucius, the Analects)* *Mengzi (Mencius)* *Mozi* *Han Feizi* *Guanzi* *Laozi (Daodejing)* *Zhuangzi* *Bingshu Sun-zi: The Art of Warfare* *Guoyu (Discourses of the States)* *Chuci (The Songs of Chu)* *Xunzi*	Spring and Autumn Warring States (770–250BC)
Huainanzi *Shiji* (Sima Qian's Records of the Historian) *Hanshu* (History of the Han)	Han (200BC–AD200)

retaining *Di*, introduced this new 'embryonic philosophy of history' which would become so fundamental to the legitimacy of every subsequent dynasty that it has been called 'the cornerstone of the Chinese Empire'.[3] As expounded by the Duke of Zhou, a younger brother of the deceased King Wu, power on earth derived from a supreme and impersonal entity called 'Heaven'; and it came in the form of a devolved 'mandate' whose term was finite and in some way contingent on the virtuous conduct of the holder.

The phrase itself – 'Heaven's Mandate' – first surfaces in a debate reported in the *Shangshu* that took place after King Wu's untimely death in *c.* 1043 BC. Wu's eldest son, the future King Cheng, was deemed too young or inexperienced to assume the reins of power immediately. A regency council was therefore preferred, and the Duke of Zhou, a consummate leader as well as the brother of the deceased Wu, duly assumed its direction with the support of a half-brother and the young king. But this triumviral arrangement was resented by several other royal brothers, who made common cause with a disgruntled scion of the defeated Shang and withheld recognition.

The Zhou, poised on the threshold of power and with vast new territories awaiting their control, could have done without a succession crisis that would rank 'as a defining moment not only for the Western Zhou but for the entire history of Chinese statecraft'.[4]

As war threatened, the young King Cheng, doubtless supervised by the doughty Duke of Zhou, consulted the ancestors by turtleshell-cracking. Cheng's grandfather Wen had done the same when the Zhou had first launched their bid for power. On that occasion Heaven had smiled on 'our raising up our little country of Zhou'; divination, in other words, confirmed the propriety of action. The same procedure now produced an equally reassuring reply; to a 'charge' about engaging the rebels, the cracked response was read as 'auspicious'. 'And so expansively I will take you east

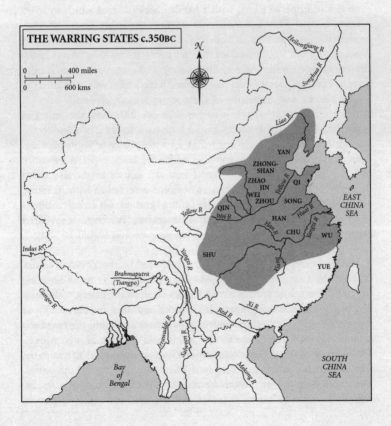

THE WARRING STATES c.350BC

to campaign,' declared the young king, 'Heaven's Mandate is not to be presumed upon; [but] the divination is aligned like this [in other words, favourably]'.[5]

War followed, and since the rebellious brothers were governing territories in what had once been Shang's central domains, the Zhou royal forces again swept east down the Yellow River, routing the enemy and not stopping this time until they reached the sea in Shandong province. An area of over 1,600 kilometres (1,000 miles) long by several hundred deep, in fact most of 'the cradle' that was north China, was now at Zhou disposal.

The victors parcelled it out among their kinsmen and commanders in the form of subordinate fiefs, many of which would become hereditary. From this division of the spoils were born the territorial units that would develop into states under the later Zhou and, later still, would provide the dynasties of imperial China with a handy checklist from which to select a dynastic name. They included, to the north of the Yellow River, Yan (near modern Beijing) and Jin, which would disintegrate into Han, Wei and Zhao; also Qi and Lu in Shandong (the first conferred on King Wen's Chiang ally, the second on the Duke of Zhou's son); and numerous lesser entities such as Tang and Song (where a contrite Shang leader was reinstated).

The history and geography of these states are not especially relevant at this point; but the way their names echo down through the centuries is notable. Most later dynasties would look back to the Zhou and to the states they had unwittingly created as a prime source of legitimisation. Besides appropriating their names – hence the later imperial dynasties of Jin, Wei, Tang, Song, etc. – great imperial houses might also claim descent from their ruling lineage or regional association with it. Either way, Zhou and its subordinate states came to embody an archaic authenticity out of all proportion to their achievements. Perceived as favoured exemplars, they conferred incontestable prestige and would be shamelessly exploited for it.

Just one exception may be noted. Established by the Zhou a century later on the steppe-land borders of Gansu province, the horse-breeding fief called Qin would seldom attract endorsement from posterity's dynastic giants. Though becoming a state, a kingdom and then an empire, Qin as a name would be little commandeered by others and, until the twentieth century, no orthodox Chinese ruler would care to be associated with it. Throughout most of history the royal Zhou so outranked the imperial Qin in heavenly kudos that they were often considered polar opposites. The Zhou, despite – or possibly because of – their tolerance of a 'feudal' federalism, were reckoned virtuous; and the Qin, with their aggressive centralism, were not. Only when patriotic nationalists revived the memory of Qin's first ever unification of China, and when Marxists and Maoists discovered the revolutionary credentials of its despotic instigator – not to mention terracotta evidence of his awesome power – would Qin cease to be a dirty word.

Following its comprehensive victory, the Zhou triumvirate headed by the Duke of Zhou founded an alternative capital near Luoyang in Henan province in what, to the Zhou, were then distant eastern regions. There, in *c.* 1035 BC after seven years as de facto regent, the wily Duke of Zhou stepped down from his management of affairs, declined to return to the ancestral capital in the west, and handed back the reins of power to the legitimate ruler, King Cheng. This act would be seen as one of magnificent abnegation and is that for which the Duke is most revered. Having steered the Zhou through their greatest crisis, presided over the creation of the kingdom, and largely formulated its heavenly rationale, the Duke could rather easily have usurped the throne. That he did not was convincing proof of superior virtue and would win him a reputation that almost eclipsed that of Kings Wen, Wu and Cheng. Historians without exception would exalt his memory and moralists would cherish his example; in *The Analects*, or 'Sayings', of Confucius the ageing philosopher is reported to have sighed: 'How I have gone downhill! It has been such a long time since I dreamt of the Duke of Zhou.'[6]

But whether the Duke really stepped aside, or whether he was pushed, is unclear. He may, it seems, have had a slightly different interpretation of the Heavenly Mandate to that of his fellow triumvirs. In another debate on the subject, he insists that the Mandate had passed from the Shang to 'the Zhou people', not just their king, and in particular to those Zhou people who, like himself, advised and instructed the king in the ways of virtue. This has been taken as a plea for a meritocracy – rule by those of proven ability and character – and it could imply greater empowerment of the bureaucracy and of enfeoffed officialdom. But it was not accepted by the Duke's colleagues, who trumped it with a reference to divination. Since only the king could consult Heaven directly, only he could enjoy the Mandate. As the chosen son of the senior Zhou lineage, he already, in a sense, embodied 'the Zhou people'. In the familial terms so dear to Confucianists he was both his people's father and 'Heaven's Son', a formulation that like the Mandate itself would be adopted by all subsequent rulers.

Yet whether this uniquely privileged status should be seen as a charter for autocracy, or whether as a check to it, would continue to be debated

– and still is. If Heaven's Son was accountable only to Heaven, he could afford to ignore advice. If, however, the Mandate depended on the virtue with which it was exercised, he needed to be more circumspect. Virtue was assessed in terms of the welfare of the state and its people. 'Heaven's love for the people is very great [says a character in the third-century BC *Zuozhuan*]. Would it then allow one man to preside over them in an arrogant and wilful manner, indulging his excesses and casting aside the nature Heaven and Earth allotted them? Surely it would not!'[7] Hence, were the ruler (after warnings in the form of portentous defeats, civil discontent or natural disasters) not to mend his ways, the Mandate would automatically slip from his grasp. It could then legitimately be claimed by someone else. Under such circumstances it could be construed not as a charter for absolutism but as an invitation to revolt. Whether or not that was his intention, the Duke of Zhou had opened a can-shaped *ding* of constitutional worms.

King Cheng, delivered at last from his ducal uncle's machinations, ruled uneventfully for over thirty years (*c.* 1035–*c.* 1003 BC). As his dying testament he left an admonition that would be long cherished and might usefully serve as an epitaph for the early Zhou: 'Make pliable those distant and make capable those near. Pacify and encourage the many countries, large and small.'[8] King Kang (r. *c.* 1003–*c.* 978 BC), Cheng's son and a contemporary of the biblical King David, heeded the advice, and while more inclined to encouragement than pacification, presided over a vast and flourishing kingdom. It was not until the reigns of his son and grandson, Kings Zhao (r. *c.* 977–*c.* 957 BC) and Mu (r. *c.* 956–*c.* 918 BC), that Zhou authority would experience its first setbacks.

Unfortunately for the historian, although avid diviners, the Zhou rarely troubled to inscribe their fire-cracked turtleshells with a written summary of 'charge' and response. But such information may have been recorded on less durable materials, for this was almost certainly the case with oracular communications conducted using a new and increasingly preferred medium. Kinder to turtles, the new medium involved a random disposition of sticks, which could be reused. The sticks were stalks of the yarrow plant or milfoil, and they were cast, perhaps like spillikins, six at a time, so that they fell to form hexagrams (six-sided figures) that the diviner then interpreted. Much lore, some art and some mathematics were involved; but it is safe to assume that the results were written down because the 'reading' of hexagrams provided the inspiration for 'The Book of Changes' (*Zhou yi* or *Yijing*, *I-ching*). This classic text, recorded in the ninth century BC, consists of verses that incorporate divinatory terms plus images that may have been those that the diviner 'read' in the hexagrams.

They also employ a technique typical of Chinese verse, and indeed literature and art as whole, which engages the reader by juxtaposing, or correlating, naturalistic images with human concerns to delightfully subtle, if sometimes obscure, effect. The same associative technique appears in another near-contemporary (but non-divinatory) classic. This is 'The Book of Songs' (*Shijing*, also called 'The Book of Odes'), on which Confucius is supposed later to have worked. The first of the 'Songs' – mostly ritual hymns, heroic verses and pastoral odes – provides a standard example of the correlational technique. The mewed call of an osprey is juxtaposed with a marriage proposal to convey, through terse imagery, onomatopoeia and pun (all largely lost in translation), a heavy sense of sexual expectation.

> *Guan, guan* cries the osprey
> On the river's isle.
> Delicate is the young girl:
> A fine match for the lord.[9]

(More than two millennia later, this same poem remained part of an educated person's repertoire. In *The Peony Pavilion*, a play written in 1598, the demure heroine experiences a sexual wanderlust when her tutor introduces her to it; or as her maid puts it to the tutor in a delightful English translation: 'Your classical exegesis/Has torn her heart to pieces.'[10])

Classics like the *Shijing* and *Yijing* reveal aspects of ritual practice and social life in early first-millennium BC China as well as the prevalence and development of literary culture. Historians, of course, would prefer something more factual and, as if to oblige, the Zhou compensated for their inarticulate oracle shells by incorporating inscriptions on their bronzes. Some of these are of considerable length and feature events or personalities known from other textual sources. They have been of great assistance in extending the chronology of the Zhou, which is famously anchored on an eclipse recorded in the texts and identified astronomically as occurring in 841 BC, 'the first absolute date in Chinese history'.

Most of the bronze inscriptions describe, or simply record, the bestowal of gifts, honours, offices, commands or lands. Taken in conjunction with stylistic changes in the bronzes themselves, with their archaeological setting and its wide distribution, and with later textual information, they confirm that, in the words of Jessica Rawson, 'the Zhou achievement was truly remarkable'. Although 'too little considered . . . [it] imprinted itself indelibly, not only on its own day, but on all succeeding generations'.[11]

LESS SPRING THAN AUTUMN

Painstaking analysis of Zhou mortuary sites and buried hoards, both of them rich in bronzes, has led Rawson to another conclusion: that an extraordinary change, indeed 'a revolution', overtook Zhou ritual practice in the first years of the ninth century BC. Quite suddenly bronze vessels became larger and more standardised in form, and they often comprised sets of identical items; their designs betrayed an interest in recreating archaic forms; their inscriptions were much more formulaic than previously; and they were accompanied by a new repertoire of bronze bells and jades.

It was a ritual 'revolution' to the extent that these changes implied a grander, noisier and more staged liturgy under firmer central control and involving greater public spectacle. Its standardisation throughout the northern 'Central Plain' must have owed something to better communications; cultivation was evidently being extended and neighbouring fiefs were beginning to abut. Moreover, the inscribed bronzes were apparently doubling as archival records, like the Shang's oracle bones, and being collected, displayed and hoarded as prestigious family heirlooms. But since they recorded royal favours, those who cherished them, and who in some cases had actually had them cast, were not their royal donors but their recipients, some of comparatively humble origin. The Zhou, in other words, were broadening their base of support while enhancing their own precedence.

Far from being a spent force then, by the early 800s BC Zhou authority, at least in ritual matters, was being projected more effectively than Shang authority had ever been. Rawson takes this to mean that the Zhou kings not only saw themselves as the successors of a unitary Shang state but 'believed . . . that the natural condition of China was such a single state' and proclaimed this political model with tenacity, despite the tensions it generated, 'within the more naturally fragmented Chinese region'.[12]

None of which is exactly contradicted by the dynastic dirge found in the written texts. Ritual rigidity need not, after all, imply political authority. The Zhou could have re-emphasised their formal precedence to compensate for military misfortunes; and their subordinate vassals could have conformed in ritual matters to disguise their political defiance. Alert to that correlational technique found in 'The Book of Songs', one should not perhaps look for explicit convergence. But it has to be said that this archaeological evidence for an ascendant Zhou is inconsistent, if not downright incompatible, with the written narrative of a declining Zhou.

According to the written sources, in 957 BC the Zhou king Zhao launched an ill-advised attack on Chu, a large tribute-paying but perhaps non-feudatory neighbour on Zhou's south-eastern border. The Zhou were roundly defeated, six armies being 'lost' while the king himself 'died' – possibly drowned, probably killed. Thirteen years later King Mu, his successor, did rather better against the 'Quan Rong', a people on Zhou's north-west frontier, but was unable to prevent the permanent breakaway of Zhou's easternmost vassals. 'The royal house declined and poets composed satires,' says Sima Qian, main author of the first-century BC history known as the *Shiji*. The next king had to be 'restored by the many lords', presumably because his throne had been usurped; and his successor must have encountered further trouble in the east, for he had occasion to boil alive the chief of Qi (in Shandong) in a cauldron.

About 860 BC – so at the height of Zhou's 'ritual revolution' – 'great Chu' took the offensive, invading Zhou territory and reaching a place called E in southern Henan. 'The [Zhou] royal house weakened . . . some of the many lords did not come to court but attacked each other.' Chu reinvaded in 855 BC, 'the many lords' continuing troublesome. The 200th anniversary of the Zhou's triumph at Muye found their young king in exile. A regency modelled on that once headed by the Duke of Zhou took over and not until fourteen years later did it stand down for the exile's son, Xuan.

King Xuan reigned long (827–782 BC) and aggressively. Vassal territories were reclaimed, tribute and trade relations with Chu may have been re-established, and western incursions by a people called the Xianyun (probably the same as the Quan Rong) were repulsed. But Zhou joy was short-lived. Heavy-handed intervention in Lu, another Shandong state, proved counterproductive, and 'from this time on, the many lords mostly rebelled against royal commands', says the *Shiji*.

The accession of King You in 781 BC was greeted by a cacophony of heavenly disgust, with a major earthquake, landslides and both a solar and a lunar eclipse. 'How vast the woe!' declared one of the Songs of such an appalling conjunction.

> The hundred rivers bubble and jump,
> The mountains and mounds crumble and fall,
> The high banks become valleys,
> And the deep valleys become ridges,
> Woeful are the men of today![13]

Implicit in all this was criticism of the king himself. As with the last of the Shang kings, any ruler facing imminent disaster had previously to have been hopelessly discredited as a favoured Son of Heaven. King You supposedly ignored all the omens, flouted tradition by manipulating the succession in order to gratify his favourite consort, and alienated his remaining vassals by repeatedly summoning them to the defence of the realm against imaginary invaders. Apparently Bao Si, the beguiling consort in question, particularly enjoyed this wheeze. But the vassals soon tired of it, and when in 771 BC the Xianyun did indeed attack, King You's cry of 'wolf' went unheeded. Left to their own devices, the Zhou were routed, their capital destroyed and their king killed.

Zhou fugitives, having hastily buried many bronzes for safe-keeping (and for the subsequent delight of archaeologists), headed east to their alternative capital at Luoyang. There, with the support of some still-loyal feudatories, King Ping, You's son, was restored and the ancestral temples reconstituted. The Zhou were not finished; over 400 years remained to them. But now creatures of their erstwhile vassals, they reigned without ruling. Once emperors in all but name, they clung henceforth to such influence as their ritual precedence afforded, like popes in all but patronage.

So ended the Western Zhou (*c.* 1045–771 BC) and so began the Eastern Zhou (772–256 BC). But because the Zhou kings would now play only a referee's role in the political mêlée, the latter is less often referred to as a dynastic period – 'Eastern Zhou' – than as a dynastic hiatus. This hiatus, a recurrent phenomenon in Chinese history which will merit attention, is divided into two parts: the 'Spring and Autumn' period and the 'Warring States' period. Both terms derive from the titles of relevant historical texts, with the 'Spring and Autumn' Annals (*Chunqiu*) covering the years 770–481 BC and the 'Warring States' Annals (*Zhanguoce*) the years 481–221 BC. Although the cut-off date between the two periods is debatable (475 or 453 BC are often preferred), basically the whole span witnessed intense competition between the multiplicity of one-time feudatories, now considered 'states', within and around the crumbling Zhou kingdom along the lower Yellow River.

During the three centuries of the 'Spring and Autumn' period there were more of these 'states', they were smaller, and the scale of conflict was contained at a not too disastrous level. Something like 148 semi-sovereign entities are mentioned in the *Zuozhuan*, a commentary on the 'Spring and Autumn' Annals; clearly, not only the Zhou but also their subordinates had been freely indulging in the fissiparous 'feudal' enfeoffment of relatives and dependants. But thanks to a process of gradual conquest and elimination, the active participants in the political tournament became fewer, larger and more formidable. The 148 dukedoms, city-states, combined townships and assorted enclaves shrank to thirty or so, and during the

'Warring States' period these would be further consolidated into seven, then three, major participants. As the contest neared its climax, the stakes grew higher and warfare more intense. 'Spring' contrived a canopy of constitutional respectability to hide Zhou's shame; 'Autumn' shredded this political foliage; and in its wintry aftermath, 'warring state' would clash with 'warring state' in a fight to the death.

The details would be enough to drown any tender narrative. An ambitious study recently contrasted this bellicose aggregation-into-empire of ancient China's 'states' with the opposite tendency in early modern Europe – the rejection of unitary empire and the entrenchment of a multi-state system as a result of equally internecine competition. But whereas the study accepted a list of eighty-nine wars involving the European 'Great Powers' during the roughly four centuries prior to AD 1815, no less than 256 wars were individually identified for northern China's 'Great Powers' during the roughly four centuries prior to 221 BC – and this after the exclusion of all purely civil conflicts and any of an external nature or involving nomadic peoples.[14]

Happily many of these wars appear to have been brief and fairly bloodless. They were also subordinate, even incidental, to the far more complex game of political alliances and stratagems that constituted contemporary statecraft. Bribe and bluff turned the tables quite as often as warfare, the wasteful nature of which, together with its unpredictable outcome, made it a recourse of last resort. No strangers to the balance of power, the Chinese 'states' set lofty standards in realpolitik. Scruple-free statesmen would later turn to the 'Spring and Autumn' Annals for inspiration; Machiavelli might have scanned them with profit. As the *Zuozhuan* ('Zuo's Commentary' on the often enigmatic 'footprints' of the annals themselves) makes clear, the heroes of the period were not halberd-wielding warriors and charioteers but strategists, schemers and honey-tongued spokesmen.

Nevertheless, a just-possible synchronism, plus the epic character of the *Zuozhuan* with its frequent battles, intrigues and debates, has invited comparison with the Homeric and Sanskrit epics. Gods are notable by their absence in the Chinese text; but counterparts for bluff Hector or lofty Priam of the *Iliad* put in an appearance, while the exploits of Chonger, a central character in the *Zuozhuan*, mirror those of Rama or the Pandavas in the Indian classics.

Chonger was the son of the ruler of Jin, a large state loyal to the Zhou which extended north from the Yellow River into Shanxi province. His chances of the succession were remote, however, his mother being a Rong (that is non-Xia or non-'Chinese') and his appearance being physical proof of this handicap; his ribs were said to be fused together and there was something odd about his ears. 'Chonger' literally means 'double-eared', a sobriquet presumably preferable to 'single-eared' but here taken to indicate some peculiarity, perhaps pendulous lobes. Sealing his fate by being implicated in a plot, in 655 BC the youthful Chonger fled into exile and so embarked on a nineteen-year saga of picaresque adventure.

Accompanied by a band of loyal and capable companions, Chonger first spent some years among the Di, another non-Xia people, and then wandered extensively throughout the Zhou states and south as far as the great state of Chu in the Yangzi basin. Useful contacts and insights were acquired and feats of statecraft performed. Also contracted were debts-to-be-repaid, scores-to-be-settled and brides-to-be-deserted – in equal measure. With a growing reputation for outspoken courage and with plentiful evidence of Heaven's favour, the prodigal Chonger returned to his native Jin on the death of his ruling half-brother and duly succeeded him as Jin Wen Gong ('Duke Wen of Jin') in 636 BC.

A year later Jin's forces restored the legitimate Zhou king after he had been temporarily ousted from his embattled enclave at Luoyang. Then in 634 BC they defeated an invading army from Chu at a place called Chengpu. It was the first battle in Chinese history that was recorded in sufficient detail for modern military historians to produce a plan of engagement showing rectangular troop concentrations and arrowed lines of advance.[15] A hundred war chariots and a thousand foot-soldiers were captured for presentation to the Zhou king, who now feted the once outcast Chonger as the saviour of *zhongguo* ('the central states') and officially recognised him as *ba*, a title that may be rendered as 'overlord' or 'protector of the realm'.

Terms like *ba*, *gong* and *zhongguo* pose a problem since they are conventionally translated into non-Chinese languages in a somewhat random fashion. *Ba*, for instance, is commonly rendered as 'hegemon', a Greek title awarded to one of the near-contemporary Hellenic city-states, usually Sparta or Athens, in recognition of its primacy and leadership. In China the 'hegemony' also changed hands; the ruler of Qi in Shandong had previously held it, and Jin would later be succeeded as *ba* by Chu, Wu, Qin and others. But in its Chinese context, the term was meaningless without the legitimacy and overall authority, albeit nominal, of the Zhou. Accepting his appointment at the third time of asking – a deferential convention – the Jin ruler made this clear: 'Chonger ventures to bow twice, touching his head to the ground, and respectfully accepts and publishes abroad these illustrious, enlightened and excellent commands of the [Zhou] Son of Heaven.'[16]

Lip-service to the Heavenly Mandate and to the idea of a single ruling lineage survived, and it set apart those who adhered to it – the so-called Xia (sometimes Hua-Xia) people – from peoples who did not, such as the Rong and the Di. In both the Greek and Chinese worlds a literate and increasingly urban society now shared a sense of superior distinction that transcended internal conflicts. The Greek states sublimated their differences at the sanctuary of Zeus at Olympia, where the first games were supposedly staged as early as 776 BC. Less famously, the Chinese states, while observing certain conventions in their cut-throat statecraft as if it too were a competitive sport, also held athletic games. Instituted by the up-and-coming state of Qin in the early 'Warring States' period, they included trials of strength, dancing, archery, chariot-racing and some sort of butting contest involving horns.[17]

While the Greek 'hegemon' serves as a rendering of *ba*, it is the 'duc' or 'duke' of the Romance languages which is invariably used to translate *gong*; hence 'Duke of Zhou' for *Zhou gong*. In similar fashion 'marquis' is used for *hou*, 'viscount' for *zi*, and so on down through the rungs of the European aristocracy and the rankings of the Zhou elite to 'esquire' or 'knight' for *shi*. This convention was adopted because social and economic relationships in ancient China seemed to conform to what European historians understand by 'feudalism'. But the analogy should not be taken too far. Zhou China and medieval Europe differed – by, at the crudest, some 8,000 kilometres (5,000 miles) and 1,500 years. Additionally Marxist historians, while insisting on a prior age of slavery under the Shang, have quibbled over just when the supposed transition to feudalism may have taken place; and others have doubted whether Chinese feudalism ever involved the contractual relationships that underpinned the European system (and led, for instance, to English barons demanding a Magna Carta).[18] But the use of 'duke', 'marquis', etc. continues, and it has led to the introduction into Chinese history-writing of other exotic and perhaps misleading terms, such as 'manorial lands' and 'seigneurial rights'.

Zhongguo is in another category. The word in Chinese consists of two characters, the *zhong* character clearly depicting 'central', 'middle' or 'inner', and the *guo* character meaning 'state' or 'kingdom'. It is in fact the name by which the Chinese still know their country today, 'China' itself being as much an alien expression to the people who live there as, until the nineteenth century, 'India' was to the people who live there. As the geographical name of the modern republic, *zhongguo* ('the Central State' or 'Central Country') appears on politically correct maps, and its twin characters feature among the six officially used to express the phrase that is translated as 'The People's Republic of China'. The same two characters, however, were once no less correctly rendered as 'the Middle Kingdom'; and before that they were used to indicate the 'central states' of the later Zhou (for *guo*, like all Chinese nouns, can be either singular or plural).

In other words, depending on its historical context, *zhongguo* can designate a small nucleus of antagonistic states in northern China or its antithesis – a vast east-Asian agglomeration of territories under a single centralised government. The term is almost as misleading as 'the Great Wall'. But promoters of a long and continuous tradition of Chinese civilisation rightly stress that only a shared sense of identity could have generated the concept in the first place. 'The central states' of the 'Spring and Autumn' and 'Warring States' periods shared a common culture; they already evinced what has been called 'a superiority complex' in relation to their less literate neighbours; and in their nominal allegiance to the Zhou and Heaven's Mandate they preserved amid the harsh realities of competitive coexistence the ideal of a more harmonious political hierarchy under a single and more effective dispensation.

THE CONFUCIAN CONVEYANCE

Through this shared world and culture of the later Zhou's 'central states' there roamed not only exiled adventurers like Chonger of Jin but merchants and craftsmen, teachers, magicians, moralists, philosophers and charlatans. It was Asia's age of itinerancy. Beyond the Himalayas the Gangetic plain also swarmed with vagrants – renunciates, metaphysicians, miracle-workers and holy men; among them were Mahavira, the founding *jina* of Jainism, and Siddhartha Gautama, the Buddha ('Enlightened One') whose teachings would enjoy a longer currency in China than in India. In both countries the multiplicity of hard-pressed states and rival courts offered avid listeners and potential patronage. Troubled times inspired a spirit of enquiry and a predisposition towards novel solutions. So too did social upheaval and the emergence of a market economy.

In northern China, social integration was already under way. In the later Zhou period the fortified cities of the Zhou's feudatory states extended their writ beyond their immediate hinterlands to incorporate less assertive communities. These were often comprised of non-Xia peoples, whom the literate Xia knew as Di and Rong (in the west and north) or Man and Yi (in the south and east). Subdued by conquest or seduced by alliance (typically including marriages like that of Chonger's mother), the non-Xia chiefs embraced the 'feudal' system of exploitation and exacted the usual tithes from whatever resources of land and labour they commanded. Under the early (Western) Zhou, agricultural exactions had taken the form of service, with the peasant labouring on a portion of his holding for his 'feudal' superior under a division of agrarian activity known as the 'well-field' system. But by the late 'Spring and Autumn' period a tax on individual holdings was steadily replacing it.

The tax was paid in kind, although at about the same time, in the sixth century BC, metallic coinage made its appearance. Foundries, once reserved for the production of ritual bronzes, had already begun turning out weapons and farm implements such as spades and ploughshares. The latter, increasingly of iron, plus the wider use of draught animals, made feasible the reclamation of heavy marginal lands, the terracing and irrigation of steeper loess slopes and the introduction of a winter sowing of wheat. The importance of the new tools may be inferred from the value attached to miniature bronze replicas of them, for it was these same pocket-rending playthings which served as the first coins. 'Knife-money', complete with blade and handle, was favoured in Qi; and more than a thousand stumpy 'spade-coins' have been found in a single hoard in Jin. They were evidently used as both a medium of exchange and a means of wealth accumulation. Trade was no longer restricted to tributary exactions and official gift presentations. By road and river commodities were being moved in bulk, while from far beyond the 'central states' came exotica like jades from Xinjiang, ivories and feathers from the south. The *Zuozhuan* mentions merchants and customs posts; the marketplace was an important feature of contemporary city-planning.

But perhaps the most crucial development is one that is less easy to isolate, for demographic change, like climate change, may be almost as imperceptible as it is decisive. The most compelling evidence comes from a recent statistical study of the *Zuozhuan*.[19] This revealed that, whereas at the beginning of the 'Spring and Autumn' period all the most active participants mentioned in the text were the sons of rulers, during the middle of the period they were mostly ministers or members of the ministerial nobility, and by the end of the period they were overwhelmingly *shi*, a term that originally meant something like 'knight' but was now applied to all educated Xia 'gentlemen' without much regard to descent or profession. Thanks to natural fertility and higher agricultural yields the population had expanded and with it the whole demographic base of Xia society.

The *shi*, later burdened in English translation with functional descriptions such as 'the literati', 'the governing class', 'the guardians of Chinese tradition' and 'the backbone of the bureaucracy', were still seeking a role in the 'Spring and Autumn' period. Birth conferred on them more in the way of expectation than privilege. The younger sons of younger sons, collaterals or commoners who had acquired an education, they coveted employment and to that end cultivated professional expertise. As policy advisers, literary authorities, moral guardians, diplomatic go-betweens, bureaucratic reformers and interpreters of omens, they represent a distinct phenomenon of the age and would become a feature of later imperial government. Though once 'knights', only a few *shi* now saw active military service; fewer still engaged in agriculture or trade. Their worth lay in words, their skills in debate, and their value in a potent mix of high-mindedness and ingenuity.

Not all *shi* embraced the competitive job market. China too had its renunciates; their teachings in favour of personal detachment, emotional vacuity, various physical disciplines and a back-to-nature primitivism would be compounded into such works as the famously demanding *Daodejing* ('The Way and Integrity Classic', *Tao-te ching*). Though compiled in the third century BC, it is attributed to one Laozi ('Old Master', *Lao-tzu*), who, if he existed, may have lived 200 years earlier. The more rewarding *Zhuangzi* (*Chuang-tzu*) of perhaps the fourth century BC is another such compilation named for its supposed author but containing many interpolations. Both works as finally put together would be in part a reaction against the teachings of Confucius, a man with 'brambles for brains', according to the *Zhuangzi*. Much later, both works would become central to the canon of Daoism (Taoism) when it emerged as a not exactly coherent school of thought in the first century AD.

Other *shi*, while welcoming the opportunity of employment, were not very successful in obtaining it. From the little state of Lu in Shandong, a bastion of conservatism once ruled by the now sidelined descendants of the Duke of Zhou, one such son of a 'gentleman' set off to make his name around 500 BC. Like his father, a military man of legendary strength who was supposed to have held a portcullis aloft, this Kong Qiu seems to have had a sturdy presence and is further credited with a physical peculiarity – always an indication of future distinction – consisting of a lump on the head; perhaps it was just a very high forehead. He was not, though, interested in warfare like his father, and despite his distinctive appearance found recognition elusive. He was gone for thirteen years, travelling through many of 'the central states', by one of which he was briefly employed. But in a stressful age, finding a patron who met his lofty standards proved difficult, and finding one who would attend to his idealistic injunctions nigh imposs- ible. Kong Qiu returned to Lu an admirable, if slightly ridiculous, failure.

'Great indeed is Kong Qiu! He has wide learning but he has not made a name for himself in any field' [scoffed a village wag].

The Master, on hearing this, said to his disciples, 'What then should I make my speciality? Chariot-driving perhaps? Or archery? I think I should prefer driving.'[20]

Occasionally sarcastic but never resentful, the man known outside China as Confucius (a Latinisation of 'Kong Fuzi', 'Master Kong') would serve out the rest of his days as a poorly paid minor official in the irrelevant state of his birth. The Buddha found a large following in his lifetime; kings revered him and when (conventionally about 483 BC but probably later) he achieved nirvana, his relics were carefully preserved and piously distrib- uted. But 'the Master', when he died in 479 BC, was mourned only by his small circle of disciples – and maybe Mrs Confucius, a lady so inconspic- uous that nothing beyond her once having given birth is known. Nor was there any Confucian cult until several centuries later, by when the facts of his life had been decently obscured by legend, and a whole corpus of texts awarded to him, most of them erroneously. Seldom has posterity been so generous; seldom has such a dismal career ultimately been rewarded with such universal esteem.

That Confucius was a formidable scholar and an inspirational mentor with a well-defined mission is more relevant. In a thumbnail autobiog- raphy, his professional aspirations receive not a mention:

At fifteen my heart was set upon learning; at forty I was no longer perplexed; at fifty I understood Heaven's Decree; at sixty I was attuned to wisdom; at seventy I could follow my heart's desires without over- stepping the mark.[21]

Like Socrates, who was born just a decade after Confucius's death, he believed that morality and virtue would triumph if only men would study. Take a town of 10,000 households, he told his followers. It would surely contain many who were as loyal and trustworthy as he, but there would be none who cared as much about learning as he. In the course of his intellectual odyssey, he may actually have written the short 'Spring and Autumn' Annals (*Chunqiu*) – he was certainly familiar with them – and he may have contributed to the compilation of other works such as 'The Book of Songs' (*Shijing*), a particular favourite. But the authorship of all such texts is problematic; their compilation in the forms that survive today resulted from several 'layers' of scholarship, not to mention dollops of blatant fabrication, spread over many centuries.

The same is true of parts of his collected sayings, known as *The Analects* (*Lunyu*), and from which the quotations above are taken. But it is thought that other parts genuinely represent what the Master said in conversation with his disciples. They thus have an identity and an immediacy that are more akin to those of the Gospels than, say, the *jataka* stories on which the Buddha's life is based. Here then is what Laozi might have called a proper 'shoe', not just 'a footprint', a recognisable voice, the first in China's history and arguably the greatest, addressing and exhorting the listener directly. Sometimes combative like an out-of-sorts Dr Johnson, the Master belies his dry-as-dust reputation, endearing himself to the reader much as he did to his disciples.

Confucius himself always disclaimed originality. Although there is little consensus about many of his key concepts – and even less about which English words best represent them – the gist of his teaching seems not especially controversial. Sons must honour their fathers, wives their husbands, younger brothers their elder brothers, subjects their rulers. 'Gentlemen' should be loyal, truthful, careful in speech and above all 'humane' in the sense of treating others as they would expect to be treated themselves. Rulers, while enjoying the confidence of the people and ensuring that they are fed and safe, should be attuned to Heaven's Mandate and as aloof and constant as the northern star. Laws and punishments invite only evasion; better to rule by moral example and exemplary observance of the rites; the people will then be shamed into correcting themselves. Self-cultivation, or self-correction (a forebear of Maoist 'self-criticism'), is the key to virtue. Of death and the afterlife, let alone 'portents, prodigies, disorders and deities', Confucius has nothing to say. It is up to the individual, assisted by his teacher, to cultivate himself. Not even he was born with knowledge; he is just 'someone who loves the past and is diligent in seeking it'.[22]

'I transmit but do not innovate. I am truthful in what I say and devoted to antiquity.'[23] For Confucius, 'the Way' was the way of the past and his job was that of transmitting it or conveying it. The mythical Five Emperors, the Xia, the Shang and above all the Zhou – these were the models to which society must return if order was to be restored. 'I am for the Zhou,' he declared, meaning not the hapless incumbent in Luoyang but Kings Wu, Wen, Cheng and Kang of the early (Western) Zhou and of course the admirable Duke of Zhou. The rites of personal conduct and public sacrifice must be observed scrupulously; more important, they must, as of old, be observed sincerely. The 'rectification of names', a quintessentially Confucian doctrine, was a plea not for the redefinition of key titles and concepts in the light of modern usage but for the revival of the true meaning and significance that originally attached to them. More a legitimist than a conservative, Confucius elevated the past, or his interpretation of it, into a moral imperative for the present.

And there it would stay for two and half millennia. It was as if history, like Heaven, brandished a 'mandate' that no ruler could afford to ignore. But this general principle soon came to transcend the particular injunctions contained in the few, if pithy, soundbites of *The Analects*. Aboard the Master's 'conveyance', and labelled as 'Confucianist' (rather than 'Confucian'), then 'Neo-Confucianist', would be loaded all manner of doubtful merchandise. History would prove more tractable than Heaven.

WARRING STATES AND STATIST WARS

By the time Confucius died in 479 BC, the 'Spring and Autumn' period was fast fading into the crisis-ridden 'Warring States' period. Already the large state of Jin, once ruled by Chonger, was disintegrating. Not until the end of the century would it be consolidated into the three states of Han, Zhao and Wei (not to be confused with the river of that name), so presenting the Zhou king in Luoyang, their supposed superior, with an unwelcome fait accompli. When he did reluctantly accept it, it is said that the bronze cauldrons of Zhou, symbols of the ancient dynasty's virtue, 'shook'. Also shaken, in fact toppled, within a century of Confucius's death was the ruling house of Qi, the largest state in Shandong. In a *fin de siècle* atmosphere 'all now took it for granted that eventually the now purely nominal Zhou dynasty would inevitably be replaced by a new world power'.[24]

The ferocious fight to the death among the strongest of the remaining states makes for grim telling. Standing armies take the field for the first time, new methods of warfare swell the casualties, and statecraft becomes more ruthless. Yet the period is by no means devoid of other arts. Stimulated by the disciples and heirs of Confucius, China's great tradition of philosophical speculation was born. It was an era, too, of startling artistic creation in which traditional arts began to break free from the constraints of ritual. And from the recent excavation of a host of contemporary texts it appears to have been an important age for medicine, natural philosophy and the occult sciences. Far from being a cultural cesspool, the 'Warring

States' period, like other interludes of political instability, sparkles with intellectual activity and artistic mastery.

Of all the tombs excavated in the late twentieth century, perhaps the most surprising were those opened in 1978 and 1981 at Leigudun near the city of Suizhou in Hubei province. South of the arena in which the 'central states' competed and nearer the Yangzi than the Yellow River, Leigudun was the capital of a mini-state called Zeng. During the 'Spring and Autumn' period Zeng had been subordinated by Chu, the great southern power that had once contended with the early (Western) Zhou and later with Chonger of Jin.

Although Zeng's rulers had retained the rank of 'marquis', the minor status of their beleaguered marquisate promised the archaeologists nothing special in the way of grave goods. It was pure luck that one of the tombs proved to be that of the ruler himself, Zeng Hou Yi ('Marquis Yi of Zeng'), who died about 433 BC. Even foreknowledge of this elite presence would hardly have prepared the diggers for the staggering array of exquisite jades, naturalistic lacquerware and monumental bronzes that were laboriously brought to the surface. Now occupying half of a palatial museum in the provincial capital of Wuchang (part of the three-city Wuhan complex), the contents of the Zeng Hou Yi tomb have been described by Li Ling, director of the 'Mass Work Department' responsible for the excavation, as an exceptional discovery 'that shocked the country and the world as well'.[25]

Leigudun's 114 bronzes weigh in at over ten tonnes, yet they 'shock' more by reason of the lacy profusion of their openwork decoration. Squirming with snakes, dripping with dragons and prickly with other sculptural protuberances, their shapes are further obscured by a fretwork of the wormy encrustation known as vermiculation. They look as if they have lain for two and a half millennia not in the ground but on the seabed and been colonised by crustacea. For this triumph of flamboyance over form – and of the lost-wax process over in-mould casting – one should not fault the marquis's taste. Sites elsewhere in Chu territory have yielded items nearly as extravagant. But at Leigudun ornamentation was taken about as far as metal-melting would permit. Chu's connoisseurs of the fanciful and intricate were already turning to lacquerware, inlay and fine silks. As the storm clouds gathered over the *zhongguo*, the courts and artisans of this south-central state would establish a tradition of cultural exuberance and eccentric exoticism that, in the plaintive Songs of Chu (*Chuci*), would long survive the political extinction of 'great Chu'.

The centrepiece of the Leigudun collection is a house-size musical ensemble consisting of sixty-five bronze bells with a combined weight of

2,500 kilograms (5,500 pounds). The bells are clapper-less (they were struck with wooden mallets), arranged according to size, and suspended in three tiers from a massive and highly ornate timber frame, part-lacquered in red and black. In an unusual but highly successful foray into figurative sculpture, bronze caryatids with swords in their belts and arms aloft stand braced to support each tier. At the centre of the ensemble the largest bell is a replacement. Its design is more elaborate than the others and it carries a dedicatory inscription to the effect that King Hui of Chu, hearing of the death of Marquis Yi of Zeng, had had this bell specially cast and sent it as an offering to be employed in the marquis's mortuary rites.

Significantly, the Chu ruler is here described as *wang*, that is 'king', a title still reserved to the fading Zhou, not adopted by other warring states until the late fourth century BC, but in use in Chu since at least the tenth century BC. Chu was evidently in a league apart from the 'central states', although its political trajectory is far from clear. Originating somewhere in southern Henan or northern Hubei, it had slowly spread to embrace an enormous arc through what is now central China from the Huai River basin to the Yangzi gorges and Sichuan. Expansion was largely at the cost of non-Xia peoples, referred to as Man, whose traditions no doubt account for Chu's distinctive cultural profile and whose incorporation may explain why the 'central states' disparaged Chu as non-Xia and so 'not one of us'.

Southward expansion had brought Chu into contact with other culturally hybrid polities outside the 'central states'. In effect the *zhongguo* 'cradle' of Chinese civilisation in the north was already being challenged by the states of 'core' China farther south. They included Wu in the region of the Yangzi delta in Zhejiang, and Yue to the south of Wu in Fujian, with both of whom Chu was occasionally at war. In the late sixth century BC, Wu had overrun Chu and obliged its king to flee to Zeng, where the then marquis had given him protection. Frustrated by this grant of sanctuary, the Wu ruler had vented his fury on an earlier Chu king, whose corpse, or what remained of it, was exhumed, publicly flogged and thoroughly dismembered. Wu's ruler was made *ba* ('hegemon') in 482 BC but nine years later was conquered by Yue. Chu thereupon retook most of its lost territory; and it is supposed that it was in remembrance of Zeng's act of mercy to his fugitive predecessor that in 433 BC King Hui of Chu caused the great central bell of the Leigudun ensemble to be cast for the tomb of Marquis Yi, the grandson of Chu's saviour.

States like Chu, Wu and Yue that were located around or beyond the perimeter of the northern 'central plain' figure prominently from the fifth century BC onwards. Their consolidation may have benefited from immigration as refugees fled from the fighting in the north, and they certainly took advantage of a wave of centralising reforms that significantly advanced state formation throughout China in the sixth to fourth centuries BC. Cause and effect are hard to distinguish in this process. To adapt a formulation used in respect of the European states in the later Middle Ages, during the 'Warring States' period 'the state made war and war made the state'.[26] Although in China the state proved a better warmonger than war did a state-monger – for the wars got worse and the states got fewer – the military imperative of mobilising all possible resources clearly depended on civil reforms that strengthened the authority of the state.

Qi in Shandong had pioneered the process and most other states followed suit, the last and most thoroughgoing reforms being those in Qin. Essentially the reforms reversed the earlier trend towards feudal fragmentation. Borderlands and newly conquered or reconquered territories, instead of being granted out as fiefs, were formed into administrative 'counties' or 'commanderies' under centrally appointed ministers and could thus serve as recruitment units. This system was then extended to the rest of the state; population registration and the introduction of a capitation tax would soon follow. Meanwhile oaths, sealed in blood, were sworn to secure the loyalty of subordinate lineages, while rival lineages might be officially proscribed. Regulations and laws were standardised and then 'published' in bronze inscriptions. Land was gradually re-allocated in return for a tax on its yield, the tax being increasingly paid in coin.

Histories, such as the *Zhanguoce* and the later *Shiji*, tend to deal with such developments in terms of personnel rather than policy. Reforms receive mention when they can be credited to a minister or adviser deemed worthy of his own biographical sketch. Viewed thus, the rivalry between the warring states includes an important element of competitive headhunting. Attracting the loftiest minds, the most ingenious strategists and the most feared generals not only improved a ruler's chances of victory but advertised his virtuous credentials (for virtue attracted expertise like a magnet) and so advanced his candidacy for the award of Heaven's Mandate.

Job-hunting *shi* in general rejoiced; and especially favoured were those savants who, while extending or rejecting the teachings of Confucius, propounded theories about authority and human motivation that included good practical insights into some aspect of statecraft or man-management. Mozi ('Master Mo', *c.* 480–*c.* 390 BC, but known only for his eponymous text), after advocating a more frugal, caring and pacific society, appended some twenty chapters on defensive tactics, they being the only kind of military activity in which a peace-loving disciple of Mozi (or a Mohist) might decently engage. Unconventional and idealistic, Mohism seems to have been most influential in the ever-eccentric Chu.

Mengzi lived about fifty years later and found employment at the court of Wei, but he too is otherwise an obscure figure. Devoted to the memory of Confucius, he fleshed out the Master's utterances into a detailed programme for reform: emulate the mythical Five Emperors and the Three Dynasties (Xia, Shang and Zhou), urged Mengzi; respect Heaven's Mandate, reduce punishments and taxes, and reinstate the 'well-field' system of land-holding; in an age of greed and violence only a ruler who abjured oppression, who cultivated virtue and consulted the welfare of the people, would be sure to triumph; likewise for society as a whole – morality would prevail if human nature was allowed to realise its basic goodness. All of which, while reassuring, made little impression on *zhongguo*'s power-crazed warlords. Only later would it win for Mengzi the title of 'second sage' in the great Confucian tradition and later still the Latinisation of his name into 'Mencius' by Rome's almost-approving missionaries.

Of far more influence, and decisive for the triumph of centralised government in the state of Qin, was a school of thought known as 'legalism'. Later histories credit, or more usually condemn, one Shang Yang, minister of Qin from 356 BC, for erecting the draconian framework of the first 'legalist' state, although it would be left to others to provide a theoretical basis for it. Like Chu in the south, Qin in the far north-west was peripheral to the 'central states' and was habitually disparaged by them as non-Xia. It had expanded into the valley of the River Wei, once the Western Zhou heartland, but its roots lay farther west and its population included large numbers of pastoral Rong. Problems of integration and defence kept Qin on the sidelines until Shang Yang, after learning his trade in Wei state, interested Qin's duke in a programme of radical restructuring. The 'county' system of direct administration was introduced, weights and measures standardised, trade heavily taxed, agriculture encouraged with irrigation and colonisation schemes, and the entire population registered, individually taxed and universally conscripted. 'Mobilising the masses' was not a twentieth-century innovation.

The carrot in all this was an elaborate system of rankings, each with privileges and emoluments, by which the indvidual might advance according to a fixed tariff; in battle, for instance, decapitating one of the enemy brought automatic promotion by one rank. But more effective than the carrot was the stick, which took the form of a legal code enjoining ferocious and indiscriminate punishments for even minor derelictions. Households were grouped together in fives or tens, each group being mutually responsible for reporting any indiscretion by its members; failing an informant, the whole group was mutually liable for the prescribed punishment. In battle this translated into a punitive *esprit de corps*. Serving members of the same household group were expected to arrest any comrade who fled, to deliver a fixed quota of enemy heads, and to suffer collective punishment if they failed on either count. Shang Yang was himself a capable general and may have led some of these conscript units (or perhaps 'neighbourhood militias') when Qin forces scored a decisive victory over the state of Wei in 341 BC. Sixteen years later Qin's duke assumed the title of 'king'. But by then Shang Yang, following the death of his patron, had fallen foul of his own penal code and been condemned to an ignominious extinction, being 'torn apart by carriages'.[27]

In practice it may have been that not all these measures were Shang Yang's. Some may have been awarded him posthumously by the back-dating beloved of historians. And they may not have been as harsh as they are portrayed; discrediting Qin and its policies would be a priority of the subsequent Han dynasty, during whose long ascendancy Qin's history would be compiled. The reforms were nevertheless sensationally effective. Besides again ravaging Wei state, in 316 BC Qin's forces swept south over the Qinling mountains into Sichuan and thus, as will be seen, secured a vast new source of cereals and manpower plus some important strategic leverage over Chu. During the last century of the 'Warring States' (*c.* 320–220 BC) Qin was more than a match for any of its rivals. It largely dictated the ever shifting pattern of alliances and it initiated about forty of the sixty 'great power wars' recorded for the period.

Visiting Xianyang, Qin's new capital, in *c.* 263 BC the philosopher Xunzi was both impressed and appalled – impressed by the decorum and the quiet sense of purpose, appalled by the lack of scholarship and the plight of the people; they were 'terrorised by authority, embittered by hardship, cajoled by rewards and cowed by punishments'. In fact the whole state seemed to be 'living in constant terror and apprehension lest the rest of the world should someday unite and strike it down'.[28] Xunzi wanted nothing to do with the place, and having previously directed the Jixia, an intellectual academy in the state of Qi, he hastened on to a more congenial post in Zhao, then one in Chu, so completing a circuit of four of the main power contenders. It was deeply ironic that it would be Han Fei, one of Xunzi's disciples, who would eventually provide legalism with an intellectually

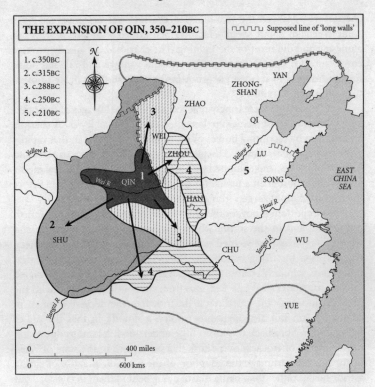

THE EXPANSION OF QIN, 350–210BC   ⊓⊔⊓⊔⊓ Supposed line of 'long walls'

1. c.350BC
2. c.315BC
3. c.288BC
4. c.250BC
5. c.210BC

N

0   400 miles
0   600 kms

respectable rationale, and another, Li Si, who as the First Emperor's chief minister would become legalism's most notorious practitioner.

At about the same time as Xunzi's visit to Xianyang, Qin abandoned the traditional policy of alliances and adopted one of unilateral expansion through naked aggression. 'Attack not only their territory but also their people,' advised Qin's then chief minister, for as Xunzi had put it, 'the ruler is just the boat but the people are the water'. Enemy forces must be not only defeated but annihilated so that their state lost the capacity to fight back. 'Here', intones the *Cambridge History of Ancient China*, 'we find enunciated as policy the mass slaughters of the third century BC.'

The slaughters were made more feasible by important advances in weaponry and military organisation. In the 'Spring and Autumn' period, military capacity had been assessed in terms of horse-drawn chariots. Besides usually three passengers – commander, archer/bodyguard and charioteer – each of the two-wheeled chariots was accompanied by a complement of about seventy infantrymen armed with lances, who ran alongside and did most of the fighting. The chariot was a speedy prestige conveyance for 'feudal' lords and provided a vantage and rallying point for the troops, but it often got stuck in the mud and was liable to overturn on rough terrain.

As centralisation increasingly relieved subordinate lineages of their fiefs and autonomy, most states supplemented these 'feudal' levies of chariots and runners by recruiting bodies of professional infantrymen that rapidly grew into standing armies. Disciplined and drilled, clad in armour and helmets of leather, and equipped with swords and halberds, the new model armies were more than a match for the chariot-chasing levies even before the introduction of forged iron and the deadly crossbow.

These important innovations seem to have orginated early in the fourth century BC and in the south, where Wu was famed for its blades and where Chu graves have yielded some of the earliest examples of the metal triggers used for firing crossbows. Never far behind any technological innovation, scholarly treatises provide evidence of warfare being elevated into an art. A *shi* called Sun Bin, also from the south, is credited with the first text in which the crossbow is described as 'the decisive element in combat'.[29] Sun Bin also mentions cavalry, a novelty in that the art of fighting from horseback was as yet little understood. A famous discussion on the merits of trousers over skirts that took place in the state of Zhao in 307 BC seems to mark the adoption of the nomadic practice of sitting astride horses rather than being drawn along behind them in chariots. But cavalry were used largely for reconnaisance and their numbers were small. Mozi, that stickler for non-aggression, manages under the rubric of self-defence to reveal the development of a much more sophisticated level of siege warfare, including the use of wheeled ladders for wall-scaling and smoke-bellows to counter tunnellers. Cities had long been fortified, but it was in the 'Warring States' period that chains of garrisoned forts linked by 'long walls' first receive mention. Partly to define territory, partly to defend it, 'long walls', bits of which would later be incorporated into Qin's supposed 'Great Wall', were perhaps the most obvious manifestation of state formation.

Universal conscription naturally meant that armies were much bigger. At the great battle of Chengpu in 632 BC each side had supposedly mobilised up to 20,000 men. By the beginning of the 'Warring States' period, armies are thought to have numbered around 100,000, and by the third century BC several hundred thousand. Battle-deaths running to 240,000 are mentioned but are presumed to be exaggerations. The slaughter was nevertheless on an unprecedented scale; the battles sometimes lasted for weeks, and prisoners-of-war could expect no mercy; their numbers, like their heads, were simply added to the body-count.

In a series of decisive campaigns accompanied by just such slaughter, Qin decimated the forces of Han and Zhao between 262 and 256 BC. The ageing Zhou king, who had unwisely thrown in his lot on the side of Zhao, was also forced to submit. According to an almost throwaway paragraph in the *Shiji*, in 256 BC this last of the thirty-nine Zhou kings of such illustrious memory 'bowed his head in recognition of guilt and offered his entire territory . . . to Qin'. 'The Qin ruler accepted the gift and sent the Zhou ruler back to his capital. [Next year] the Zhou people fled to the east and their sacred vessels, including the nine cauldrons, passed into the hands of Qin. Thus the Zhou dynasty came to an end.'[30]

Ten years later, in 246 BC, there succeeded to the Qin throne a thirteen-year-old boy 'with arched nose and long eyes, the puffed out chest of a hawk, the voice of a jackal . . . and the heart of a tiger or a wolf'. At this stage he was known as King Zheng of Qin. A quarter of a century's ruthless campaigning would see the remaining 'warring states' eliminated and the same King Zheng arrogate to himself the Zhou's Heavenly Mandate and assume the title of Shi Huangdi, 'First Emperor'.

Contrived in bloodshed, China's tradition of empire would endure, often broken but never abjured, from this 'First Emperor' in the third century BC until the film-famous 'Last Emperor' of the twentieth century AD. A milder young man wearing thick spectacles, dark suit and silk tie, the last of China's emperors, like the last of its Zhou kings, would 'flee to the east'. Having first abdicated and then been deposed, he would slip away from Beijing's Forbidden City in 1924 to place his person at the disposal of the Japanese invader.

3

THE FIRST EMPIRE

C. 250–210 BC

STONE CATTLE ROAD

ALTHOUGH *QIN* SHI HUANGDI (the Qin 'First Emperor') is invariably described as the architect of China's earliest integration, his achievement was not quite as remarkable as might be supposed. The Qin edifice would last barely a generation, after which the empire would have to be laboriously reconstructed; it covered little more than 'core' China, and that not entirely; and although the First Emperor certainly outdid all his predecessors in aggressive universalism, his success was largely down to others. Shang Yang and his 'legalist' associates had devised the interventionist framework of what amounted to a totalitarian state; various rationalists and ministers continued to fine-tune this machinery: and it was the kings of Qin prior to the First Emperor who had instigated the policy of expansion and had substantially realised it while assembling the resources for its completion.

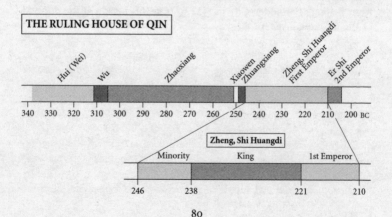

THE RULING HOUSE OF QIN

Hui (Wei) · Wu · Zhaoxiang · Xiaowen · Zhuangxiang · Zheng, Shi Huangdi First Emperor · Er Shi 2nd Emperor

340 330 320 310 300 290 280 270 260 250 240 230 220 210 200 BC

Zheng, Shi Huangdi

Minority · King · 1st Emperor

246 · 238 · 221 · 210

In *c.* 330 BC – so a century before King Zheng of Qin assumed the title of 'First Emperor' – his great-great-great-grandfather King Hui of Qin had allowed his attention to wander away from the east, from the lower Yellow River and its ever 'warring states', to focus on an inviting but remote and apparently unattainable prospect in the far south-west. There, over the switchback mountains of the Qinling range (now a last redoubt of the Giant Panda), across the valley of the upper Han River, and beyond the misty Daba Hills, lay what one scholar calls the 'land of silk and money'.[1] This was Sichuan, the great upper basin of the Yangzi that is today the country's most populous province. Two administrations then controlled it – as indeed they do now following a 1997 bisection of the province: Ba in the south-east roughly corresponded to the modern Chongqing region and Shu in the centre to the modern Chengdu region.

Neither Shu nor Ba figure much in the 'Spring and Autumn' or the 'Warring States' Annals. Distance, gradients and climate conspired to isolate Sichuan from the Yellow River states, while the Sichuanese peoples were deemed too alien and uncultured to participate in the cynical manoeu-vrings and bloodlettings of the high-minded Xia. Outside this charmed circle, the great bell-casting southern state of Chu had on occasion pushed up the Han and Yangzi valleys into Ba; but it was Shu which was the larger of the two Sichuanese states, the more cohesive and the richer (if one may judge by the opulence of its earlier occupants as revealed in the sacrificial pits at Sanxingdui). It was also the nearer to Qin's homeland in the Wei valley, though even by high-flying crow the distance between Xi'an, near where was situated the Qin capital of Xianyang, and Chengdu is a good 500 kilometres (310 miles).

King Hui of Qin had nevertheless established cordial relations with his distant neighbours. He exchanged presents with the king of Shu, encour-aged small-scale trade with his kingdom and nursed big-scale designs upon it. Access remained a challenge, but according to a later and scandalously slanted account, he sought to resolve this problem by adopting a ruse of which gift-bearing Greeks would not have been ashamed. Five life-size stone cows – rather than a wooden horse – were commissioned and, when sculpted to naturalistic perfection, were mischievously embellished by spattering their tails and hindquarters with gobs of purest gold. The herd was then put to grass where emissaries from Shu might observe it and reflect.

Shu people being, even by Qin's doubtful standards, unenlightened in the ways of civilisation and so somewhat credulous, the emissaries reported this remarkable phenomenon to their king; and he of course, excited by the idea of an unlimited supply of gold cowpats, indented for 'the stone cattle' as a gift. King Hui of Qin assented. But because of the impossibility of hauling such a herd up the scree-trails and panda-paths of two major mountain ranges, he graciously offered first to construct a suitable drove road. The king of Shu applauded and the work began.

Whatever its origins, this 'Stone Cattle Road', of which archaeologists have since uncovered some convincing traces, was a major undertaking and the first of Qin's great civil-engineering feats. It was also a revolutionary departure in 'warring states' strategy and the earliest mountain highway in China. Like the trans-Himalayan jeep-track that linked Xinjiang with Pakistan (until Chinese engineers obligingly replaced it with the 1970s Karakoram Highway), much of the new road was of carpentry. Where modern engineers would cut or tunnel, the makers of 'Stone Cattle Road' traversed. (Not even in China had the blast of gunpowder yet been heard.) It teetered along galleries cantilevered out of the sheer hillsides. Holes were bored horizontally into rock faces and plugged with sturdy poles that projected far enough to accommodate the planking of the carriageway. Elsewhere rivers were bridged and forest felled. King Hui's solicitude for the cattle's safe passage could not be faulted; and in time his counterpart in Shu welcomed the stone herd to Sichuan's lushest pastures – and then returned it. There was no ill feeling; it was just that the ruminants failed to perform as expected.

Not so easy to repel, though, were the heavily armed and armoured Qin storm-troopers with their chariots and supply wagons who followed along 'Stone Cattle Road'. Clattering over the planked galleries, Qin's forces invaded Shu in 316 BC. On the flimsiest of dynastic pretexts, King Hui of Qin had abandoned his bluff and now put his road to the purpose for which it had all along been intended. Comprehensively outwitted in the hills, Shu was easily outfought on the plains. After consecutive defeats, its king fled, while the ruler of neighbouring Ba was taken captive. Save for slivers of territory in the south and the east (where Chu retained an interest) all of cultivable Sichuan was at the mercy of the king of Qin. It was the largest territorial acquisition in China since the Western Zhou had overrun the Shang domain following the *c.* 1045 BC battle of Muye.

Only elsewhere in Asia had a comparable feat of arms been recorded. Just ten years earlier Macedonian infantry had erupted into India in similar fashion. Without the benefit of a mountain highway Alexander the Great had led his men on a circuitous route through the Hindu Kush before descending to no less promising victories in the basin of the upper Indus. *Panj-ab*, meaning the 'five-rivers' tributary to the Indus, lay at Alexander's mercy much as *Si-chuan*, meaning the 'four-rivers' tributary to the Yangzi, did at King Hui's mercy. Yet in the case of the would-be world-conquering Alexander, there the odyssey had ended. His Indian escapade proved to be no more than a historical hiccup. Within a year he was gone, and within three he was dead. His arrangements for India's richest province collapsed as soon as he withdrew; so did much of his army as thirst took its toll on the desert march back to Babylonia; and within the subcontinent his incursion left so little impression that no surviving Indian source contains so much as a mention of it.

The Chinese outcome was very different. It brought Sichuan within the ambit of Xia culture and so, imminently, of Chinese empire – where it would remain. For Qin, if not for Alexander, victory marked a point of no return. The conquest had doubled Qin's territory and elevated its status from that of 'warring state' to warring superstate. There could be no question of relinquishing a land as rich in minerals as it was in cereals, as well served by rivers as it was by climate, and as advantageous strategically as it was economically. Rebellions were ruthlessly suppressed, and after a brief experiment in feudal dyarchy, directly administered 'counties' and 'commanderies' were carved out across the country. Qin methods of registration and recruitment were imposed, the 'legalist' tariff of rewards and punishments was introduced, and weights, measures and calendar were standardised. At Chengdu the massive walls, said to have been 23 metres (75 feet) high by 6.4 kilometres (4 miles) long, of a new provincial stronghold soon proclaimed Qin's permanent intent. Compounded as usual of layered earth that had been tamped between wooden shuttering into the concrete-like *hangtu*, the fortifications left deep excavations, or borrow-pits, scattered about the Chengdu plain which were large enough, when flooded and stocked, to feed the city on fish. However demanding and intrusive, Qin rule was not indifferent to the welfare of the 'black-haired commoners'; on the docility of the masses depended their mass mobilisation.

Meanwhile, across 'Stone Cattle Road' and other hastily constructed roadways poured pioneers from Qin's harsher climes in the Wei and Yellow rivers – land-hungry colonists, corvée-serving conscripts, labour-sentenced convicts, mineral-seeking prospectors and career-in-crisis exiles. 'Of all the regions [that would be] unified by Qin, Shu underwent the longest and most sustained transformation,' writes a persuasive champion of the process.[2] Comparatively undisturbed for eighty years, Qin here had a chance to field-test the policies and experiment with the projects that would characterise its all-China dominion.

The 'land of silk and money' lay ripe for development. In addition to linens and other fabrics, Sichuan's vast silk output, especially of brocades, would provide both a tradeable commodity and, when packed in bales of standard weight, a convertible currency. More recognisable coinage came from the great mineral deposits to be found throughout the province and that of neighbouring Yunnan. Here 'making money' meant just that. Mined, minted and managed locally, copper coins, now of a more familiar and pocket-friendly shape, filled the coffers of Qin, and to judge by their ubiquity at contemporary grave sites found ready acceptance among the ancestors. Salt and iron-ore deposits were also extensively worked, both of them under state direction but with ample scope for private initiative. The salt brought in wealth; the iron was wrought into tools and weaponry.

Cereal production, the mainstay of every settled economy and the measure of its success in that it governed the availability and mobilisation of manpower, received the highest priority. Cadastral surveys were conducted, a grid of plots interspersed by paths and dykes was imposed, and much land was re-allocated. If one may judge from the scant documentation, the state even attempted to dictate what crops were planted and when. This may have applied especially to newly irrigated land; for in *c.* 270 BC Li Bing, as the Qin governor of Shu, conceived a means of partially diverting the Min River (one of *Si-chuan*'s 'four rivers') into the Chengdu plain.

Li Bing's Dujiangyan system of weirs and races was extremely ambitious. The labour requirement can only be guessed at, but both deep-cutting and hill-contouring were involved, plus some bridge-building and an elaborate distribution network. 'The largest, most carefully planned public works project yet seen anywhere on the eastern half of the Eurasian continent', it reduced the danger of floods, provided a commercial waterway, and in time converted central Sichuan into the great rice-bowl of inland China.[3] It also made Li Bing himself into a legend, and though now enveloped in the steel and concrete of later improvements, the scheme survives to this day. In fact it is a UNESCO World Heritage site. Like 'Stone Cattle Road', Li Bing's Min River waterworks anticipated the later earth-moving feats of the First Emperor. But unlike them, it would be neither forgotten, like the First Emperor's tomb, nor misconstrued, like his wall. If China had its own 'seven wonders of the ancient world', Li Bing's waterworks would be one of them.

While Li Bing was busy with his sluices, Zhaoxiang, the longest-reigning king (306–251 BC) of the now resource-rich Qin, had already been flexing his new military muscle. Primed on Sichuan's growth steroids, Qin burst from the blocks of Sichuan's strategic location. Command of the upper

Han and Yangzi valleys constituted a direct threat to any state or states based on their middle and lower reaches: and this, in the third century BC, meant the great southern state of Chu. As early as King Hui's time, while debating the pros and cons of building 'Stone Cattle Road', a Qin minister had observed that of all the 'warring states' only Qin and Chu had the resources to prevail over the rest. By the 280s BC the pressing question was simply which had the resources to prevail over the other.

At around the time that Qin's forces had been subduing Sichuan, Chu's had been subduing Yue. Yue was even farther from the Yellow River and its 'warring states' than Sichuan. It lay south of the Yangzi delta and adjacent to Wu, a state on and about the delta itself that had been the scourge of Chu back in the sixth century BC when the marquis of Zeng had offered sanctuary to Chu's king. Courtesy of what amounted to an interstate food chain, matters had been getting slightly simpler. Wu had been devoured by Yue in the early fifth century BC, and then Yue (including Wu) had been overrun by Chu in the late fourth century BC. Naturally if Chu (now including Yue and Wu) were to succumb to Qin, the entire Yangzi valley, including its far-reaching feeders such as the Han River, would be united. Qin would be practically invincible, two-thirds of 'core' China would be under its rule and, quite incidentally, an excruciating era of same-sounding states would be nearly at an end.

Well aware of the threat posed by Qin's outflanking move into Sichuan, Chu had first tried to cobble together an anti-Qin alliance. When this failed, in c. 285 BC a Chu force thrust up the Yangzi, pillaged in Ba and Shu and then veered south into either Guizhou or Yunnan province. The geography is uncertain but the motivation is clear: to outflank the outflanker. Qin responded with a countermove that severed this Chu tentacle. Cut off in the far south-west, the Chu expeditionary force settled down among the indigenous people, and while advancing the process of casual cross-culturation, played no further part in the tug-of-war between Qin and Chu.

Seizing the moment, in 280–277 BC Qin hit back with a pincer movement involving two amphibious advances, one down the Han valley and the other down the Yangzi. The first struck deep into Hubei province and captured both the Chu capital and the ancestral tombs of its kings. The second ended Chu influence in Ba and secured the Yangzi down to below its famous gorges. Chu never recovered from these twin disasters. The loss of territory was severe, and the subsequent drift of Chu's domain towards the coast and Shandong should be seen as less in the nature of compensation, more of dissipation. Worse was the loss of prestige and legitimacy.

Deprived of his capital and unable to perform the sacrificial rites at the tombs of his ancestors, Chu's king had clearly forfeited Heaven's favour. In terms of moral authority as much as military clout, his state could no longer be regarded as a serious contender for supremacy.

Yet Chu would stagger on for another fifty years before finally being extinguished; nor was it even then forgotten. To cries of 'Great Chu shall rise again', it would do just that when the Qin experiment in empire foundered. From Chu would come the contenders for a new dynastic dispensation; and under one of them, the founder of the Han dynasty, its softening southern mix of extravagant expression, encrusted artistry, shamanic mysticism and lachrymose verse would colour the mainstream of northern Chinese culture. Once regarded by the Yellow River's 'warring states' as uncivilised 'barbarians', both Chu and Qin pursued trajectories that converged on the 'central plain', so belying the idea of all political power and high culture radiating outwards from it. The dynamic was as often centripetal as centrifugal; 'Chinese civilisation' was as much compounded as diffused.[4]

Unlike Chu's king, King Zhaoxiang of Qin must have been vastly encouraged by the success of his arms in Hubei. Qin's star was clearly in the ascendant; its resources had been further augmented; and from the middle Yangzi to distant Shanxi its territories now wrapped themselves around the Yellow River's 'warring states' in a maw-like embrace. But despite every strategic advantage, King Zhaoxiang's final trumphs were dearly bought. As already noted, appalling slaughter accompanied the defeat of Zhao, Wei and Han (the Jin successor states) in the 250s BC. Even the 256 BC overthrow of the ancient house of Zhou was not without its bloody aftermath in that six years later the last Zhou king, now a pensioner of Qin, was put to death on suspicion of plotting a comeback.

In the previous year, 251 BC, but of natural (if long-overdue) causes, old King Zhaoxiang of Qin had himself died. In quick succession his son and then his grandson succeeded. When the latter died in 247 BC, the succession passed to this latter's presumed son, the thirteen-year-old Zheng, who would become the First Emperor. But because of his age, Zheng did not actually take up the reins of power – or 'receive the cap of manhood and put on the girdle and sword' – until 238 BC.

Royal longevity being an important factor in the stability of any dynasty, this interlude of seldom uncontentious successions, plus a nine-year minority, could well have been fatal to Qin's prospects. Disappointed court factions mounted rebellions, outlying 'commanderies' wavered in their allegiance, and the surviving 'warring states' hastened to take advan-

tage. But fortune, no less than unrivalled wealth and a compliant populace, favoured Qin. The rebellions were suppressed and the external
attacks heavily punished. 'At this time', says the *Shiji*, referring to Zheng's
accession in 246 BC,

> Qin had already annexed the regions of Ba, Shu and Hanzhong [the
> 'middle Han' river] and extended its territories to Ying [the Chu
> capital], where it set up Nan ['Southern'] Province. In the north it
> had taken possession of the area from Shang province east, which
> comprised the provinces of Hedong, Taiyuan and Shangdang, and
> east as far Xingyang . . . setting up the province of Sanchuan.

These northern acquisitions extended up to the steppes of Mongolia and
gave Qin command of more than half the lower Yellow River basin. They
were further extended during Zheng's minority as Qin generals took some
thirty more cities and set up yet another new province.[5]

Thus when young King Zheng came of age in 238 BC, Qin was in effect
already supreme. It possessed over half of its future empire and regarded
most of the surviving states as inferiors or vassals. Apart from the massacre
of a suspiciously approximate 100,000 in Zhao in 234 BC, the *Shiji* is unusually reticent about casualties during this final phase of unification.
Presumably they were not significant. Zheng himself characterised his
campaigns as essentially corrective – 'to punish violence and rebellion'.
The object was no longer annihilation but annexation. Han and Zhao's
submission was followed by that of an already fractured Wei in 225 BC, of
the displaced and enfeebled Chu in 223 BC, and finally of Yan in the extreme
north-east and Qi in the Shandong peninsula in 222–221 BC. 'Thanks to
the ancestral spirits, these six kings have all acknowledged their guilt and
the world is now in profound order,' gloated the victor.[6]

It remained only to mark the achievement by a suitable upgrading of
King Zheng's title. Deliberations were held and a form of words meaning
'Greatly August One' was proposed. Zheng, acutely aware of his newly won
precedence, had a better idea. 'We will drop the "Greatly", keep the "August",
and adopt the title used by the emperors of high antiquity [that is the
mythical Five Emperors], calling ourselves Huangdi or August Emperor.'

An official proclamation immediately confirmed the new designation:
from now on there were to be no more posthumous names; emperors
were to be known only by the numerical titles they inherited. 'We ourselves
shall be called First Emperor [*Shi Huangdi*], and successive generations of
rulers shall be numbered consecutively, Second, Third, and so on for 1000
or 10,000 generations, the succession passing down without end.'[7] But

posterity would decline to be bound by this ruling. One of the First Emperor's most sensible innovations proved to be one of his least regarded; the sequence would stop at 'Second Emperor'.

QIN'S CULTURAL REVOLUTION

On his accession a ruler's first responsibility was to his lineage – past, present and to come. In honouring his ancestors he anticipated his becoming one of them and so demonstrated the legitimacy of his succession and that of his heirs. To this end, plans for a suitably imposing tomb for the then teenage Zheng had been drawn up as soon as his father's funerary rites were consummated. The plans were probably revised and extended as he advanced to manhood, kingship and august emperorship, by when a truly spectacular funerary work was in prospect. Meanwhile his parents were exalted, with his father being given the accolade of 'Grand Supreme August [One]', despite the ban on posthumous titles. His mother, who was still very much alive, posed a different problem. She had first to be rehabilitated, in fact rescued from an infamous affair that threatened the very legitimacy that the young emperor was so determined to emphasise.

It so happened that during Zheng's minority the state had been run by a group of veteran statesmen and generals under the direction of the able Lu Buwei, chancellor to Zheng's father. Unusually, indeed scandalously by the standards of Confucian 'gentlemen' accustomed to regard influence as their own prerogative, Lu Buwei owed his position not to scholarship but to trade. Though a highly successful businessman, he still ranked as a merchant, one of the most despised professions throughout the Xia states and a heavily penalised one under Qin's 'legalist' regulations.

Contempt for such an upstart may account for the *Shiji*'s decidedly racy biographical note on Lu Buwei. Like most of Qin's ministers, he was not a native of that state, and before arriving there in *c.* 251 BC had enjoyed the favours of a celebrated concubine. Her name is not mentioned, only her 'matchless beauty and great skill in dancing', which attracted other admirers, including the then crown prince of Qin. The crown prince prevailed on Lu Buwei to part with her, 'she concealed the fact that she was already pregnant', and her baby, a son born in the fullness of time, had therefore been assumed to be the offspring of the Qin crown prince. Meanwhile the crown prince had succeeded as king of Qin; the matchless concubine had been recognised as his official consort; and her infant had been declared heir apparent. This was the young Zheng. If the story was true, the future First Emperor was an impostor. Illegitimacy could, and had been, rectified by making his mother a royal consort; but there could be no redemption for the issue of a barely mentionable relationship between a common concubine and a market trader.

Nor was that the end of the affair. When the thirteen-year-old Zheng succeeded on the death of his father, his mother, now Dowager Queen and soon to be Dowager Empress, resumed her relationship with Lu Buwei. He, though, seems to have tired of her attentions and grown anxious lest the affair become public.

> He therefore searched about in secret until he found a man named Lao Ai who had an unusually large penis, and made him a servant in his household. Then, when an occasion arose, he had suggestive music performed and, instructing Lao Ai to stick his penis through the centre of a wheel made of paulownia wood, had him walk about with it, making certain that the report of this reached the ears of the Queen Dowager so as to excite her interest.[8]

It did. Her Majesty's interest was royally excited and Lao Ai, the stud, found himself the unwitting beneficiary of this none-too-subtle ploy. Accused of some misdemeanour, he was sentenced to a mock castration (only his whiskers and eyebrows were removed) and then consigned to the Queen Dowager's apartments as a certified eunuch. 'She grew to love him greatly,' says the *Shiji*, as well she might considering he was not a eunuch at all. Ever by her side, Lao Ai was showered with gifts, acquired an entourage of several thousand and became a power in the land. When the Queen Dowager found herself pregnant again, the couple discreetly retired to the country. Their chances of living happily ever after received a setback, however, when in 238 BC their sons (there were two) were identified as a threat to the succession. The just-enthroned King Zheng ordered an investigation and 'all the facts were brought to light, including those that implicated the [now] prime minister Lu Buwei'.[9]

Lu Buwei found others to plead his cause. But the unfortunate Lao Ai raised the standard of revolt. His forces were easily defeated, his family annihilated, 'several hundred heads were cut off in Xianyang', and the rest of his supporters – some 4,000 families – were transported to Sichuan. Lao Ai himself was torn apart by carriages, their wheels no doubt of paulownia wood. The Queen Dowager and Lu Buwei were merely banished from court. But in 235 BC a pardon saw Her Majesty's return to Xianyang, while Lu Buwei was consigned to exile, also in Sichuan. Fearing this was the prelude to a death sentence, the merchant prince 'drank poison and died'.

The *Shiji* spares no detail in the telling of the affair. There is, though, some doubt about the extent to which Sima Qian, the *Shiji*'s main author, was responsible. Throughout his text, the 'Grand Historian' paints a somewhat ambiguous picture of the First Emperor. Writing under the Han dynasty just over a century later, he had every reason to denigrate Qin; the Han founder had overthrown the house of Qin, whose one credible emperor must therefore be shown as lacking in the legitimacy and virtue on which Heaven's Mandate depended. Sima Qian accordingly quoted with approval a long diatribe against the First Emperor. He was 'greedy and short-sighted', dismissive of advice and precedent, ignorant of the masses, and 'led the whole world in violence and cruelty'; his laws were harsh and his conduct deceitful – all of which, though excusable in the context of Qin's seizure of power, was not conducive to the establishment of a just and permanent empire. The First Emperor's main fault, therefore, was that of 'not changing with the times'.[10]

On the other hand, as will be seen, Sima Qian had excellent reasons of a delicate nature for not gratifying his Han patron. He may therefore have been reluctant to demonise the preceding dynasty. In fact he gives it as his own opinion that, though 'Qin's seizure of power was accompanied by much violence, yet [the Qin dynasty] did manage to change with the times and its accomplishments were great'.[11] Taken in conjunction with certain linguistic incongruities in the relevant section of his text, this has led scholars to suppose that the story of Lu Buwei being the father of Zheng was added later by others keen to ingratiate themselves with the Han. Yet the account of the rise and fall of the wretched Lao Ai appears genuine enough. Like later emperors, the first emperor found that he could best demonstrate his legitimacy by disposing of all who might question it.

Another telling preliminary to the First Emperor's personal reign was his announcement, immediately after assuming the imperial title, that Qin 'ruled by the power of water'. This was a reference not to the success of Li Bing's Sichuan sluices but to the 'Five Phases' (or sometimes 'Five Powers' or 'Five Elements'), whose sequential ascendancy supposedly controlled the course of history. While Confucians attributed a dynasty's power to Heaven's Mandate, others of a less orthodox (or more Daoist) persuasion attributed it to one of the five elemental Phases/Elements – earth, wood, metal, fire and water. Lending potency to successive dynasties, these phases rotated in an endless cycle based on the idea that each overcame its predecessor; thus wood floated on water, metal felled wood, fire melted metal, water quenched fire, earth dammed water, and so on. Since the Zhou had apparently espoused fire, the Qin must adopt that which overcame it; thus 'the power of water now began its period of dominance', says the *Shiji*; and since, to the credulous ruler, a whole school of 'Five Phases' philosophy was now available, Qin's adoption of the new element had significant ramifications.

For to each of the Five Phases/Elements was awarded an auspicious correlate from among the colours, the numbers, the seasons (an extra one was added) and much else besides. In the case of water, the appropriate colour was black, the number was six, and the season was winter. Winter was also the cruellest season, a time of darkness, death and executions (which were held over until then). Through no fault of his own other than that of endorsing a widespread tradition, the First Emperor's destiny was tied to watery associations that, especially for those living in the Yellow River's flood-prone 'central plain', were of the grimmest. Even if he had been the most indulgent and fun-loving of princes – which he was not – the First Emperor's reign could scarcely have engendered either fond feelings or lustrous associations.

He nevertheless embraced his watery lot with typical thoroughness. He himself wore black, while his troops in black armour issued from black-flagged fortifications beneath black-emblazoned standards. Obviously the Yellow River had to be renamed. But as Sima Qian explains, because it was credited with being the source and embodiment of all water, merely calling it the 'Black River' was not good enough. Rather did it become *te shui*, 'the Water of Power'. The number six posed no problem. The inter-locking tally-sticks that signified an imperial commission (the emperor kept one half, the commissioned official the other) were ordered to be six 'inches' long. Likewise official caps became six 'inches' wide; and the length of a 'pace' was calculated as exactly six 'feet' (it was a double pace, or two strides). Six 'feet' was also the prescribed width for official carriages, which were to be drawn by six horses, presumably black ones. When similar specifications were extended to chariots and carts, six 'feet' became the standard gauge for Chinese wheel ruts, so ensuring a tram-like ride on the empire's deeply scored highways. The calendar was also realigned and recalibrated. This was a ritual responsibility for every new ruler but one that, in this case, saw the New Year and its celebrations being put back to the tenth month so that they coincided not with the solstice or the beginning of spring but with the onset of winter.

Such meticulous attention to detail, to quantification, standardisation and regulation, advertised dynastic regard for the 'Five Phases/Elements' while according neatly with what was the most obvious feature of the legalist state. It was once supposed that oppressive laws, accompanied by their tariff of graded rewards and draconian punishments, were what distinguished legalism. But the 1970s recovery of a cache of bamboo documents from a tomb outside Wuhan deep in what had been Chu territory (Hubei province) prompted qualification. In part constituting a local official's handbook of Qin statutes and legal practice, the documents did not exactly dispel the idea of a ferocious justice. Under some circumstances the theft of a single coin could result in the amputation of a foot, plus tattooing of the torso (a particularly degrading form of disfigurement) and hard labour. But straight fines or short spells of unpaid corvée service appear to have been the more usual punishments; and whatever the case, justice was anything but arbitrary. The nature of the offence, the degree of intent, any extenuating circumstances, and the bureaucratic procedures to be observed throughout the legal process, were minutely addressed even for misdemeanours of little apparent consequence. Likewise statutes dealing with agriculture clearly listed not only the different types of cereal crop to be sown but the quantity of seed required to sow a given area with each. Reports on the state of the fields were to be submitted whenever there was anything to report – when it rained, when it didn't rain, when pests were detected and so on. There were also annual prizes for the overseer, stockman and labourer responsible for the district's best ox, plus of course penalties for the worst (typically two months corvée).[12]

As originally in the state of Qin, then in Sichuan, in conquered parts of Chu, Wei and Zhao, and now throughout the empire, the emphasis was on 'efficiency, precision, and fixed routine in administrative procedure . . . [plus] exact quantification of data, and attention to the improvement of agricultural production and conserving of natural resources'.[13] Households were registered for taxation purposes, and the population organised into grouped families for military and civil conscription. All newly acquired territories were reconstituted as directly administered 'commanderies', of which there were thirty-six in 221 BC, each of them further divided into 'counties'. Lest the former ruling families of the no longer 'warring states' cause trouble in the commanderies, their scions were summoned to the Qin capital at Xianyang and installed in replicas of their erstwhile palaces under the watchful eye of the emperor. Meanwhile their armies were disbanded and all surplus weapons melted down; the metal was recast not into ploughshares but into twelve colossal pieces of statuary, all of them later rendered down for other uses. Qin's copper coins fared better. They became standard tender throughout the empire, and their design – flat and circular with a square hole in the middle so that they could be easily strung together – would last more than two thousand years. The standardisation of weights and measures was also extended throughout the empire, heavy penalties being prescribed for any variation beyond an acceptable factor that was carefully specified in the case of each measurement.

To ensure universal implementation of these orders and to promote bureaucratic efficiency, it remained only to standardise the script in which they were written and read. In the course of the first millennium BC the so-called 'Large Seal' script of the Shang and Zhou had acquired local characteristics in the various 'warring states'. Moreover, in states outside the 'central plain', such as Shu and Chu, some still-undeciphered fragments of pictography suggest a regional challenge from quite unrelated writing systems. The First Emperor's introduction of what came to be known as the 'Small Seal' script was designed to counter all such diversity. It involved eradicating obsolete or offensive characters, simplifying and rationalising others, and standardising each and every one. Although destined for an early and more lasting revision by Han scholars, 'Small Seal' script established the principle of a written language that was common to the literate elite throughout the empire regardless of spoken dialects, and which was recognised as the medium of both government and scholarship. It was a principle of incalculable significance. Regional distinctions were thereby subsumed, although social distinctions, particularly as between the lettered classes and the unlettered, were engrained. Without this standardisation China's bureaucrats would today need as many interpreters as the European Union; and that claim to several thousand years as a single 'continuous civilisation' would scarcely be sustainable, or even enunciable.

Such measures, accompanied by a programme of gargantuan public works that would dwarf 'Stone Cattle Road' and Li Bing's waterworks, secured the cause of integration more effectively than mere conquest and ensured its survival beyond the fall of Qin. There was no precedent for such a vast and substantially non-Xia empire comprising not only the Yellow River basin but Sichuan, the Yangzi and much of southern China and Inner Mongolia. In applying to all of it without distinction the same standards of administrative control and mass mobilisation, the First Emperor seems to have been aware that he was breaking new ground. In a series of inscriptions, whose texts were faithfully recorded by the historian Sima Qian, the emperor dwelt more on his administrative than his military achievements.

In his twenty-eighth year [219 BC] the August Emperor made a new beginning.

He adjusted the laws and the regulations [and set] standards for the ten thousand things . . .

The merit of the August Emperor lies in diligently fostering basic concerns, exalting agriculture, abolishing lesser occupations, so the black-headed people may be rich.

All under Heaven are of one mind, single in purpose.

Weights and measures have a single standard, words are written in a uniform way.

Wherever sun and moon shine, where boats and wheeled vehicles bear cargo, all fulfil their allotted years, [and] none do not attain their goal.

To initiate projects in season – such is the August Emperor's way.

Empire, a product of surplus resources, new technologies (metallurgical, agricultural and military) and individual initiative, had already swept through other parts of Asia. Darius and Xerxes of the Persian Achaemenid dynasty had created a territorial colossus stretching from the Aegean to the Indus in the late sixth century BC; Alexander of Macedon had briefly exceeded it in the fourth century BC; and in the early third century BC, while Qin was flexing its muscles in Sichuan prior to China's first 'unification', the Maurya dynasty of Pataliputra was effecting a first 'unification' of India.

Ashoka, the third of the Maurya emperors and a near-contemporary of *Qin* Shi Huangdi, also favoured stone-cut inscriptions. Gouged into India's bedrock or neatly engraved on monolithic stone columns, they have lasted better than the First Emperor's stelae, of which only one remaining fragment is reckoned authentic. On the other hand the Indian empire they memorialised would vanish within a decade of Ashoka's demise, while the Chinese empire of *Qin* Shi Huangdi would be reconstituted as the long-lasting Han empire and would survive, in principle when not in practice, for over 2,000 years.

Similarly, history's verdict on the two emperors could not be more different. Ashoka is revered as a benevolent reformer who renounced violence, championed monasticism, proclaimed a universal dharma and dispatched evangelists instead of armies. By contrast, *Qin* Shi Huangdi is seen as the worst of tyrants, an 'oriental despot' at the helm of a

totalitarian state, by nature violent, superstitious and prone to megalomania. Yet his inscriptions claim that he too 'brought peace to the world',
'implemented good government', 'showed compassion to the black-headed
people' and 'worked tirelessly for the common good', not to mention decom-
missioning weapons and administering justice without favour or remorse.
They in fact contain sentiments from which Ashoka would not have shrunk
plus phrases which in translation seem to mimic those of the Maurya.

But because so little is known of Ashoka beyond what is contained in
his inscriptions, he is usually taken at his own evaluation. The First Emperor,
because so much is known of him from other sources, is not. Falling victim
to a prolific historiographical tradition that would habitually disparage
ephemeral dynasties and which was gravely offended by some of his actions,
the First Emperor, were he to have emerged from his underground
mausoleum, would have found his stone-cut words ignored. He might then
reasonably have complained about double standards; for had works like
the *Shiji* and those based upon it been destroyed and only his epigraphy
survived, history might have been as kind to him as it has to Ashoka.

In 213 BC the destruction of other texts constituted the incident mainly
responsible for consigning the First Emperor's reputation to abiding
ignominy – abiding, that is, until Red Guards tore a leaf from his book,
so to speak, in the late 1960s and thus helped to rehabilitate China's first
cultural revolutionary. For though his reformation of the script was
welcomed by the literate, the First Emperor showed nothing but contempt
for traditional scholarship. History was there to be made, he seemed to
say, not to be repeated. To those who prattled about the grand old Duke
of Zhou and Heaven's Mandate, he extended neither respect nor favour;
and when they continued to snipe at the legalist emphasis on law rather
than precedent, and on a ruler's strength rather than his virtue, the literary
pogrom of 213 BC was his typically unequivocal response.

After Lu Buwei, the merchant-minister who was probably *not* the First
Emperor's father, fell from grace in 238 BC, he had been replaced in the
imperial favour, and eventually as chancellor, by another upstart. Described
as 'a man from the black-headed people of the lanes and alleys', this was
Li Si, whose twentieth-century biographer considers him the *éminence
grise* behind the First Emperor's throne and calls him 'China's First
Unifier'.[14] An arch-practitioner of legalism and probably the composer of
the emperor's triumphalist inscriptions, Li Si had once studied under the
philosopher Xunzi. So had Han Fei, legalism's most eloquent exponent.
Both Li Si and Han Fei then embraced a scruple-free code that was
anathema to their mentor but welcome enough in Qin, a state of which

the philosopher had been highly critical. One can only suppose that the quality of Xunzi's instruction left something to be desired.

In the assault on tradition Han Fei led the way, famously satirising Confucian scholars as 'stump-watchers'; for according to Han Fei, in urging the emperor to adopt the ways of the ancients, such scholars would have His Majesty behave like a doltish farmer who, chancing to see a rabbit collide with a tree stump, lays down his plough and spends the rest of his days watching the stump in expectation of repeat pickings. In other words, past precedent was no guide to present exigencies, and the state could ill afford scholars who preached such nonsense. Since they neither tilled nor fought, such pedants were parasites. Their elegant phrases undermined the law and their disputatious counsels left the ruler in two minds. If indulged, they would assuredly bring ruin, wrote Han Fei.

> Therefore in the state of an enlightened ruler there are no books written on bamboo strips; law supplies the only instruction. There are no sermons on the former kings: the officials serve as the only teachers. And there are no fierce feuds involving private swordsmen; cutting off enemy heads [in battle] is the only deed of valour. When the people of such a state speak, they say nothing in contradiction of the law; when they act, it is so as to be useful; and when they perform brave deeds, they do so in the army.[15]

Legalism, which is also sometimes called 'Realism', 'Rationalism' and 'Modernism', was nothing if not pragmatic. Only scholarship that strengthened the state, like that of the legalists themselves, was admissible. When in 213 BC a Confucian scholar suggested to the emperor that, since he was now all powerful, this might be the moment to revive the Shang and Zhou tradition of rewarding loyal kinsmen by granting them fiefs, it was Li Si's turn to reach for the pen (actually the writer's brush). Fief-granting had proved an unmitigated disaster, he memorialised. 'Feudal' rulers had risen against their superiors, and they had been encouraged to do so by scholars who pillaged antiquity to confuse the issue and disparage present authority. Now these same 'adherents of personal theories' would have Qin repeat the mistake. They were criticising the emperor's territorial arrangements, forming cliques and undermining his authority. They must be stopped.

> I request [then] that all writings, the [*Books of*] *Odes*, *Documents* and the sayings of the hundred schools of philosophy be discarded and done away with. Anyone who has failed to discard such books within thirty days ... shall be subjected to tattooing and condemned to

'wall-dawn' [i.e. hard] labour. The [only] books to be exempted are those on medicine, divination, agriculture and forestry.[16]

The emperor concurred; and so began the great bamboo-book-burning of 213 BC. It was followed, according to later sources, by a purge in which some 460 scholars were either executed or buried alive. A far-fetched explanation offered for this second assault may simply disguise the need to halt any oral, as well as written, transmission of the texts. To a people who distinguished themselves from others on the basis of their historical awareness and essentially literary culture, the book-burning and the persecution of scholars were devastating blows. Popular sentiment would never forget them, scholarship never forgive them.

Yet the impact was certainly exaggerated. Books at the time were not numerous; nor were readers; and bamboo, though it burnt fiercely enough, also lasted well in concealment. Total suppression was probably impossible. In fact, give or take some of those 'hundred schools of philosophy', even the works specifically mentioned by Li Si survived. The historical records of Qin were exempted from destruction, and while those of the other 'warring states' were indeed depleted, the imperial archive is said to have retained copies of most ancient texts, including the Confucian classics. Several scholars have argued that a greater loss was sustained seven years later when Xianyang's palaces, including the imperial archive itself, were ransacked by Qin's victorious opponents.[17] It could be another case of Qin's reputation being burdened with the sins of its successors.

Seemingly the idea in 213 BC was not to abolish history and literature but to restrict access to them and so, as the *Shiji* puts it, 'to make the common people ignorant and to see to it that no one in the empire used the past to criticise the present'.[18] Yet the result was exactly the opposite: for in an effort to make good the supposed losses, Han scholars would scrutinise what survived even more intently. 'Thus, if anything, its practical effect was to strengthen the tendency decried by Li Si of looking backward rather than toward the present.'[19] In short, Qin's 'cultural revolution' entrenched the culture it was supposed to discredit while discrediting the revolution it was supposed to entrench.

CRUMBLING WALL, HIDDEN TOMB

That the dynasty responsible for first uniting much of what we now call 'China' should have crowned its achievement by lending its own name to its territorial creation seems logical enough. 'Qin' (pronounced 'chin') gave us 'China' – or so it is said. The word first found its way into the Indo-Aryan languages of Sanskrit and ancient Persian as 'Sina' or 'Cina', from them into Greek and Latin as 'Sinai' or 'Thinai', and from them into French and English as 'Chine' and 'China'. Spin-offs like 'sino'-phile and 'sini'-fication were coined from the same pedigree by 'sin'-ologists. In the most satisfying of equations, Qin is revealed as China's etymological ancestor as well as its imperial ancestor; and a centralised empire with a distinctive culture becomes the defining characteristic of both.

But unlike *zhongguo*'s flexible equation with 'Central States', 'Middle Kingdom' and then 'Central Country', the etymology of 'Qin = China' is far from straightforward. Sanskrit's adoption of the 'sin'/'cin' root seems to predate the rise of Qin; it could, in that case, derive from Jin (pronounced 'zhin'), the hegemonic state headed by Chonger in the seventh century BC. Much later, the Graeco-Roman world in fact knew two Chinas: Sinai/Thinai and Seres (or Serica), both of which exported silk but were not thought to be the same place. Medieval Europe then added yet another, Cathay. This was the country that Marco Polo claimed to have visited. Polo seldom mentions anywhere called 'Chin' (or 'China') and then only as a possible alternative name for 'Manzi', which was the southern coastal region.[20] In this restricted sense 'Chin'/'China' was used by Muslim and then Portuguese traders, but it figured little in English until porcelain from this 'Chin' began gracing Elizabethan dinner tables. Shakespeare caught the mood in *Measure for Measure* with mention of stewed prunes being served in threepenny bowls and 'not China dishes'.[21] After long gestation, china (as porcelain) was lending currency to China (as place) – just as in Roman times *seres* (the Latin for 'silk') had led to the land itself being called 'Seres'. Ultimately, then, it was contemporary crockery from the south of the country, not an ancient dynasty from the north, which secured the name of 'China' in everyday English parlance and led, by extension, to the term being applied to the whole empire.

Appropriately enough, Qin was acquainted with this later, southern, 'Chin'. In the wake of his victory over Chu (including Wu and Yue) the First Emperor extended his conquests deep into the extreme south of the country. They seem to have embraced Guangdong province and parts of Guangxi and Fujian (which together formed Marco Polo's 'Chin'), plus on paper at any rate what is now northern Vietnam. But uncertainty surrounds not only the extent of these acquisitions but also their timing. If, as the *Shiji* has it, Qin's successful southern campaign was in 214 BC, this was only four years before the First Emperor's untimely death and the rapid disintegration of his empire. Three new commanderies are said to have been established in the south, but since all would have to be reconquered by the Han dynasty, it must be doubtful whether Qin's control was fully effective. Whatever its extent, the First Emperor's southern dominion was fleeting.

As in Sichuan, though, it was notable for the cutting of an important canal. This linked a southern tributary of the Yangzi to a northern tributary of the West River, which itself debouches into the estuary of the Pearl River near Hong Kong. Designed in 219 BC to facilitate a southern advance and to provide an inland waterway through Hunan to Guangzhou (Canton), the canal would be much realigned but, like Li Bing's waterworks, still exists. In the same year, the emperor himself reached the southernmost point of his imperial travels when he turned back somewhere just short of the proposed canal in the vicinity of Changsha. At the time the hill country to the south had not yet been secured, which should have been a good enough reason for heading north again. But the *Shiji* offers a different explanation, indeed one that seems designed to reveal an imperial trait which was of growing concern to ministers such as Li Si and to the whole Qin court.

Apparently the emperor was much drawn to hilltops. His inscribed stelae were usually positioned on them and he liked to climb them in person. But on an eminence near Changsha his progress was halted by what sounds like a tornado. Taking this as a personal affront, he excused the wind but blamed the hill, ordering it to be stripped of trees and painted red. Three thousand convicts were put to work immediately. Since 'red was the colour worn by condemned criminals'[22] and clear-felling the nearest thing to limb-by-limb amputation, it is evident that the hill was being punished for *lèse-majesté*. Delusions of more than mere grandeur were afflicting the emperor: a sense of transcendence had overcome him; 'all under Heaven' was his, and that included natural features. When some 2,200 years later Comrade Mao's Long Marchers sang songs about 'painting the countryside red', they may not have been aware of this ominous precedent.

More significant, because it resulted in the construction of the so-called Great Wall, was the empire's extension northwards. Sima Qian's *Shiji* continues to be vague about the geography and chronology, but it seems that the First Emperor's conquests extended right along the northern perimeter of the erstwhile 'warring states' and that these conquests were undertaken continuously throughout his eleven years as emperor (221–210 BC). As in Sichuan, colonists were speedily dispatched to the newly conquered territories; and frequent mention of these deployments provides a few clues as to the advance. So does the alignment, insofar as it can be established, of the Qin wall, part of which was much farther north than most of its successors. On this basis, the First Emperor's forces look to have mounted a three-pronged advance, pushing north of west to Lanzhou in Gansu province, north of east to the edge of the Korean peninsula, and due north across the Ordos, an undulating desert wilderness within the Yellow River's great northern loop, towards Mongolia.

The last advance, that due north across the Ordos, is the only one of which Sima Qian has much to say – and most of that in the course of a biographical note on Meng Tian, the Qin general responsible. Meng Tian was sent north with either 100,000 men or 300,000 men, probably in 221 BC, to disperse the Rong and Di peoples and take control of the Ordos. Once established there, he set about building walls. At a time when in Europe Hannibal was overcoming the natural frontier that was the Alps, Meng Tian determined to construct an artificial frontier. Its line reportedly covered a distance of 10,000 *li* (*c.* 5,000 kilometres – 3,000 miles) from Lintao (near Lanzhou) to Liaodong (east of Beijing); and initially it ran north across Ningxia province until, on reaching the Yellow River, it followed round that river's great northern bend. Thereafter Sima Qian says nothing about its alignment; nor does he anywhere mention its purpose. He did, though, visit the scene of Meng Tian's labours, albeit a century later. On site he seems to have been as much impressed by the 850 kilometres (530 miles) of road that Meng Tian had constructed up through the badlands of the Ordos as he was by the wall itself.

> I have travelled to the northern border and returned by the direct road. As I went along I saw the outposts of the long [i.e. Great] wall which Meng Tian constructed for the Qin. He cut through the mountains and filled up the valleys, opening up the direct road. Truly he made free with the strength of the common people.[23]

From this it would seem that Meng Tian's 'Great Road' involved more engineering than his 'Great Wall'. The former is said to have been 'cut through the arteries of the earth', while the latter 'followed the contours of the land . . . twisting and turning' and 'used the mountains as defence' and 'their defiles as frontier posts'.[24] If Sima Qian's 10,000 *li* are to be taken literally, the wall was certainly longer than the road. On the other hand it is generally accepted that Meng did not start his wall from scratch. Wall-building, both as a demonstration of exclusive sovereignty and as a defensive precaution, had been practised by the 'warring states' for at least a century. In places Meng Tian had merely to repair these existing stretches and connect them up.[25]

The term used in Chinese literature for Meng Tian's wall, as for the 'Great Wall' of later fame, is *changcheng*, literally meaning 'long wall' or, as with *zhongguo* ('Central States'/'Middle Kingdom'), 'long walls'. Cities, palaces and even villages might be surrounded by *changcheng*. Thus according to another interpretation, Meng Tian's wall was not in fact a continuous construction but a succession of the 'outposts' observed by Sima Qian, each surrounded by its own *changcheng*.[26] This would certainly help to explain why Qin's *changcheng* receives so little mention in later history and also why it was (or they were) apparently so ineffective as a defensive rampart. If the textual context provides a clue, the section north of the Ordos was more offensive than defensive. As the culmination of a major advance and as accommodation for a permanent garrison in what had previously been Rong and Di country, the wall was (or the walls were) meant to consolidate Qin aggression rather than forestall non-Qin incursion.

Needless to say, walls, outposts, watchtowers and whatever else may have been involved were constructed of *hangtu*. Layers of brushwood were sometimes incorporated into the tamped-down earth, but dressed stonework like that of the sixteenth-to-seventeenth-century Ming wall was not even contemplated. Though *hangtu* structures last long underground, above ground they are no match for the sandstorms, extreme frosts and occasional floods of twenty centuries. Archaeologists have identified only a few stretches of Qin wall, mostly in Gansu. Yet screeds have been written about the enterprise, and some startling statistics have been deduced as to the millions of men (they served in rotation) required to shift the trillions of tons of earth necessary for 10,000 *li* of chariot-width wall. The loss of life is reputed to have been horrific, although whether it resulted from the climate and conditions of service on the northern frontier, from the ancillary roadworks as implied by Sima Qian, or specifically from wall-building is not clear. Walls certainly got a bad name; so did Meng Tian and the First Emperor as those responsible for the most notorious example. But of late, scholarship has been chary of such deductions. It is more inclined to demolish the whole concept of a 'Great Wall' and to diminish the scale and significance of Qin's pioneering effort.

This is in marked contrast to the indulgent treatment now afforded to Qin's other extravaganzas. Stone Cattle Road, Li Bing's irrigation works, a similar scheme on the Wei River, the Hunan canal and Meng Tian's road have all been archaeologically authenticated. Other Qin highways have been charted, their combined length coming to something well in excess of Gibbon's estimate for the entire road network of the Roman Empire.

But until recently the colossal dimensions of the emperor's new Opang (Epang, Ebang) palace (675 by 112 metres – 740 by 120 yards), the labour force required to excavate his tomb (700,000 men) and the almost incredible features ascribed to that lost mausoleum had occasioned only suspicion. Then in 1974 came the discovery of 'the terracotta army'. The 'grave' doubts evaporated. An emperor who could join his ancestors at the head of an entire life-size army was capable of anything.

The dimensions of the Opang palace, though probably exaggerated, no longer seem quite so excessive; the scale of the imperial tomb, its location in Xianyang having finally been discovered, prompts excited speculation; and more generally the First Emperor's alleged eccentricities are no longer airily dismissed as the self-serving exaggerations of later historians in thrall to a different dynasty and an adverse historiography. The emperor's devotion to the theory of the Five Phases/Elements – and water in particular – seems less far-fetched; and Sima Qian's account of the various imperial peregrinations, including the mountain encounter at Changsha, can more readily be taken at their face value.

Although the First Emperor seems never to have led his forces in battle – few emperors would – he made five extensive tours. The Zhou kings had occasionally done the rounds of their feudatories, and future emperors, especially the *Qing* Kangxi and Qianlong emperors, would make the grand tour a centrepiece of imperial ceremonial. It is assumed that, like them, the First Emperor travelled to see and be seen, to exercise political over-sight and be observed performing ritual ceremonies. No doubt troops were inspected and local officials interrogated; certainly orders were issued for the settlement of new colonies and the construction of new public works. But to what extent the emperor actually engaged with his subjects on these occasions is uncertain.

According to Sima Qian, he was often rather particular about not being seen. In 219 BC, on a first visit to Mount Tai in Shandong, the most sacred of summits, he completed the ascent alone and performed whatever rites he deemed appropriate in secret and without any record being made of them. Seven years later, on the advice of a man who was pandering to his hopes of longevity, he furnished each of his palaces with what might be required in the way of entertainment and female company, and then linked these establishments with covered ways and walled corridors. His where-abouts were thereafter to be kept a closely guarded secret whose revela-tion was punishable by death. A couple of bungled assassination attempts may have made him paranoid; no less plausibly he was embarking on what, for one who was already master of 'All-under-Heaven', was the ultimate challenge: mastering mortality. For just as climbing hills excited his sense of commanding the physical world, so removing himself from public sight was supposed a step towards transcending the passage of time.

Death, says Sima Qian, was made a taboo subject, with any talk of it being punishable by the same – now unmentionable – fate. Sorcerers, magicians and miracle-men with a working knowledge of eternity were summoned for examination. No expense was spared in obtaining the life-prolonging elixirs they recommended – but which may in fact have poisoned him – nor in countering the portents of mortality that surfaced with disconcerting frequency. More encouraging news came from Shandong province, long a repository of the arcane as well as the orthodox. It concerned a mountainous archipelago in the Yellow Sea where immortality, or a means of obtaining it, was reputed commonplace. The emperor determined to investigate.

Four of his five grand tours included a sojourn by the sea, whose immensity must have impressed someone from landlocked Qin and especially one whose rule depended on 'the power of water'. On the second tour, in 219 BC, he dispatched an expedition to discover the immortals in their so-called Islands of Paradise. Since the chosen explorers consisted of 'several hundred boys and girls', he seems to have anticipated the voyage being a long one. He was right; they never returned. Later legend insisted that they had in fact made a landfall in Japan and stayed there. A second expedition was dispatched in 215 BC. This did return but without news of the elusive islands. A third expedition was planned in 210 BC though apparently delayed until a large fish could be eliminated. This was more probably a sea monster – the emperor had had a dream about it destroying his fleet. He therefore took to carrying a crossbow as he continued up the coast and eventually had the satisfaction of shooting dead just such a creature. It was his last victim. Days later he himself died.

Most of which could, again, be fabrication. Though unworthy of such an esteemed historian as Sima Qian, it could have been inserted in the *Shiji* by others after Sima's death. Yet a century later a very similar interest in immortality and in locating the 'Islands of Paradise' would obsess the Han emperor Wudi, and in his case it is too well attested to be dismissed. The Shang kings had submitted their dreams to oracular scrutiny; they and the Zhou had had to face down monsters. Indulging ideas that posterity might consider fanciful, or tastes it might consider excessive, amounted to an ancestral prerogative. Whatever legalist logic or Confucian morality might make of such foibles, they were probably widespread in an age riddled with cults and rife with superstition.

Nowhere are the First Emperor's fantasies better demonstrated than in Sima Qian's description of his tomb. The site having been selected when he first came to the throne, by the time of his death a veritable mountain had been constructed upon it. Round about, beyond its double walls, were laid out the subterranean chambers in which replicas of his army and other mortuary accompaniments would be ranged. Human sacrifice as part of the funerary arrangements had not yet been abandoned. Consorts and concubines who had borne the emperor no children were ordered to join him in death, along with perhaps thousands of craftsmen and labourers whose intimate knowledge of the burial chamber might prejudice its security. But in Chu, and by now in Qin, clay effigies were increasingly preferred to still-serviceable humans as grave goods. They cost less, lasted longer, and when mass produced like the First Emperor's terracotta warriors, could be replicated ad infinitum.

The 700,000 colonists sent to work on the tomb were housed near by. There too were located their stores, furnaces, kilns and assembly lines. A similar complex, scattered somewhat farther afield, is growing up today, such is the demand for terracotta replicas and souvenirs from what is becoming China's foremost visitor attraction. But two thousand years ago Sima Qian had words only for the centrepice of the necropolis. Deep beneath the mountain itself was the emperor's great domed burial chamber.

> They dug down to the third layer of underground springs and poured in bronze to make the outer coffin. Replicas of palaces, scenic towers, and the hundred officials, as well as rare utensils and wondrous objects, were brought to fill the tomb. Craftsmen were ordered to set up cross-bows and arrows, rigged so that they would immediately shoot down anyone attempting to break in. Mercury was used to fashion imitations of the hundred rivers, the Yellow River and the Yangzi, and the seas, constructed in such a way that they seemed to flow. Above were representations of all the heavenly bodies, below, the features of the earth. Whale oil was used for lamps, which were calculated to burn for a long time without going out.[27]

Until 1974, when some well-diggers chanced to shovel down into those chambers teeming with clay warriors whom Sima Qian had not even deemed worthy of mention, all this too was considered fanciful. No grave could possibly contain towers and palaces, seas of mercury, a cartographic model of the kingdom and a replica of the sky at night. The tomb had reportedly been ransacked and destroyed on several occasions, most immediately within five years of the emperor's interment. The shattered condition of the terracotta troopers seemed to bear this out. Laboriously reconstituted and remustered, they, and not the tomb itself, whose location was still uncertain, became the stars of late-twentieth-century Chinese archaeology.

Yet since that 1974 discovery, barely a year has gone by without further revelations from the great necropolis outside Xianyang. More pits containing more warriors have been opened. Others have yielded skeletons, half-life-size carriages and life-size bronze replicas of geese and cranes. One is supposed the tomb of the First Emperor's grandmother. Meanwhile the location of the main burial chamber has been pinpointed about a kilometre from the warrior pits beneath its now greatly eroded mountain.

At the time of writing (2008) the tomb remains unopened, its secrets unrevealed. Officially it awaits the development and approval of techniques and treatments that will ensure the preservation of its contents. Conflicting authorities – scientific and archaeological as well as party, provincial and central – may also be involved. As with the Tarim Mummies, national caution excites international impatience. But no one can accuse the authorities of not whetting archaeological appetites. Surveys, scans and probes have established that the great cavity of the burial chamber is still intact, neither choked with infill nor submerged in water. Traces of mercury, presumably from the seas and rivers that flowed so ingeniously across the emperor's replica domain, have been detected; and their distribution has been scanned and charted to produce an almost recognisable map of China. The roof's planetarium may still twinkle, the crossbows stand ready to fire, and among 'the hundred officials' a life-size Li Si could be waiting, bookless, by his patron's nested coffins. Within the chamber, there may still reign that minutely regulated peace and order on which the First Emperor so prided himself in his inscriptions; but without, all semblance of decorum had been shattered almost before he was laid to rest.

4

HAN ASCENDANT

210–141 BC

QIN IMPLODES

NEARLY ALL THAT IS KNOWN OF the First Emperor and his book-burning chancellor comes from a book. In a culture as literary and historically minded as China's, biblioclasts needed to beware; books had a way of biting back, and sure enough, both emperor and chancellor would be badly bitten. Ostensibly Sima Qian's *Shiji*, one of the most ambitious histories ever written, was a direct response to the First Emperor's assault on scholarship. Sima Qian saw his task as salvaging what he calls 'the remains of literature and ancient affairs scattered throughout the world' as a result of the Qin proscription, and then organising and presenting them in a form that would edify and instruct future generations.[1] Confucius had expressed the same idea at a time when the 'warring states' were going to war, and like him, Sima Qian considered his role to be that of 'transmitter', not creator. But since all the earlier annals and commentaries ('Spring and Autumn', *Zuozhuan*, *Zhanguoce*, etc.) stopped short of the Qin unification, and since later histories would start with the first Han emperor, the *Shiji* would be the only work to deal with the intervening Qin triumph and implosion. By happy coincidence, the most dramatic upheaval in early China's history is covered exclusively by its foremost historian.

Written about a hundred years after the fall of Qin, the *Shiji* (usually translated as 'Records of the [Grand] Historian') is by no means limited to that period or to what might then have been regarded as the recent past. Its 130 chapters span some 3,000 years, a remarkable perspective in a work of the second-to-first centuries BC. When later enshrined as the first of the eventually twenty-four 'Standard Histories' (one for each 'legitimate' dynasty) it served as a sort of 'Book of Genesis', beginning the narrative of China's history and carrying it forward from its myth-rich dawn

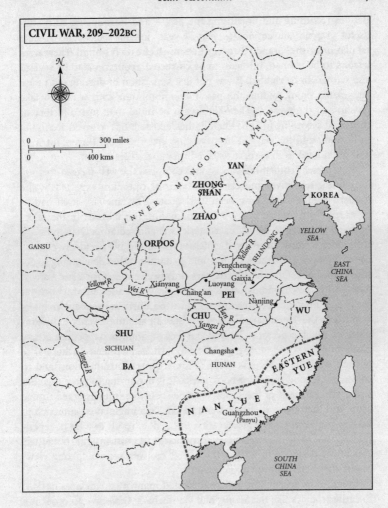

CIVIL WAR, 209–202BC

Not simply a dynastic record, then, it is not simply a history either.

and the Five Emperors, through the Three (royal) Dynasties of Xia, Shang and Zhou, including the 'Spring and Autumn' and 'Warring States' periods, and on to the Qin and Han. Although it set the pattern for all the later 'Standard Histories', it is in fact the only one that deals with more than a single dynasty.

Not simply a dynastic record, then, it is not simply a history either.

Besides recording and organising the past – and introducing such still-useful graphic conventions as year-by-year timelines and state-by-state tabulations – the 'Grand Historian' had much else on his mind. There were lessons to be learned, mistakes to be corrected, reputations to be revised and wrongs to be righted. It was not just a question of dishing out praise and blame or of raiding the past for ammunition with which to take potshots at the present. The *Shiji* was to be more than just 'a history of the world according to Sima Qian', rather 'a history of the world according to history'; and the ways of history being, like those of Heaven, intricate and often hard to discern, it required very special treatment.

To represent something so vast and complex, the well-flagged themes, long linear narratives and clanking chains of causation expected by the modern reader would have been inadequate. The language itself had to be exact; truth and accuracy were paramount. But latitude in the selection and ordering of the factual material still allowed Sima Qian to nudge the reader towards his desired conclusions. So did his decidedly creative use of dialogue and dramatisation; and so did the rather demanding structure of the book. Of those 130 chapters, only twelve comprise 'Basic Annals'. Along with the chronological tables, they provide a useful framework yet make for unsatisfactory reading without the thirty subsequent chapters devoted to the 'Hereditary Houses' (or 'states') and the seventy to biographies of notable persons. To find out exactly what is happening at any given moment – and more especially why – the reader needs to familiarise himself with the entire text (four to six volumes in translation) and to command a good supply of bookmarks. It is like trying to piece together a play with, instead of the script, a sequence of the lines assigned to one actor and then those to another and so on. This fragmented approach in no way prejudices the *Shiji*'s veracity; but it does result in a lot of repetition and not a few inconsistencies, some no doubt unintentional but others apparently designed to hint at the mixed motives and conflicting viewpoints that beset all human endeavour.

In addition, recent studies have detected many of the devices noticed in earlier classics like the *Shijing* and Confucius's *Analects* – an obsession with names and their 'rectification', meanings implied by allusion and the 'correlation' of apparently unrelated materials, and that emphasis on faithful transmission rather than innovation. But perhaps the most intriguing insight is that which interprets the *Shiji* as being a rival to the First Emperor's tomb in that it too represents a model, or microcosm, of the world as then known. Here, albeit in prose, the heavens and their constellations are also represented, and likewise the empire's rivers and waterways, its geographical divisions and its clustered high officials. As Grant Hardy puts it:

> The First Emperor's tomb was an image of the world created and maintained by bronze – the force of arms – whereas Sima Qian's *Shiji* offered an alternative depiction of the world, inscribed on bamboo slips and regulated by scholarship and morality . . . If Sima's creation could not match the First Emperor's in political power, it far surpassed it in influence, and eventually the famous mausoleum was known and understood by the place it held in Sima Qian's all encompassing bamboo-world.[2]

On the other hand if, when the mausoleum is opened, its furnishings are found to exceed or contradict Sima's description, it may be the First Emperor who has the last laugh. Already the 'terracotta army' has added an unsuspected military dimension. Further finds – imagine the consternation if they include books – could confound not only the Grand Historian but a hundred generations of subsequent historians.

If the First Emperor's innermost coffin is found intact, it may even be possible to discover what he died of. But until then 'the bamboo record' must suffice. In 210 BC the First Emperor was still in his forties and apparently fit enough to undertake another tour of his domains. Only days before his collapse he was out shooting sea monsters on the Shandong shore. The suggestion that he was a victim of poisoning therefore seems plausible. But if this was the case, the dose was probably self-administered; for in the potions prepared for him by the experts in immortality the vital ingredient was cinnabar. A mineral rarity, cinnabar came largely from Sichuan and was used as a pigment, most notably to impart a ruddy shade of vermilion to the ink reserved for emperors. As a crystalline form of mercuric sulphide, it is also toxic, and when ingested in quantity, fatal. Gulping down the draughts that promised eternal life, the First Emperor may have been inviting a rather sudden death.

According to Sima Qian, at the first hint of indisposition Meng Yi, the chief minister and brother of the wall-building Meng Tian, had been sent post-haste from Shandong to organise 'sacrifices to the mountains and rivers', presumably for the emperor's recovery. That left the imperial cavalcade in the charge of Li Si, the book-burning chancellor, assisted by Zhao Gao, a eunuch who held the important post of chief of the imperial carriages, plus Prince Huhai, the emperor's youngest son. When the emperor expired just days after Meng Yi's departure, Li Si proved uncharacteristically indecisive. Instead it was Zhao Gao who took the initiative.

The eunuch had a score to settle with the Meng brothers; Prince Huhai, a callow youth with no redeeming qualities other than his parentage, was conveniently to hand; and Li Si, who must by now have been in his sixties, was rather easily talked into manipulating the succession.

The dead emperor's written testament appointing another son as his heir was accordingly suppressed. So too was report of the death itself, for it was vital that the plotters reach Xianyang and secure the reins of power before the news of the emperor's demise encouraged others to thwart them. The cavalcade therefore rumbled on towards the capital as if nothing had happened. Meals for its reclusive principal were delivered to his carriage as usual, while a wagon of fish was positioned near by to counteract the stench of rotting emperor.

On regaining the capital, the plotters swung into action. Prince Huhai was proclaimed the emperor's designated heir and installed as the *Qin* Second Emperor. The First Emperor's preferred heir was then charged with treason and, in forged orders from his father, commanded to commit suicide – which, being a truly filial son, he did. Then the Meng brothers were censured for opposing these arrangements and detained until such time as Meng Yi could be executed and Meng Tian obliged to take poison.

These events were accompanied by a reign of terror that, as described by Sima Qian, must have made the dead emperor's heavy-handed administration seem almost benign. 'Make the laws sterner and the penalties more severe,' urged Zhao Gao. 'See that those charged with a crime implicate others and that punishments extend to the families of the criminals. Wipe out the chief ministers and sow dissension among their kin.' With the scheming eunuch acting as grand inquisitor, twelve princes and ten princesses were dismembered in the Xianyang marketplace. Those implicated with them together with their 'three degrees of relatives' – traditionally parents, siblings and offspring – suffered a similar fate but were 'too numerous even to be counted'. New laws and harsher punishments were promulgated. Taxes and levies were increased, and yet more forced labour was marched off to work and die on still-incomplete projects such as the Opang Palace and the northern frontier's walls. 'Each man began to fear for his own safety,' says Sima Qian, 'and those who longed to revolt were many.'[3]

Rebellion in fact broke out within six months of the First Emperor's death. It had already spread through the eastern commanderies when in the following year (209 BC) Li Si became the next victim of note. Shunned by the witless new emperor, 'China's First Unifier' was duped by Zhao Gao, tortured until he confessed to treason, and then condemned to undergo 'the five penalties'. These consisted of tattooing, amputation of ears, nose, fingers and feet, flogging, beheading and public exposure of the severed head. For good measure, Li Si's torso was also cut in two at the waist. Few destroyers of books can themselves have been so comprehensively shredded.[4]

Meanwhile Zhao Gao had begun gunning for his imperial puppet. In anticipation of the fable about 'The Emperor's New Clothes', His Majesty was invited to accept the gift of a horse that was in fact a deer. When he made some remark to that effect, Zhao Gao and other attendants corrected him: all agreed it was a horse, and they further pretended concern that His Majesty might be labouring under a delusionary condition. The Grand Diviner then confirmed that there had of late been some liturgical short-comings in the imperial performance of the ancestral rites. The Second Emperor was advised to withdraw from public life to fast and purify himself.

While thus secluded, a hostile force invaded his place of retreat. Zhao Gao declared it to be the advance guard of a rebel army (it was of course nothing of the sort, just his own carefully drilled cohorts) and advised the young emperor to pre-empt capture and execution by taking poison. After further prompting and not a little threatening, the emperor obliged. Zhao Gao himself then seized the imperial seals.

This, however, was too much for the other officials and much too much for Heaven, which made its feelings felt with three hefty earth tremors. Zhao Gao therefore turned to a grandson of the First Emperor, who, though reluctant to accept the throne, did the next best thing: he had Zhao Gao murdered. By now it was 207 BC, only three years since the First Emperor's death but long enough for his entire empire to be up in arms. As an inheritance it was not worth the risk of acceptance; in fact the grandson may already have been in touch with the rebels. Within three months they would be entering Xianyang itself.[5]

PAWN TO KING

'Rebellion' would seem a misnomer for the groundswell of protest that greeted the Second Emperor's excesses. There was an element of restora-tion about the uprising, of reinstating the old 'warring states', plus a strong sense of righteous obligation in overthrowing an imperial house that had so patently forfeited Heaven's favour. To be fair, it is doubtful whether Qin ever really laid claim to such a thing. The First Emperor's inscriptions scarcely mention Heaven, let alone the Mandate; and if they were drafted by such a rabid legalist as Li Si, this is hardly surprising. But in Confucian terms, legitimacy now lay firmly with the anti-Qin forces and would continue to do so throughout the next seven years of civil war.

Sima Qian deals with this confused period exhaustively, recounting the marches and counter-marches, the engagements and intrigues in remorseless detail, but always from the perspective of the contending 'rebel' camps, not of the blood-spattered Qin court at Xianyang. Larger-than-life personalities emerge from the mêlée and hint at major issues. What might otherwise have seemed like a brief and belated throwback to the 'Warring States' period is portrayed as a seminal moment, a historical watershed and a Grand Historian's grand opportunity. China's political future was being decided and its official ideology forged. The Han empire that resulted would enshrine features of Chinese culture that would be revered ever after and lend compelling substance to the idea of a continuous civilisation.

Of all the issues involved in the power struggle – territorial, dynastic, philosophical and fiscal – perhaps the most surprising was social, in that dissent swelled from the lowest ranks of society. Resistance to Qin rule proved to be not just popular but populist. In his determination to mobilise the manpower of the empire, the First Emperor had established a direct relationship between the centralised government and the localised governed. Wrenched from mass oblivion, the black-haired commoners had been dragooned into participating in the historical process. Millions had been uprooted to fight, labour or colonise on the empire's behalf. Millions more had been obliged to support this effort through heavy taxation and collective liability backed by ferocious penalties. Their woes were shared and their fears real. While nationalists would later applaud the First Emperor's efforts at unification, and while Maoists would approve his autocratic efforts in mass mobilisation, orthodox Marxists would be more gratified by the anti-Qin response and its early evidence of peasant revolt and class consciousness.

The first challenge came from a ploughman of the erstwhile state of Chu, who was called Chen She. Ordered to the frontier with a gang of conscripts in 209 BC, Chen She calculated that the heavy rain was making it impossible for them to reach their destination on schedule and that since they would therefore be treated as deserters, they might as well as desert. A colleague agreed and, by dint of some supernatural trickery, convinced the other conscripts to join them. The cry of 'Great Chu shall rise again' was first heard coming from a spookily lit shrine at dead of night; it was followed by the refrain 'Chen She shall be a king', the very words that one of the conscripts had just found written in imperial cinnabar on a piece of silk miraculously preserved inside the belly of his fish supper. As portents went, these were both explicit and imperative. The conscript gang was transformed into a band of rebels, quickly snowballed into an avenging army, and then, as others followed Chen She's example, became the vanguard of a great anti-Qin coalition. Chen She resurrected the ancient state of Chu and declared himself its king. Other pretenders followed suit north of the Yellow River in erstwhile Yan, Zhao and Wei.[6]

Sima Qian would dub Chen She 'the Melancholy King'. Accustomed to history's neglect of the common man, the Grand Historian was intrigued how someone 'born in a humble hut with tiny windows and a wattle door, a day labourer in the fields and a garrison conscript, whose abilities could not match even the average', could yet 'step from the ranks of the common soldiery, rise from the paths of the fields and lead a band of a few hundred poor and weary soldiers in revolt against ... a great kingdom that for a hundred years [i.e. since Qin's acquisition of Sichuan] had made the ancient eight provinces pay homage at its court.' The only explanation had to be that offered by Confucians: Qin had failed to rule with righteousnesss and humanity and had failed to realise that the qualities required of a ruler were not those of a conqueror. Thus Chen She had only to ride a wave of righteous protest. But when he too proved a neglectful ruler, he was himself engulfed by this wave, in fact murdered within the year by one of his own retainers. Melancholy indeed, mused the Grand Historian.[7]

A new breed of leader now emerged, the foremost example being Xiang Yu. Another native of Chu but an aristocrat rather than a commoner, descended from a long line of Chu generals, Xiang Yu towered above his contemporaries in both physique and accomplishment. He was foul of temper but fearless in battle, and his men worshipped him. Though historians nurtured in the literary and bureaucratic tradition found nothing remotely romantic in battlefield antics, Xiang Yu would prove an exception. Sima Qian called him arrogant, deceitful and ungrateful, yet could neither disguise his admiration nor resist the sort of detail calculated to enhance a heroic reputation. Xiang Yu strides from the pages of the *Shiji* like no other warrior; and it is testimony to the *Shiji*'s influence that he is still sometimes hailed as the most accomplished general in the whole of Chinese history.

Scenting a once-in-a-lifetime opportunity, other leaders emerged from the masses more like Chen She. Liu Bang of Pei, a district in the north of what had been (and was again) Chu, had also fallen foul of the Qin authorities and taken to brigandage. But while the melancholic Chen She had

had to contrive his own portents, and while the mighty Xiang Yu was well enough endowed to manage without them, Heaven of its own volition showered the young Liu Bang with auspicious signs and lucky encounters. Dragons – of all animals the most closely associated with power and celestial favour – featured in many of these manifestations. His mother had conceived him by a dragon, another hovered over him when he slept, and his well-whiskered features were sufficiently dragon-like to excite physiognomists (they foretold your future from your face), one of whom, a certain Lü, was so impressed that he gave him his daughter in marriage. Thus does the Grand Historian waste no time in flagging the future founder of the Han dynasty and his influential consort. Readers are not to be misled by Liu Bang's limited education, his boorish behaviour and indifferent military record. Heaven's favour would more than compensate.

Following the death of Chen She, it was the inspirational Xiang Yu who quickly made a name for himself as a commander. He then took over the reconstituted kingdom of Chu, first as the power behind the puppet throne, then as king and eventually as *ba* ('hegemon' or 'protector') over a cluster of satellite states. The dragon-blest Liu Bang of Pei, his gang having grown to an army, allied himself with Xiang Yu and his Chu forces. In 207 BC, the year in which the Second Emperor committed suicide and Zhao Gao was murdered, the armies of the now commander-in-chief Xiang Yu inflicted a succession of heavy defeats on the Qin forces, driving them back to the hill passes that guarded the Qin stronghold along the Wei River. 'The war-cry of Chu shook the heavens, and the men of the other armies all trembled with fear,' says Sima Qian.[8]

Meanwhile Liu Bang of Pei led his men west by way of the Han valley and then north towards Qin. Finding the passes from this direction less well defended, he opened contact with the Qin court at Xianyang, learned of the fall of the Second Emperor, and received some encouragement from the First Emperor's grandson, who was now the would-be (or more precisely 'would-rather-not-be') 'Third Emperor'. Without consulting his allies, Liu Bang then marched on the capital and took it.

As his superior commander, Xiang Yu was furious. He too thrust towards Xianyang and, threatening to exterminate both the enemy and his ally, encamped his 400,000 men within a day's march of Liu Bang's 100,000. It was not just a question of Liu Bang's insubordination. Rumours of his having made a deal with Xianyang were rife, and they seemed to be borne out by the extraordinary clemency Liu Bang had shown towards Qin's people and their would-rather-not-be emperor. Such restraint suggested that Liu Bang was both currying favour in Qin and cultivating a reputation for superior virtue, as sure a sign of imperial ambitions as the celestial dragons and tigers that were reported circling over his camp.

To fend off a clash of Qin's joint conquerors, a reconciliation was attempted by go-betweens. Liu Bang reported to Xiang Yu in person; but even as the liquor flowed and loyalties were reaffirmed, weapons were being fingered by their jumpy retainers. Pretending a weak bladder, Liu Bang excused himself, left the audience tent and failed to return. On learning that he had in fact been smuggled back to his own army in safety, Xiang Yu fell into a towering rage. (Sima Qian has him fuming rather often.) Such wrath could be assuaged only by turning on Xianyang, massacring its inhabitants, torching its palaces and archives (so probably burning more books than Li Si), murdering the now would-definitely-not-be 'Third Emperor', and in one of the *Shiji*'s several versions of this grisly episode, 'desecrating the grave of the First Emperor' – which could account for the shattered state of 'the terracotta army'.

This action of Xiang Yu's was particularly reprehensible in that the city had already surrendered, albeit to his rival; and Xiang Yu now compounded his mistake with a string of others. Instead of establishing himself within the natural stronghold that was the state of Qin, he headed back east; trouble was brewing in Shandong, his men were homesick, and Chu's new capital at Pengcheng awaited its hero. In his absence, the state of Qin was divided into four lesser kingdoms, with Liu Bang being fobbed off with its outlying commanderies in Ba and Shu (Sichuan) plus the neighbouring upper Han valley. Xiang Yu seems to have assumed that, since Sichuan was notoriously a place of exile, relegating his rival to this far-flung region beyond the Qinling range would keep him out of mischief. Liu Bang, or 'the King of Han' as he was now to be styled, saw it more as a lucky escape and a safe refuge. To make doubly sure that he was not pursued, he dismantled the carpentry of Stone Cattle Road and other mountain trails behind him.

From this 206 BC appointment of Liu Bang of Pei as king of Han, the Han dynasty would date its foundation and take its name; but it would be another four years of strife and appalling bloodshed before the Han king became the Han emperor. For no sooner had Xiang Yu marched east than Liu Bang marched north again, replacing the mountain road and retaking the Qin heartland.

The titanic struggle that now unfolded would achieve epic status. Thanks to Sima Qian, the protagonists would win such fame that references to the spirit of Xiang Yu or the stamina of Liu Bang would come to rate as conversational clichés. To this day, Chinese chessboards often indicate that one

FROM QIN TO HAN, 220–87BC

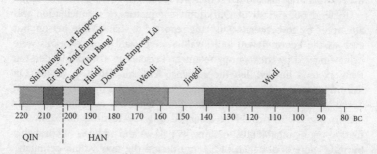

end is for 'Han' rather than 'black' and the other for 'Chu' rather than 'white'.[9] The rules of combat, such as they were, were mutually understood; move by move the game must progress until a king was toppled. But the odds were evenly stacked, and though fortunes would fluctuate, the outcome remained uncertain till the bitter end.

Liu Bang made the opening move. With a secure base in Qin and with the unlimited resources of Sichuan to draw on, he was in the same enviable position as the Qin kings of the 'Warring States' period. At the head of an army that had suddenly grown to a no doubt exaggerated 560,000 men, he swept east and took the Chu capital of Pengcheng. Meanwhile Xiang Yu, whose kingdom was more vulnerable to attack from the rear, was quashing opposition far to the east in Shandong. Greeting the news of Liu Bang's onslaught with his customary outburst, Xiang Yu headed to the rescue. Despite a march of several hundred kilometres and only 30,000 men, he drove back the enemy, reclaimed Pengcheng and won two resounding victories – such was his undoubted genius as a field commander.

Liu Bang should have been captured at the second Pengcheng battle. But surrounded on all sides and with no hope of relief, he was saved by a dust storm. Day turned to night and he escaped in the confusion; Heaven had not forgotten him. His family were taken prisoner and his great army virtually annihilated, but he fought on. Twice more he was surrounded and twice more escaped. A lull while Xiang Yu marched off to quell more unrest on his eastern seaboard allowed Liu Bang to recoup his strength. Provisions and men reached him from Sichuan and Qin down the Wei and Yellow rivers; other hastily recruited forces were sent to stir up trouble behind the Chu lines and to intercept supplies.

By the time Xiang Yu returned to the front in 203 BC, a military stalemate had set in. To break it, Xiang Yu first threatened to kill Liu Bang's captive father, then offered to settle matters in personal combat with Liu Bang himself. Liu Bang failed to rise to either challenge. Time, as well as Heaven, was now on Liu Bang of Han's side. While his resources were being constantly replenished from Sichuan and Qin, Xiang Yu's troops were tiring, their supplies failing and their strength being sapped by constant trouble from Chu's supposedly subordinate states. With Xiang Yu away putting down yet another such revolt, Liu Bang experienced a rare taste of victory. It was short-lived. Again Xiang Yu came dashing to the rescue and again Liu Bang withdrew rather than risk battle with an apparently invincible foe.

Both sides repeatedly accused one another of treachery; there was in fact little to choose between them in this respect. Even Sima Qian, a Han subject who had necessarily to uphold the reputation of the Han founder, had no intention of thereby damning the great Xiang Yu of Chu. Mean, violent, vain and distrustful the Chu king undoubtedly was, declared the Grand Historian, while all the time depicting a dazzling hero for whom nothing less than a climax of high tragedy would suffice, plus – as he warmed to his task – some of the purplest passages in the whole of the *Shiji*.

In late 203 BC the mutual insults gave way to ceasefire overtures. Both rulers agreed to withdraw; Xiang Yu surrendered Liu Bang's family; and the empire was tentatively divided along the north–south line of a canal between the Huai and Yellow rivers. Xiang Yu's Chu retained all to the east, Liu Bang's Han all to the west. A relieved Xiang Yu at last pulled back. But an encouraged Liu Bang went after him, harrying the Chu van and picking off stragglers. What should have been a victorious homecoming for Xiang Yu's men began to assume the appearance of an undisciplined rout. Liu Bang pressed ever harder and his forces grew by the day. Lukewarm supporters flocked to his standard on the promise of fiefs that he might now actually be able to deliver. So did deserters from the disillusioned ranks of the enemy.

The last great battle was fought at a place called Gaixia in northern Anhui. Outnumbered three to one, Xiang Yu's forces were finally overwhelmed and he himself surrounded, 'his soldiers being now few and supplies exhausted'. That night Xiang Yu could not sleep, reports Sima Qian. From the Han encampments came the sound of music. They were singing the songs of Chu. Was it possible, asked Xiang Yu, that so many men of Chu had already defected?

Then he rose in the night and drank within the curtains of his tent. With him were the beautiful Lady Yü, who then enjoyed his favour and went everywhere with him, and his famous steed 'Dapple', which he always rode. Xiang Yu, now filled with passionate sorrow, began to sing sadly. [His song was of how the times were against him, of Dapple's exhaustion and of what would become of 'Yü, my Yü'.] He sang the song several times and Lady Yü joined with him. Tears streamed down his face, while all those about him wept and were unable to lift their eyes from the ground. Then he mounted his horse and with 800 brave riders beneath his banner, rode into the night, broke through the encirclement to the south, and galloped away.[10]

The chase resumed. By the time Xiang Yu reached the Huai River, his 800 men were reduced to a hundred. As he approached the Yangzi, they were down to twenty-eight. Promising them three last victories, he was as good as his word. Thrice they charged against impossible odds and each time they broke through the Han ranks. It was Heaven which was destroying him, said Xiang Yu, and 'no fault of my own in the use of arms'.

On the Yangzi – it was just west of Nanjing – a boat was waiting. Safety beckoned. It was from across the river in erstwhile Wu that he had set forth eight years earlier. He still had supporters there; he could yet rule there. But 'how can I face them again?' he asked. 'How could I not feel shame in my heart?' So saying, he dismounted, and presenting 'Dapple' to the kindly boatman, turned back and strode on foot towards the Han host.

In the final scuffle Xiang Yu killed 'several hundred', according to Sima Qian, while suffering 'a dozen wounds'. Faint and bleeding, he then recognised an old acquaintance who was now a Han cavalry officer. His last words were spoken soldier to soldier.

'I have heard that Han has offered a reward of a thousand catties[11] of gold and a fief of ten thousand households for my life,' said Xiang Yu. 'So I will do you a favour!' And with that he cut his own throat and died.[12]

JADED MONARCHS

On 28 February 202 BC, with Xiang Yu dead and Chu subdued, Liu Bang of Pei 'assumed the position of Supreme Emperor'. At this point in his narrative Sima Qian ceases calling him 'the king of Han' ('Liu Bang' and

'Lord of Pei' had long since been dropped) and switches to his posthumous imperial title of Gaozu. History would adopt this title exclusively, commemorating him as *Han* Gaozu, 'the Han Great Progenitor' (or sometimes *Han* Gaodi, 'the Han Progenitor-Emperor'). The first commoner to rise to the dizzy heights of emperor, he would be the last for 1,500 years. Founding a dynasty from such obscurity was no small achievement, and the Grand Historian, writing at a time when the strongest of all the Han emperors occupied the throne, acknowledged a remarkable lineage by hailing its imperial progenitor.

Yet in 202 BC the future of the Han dynasty, and that of China as a unitary empire, was far from assured. The territorial colossus amassed by Qin had been so severely shaken that the chances of the Great Progenitor's progeny controlling the most extensive and enduring of all ancient China's imperial constructs looked remote indeed. South of the Yangzi watershed Han's writ scarcely ran at all; it was contested in the east and north, and vigorously repudiated on the northern frontier where the Ordos region, so laboriously fortified by the wall-minded Meng Tian, was quickly abandoned.

A long reign would have helped, but *Han* Gaozu lived only seven more years (202–195 BC), most of these being spent suppressing rebellions and fending off incursions. Helpful too would have been a strong successor; instead he was followed by a timid teenager (who was at least his son), then two infants (who were probably not his grandsons). Falling an early prey to the palace intrigues that attended every minority, by 190 BC Han authority was being wielded, and the throne effectively usurped, by the Dowager Empress Lü, Gaozu's bride from the days when he was a nonentity in Pei. Qin's imperial phase had lasted a paltry fifteen years; Han's looked likely to last only slightly longer.

All along there had been something less than convincing about Liu Bang's rise to power. As he candidly admitted, success had been achieved despite his capabilities rather than because of them, and at the expense of some hefty compromises. To win support he had had to appear to repudiate Qin repression. That meant dismantling the legalist state, disowning its penal authoritarianism, lessening the burdens of taxation and conscription, and cultivating a more consensual ideology and a more approachable persona. Yet without unchallenged authority, strict regulations and access to unlimited manpower and revenue, an effective government was scarcely possible. It was the old problem of the tactics and behaviour appropriate to winning an empire being unsuited to ruling it. Gaozu must needs 'change with the times'.

His personal reformation was gradual. The hard-drinking habits of a life in the field continued. The emperor liked nothing better than a bacchanalia of brimming cups, earthy jokes and clumsy horseplay in the company of cronies from Pei. Heavy drinking meant frequent 'visits to the toilet' (as Sima Qian's English translator puts it), where bad things happened; people didn't come back, they got slandered in their absence, cornered by 'wild bears' or, in the case of one young lady, cornered – then urgently 'favoured' – by the emperor. Toilets were not nice places. Then as now, the excrement was collected for manuring the fields; along with adjustable ploughs and the development of a seeding machine for drill sowing, this is thought to have contributed substantially to increased agricultural yields under the early Han. The dung accumulated beneath the privy in a noisome pit. Here rootled hogs and briefly, in 194 BC, 'the human pig', described as a blind, dumb, demented creature without ears, feet or hands but of a distinctly womanly form. This was the once lovely Lady Chi after the Dowager Empress Lü had finished revenging herself on one whose only crime was to have given birth to an imperial contender. 'Empress Lü was a woman of very strong will,' says Sima Qian. Huidi, her teenage son who had just been enthroned as Gaozu's successor, was so horrified by Lady Chi's fate that he too then 'gave himself up each day to drink' and played no further part in affairs of state.

Sima Qian's *Shiji* treats of the Dowager Empress Lü in its section on 'Rulers', as if it was she who was Gaozu's successor, while Huidi ('Emperor Hui', the di suffix signifying 'emperor') gets no separate treatment, just occasional mentions. From Gaozu's death in 195 BC until her own death in 180 BC, the dowager empress most emphatically ruled while emperors barely reigned. Huidi's only achievement was to encourage Shusun Tong, the dynasty's expert on ceremonial and ritual, in the elaboration of a Han dynastic mystique.

A noted Confucian scholar with a large following, Shusun Tong had joined Gaozu in his 'King of Han' days, had then stage-managed his enthronement, and thereafter set about introducing some decorum into the imperial court. This was not easy. Gaozu was so contemptuous of formal erudition that he was known to snatch off the cap of the nearest scholar to use as a chamber pot. Yet while informality was all very well in reaction to Qin sobriety, even the emperor was irked when drinking companions burst in on his lovemaking. What was needed, said Shusun Tong, were rules of protocol and court ritual. The emperor somewhat doubtfully agreed. 'See what you can do, but make it easy to learn . . . it must be the sort of thing I can manage.'

A task force of scholars was assembled, the texts duly scanned, and a month spent practising the new choreography in a specially built pavilion. When Shusun Tong was ready, he invited Gaozu's approval. A sigh of relief greeted the emperor's 'I can do that all right'. The new ceremonial was immediately introduced, and at the 199 BC New Year's celebrations, when nobles and officials from all over the empire came to pay court, 'everyone trembled with awe and reverence'. Gaozu at last 'understood how exalted a thing it is to be an emperor!'[13] Shusun Tong was rewarded and, during Huidi's reign, he devised and orchestrated the ancestral rites to be accorded to the deceased 'Great Progenitor' and his successors.

But it was one thing to indulge Confucian ideas of ritual and decorum, quite another to embrace Confucian notions of rulership. Gaozu was too busy shoring up his authority to set an example of moral excellence; arguably his empire was too unruly to respond to it. Laws and taxes were essential, not least because, without them, there would be no point to the amnesties and remissions with which he and his successors rewarded loyalty and assuaged resentment. Though Han emperors were more inclined to listen to advice, Qin's autocratic legacy was not in fact repudiated. *Han* Gaozu made special provision for the maintenance (and perhaps the restoration) of the First Emperor's tomb and for the conduct of his ancestral rites. The legalist framework of government – registration and rankings, group responsibility, a tariff of punishments and rewards, universal taxation, corvée and conscription – was retained *in toto*; and though somewhat relaxed in practice, it would remain fundamental to Chinese empire.

The relaxation was most notable during the reigns of the scholarly *Han* Wendi (r. 180–157 BC), one of Gaozu's sons who became emperor when the Dowager Empress Lü died, and that of the filial *Han* Jingdi (r. 157–141 BC), who was Wendi's son. But if a Confucian gloss was later given to this leniency, it was only partly thanks to their employing notable scholars, some of a Confucian bent, and more obviously because in retrospect the whole half-century from Gaozu's death to that of Jingdi came to be seen as a golden age. Relative peace prevailed, although at some cost in respect to the northern frontier, as will be seen; harvests were generally good, a sure sign of celestial favour; and remissions and pardons were frequent. Wendi's virtue was 'of the highest order', concluded Sima Qian, who even found a good word for Dowager Empress Lü: during her 'reign' 'punishments were seldom meted out and evil-doers were few; the people applied themselves to the work of farming; and food and clothing became abundant'.[14]

Jingdi's moment of glory came in 154 BC when six kingdoms rose in revolt and were defeated. The trouble dated back to Gaozu's reign and was a legacy of his war with Xiang Yu. At the decisive battle of Gaixia in Anhui, the victors had been the Han generals. It was their forces which had over-powered Xiang Yu's while, in Sima Qian's words, 'the King of Han followed behind'. Doubtful whether Liu Bang would ever defeat his rival, the generals had risked their troops only after being promised substantial kingdoms by way of reward. When the same generals had urged Liu Bang to assume the emperorship, they had done so partly in comformity to a traditional formula for such occasions, partly because it really mattered to them; for as they explained, 'if our king does not assume the supreme title, then all our own titles will be called into doubt'.[15] Thus, when the king of Han obliged and stepped up to the imperial throne, a clutch of far from submissive generals clambered on to royal thrones of their own.

The new dynasty required an imperial capital to accommodate its ancestral tombs and temples, not to mention its court and administration. Emulating the Eastern (Later) Zhou, Gaozu had lit on Luoyang, which was well sited in the heart of the Zhongyuan ('central plain') between Qin and Chu. But no sooner had he settled there than he was persuaded to remove to a remoter but far more defensible site at Chang'an in the western fastness of Qin (it was near Xianyang at the modern Xi'an). Luoyang had been revealed as a death-trap, for in rewarding his generals Gaozu had relinquished direct control over much of its hinterland. He had in fact alienated practically all the territories that had been awarded to Xiang Yu when in 203 BC the exhausted rivals had partitioned the empire between them. Thus the entire eastern half of what had been the First Emperor's domain had been parcelled out as ten kingdoms, with only the western half remaining as directly administered commanderies. In effect victory had been bought at the cost of reinstating the discredited system of heredi-tary 'feudal' enfeoffment, plus all that it implied in terms of diminished imperial authority. Luoyang and the pitiful fate of its last Zhou emperors may have served as a reminder.

Though the work of clawing back these enfeoffed kingdoms had begun immediately, they remained a threat, and the task would not be completed for the best part of a century. Gaozu's efforts concentrated on a change of personnel. Erstwhile generals and other potential challengers were grad-ually replaced as kings by less bellicose members of his own family. Empress Lü continued the process by installing members of her own family. Wendi, in replacing them, took the opportunity to break up some kingdoms and reclaim others. The 154 BC revolt suppressed by Jingdi provided a further opportunity for undermining the kingdoms. All of this forestalled a relapse into the chaos of the 'Warring States' era, although so long as kingdoms rejoicing in illustrious names like Qi, Zhao, Yan and even Chu survived, the integrity of the empire remained compromised.

Dynastic history tends to portray these Han kingdoms, or 'sub-kingdoms', as recalcitrant satellites vainly contesting a manifest imperial destiny. Archaeology once again provides a corrective. Several royal tombs of the early Han period have been discovered; and until the day when *Qin* Shi Huangdi's great mausolem is opened, they afford the most striking glimpse of ancient China's material culture. Admittedly subterranean chambers are less exciting than Graeco-Roman colonnades. But stone was scarce in much of China. The population was concentrated on the alluvial flood-plains where construction meant *hangtu* footings and wooden superstructures. Buildings of several storeys slung with saddle-back roofs and upcurled eaves are depicted in tomb paintings and described in texts. They look spectacular. But timber rots and brickwork crumbles. Save for extensive foundations, such as those traced at the new imperial capital of Chang'an, and a few glazed roof tiles, very little survives.

Yet if China's landscape is short on ancient monuments, compensation lurks beneath. Courtesy of a mental outlook that avidly embraced the afterlife, ancestors were cherished not just as loved ones but as progenitors deserving of the Confucian respect due to all parents, and as intermediaries in any dealings with the spirit world. Their tombs were carefully prepared. The deceased were interred in as pristine a condition as possible (cremation would have been even more dishonourable than dismemberment or mutilation); and to meet their ongoing needs in terms of comfort, sustenance, status and diversion, they were provided with the accoutrements they had enjoyed in life. In this sense every tomb reflected its occupant's lifestyle and became, like the First Emperor's, a microcosm of the material world that he or she had relinquished.

The tombs of the Han kings were no exception; they may be taken as providing reliable evidence of the resources and tastes of their royal occupants. When in 1968 some soldiers of the People's Liberation Army discovered what proved to be the tombs of the king and queen of Zhongshan (a Han kingdom in Shanxi), it was the royal couple's jade suits which excited the most interest. A dazzling hoard of silks, lacquerware, figurines and inlaid bronzes also impressed the fatigues-clad militiamen; but for sheer extravagance the jade tailoring was in a class of its own. Discoveries elsewhere of Han-period jade suits in various stages of disintegration have since ensured pride of place in many of the country's museums for what may be the world's only stone clothing.

Each tight-fitting suit covered its corpse entirely, including face, feet and fingers, like a suit of armour. Jade was supposed to have preservative qualities, presumably more spiritual than chemical, that were effective only if no part of the body remained exposed. But though appearing to be a single garment, each outfit was typically a fourteen-piece suit including matching gloves, footwear, face-mask, separate sleeves and helmet. Like the armour of the 'terracotta warriors', all these items were made up of small and precisely butted rectangular plates, some two to three thousand jades per suit, each sewn to its neighbours using thread of either gold, silver or silk. Not even the pharaohs dressed their dead in jade-mail stitched with gold. Whether assessed in terms of craftsmanship, weight or value, such tailoring testifies to an opulence and patronage beyond the means of most 'satellite kings' – and possibly even emperors.

At Changsha, the capital of another kingdom created by Gaozu for one of his generals (but this time south of the Yangzi in Hunan), no royal tombs have been discovered. A mound excavated at Mawangdui in the city's outskirts in the 1970s, however, was found to conceal comparable treasures within the gargantuan nested coffins of the kingdom's chancellor, otherwise the marquis of Dai (d. 186 BC), of his wife the Lady Dai, and of a literary gentleman thought to be their son. Not being kings, none of the family merited a jade suit, although more mundane methods of preservation – such as carefully sealing the coffins against damp and bacteria – had served one of the deceased well. After 2,100 years, silk-wrapped and swaddled in her innermost coffin, the Lady Dai was found to be intact, albeit phenomenally aged and in dire need of a hairdresser. Unlike the Tarim Mummies, her corpse was not desiccated; her joints could be moved and her flesh was responsive to a gentle poke. A post-mortem revealed her medical history, plus '138 and a half seeds' still lodged in her digestive system; the Lady Dai had last snacked on musk melon.

The furnishings of her tomb are known in some detail because among them were found bamboo slips containing a complete written inventory. This listed, for instance, not only the various receptacles that were unearthed in her dining area but the delicacies that once filled them; seven kinds of meat are mentioned, with cooking suggestions, and two of ale, one unfermented and the other perhaps a stout. Exquisitely painted silks decorated the walls of the chamber and a T-shaped silken banner was draped over the innermost coffin. Miraculously preserved, the banner appears to depict an elderly Lady Dai bent over the walking stick that was found among her grave goods. Below her a feast is in progress complete with some of the first chopsticks to be depicted; above, a celestial concourse awaits her spirit.

Painted T-shaped silk banner from Mawangdui, Changsha (Hunan). Excavated in the 1970s, Mawangdui's three tombs yielded a dazzling array of artefacts. The banner was found draped over the innermost coffin of the Lady Dai (d. c.150 BC), a contemporary of the Former Han empress Lü.

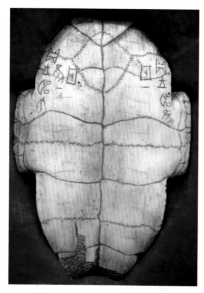

Left Inscribed turtle plastron from Anyang (Henan). The authenticity of the Shang dynasty (c.1600 BC–c.1045 BC) was substantiated through study of the written characters inscribed on such shells. Early evidence of a written tradition, they record oracular responses obtained from the cracking of the shells when subjected to heat.

Middle Elongated bronze figure from a sacrificial pit at Sanxingdui in Sichuan. Dated to c.1200 BC, this nearly two-metre-tall figure remains a stylistic anomaly. Such finds suggest that technically sophisticated cultures flourished beyond the parameters of the Yellow River's classic 'Three Dynasties' (Xia, Shang and Zhou).

Bronze vessel (a *zun* with pan) from the tomb of the Marquis of Zeng (d. 433 BC) in Hubei. The casting of often colossal bronze vessels was one of the supreme achievements of ancient China. None were more encrusted with decoration than those found in the 'warring state' of Chu, to which Zeng was tributary.

The 1974 discovery of the *Qin* First Emperor's 'terracotta army' was probably the greatest archaeological find of the twentieth century. Thousands of warriors and hundreds of horses are now on display at the site near Xi'an. More exotic artefacts, like four-horse chariots in bronze chased with silver and gold, have since been excavated, and the main chamber of the emperor's tomb has still to be opened.

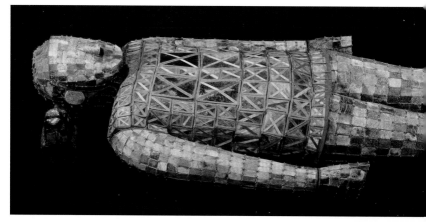

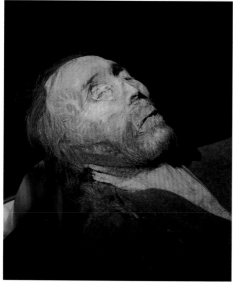

Above Jade burial suit of Princess Tou Wan. In the Han period (c.200 BC–AD 220) royalty were often buried in tailored jade. Besides advertising the rank of the deceased, jade was supposed to have preservative qualities. Each suit consists of hundreds of platelets, like the armour of the 'terracotta warriors', that were knotted together with silk, silver or gold thread.

The so-called 'Tarim Mummies' from the deserts of Xinjiang caused an archaeological furore when identified as not just un-Chinese but decidedly European. Though the origins, language and technologies of this 'Charchan Man', or 'Ur-David', are still uncertain, it seems that in the first two millennia BC much of what is China today was populated by non-Mongoloid peoples.

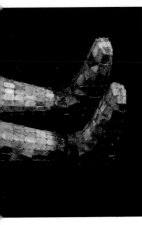

Below Though typical of the structures associated with the long northern frontier, these fortified remains are not those of the Great Wall but of a military granary. Located near Dunhuang in the Gansu corridor, they date from the Later/Eastern Han dynasty (AD 25–220).

The Three Kingdoms period (AD 220–265) is best known as the setting for the later *Romance of the Three Kingdoms*. A scene from this enduringly popular novel is here depicted on a lacquer-coated box of the Ming period.

Under the Tang dynasty (618–907) imperial China stretched out along the Silk Road to achieve its greatest extent. Even the peoples of Mongolia, Kazakhstan, Kyrghystan and Uzbekistan tendered tribute, typically in horses (seen here being ridden by their escorts in a silk painting of the Song dynasty). Central Asia's bloodstock was prized, its sports (like polo) were adopted and its fashions aped. Ceramic figurines of the period depict elaborate female head-dresses and booted cameleers with noses of most un-Chinese proportions.

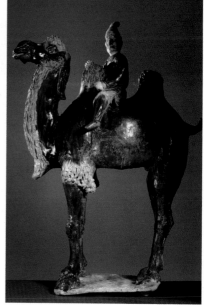

Seventeenth-century Tibetan fresco of the Buddha's First Sermon. Buddhism reached China in the second century AD, some five hundred years after the Buddha lived and preached in India. It spread rapidly during the long 'Period of Disunion' (220–581) and thereafter enjoyed imperial patronage under the Sui and Tang dynasties.

The 'Ancestor Worshipping' cave at Lungmen (Longmen) outside Luoyang in Henan was commissioned in the 670s by Empress Wu, wife of *Tang* Gaozong and China's only female 'emperor'. The tradition of rock-cut images of the Buddha had come from India by way of Afghanistan (Bamian) and Xinjiang.

南無如來一躯
意為亡弟知球三七
齋畫造慶讃供養

Traffic along the mountain-and-desert trails known as the Silk Road was two-way. Buddhist missionaries heading east into China were soon complemented by Chinese pilgrims heading west for India. Most passed through Dunhuang in Gansu, from where came this ninth-century silk painting of a travelling monk.

The tomb contained no manuscripts on silk. These came only from the supposed son's tomb and included two uncorrupted versions of Laozi's *Daodejing*, hitherto unknown works on medicine, astronomy and divination, a sex manual, and some historical fragments of which even Sima Qian seems to have been unaware; they must have been lost to scholarship in the decades between the burial and his writing the *Shiji*. Predating the textual hoards previously discovered along the Silk Road, the Mawangdui collection should indeed prove 'of monumental importance to historians in their reconsideration of ancient Chinese history'.[16] In the same tomb were also found three of the earliest scale maps yet known. Evidently the result of careful survey and intended for military reference, one presents a topography that is still recognisable provided it is inverted; the Chinese preference was for south at the top of a map and north at the bottom. It covers the sensitive border region comprising the southern half of Changsha kingdom and the northern half of Nanyue.

Nanyue ('Southern Yue') was a Han kingdom with a difference: it owed nothing to *Han* Gaozu and had imperial pretensions of its own. Corresponding roughly to Guangdong province plus neighbouring parts of Guangxi and northern Vietnam, its capital was at Panyu. This was the then name for the metropolis of Guangzhou (Canton), in the heart of whose international district were exacavated in 1983 yet another Han-period royal tomb and, in the 1990s, the remains of the royal palace gardens.

The tomb is that of King Wen, the second in the Nanyue succession and not to be confused with his contemporary *Han* Wendi, the emperor in Chang'an. In accordance with his rank, Nanyue's King Wen was buried in a jade suit; it did nothing for the preservation of his corpse, although his many-chambered tomb is interesting. It represents in miniature the layout of his palace, with public rooms to the fore (banqueting hall in the east wing, treasure store in the west wing) and private apartments to the rear (including a chamber for those servants who accompanied him in death and another for concubines similarly 'honoured'). Both Han and native Yue productions figure among the furnishings, along with African ivory, frankincense from southern Arabia and a circular silver bowl with lid that could be Persian. Then as now, the wealth of Panyu/Guangzhou stemmed from its Pearl River frontage on the South China Sea. Backed by the Nanling mountains, Nanyue seemed to have eluded Han ambitions and to be enjoying the perks of its balmy climate spiced with whatever foreign fancies came its way.

The Yue people are thought to have been Malayo-Polynesian rather than Mongoloid like the Xia Chinese. In northern China they were invariably deplored for their alien customs (e.g. banana leaves for plates) as much as for their steamy hillsides and malarial swamps. When the First Emperor extended his sway into the region, it was not a popular destination; only 'fugitives, reprobates and shopkeepers' were sent to settle there. Qin's short-lived administration had been skeletal, and when the emperor died, it broke away. A Qin official, taking his cue from the melancholy Chen She's uprising, had declared Nanyue an independent kingdom and himself its first king.

This was Zhao Tuo, otherwise King Wu of Nanyue. For ten years he was left in peace, *Han* Gaozu 'having enough to do to take care of internal troubles', according to Sima Qian. But in 196 BC the Han emperor sent a trusty troubleshooter, the Confucian ideologue Lu Jia, to talk King Wu into acknowledging Han supremacy. The king obliged in return for recognition of his assumed title, then reneged over a trade dispute. A Han embargo on iron sales, a strategic commodity since it was used for weapons, brought protests, followed by recrimination: King Wu declared himself an emperor, and troops sent south in 183 BC by the Dowager Empress Lü failed to quash this presumption. On the contrary, Nanyue's troops began overrunning neighbouring territories. Their sovereign now rode in a carriage with a yellow canopy and issued his own 'edicts', both of these being imperial prerogatives.[17]

Sima Qian has Nanyue's first king (and self-made emperor) dying in 137 BC. This seems unlikely; for if, as he says, King Wu was a magistrate under the First Emperor, he would have been at least a hundred and have outlasted two Qin and six Han emperors. More plausibly it was his successor, he whose jade suit now lies in the Guangzhou museum, who received the troubleshooting Lu Jia a second time and undertook to renounce the imperial style and send tribute to Chang'an. This was during *Han* Wendi's reign and should have ended the matter; but unlike Qin's incorporation of the Chinese 'Midwest' in Sichuan, the Han incorporation of its 'Deep South' dragged on.

Two more kings of Nanyue occupied the throne in Panyu before trouble broke out again. By then, from Chang'an the mighty *Han* Wudi, son and successor of Jingdi, was transforming Han's patchwork dominion into a dynamic east-Asian empire. The much-fragmented 'feudal' kingdoms had been reduced to impotence and obliged to accept imperial appointees as their chancellors, or prime ministers. This innovation went down badly in Nanyue when it was introduced in 113 BC. No Nanyue king had as yet actually visited Chang'an to offer tribute; and when a pro-Han faction in Panyu persuaded the young king to do so, the country rose in revolt under its existing chancellor. Han envoys and supporters were massacred, an avenging force from Chang'an repelled.

The Han empire, which had just opened a grand salient into central Asia, was being humbled by 'barbarians' at its back door. *Han* Wudi could no longer trifle with the situation, and suasion having failed, only force remained. In 112 BC no less than four expeditions converged on Panyu by river and sea. The 'General of the Towered Ships' at the head of 20,000–30,000 men got there first. Joined by the 'General Who Calms the Waves', he stormed Panyu at night and, come dawn, the city surrendered. 'Thus five generations, or ninety-three years after Zhao Tuo first became king of Southern Yue, the state was destroyed.'[18] Sima Qian, then at work on his *Shiji*, felt nothing but satisfaction. There would be no more kings of Southern Yue, nor of Eastern Yue (in Fujian), which suffered a similar fate the following year. By the end of 111 BC all of mainland southern China plus the island of Hainan and the Red River valley of northern Vietnam were finally incorporated into the empire.

5

WITHIN AND BEYOND

141 BC–AD 1

HAN AND HUN

AMONG FUGITIVES FROM HAN JUSTICE IN the second century BC there was a saying that, if all else failed, they could always go 'Northward to the Xiongnu [or] Southward to the Yue'. Of these the first was generally preferred, the Mongolian steppe-land of the Xiongnu being more congenial than pestilential Southern Yue. But for the authorities in Chang'an, the problem was the same: permeable border zones, with unpredictable enemies beyond and fickle dependants within, were incompatible with a well-regulated empire. In the far north, as in the deep south, the frontier had taxed the resolve of *Han* Gaozu and his successors and would only be settled, after a fashion and at great cost, in the reign of *Han* Wudi.

Wudi succeeded *Han* Jingdi in 141 BC. Fifteen at the time, he was still on the throne when he died at the age of sixty-eight. One of the longest and most eventful reigns on record (141–87 BC) benefited greatly from continuity, then fell victim to it. Opinion of Wudi's rule has always been divided. He was either 'an outright autocrat' who subverted the authority of his ministers to 'direct the government in person', and so become 'perhaps the most famous of all Chinese emperors'; or he was a palace cipher, scarcely able to control his own household, who 'took no part in the military campaigns for which his reign is famous' and was so oblivious of their cost that his tenure was in fact 'a calamity for China'.[1] While the emperor busied himself with matters of ceremony and ritual and dabbled in the arts, state initiatives seem often, but not always, to have come from ministers, counsellors or generals; and once approved, their execution was entrusted to the same functionaries.

This was in accord with Confucian teaching. Emperors were not supposed to toil day and night over cartloads of bamboo documentation as the Qin First Emperor was said to have done, nor to take the field with troops and drinking companions like *Han* Gaozu. Setting an irresistible example of righteousness and humane conduct required Heaven's Son to stand aloof, and with his authority unimpaired by legislative niceties and executive responsibilities, cultivate a state of impassivity.

The condition was known as *wuwei*, a Daoist term variously translated as 'doing nothing', 'suspended animation' or 'surcease of action'. The sage ruler 'does nothing (*wuwei*)', says Laozi, 'and there is nothing that is not brought to order'.[2] This was possible because in an ideal world the moral example set by the emperor was thought to create an attractional effect, like a magnet. By it, society as a whole was automatically orientated on the path of righteousness, so eliminating the need for laws and punishments, and by the same force the ablest and most upright of subjects were drawn ineluctably into the emperor's ambit of service. His Celestial Majesty might then 'do nothing' in the knowledge that, with such paragons at the helm, nothing would not be 'brought to order'.

There was a danger, though: cynics might be tempted to judge the excellence or otherwise of the emperor by the calibre of his officials. Discovering and selecting men of unimpeachable distinction and ability was critical, and it could usefully be advanced by some intelligent recruitment. Time and again the records include edicts urging officials throughout the empire to seek out promising candidates for office and send them to Chang'an. The practice had started back in Zhou times but assumed much greater urgency under the Han as the administration grew in size and complexity. *Han* Wudi increased the frequency of these recruitment drives, while standardising the selection process by the introduction of a question-and-answer element. Qualification by examination, a cardinal feature of the later imperial bureaucracy, would follow. Even a questionnaire required a syllabus and a panel to mark the submissions. The panel was set up as an academy of scholars, of whom there were fifty in 136 BC, though the number soon increased; and the syllabus entailed these academicians selecting and interpreting a canon of suitable texts, initially five, all of them either favoured by Confucius ('Book of Changes', 'Book of Songs', 'Book of Rites') or attributed to him ('Book of Documents', 'Spring and Autumn' Annals). In effect an embryonic 'Confucianism' based on writings associated with Master Kong was acquiring, through state endorsement, an institutional substance and a veneer of orthodoxy.

But in the practice of government Wudi favoured concepts and policies more in keeping with those promoted by the Qin First Emperor. Wudi too travelled extensively, refined and consummated the sacrificial rites to be conducted at various sacred summits, and became obsessed by life's transience and the lure of the immortals in their Paradise Islands of Penglai. Since *Han* Gaozu had neglected to realign his new dynasty with one of the Five Elements (or Phases), in 104 BC Wudi made good the deficiency. The calendar was revised, a Grand New Beginning announced, and 'earth', the element that overcame Qin's 'water', acclaimed as that by which Han ruled. Its complementary colour was yellow and its appropriate number five, though it does not appear that wheel gauges were altered accordingly. The dynasty was thus belatedly synchronised with the waxing and waning of the elemental Phases, and the legitimacy of its having supplanted Qin affirmed in terms, not of the Confucian's beloved Mandate, but of an esoteric theory more often associated with Daoism.

There is no evidence of legalist precedent being invoked by Wudi to restore the full severity of the First Emperor's laws and punishments; but the courts were busier and the convict population greater than at any other time under the early Han. Taxes were increased; state monopolies of iron and salt (in 119 BC) and liquor (98 BC) were introduced to raise additional revenue; and convicts, slaves (usually prisoners of war or debt defaulters), conscripts and corvée labourers were mobilised on a massive scale. Roads, flood prevention schemes and imperial monuments accounted for some of this activity; so did the newly 'nationalised' foundries and salt-workings, in which unpaid labour was the norm (it would today be called 'slave labour'). But the main reason was war. 'Wu-di' means 'The Martial Emperor', and though he seems seldom to have inspected his troops and never to have led them in battle, his reign was one of incessant campaigning, mostly in that great wilderness, devoid of familiar place-names and features, that lay on and beyond the northern frontier.

Here, in an arc extending from the Korean peninsula to Xinjiang, across thousands of kilometres of forest, steppe and desert, China's sedentary agriculture blended into a harsh and interminable realm of nomadic pastoralism. As in Africa and the Middle East, the relationship between 'the desert and the sown' was an uneasy one, potentially beneficial to both but fraught with mutual misunderstanding and suspicion. In east Asia, distinctions in lifestyle and culture between the windswept nomad encampments and the huddled farming hamlets were compounded by differences of race (though this may have been more perceived than real), governance, language, literacy and much else that each held dear in the way of accomplishment. China, 'the land of caps and girdles', as Sima Qian calls it, was one thing; the *yi* ('barbarian') country, a land of pelts and trousers, quite another.

But if the social and economic distinctions were clear cut, the vegetational divide was anything but. Cultivation fingered into the steppe; shifting sands invaded the crops. Irrigation could transform desert as dramatically as desiccation could terminate farming. Extensive grazing grounds interrupted the patchwork fields to the south; rich oases dotted the western deserts. While the rivers were few, their watersheds indeterminate and their valleys too agriculturally valuable to be turned into frontiers, the mountains were far, their contours generally surmountable and their directional trends unhelpful. The demarcation of a frontier, let alone its regulation, looked impossible across such terrain and would tax imperial China for centuries.

The Qin First Emperor had not been deterred. His Qin forebears had long experience of dealing with their nomadic neighbours, and Meng Tian's great push into the Ordos of *c.* 218 BC had been conducted so as to secure, once and for all, Qin's northern and north-western flanks. The resulting network of forts, watchtowers, walls and roads – the 'Great Wall' of later tradition – might have served well had it been maintained. But the costs were prohibitive, and the years of civil war that followed the death of the First Emperor proved fatal. Troops had been withdrawn, colonists drifted back to the south, and the 'forward policy' was abandoned.

Arguably, though, it was the original advance into the Ordos and neighbouring steppe to the east and west which was of more consequence. Deprived of valuable grazing, and with informal trade across the new frontier restricted, the herdsmen beyond it for once made common cause. Effective leadership came courtesy of the Xiongnu, a tribe or lineage that rapidly became the nucleus of a great confederacy. Under Maodun, a young Xiongnu prince who slew his father to claim the title of *shanyu* (*chanyu*), or king, in 209 BC, the Xiongnu confederacy swept east, west, south and north, routing Chinese and non-Chinese alike. *Shanyu* Maodun reclaimed all the lands taken by Meng Tian and penetrated deep into what are now Hebei and Shanxi provinces. Thus, while Liu Bang and Xiang Yu had been fighting to the death on the banks of the Yangzi, Maodun had made free with the northern commanderies and 'was able to strengthen his position, amassing over three hundred thousand skilled crossbowmen', according to Sima Qian.

In English 'Xiongnu' is sometimes rendered as 'Hun'. As to whether these two words really represent the same original when mangled by Chinese and Latin pronunciation, there is, however, no consensus; learned opinion blows one way then the other, like the wind across the Eurasian steppe. Certainly the Huns who invaded Europe were nomadic pastoralists like the Xiongnu. They too fought on horseback, terrorised an empire and had to be bought off at great expense. But that was centuries later and half a world away. Judged by the few words that have been identified, the Xiongnu spoke a Siberian language and may well have come from there. Equating them with the Huns of European history is useful only insofar as any mnemonic signage, however dubious, is welcome when negotiating the unfamiliar wastes of inner Asia's remote past.

Since the steppe peoples left no account of their affairs and were said to be illiterate, nearly all that is known of them comes from Chinese sources. But without much in the way of prior records, a historian like Sima Qian had to rely on quizzing contemporaries with frontier experience, collecting observations of his own and using his imagination. The last unexpectedly extended to representing the nomadic point of view; for his early foray into anthropology and for his supposed 'barbarian' sympathies, the Grand Historian has been complimented.[3]

The *Shiji*'s section on the Xiongnu themselves is far longer and more informative than that on Nanyue. Evidently the steppe confederation presented Han statesmen with something more than the threat of dynastic and military embarrassment. It was a confrontation in which the empire's future extent was being projected and its identity forged. With uncanny foresight Sima Qian seems to have surmised the course of subsequent history and anticipated the part that would be played in it by later frontier peoples – Tibetan, Khitan, Turk, Mongol and Manchu to name but a few. In measuring *zhongguo*'s centrality, stability and cultural superiority against a nomadic 'other' of marginal, itinerant and barely literate pastoralists, the Grand Historian set an historiographical convention that would become an historical reality. Han versus Hun was just round one.

Sima Qian conveys this idea by treating the Xiongnu as a recurrent phenomenon prefigured by those non-Xia indigenous peoples such as the 'Rong' and 'Di' who had been assimilated in Zhou times, and by quoting the stereotypical opinions of his contemporaries. In Chinese, the term 'Xiongnu' was explained as meaning 'Furious Slave'. They were commonly compared to wolves and other predators. A visitation from the Xiongnu was 'like a flock of birds' descending on a cornfield. They came 'like a sudden wind' and left 'like a mist' but 'with the speed of lightning'. Among such 'barbarians', aggression and avarice were inherent and, without long exposure to the refinements of civilisation, nigh incorrigible. The Han would need to be patient, even magnanimous, to overcome them.

Han Gaozu, when not chastising his kings (several of whom had indeed fled 'northward to the Xiongnu'), had led a personal crusade to expel the Xiongnu in the winter of 200 BC. It did nothing to redeem his military reputation and ended in disaster. Frost-bitten and outmanoeuvred by the

Xiongnu rough-riders, the Han forces had been surrounded at Pingcheng, a place near Datong on the Shanxi/Inner Mongolia border. The emperor himself would have been captured but for the intercession of *Shanyu* Maodun's queen, who urged clemency as a basis for negotiation. Gaozu and his forces were permitted to beat an ignominious retreat, and after further defections and incursions, the first in a series of treaties that would last for sixty years had been signed in 198 BC.

Known as 'peace-through-kinship' (*heqin*) treaties, their terms were unflattering to Han sensibilities. The Xiongnu were accorded equal, or 'brotherly', status; and in return for an undertaking to curtail their incursions, the *shanyu* was to receive an imperial bride and an annual gift of silks, grain and 'other foodstuffs'. Effectively tribute, these gifts could also be supposed a bribe or even an investment in that the Xiongnu might become addicted to Chinese products, then dependent on them. Likewise scruples over the export of an imperial princess were stifled by hopes of her giving birth to a half-Han *shanyu*, or at least exerting a favourable influence on Xiongnu policy. Face could always be saved; but the facts spoke for themselves. In retrospect, imperial China's first international commitments in the second century BC bear an uncanny resemblance to its last in the nineteenth century AD; though ostensibly between equal parties, both were decidedly 'unequal treaties'.

With each treaty renewal, the size of the annual tribute/bribe payable to the Xiongnu increased; gold, ironware and liquor were added, while the grain and silk components soared to astronomical proportions. Nor did the Xiongnu incursions in fact cease. They were on a lesser scale but just as frequent, those responsible often being Han renegades or tribal affiliates over whom the *shanyu* exercised little control. Han resentment grew proportionately. It had peaked in 192 BC when a communication from *Shanyu* Maodun to the Dowager Empress Lü mischievously suggested that, since both had been widowed and were of a certain age, they might find agreeable consolation in one another's company. This was too much for the dowager empress, who was all for calling out the army. Cooler counsels prevailed, however; indeed, the final response from one of a normally vain and vindictive disposition plumbs the depths of abasement:

> My age is advanced and my vitality is diminished [wrote the dowager empress]. Both my hair and teeth are falling out, and I cannot even walk steadily. The *shanyu* must have heard exaggerated reports [of me]. I am not worthy of his lowering himself. But my country has done nothing wrong, and I hope that he will spare it.[4]

Another reading of the *shanyu*'s original letter interprets his desire 'to exchange the things that I have for the things that I do not have' as referring not to caresses but trade.[5] If this is correct, it introduces a factor that would soon become central to Han–Xiongnu relations. For the Han policy of making the Xiongnu reliant on Chinese produce was paying off. In subsequent negotiations, access to the markets that had sprung up along the frontier is mentioned among the Xiongnu demands as often as tribute, and its refusal would become highly provocative.

Despite frequent setbacks, *Han* Wendi and *Han* Jingdi had continued the 'peace-through-kinship' policy. Nostalgia for a Han golden age in the first half of the second century BC would owe much to this costly calm before the storm. Meanwhile *Shanyu* Maodun's successors greatly extended their Xiongnu empire, especially to the west, where the Yuezhi people were driven out of the Gansu corridor and Xinjiang to beyond the Pamirs. This prompted a suggestion, credited to the teenage Wudi, for a Han envoy-explorer to try to make contact with the Yuezhi and sound them out about an anti-Xiongnu alliance. A palace official called Zhang Qian volunteered for the task and in *c.* 138 BC, accompanied by a servant who was good at bringing down game, plus a small military escort, this explorer Zhang disappeared into the desert sunset. He was soon intercepted and taken captive by the *shanyu*'s troops. How would the emperor feel, asked the *shanyu*, if the Xiongnu sent emissaries traipsing across China to open diplomatic relations with Nanyue? The mission was an affront to Xiongnu sovereignty and Zhang was to be detained by them indefinitely.

He would in fact escape, but not until ten years later. Resuming his journey, explorer Zhang then vanished into the unknown a second time. He had probably been completely forgotten when in 126 BC, thirteen years older, geographically wiser than any contemporary and lately escaped from yet another spell in Xiongnu captivity, he and his huntsman-companion came trotting back into Chang'an. By then Han–Xiongnu relations had plummeted into all-out war. Nothing would be more timely than central Asian intelligence from an intrepid traveller who deserves recognition as both the pioneeer of the 'Silk Road' and the first to play the 'Great Game'.

On the other hand, nothing would be more challenging than discoveries with a shock value comparable to those that awaited Columbus. For according to explorer Zhang, Han China was not alone in the world: out there, there were other 'great states', as he called them. Their people lived in cities; and they too 'kept records by writing', an extraordinary revelation. They 'made their living in much the same way as the Chinese'; and shockingly, they were quite unaware that *zhongguo*, now taken to mean 'the Middle Kingdom', was anywhere near the middle.

EXPLORER ZHANG AND THE WESTERN REGIONS

After coming of age, in 135 BC *Han* Wudi had signed another 'peace-through-kinship' treaty with the then *shanyu*. The matter had sparked a heated debate in Chang'an, and this had flared again in 134 BC when, with Xiongnu suspicions disarmed by the latest tribute bonanza, prospects for a surprise counter-strike, not to say a perfidious one, seemed particularly favourable. Old arguments were rehearsed, revenge of Gaozu's defeat at Pingcheng was reinvoked, and Wudi now sided with the hawks; an elaborate plan was approved for luring the *shanyu* into an ambush in the town of Mayi (in northern Shanxi).

This time there was no disaster, just dismal failure. The Xiongnu got wind of the trick, wheeled about, vanished into the steppe, and repudiated the treaty. Five years of 'phoney war' ensued. Xiongnu raids continued but so did the frontier markets, at which cross-border trade flourished as never before. It was all part of the plan. In autumn 129 BC, when the markets were at their busiest, Han armies swooped on four of them. Despite the element of surprise, only one attack was moderately successful. Xiongnu losses were put in the hundreds, Han's in the thousands, and Pingcheng remained unavenged. But two years later Wei Qing, brother of the emperor's favourite consort and one of half a dozen charismatic generals to emerge at this time, redeemed the *Qin* First Emperor's conquests by retaking the Ordos. It was 'the first major setback for the Xiongnu since the days of Maodun'.[6] Qin's 'Great Wall' defences were reoccupied and settlements re-established on either side of the Yellow River's northern bend.

This brought retaliation from the Xiongnu both east and west of the new salient and was followed by devastating countermoves from the Han. Throughout the 120s BC scarcely a year passed without ever larger Han expeditions probing ever deeper into Xiongnu territory. By 119 BC they were pushing north right across the Gobi desert into Outer Mongolia and north-west through Gansu to Ningxia. Han armies were now matching the Xiongnu for mobility and could support themselves in the field for several months. New commanderies, crammed with labour camps and soldier-settlers, ensured the security of the 'Great Wall' frontier, while Xiongnu losses, especially of livestock and pasturage, induced dissent within the nomadic confederation. The consequent defections may partly account for the improved performance of the Han forces as these new allies were deployed against their erstwhile comrades.

Success was real, but the price high. Sima Qian follows official practice by 'scoring' each engagement as if it were a rubber of bridge, or an exam paper. From his totting up of the hundreds of thousands of troops involved, the tens of thousands slain, the numerous generals and chieftains captured, and the vast herds of sheep, cattle and horses corralled, it appears that, for the Han, acceptable losses ran as high as 30 per cent and sometimes reached 90 per cent. If anything, the Xiongnu fared better in this respect – and they needed to; for while Han resources of manpower and provisions were practically inexhaustible and constrained only by the logistics of deployment, nomadic numbers were finite, their livelihood in terms of flocks and herds was vulnerable, and their only asset lay in the limitless terrain.

Having reclaimed the northern frontier and scattered the enemy, the Han might have scaled down their operations after 119 BC. That they would do no such thing looks to have been due to the intelligence-gathering of explorer Zhang. For although the exact chronology is uncertain, it seems to have been at about this time that his information on central Asian affairs was reviewed, he himself re-examined, and a new direction given to Han's expansionist momentum. Instead of pushing ever farther north into the unrewarding wastes of Mongolia, Chang'an's troops would veer west and set their sights on the flourishing states of central Asia, as reported by Zhang.

Initially Zhang's discoveries had served as a distraction. In the course of his western odyssey, the explorer had crossed the deserts of Xinjiang, scaled the bleak Pamirs and descended to both the Syr Darya (Jaxartes River) and Amu Darya (Oxus River). The region along the former was called 'Dayuan', otherwise Ferghana and now eastern Uzbekistan, that along the latter 'Taxia', otherwise Bactria or northern Afghanistan. Since the Yuezhi had just overrun Bactria, they showed no interest in returning east of the Pamirs to oblige Chang'an in its feud with the Xiongnu. Their future lay south of the Himalayas, where they would be known as the Kusana (Kushan), would found one of northern India's greatest empires, and in the first century AD would repay Zhang's visit by sending to China the first Buddhist missionaries. But as yet ignorant of 'the Enlightened One', the Yuezhi in the early 120s BC opened explorer Zhang's eyes only to the importance of the strange world into which he had blundered.

Had it not been for his decade-long detention by the Xiongnu, Zhang would have found Greek-speaking kings with names like Euthydemus and

Menander still ruling in Bactria. Relics of Alexander the Great's expedition, these Bactrian kings had been ejected by the Yuezhi in 130 BC, just months before Zhang's arrival. Their magnificent gold and silver coinage was still in circulation and surprised Zhang by its novel use of portraiture. Each coin, he reports, 'bore the face of the king [and] when the king died, the currency was immediately changed and new coins issued with the face of his successor'. Such a practice had never been known in China; since it could be construed as ennobling commerce and demeaning the sovereign by association with it, nor would it be.

West of Bactria stretched the great kingdom of 'Anxi', otherwise Parthia or Persia (Iran), where the Seleucids, also legatees of Alexander's empire, had earlier been overthrown by the Parthian Arsacids; this Anxi extended to what Zhang calls 'the western sea', which is thought to be the Gulf rather than the Mediterranean. East of Bactria, the kingdom of 'Shendu' was of more interest. While exploring the Bactrian bazaars, Zhang had noticed 'cloth from Shu [Sichuan] and bamboo canes from Qiong [also in Sichuan]', both of which were said to have been imported via 'Shendu'. Although some of explorer Zhang's place-names are hard to identify, there is no question that 'Shendu' was India; its inhabitants 'rode elephants into battle' and even the Romans knew the country as 'Sindu' (after the Sind, or Indus, River). Since it was said to be several thousand kilometres east of Bactria, Zhang reasoned that it must 'not be very far away from Shu'. Silk cloth and bamboo canes must therefore be reaching India direct from China's extreme south-west.

Of all Zhang's revelations, this was the one that had at first excited the most interest in Chang'an. As his ten years of Xiongnu captivity had demonstrated, access to central Asia was as yet fraught. Across the deserts of Xinjiang the Xiongnu controlled the route north of the 'Great Swamp' (nowadays the salt desert of Lop Nor), while Xiongnu allies, the proto-Tibetan Qiang, controlled that south of it. Only the cane-and-silk route from Sichuan to India and Bactria looked to offer a way of circumventing both. When Zhang had proposed that he lead a secret expedition to explore it, 'the emperor was delighted'.

This must have been in *c.* 125 BC, the year after Zhang's return from 'the western regions'; for by 123 BC the explorer was back again, the south-western route having proved a cul-de-sac. There was indeed some unofficial trade between Sichuan and India; and Zhang stressed the importance of an intervening kingdom called 'Dianyue', whose people also rode elephants; it was probably Burma. But the hillsmen of Yunnan, between Sichuan and Burma, had been unimpressed by the affable Zhang, opposed his progress and murdered his colleagues. Further efforts would require military support, and this would not be forthcoming until twelve years later. Coinciding with the storming of Panyu (Canton) and the subjugation of Nanyue, Han troops would then force their way into Yunnan. Sima Qian, the 'Grand Historian', accompanied them, certainly as far as the now provincial capital of Kunming. But farther to the south-west their progress was halted in the vicinity of the Lancang (upper Mekong) River. The perpendicular terrain, as much as the population, would in fact keep the silk-and-cane trail shrouded in mystery for centuries. Only with the construction of the Burma Road in the run-up to the Second World War would a serviceable trade route finally link China and India over the dripping passes at this extremity of the eastern Himalaya.

Meanwhile Han operations against the Xiongnu had continued. In 121 BC they had been rewarded with the surrender of one of the *shanyu's* subordinate kings, who brought with him 40,000 men and control of the Gansu corridor. Then known as Hexi ('west of the [Yellow] river'), this vital neck of cultivation was secured, settled (700,000 were compelled or induced to remove there) and fortified over the next few years to as far as the Jade Gate (*Yumen*), the terminal of the extended 'Great Wall' near Dunhuang. The Han now had the equivalent of 'a covered way' leading into Xinjiang. It was this that led to explorer Zhang's recall from obscurity in *c.* 119 BC (in the interim he had been demoted and nearly beheaded as a scapegoat for a recent defeat by the Xiongnu), and to his again being quizzed about 'the western regions'.

According to Zhang, all the kingdoms of the far west so valued the produce and political endorsement on offer from Han China that they could be induced to accept some kind of feudatory status. The more martial peoples of Ferghana and other northern states would be keen to join the Han against their common Xiongnu enemy; and the more commercial peoples of Bactria, Parthia and India would comply with tributary conventions if they could be assured of Chinese trade. In this way, argued Zhang (or perhaps the Grand Historian on his behalf), all could be brought within the Han scheme of things. The emperor would be gratified by a constant stream of exotic products and visitors, 'his might would become known throughout all the lands within the four seas', and in time their rulers would 'acknowledge themselves our foreign vassals'.[7]

It is noteworthy that neither trade nor alliance was seen as an end in itself; arguably they never would be, at least for as long as the Chinese empire lasted. Both were perceived as inducements whereby the lands discovered by explorer Zhang could be satisfactorily fitted into a traditional scheme of sino-centric geography. Modelled on the cosmos, this conceived of 'All-under-Heaven' being disposed in rings of concentric dependency that radiated outwards from the universal sovereign (that is, the Han emperor) and which shaded from the directly administered commanderies of the empire itself to its less directly ruled kingdoms, various indirectly ruled tributary states on the frontier, and finally feudatory dependants beyond it.

Resourceful as ever, in *c.* 119 BC Zhang responded to the emperor's renewed interest with another master plan. Bactria this time took a back seat in it. The priority was to secure Xinjiang and its transit routes. Deprived of Chinese grain and manufactures, the Xiongnu had been resupplying themselves from Xinjiang's oases. Each a small city-state, the oases had made Xinjiang what Zhang called 'the right arm of the Xiongnu'. It must be 'cut off', and he knew just the people to do it. They were the Wusun, a tribe that had fallen out with the Xiongnu and, like the Yuezhi, been displaced by them. Now established somewhere in the north of Xinjiang (perhaps in the vicinity of modern Urumqi), they would be flattered by Han overtures and easily bribed into an offensive alliance. 'The emperor approved of this suggestion,' reports Sima Qian.

Reinstated in high office, in 115 BC explorer Zhang readied himself for a last odyssey into the land of ruddy cheeks and bushy beards, of fat-tailed sheep and shaggy camels with wobbly humps. To the emperor it must have sounded like a realm of make-believe, albeit an expensive one. Gifts comprising 'gold and silks worth a hundred billion cash' and 'tens of thousands of cattle and sheep' were entrusted to Zhang, along with an escort of 300 and a staff sufficient to supply ambassadors to all the countries beyond.

As an arena for imperial expansion, inner Asia has somewhat improbably been called 'the rough equivalent of the Mediterranean Sea' in Graeco-Roman history.[8] Though as dry as the Mediterranean is wet and as harsh as it is balmy, the sands of what was later known as Turkestan glowed at sunset like 'the wine-red sea' and did indeed produce grapes; Zhang had earlier noted that they were fermented into a fine liquor that improved with age; and it was from Xinjiang that the vine would speedily be introduced into China. More to the point, the trading oases lay strung around the desert like an archipelago of islands. Inexperienced voyagers could safely navigate from one to another; and autonomous but vulnerable, they could then serve as ports of call and supply or as permanently garrisoned strongholds. The key to the wider world beyond lay in securing the 'sea-ways' of Xinjiang.

Zhang led his men with the confidence born of long years of hard travel. The Wusun were located, their strength ascertained, and his gifts well received. Interpreter-guides were provided for his envoys to Bactria, India, Parthia, Ferghana and Sogdiana (the later Samarkand). But the Wusun faced a leadership crisis and were ill informed about the might of Han China. Before committing themselves to an alliance, they preferred to send their own envoys to the Han court. Zhang accompanied them back to Chang'an. He had the satisfaction of seeing 'their appreciation of Han considerably enhanced' and of receiving the various delegations that his envoys to the other central Asian states would escort back to Chang'an.[9] When Zhang died, probably in 113 BC, he was hailed as the pioneer 'who had opened the way' to the Western Regions. 'All the envoys who journeyed to these lands in later times relied upon his reputation to obtain a hearing. As a result of his efforts, the foreign states trusted the Han envoys.'[10]

But Han comings and goings across Xinjiang were not trusted by the Xiongnu, who during the last decade of the century mounted major assaults on both the Gansu corridor and the northern frontier. These were counter-productive with regard to the Wusun, who, stampeded by Xiongnu threats, soon embraced the Han alliance envisioned by explorer Zhang. Signed in 105 BC, the treaty was not so much one of 'peace-through-kinship' as of 'war-through-kinship'. *Han* Wudi got 1,000 horses, a willing feudatory and a doughty defender of Han interests in Xinjiang and beyond, while the Wusun welcomed lavish gifts, a powerful patron and a tearful imperial bride.

This Princess Xijun and her sizeable entourage proved the most influential element in the package. Married to a grey-bearded Wusun leader, then to his grandson – with neither of whom she was able to converse – the princess yet exercised considerable influence among her new kinsmen and would on occasion act as the Han emperor's representative. But she never became reconciled to her fate and famously composed a song that would be remembered long after the Wusun themselves had been forgotten. The song tells of Princess Xijun's exile in 'a strange land on the other side of heaven', where her house was a tent of felts, and her food just 'meat with fermented milk as a sauce'. 'I live with constant thoughts of my home,' sang the princess, 'my heart is full of sorrow. I wish I were a yellow [-beaked?] swan winging back to my home country.'[11] The song is included in the *Hanshu*, the second of the 'Standard Histories' (so sequel to Sima Qian's *Shiji*), which was compiled by members of the Ban family. One of them was Ban Zhao, the sister of the main author; and it was surely she, a noted scholar in her own right and in this case a peculiarly sympathetic one, who was responsible for incorporating so poignant a reflection of the homesick plight of a Chinese bride.

While the princess was accustoming herself to life in a yurt, operations to secure the Xinjiang route had continued. Though by no means an unqualified success, in 104 BC they were sufficiently advanced for the dispatch of a military expedition to the capital of Ferghana (it lay between Khojend and Samarkand). This was much the most ambitious foray made by the Han into central Asia, both in terms of distance (about 4,000 kilometres – 2,500 miles – from Chang'an) and of troops (6,000 cavalry and over 100,000 infantry). Its purpose was twofold: to punish Ferghana for its reluctance to be drawn into a subordinate relationship with Chang'an, and to obtain some of its famously 'blood-sweating horses'. Equine bloodstock, always an important item in nomad–Han trade, was a speciality of the region and would long remain so. Li Guangli, the general who commanded the expedition, was anticipating William Moorcroft, superintendent of the English East India Company's stud farm, who in the 1820s would spend six years tracking the finest stallions in Asia to exactly the same region and so launch European participation in both the exploration of central Asia and the 'Great Game'.

Moorcroft would die on his quest, and at first Li Guangli fared only slightly better, being defeated by the terrain as well as the enemy. Returning to Dunhuang in disgrace, he was refused re-entry into Han territory and sent back to Ferghana in 102 BC to try again with augmented forces. This time he succeeded. He won a string of victories, obtained the king of Ferghana's head (his subjects had decapitated him), commandeered 3,000 assorted horses, and left the neighbouring states in no doubt as to the seriousness of Han intentions. After such a demonstration 'all the states of the Western Regions were shocked and frightened', says the *Hanshu*.[12] Most of the Xinjiang oases now sent missions to Chang'an, and Bactria and Parthia would follow suit.

But the cost of the exercise had been all too commensurate with its achievement. Of the over 100,000 men who had marched out of Dunhuang with Li Guangli, only 10,000 straggled back. Even Han China could not long sustain human losses on this scale, nor the financial expenditure involved in winning allies like the Wusun. The new state monopoly on liquor probably produced as much resentment as revenue, and voices were increasingly raised in protest over expansionist policies that, while impoverishing the whole empire, gratified only the imperial court.

Among these voices, though somewhat tentatively, was that of Sima Qian. In 99 BC, when the Grand Historian had been working on his *Shiji* for about seven years, a general called Li Ling served under Li Guangli's command in an expedition against the Xiongnu during which Li Ling suffered defeat and was forced to surrender. Li Ling's courage was not in question; with just 5,000 infantry, a ridiculously inadequate force, he had fought on for weeks against impossible odds until not an arrow was left. Sima Qian knew Li Ling and respected him, although he says he was not a particular friend. In interceding with the emperor on his behalf, the Grand Historian meant only 'to broaden His Majesty's views' and counteract the calumnies of others. But somehow 'our Enlightened Ruler did not wholly perceive my meaning'. Sima Qian was accused of trying to exonerate Li Ling in order to disparage the great Li Guangli. This in turn was construed as an attempt to deceive the emperor, a capital offence.[13]

Faced with such a charge an official was expected to commit suicide. His honour would thereby be partially redeemed, the emperor would be unimplicated in his fate, and the laws and punishments would remain in utopian abeyance. For in the Confucian ideal, officials attracted by the magnetic effect of the emperor's moral example were supposed to be sufficiently righteous and high-minded to recognise their guilt and penalise themselves. Not to do so would be to acknowledge their inadequacy for office in the first place and so cast a slur on the judgement and moral calibre of the emperor, a surefire way to a death yet more painful.

Except as a delaying tactic, it was pointless to plead one's innocence. Imprisonment pending trial was a euphemism for torture pending confession; the trial itself was intended merely to hear the confession and award punishment; and for an accused to be exonerated was almost unheard of. But of late there had arisen a custom whereby an accused might, at great expense, purchase commutation of a death sentence into something less draconian, such as demotion or exile. This was what explorer Zhang had done when disgraced in battle with the Xiongnu. The practice seems to have been favoured by *Han* Wudi as a means of raising revenue and was much abused for this very purpose.

Grand Historian Sima Qian declined both these options. He could neither raise the necessary funds for commutation nor resign himself to a suicide that would mean leaving his great work unfinished. His father had started the *Shiji* and had entrusted him with the task of completing it. 'How can I, his son, dare to neglect his will?' he asked. Filial piety as well as personal attachment dictated that he persevere. And though horrible to contemplate, there was in fact a third option. Worse than suicide, more disgraceful than execution, and too humiliating to be named in the long letter he wrote explaining his decision, it would at least permit him to finish his life's work.

This extreme penalty, 'the punishment of rottenness' as it was called, involved a short detention in 'the silk-worm chamber', a cell reserved exclusively for judicial castrations. After repeated beatings and the inevitable confession, Sima Qian saw his final emasculation as an abject surrender, just like Li Ling's. 'Together we became a sight for all the world to laugh at in scorn. Alas, alas! Matters such as these, it is not easy to explain in detail to ordinary people.' The physical shame, the ignominy brought on his ancestry and family, and the contempt in which he was popularly held for the rest of his life drew from the Grand Historian a bitter outpouring. Such was the price of scholarship, such the debt that posterity owes for the first and finest of China's Standard Histories.

> When I have truly completed this work, I shall deposit it in the Famous Mountain. If it may be handed down to men who will appreciate it, and penetrate to the villages and the great cities, then though I should suffer a thousand mutilations, what regret should I have?[14]

By the time of his death he had brought his great work up to the reign of *Han* Wudi. He had also included enough innuendoes to alert posterity to both the emperor's failings and his own likely bias. Whether he actually outlived his tormentor is not certain.

ADMINISTERING AN EMPIRE

The Han empire had reached its greatest extent around 90 BC. Nanyue (including all of northern Vietnam), Hainan Island (though this was abandoned in 46 BC), parts of Yunnan, all of Gansu, the trans-Xinjiang 'seaways' and many of that province's oasis cities could now be counted as Han territory. In addition, new commanderies had been established in the extreme north-east to include much of Manchuria and north Korea; and farther afield, feudatory or tributary relations had been established with the Wusun and many of the central Asian states. No significant additions would be made by the Han after Wudi's 87 BC death, nor by any subsequent dynasty until some eight centuries later.

The Xiongnu had been reduced from a threat to a nuisance. Their confederacy splintered; a new treaty was signed with one of its segments in 51 BC, and large numbers of these subdued Xiongnu settled on marginal lands within the frontier. Border alarms now as often involved Qiang from the Tibetan plateau, or a people called the Wuhuan from the Manchurian

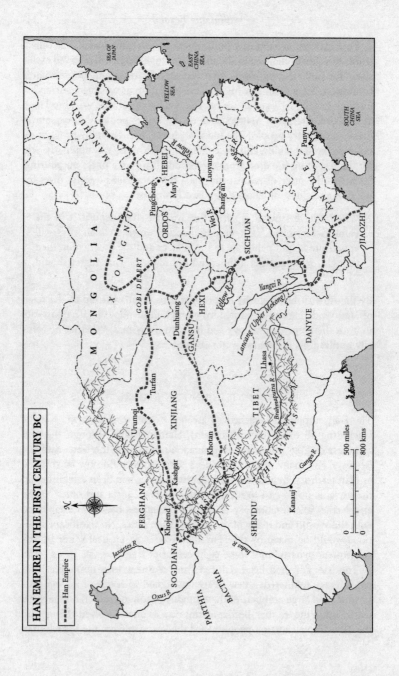

HAN EMPIRE IN THE FIRST CENTURY BC

- - - - Han Empire

N

SEA OF JAPAN

EAST CHINA SEA

YELLOW SEA

SOUTH CHINA SEA

MANCHURIA

MONGOLIA

XIONGNU

GOBI DESERT

Pingcheng
Mayi
HEBEI
Luoyang
Yellow R
Chang'an
Wei R
ORDOS
Yan R
Yangzi R
SICHUAN
Panyu
JIAOZHI

Yellow R
HEXI
GANSU
Dunhuang
Yangzi R
Lancang (Upper Mekong)
DANYUE

XINJIANG
Turfan
Urumqi
Lhasa
TIBET

Kashgar
Khotan
KUNLUN
Brahmaputra R

FERGHANA
Khojend
PAMIRS
HIMALAYAS
Ganges R
Kanauj

SOGDIANA
Jaxartes R
SHENDU

PARTHIA
BACTRIA
Indus R

Oxus R

500 miles
800 kms

steppe-forest. Instead of expansion, Chang'an pursued a policy of consolidation through colonisation. Under Wudi's successors, it would increasingly become one of retention, then retraction, as intrigue overwhelmed the empire from within. The dynastic cycle had reached its zenith.

Elsewhere it was empires which rose and fell – Persian, Greek, Indian and Roman. In China it was dynasties. Empire remained a constant. Heaven's Mandate might be transferable but its terms were fixed; there could be but one legitimate emperor, one 'Son of Heaven'. Though variable in extent and often flatly contradicted by political realities, imperial authority was becoming as inseparable from the notion of Chinese identity as was its self-consciously literate culture. Courtesy of Han, of its centralising and staying power, and of its statesmen, generals and scholars, '*zhongguo*' was being mentally and physically reconfigured as the emphatically singular 'Middle Kingdom' or 'Central State'.

Rome's near-contemporary empire was comparable in size and would last several centuries. But China's would weather the millennia. Many explanations – geographical, psychological, even genetic – have been offered for the contrasting fortunes of the two empires and for the different political orders to which they would give rise – fragmentary and increasingly consensual in the case of Europe's nation-states, unitary and increasingly authoritarian in the case of China's empire. Explanations that emphasise imperial China's more effective administrative structure and its more flexible ideology are certainly not the most exciting. Yet they carry conviction; and both – the administrative machinery and its ideological lubricant – were honed under the Han.

The Han bureaucracy has been called by one of its recent exponents 'the most impressive form of government that as yet had been devised in the world'.[15] It was both pervasive and intrusive, insistent on participation, not unresponsive, but oblivious of representation. The entire population, 57.6 million as deduced from the first surviving count of AD 1–2, was registered among some 12 million family households. These were grouped into mutually responsible units of five or ten as in Qin times. The family groups were organised into hamlets, each with a headman, and the hamlets into communes, each with a chief. Neighbouring communes constituted a district or county, neighbouring districts a prefecture, and neighbouring prefectures a commandery (or one of the now few and much-reduced subsidiary kingdoms).

All the last three administrative units were manned by salaried officials who had been chosen on merit and posted from outside to avoid any local conflict of interest. Their functions were not simply extractive. Besides being responsible for registration and judicial duties, they organised relief and public works (roads, bridges, dams, granaries), regulated local markets and manufactories, and oversaw public order and security. Of the revenue they collected through taxation, whether in coin or kind, only part was remitted annually to the central government, the rest being retained for local expenditure. The same was true of the labour levies for civil and military service. Conscription (typically two years' service for every adult male) and corvée labour (one month per year) did not normally mean transportation to the northern frontier or labouring on one of Chang'an's imperial extravaganzas; terms were mostly served within the district or prefecture and to some mutually beneficial purpose, such as suppressing banditry or improving irrigation.

In 5 BC the total number of bureaucrats serving in both central and local government was estimated at over 130,000. Office was open to those with the requisite education or attributes, and as is the way with civil services, all posts were graded into a hierarchical pecking order that cut across departmental divisions. Pay scales conformed to this grading, although the values given to each rank as expressed in 'bushels' were survivals from a coinless past and had little to do with current pay equivalents.

Not even the emperor's several thousand concubines and handmaidens were exempt from the system. By the beginning of the first century AD they too had been bureaucratised with ranks equivalent to those in government. Thus a 'Brilliant Companion' enjoyed the same status as the Chancellor, who was one of the highest officials in the land with a '10,000 bushels' ranking; a 'Beautiful Lady' was ranked at 2,000 bushels, a 'Compliant Lady' at 1,000 and a 'Maid for All Purposes' at 300. Mere 'Night Attendants' and 'Soothing Maids', at 100 bushels, held roughly the same rock-bottom rank as 'Accessory Clerks'.

It was the same throughout the emperor's household and those of the empress and the heir apparent. The 'Prefect Grand Butcher', his assistants and apprentices, forty-two in all, were also ranked, although their bloodied subordinates who did the actual cutting and dicing were not; in 70 BC, by way of an economy measure, the latter's number was reduced to 272.[16]

Neither the butchers and other provisioners nor the women of the bedchamber were employed merely to gratify a gargantuan imperial appetite. Both served a dynastic function. The ladies carried a heavy responsibility for the future of the imperial lineage, while the provisioners supplied the needs of its past, their prime carcases and first pickings being destined as sacrificial offerings to the ancestors. Conspicuous extravagance was an accepted measure of majesty, for the dead as for the living. Ancestral shrines had their own staffs for attendance on the deceased and for the maintenance of the tombs and their surroundings. Whole tomb towns, endowed and populated for the purpose, sprang up in their vicinity. According to the *Hanshu*, by the time of *Han* Yuandi (49–33 BC), there were over 200 ancestral shrines tended by some 57,000 officials, at which, in the course of a year, 24,455 meals were ritually served.[17]

Faithful service or imperial favour might lead to an advance in rank, but rankings were not a sure guide to professional competence or influence, only to social status. For the able, the ambitious or the well endowed, the system itself provided a genuine chance of recognition. Patronage and nepotism, though normal, rarely resulted in a post becoming hereditary. Although Sima Qian, for instance, had succeeded his father as Grand Astrologer (the Han equivalent of Grand Diviner), this was thanks not to inheritance but to a paternal apprenticeship for this highly specialised function, 'the most versatile and technically trained . . . in the entire central government'.[18] (At the time, there was no such office as 'Grand Historian'; the term, though adopted by the author of the *Shiji*, became a title with a ranked office only when Ban Gu was officially encouraged to undertake the authorship of the Han dynastic history (*Hanshu*) in the late first century AD.)

The hierarchy of rankings provided a bureaucratic framework, but individual titles, ranks and responsibilities, both in central government and local government, changed with bewildering frequency. Neat flow-charts showing the most senior 'Three Excellencies' (typically Chancellor, Commander-in-Chief and Grand Minister for Public Works) atop the 'Nine Ministries' (Master of Ceremonies, Superintendent of the Household, Commandant of Justice, various treasurers, etc.), with each ministry then branching into its various subordinate bureaux, can be misleading. The system was far from static. And responsibility was as often divided as delegated: for all officials were subject to vigilant scrutiny from a separate censorate, registry, auditor or inspector. Direction might come from above, but correction came from beside or even below. 'Parallel administration' was an accepted feature of government long before its reinvention by the Chinese Communist Party.

Sometimes a post would be shared by two officials; sometimes posts were paired, with an official 'of the Left' being matched by one 'of the Right'. More typically whole hierarchies were duplicated. The 'Prefect Grand Physician' and his staff of assistants and pharmacists were observed by the 'Inspector of the Grand Physician' with his own staff of assisting, attending and apprentice physicians. In the commanderies and kingdoms, teams of inspectors, sometimes called 'shepherds', roamed their flocks with bated writing-brush as they scrutinised the local administrations in search of improprieties. Yet merit, no less than misdemeanours, had to be reported; failure to do so could result in the censors themselves being censured. It was a system of checks and balances, worthy in every way of a civilisation that would invent the world's first mechanical timepiece.

The emperor himself was not exempt from correction. Confucius had been adamant that senior officials, possessed by definition of the highest moral character, were duty bound to admonish the emperor as well as advise him. They did so obliquely, often fearlessly, and sometimes to effect. For example, while Heaven might sound an ominous warning with flood and famine, it was up to local officials to report such occurrences, ministries to mitigate them, astrologers and others to interpret them, and senior counsellors to bring them – or not bring them – to the emperor's attention and urge unpalatable correctives. Autocracy was thus checked by bureaucracy. Ideally it was balanced by it; occasionally it was overbalanced by it.

Much depended on the character of the emperor. *Wuwei* rulers such as the possibly aloof Wudi and his pacific successors *Han* Zhaodi (r. 87–74 BC, *Han* Xuandi (r. 74–49 BC) and *Han* Yuandi (r. 49–33 BC) were well suited to the system. All the latter (the Han emperors 'Z', 'X' and 'Y' for those allergic to assonance) won warm praise in the pages of the *Hanshu*. Xuandi so epitomised the ideal of the responsive ruler that his reign 'could be called the renaissance [of the dynasty]', while Yuandi was 'broad-minded and had his inferiors express themselves completely'.[19] These 'Z-X-Y' decades of the mid-first century BC were marked by retrenchment after the extravagant expenditure of Wudi's long reign. 'All within the four seas were exhausted,' says the *Hanshu*, 'the population having been reduced by half' as a result of Wudi's foreign adventures. But thanks to corvée exemptions, tax reductions and various amnesties and economies, the people now rediscovered 'rest and repose' and 'became opulent'. Harvests were good, and Heaven held its devastating hand to smile on all that lay under it.

But a dictator like the Qin First Emperor (he of the 'terracotta army' and tantalising tomb) had obviously not welcomed officials who were given to 'expressing themselves completely'. His book-burning minister Li Si had habitually tendered advice only after ascertaining that it was likely to prove acceptable or ensuring that it first came from someone else. Emperors of an independent character were a liability. Bureaucrats and palace officials must either conspire to corrupt them with dissolute distractions or simply bide their time. Worse still, though, was no emperor at all, or one too young or incompetent to appreciate his role. Regents and empresses might then fill the vacuum, fighting among themselves, and placing the entire bureaucracy under enormous strain as they vied for its support or strove to short-circuit it.

This was what happened as the first century BC ground towards its end. It can hardly have been a surprise. Succession crises had dogged the Han ever since the death of their 'Great Progenitor' (*Han* Gaozu). The feisty Dowager Empress Lü had then manipulated the succession with a view to replacing the house of Han with her own Lü clan; and this seems to have set a precedent for similar manoeuvres by virtually every subsequent empress and her supporters.

Since an empress was by definition either the would-be mother, or the mother already, of a potential heir apparent, such jockeying should not have threatened the succession. But as in the bureaucracy, so in the palace – duplication complicated matters. Rarely could it be assumed that an empress was for life; they came and went with dismal frequency. They might fail to produce a male heir, be eliminated by a rival, implicated in a plot, find another's son preferred to their own, or simply fall from imperial favour. Delectable replacements from the ranks of all those 'Brilliant Companions' and 'Compliant Ladies' could be insistent and hard for an emperor to resist, especially if they had a promising heir apparent already in tow. Dowager empresses further complicated matters. As well as being experienced in palace intrigue and less vulnerable to imperial fancy, the dowagers retained great influence as residuary legatees of their husbands' heavenly authority and as the mothers or grandmothers (in which case they were grand dowager empresses) of incumbent emperors.

Another succession-related crisis had darkened the last days of *Han* Wudi's long reign. In 91 BC his empress, née Wei, had been implicated in a case of witchcraft. The origins of this affair are unfathomable, though its ramifications were horrific. Her son, the heir apparent, took up arms against his father, the ageing Wudi; Chang'an was plunged into civil war; and eventually almost the entire Wei clan was eliminated, including a chancellor, an inordinate number of generals, the heir apparent and the Empress Wei herself. But the proposed substitution of another favoured consort, plus son, met with much the same outcome; another chancellor was toppled and more generals disgraced, Li Guangli, the conqueror of Ferghana, among them. The Wei purge was then reviewed, mistakes were acknowledged, and the few surviving members of the clan reinstated. They included a toddler, the grandson of the rebellious heir apparent, who would one day reign as

Han Xuandi, plus a stern and rather intimidating figure, the nephew of the deceased Empress Wei, called Huo Guang.

As Wudi's health declined, Huo Guang emerged as a capable minister and stabilising influence. A new heir apparent, Wudi's son by yet another consort, was soon in place, although when the emperor died in 87 BC, this Zhaodi was still only seven. Fortunately Wudi had made his wishes clear. Bypassing the 'Three Excellencies' (Chancellor, Commander-in-Chief and Grand Minister of Public Works), he had appointed what would in effect be a regency triumvirate headed by Huo Guang. Lest his meaning was still unclear, he had also presented Huo Guang with a specially commissioned painting that depicted the grand old Duke of Zhou, every Confucian's hero, offering kindly guidance to the young King Cheng back in the early days of the Western (or Former) Zhou around 1043 BC.

To this challenge of emulating a revered figure from nearly a millennium earlier Huo Guang rose with almost indecent confidence. He exercised complete authority, buttressed it by supplying young Zhaodi with one of his granddaughters by way of an empress, and then when Zhaodi, still heirless and barely twenty, mysteriously died, shrugged off the inevitable suspicions and set about finding another compliant emperor. In this tortuous endeavour he was much assisted by the authority that reposed in the now dowager empress, who was otherwise his fifteen-year-old granddaughter.

As a first move, Wudi's only remaining son was cold-shouldered, probably because, being more than twice the age of Zhaodi, he would have had little need for a regent. Instead, one of Wudi's grandsons was summoned to Chang'an. According to the *Hanshu*, this young man responded to the call too promptly and then embraced his heavenly perks much too enthusiastically. The palaces rang with song and ribaldry when they should have been in mourning; Zhaodi's womenfolk were liberally favoured while their former lord yet lay in state; and more credibly, the new emperor showed vindictive tendencies towards any who criticised his conduct. Sensing imminent danger as much as insupportable disrepect, Huo Guang moved quickly. Within a month the young man had been deposed by an edict issued on the authority of the little dowager empress. Another directive summoned Bingyi, the same great-grandson of Wudi and his Empress Wei who as a toddler had escaped the witchcraft purge of seventeen years earlier and was now (74 BC) installed as *Han* Xuandi.

For Huo Guang it was a case of 'third emperor lucky'. The grateful Xuandi proved a model ruler and showered him with precious gifts, including the revenue and service obligations from an unprecedented

17,000 households. He also ensured that Huo Guang retained an unassailable position until, after a short illness, in 68 BC the great facilitator finally died of natural causes – itself a privilege seldom enjoyed by the most senior officials, especially those who dabbled in the succession. Huo Guang's funeral was the grandest ever witnessed for someone of less than imperial rank. Xuandi himself attended; and, says the *Hanshu*, among the emperor's parting gifts was the investiture, redolent of royalty, of a sea-grey suit of tailored jade.

CONFUCIAN FUNDAMENTALISM

Though *Han* Wudi had so warmly recommended the tutelary role played by the long-dead Duke of Zhou, he seems not to have approved of some of the duke's ideas on imperial authority – ideas such as virtue being essential to legitimacy, moral excellence being the best guarantee of an orderly society, and the Mandate being both contingent and transferable. On the contrary, Wudi, and then Huo Guang, continued to uphold the need for authority to be beyond dispute, for laws to be strictly enforced, punishments vigorously inflicted, and service universally exacted. The severity of Qin and its legalist exponents was invoked without embarrassment, while the Confucian habit of harping on the past and emphasising the 'magnetic' attraction of moral rectitude was ridiculed as hopelessly impractical.

But a reaction was soon under way. *Han* Xuandi, and more especially his son *Han* Yuandi, presided over a surge in Confucian remorse for the excesses of Wudi's reign. By the end of the century, appalled by the example of Huo Guang's exercise in dynastic manipulation and carried along by this swelling tide of reaction, a much-ridiculed figure would be embarking on a unique experiment in what might tentatively be called Confucian fundamentalism.

Evidence for this turning of the ideological tide is to be found both in the *Hanshu*'s approval of the economies and retrenchments undertaken during the 'Z-X-Y' years, and in an almost unique document that recounts an official consultation of the period. As per its unappetising title – 'Discourses on Salt and Iron' – this document ostensibly deals with a discussion of the government monopolies in salt, iron and other commodities. True to the traditions of Chinese literature, it is not, however, entirely what it seems. In fact ranges very much wider, being part of an official inquiry into the plight of the nation. Similarly, though the monopolies in question dated from *Han* Wudi's reign, and though the consultation itself was held in 81 BC in *Han* Zhaodi's reign, the surviving account of the debate dates from *Han* Xuandi's reign. It was thus composed as much as twenty or thirty years after the event.

It could have been based on an original transcript and intended as a belated record of the debate, or perhaps it was simply undertaken as an academic exercise; but much of its interest lies in the mid-first-century BC context in which it was written. Throughout the discusssion, official spokesmen are called on to defend the government's hard-line policies against the criticisms of articulate opponents. These government spokesmen have since been designated 'modernists' and their critics 'reformists', although neither can be regarded as advocating an exactly progressive agenda; it was more a case of conservative pragmatism versus reactionary idealism.[20]

The modernists rehearsed legalist arguments: people are naturally lazy and need to be coerced; laws are worthless if not enforced; monopolies are beneficial to both state and consumer; taxes and labour service are essential for security and social betterment; expansion and trade likewise; and government is about everyday realities, not abstract theories. The reformists, on the other hand, followed Confucian thinking to disagree on all counts: the people should be left to get on with their work, which was agriculture, not state service or manufacturing or moneymaking; foreign adventures, whether military or commercial, were unproductive; state-run industries were inefficient and produced shoddy goods; and the government should step back on all fronts, cut down on extravagance, cultivate a social conscience, and restore the balance between *yin* and *yang* by promoting rectitude and emulating the more benign policies of ancient times. Somewhat perversely, then, 'the modernists' were defending the status quo and 'the reformists' advocating a return to the distant past.

Very little came of the discussion. The state-run monopoly of salt was retained, that of iron withdrawn only in respect of manufactories in Chang'an itself, and that of liquor only in respect of the provinces (where it had probably been ineffective anyway). Yet throughout the debate it was the hard-line modernists who were repeatedly reduced to silence, while the Confucian reformists enjoyed triumph after triumph; they required fewer speakers than their opponents, their arguments received greater coverage, and they usually got the best lines: officials without a good grounding in the classics were described as like landlubbers 'putting to sea without oars', and dispatching expeditions against the Xiongnu was as unproductive as 'fishing in the Yangzi without a net'. The Qin emperors and their legalist advisers were repeatedly rubbished for having fallen

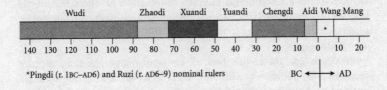

FORMER/WESTERN HAN SUCCESSION, 87BC–AD9

| Wudi | | Zhaodi | Xuandi | Yuandi | Chengdi | Aidi | Wang Mang |

| 140 | 130 | 120 | 110 | 100 | 90 | 80 | 70 | 60 | 50 | 40 | 30 | 20 | 10 | 0 | 10 | 20 |

*Pingdi (r. 1BC–AD6) and Ruzi (r. AD6–9) nominal rulers

BC ← → AD

beneath the weight of their own oppression; yet the Zhou and their peerless duke emerged unscathed. Thus the whole exercise was portrayed as a victory for the Confucian 'reformists', though in 81 BC it had probably been nothing of the sort. But by 40 BC, when this record of the debate was recorded, their arguments were being vindicated and Confucian reformism was indeed about to triumph.

This important trend owed little to the personal influence of the emperors, who followed one another in quick succession during the last half of the century. *Han* Yuandi (r. 49–33 BC) liked serious music, displayed moderation in all things, and was often ill. The economies associated with his reign were largely the work of his reformist officials. So was the very cold reception accorded to Chen Tang, a military officer in Xinjiang whose prompt action had resulted in a crushing defeat of the Xiongnu in 36 BC. Chen Tang's escapade had taken him west as far as Sogdiana (Samarkand) and had certainly upstaged Li Guangli's ponderous successes in the same region seventy years earlier. But because of the urgency of the situation, Chen Tang had had to act unofficially and on forged authority. Given the favourable outcome, this might have been overlooked had opinion still favoured a forward policy. But it did not; central Asia was no longer considered a priority, foreign adventures found no precedent in the now fashionable history of the Zhou kings, and Chen Tang was lucky not to be executed.

The famously abstemious *Han* Yuandi was extravagant only in the matter of empresses. He had three, all of whom produced male heirs whose descendants would be involved in the succession. Wang Zhengjun, the last of the three and another of those empresses with ambitious relatives and a far more imperious character than her easy-going husband, bore him *Han* Chengdi (r. 31–7 BC), his successor. Chengdi liked erotic music, had a habit of absconding from his apartments to pass incognito among the low-life of Chang'an, and was content to let his mother's family run his empire. This the Wangs did; and they being reform-minded Confucians devoted to the interventionist example of the Duke of Zhou, the official bureaucracy found itself increasingly sidelined by an 'inner court' or 'palace secretariat' that was closer to the emperor and more readily packed with Wang supporters.

Proposals current at this time of revisionist experiment included a suggestion for doing away with the coinage in favour of an economy based on kind, and another for imposing a ceiling on wealth and landholdings so that the surplus could be redistributed to the peasantry. Meanwhile scholars busied themselves with an exegetical sifting of the Confucian classics, in which they doubtless found more clues to life as so gloriously lived a thousand years earlier. Save for the stream of alleged scandals and atrocities emanating from the inner sanctums of the imperial palaces, the dawning of a brave old world seemed imminent.

This received an unexpected setback when in 7 BC the still-heirless Chengdi died and was succeeded by *Han* Aidi, his half-nephew (r. 7–1 BC). Dowager Empress Wang suddenly found herself powerless. Wang Mang, her impressive great-nephew and currently the fifth Wang to hold the supreme 'Inner Court' office of Marshal of State, was relieved of his powers. A new faction comprised of rival dowagers with their own Marshals of State took over. The reformist cause had fallen from favour.

The eighteen-year-old Aidi is credited with much ambition. But he suffered from some chronic form of arthritis and, ominously for the succession, 'cared neither for music nor women'. 'At times he watched boxing, archery and military sports,' says the *Hanshu*; at others he fawned on a dashing young officer called Dong Xian.[21] Made Marshal of State at the age of twenty-one, Dong Xian hosted a reception for a visiting *shanyu*, who was taken aback by his youth and inexperience. Dong Xian might have risen even farther; at one point the emperor actually proposed abdicating in his favour. This, however, was too outrageous a suggestion even for Aidi's dowagerial sponsors. All factions for once united in vetoing it.

It would be gratifying to report that Aidi reached AD; sadly he just failed, dying of arthritis in 1 BC. Another successor was rapidly plucked from among the long-dead Yuandi's descendants by the Grand Dowager Empress Wang, Yuandi's now eighty-something widow. And on her authority and his own insistence, Wang Mang, her nephew and the Wang family's leading light, was restored as Marshal of State and regent for Pingdi (r. 1 BC–AD 6), the nine-year-old emperor. The much-quoted precedent for Wang Mang's ascendancy was of course that of the Duke of Zhou taking young King Cheng under his wing as revised by the glum Huo Guang during *Han* Zhaodi's reign.

The zealously 'reformist' Wangs were back in control; and thanks to several timely demises, some of them natural, they were now virtually unopposed. Quite by chance, what would have been Christendom's year o (if the Gregorian calendar had not omitted it) would be 'Year Zero' for the Confucian 'commonwealth'. The much-misunderstood Wang Mang was about to introduce an instructive experiment in reactionary reform.

6

WANG MANG AND THE HAN REPRISE

AD 1–189

A ONE-MAN DYNASTY

AS THE LAST CENTURY OF THE pre-Christian era wound down, any *fin de siècle* forebodings troubled China more than they did the Mediterranean world. Rome was entering its Augustan age; peace had been restored after the civil strife of the triumvirate period, Octavian was being hailed as both emperor ('Caesar') and deity ('Augustus'), and the legions were about to triumph from Scotland to the Yemen. But in China the celebrations were over; retrenchment was the order of the day. Han troops would never again tramp across the high Pamirs into central Asia, nor take for granted Vietnam, whose first of many 'wars of independence' was about to erupt. In Chang'an the great public spectacles of *Han* Wudi's reign – military parades, tribute receptions and athletic meetings like those of Qin – had been either scaled down or abolished. Imperial hunting grounds were being neglected; stables stood empty as the emperor's equestrian establishment was halved. Hundreds of musicians and dancers had been dismissed as surplus to ritual requirement. The textile workshops in Shandong that had supplied the court with robes and furnishings had been shut down completely.

By AD 1 the Han dynasty had been in power for over two hundred years. *Han* Gaozu (the 'Great Progenitor') had reunited the empire, and under *Han* Wudi its borders had been so extended as to negate any immediate threat of incursion. Between and since, several model emperors had presided over long periods of peace, prosperity and progress. The cap-doffing 'Confucian' scholars so despised by the 'Great Progenitor' had become the pride of his progeny; and in the hands of such cultured bureaucrats, the administration comfortably controlled a population as large as that in thrall to Rome. The august Octavian, who was making administrative reform his own priority, would have despaired had he had any inkling of the intricate checks and balances of the Han bureaucratic apparatus.

But of late it did seem that the Han dynasty had enjoyed less in the way of celestial favour. From the mid-first century BC discouraging portents had begun to outnumber the encouraging ones, and by *Han* Chengdi's reign (33–7 BC) their message, as interpreted by Confucian reformists, amounted to a disturbing indictment. Summarising the situation in his translation of the Ban family's *Hanshu*, editor Homer Dubs calls this cata-logue of catastrophes 'unique': 'fires, comets, eclipses, fogs, flies, droughts, floods, earthquakes, avalanches, murders, meteors, and thunders dot the pages of the [*Hanshu*'s] chapter [on Chengdi], few years being without several such visitations'.[1] Not even the reviled Qin First and Second Emperors had been quite so afflicted with ill omens. Dynastic change was in the stars, on the breeze and underfoot.

Omens could of course be contrived, exaggerated or misinterpreted, but an incontrovertible sign of celestial displeasure was the lack of legit-imate heirs. Three successive emperors had failed to produce direct succes-sors. Short of advertising the Mandate for tender, Heaven could scarcely have made its disquiet clearer. Heirs being as important as ancestors, a dynasty that failed in this fundamental responsibility was in dire jeopardy. It was alleged that Chengdi had in fact sired two boys by a concubine; if so, they had been murdered to oblige a more favoured consort who herself then failed to bear a son. Aidi certainly had no heirs; he was not so inclined. And likewise poor little Pingdi, for he never quite attained puberty. Following the example of Huo Guang as regent for *Han* Zhaodi, Wang Mang provided Pingdi with one of his daughters as empress; but in AD 6, when he was still only fourteen, Pingdi fell ill and died.

By now all of *Han* Yuandi's male descendants had been exhausted. It was therefore a question of going back another generation to *Han* Xuandi and selecting a candidate from among *his* male descendants. Of these there were many and of all ages; five of them had been enfeoffed as kings according to the *Hanshu*, and forty-eight as marquises. But Wang Mang was unimpressed by this royal regiment. In opting for its most recent recruit, a one-year-old babe who was named Ruzi ('the infant prince'), he claimed to be acting in accordance with a doubtful tradition that required a new emperor to come from the generation after that of his predecessor. With copious references to the Duke of Zhou's impeccable example, to Confucius's endorsement of it ('I am for the Zhou') and to his own recent

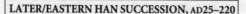

LATER/EASTERN HAN SUCCESSION, AD25–220

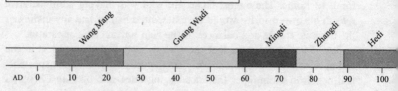

appointment as 'the Duke Giving Tranquillity to the Han Dynasty', Wang Mang contrived his advance from regent for the deceased Pingdi to regent and acting emperor for the mewling Ruzi (AD 6).

He pledged to stand down when Ruzi came of age, but the choice of so young a prince left little doubt that the now acting emperor was bent on becoming the next actual emperor. Favourable portents said as much, some of them so bluntly that they should perhaps be seen more as ritual reassurance than as an exercise in public deception; they included a prophetic letter sealed within a copper casket, an inscription hidden in a rock, and a very vivid dream reported by a Han relative. Auspicious items of tribute received at about this time – a live rhinoceros, a white pheasant and 'a stone ox from Ba' (in Sichuan, where the fashion for carved cattle apparently continued) – provided further encouragement. Most convincing of all was the ease with which objectors were being silenced and Han loyalists confounded. Heaven's approval of Wang Mang was being made manifest through the empire's concurrence.

The Wangs already enjoyed powerful support built up over three generations. In addition, Wang Mang himself was backed by fellow Confucian fundamentalists who welcomed the idea of a scholar-sage in their own image replacing an apparently compromised lineage. Heaven's intentions with regard to the Mandate seemed clear enough; and the chances for a peaceful transfer, the first on record, looked good. Hence it was that, after a decent interval full of encouraging memorials, on 10 January AD 9 at the tomb-temple of *Han* Gaozu, and with the blessing of the now eighty-something Grand Dowager Empress Wang, Wang Mang formally 'accepted the resignation' of the Han and was entrusted with the imperial seals. Little Ruzi was returned to the nursery none the worse for his two years as heir apparent, and the new emperor issued his first proclamation.

> By portents and credentials, designs and writings, a metal casket and a written charter, the gods have proclaimed that they entrust me with the myriad common people of the empire . . . [*Han*] Gaozu received

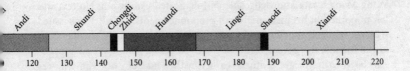

a mandate from Heaven and has transmitted the state [to me by] a writing on a metal charter. I wear the royal hat and ascend the throne as the actual Son of Heaven. It is fixed that the title [of my dynasty] in possessing the empire shall be Xin.[2]

'Xin' means 'new', and perhaps this is what Wang Mang intended. But a 'New Dynasty', besides being a statement of the obvious, scarcely chimed with its founder's Confucian purpose of restoring the old. More convincingly, editor Dubs derives 'Xin' from Xin-du, the fief of which Wang Mang was marquis. Just as Liu Bang (*Han* Gaozu) had named his dynasty after his prior kingdom of Han, so Wang Mang was naming his after his marquisate of Xin-du.[3] As ever, it was precedent, not expediency, which mattered most to the one-man dynasty that was Wang Mang.

Practically everything that is known of Wang Mang's reign comes from the *Hanshu*. None of it is favourable, and nor could it be; for Wang Mang had to be discredited in the historical record. His overthrow in AD 23, the restoration of the Han in AD 25 and the two more centuries of Han rule that would follow meant that he could be portrayed only as a usurping impostor. Instead of occupying his place after Pingdi in the *Hanshu*'s chronological annals of the emperors, he is relegated to a biographical memoir at the end of the text. Lack of legitimacy was meant to be inferred from this and would never subsequently be questioned; the Xin dynasty was forever banished from imperial China's legitimate dynastic succession.

Historiographical convention demanded that Wang Mang be exorcised; therefore he must first be demonised. On page after page he is caricatured as an unctuous and manipulative hypocrite whose vanity and indecision were as disastrous for the empire as they were for himself. Parsimonious or extravagant, indulgent or vindictive, aggressive or conciliatory, his every action is seen purely in personal terms and condemned as a failure of character. The Ban family, who compiled the *Hanshu*, had good reasons of their own for bad-mouthing Wang Mang: he had dismissed one of them from office, and they were writing under the restored Han, to whom the

Bans were indebted and Wang Mang was anathema. But there may, too, have been an ideological consideration. For it could hardly be denied that Wang Mang was a knowledgeable and dedicated Confucian. No text was left unquoted in his memorials and pronouncements; no edict was issued without some compelling reference to the past, especially to the Zhou kings. Indeed, the *Zhouli*, a text of the third century BC that had supposedly been written eight centuries earlier by the Duke of Zhou himself, was now accorded classic status. Wang Mang's reign, according to the modern historian Ch'en Ch'i-yün, 'marked the climax of Han Confucian idealism'.[4] But how then could it have gone so disastrously wrong? Since Confucianism could not possibly be to blame, the fault must lie in Wang Mang himself. Confucius had emphasised that, in setting an example of righteousness and benevolence, the ruler must be sincere. Obviously Wang Mang was not. His ideas might be sound and his scholarship formidable but, according to the *Hanshu*, they were fatally compromised by a venal and cynical nature.

At first all had gone well. In a flurry of directives, slavery (though never that common) was abolished, the sale of land was forbidden, orders were issued for the break-up and redistribution of large estates, and there was a move towards the restoration of the Zhou's idealised 'well-field' system of peasant landholdings (whereby eight families each held an equal area of land within a ditched grid, somewhat like a boxed 'noughts-and-crosses' graph, the spare square in the middle being held in common). These were brave initiatives aimed at redressing inequality and reinstating a traditional economy based on a self-sufficient peasantry. They ought to have won the approval of both precedent-minded historians and later social reformers. But in fact even twentieth-century revolutionaries would be little tempted to rehabilitate Wang Mang. Chiang Kai-shek, the Nationalist leader, would deplore the Marxist construction that could be put on the egalitarian 'well-field' system. Marxists were equally uncomfortable with it because of its 'feudal' context.[5]

Indifferent to the future, Wang Mang pushed ahead with reviving the past. The rankings system was rejigged, all ranks renamed, old nobilities reintroduced, and old names preferred for all existing posts in the administration and for all the provincial commanderies and counties. The calendar was readjusted, the time of day recalibrated, and the geography of China rectified so as to conform with a traditional concept of 'all within the four seas'. This meant, for instance, conflating Qinghai's Lake Kokonor into an ocean and naming both it and its near-Tibetan hinterland as 'Xihai', 'the Western Sea'.

No one could accuse the new emperor of dragging his feet. 'By nature irascible and irritable,' according to the *Hanshu*, 'he would not content himself with *wuwei* ['inaction'] . . . he always wanted every [initiative] to be in accordance with ancient practices, and sought some classic text as authority'. Confucius had demonstrated how, by studying the canonical texts and cultivating benevolence, a just moral order might be restored. But Confucius had been denied the chance of actually putting his ideas into effect. Wang Mang now had that chance. To create a Confucian utopia, or *taiping* (an era of 'heavenly peace' as outlined in the *Zhouli*), a prerequisite was the 'rectification of names'. Getting the names of things right was as important as the precise orientation and orchestration of ceremonies, or the synchronisation of the calendar with the seasons and the lunar phases. If names corresponded to their anciently ordained realities, cosmic order would be restored, the forces of *yin* and *yang* would be brought into equilibrium, the Five Elements/Phases correctly aligned, and Heaven's favour ensured.

Conversely, inappropriate names could only bring disaster. When the troops fared badly, it must be because their generals were handicapped by operational misnomers. Likewise when civil unrest broke out, the affected commanderies obviously needed to be reconfigured and their names revised – again. Wang Mang took full responsibility. 'He pondered deeply' and invariably concluded that 'the blame lies in titles not being correct'. On one occasion, he elevated two of his sons to royal status in the belief that Heaven required reassurance about the Xin dynasty's succession; as he explained, 'in this way, without [the empire], the barbarians of the four quarters will be driven away and, within, *zhongguo* will be pacified'.[6]

But while the effect of these changes was more bewildering than disastrous, his economic policies were potentially catastrophic. His four reformations of the coinage (including the reintroduction of archaic currencies such as 'spade-money' and cowrie shells), his 'Five Equalisations' (designed to stabilise prices and provide rural credit) and his 'Six Monopolies' (forest produce was added to the usual list of iron, salt, liquor, etc.) may have been well intentioned. Although state monopolies had been a Confucian target in the *Discourses on Salt and Iron*, all these measures could be seen as discouraging speculative enterprise in favour of honest small-scale farming, the bedrock of Confucian economics. But in practice they caused chaos and distress. Most were swiftly adjusted or rescinded, though not before corrupt officials, hoarders and counterfeiters had had a field day.

Naturally Confucian studies were heavily promoted. The imperial academy opened its doors to ever more examination candidates and ever more examining 'erudites'; a colony with housing for 10,000, a market and a granary were established for them in Chang'an. The now six (with the addition of the *Zhouli*) classic texts were further scrutinised and collated, various commentaries on them assessed, and an official 'libationer' enjoying the highest of bureaucratic rankings was appointed for each text. It is said that the practice of conferring honorary titles on Confucius himself dates from this period and likewise the worship of his memory.[7]

Few of these policies were entirely novel. Nor, as will be seen, were Wang Mang's external dealings with the Xiongnu and the Qiang anything like as naive as the *Hanshu* implies. Even the cumulative effect of so much change might not have been disastrous had Wang Mang been granted the time to implement his ideas and, where necessary, moderate them. In AD 11 he was in his late fifties, and despite the necessarily repulsive portrait offered in the *Hanshu* (bulging eyes, hoarse voice, pigeon chest, etc.), he was apparently in excellent health. But in that year his nemesis was decreed; all prospects of successful reform were dashed by one of the greatest cataclysms to which China has ever been subject.

First there was a plague of locusts along the Yellow River. It was nothing unusual. A bounty was offered to locust hunters, so many cash (the basic copper coin) per pound being paid out for squashed insects just as, in the no less lowering times of Chairman Mao's 'Great Leap Forward', a few *fen* per dead sparrow would be offered to conserve grain stocks and stave off famine. Seemingly there is nothing quite like impending catastrophe to bring out the esteem in which autocrats hold the death-defying capabilities of the masses.

Then came the flood. The *Hanshu*, in its determination to implicate Wang Mang, is somewhat sparing of the details:

> . . . the Yellow River broke its banks in Wei commandery, overflowing several commanderies from Jinghe eastwards. Previously Wang Mang had been fearful that it would break its banks and injure the graves of his ancestors. But the flood went eastwards and they were not troubled. Therefore he did not dike it.[8]

To be fair, few were the years in which the Yellow River or its tributaries failed to flood. Heavy rains turned the river's upper waters into a raging soup of Tibetan shales and Mongolian loess that, distributed by sluice and duct throughout the river's lower basin, accounted for the high fertility of the Zhongyuan ('central plain'). But as the river's flow there slowed, so did the silt sink to the bottom and the bottom thus rise to the top. Water levels regularly rose above those of the surrounding countryside and had obliged many previous emperors to divert labour to levee-building and diking. Wang Mang himself had already grappled with the dislocation caused by one such flood during Pingdi's reign, when the river had spilled from its normal course south of the Shandong peninsula and wandered farther south to join the Huai River. But the great flood of AD 11–12 took it in the opposite direction. A wall of water cut a wide swathe across the densely populated plain and diverted the entire river from its southern outlets to a new delta several hundred kilometres away to the north of the Shandong peninsula.

The *Hanshu* says little of the lives that were lost, the livelihoods destroyed, the anarchy that directly resulted, or the loss of revenue and manpower suffered by the government. But by collating these floods with the extant population data, Hans Bielenstein, an authority on the period as well as a Wang Mang apologist, has deduced massive disruption throughout the empire's heartland, followed by widespread civil disorder and a major population drift westward and southward away from the devastated areas into the valleys of the Huai, Han and Yangzi rivers. 'Unrest sprang up along the migration routes, where starving peasants banded together to take food by force,' says Bielenstein. '. . . [In Shandong] the peasant bands grew and eventually merged into a large, poorly organised, but nearly invincible army.'[9] The *Hanshu* calls these desperate militias 'the Red Eyebrows' (after the minimal insignia they daubed on their foreheads) and ascribes their rebellion to Wang Mang's misrule. Imperial forces sent east to quell the trouble failed to do so. By AD 22 the rebels were still advancing on all fronts with some sections streaming west towards Chang'an.

They were not the only ones taking advantage of the post-flood chaos and the empire's plight. In the far north the Xiongnu and Wuhuan were threatening the frontiers, while in southern Henan and Hubei (once the heartland of Chu and the locus of anti-Qin revolt) more peasant unrest was being eagerly championed by disaffected members of the rural gentry, some of them junior members of the Han lineage. While the Red Eyebrows remained true to their populist roots, these Han-led peasant armies claimed a troubling legitimacy by espousing the restoration of the previous dynasty and finding plentiful portents for Heaven's rejection of the present one. In AD 23 they took Luoyang and set up there a Han scion as the 'Gengshi ('New-beginning') emperor'.

Wang Mang, too, was dismayed by Heaven's inexplicable censures. As he lurched between defiance and clemency, enemies closed in on Chang'an and supporters either deserted or were purged. Intensifying his textual studies, the emperor dug out promising precedents and came up with yet more names. If the *Hanshu* may be believed, he also appealed for experts in unconventional warfare to come to the aid of the empire. A suggestion for a pontoon bridge composed of swimming horses was explored, as were appetite-suppressing pills as a lightweight alternative to military rations. The reconnaisance service offered by a man who claimed that he could fly sounded particularly promising. The aviator constructed his wings from the pinions of a large bird, 'connected them by pivots', and having covered his body with more plumage 'flew several hundred double-paces', says the *Hanshu*, 'then fell'. Editor Dubs, in a deadpan footnote, suggests that an eminence may have served as a launch pad and that 'this is perhaps the earliest authentic account of human flight'.[10]

An alternative reading of the frantic experimentation that characterised the last days of the Xin might suggest that Wang Mang was at his wits' end. He took to a diet of ale and shellfish, 'read only military books', and slept at his writing stool. By the time Chang'an fell to the first peasant army, he was too weak to walk. With fire raging through the Weiyang Palace he was carried to a moated tower outside the city. The *Hanshu* conjures up a Nero-like scenario with the emperor surveying the devastation from the tower's topmost parapets; King Lear might be nearer the mark. A litany of new titles, such as 'The General-Causing-Great-Waters-to-Run-So-Extinguishing-Any-Fire-that-has-Arisen', proved ineffective. So did a written appeal 'in more than a thousand words' that Wang Mang addressed personally to Heaven and accompanied with heart-rending lamentations.

Surrounded by the attacking mob, a thousand faithful supporters offered stout resistance until their arrows ran out. The mob then forded the moat and, just as the light was fading in the western sky, scaled the tower. Wang Mang fell in the crepuscular slaughter, his corpse being decapitated and dismembered on the spot. Dozens died in the fight to secure gory souvenirs, reports the *Hanshu*, and in so doing, repeats exactly the characters used by Sima Qian, the Grand Historian, to describe the fate of Xiang Yu on the banks of the Yangzi two centuries earlier. The penalty for opposing the Han was the same; so was the phrasing appropriate to such a crime.[11]

ACROSS THE WATERSHED

Recent scholarship, though united in suspicion of the *Hanshu*'s caricature of Wang Mang, is far from unanimous about the effect of his policies. As an experiment in the reordering of an empire, they had undoubtedly failed.

Confucian remedies, culled from an often defective tradition or lifted from the more contentious *Zhouli*, and then literally interpreted and slavishly applied, had proved no panacea; a hallowed past could not be resuscitated simply by replicating its institutions and its nomenclature. Although the idea of a utopian *taiping* based on the Confucian texts would appeal to later usurpers (and most notably to those nineteenth-century insurgents who actually adopted 'Taiping' as their title), it ceased to engage the orthodox. For them, using Confucianism as a crude political blueprint was a mistake. The zealotry so evident among Confucian 'reformists' in the first century BC would become notably more restrained in the first centuries AD. Gentlemen-scholars would often shun politics altogether to savour the simple life of the countryside or retreat into the metaphysical undergrowth of those nonconformist practices and beliefs associated with Daoism.

Confucianism as a moral code, however, was a different matter. Arguably, Wang Mang's apparent obsession with style over substance – with mimicking outward forms instead of cultivating inward virtues – entrenched what one scholar has aptly termed 'the Confucian persuasion'. The Chinese language has no personalised noun corresponding to the English word 'Confucianism'. *Ru*, the character which is so translated, means something much more general like 'learned gentility' or simply 'dilettante-(ism)'. Lacking the specifics of either a political philosophy, a personal ideology or an organised religion (except insofar as Confucius himself became a cult figure), 'Confucianism' is best seen as the text-hallowed brand of learning elaborated by Master Kong and his followers to advance a unique 'moral perspective'.

This moral perspective, or 'persuasion', embraces all social, cultural and political relationships. It disposes them in an ordered hierarchy and ordains the behaviour appropriate to each. Son and father, student and teacher, subject and ruler – all are locked into morally binding one-to-one relationships which, though notionally reciprocal, in practice hinge on the deference and devotion required of the junior partner – the son, student, subject. So too with wife and husband, family and ancestors, feudatory and sovereign, and so on. For those of 'the Confucian persuasion', ethical precept governs all, and no aspect of domestic life, professional affairs or government policy can be discussed without reference to it.

This was especially true in the serried ranks of the bureaucracy, a service composed entirely of *ru* (in the sense of 'Confucian scholars') recruited for their proficiency in *ru* (in the sense of 'the Confucian classics'). Nor would the troubled times ahead change this. Though intellectually challenged by Buddhism and Daoism, and somewhat marginalised by the patronage these 'religions' attracted as well as by the rise of militarism, the Confucian persuasion would yet stand its ground wherever peace pertained and civil government flourished. 'Disdained by ruthless monarchs,' writes the late Arthur Wright, 'thwarted by palace intrigue, circumvented by eunuch power, undone by venality in their own ranks, China's bureaucrats nevertheless persisted in their efforts to infuse the politics of the realm with the principles of Confucian morality.'[12]

Here, then, may be detected another of those great civilisational continuities. Though less obvious than an elegant literacy, or the primacy awarded to history, to the membership of an agrarian society surrounded by more nomadic peoples, and to imperial integration as the political norm, 'the Confucian persuasion' yet underpinned all these conceits and would prove no less enduring.

Wang Mang's 'fundamentalism' did not discredit the principles of Confucianism, and neither can his reactionary reforms be held primarily responsible for the chaos that engulfed the empire during and after his reign. Rather was it the social and economic upheaval, the mass migrations and the breakdown in law and order that resulted from the flooding of the Yellow River. Destitution being the most compelling of dictators, probably no emperor could have controlled the situation. A form of government devised for a settled agrarian population was in deep trouble the moment villagers turned vagrants and farmers took to brigandage. With the fields obliterated and the registered householders no longer at home, the revenue failed and the corvée collapsed. Central authority was itself undermined. It was this dislocation which encouraged a host of contenders for the Mandate in the AD 20s, sustained numerous other rebellions of a more peripheral nature, and encouraged landed clans in the core provinces to exploit the situation by augmenting the size of both their holdings and their followings. The Han would have to come to terms with all these groups. Restoration would entail as much in the way of compromise as conquest, and this in turn would leave the dynasty a prey to the factional struggles that would eventually engulf it.

A watershed in more ways than one, Wang Mang's chaotic reign had divided the Han era in two. Just like the Zhou kings of old, the restored Han of the first century AD would seek to put recent reverses behind them by choosing a new setting for their imperial capital. They too forsook the marginal but easily defended Wei valley in Shaanxi (once the homeland of Qin as well as Zhou and where stood Chang'an) in favour of the more easterly city of Luoyang, close to the Yellow River and at the heart of the central plain in northern Henan. Such a move had been meditated by *Han*

Gaozu, often mooted since, and recently anticipated by the Han claimant known as the Gengshi ('New Beginning') emperor. At the head of an army from southern Henan, in early AD 23 this Gengshi emperor had successfully challenged Wang Mang's forces only to find his 'new beginning' brought to an early end. Overwhelmed by a starving horde of Red Eyebrows as they streamed west to Chang'an, in AD 24 the Gengshi emperor was deposed, then murdered. For a second time, and then a third, Chang'an was burned and its palaces and ancestral tombs ransacked. In preferring Luoyang to this charred devastation, the next Han claimant would bow as much to necessity as strategy. No less pragmatic, history also views the Han's eastward move as a watershed. Mimicking the chronological division of the Zhou, it knows the Han emperors of Chang'an who preceded Wang Mang as the 'Former' or 'Western' Han, and their distant cousins in Luoyang who succeeded Wang Mang as the 'Later' or 'Eastern' Han.

But in AD 24 the succession was far from assured. Would-be emperors were lining up all over the place. In what he calls 'a crowded field', Bielenstein notes eleven contenders who actually declared themselves imperial runners. At least one rode with the vagabond Red Eyebrows and another with the dreaded Xiongnu. Some were regional warlords, two of the most powerful being Gansu-based rebels who had risen against Wang Mang, while the most enduring was a Wang Mang loyalist in Sichuan. Nearly all claimed Han descent, usually as sixth-generation descendants of *Han* Jingdi (r. 157–141 BC), the grandson of the 'Great Progenitor'. But of these Han claimants, the most forward, the Gengshi emperor, had made an early exit and the most able had been eliminated in a feud. There remained the latter's younger brother, an unrated contender called Liu Xiu. He nevertheless assumed imperial rank in AD 25 and thereafter displayed unsuspected qualities to outwit all rivals and, as *Han* Guang Wudi, become the recognised founder of the Later Han dynasty.

None of this was achieved overnight. In general, the Later Han would prove less adventurous than the Former Han and far more prone to crises. The official histories award them a generous two centuries (AD 25–220); but their first eight decades were characterised by laborious reconstruction, the next eight brought a painful unravelling, and the last four saw them reduced to a pitiful irrelevance. When later writers sang of the glories of Han, they almost invariably had in mind the Former or Western Han, not the Later or Eastern Han.

Han Guang Wudi's thirty-two-year reign (AD 25–57) was devoted entirely to re-establishing the dynasty. The reconstruction of Luoyang and its elevation into a capital worthy of All-under-Heaven's ruler was as crucial to this process as the suppression of revolt. More regular in its grid-like configuration than Chang'an, Luoyang's walled and gated inner city would comprise an area of 10 square kilometres (4 square miles). In accordance with hallowed principle, the domestic establishment of the always 'south-facing' emperor was located in its northern palace with government offices in its southern palace. The two were linked by a 3-kilometre (2-mile) screened walkway that bisected the inner city. Extensive suburbs sprawled outside the great walls; though of tamped earth, or *hangtu*, 'the walls still measure up to ten metres in height today'. Bielenstein makes the city inferior only to contemporary Chang'an and Rome in terms of size, and claims that its population of 'no less than half a million' exceeded either.[13]

In defeating his many rivals, *Han* Guang Wudi displayed an aptitude for military command that was rare among emperors, plus a confidence in his subordinate generals that was almost unprecedented. Internal revolt was dealt with first. The Red Eyebrows, much reduced by a hard winter in Shaanxi and a sound drubbing from one of the Gansu warlords, were forced to surrender in AD 26. Other revolts in the central plain and Shandong were largely quelled by AD 30 and Gansu brought to heel by AD 34. Two years later Sichuan (or 'Shu', for its self-declared emperor had resurrected the name of the kingdom extinguished by Qin three centuries earlier) finally surrendered. Fire-belching dreadnoughts, rather than stone cattle, this time proved its undoing. In a notable campaign a Han naval force sailed up the Yangzi, ignited Shu's floating battlements, which spanned the river just below the gorges, and then blazed a trail to Chengdu, the Shu capital.

The outlying regions of the Former Han's once sprawling empire took longer to reclaim, mainly because they were slower to revolt. It is customary to follow the *Hanshu* in blaming Wang Mang for their loss. His passion for rectifying names is supposed to have antagonised the *shanyu* (king) of the Xiongnu; and in the same spirit of insensitive superiority he may have reneged on existing trading arrangements. 'Seldom can a man have been so consummately deceived by his own propaganda,' writes a generally sympathetic authority.[14] Yet *Han* Guang Wudi would treat the *shanyu* no less contemptuously than Wang Mang, and it was only after a later spat in the AD 30s that the Former Han commanderies along the northern frontier were abandoned. The same was true elsewhere. Contact with the Western Regions (that is Xinjiang) was lost not during Wang Mang's reign but in the course of the civil war that followed it; trouble with the 'proto-Tibetan' Qiang peoples of the Kokonor region of Qinghai, whom Wang Mang had subdued, re-ignited only as his authority failed; and the revolt in Vietnam did not break out until sixteen years after his death.

The reconquest of these regions owed much to the great Ma Yuan, head of a powerful landed clan in the Wei valley, who besides tendering advice that stabilised the currency after Wang Mang's experiments was one of the most successful Later Han generals. In fact General Ma would become a cult figure; in some parts of China there are still temples dedicated to his memory. When offering his services and the allegiance of his family to *Han* Guang Wudi in AD 28, General Ma was revealingly frank. 'In present times', he explained, 'it is not only the sovereign who selects his subjects. The subjects also select their sovereign.'[15] The emperor apparently accepted this, and Ma's faction duly became one of a handful that exercised enormous influence at court throughout the Later Han period.

Meanwhile, far to the west, Ma himself began grappling with the proto-Tibetan Qiang people. Between AD 35 and 39 he subdued the region from modern Xining to Kokonor and settled vast numbers of Qiang along and within this sector of the frontier. It was hoped that they would become taxable subjects as they forsook pastoralism in favour of sedentary farming; and for twenty years peace did indeed return to the area. But here, as along the northern frontier, a generation of instability had already prompted an exodus of the existing population. The ingress of non-Chinese only slewed the population balance still further, so that even within striking distance of Chang'an concentrations of Qiang and Xiongnu numerically challenged those indigenous descendants of the erstwhile Xia and Qin who may now be called 'Han Chinese'. This would have unexpected consequences; the Qiang problem, unlike the Qiang themselves, was anything but settled.

General Ma's next assignment could hardly have been farther away. In AD 40 revolt broke out in the south of Nanyue, or what is now northern Vietnam. For Ma it meant crossing the whole of China, exchanging near-tundra for tropics, raising a new army, and adapting the tactics of frontier patrolling to jungle warfare. The trouble was again ethnic, although it would acquire strong nationalist overtones. The indigenous Yue had risen against Han rule and more especially against Han immigration into the Red River basin. Whereas in the north of China Han settlers were retreating, in the south they were encroaching; a great population drift that over the next several centuries would change the whole pattern of Chinese demography was gathering pace.

Untroubled by such trends, Ma marched into Vietnam with over-whelming force, his supplies followed by sea from Guangdong, and the revolt was all over by the end of AD 43. But the written character for 'Yue' being read as 'Viet' in Vietnamese, and leadership of the Yue having fallen to two wildly courageous sisters (called Zheng in Chinese, Trung in

Vietnamese), it was inevitable that later Vietnamese patriots would hail the revolt as the first 'national uprising' of an all too often oppressed people. Heavily romanticised, the story of Viet resistance to General Ma became a national epic rich in detail. It tells how one of the Boadicea-like Trung sisters rode into battle on elephant-back with her breasts flung over her shoulders like saddlebags – an arrangement that could be editorially glossed as the earliest authentic reference to the halter-neck top, or perhaps the brassiere. Chinese sources credit General Ma with extending to the Yue/Viet the opportunity of peaceful assimilation to Chinese ways and an end to their incorrigible tribalism. Certainly northern Vietnam under-went intensive sinicisation; and despite constant troubles, the next 'national uprising' would be a long time coming. In fact the Red River valley would remain under some form of Chinese rule for all of the ensuing millen-nium. But the Vietnamese prefer to forget this hiatus in their national struggle, and not surprisingly, temples dedicated to Ma Yuan are notably absent in Hanoi.

No sooner had General Ma reported back to Emperor *Han* Guang Wudi in Luoyang than he received another troubleshooting assignment, this time to the northern steppe-land on the Shanxi–Inner Mongolia frontier. There and throughout the 'Great Wall' borderlands the Xiongnu had taken advantage of the recent civil strife to stage a remarkable come-back. Partly through their own efforts, partly thanks to the erratic support of renegade Chinese warlords and of the nomadic Wuhuan and Xianbei peoples of the north-east, the Xiongnu had recovered practically all the territories once ruled by the great *shanyu* Maodun. Raiding parties were reaching what remained of the Former Han's ancestral tombs near Chang'an and, far to the west, were threatening the ever loyal Wusun. The Ordos was back in Xiongnu control; so, to the west of it, were many of the oasis-cities of northern Xinjiang and, to the east of it, even the arable parts of Shanxi and Hebei.

The last of these was General Ma's new theatre of operations. In AD 45 he set up headquarters west of where Beijing now stands. From there he marched north to Mongolia. But the Xiongnu evaded him, and in what was supposed to be a surprise raid on their Wuhuan allies, Ma himself was surprised. He lost a thousand cavalry, and though he remained in the region for another year, he did not again take the offensive. This could be because he did not need to. For in AD 46 the *shanyu* died, the succession was disputed, and the Xiongnu became the prey of their Wuhuan allies. 'From the Chinese point of view', writes Rafe de Crespigny, an authority on the northern frontier, 'there was hardly any purpose in an aggressive policy while their enemies were carving one another up in such a satisfactory fashion.'[16] Far from disgraced, General Ma moved on again. He would live to fight and die while suppressing yet another insurrection, his fourth, in northern Hunan.

Though by no means the end of the Xiongnu people as a frontier presence, the ructions over the *shanyu*'s succession in AD 46–49 sounded the death-knell of the Xiongnu state. Repeating events of exactly a hundred years earlier, in AD 51 one *shanyu* claimant finally turned to Luoyang for support and tendered his allegiance, plus a modest tribute. In return he received Han recognition plus decidedly less modest gifts – 10,000 bales of silk fabric, 2.5 tonnes of raw silk, 500,000 kilos of rice and 36,000 head of cattle. Tributaries never came cheap; in fact the *shanyu* of these 'Southern Xiongnu', in trading kowtows for commodities, and sovereignty for security, may have struck a better bargain than his ancestors under the old 'peace-through-kinship' treaties. Moreover, the gifts were just the first instalment of what was in effect an annual subsidy. By AD 91 the Southern Xiongnu were estimated to be costing the Han exchequer 100 million cash per year.

Nor were they the only beneficiaries of the Later Han's policy of accommodation on the frontier. The Wuhuan and, on occasion, the Xianbei were also handsomely paid for assisting the Han, whether against the still-hostile 'Northern Xiongnu' or against one another. Perhaps as many as 3 million Wuhuan were eventually settled within the frontier. The Han army welcomed the addition of their fearsome cavalry, while the Wuhuan welcomed a subsidised existence like that of the Southern Xiongnu. It was different with the Xianbei (Xianbi, Sarbi). Having assisted the Han in driving off the Northern Xiongnu in AD 91, they proceeded to fill the Mongolian void left by this Xiongnu exodus. By the second half of the second century AD the Xianbei headed a new nomadic confederacy that would pose an even greater threat to the Later Han than had the once united Xiongnu.

All these frontier peoples merit more consideration than the mostly Chinese sources permit. Tomb paintings discovered in Inner Mongolia portray them as shaven-headed, sometimes with a Mohican tuft, and shabbily dressed. The Wuhuan and Xianbei seem to have originated in eastern Mongolia or western Manchuria, though their ethnic identification as 'proto-Mongol' is more tentative than that of the Qiang as 'proto-Tibetan'. They lived in tents, herded livestock and were good on horseback. More critically, as a result of Luoyang's accommodating policies, they (plus the Qiang) came to occupy vast areas within the north, north-west and north-east frontiers of the Later Han empire.

For the Han they were a mixed blessing. Tributaries had been won, and the northern frontier had been returned to where it had stood under the Early Han. But the cost was great. It was argued that subsidies were cheaper than the military campaigns and garrisons that would otherwise be necessary. Yet incorporating alien populations that resented discrimination from their Han neighbours (though in many areas they outnumbered them) would have devastating consequences. Though initially illiterate and alien to all that constituted Chinese civilisation, the Qiang, Xiongnu, Wuhuan and Xianbei would come to play a decisive role in the post-Han period. In that age of warring kingdoms, they, just like the men of Chu and Qin in the earlier 'Warring States' period, would be invited into the central plain as mercenaries and then power-brokers. Insinuating themselves among the peoples who today consider themselves Han Chinese, the alien 'tributaries' would infuse the indigenous mainstream. Thereafter the flow of China's history would be as much theirs as that of their erstwhile Han enemies.

As for the 'Western Regions', that appendage of island-oases and intersecting silk-ways beyond the Gansu corridor in Xinjiang, the Later Han were ambivalent. For nearly half a century (AD 25–73) no attempt was made to reclaim the area. Suche (Yarkand), the principal kingdom in the extreme south-west of Xinjiang, attained a brief hegemony over the other oasis-states, but the Northern Xiongnu were soon raiding and trading at will throughout the region. Colonies established by the Early Han remained in a state of siege – if they remained at all; and the 'Jade Gateway' to the Silk Road near Dunhuang was more often barred than open. None of this, however, prompted speedy action. For in retrospect those long-distance exchanges of the previous century, which the Chinese had habitually characterised as tribute and the tributaries as trade, looked less worthwhile. At one point the two-way traffic along the silk trails had grown so heavy as to be almost continuous. Yet its prestige value to the Han court had declined. The system, it seems, was being too much abused.

The point was well made in a report on relations with Kashmir. Here was a country, south of Xinjiang and on the other side of two of the world's highest mountain chains, that was clearly beyond the reach of Han arms. It was almost beyond the reach of Han emissaries. Supplies were unobtainable on the mountain trails, a military escort was essential to discourage bandits, and such was the effect of the extreme altitudes that the Kun Lun and Karakoram mountains were known to the Chinese as 'the ranges of the Greater and Lesser Headache'. For long stretches the trail – it probably followed the Hunza, Gilgit and Indus rivers – narrowed to ledges less than 45 centimetres (18 inches) wide. Travellers had to rope themselves together. 'The danger of the precipices beggars description,' said the report. Yet for the best part of a century substantial missions had been scrambling back and forth, often annually, to pledge fealty on behalf of the Kashmiris and to confer titles on behalf of the emperor. In both directions they also carried merchandise – woollens, embroidery and Indian produce from Kashmir, large consignments of silk from China. Secure in their Himalayan fastness, the Kashmiris brooked no interference in their internal affairs and massacred one Han mission that tried. But apologies had followed, the protestations of loyalty continued, and the exchanges had resumed. Inveterate traders to this day, the Kashmiris were clearly using the Han tributary system and the protection that it afforded to conduct purely commercial activities. As the report puts it, 'envoys sent out on missions to carry the commands of the emperor' were being diverted 'to escort the merchants of the barbarians'.[17]

It was not tribute or trade which tempted the Han back into Xinjiang but the Xiongnu. In AD 73, 74 and 77 military expeditions launched from Gansu against the Northern Xiongnu pursued them deep into Mongolia and reoccupied the northern Xinjiang oases of Turfan and Hami. Ban Chao, the brother of the *Hanshu*'s authors, took part in these forays, and it was he who in the AD 90s famously led a series of further expeditions that re-established Han supremacy throughout Xinjiang. As Protector-General of the Western Regions, an office defunct since the conquests of the Early Han, Ban Chao supervised the resettlement of Han colonies along the silk routes and renewed contacts with the states of central Asia. In AD 97 a mission under his subordinate, Kan Ying, was dispatched to 'Da Qin', a distant realm with an apparently insatiable appetite for Chinese silk. It was probably the Roman empire, albeit its eastern provinces. Sadly the encounter that might have resulted was pre-empted by the mission's detention in Parthia, whose merchants, like those of Sogdiana (Samarkand), had a vested interest in excluding competitors from the overland trade.

Han horizons, which had been at their most expansive in the early first century BC under the Former Han, seemed to be reopening in the late first century AD under the Later Han. On the other side of China in North Korea, twentieth-century discoveries of richly endowed Han tombs have substantiated a patchy textual record of conquests and commanderies in the Korean peninsula which date from *Han* Wudi's time. But with no external threat from this quarter, Han pretensions ebbed and flowed without provoking much comment. Their effect was more notable in terms of acculturation. Confucian values and useful Chinese achievements, such as literacy and paper-making (developed in the first and second centuries AD), passed down the Korean peninsula and across the Tsushima Strait. In AD 57, and again in 107, Luoyang entertained its first recorded visitors from Kyushu in the Japanese archipelago. At almost exactly the same time, Han texts make their first mention of a revered teacher who was called 'Fo' in China but 'The Buddha' in India. From the Sea of Japan to the Ganges and the Tiber, Han China's horizons now spanned the Eurasian landmass.

They soon retracted. The Han administrations in Korea were forced back into Liaodong province in the early second century AD, and all the Western Regions were abandoned – again – soon after. The main reason in the case of the latter was the cost of maintaining so many tributary statelets and far-flung colonies. But renewed trouble with the Qiang in the Gansu corridor threatened access to the region and was a contributory factor. The Qiang revolts came thick and fast. By AD 168 the Han had been forced to withdraw from three of Gansu's commanderies, so narrowing its famous 'corridor' to little more than a crack. Proposals to withdraw completely from the whole of eastern Gansu were canvassed but met with strong resistance, most notably from Gansu itself. When in AD 184 the whole region erupted again in rebellion, its Han population would make common cause with their Qiang and Xiongnu neighbours. One rebel group even adopted the title 'Ping Han', meaning 'Pacifying the Han'. The dynasty itself now became the target, and under Dong Zhuo, one of Gansu's king-making leaders, this Gansu revolt would 'play a key role in the decline and fall of the Han empire'.[18]

DECLINE AND FALL

As with the later Roman emperors, so with the Later Han emperors: few merit mention for what they did and not many for what was done in their name. After AD 88 the succession passed to a motley collection of infants, invalids, weaklings and imbeciles; though castigated in the Standard Histories, they seem more deserving of pity than censure. Their dates help to break up a substantial passage of time, but seldom can a change of emperor be taken to indicate a transfer of power or an adjustment in policy. Power changed hands between factions, not emperors; policies, where discernible, were dictated by events.

Much as the founding of the Han dynasty (in 206 BC) had been made to predate the installation of its first emperor (in 202 BC), so the formal demise of the dynasty (in AD 220) substantially postdates the empire's actual disintegration (in AD 184–89, if not earlier). Dynasties and their empires would quite often not be coterminous. The Standard Histories, in emphasising a dynasty's maximum span, sought to obscure the usually shorter duration of its effective empire. Adding a bit at either end – one might call it dynastic elastication – gave the desired impression: integrated empire was meant to seem the long-lasting rule, division the short-lived exception. Commissioned by the court and written by scholars from the central bureaucracy, the histories betray a vested interest in magnifying and prolonging central authority, plus a natural bias towards events and intrigues at court. A Luoyang perspective on the rest of the empire is standard.

But as seen from, say, Sichuan, Shandong or the Yangzi, let alone the border regions, things looked different. Never were the Later Han untroubled by insurrection, and only in the three decades after *Han* Guang Wudi (so AD 58–88) was the dynasty spared major regional or 'religious' revolts led by would-be emperors. In one year, AD 145, no less than three rebel emperors took the field; four others followed their example over the next decade. There were possibly as many competing emperors during the two centuries of the Later Han's unitary empire as during any two centuries of the ensuing 'Period of Disunion'.

The internecine intrigues and bloodlettings at the Later Han court reflected this strife in the wider empire, as well as encouraging it. At first all had gone well. After *Han* Guang Wudi's death, his son and then grandson continued to manage the competing factions at court with some success. *Han* Mingdi (r. AD 58–75) chose a daughter of General Ma Yuan as his empress, so appeasing the powerful Ma clan of the north-west while confounding its rivals, some of whose members were executed or exiled. On the other hand, *Han* Zhangdi (r. AD 75–88) chose a consort from the rival Dou grouping from Henan, which led to the downfall of the Ma clan, some of whose protégés were jailed and/or committed suicide.

The casualty rate was not exceptional; imperial favour was ever fickle, and dismissal was commonly attended by death. Moreover, both emperors managed the fraught issue of the succession rather well considering that neither of their empresses actually bore them sons. Normally this would have left an empress vulnerable to being replaced by some 'graceful lady' who did give the emperor a son; this might in turn bring the disgrace of the incumbent empress plus the downfall – or worse – of her clan. But such an eventuality was pre-empted in both these cases. *Han* Mingdi's empress wisely co-opted into her own faction an imperially favoured mother-to-be and promoted the suitability of the latter's son as if he were her own. *Han* Zhangdi's empress went one better by championing in similar fashion two sisters, the Ladies Liang, one of whom duly gave birth to the future *Han* Hedi (r. AD 88–106). There was, however, risk in such an arrangement: the mother of the heir apparent might renege on it, turn the emperor against his empress and supplant her as consort and her clan as power-brokers. This is precisely what the Ladies Liang would eventually do. Better by far, then, indeed the ideal arrangement, was for the emperor to choose in the first place an empress whose attributes included a delectable sister. That way the same family got two bites at the cherry of providing a male heir and so of retaining its influence into the next generation. As an insurance policy, the empress-plus-sister combination would later become something of a commonplace.

Han Hedi's accession in AD 88 introduced another complication, namely a minority, for he was barely nine years old. In accordance with a tradition that extended back through the Dowager Empress Wang (wife of *Han* Chengdi and aunt of Wang Mang) to the Dowager Empress Lü (wife and virtual successor of the 'Great Progenitor' *Han* Gaozu), this opened the way for the exercise of power by the now Dowager Empress Dou, the widow of Hedi's deceased father. It also meant appointing a regent who, like the revered Duke of Zhou, might shoulder the burden of rule while, like Wang Mang and Huo Guang, shamelessly manipulating the succession. Naturally the Dowager Empress chose as regent one of her brothers, Dou Xian; and thus by AD 90 it was the Dou clan who appeared to be in a position of unassailable power.

It lasted only a couple of years. In early AD 91 *Han* Hedi was deemed to have come of age and duly assumed the imperial cap and insignia. Eighteen months later, with the advice and active encouragement of the senior palace eunuch, Hedi effectively staged a coup against the Dou clan and their suffocating attentions. Dou Xian and his brothers saw fit to kill themselves; numerous supporters, including Ban Gu, the main author of the *Hanshu*, were executed; and the dowager empress, though spared, was removed from public life.

Hedi, however, had his own succession problems. One empress, then another, failed to bear him a son. When he died in 106, it was the second of these, the empress (now dowager) Deng and her inevitable faction, who selected as his successor *Han* Shangdi (r. 106). At the time Shangdi was just three months old and not destined to get much older. He died before his first birthday and was replaced by *Han* Andi (r. 106–125). Andi, at twelve, could be considered a veteran. His coming of age was imminent, and with it the chance of an emperor actually ruling and deciding the succession for himself. Unfortunately Andi managed neither of these goals. He was weak and incompetent, and his only claim on posterity's attention is as, by general consent, 'the worst sovereign of the two Han dynasties'.[19] It was during his reign that the Western Regions were abandoned, the Qiang resumed their offensive and the more immediate empire was again beset by natural disasters.

By now a pattern was emerging. Emperors, instead of managing their support, were more often being managed by it. Of the contesting elements in the dynastic free-for-all that would characterise the last days of the Later Han, all bar one – the military – were in place. Of these elements the bureaucracy as it had existed under the Former Han continued to operate but was not the most important contender. Rather did it provide a source of patronage. Its senior posts were treated as sinecures, given as rewards, and by the late second century AD openly sold to the highest bidder. The bureaucracy's executive functions were increasingly usurped by a separate palace secretariat which, as the 'Department of Affairs of State', would exercise supreme executive authority and acquire its own bureaux, or 'boards'. Under the Later Han it was staffed by men whose main qualification for office was not a knowledge of the classics but proximity to the emperor or his acting surrogates.

Meanwhile the bureaucracy's wider administrative responsibilities were being circumscribed by intervention from above and fragmentation from below. More and more land, along with its produce and population – in effect the empire's tax base – was being partially alienated in the form of heritable kingdoms (for imperial cadets) and more especially marquisates (principally for the relatives and supporters of contending empresses). Individually the old commanderies and counties were thus shrinking, while collectively they were being subordinated to a superior structure of provinces or regions (*zhou*). Originally these provinces comprised the circuits covered by the inspectors ('shepherds' or censors) who oversaw the bureaucratic machinery. But in time, inspectorates became permanent, were based in their own 'provincial' capitals and acquired their own bureaucratic and, as of AD 180, even military establishments. Thus the dozen or so provinces, though divided into commanderies and counties, pocked by kingdoms and marquisates and perforated by peripheral feudatory dependencies, now constituted the primary divisions of the empire. Once under military command, they would constitute the power bases from which contenders would finally challenge and overthrow the Han.

More active than the bureaucracy in the pursuit of reward and influence was that parallel world of carefully supervised rank-holders inside the imperial harem. An emperor enjoyed the services of hundreds, often thousands, of young women. Like the bureaucrats, they were recommended to court either by their families or local officials and then selected by examination. Though the examination involved no written submission, it was of a thorough and intimate character, special attention being paid to the flawless nature of the girl's complexion, figure, physique and virginity, as well as to her deportment, accomplishments and the repute of her family. 'Skin white and fine . . . belly round, hips square, body like congealed lard and carved jade, breasts bulging and navel deep enough to take a half-inch pearl,' reported one examiner, 'no piles, no blemishes, no moles and no sores, nor defects in the mouth, the nose, the armpits, the private parts, or the feet.'[20] A family's fortunes might be riding on the outcome. If the candidate was selected and duly 'favoured' by the emperor, rank, office and honours would flow to her relatives. If she bore him a son, these rewards would be upgraded and her status within the imperial household dramatically enhanced. To be a candidate for empress, powerful support counted for more than a love-struck emperor. But the rewards could be worth it; sons being scarce among the Later Han, a chance to influence the succession beckoned.

The Standard Histories nevertheless tell of emperors so distracted and besotted by their womenfolk that they habitually neglected the call of duty and ignored the plight of the empire. Consorts and dowagers are portrayed as inherently devious and spiteful, devoid of any sense of duty, and largely responsible for the endless intrigues and purges. This was explained in cosmic terms as *yin*, the passive female principle, being in disastrous ascendancy over *yang*, its active male opposite or complement. All of which not only reeks of gender prejudice – we know of only one female Han historian – but is open to serious doubt on other grounds.

Ban Zhao, that one lady historian, was she who completed the *Hanshu* after the execution of her brother Ban Gu. She also wrote another work entitled *Lessons for Women*. The lessons were scarcely empowering. A woman's role was one of willing and vigilant subservience to family, husband and in-laws; her attention should be directed to personal hygiene and chaste conduct; appropriate activities included sewing, weaving and light kitchen duties. But the author did register a plea for equality of education, and from about AD 100 Ban Zhao herself acted as tutor and adviser to *Han* Hedi's second consort, the empress and then Dowager Empress Deng. How far Ban Zhao influenced her pupil is not known, but it seems unlikely that empresses, who were often little more than children when they took an emperor's fancy, can themselves have been mistresses of the Machiavellian arts. More plausibly, when young they served as decorous tools in the hands of their families and when older as dynastic scapegoats at the disposal of Confucian scholarship.

Better understanding of the role played by women under the Later Han, and of the importance of the bridal chamber as a portal to social and political advancement, owes much to the gender-conscious scholarship of recent times. In similar fashion, the total disregard of the toiling peasantry as other than a productive but unpredictable phenomenon, like the weather, has been rectified by historians raised in the traditions of proletarian revolution. But the same affirmative treatment has yet to be extended to another influential and characteristic component of court life, the eunuchs.

In phrases like 'the evils of eunuchry', the stereotype of a manipulative and corrupt fraternity of falsetto felons still haunts the textbooks, uncorrected by any latter-day lobby of emasculated revisionists.[21] It originated in the *Hanshu* and subsequent Standard Histories, where castration is taken to be contemptible, with words like 'capon' and 'gelding' getting an airing. Worse than the physical mutilation, though, was the renunciation of Confucian values implied by a condition that eliminated the possibility of descendants. For the chance of an easy life overseeing his masters' breeding stock of consorts and concubines, a eunuch was thought to have ducked his own reproductive responsibilities and severed the continuum of his lineage. It was tantamount to apostasy. There would be neither heirs to perform his funerary rites nor descendants to honour him and provide for his ancestors. One who so brazenly flouted all that society held dear must expect to be treated as a pariah.

At a time of intense factionalism, when control of the realm was being contested within that part of the Luoyang palace complex reserved for the emperor's women, the access and influence enjoyed by eunuchs would be crucial. Since eunuchs are little mentioned prior to the Later Han, it is often assumed that their prominence was in fact a product of the period. But this may appear the case simply because most prior history was derived from the *Shiji*, whose completion had of course cost its author his own masculinity. As a eunuch himself, the Grand Historian had been disinclined to advertise the menial role of others so afflicted, or to heap disparagement and blame upon them. He was, too, painfully aware that castration could be a punishment rather than a career move, and that as a father himself prior to mutilation, it did not in fact preclude the possibility of descendants. Even eunuchs-from-childhood could acquire children through adoption. The practice was common, and under the Later Han, eunuch 'fathers' won the right to pass on their ranks and offices to these adopted heirs.

When in AD 125 *Han* Andi died having neither asserted the authority of the throne nor made any clear provision for the succession, his childless empress took the now familiar step of raiding the palace crèche. But her selection of an infant so insignificant that not even his identity is recorded misfired. For this '*Han* Anon-di' (for want of a better name) died within the year; and before another babe could be snatched from his wet-nurse, a palace coup brought the installation of Andi's only son (albeit by a concubine), the eleven-year-old *Han* Shundi (r. 125–144). The coup, accompanied by the usual executions and suicides, was important in that it was the first to be engineered by eunuchs. Moreover the eunuchs had shown a clear preference for a candidate with a reasonable chance of attaining adulthood and so of dispensing with the heavy-handed supervision of Dowager Empress Deng and her faction. Shundi would be grateful; and thereafter the palace eunuchs would often shore up imperial authority against the encroaching tide of kingmakers, whether dowagers, regents, bureaucrats or generals.

Such loyalty to the dynasty might have won the eunuchs more favourable treatment from posterity had they not, like everyone else, then rewarded themselves by extracting grants and honours from the emperor and by engaging in the factional merry-go-round. Shundi's installation brought marquisates for eighteen eunuchs, plus a return to power for the Liang faction, one of whose ladies became empress. Through a succession of regents and imperial brides, the Liangs hung on to power until AD 159. Meanwhile emperors came and went, most of them being toddlers with a suspiciously short life expectancy. In fact not one of the last nine emperors of the Later Han was an adult at the time of his accession.

A major earthquake in AD 133 and a drought in AD 134 heralded disturbances in the far south, Xianbei raids in the north and revolts in Gansu. All were seen as bad omens and triggered the post-AD 145 rash of rebel emperors, plus the usual scholarly doubts about the Mandate and the dynasty's future. These were not allayed when an emperor, *Han* Huandi (r. 146–168), actually managed to reach manhood. For like *Han* Hedi, Huandi resented his matronly minder and soon moved against her whole Liang faction. Largely with eunuch support, the Liangs were ousted amid the usual bloodletting. Huandi then chose as bride – or more accurately was chosen as groom for – a Deng damsel, quickly followed by a Dou damsel. But the jinx continued. When Huandi died, not one of his empresses had borne him a son; nor had he nominated a successor. The succession was up for grabs again, and in time-honoured fashion the twenty-year-old Empress Dou set another child on the throne, confirmed her father as regent, and so reinstated the great Dou clan of the north-west.

Regent Dou then plotted the overthrow of the eunuchs, who were by now sufficiently entrenched to menace any faction's monopoly of power and patronage. The plot, a none-too-subtle scheme involving the execution of every eunuch at court, leaked out. Forewarned, the eunuchs closed ranks, commandeered the young emperor and the dowager empress, and on their authority deployed troops to secure Luoyang's twin palaces and the walkway between them. Regent Dou and his supporters also called on the military. The opposing forces confronted one another, traded insults and bellowed threats. There was no actual fighting on this occasion; Regent Dou's men deserted him, and he and his supporters, plus their extended families – perhaps a few hundred in all – were subsequently either killed or committed suicide. With the deployment of troops within the capital, a dangerous new precedent had been set.

The new emperor was *Han* Lingdi (r. 168–189), a rival to *Han* Andi for the title of the dynasty's worst. Though he achieved his majority in 171, he remained a hopeless dependant on eunuch support throughout his reign. With the fall of the Dou, the eunuchs instituted proceedings against Dou partisans within the bureaucracy. This brought a bloody purge of the offending clique and something called the 'Great Proscription'. When required to authorise it, the thirteen-year-old emperor dared to ask what was meant by a 'proscription' and what exactly was a 'clique'. It was explained that the one excluded from office the other, clique members being all those related in any degree to the purged officials. Later extended, this bar on family-based factions effectively reserved to the eunuchs and their henchmen a lucrative monopoly of all senior posts within the palace secretariat and the old bureaucracy.

Resentment of the Great Proscription and of the eunuchs' flagrant abuse of power mounted throughout the AD 170s. In the provinces the tide of local revolt and vocal disaffection refused to ebb; the south was again in turmoil; and the entire northern border was at the mercy of a Xianbei confederacy led by Tanshihuai, a nomadic leader in the great tradition of Maodun and the later Chinggis Khan. Yet all these were as nothing compared to the mass uprising that occurred in AD 184. 'In a few weeks the whole empire joined in rebellion and the capital was in fear and trembling,' says a digest of the Standard History.[22]

Not unlike the Red Eyebrows in the reign of Wang Mang, this so-called 'Yellow Turbans' movement sprang from deep-seated grievances over agrarian distress and administrative corruption. But its focus and energy came from its leader's command of magical powers and miraculous cures. They made credible his promise of a new age of peace-and-plenty and filled his followers with a quasi-religious zeal. More ominously – and omens, all ill, were indeed being reported even more frequently than uprisings – the Yellow Turbans pretended no loyalty to the Han; on the contrary, the overthrow of the dynasty and its adherents was their declared objective.

In happier times, such a challenge might have led to a closing of ranks in Luoyang. Instead it found court and government totally unprepared. The movement quickly infiltrated the city, where a thousand Yellow Turbans were hunted down, while outside it the massing of the rebels served only to heighten the tension at court and militarisé the whole empire. Since the commandery militias were no match for such a mass assault, regular troops were for the first time entrusted to the provincial inspectorates. Simultaneously expeditionary forces were dispatched from Luoyang, so providing some basis for another innovation of the period, a eunuch army, or rather a palace guard under eunuch control. As in the dying days of Wang Mang, the tussle for command saw hastily appointed generals assume elaborate titles before taking the field. From Gansu to Shandong, armies proliferated, their loyalties often doubtful. The Turbans, though occasionally defeated, proved hard to eradicate; the generals, though claiming victory, proved reluctant to disband.

In AD 189, with the rising far from over, *Han* Lingdi sickened and died. The inevitable succession crisis could hardly have come at a worse time. Dong Zhuo, a tough-talking Gansu warlord who had been conducting operations in the east, had refused to stand down. Rather did he advance with his army to within a day or two's march of the capital, there to await developments. Happily Lingdi had left two sons, aged thirteen and eight, by different empresses. But though this in itself was no mean achievement, he had declined the responsibility of naming either as his successor. The choice therefore lay with the eunuchs, who, despite lifting the Great Proscription in the face of the Turbans' revolt, still controlled the main offices of state.

The eunuchs opted for the elder and decidedly dimmer of the two boys. He was duly enthroned as *Han* Shaodi (r. AD 189); his mother, a butcher's daughter, became the dowager empress and her brother the effective regent. The arrangement mirrored that of AD 168, recalled the pogrom that had then brought the eunuchs to power, and induced a complementary reaction. The regent, egged on by one of the ever-contending factions, plotted to eradicate the eunuchs. Again the eunuchs got wind of the plot. But by then the plotters had already summoned military support, including Dong Zhuo and his lurking army. Though the eunuchs succeeded in tricking and decapitating the regent, it was their only success. Trapped and then assailed within the Luoyang palace complex, they withdrew from the southern palace up the covered way to the northern palace. With them went the young *Han* Shaodi and his half-brother. Dong Zhuo remained just outside the city, coveted by all and contemptuous of all. There were enough troops within the city to complete the task. Fire broke out in the southern palace, and in the smoke and the carnage, the eunuchs, some two thousand of them, were massacred to a man. Meanwhile the imperial half-brothers had been mysteriously spirited away.

It was thought they were loose in the countryside; but to generations of later Chinese they had in fact slipped over the historical horizon into the kinder realms of fiction. For it is at this point, with the last of the Later Han at large in an empire that was no longer theirs, that the *Romance of the Three Kingdoms*, one of the greatest works of Chinese historical fiction, begins.

'When Lingdi closed his eyes on 13 May 189, in a sense the whole traditional empire died with him,' writes a contributor to the *Cambridge History of China*.[23] A new era, 'the Period of Disunion', was dawning. Its history would be painful; yet romance would make it palatable, even popular. The *Romance of the Three Kingdoms* has much the same relationship to factual history as the Arthurian legends or the plays of Shakespeare. Its heroes command greater recognition than all the Later Han emperors put together, and its pacy tone betrays a keen sense of narrative suspense. Thus each of its 120 chapters ends with the same formula; a cliff-hanging interrogative is followed by a standardised injunction: 'What then had become of the Han princes? READ ON.'

7

FOUR HUNDRED YEARS
OF VICISSITUDE
189–550

THREE KINGDOMS AND THE RED CLIFFS

LOATH TO CAST OFF INTO A mounting tide of dynastic turbulence, traditional histories of China cling to their Han moorings long after logic
dictates otherwise. The Yellow Turbans' revolt of 184, and the military
response it elicited from sundry power-brokers and provincial leaders, had
shattered the empire throughout its heartland; then in 189 the massacre
of the eunuchs had left the person of the Han emperor without the support
of the one group that was wholly dependent on imperial authority and
generally supportive of it. There would be no going back for either empire
or emperor. As of the 180s the issue was one of transition. The continued
presence of a Han 'Son of Heaven' merely extended a fig-leaf of legitimacy
to those bent on replacing him. In an analogy first used during the great
civil war between Xiang Yu and Liu Bang (*Han* Gaozu) and now back in
vogue, 'the deer was loose'. Heaven's Mandate had broken cover; the chase
was on.

First off the mark was Dong Zhuo, the truculent Gansu warlord who
at the head of his troops had been observing events from outside Luoyang
with ill-disguised relish. Receiving word of the whereabouts of the boy-
emperor and his half-brother, he intercepted them. Apparently they had
been smuggled out of the palace at dead of night, and 'proceeding by
the light of glow-worms', had blundered about the countryside till they
found and commandeered 'a commoner's cart'. The detail of this escapade,
as reported by the younger and brighter of the two boys, made a deep
impression. Dong Zhuo decided that the boy had more to recommend
him as emperor than his speechless half-brother, and by browbeating all

opposition and citing the example of Huo Guang's juggling with *Han* Wudi's grandsons in 74 BC, he contrived the switch immediately; *Han* Shaodi was deposed and his half-brother instated as emperor. Posterity, on the other hand, would become fixated on the idea of Heaven's Sons jolting along the byways of Shanxi as nocturnal carters. It became a quintessential image of fallen majesty.

As *Han* Xiandi, the younger boy would reign, if not rule, unchallenged for the next thirty years (189–220). His deposed half-brother was quietly murdered; other Han claimants simply failed to materialise; there was, indeed, little for them to claim. The last of the Later Han thus managed a longer reign than any of his predecessors except the first. Irrelevance, plus imminent extinction, had finally eased the dynasty's chronic succession problems.

Initially *Han* Xiandi, the new boy-emperor, remained under Dong Zhuo's iron control. No favourite of the historians, Dong Zhuo is portrayed as 'cruel', 'vindictive', 'relentless in his punishments', and outrageously disrespectful. Such conduct neither mollified opponents nor deterred revolt. 'Bandits and rebels had sprung up everywhere,' says the *Zizhi Tongjian*, an exhaustive history which, though written in the eleventh century, incorporates third-century sources that have since been lost. Many of these rebel bands owed their inspiration to the Yellow Turbans; some had 30,000–40,000 armed men; and their leaders rejoiced in blood-curdling nicknames such as 'Ox-horn Zhang', 'Poison Yu', 'Zuo of the Eighty-foot Moustache' and 'Big Eyes Li'.[1]

Such groups, though, were small-fry compared to the great landed lineages and factions who, while protesting loyalty to the Han, resented Dong Zhuo's pretensions and in 190 began to mobilise against him. With strong provincial power bases and the wherewithal to attract able advisers and inspirational commanders, these clans cheerfully harked back to the 'Spring and Autumn' and 'Warring States' periods. Archaic entities like Shu (Sichuan), Wei (southern Shanxi), Wu (lower Yangzi) and Chu (Huai River and mid-Yangzi) were revived to gratify their territorial ambitions. The strongest among them openly aimed at restoring the office of *ba*, or 'hegemon', with a view to proffering the protection once extended to the powerless Later Zhou to the now equally powerless Later Han.

Threatened by all these forces, Dong Zhuo decided to abandon Luoyang. He would withdraw 'west of the passes' to the old capital of Chang'an in the Wei valley, a more defensible position and one nearer to his own power base. He claimed to be following *Han* Gaozu's example of 209 BC; new dynasties (Shang, Zhou, Qin and Han) had invariably arisen in the west;

perhaps he hoped to emulate them. But if that was the plan, it never reached fruition. Emperor and entourage were sent on ahead to Chang'an; Luoyang was then ransacked and burnt to the ground by Dong Zhuo's forces, its population, still perhaps half a million, being herded west at sword-point. Thousands fell by the way, and the survivors had barely begun reclaiming Chang'an when they were plunged into more confusion. For in 192 Dong Zhuo was assassinated by his own bodyguard.

The next four years brought no respite from the bloodshed and destruction. Chang'an was repeatedly sacked by avenging armies and ravaged by famine. Detachments of locally settled Qiang and Xiongnu joined in the sport at the invitation of the competing warlords. The imperial court was just part of the spoils. Passed back and forth like an awkward orphan, 'lodged among thorns and wattles' and 'wandering without shelter', the emperor came of age, accepted an empress and was eventually offloaded back in the ruins of Luoyang. From there he was whisked farther east to Xu. A coastal province adjoining Shandong, Xu was in a region dominated by the wily Cao Cao. As of the year 196 *Han* Xiandi and his entourage were under the Cao family's protection, and would remain so.

The young emperor served his new minders well. On Cao Cao he conferred the title duke of Wei in 213 and king of Wei in 216, so endorsing what would be the largest of the 'Three Kingdoms' into which the empire was fracturing. Better still, it was in favour of Cao Pi, son and successor of Cao Cao, that *Han* Xiandi finally abdicated the imperial throne in 220. Easily persuaded and generously compensated, the last of the Han seems to have lived much happier ever after. Meanwhile the Cao family's Wei dynasty ensconced themselves in a rebuilt Luoyang. After such an amicable handover, they could reasonably claim to be in enjoyment of Heaven's favour, in possession of the Mandate, and *in situ* as the sole legitimate successors of illustrious Han.

But the claim did not go unchallenged. The revolt of the Yellow Turbans, and the upheavals that had racked the empire ever since, had proved the ruin of some established families, yet the making of others. As ever, social mobility thrived on political instability. Bold warriors, ingenious strategists, accomplished administrators and persuasive scholars could take their pick of patrons eager for whatever advantage they offered. Handsomely rewarded with revenue assignments and commands, the more able among the newcomers amassed territories, attracted their own followings and then typically either supplanted their erstwhile patrons or split from them. Most were of comparatively obscure origins; charisma, dynamism and evidence of divine favour were what counted. Cao Cao's father was said to have been the adopted son of a palace eunuch; 'there was no way of telling his family origins', says the *Zizhi Tongjian*, 'though ... even in youth he was clever and ingenious'.[2] Yet by mobilising numerous cousins and by fathering some twenty-five sons, at the time of his death in 219 Cao Cao headed a clan that was a match for any.

Much the same could be said of the founders of the two other kingdoms of the 'Three Kingdoms' period. The Sun family had a slightly more distinguished pedigree but again owed its success to ability rather than birth. From the east, Sun Ce had contested Dong Zhuo's 189 manhandling of the Han succession. Then Sun Quan, his near-invincible brother and successor, reconstituted the region of Wu in the lower Yangzi basin as the second of the Three Kingdoms. Appointed king of Wu by *Han* Xiandi and

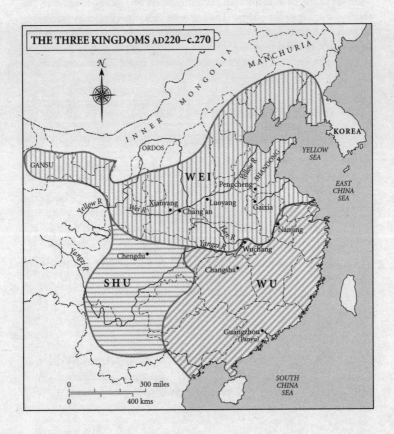

THE THREE KINGDOMS AD220–c.270

later, in a belated response to Xiandi's abdication, declaring himself to be the legitimate emperor, Sun Quan extended his Wu dynasty's authority throughout all China-below-the-Yangzi (including northern Vietnam).

Retrospectively Wu came to be seen as the first of the difficult but distinguished succession of Yangzi-based 'southern dynasties' that would last, on and off, for a millennium. But at the time, Wu's claim to legitimacy was the weakest of the Three Kingdoms. It was only when these later southern polities afforded a haven to fugitives from alien rule in the north, and so became redoubts of traditional Han culture, that their aura of authenticity would reflect favourably on Wu as the first imperial dynasty to be based on the Yangzi rather than the Yellow River.

Clever and relentless campaigners as Cao Cao and Sun Quan were, they were yet upstaged as inspirational commanders by Liu Bei, founder of the third of the Three Kingdoms. The histories describe Liu Bei as exceptionally tall with arms that reached to his knees and eyes that could see round to his ears; more prosaically 'he was a man of great ambitions but few words'.[3] The central character in the *Romance of the Three Kingdoms*, he

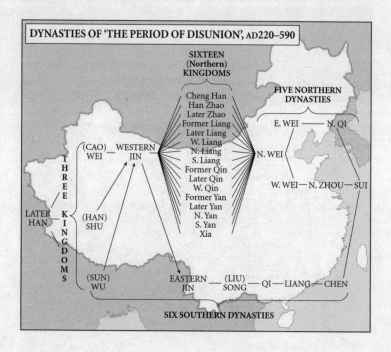

DYNASTIES OF 'THE PERIOD OF DISUNION', AD220–590

SIXTEEN (Northern) KINGDOMS

FIVE NORTHERN DYNASTIES

Cheng Han
Han Zhao
Later Zhao
Former Liang
Later Liang
W. Liang
N. Liang
S. Liang
Former Qin
Later Qin
W. Qin
Former Yan
Later Yan
N. Yan
S. Yan
Xia

E. WEI —— N. QI

(CAO) WEI   WESTERN JIN

N. WEI

W. WEI — N. ZHOU — SUI

THREE KINGDOMS

LATER HAN

(HAN) SHU

(SUN) WU

EASTERN JIN   (LIU) SONG — QI — LIANG — CHEN

SIX SOUTHERN DYNASTIES

strides from the page a ready-made hero flanked by two devoted brothers-in-arms (Zhang Fei and Guan Yu, the latter another Herculean figure who would later be deified as Guandi). None was handier with the sword, nobler of intention or better loved than Liu Bei. But his path to glory was long and chequered. Poor and fatherless, he had sold sandals as a child and then enlisted with a military commander in the far north-east. As a mercenary leader drifting through the crumbling empire in the 190s, there can have been little to distinguish him from the likes of Poison Yu and Big Eyes Li.

He was mostly victorious, and his following grew with his reputation. In 197 he joined Cao Cao but soon turned against him and in 201 repaired to Sichuan. Cao Cao then swept all before him in the north and seemed intent on making Sichuan his next target. But fatefully in 208 Cao Cao opted for a southern offensive against Wu; to oppose him, Liu Bei and Sun Quan of Wu joined forces; and at the Red Cliffs, a point on the Yangzi near its confluence with the Han River (and now within the great conurbation of Wuhan), the forces of the north and south finally collided in one of the most decisive battles of the millennium. 'The key to the history of the period,' according to one historian, 'the battle [at the Red Cliffs] decided the question of [China's] unity or division.'[4]

Thanks to the Standard Histories, and more especially to derivative works like the *Romance of the Three Kingdoms* and the countless poems, dramas, operas and comic strips based on it, the battle at the Red Cliffs is better known than any other in pre-modern Chinese history. Vast troop numbers are mentioned, and their deployment in a pre-battle game of bluff and counter-bluff has been carefully studied. But waged along the Yangzi, it was essentially a naval encounter, and like most Chinese battles, hinged on a single manoeuvre.

To cross the river, here about a kilometre wide, Cao Cao had chained together a bridge of boats and, preparatory to floating it across the stream, had moored it alongside his camp-cum-landing-station below the Red Cliffs on the north shore. On the south shore a smaller Wu force awaited the arrival from downstream of the main Wu fleet under Sun Quan. Liu Bei's allied force was encamped a short distance upstream. It was early January (209), a month of cold north-westerlies that favoured Cao Cao in the lee of the north bank.

Then one night the wind swung round to the south-east and a small fleet put out from the southern shoreline. With sails filling, it winged through the darkness towards Cao Cao's base. Lookouts there reported its approach, but no alarm was sounded. Defectors were expected; and anyway these were not many-masted warships but lightly manned yawls (or their junk equivalents). Cao Cao's northern forces were thus quite unprepared for the pyrotechnics when, within hailing distance, fuses were lit below decks, hulls crammed with oil-soaked tinder ignited, and the oncoming fleet became a wall of fire.

> The fire was sped by the might of the wind, and the boats homed in like arrows in flight. Soon smoke and flame screened off the sky. Twenty fiery boats rammed into the naval station. All at once Cao's ships caught fire and, locked in place by their chains, could not escape.[5]

Though the flames spread from the ships to Cao Cao's camp, most of his landward troops did in fact escape. But in doing so, they discovered the purpose behind the earlier deployments; for all retreat was cut off, and in a series of ambushes the northern army, already weakened by exhaustion and disease, was practically annihilated. Cao Cao was captured, then quickly released; his captor happened to owe him a favour. But he never again invaded the south. Indeed, it was Sun Quan who advanced, moving his capital to a city within sight of the Red Cliffs that he named Wuchang. (He later moved downriver, and farther north, to where Nanjing now stands.) As for Liu Bei, after more adventures he returned to Sichuan, there to found the third of the Three Kingdoms. Inevitably it was known as Shu. And thus as Shu, Wu and Wei, the intrepid adversaries of the Red Cliffs, and then their descendants, would continue their three-sided vendetta for control of China for another half-century.

Apart from heroic stature, Liu Bei possessed an asset that had not been much noticed in his youth: he had a doubtful claim to very distant descent from *Han* Jingdi (r. 157–141 BC), the Former Han emperor from whom *Han* Guang Wudi, founder of the Later Han, had also traced his descent. This connection lent credibility to Liu Bei's 219 elevation as king of Shu (under the Later Han, kingship had been reserved exclusively for members of the Han family) and it became of special interest when, a year later, Cao Pi, son of Cao Cao of Wei, was reported to have replaced *Han* Xiandi as emperor. The news, by the time it reached Sichuan, may have become garbled, or perhaps Liu Bei simply misrepresented it. For he announced that *Han* Xiandi had in fact been killed and that Cao Pi was a usurper, but that the Han dynasty, far from being defunct, need only switch to another line of descent to find a successor – just as it had when the Later Han came to power. Indeed, following the usual rash of omens and impeccably argued entreaties, Liu Bei was persuaded that he himself was the lineal descendant chosen by Heaven. He performed the imperial rites of initiation, his ministers extended their whole-hearted support – in the terminology of the time, they were happy 'as ducks in duckweed' about it – and from then on Liu Bei, and then his son, reigned as the sometimes designated 'Han-Shu emperors' in Sichuan.[6]

But for Liu Bei of Han-Shu, as for Cao Pi of Wei and Sun Quan of Wu, acting the local emperor was no substitute for universal sovereignty. The assumption of imperial status prior to the conquest of the whole empire, though supposedly prophetic, proved merely provocative. Mocked by the Qin and Han traditions of unitary rule, none of the new dynasts could be confident of his legitimacy until he had eradicated the others. Only then could Heaven's favour be taken as manifest, the dynastic changeover as complete, and posterity's approval as assured. In effect, all three would-be dynasties were condemned to fight on, so squandering their resources and alienating their subjects. To any but an already supreme ruler, the legacy of empire could be more curse than blessing.

The same could be said in respect of the historiographical tradition. Imperial history being premised on the idea of a single and near-continuous line of legitimate dynasties, later historians would feel obliged to prefer the claims of one of the Three Kingdoms over the other two. Thus the Standard Histories of the period written under the later Jin dynasty favour the Cao's Wei dynasty, whom the Jin succeeded; so do other works written under the patronage of later northern dynasties, the *Zizhi Tongjian* being typical; all emphasise control of the empire's core region along the Yellow River as essential in any claim to legitimacy. But histories written under the dispensation of the southern dynasties generally prefer the claims of Liu Bei's Shu, or Han-Shu, dynasty. To them the superior virtue of a ruler like Liu Bei, plus his lineal descent from the illustrious Han, counted for more than geography. Thus it is that the *Romance of the Three Kingdoms*, which was based on a southern reading of events, makes Liu Bei its hero and emphasises his Heaven-favoured attributes. The crucial change of wind, for instance, that led to Cao Cao's defeat at the Red Cliffs is seen not as a meteorological freak but as evidence of how Liu Bei's virtue attracted the very best advisers, one of whom specialised in arranging these things direct with the gods.

Though there is much uncertainty about the authorship of the *Romance*, it has been argued that if, as seems probable, it was first written in the fourteenth century, it should also be read as a rejection of the then crumbling Mongol (or Yuan) dynasty by supporters of the incoming Ming dynasty. In this context it becomes a plea for the indigenous values and traditions of the Han – the people as well as the dynasty – against the claims of alien invaders from the north. By retrospective association, Cao Cao and his Wei dynasty get unjustly tarred as non-Han usurpers; and the greatest of national epics finds itself conscripted as nationalist propaganda. As ever, the writing of history, even of historical fiction, was itself a political act.

DAO AND THE CELESTIAL MASTERS

The *Romance of the Three Kingdoms* begins with one of the most-quoted aphorisms in China's history: 'the empire long united, must divide: long divided, must unite'. A thousand pages (in translation) later it ends, give or take a paragraph, with the same phrasing reversed: 'the empire long divided, must unite; long united, must divide'. So it had; so it would. Long united under the Han, it had divided; long divided under the Three Kingdoms, it must unite. In 263 Liu Bei's Shu, or Han-Shu, dynasty was finally conquered by the Cao family's Wei dynasty. Two years later the Wei were themselves toppled by Sima Yan, a power-broker whose family had been pillars of Wei since Cao Cao's day. And in 280 this Sima Yan's new Jin dynasty finally extinguished the Sun family's Wu dynasty in the south. China was again united.

But not, in this case, long united. As rulers of all China, the Sima family's Jin (or 'Western Jin') dynasty scarcely outlasted the one-man Xin dynasty of the much-maligned Wang Mang in the early first century. Within a decade it was overtaken by civil war and invasion, and within a generation the Jin had been driven from Luoyang (311), then Chang'an (316), into prolonged exile south of the Yangzi. There they would reign (317–420) as the 'Eastern Jin', their capital at Jiankang (Nanjing) being east, as well as south, of Luoyang and Chang'an.

The *Romance of the Three Kingdoms*, by ending on an upbeat note of unity restored by the Jin in 280, thus gives a highly misleading impression. Successful reintegration was still three centuries away. The 'Period of Disunion', having begun with the empire's tripartite division into the Three Kingdoms, would in fact grow more disunited. The long-lasting 'South–North' (Nan–Bei) division of the country would find the south (with its 'Six Dynasties') and the north (with its 'Sixteen Kingdoms', then its 'Five Northern Dynasties') themselves subject to fragmentation and frequent dynastic change. For a kaleidoscope of kingdoms within an erstwhile empire, not even medieval Europe would surpass post-Han China.

Through this taxing era, the student of imperial affairs, instead of grappling with a quickfire succession of emperors, does well to keep track of whole dynasties. Sheer frustration with its ephemeral polities, plus an understandable reticence on the part of those committed to the primacy of an indivisible Chinese state, have led to the period being dismissed as the equivalent of Europe's 'Dark Ages'. Just as the grandeur that was Rome gave way to barbarian invasion, political fragmentation, religious superstition and a decline in urban life, so seemingly did the might that was Han. But the dates do not quite coincide: China's eclipse was ending when Europe's much longer occlusion was just beginning. And for China, if not for western Europe, division and incursion proved culturally and socially stimulating rather than stultifying.

It had happened before. Endemic strife in the 'Spring and Autumn' and 'Warring States' periods had excited the speculation and created the opportunities that in retrospect had transformed that era of instability and division into a golden age. It was, after all, the time-frame of Confucius, Mozi, Laozi and 'the hundred schools of thought', of exuberant grave goods, big bronze bells and the plaintive songs of Chu. Subsequent stability and cohesion under the Qin and Former Han had been productive of public works (roads, palaces, walls, irrigation, reclamation and colonisation schemes), plus much fine, if orthodox, scholarship. But bureaucratic rule and unchallenged sovereignty had been no guarantee of creative excellence or devotional innovation. Now, once again, supposedly negative factors such as political disarray and social dislocation proved more effective catalysts. Far from 'dark', the post-Han age of disunion is illumined by dazzling literary achievements, by the emergence of Daoism as an indigenous counterpoint to Confucian orthodoxy, and by the adoption of Buddhism, the greatest religio-cultural import in the history of pre-modern China. The resulting syntheses, accommodated and encouraged within a reunited empire, would largely account for the never surpassed magnificence of the imperial Tang (traditionally 618–907).

Han-period verses, known as *fu*, read like nothing so much as rollicking catalogues. Virtuoso exercises in vocabulary, and often concerned with the natural world, they may actually have been intended for lexicographical reference. Commissioned and adjudged by the court, *fu* exalted the emperor and idealised imperial set-pieces – palaces, parks, receptions, hunts – with few concessions to any harsher reality. Though they gratified dynastic pride and served educational and propaganda purposes, they left little scope for personal expression. This changed with the fall of the Han. The transitional period (*c.* 190–220) had witnessed an unprecedented burst of literary activity which was sustained during the rest of the Three Kingdoms period and on into that of the Six (southern) Dynasties. *Fu* became more expressive, and with the development of new forms in both prose and poetry, especially the verses known as *shih*, 'literature as literature came into its own'.[7] Without entirely renouncing didactic and dynastic responsibilities, writers looked on the past anew and began to convey a sense of their own troubled time and of their responses to it. Escaping from Chang'an after the murder of Dong Zhuo (the warlord who had intercepted the young Han princes and then swapped one for the other), Wang Can wrote a poem called 'Seven Sadnesses'.

> Once out the gate, nothing to see,
> Just white bones covering the plain,
> A starving woman on the road
> Embraces a child and abandons it in the grass.[8]

In this extract the poet achieves his effect by zooming, like a camera, from the wide-angle devastation to the close-focus tragedy; pathos lies in the sharpening detail: so does the bite of criticism. Writers were beginning to respond to their own need for expression rather than to the eulogistic requirements of imperial patrons. Aesthetic considerations were prevailing over mere verbal exhibitionism.

'Literature is indeed the great profession by which the state is governed, the magnificent action that leads to immortality ... Life and glory last only a limited time, unlike literature which lasts forever.'[9] So wrote not some slighted versifier but *Wei* Wendi, the emperor himself, this being the title taken by Cao Pi after *Han* Xiandi abdicated in his favour. As literary patrons, the Cao family collected existing texts and commissioned compilations of them. A new penal code that digested the juridical pronouncements of the Han and anticipated major legal compilations under the Jin and Tang should perhaps be seen in this context – though it also served to assert the always draconian punishments that awaited the malefactor. Such compilatory work was often of a more literary nature, and Cao Cao and Cao Pi were themselves notable writers. The latter is best known for his prose criticism. Bemoaning the loss of literary colleagues in an epidemic of 217, he undertook to edit their collected works and, in so doing, aired the idea of *qi*, in the sense of an individual's inspiration and style, as something innate and quite distinct from talent. Both Caos also penned poems of their own. Cao Cao preferred contemporary themes in which he expressed sympathy for the plight of the Han, as in the allusively titled 'Dew on the Shallots'. Cao Pi famously wrote rhapsodies in which his voice is that of a maiden bemoaning the absence of her lover, possibly also in reference to the fallen Han. Both were upstaged by another member of the family, the prolific and influential Cao Zhi, who is sometimes rated among China's greatest poets.

The warmth of Cao (or Wei) sentiment for the Han, and the unusually bloodless nature of the dynastic changeover, are worth noting. Cao Pi and his advisers had given much thought to the legitimisation and staging of the dynastic transition. A stele, of which there survive some fragments as well as rubbings of the original text, was inscribed to mark the occasion; and the manifestations and precedents cited on it would provide something of a charter for the upstart dynasties that followed.

Although Cao Cao, as effective regent for *Han* Xiandi, had invoked the tutelary examples of Huo Guang and the Duke of Zhou, Cao Pi, in replacing *Han* Xiandi, obviously needed a different frame of legitimising references. According to those who supposedly bombarded him with pleas to accept the Mandate, the situation little resembled that under the Former Zhou (when the grand old Duke of Zhou had exercised power without coveting the emperorship) but closely paralleled that under the remoter, not to say mythical, Five Emperors with whom the whole dynastic pedigree had supposedly begun.

In those far-off days the succession had passed not from father to son in lineal descent but from one imperial incumbent to the next on the basis of merit. When an emperor recognised someone of manifestly superior virtue, he simply and selflessly abdicated in his favour. Clearly this was just the principle required to legitimise Cao Pi's elevation. Yet since only the last of the Five Emperors had contravened the practice to name his son as his successor and so found his own dynasty (the Xia), it boded ill for Cao Pi's descendants; on identical grounds – virtue over birth – the Sima family would overthrow the Cao's Wei dynasty to found their own Jin dynasty; and subsequent regimes in both the north and south would follow this example. The idea that the Mandate belonged to the meritorious proved inherently destabilising.

An additional feature of Cao Pi's stele inscription is its citing of neo-revelatory texts and other unconventional data – omens, divinations and predictions – that were outside the Confucian tradition. All have been identified as Daoist, so making the accession of Cao Pi and his Wei dynasty what one writer calls 'the first in a long tradition [involving the] Daoist legitimation of emperors'.[10] In the late second and early third centuries Daoism was at last emerging as a distinct 'persuasion'. A Daoist canon was being collated and Daoist leaders, like those of the Yellow Turbans, attracted vast followings. Although the 184 revolt of the Yellow Turbans had been speedily suppressed, erstwhile adherents played an important role in the strife of the Three Kingdoms period with one group in particular establishing a martial theocracy in Hanzhong on the mountainous north-east border of Sichuan. There, as 'the Celestial Masters' or 'Five Pecks' movement (each household contributed five pecks of grain to the common good), they held out for several decades; and when in 215 they finally succumbed to Cao Cao, it was on terms so agreeable that a Wei–Daoist accommodation has been inferred. Most members of the sect removed en masse to the more favoured Xu, where their leaders were rewarded with fiefs and titles. They then obligingly revealed arcane communications and texts that foretold how the next emperor would be 'a princeling of Wei'. And thus Cao Pi, being just such a one, finally overcame his feigned scruples and assumed the emperorship.

In an age that was as notable for natural calamities as political upheavals, the great reassurance of supernatural intercourse and esoteric revelations is understandable. At a popular level the Celestial Masters plied their followers with medicinal cures and offered various forms of psychological encouragement, plus a degree of social welfare and gender equality, and the ultimate promise of *taiping* or 'heavenly peace'. At a higher level, Daoist 'science' tickled aristocratic fancies with alchemical experiments and with potions and exercises designed to ensure longevity or transcendence. And at the dynastic level Daoist revelations and predictions augmented those of court astrologers and calendrists as a source of legitimisation; highly regarded, carefully studied and easily manipulated, such forecasts 'served a function not entirely different from that of economic indicators in a modern nation [state]', suggests one authority.[11]

Daoism in operation was pervasive and obvious. However, defining Daoism is not so easy. One writer has described it as a religion that is 'not afraid of incoherence'. Loosely the term has sometimes been applied to almost any indigenous practice or doctrine not obviously either Confucian or Buddhist. In this catch-all sense Daoists could be followers of shamans, miracle-workers and mediums, subscribers to any of a myriad of local cults, practitioners of various physical, psychic and sexual disciplines, political and social renunciates in general, anyone who cultivated the *Laozi*'s state of *wuwei* (non-action), members of martial arts fraternities, and/or supporters of just about any movement of social protest with a millenarianist agenda. Admittedly this is not very helpful. Buddhists would also be associated with many of these practices. Moreover the simple formula 'Daoist = non-Confucian + non-Buddhist' may in fact be misleading, since the very terms imply a degree of confessional exclusivity and personal commitment which, though familiar enough to anyone imbued with the Judaeo-Christian tradition, was yet quite alien to Chinese thought.

In China no doctrine, revelation or mode of conduct was credited with a monopoly of truth, nor was any accounted complete in itself, for the simple reason that none was that clearly defined. Confucians (*ru*) had always dabbled in Daoist practices; indeed, in the post-Han period Confucian studies became heavily influenced by both Daoist and Buddhist texts. Daoists in turn usually subscribed to the core Confucian values, while Daoist communities became deeply indebted to Buddhism for such organisational features as a clergy and institutionalised monasticism. Scholarly debate might rage between the 'schools', but it was not unusual for the participants in their personal lives to combine elements of all three 'religions'. Discrimination and strife, when they occurred, owed little to doctrinal differences and were invariably prompted by economic or political considerations.

If, as a recent exponent claims, Daoists are best characterised as those 'who agreed that they should refine and transform themselves to attain full integration with life's deepest realities', then 'it was not until about [AD] 500 that certain people began to become "Daoists" in a coherent social sense'. Only then did there emerge communities self-consciously dedicated to such a lofty pursuit.[12] But the concept – or enigma – that was *dao* itself was much older; and it usually connoted not a school of thought but a state of transcendent integration or some approach conducive to attaining it. Though invariably translated into English as 'the Way', it has been suggested that, but for Charles Wesley, a more helpful rendering of *dao* would be as 'the Method', and so Daoism as 'Methodism'.

As ever in China, the decisive development is to be found in the written tradition. By the third century the core Daoist texts, especially the *Laozi* (or *Daodejing*) and the *Zhuangzi*, had been around for hundreds of years and appeared heavily corrupted. It was the work of collating, editing and reinterpreting them, of adding substantially to this corpus, and of compiling the first comprehensive canon of Daoist texts, which was undertaken in the third to sixth centuries. This, plus the disturbed conditions of the age, stimulated new Daoist schools of thought and contributed to the dissemination of Daoist teachings. When the Jin court fled south in 317, Daoist scholarship went with it, with more Daoists accompanying a later Jin exodus from Sichuan. In the aristocratic ambience of the southern dynasties, Daoism flourished. In the Hangzhou region of Zhejiang in 399 it inspired another Celestial Masters revolt, born like that of the Yellow Turbans out of popular discontent and suppressed just as bloodily. But twenty years later it was a general who had been hailed as a Daoist messiah who overthrew the Jin to found the Liu Song (420–479), the third of the south's Six Dynasties. At about the same time, in the north, a Daoist Celestial Master gained such an ascendancy over an emperor of the Northern Wei dynasty (389–535, and not to be confused with Cao Pi's earlier Wei) that his rule has been dubbed 'a Daoist theocracy'.[13]

Thanks to the efforts of scholars during the centuries of disunion, Daoism won a degree of doctrinal cohesion, academic respectability and institutional substance. Court and aristocratic circles endorsed it; Xiongnu and Xianbei warlords found in it, as they did in Buddhism, shamanic elements more agreeable to their own devotional traditions; and as a vehicle of social protest it retained its grassroots appeal and its explosive potential. Daoism had finally 'become a visible presence in Chinese history and society', both all-pervasive and long-abiding.[14] Indeed, the textual work on Daoism continues even today, spurred on by new discoveries such as fragments of the first Daoist canon found at Dunhuang in the early twentieth century and the bamboo texts of the *Laozi* subsequently unearthed at Mawangdui.

ENTER THE ENLIGHTENED ONE

While Daoism profited from its indigenous credentials, it would be wrong to infer that Buddhism must therefore have been handicapped by its foreign provenance. Objections would certainly be raised on this score and the superiority of Chinese culture frequently reasserted. But the sensational spread of Buddhism in the third to sixth centuries – the 'Period of Disunion' – utterly belies the idea of Chinese civilisation being unreceptive to extraneous ideas. If Daoism then prospered, Buddhism triumphed. China became a Buddhist country and would remain so for centuries, its Buddhist community outnumbering even India's. Monasteries by the thousand dotted the cities; rock-cut shrines, tiered stupas ('pagodas') and colossal Buddha figures graced the countryside. Society and the visual arts were transformed; commercial and cultural intercourse with the rest of Asia flourished. From Xinjiang to Shandong and Guangdong wealth and manpower were lavished on devotional endowments, and wherever peace prevailed, robed monks and nuns mingled with the gowned scholars of Confucian orthodoxy. Notions of enlightenment, compassion and the sanctity of life softened learned discourse, if not political ambitions. The drone of prayer, borne on the breeze, consoled an age made frantic by the staccato clash of arms.

Yet the process of introduction and naturalisation was slow and fraught. The Buddha had lived and taught in northern India around the fifth century BC, but not until 500 years later does a recognisable reference to him surface in Chinese history. A Han prince, who had been enfeoffed as the nominal king of Chu by *Han* Guang Wudi, founder of the Later Han, is described in the *Houhanshu* ('History of the Later Han') as 'fasting and performing sacrfices to the Buddha'; the year was AD 65, the place Pengcheng (Xiang Yu's one-time capital in Jiangsu), and the prince a Daoist devotee. At the time the Buddha seems to have been revered, along with Laozi, as a co-opted member of the Daoist pantheon rather than as the embodiment of an alternative doctrinal 'Way'. There is no mention of the enormous body of literature – devotional, metaphysical and organisational – that 500 years of Buddhism in south Asia had generated. And Pengcheng being on a trade route that leads to Luoyang not from central Asia but from the China coast, it is possible that the cult had reached the Later Han empire by sea. Buddhist communities were already established in south-east Asia; and the Buddhist symbols (lotus flowers, elephants, etc.) found among the second-century relief carvings at Kongwangshan on the seaboard of Jiangsu appear to substantiate this routing.

Half a century later a travelling official, who was also a noted poet, described an evening of revelry at Chang'an, the erstwhile Han capital. It included a performance by some gorgeously attired dancing girls who quite bewitched the assembled company. 'One look at them would make one surrender a city,' raved the poet-official; you couldn't help but be captivated; not even someone 'as upright as a Buddhist Sramana', he wrote, could be immune.[15] A *sramana* being a resident of an *asrama* (ashram), this seems to be one of the first references to Buddhist monasticism in China. By the beginning of the second century Buddhism was evidently recognised in China as a distinct and somewhat other-worldly religion; a few key terms, such as *sramana*, had made the transition from their original Sanskritic language into Chinese; and in Chang'an, and probably Luoyang and other cities, Buddhist communities were already established.

By the end of the second century, worship of the Buddha at richly endowed provincial centres is attested – and a clue to the popularity of the new cult afforded – by a reference in the Standard History of the Three Kingdoms period. There it appears that in *c.* 193 a man called Zhai Rong was put in charge of grain shipments in central Jiangsu, and instead of remitting the revenues from this lucrative assignment, appropriated them to set up a Buddhist community. He may have been a sincere seeker of enlightenment, but from the embarrassed disclaimers of later times it seems more likely that he belonged in such disreputable company as contemporaries like Ox-Horn Yang and Poison Yu. A vast 'temple' – which from mention of its layered 'umbrella' finial may have been a stupa – was erected, monastic buildings capable of accommodating 3,000 monks were attached, and a gilded statue of the Buddha was arrayed in silks and brocades and occasionally given a ritual bath. Buddhist adherents from far and wide were summoned to the site; others were simply drawn there by Zhai Rong's offer of exemption from corvée in return for attendance.

> Whenever the bathing of the Buddha was to be performed, [Zhai Rong] always had great quantities of wine and food set out, and mats were spread along the road for a distance of [several kilometres]. To enjoy the spectacle and the fare, some ten thousand came and the expense ran to millions [of cash].[16]

All of which, while ostensibly admirable (if ill informed about Buddhist strictures on alcohol), had the desired effect. Zhai Rong acquired a large and devoted following that, stiffened with troops, would support his subsequent and mercifully brief career as a murderous warlord. 'For obvious reasons,' writes Erik Zurcher, author of the seminal work on the Buddhist 'conquest' of China, 'Zhai Rong never became the ideal prototype of the liberal donor . . . [and] in Buddhist sources he is practically never referred to.'[17]

Meanwhile a trickle of Buddhist texts had begun appearing in Chinese translation. The challenge of translating abstract and often esoteric terms from an alphabetic, grammatically complex and highly inflected language like Sanskrit into the letter-less, uninflected and starkly concise written language of China posed almost insuperable problems. Christian missionaries would encounter something similar when trying to convey to Chinese catechumens the mysteries of, say, the Trinity or transubstantiation. Key ideas like 'dharma' and 'nirvana', which the Indic world took for granted, were hard for the Chinese to fathom, though Daoism sometimes provided a solution, albeit at some damage to the original. Thus *wuwei*, for instance, was used for 'nirvana', and *dao* not only for 'enlightenment' but also for 'dharma' and even 'yoga'. Other ideas, such as monastic celibacy and reincarnation, were simply offensive to a society in which procreation was seen as a moral duty and ancestors were cherished as spirits immune from the hazard of rebirth. While Confucianism harped on the individual's duty to family and state, Buddhism signposted a path to salvation that neatly bypassed both.

Additionally the first texts to reach China were not necessarily the most revealing; nor were the missionaries who endeavoured to expound them always any better equipped intellectually than they were linguistically. That the main missionary drive came overland from India and the central Asian states by way of the silk routes is certain. Trade with the west had not been diminished by the Later Han's retraction from the Western Regions. Moreover archaeology is positively eloquent in the matter, with a long trail of Buddhist sites, inscriptions, sculptures, documentational hoards and paintings extending from north-west India round or through the western Himalaya and then from Parthia, Afghanistan and Sogdiana (Samarkand) to Xinjiang, Gansu and Luoyang. In the second half of the second century, the ten missionaries known to have been operating in the Jin capital at Luoyang comprised two Parthians, two Sogdians, three Indians and three Yuezhi (from Afghanistan and what is now Pakistan, where the Yuezhi were known as Kushans).

Buddhism and long-distance commerce went hand in hand. In India merchants had derived encouragement from the Buddhist disregard of caste strictures on the freedom of movement; in China the Confucian contempt for traders and commerce in general disposed the mercantile classes towards Buddhism as a respectable alternative. In both countries, the merchant community reciprocated, proving generous benefactors as well as extending hospitality and protection to missionaries. Zhai Rong's stupa-cum-monastery in Jiangsu sounds remarkably like the slightly older complex at Sanchi (near Bhopal in Madhya Pradesh), whose inscriptions actually record the names of its merchant donors. More certainly the remarkable fourth-century cave paintings at Kizil (near Kuqa in Xinjiang) mimic those of Ajanta (in Maharashtra on the road to India's west coast) and include a telling scene of the Buddha lighting the way for a one-man caravan. Produced by the same quasi-fresco technique and probably contemporary, the narrative scenes and interlocking designs at Kizil and Ajanta, though half a continent apart, are thought to be the work of artists who were either from the same school or in possession of a common crib.[18]

Buddhism, with its itinerant imagery ('the Wheel' of dharma, the 'Eightfold Path', the Middle 'Way'), was on the march again. During the first to third centuries – and especially under the patronage of the Yuezhi/Kushan rulers whose empire extended from India and Afghanistan to Khotan in southern Xinjiang – the proselytising impetus of Ashoka's age resumed. Ashoka had convened the First Buddhist Council in the third century BC; some time in the second century AD the Kushan emperor Kanishka convened the fourth; and it was in the course of its deliberations that doctrinal differences led to the schism between what would become known as the Mahayana and Theravada (or Hinayana) schools.

The dispute intrigued China's Buddhist scholars, and both schools were initially represented there. But throughout the regions north of the Himalayas it was the more accessible Mahayanist teachings which eventually prevailed. Mahayanists offered better odds on achieving Enlightenment; even the laity stood a chance. Additionally they laid great stress on devotional aids, including depictions of the Buddha and scenes from his life-story; often executed in stone and influenced by Hellenistic models, these typified the Indo-Asian style known as Gandhara that inspired China's Buddhist iconography. And crucially, Mahayanists deified not only the Buddha himself but a host of other Enlightened Ones, known as Bodhisattva (in Chinese *busa*), who included Amitabha ('the Buddha of the Western Paradise' to the Chinese), Avaloketiswara (who changed sex to become the female 'Guanyin' in China) and Maitreya (the Chinese 'Miluo', or 'Future Buddha'). All such Bodhisattva having postponed their nirvana, they were available to help the seeker along the Way; the teachings and mythologies attributed to them – penances undertaken, powers obtained and wonders worked – formed a substantial part of both the textual corpus and the missionary's arsenal; and the ceremonies and rituals appropriate to their worship served as a focus of popular devotion.

By the year 311, when the Jin fled Luoyang before a Xiongnu onslaught, there and in Chang'an some 180 Buddhist establishments were reportedly flourishing and there were nearly four thousand monks. Early communities in the provinces, such as Zhai Rong's in Jiangsu, had been joined by others as far afield as Vietnam, where the overland Buddhist *acharya* (disciple) from north India and central Asia met the seaborne apostolate coming from peninsular India and Sri Lanka via south-east Asia. In the Yangzi region, under the patronage of Sun Quan and his successor in the 'Three Kingdoms' state of Wu, Indian and Yuezhi missions had won both scholarly acceptance and aristocratic attention. At the Wu, and then Eastern Jin, capital of Jiankang (later Nanjing) silk exports and an inward trade in the exotic produce of south-east Asia sustained a lavish lifestyle and a hothouse intellectual climate. The city would retain its fame as a centre of the loftiest and most speculative Buddhist and Daoist debate throughout the 'Six (southern) Dynasties' period.

Everywhere the quality of translations had greatly improved. This was thanks in large part to the labours of Dharmaraksha (*c.* 230–307). The son of a Yuezhi merchant domiciled in Dunhuang (Gansu), Dharmaraksha had received a Chinese education and, proving a consummate linguist, had undertaken the translation of over 150 Buddhist texts; according to his biographer, 'he contributed more than anyone else to the conversion of China to Buddhism'.[19] Chinese scholars were now alert to a literary and speculative tradition that for its richness and prolixity rivalled their own.

Following a brief reassertion of suzerainty over the rulers of Xinjiang by the first (Western) Jin emperor, religious traffic on the Silk Road had become a two-way affair with Chinese Buddhists – Dharmaraksha among them – heading for Khotan, Kashmir and beyond in search of texts, relics and spiritual guidance. Meanwhile the stupa – originally a reliquary mound that had become Buddhism's most characteristic monument and which in India was typically a hemispherical dome atop a low pedestal – had in China begun to shoot upwards, incorporating the tiled eaves and multiple storeys of the indigenous architectural tradition to assume the tiered and tapered profile of the classic 'pagoda'.

By the fourth century, then, Buddhism had cast its slender shadow across the land. But it had yet to overlay every rural fortress and hilltop hermitage. The 'Way' of the *Laozi* and the 'Eightfold Path' of the Buddha were not yet so nearly indistinguishable as to raise the question of which had 'conquered' which. And Buddhism had still to forge a relationship with the secular power that would elevate it into, if not a state religion, then a religion of state. For that, it would be indebted to other waves of alien 'conquest', as inarticulate and confrontational as the *acharya*'s were literate and accommodating.

INTO THE ABYSS

For sheer immediacy, plus a touching glimpse of one man's dismay in the face of overwhelming historical events, nothing can beat the letter written from somewhere in northern China in the year 313 by a foreigner called Nanai Vandak. The letter is on paper, one of the earliest examples of its use for correspondence. With other mail, and still in the postbag in which it had been abandoned some sixteen centuries earlier, it was acquired in 1907 by the archaeological explorer Aurel Stein while he was controversially uplifting ancient scrolls by the donkey-load from the caves of Dunhuang. How the postbag had come to be parted from its postman in the first place is not known; nor is it certain to where the letter was addressed. But from its tone and content it is assumed that Nanai Vandak was a commercial representative, probably a Sogdian or Persian, they being major contractors in the overland silk trade; and that the letter was in the nature of a report to his superior, perhaps in Samarkand. The year of its writing, 313, is the crucial part. Nanai Vandak had news from China of no small importance. The Jin capital of Luoyang had for some time been under intermittent siege, many of its defenders had deserted, and those who remained had little to eat. But more than a year after the event, the writer's disbelief at the city's ultimate fate was still almost palpable.

> ... And, Sir, the last Emperor – so they say – fled from [Luoyang] because of the famine. And his fortified residence burnt down, and the town was [destroyed]. So [Luoyang] is no more, [Yeh] is no more! ... They pillaged up to N'ymn'ymh and up to Ngap, these Xiongnu who yesterday had been the Emperor's property! ... And, Sir, if I wrote you all the details of how China fared, it would be [a catalogue] of debts and woe. You will have no wealth from here ...[20]

Though evidently not an eyewitness to all these events – and though his account still perplexes posterity with its rendering of Chinese place-names – Nanai Vandak had gauged the scale of the disaster well. With the flight of the Jin court and the destruction of Luoyang by the Xiongnu, 500 years of Chinese empire had come to an end. It was one of history's more emphatic breaks. Arthur Waley, the great twentieth-century sinologist and translator, likened the fall of Luoyang in 311 to the sack of Rome by the Goths in 410;[21] Erik Zurcher, following the Franco-Hungarian orientalist Etienne Balazs, simply dubbed its perpetrator 'the Attila of Chinese history' – a tag of no mean consequence considering the number of contemporary contenders.[22]

Luoyang had of course been sacked before, yet rebuilt. The Later Han were long gone, yet Wei and then Jin had risen from their ashes; indeed, it was the Jin who had briefly 'united the empire long divided'. But now it was different. The victors were Xiongnu, not Chinese, their apparent aim being to despoil China, not reconstruct it. In 311 the world's second-largest city had been laid waste, and its oldest empire terminated, by a horde of unlettered tent-dwellers.

Arguably the Jin had brought the catastrophe on themselves. Their fragile reunification after the Three Kingdoms period had been achieved at a high cost to central authority. Kinsmen had been rewarded with military commands over semi-autonomous districts; and when Sima Yan, founder of the dynasty, had died in 290, these royal princelings had predictably vied for control of his successors. The so-called 'War of the Eight Princes' (290–311) had served to thin the ranks of the Jin contenders while devastating the empire for which they contended. Fierce competition for military recruits snatched the farmer from his fields and the herdsman from his herds. Serviceable cattle and available food-stocks were commandeered by military provisioners. Seed went unsown, grass ungrazed, coin unminted, taxes unpaid.

In their desperation, thousands took to crime, tens of thousands took to the hills, hundreds of thousands just took to the road. The press of vagrants and migrants then destabilised the provinces through which they straggled; government collapsed; locality warred with locality. The formulaic phrasing used in the Standard Histories may for once have had some substance: 'the rivers filled with floating corpses, bleached bones covered the fields', says the *Jin History*. 'There was much cannibalism. Famine and pestilence went hand in hand.'[23]

Fortune favoured those whose roving habits, social organisation and sense of a distinct identity, not to mention their equestrian skills and horses, could most readily be translated to military advantage. Xiongnu, Xianbei, Qiang and other tribal groupings who were already settled within the empire were sought as auxiliaries, and whether willingly recruited or driven to take up arms by the recruiters were well represented among the contending forces. Other tribal confederations from beyond the northern frontier, drawn into the fray as allies, stayed on as predators. All the frontier peoples had grievances of their own, not least that of diminished status. Once honoured guests and respected allies of the Han, they had gradually been demoted to what Nanai Vandak calls 'the property' of the Jin. 'From being princes and nobles we have descended to the same level as ordinary registered households of commoners,' complained one Xiongnu leader.[24] The good old days of massive Han subsidies were fondly recalled; and it was a descendant of one of the ancient 'peace-through-kinship' unions between a *shanyu* and a Han princess who led the advance on Luoyang in 310.

This Liu Yuan, though unquestionably a Xiongnu, had adopted the name (Liu) of the imperial Han and actually designated himself 'king of Han'. Like that other latter-day 'king of Han', Liu Bei of the 'Three Kingdoms' period, he hoped to use the connection to rally support from contemptuous Chinese subjects. But he died before his mainly Xiongnu forces could take Luoyang. The honours fell to his successor, Liu Cong, 'the Chinese Attila'. Ten thousand defenders are said to have been slaughtered in the final assault, a modest figure by Chinese standards which may reflect earlier desertions. If the descriptions of a city already choked with dead bodies are to be believed, Liu Cong's incendiarists may even have done it a favour.

Chang'an soon shared Luoyang's fate – twice. Meanwhile the Jin emperor was captured and later killed. So was his successor. That left Sima Rui, a distant cousin stationed on the far-off Yangzi, to claim the emperorship and revive the dynasty. He did so, albeit only in the south, as founder of the Eastern Jin, and was there soon joined by at least a million, perhaps several million, who fled from the north to escape the mounting chaos. Aristocratic émigrés joined destitute refugees in the mass exodus. Entire districts upped sticks, followed their local leaders south, and there settled under the same district administration with the same name. Though there would be friction with both prior settlers in the south and with the region's indigenous peoples, northerners would provide the southern court with its most distinguished scholars, its later dynasts and its most effective, if not entirely reliable, troops. In a strictly demographic sense, there was thus some substance to the southern dynasties' claim to be the heirs of Han. Hopes of returning north never flagged; and at court, standards of conduct, scholarship and ritual were zealously maintained against just such a day.

This was in marked contrast to the dismal state of affairs in the north. There the 'Sixteen Kingdoms' period (traditionally 304–439) was under way. Of these sixteen kingdoms' sixteen dynasties, some followed one another in an orderly chronological succession but most crowded abreast in a jostle of competing entities. The result of internecine squabbling and fragmentation among the rampaging tribes, all these regimes were fundamentally unstable, being incapable of reactivating the depleted administrations they had inherited, despised by their Chinese bureaucrats and subjects, and all too ready to resort to coercion.

Perhaps the most feared was the Jie or 'Later Zhao' dynasty of Shandong and Hebei. It was founded by a Xiongnu one-time slave and outlaw called Shi Le (r. 319–33). Shi Le, though he knew neither scruples nor letters, was yet a gentleman compared to Shi Hu (333–49), his successor. The reign of

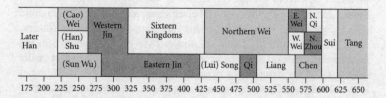

'PERIOD OF DISUNION' SUCCESSION, AD 220–600

Later Han	(Cao) Wei	Western Jin	Sixteen Kingdoms	Northern Wei		E. Wei	N. Qi	Sui	Tang
	(Han) Shu					W. Wei	N. Zhou		
	(Sun Wu)		Eastern Jin	(Lui) Song	Qi	Liang		Chen	

175　200　225　250　275　300　325　350　375　400　425　450　475　500　525　550　575　600　625　650

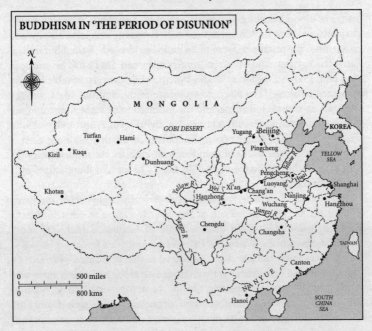

BUDDHISM IN 'THE PERIOD OF DISUNION'

Shi Hu, charitably described as a psychopath, was 'one of unprecedented terror'.[25] On falling out with his own heir apparent, he is said to have had the young man killed along with his consort and their twenty-six children, and then to have had them all buried in the same coffin; their over two hundred retainers shared the same fate, though not the same coffin. To such monsters a doctrine enjoining non-violence and respect for life in all its forms should have been cause for ridicule, tending to rage. Yet it was under the patronage of precisely these Xiongnu tyrants that Buddhism in the north made its most dramatic strides.

Fotudeng, a missionary and miracle-worker from Kuqa (Kuche, Kucha) on the Silk Road who had once studied in Kashmir, reached the Yellow River in 310. Forseeing the outcome of the siege of Luoyang – he was also a seer – he secured an interview with Shi Le, then one of the city's assailants. Since he knew 'that Shi Le did not understand profound doctrines and would respect only magical powers as evidence of the potency of Buddhism', Fotudeng filled his begging bowl with water and conjured from it a bright blue lotus.[26] Greatly impressed, the Xiongnu leader, and later his blood-curdling successor, adopted Fotudeng as their 'court-chaplain' and took Buddhism as their cult. Fotudeng's remarkable powers, rather than his teachings, were often called to the aid of the Shi family's Later Zhao dynasty and were handsomely rewarded. Shi Le had his younger sons educated in a Buddhist establishment, while the unspeakable Shi Hu arrogated to himself the title 'Crown Prince of the Buddha'. Mass conversions, an enormous following, and the foundation of some nine hundred monasteries, nunneries and temples are mentioned. From such dubious dealings with the secular power, Buddhism in north China acquired a popular base. In the words of Fotudeng's biographer, the miracle-working monk 'used the patronage of the Shi family to lay the foundations of a Buddhist church'.[27]

But whether Fotudeng was quite as doctrinally negligent, or the Later Zhao quite as easily impressed, as the records suggest is open to doubt. Fotudeng's disciples would include some of Chinese Buddhism's most outstanding scholars. When the Later Zhao kingdom fell apart in 349 – four princes were enthroned and murdered in that year alone – Fotudeng's disciples fanned out across the north from Shandong to Sichuan and gravitated south as far as Guangdong. One of them, the monk Dao'an, became the greatest exponent, translator and organiser in the early history of Chinese Buddhism; and of his disciples several assisted Kumarajiva, another native of Kuqa, in the most ambitious of all translation projects in terms of quantity and fidelity. Yet all such luminaries continued to revere Fotudeng's memory, which would suggest that he was more than a mere showman and miracle-worker.

As for the Xiongu, they certainly viewed Fotudeng as some superior kind of shaman whose skills as a doctor, rainmaker, seer and political analyst were worth cultivating. But as Shi Hu explained, they also appreciated the peculiar advantages of Buddhism. 'Buddha, being a foreign [or outsiders'] god, is the very one we [as outsiders] should worship,' he declared in the course of an edict urging Buddhist devotion;[28] on similar grounds, Buddhism would be encouraged by later incomers such as the Mongols and Manchus. Additionally, its universalist message, extending the chance of release from suffering to all peoples regardless of race, gender or education, was in marked contrast to the narrow social remit of Confucianism. In effect Buddhism offered to semi-literate herdsmen a source of identity and legitimacy denied them by the lofty standards of Confucian scholarship; and by sidelining the precedent-bound rituals of the *ru*, it brought these alien rulers into direct touch with the less educated mass of their subjects, Chinese and non-Chinese, among whom northern Buddhism now found its greatest following.

Most of the 'Sixteen Kingdoms', though ruled by non-Chinese and dominated by their tribal followings, acknowledged the necessity of enlisting the support of the Chinese masses who constituted the majority of their subjects. To this end they paid lip-service to Han traditions, experimented with bureaucratic government and adopted illustrious dynastic names. As well as two Zhao dynasties, there were several Wei, Yan and even Qin dynasties. Based like its original namesake on Chang'an and the Wei valley, the first of these Qin dynasties (351–86) was an unlikely contender for power. Ethnically the latter-day Qin were *Di*, a tribe of semi-sedentary shepherds and goatherds from the Tibet/Sichuan frontier rather than full-blooded horse-and-camel-rearing nomads from the Mongolian steppe. They had no tradition of concerted action and were 'governed by a rather large number of independent petty chiefs'.[29] They nevertheless adopted the expansionist policies associated with the Qin of old; and partly thanks to a fragmented resistance that badly underestimated them, partly to intelligent accommodations with the more formidable Xiongnu and Xianbei, the Qin had by 381 successfully reunited all of northern China.

In the process Qin forces had seized Sichuan from the Eastern Jin and then threatened the north–south division of the country by advancing on the rest of the Eastern Jin empire in the Yangzi basin. The city of Xiangyang on the Han River was captured and Jiankang, the great southern capital, exposed. When the Jin retook Xiangyang, the Qin responded in emphatic fashion, fielding an incredible 270,000 cavalry and 600,000 infantry for a two-pronged advance on the south – one prong via Henan and the Huai River and the other via Sichuan and the middle Yangzi. But in 383, beside the Fei River, a tributary of the Huai, disaster struck the Qin. The eastern army suffered a mysterious but catastrophic defeat that effectively ended not only the whole offensive but Qin's all-too-brief dominion.

This so-called battle at the Fei River, though less convincing than that at the Red Cliffs, is another of those north–south engagements credited with being decisive for the future of China. Qin's bubble had been burst. The southern court at Jiankang (Nanjing) had survived its hour of peril and would linger on for another two centuries of cultivated discourse and confused politics. In 385 southern forces actually attempted their own reunification and reached the Yellow River before withdrawing. Over the next thirty years the Jiankang government was repeatedly rocked by insurrections, yet no northern dynasty sought to take advantage; and it was the same when in 420 the last Eastern Jin emperor conceded the Mandate to his general Liu Yu, founder of the southern Liu Song dynasty. While the 209 battle at the Red Cliffs had consigned the once united empire to being long divided, the 383 battle at the Fei River confirmed that long divided meant longer than a couple of centuries. 'In the aftermath of the collapse of the Former Qin [so called because it was succeeded in the north-west by a Qiang kingdom that adopted the same dynastic name] the north was more politically fractured than it had been at any time since the fall of the Western Jin.'[30]

LUOYANG AGAIN

The details of the Fei River battle as relayed by the Standard Histories have been much debated. Suffice it to say that a combination of minor engagements seems to have culminated in a massive communications failure. The Qin forces misread their general's cunning plan to lure the enemy across the river and took his failure to attack as evidence of a prior reverse of undisclosed magnitude. They therefore not only held their fire, as ordered, but withdrew. Retreat then turned to rout. The Qin thought they had lost a battle that had not as yet been fought; and their imperfectly integrated associates and allies, putting self-preservation first, simply dispersed. The mighty force had not so much been defeated as dissolved.

The idea of 'dissolution' may be appropriate because, however unconvincing the details of the 'battle', water seems to have played a major part in it. Indeed, the Fei River affair may be taken to illustrate the widening gulf between military deployment as understood in the north and in the south. In the south nearly all warfare involved ships. Troops, mostly infantry, were moved by river, lake, canal or coast, and campaigns were planned around these lines of advance. Roads were few. The terrain was hostile to baggage trains, the malarial climate was lethal to men on the march, and both were bad for horses. Scarcer here than water buffalo, horses found the grazing unnutritious and the going treacherous. Breeding them, too, was problematic; offspring born anywhere south of the Yellow River were reckoned second rate, and most cavalry mounts had to be imported from the steppe. Thus the southern armies, while they could give a good account of themselves among the bamboo brakes and rushy waterways of their native land, were at a major disadvantage when they ventured on to the windswept plains.

It was the other way round in the north. There mounted warfare and draught transport were everything. From Shaanxi, Gansu and the steppes came the swiftest and sturdiest horses in Asia. Peoples like the Xiongnu and Xianbei rode from infancy. They herded and hunted from horseback, and with bow and blade they fought from horseback. Bloodstock remained the mainstay of their economy. The northern plains, no less than the adjoining steppes, were an equestrian arena.

But while the saddle was proverbially 'the nomad's throne', as of the early fourth century the rider seems to have sat it more firmly. Saddles themselves became more substantially padded, were tailored to horse and rider, and were fitted with leg guards; the *c.* 300 introduction of the stirrup – one of those obscure inventions credited with changing the world – afforded the rider a much steadier platform from which to loose an arrow or launch a lance; and both riders and horses came to be encased in increasingly heavy body armour. Although the crossbow, with various refinements, remained the weapon of first choice, it was less effective against steel-plated knights on leather-padded steeds. A charge by this tank-like cavalry carried all before it and may partly account for the fortification in this period not only of royal residences but of rural homesteads and villages. Yet in the south such equestrian developments availed the invader not at all. Horses on boats were hard to manage; and in paddy fields and swamps the overladen panzers sank to a soggy standstill. One reason why the north–south division of the country lasted so long could simply be that neither party possessed the military means to overrun the other.

Evidence for the use of the stirrup and horse armour comes from contemporary paintings and figurines of helmet-hooded Xianbei on stiffly skirted chargers. It was fearsome offensives by just such troops of a Xianbei confederation from beyond the northern frontier which ended the 'Sixteen Kingdoms' free-for-all. The Tabgach (in Chinese 'Tuoba'), the confederation's main tribal component, first fell out with allies in the plains of the north-east. Following a row over a consignment of horses, the Xianbei swooped down to settle matters, and as 'the Northern Wei' (386–534), the Tabgach leadership then steadily eliminated Xiongnu, Qiang and other dynastic rivals. By 439, from their capital at Pingcheng (Datong in northern Shanxi), they had reunited all China above the Huai River.

The sway of this Tabgach/Tuoba 'Northern Wei' dynasty, the first and much the most important of the so-called 'Five (northern) Dynasties', would last nearly a century. Its four short-lived successors (making up the 'Five Dynasties' sequence) would then swiftly succumb to the Sui; and it was the Sui's two emperors who, not before time, would ring down the curtain on the testing 'Period of Disunion' and usher in the great era of Tang. Another golden age was imminent; and lustre being long in the buffing, its harbingers may be sought among the Northern Wei.

In administering an empire – or half of one – the Northern Wei faced the same problems as their predecessors from the tribal world: basically it was a question of how to retain the loyalty and cohesion of forces that were substantially non-Chinese, while inducing subjects who were now overwhemingly Chinese to reactivate the administration, resettle the land and so restore the flow of foodstuffs, manpower and revenue. Positive discrimination helped to reassure the Xianbei population. Known as *guoren* ('people of the [Tabgach] states', or 'compatriots'), they were treated as a ruling class with their own ranking system. They retained their native customs and language, enjoyed numerous privileges and tax exemptions, and had a monopoly of military appointments. Large numbers settled in the vicinity of the capital; others patrolled the northern frontier up to the Gobi desert, where a network of forts was built.

Ideally the *guoren* would be supplied and supported by the empire's Han Chinese subjects. Labour of a servile nature was readily available; large numbers of enslaved captives and convicts were brought to the capital and used for public works, military supply and the cultivation of state lands. But it was not so easy to attract unenslaved, and so taxpaying, agriculturalists back to work on long-deserted holdings. The overall decline in population during the 'Period of Disunion' has been put as high as 30 per cent. Especially marked in the north, where emigration continued to take a heavy toll, depopulation induced victorious regimes 'to place greater value on the control of persons than the control of territory' and to treat cultivators as the spoils of war.[31] Large numbers were indeed resettled, usually within reach of the capital; but many decamped at the slightest provocation, and as the pace of conquest slowed, so did the supply of new settlers. To increase the agricultural yield, the Northern Wei would have to devise inducements and incentives for the cultivator, including a permanent and equitable system of land tenure.

Vouchsafed a longer dominion than any of their post-Han predecessors, the Northern Wei had ample time to acclimatise politically and to experiment. As under previous regimes, Buddhism served as a source of legitimisation and as a bridge over the ethnic divide between non-Chinese and Chinese. But it was also harnessed more directly to the interests of the state. A branch of the bureaucracy took over the regulation of Buddhist affairs; and the difficulty of Buddhist clergy owing obedience to their monastic superiors rather than to the imperial authorities was overcome by elevating the emperor above the clergy as a titular Bodhisattva. A similar move in the south saw Wudi (r. 502–49) of the Liang dynasty, the last but one of the Six (southern) Dynasties, assume hybrid titles such as *Huangdi Busa* and *Busa Tianzi* ('Imperial Bodhisattva', 'Buddhist Son of Heaven').

Potential disloyalty, if not subversion, was only one of many criticisms voiced of Buddhism at the time, all being indicative of its now pervasive presence. With manpower in short supply the monasteries were especially vulnerable on the grounds that they provided a safe haven for idlers and tax-dodgers. Not only monks but all those who laboured on the vast monastic estates were exempt from taxation, conscription and corvée. So were the estates themselves, their produce and income going to support and enrich the clerical community and enhance its standing. State projects and revenues suffered as a result. The colossal Buddha figures and caves still extant at Yugang (near Pingcheng) and Lungmen (near Luoyang), for instance, were hewn from the rock by tens of thousands of labourers who might otherwise have been employed on works of public utility.

Such criticisms, and there were many others, had already surfaced in the south in 340 and 403. In the north they found favour with the Northern Wei emperor known as Tai-wudi (r. 424–52), who completed the dynasty's conquests. Falling under the influence of a Daoist Celestial Master, the emperor was ceremonially installed as 'the Perfect Lord of Great Peace [*taiping*]' and presided over a veritable Daoist revolution in the inner circles of power. Buddhist monks and other leaders of popular cults were purged in 444 and, not for the last time, Buddhism itself was proscribed in 446. Although support for the move was forthcoming from the alienated Han gentry, all this was too much for the Xianbei military, who found their monopoly of high office threatened, and much too much for the emperor when he discovered that a Daoist-influenced rewriting of the dynasty's history disparaged his nomadic ancestry. The proscription was accordingly relaxed around 450, repealed after Tai-wudi's 452 assassination, and completely reversed when from 465 the formidable Dowager Empress Feng gradually took over the reins of power.

'Few rulers in history have made more thoroughgoing attempts to change their subjects' lives than did the dowager and her step-grandson Xiao-wendi,' writes one authority.[32] Not only was Buddhism reinstated, the dowager herself being a lavish patron, but in a series of decrees spread over thirty years the whole trajectory of the regime was reversed. The Xianbei were now to abandon their distinctive language, dress and customs, and through intermarriage and education to become sinicised. The Northern Wei, from representing a steppe hegemony over the northern plains, would pursue a northern plains dominion over the whole of China. And instead of autocratic military rule, a bureaucratic civilian government like that of the Early Han was to be encouraged, agriculture favoured and the ethnic divide between rulers and ruled bridged by the blending of Han and non-Han.

In the short term this experiment failed, just like Tai-wudi's Daoist experiment. But it had profound consequences. Indeed, 'the effects of the series of decrees from 472 until . . . 499 on China for the next three centuries were to be immeasurably great'.[33] For instance, the incentives now offered to all taxpaying agriculturalists included a fixed entitlement to both farmland and mulberry groves (for silkworms), with additional acreage depending on the number of women, slaves and livestock attached to each household. An 'equal-field system', it was intended, like the old 'well-field system', as an equitable division of land by the state which would form a basis for registration and taxation. But the holdings were considerably bigger than of old, and part of each, notably that required for mulberry trees or other cloth-yielding crops such as hemp, was hereditary. In other words, there was enough here to make the cultivator think twice before vacating whenever famine or disturbance threatened. Something similar had been attempted by the Cao Wei and Western Jin dynasties; but it was this Northern Wei version that would be adopted by the Sui and Tang. It would last until the mid-eighth century, at which point 'Chinese attempts at state regulation of land finally came to an end and were not effectively renewed . . . until the communism of the twentieth century'.[34]

In theory no state-allocated land (other than that for mulberry trees) could be disposed of or inherited. Yet almost immediately both these practices became commonplace. As larger landholdings were consolidated, the 'equal-field system' became decidedly unequal and in fact helped to sustain a new class of landed proprietors. Even Xianbei warriors seem to have been attracted by the system, and wherever the reforms were effective and the tenure could be made hereditary, powerful landowning clans of now mixed descent took root. From this milieu of military men turned landowners, and of non-Han turned Chinese, would come most of the leading figures of the sixth and seventh centuries. An ethnic and social accommodation – Chinese historians might prefer 'assimilation' – was under way. Like Buddhism, it would be instrumental in underpinning the eventual reintegration of the empire.

Central to the new policies devised by the Dowager Empress Feng and continued by Xiao-wendi was the 493 removal of the imperial capital. From Pingcheng, a place on the verge of the Mongolian steppe that had proved difficult to supply with grain, let alone luxuries, it was to be transferred to the still-devastated Luoyang, a site well served by road and water transport, at the centre of the great northern plain, and steeped in imperial associations. After much discussion and in the face of considerable disquiet, the move had to be made as if by accident. While leading south an army to assail the Qi, fourth of the Six (southern) Dynasties of Jiankang (Nanjing), the emperor engineered a halt near the site of the old Han, Wei and Jin capital. Incessant rain had already dampened martial spirits, and it now led to pleas to abandon the whole campaign. The emperor, feigning reluctance, agreed on condition that the army stay put and begin reconstructing the city.

So it did; and after nine years of rebuilding and a massive population transfer, a great city once again graced the northern bank of the Luo River. The new Luoyang covered an area of over 18 square kilometres (7 square miles) and accommodated more than half a million people and 1,300 monasteries. It witnessed scenes of magnificence barely rivalled by its predecessors, it hosted further developments in Buddhist scholarship, it minted the first new coinage for a couple of centuries – and it lasted for all of a generation. Not wilfully destroyed this time, merely evacuated, by 535 Luoyang was again a ghost town.

The move from Pingcheng had always been resented, most notably by the Xianbei garrisons on the northern frontier. The policy of sinicisation and the favour being shown to Han bureaucrats proved the final straws. The northern Xianbei troops rebelled and the Northern Wei empire split. Other tribal groupings hastened to join in the fray; in 534 the last Northern Wei emperor was deposed; and in the same year Luoyang's population was removed to a new capital. From the flurry of ferocious infighting between the short-lived dynastic successors of the Northern Wei would emerge the dynamic instigator of China's second attempt at an enduring integration.

8

SUI, TANG AND
THE SECOND EMPIRE
550–650

INTERCALARY CONJUNCTION

BEFORE CHINA'S ADOPTION OF THE STANDARD Gregorian calendar in 1912, each month of the Chinese year lasted twenty-eight to twenty-nine days, that being the duration of the moon's cycle. But since 28/29 days x 12 months comes to somewhat less than the 365 days of the solar year, the Chinese calendar, like other luni-solar calendars, needed a way of accommodating the difference. The Julian and Gregorian calendars manage this by extending the duration of most months to thirty or thirty-one days, so spreading the differential throughout the year. But in China, as in pre-Julian Rome, the moon-length month remained standard. Instead, the luni-solar difference was taken up by the introduction, every eighteen months or so, of an additional month.

When to introduce this 'intercalary' month was a matter of deep concern and elaborate computation, for on the exact harmonisation and synchronisation of the terrestrial world with that of the cosmos depended just about everything – virtue, longevity, health, prosperity, justice, dominion and immunity from disasters. Like other essential ongoing corrections – to the name of the year-period, the setting of the hours, the timing of the seasonal rites, the musical pitch of the ritual pipes – it was ultimately an imperial responsibility. Outstanding emperors, especially those who founded a dynasty or achieved much in their own right, were thought to have been well advised in such matters; bad emperors were generally supposed to have neglected or manipulated them.

This idea of fraught but cathartic interludes in which human affairs were realigned with the rhythms of the cosmos could be extended to the dynastic succession itself. Some dynasties lasted long; others barely survived a few turbulent decades – it was as if they had been inserted to fill a hiatus or give a new direction. The Former Han had been preceded by the intrusion that was the First Emperor's Qin dynasty, and the Later Han by the 'blip' that was Wang Mang's Xin dynasty. A pattern was apparent; and since the succession of dynasties was supposed to mimic the cycles of the planets, some Chinese historians embraced the possibility of 'intercalary' dynasties. Thus Qin and Xin could be seen as necessary, if traumatic, correctional preludes that had brought Former Han and Later Han into propitious harmony with the cosmic forces.

The task of what he calls 'making a distinction between the orthodox and the intercalated status [of dynasties]' was one that eventually defeated Sima Guang, the eleventh-century author of the *Zizhi Tongjian* (and not to be confused with Sima Qian, the second-to-first-century BC 'Grand Historian' who wrote the *Shiji*). In the post-Han period there were just too many dynasties for Sima Guang to decide which were intercalary and which, if any, were not. Yet the title of his all-embracing history, which translates as something like 'A Comprehensive Mirror for Aid in Government', seems to endorse the idea of history 'reflecting' the cosmic cycles.[1] And in common with all Chinese historians, Sima Guang continued to subscribe to the belief that each individual dynasty did indeed conform to a cyclical pattern. Planet-like again, every dynasty ascended and declined, waxed and waned, shone and faded. Strong and virtuous emperors usually came early in the succession; weaker and worse ones usually came towards the end. Indeed, 'the bad-last emperor', a necessary conjunction if the Mandate was about to be forfeited, features so frequently in the Standard Histories as to be considered a convention of history-writing. As with the 'vindictive empress' and the 'scheming eunuch', the dismal deeds and delicious improprieties credited to such stereotypes should be approached with caution.

Moreover Sima Guang did not entirely abandon the idea of dynasties themselves being intercalary. It might not be applicable in respect of the localised dynasties of the 'Period of Disunion', but with the return to a wider dominion in the late sixth century it was about to be demonstrated in the most satisfactory fashion. For before the Tang dynasty could embark on its long and glorious career, another short and dramatic intercalary prelude would serve to bring the country back into what dynastic historians regarded as its natural trajectory. This was as a unitary empire; and the dynasty responsible was the Sui.

There were only two Sui emperors, their combined reigns lasting just thirty-seven years (581–618), but for maniacal energy and solid achievement it is hard to find their equal in the later history of the empire. Rather one must look, as they did, to the past. Just as the mighty empire of Han had relied on the administrative structures, legal constraints, mobilisational capacity and awesome reputation generated by the Qin First Emperor, so the empire of Tang would scarcely have flourished without the conquests, institutions and infrastructure bequeathed it by the Sui. And yet, since neither Qin's controversial reputation nor any hint of 'intercalated status' could be entertained by a dynast ambitious for his lineage, it was not the example of Qin which inspired the Sui but that of Han itself. As will be seen, the dynasty that the Sui regarded as traumatic and transitional was the one they replaced. Intercalary interludes, like 'bad-last' emperors, were always someone else's.

When in 534 the newly rebuilt Luoyang had been forcibly evacuated, it was on the orders of a warlord called Gao Huan. Himself Chinese but from the northern frontier and married to a Xianbei, Gao Huan then ruled in the name of several short-lived Northern Wei descendants (known as the Eastern Wei) from a more defensible capital at Ye in the south of Hebei. Luoyang was thought too exposed because to the west another warlord of pure Xianbei descent called Yuwen Tai ruled in the name of more puppet emperors of Northern Wei descent (there known as the Western Wei). In time-honoured fashion, both these Wei remnants were soon removed, with Gao Huan's successors in the east reigning as the Northern Qi (551–77) and Yuwen Tai's in the west as the Northern Zhou (557–81). (They called themselves just 'Qi' and 'Zhou', of course, all the 'northerns', 'easterns' and 'westerns' having been added later for the convenience of historians.)

The Northern Qi in the east was the more sinicised of the two regimes and may be seen as continuing the ethnic assimilation of Han and non-Han promoted by Dowager Empress Feng and Xiao-wendi of the Northern Wei. But it was Yuwen Tai's Northern Zhou dynasty based in Chang'an which, though initially the weaker of the two, proved the more innovative and dynamic. According to one historian – admittedly not a Chinese one – this largely non-Han regime, headed by a Xianbei elite many of whom spoke no Chinese at all, 'was the anvil on which were forged the structures of power – the economic, political and military institutions – upon which [the Sui-Tang] monolith grew'.[2] In fact the Northern Zhou actually fashioned that monolith to the extent that they reunified the north, added to it the ever vital resource-base of Sichuan, revived claims to Gansu and some of the oasis-cities beyond, and ennobled a man whose son, as *Sui* Wendi, would complete the process of reunification. Just as the dukes and kings of Qin in the 'Warring States' period had developed centralised bureaucratic structures and mobilised massive armies for the career of conquest that made possible the Qin, and then Han, empires, so it was the little-honoured innovations of the Northern Zhou which made possible the better-known triumphs of Sui, which in turn underpinned the glorious Tang.

One day in 535 Yuwen Tai, already the power behind the Western Wei throne, was out fishing with friends near Chang'an. In what must have been a novel sport for men from the desiccated northern frontier, the anglers chose a stretch of water that looked to have been man-made. Curious about its origins – it probably dated from the Former Han – Yuwen Tai sought information. A local man called Su Chuo was produced, and he proving a fund of information, the Xianbei warlord took more delight in his antiquarian 'catch' than in the fishing. He kept Su Chuo talking for the rest of the day and well into the night. Besides information about 'the vestiges of the rise and fall of successive dynasties', he learned of 'the way of orderly government . . . the way of emperors and kings' and of the political teachings of ancient sages like the legalist Han Fei. Curiosity and an open-minded pragmatism being among the finer qualities of the non-Han incomers, Yuwen Tai was intrigued. He co-opted Su Chuo as his fiscal adviser and also entrusted him with the task of devising a legitimising ideology for the new regime, a role in which subsequent Northern Zhou rulers would retain him.[3]

Su Chuo's approach to the problem of how to make non-Han rule more palatable in northern China was to present it not as a compromise with the surviving traditions of the Han Chinese but as a reversion to the pre-Han, and of course pre-Buddhist, purity of those traditions. In other words, he would out-orthodox the orthodox. Like Confucius, he harked back to the age prior to the 'Warring States' period when society supposedly conformed to the highest ideals of Confucian decorum and duty. Hence the choice of 'Zhou' as the dynastic name; hence his putting into Yuwen Tai's mouth sentiments and speeches culled from those credited to the Duke of Zhou; and hence his promotion of the *Zhouli* ('Rites of Zhou'), a contentious text, also sometimes credited to the Duke of Zhou, that described the life and times – and more especially the life and terms – of that Elysian age.

The *Zhouli*, it may be recalled, was also the text so slavishly adopted by Wang Mang in the early first century AD. Once again the long-forgotten nomenclature of Zhou times was resurrected; edicts were issued in the archaic Chinese of that period and all officials compelled to learn it; a handy catechism comprising the Six Articles of the new dispensation had also to be memorised by heart; and the 'equal-fields system' of land tenure, though introduced by the Northern Wei, was retained as a fair approximation to the ancient 'well-field' grid of equal peasant holdings. Naturally Buddhism and Daoism were frowned on and both were eventually proscribed.

Whether such affectations endeared the foreign elite to their Chinese subjects is, however, doubtful; for when the duke of Sui, a member of that elite, rose against the Northern Zhou in 581, one of his first moves would be to reject the whole exercise. In effect, Confucian 'fundamentalism' probably served the Northern Zhou no better than it had Wang Mang. On the other hand, it served their successors rather well, in that abolition of such an inconvenient model not only enhanced their credibility but threw open the ideological arena for other political exemplars from the past.

More practical and much more productive were the Northern Zhou's recruiting initiatives. When they first arrived in Chang'an, Yuwen Tai and his Xianbei followers mustered an effective but not numerous cavalry. To hold off repeated attacks by the Eastern Wei/Northern Qi, they needed to organise local recruitment, enlist the loyalty of various rural militia, and raise both the standing of military men and the standard of military training. This they did so successfully that by 550 the records speak of 'Twenty-four Armies' and by the early 570s of 100,000 men under arms. The Gansu corridor was successfully subdued by 549, and after the collapse of the Liang dynasty in the south, Sichuan and then the Han River basin were taken in the 550s. Northern Zhou territory now reached to the Yangzi. To complete the reunification of the north it remained only to overwhelm the Northern Qi in Shandong and Hebei, a feat that was achieved in 577 with a massive force put at 570,000.

But just how this turnaround in the size and cohesion of the Northern Zhou's military machine was effected is far from clear. The key development is thought to have been the institution of *fubing* ('territorial forces' or 'militia forces'). These *fubing* would famously become the backbone of the Sui and Tang armies and attract much later comment, none of which has helped to clarify their genesis. Under the Northern Zhou most *fubing* were probably infantry rather cavalry, Han Chinese rather than non-Han, and volunteers rather than conscripts, having been lured into service by exemptions from taxation and corvée. Yet there were numerous exceptions: conscription was by no means abandoned; some *fubing* may have originated in units previously recruited by local magnates and then incorporated into the 'Twenty-four Armies'; the enormous numbers of horses mentioned show that cavalry, both light and heavy, remained crucial; so did the recruitment of non-Han forces; and in the north, as in the south, there is evidence for the growth of military professionalism and a martial culture. Long-term enrolment, with military families or groups of families providing recruits from one generation to the next, is evident; and the growth of an *esprit de corps* may be inferred from the news that, as of the 570s, the Twenty-four Armies 'began to perform guard duty by rotation in the environs of the imperial palace, an important feature of the *fubing* system under the Sui and Tang dynasties'.[4]

But perhaps nothing contributed more to this steady build-up than the success it generated. Victory brought reward to all – grants, amnesties and booty to the rank-and-file, honours, emoluments and more booty to their commanders, and additional manpower and foodstuffs to the regime. Expansion created its own momentum; and there seemed no limit to it. For the conquests of the Northern Zhou, reaching from the Liao River in Manchuria to Gansu, Sichuan and the upper Yangzi, had not just reunited the north but had thrown a cordon round the breakaway southern empire based at Jiankang (Nanjing) on the lower Yangzi.

By the sixth century Jiankang, the capital of all the southern dynasties, had grown into 'the largest city of the age' with a population of around a million. Commercially and intellectually it shamed the northern capitals of Chang'an, Luoyang and Ye.[5] In its markets the silks and hardware of the north met the spices, pearls and feathery exotica of Vietnam and southeast Asia. Beside the Yangzi, and scattered over the wooded slopes behind, some seven hundred Buddhist establishments maintained the highest standards of exegesis, while at court piety vied with conversational finesse and the grossest indulgence.

Yet for the powdered scholars dissecting the finer points of the Lotus Sutra, as for the rouged poets rhapsodising over the almond blossom, a nasty shock awaited. The long reign of the ultra-pious *Liang* Wudi (r. 502–49) was interrupted by a crescendo of rebellions that climaxed in 548 with Jiankang itself capitulating after a four-month siege. Brocaded aristocrats, deserted by their retainers and unacquainted with the mechanics of cooking, were said to have starved to death in the lacquered luxury of their own apartments. The city was sacked with appalling brutality; and when order was restored in the 550s, the new Chen dynasty (557–89) ruled a reduced and enfeebled southern empire. It was further circumscribed by a defeat at the hands of the Northern Zhou in late 577. As of that date, 'to any northern statesman . . . the Chen must have looked like an easy conquest'.[6]

Only a dynastic crisis in the north delayed the inevitable. In 579 the Northern Zhou emperor died. He was succeeded by Crown Prince Yuwen Pin, a pathological libertine in whom the attributes of 'bad-last' emperor assumed monstrous proportions. Bingeing from the sacerdotal vessels reserved for the ancestors, he flouted the rites, chastised his womenfolk, violated the wife of a kinsman, and beheaded those even suspected of disapproval. His one asset was his father-in-law, the duke of Sui, a man of mixed ethnicity and a veteran of the wars with the Northern Qi who was indeed, as per his title, a 'Pillar of the State'.

When in 580 Yuwen Pin suffered a stroke and died of natural causes, the duke of Sui engineered his own appointment as commander-in-chief and regent for Pin's seven-year-old successor. Events then took a predictable course. Rebellions were quashed, the Yuwen clan was steadily eliminated, and pleas for a new dynasty, supposedly emanating from the young emperor and backed by all manner of portents and predictions, rained down on the duke of Sui. In 581, with a show of the utmost reluctance, he accepted the incumbent's abdication and assumed the Mandate. Soon after, the suspicious demise of the ex-emperor brought the number of Yuwen kinsmen purged in the changeover to exactly sixty.

Five years of consolidation and inclusion ensued. *Sui* Wendi (that being the temple-name adopted by the once duke, now emperor) embarked on an important programme of administrative reform that, in reinstating the institutions of the Han empire, brought into government far more Han Chinese than non-Han. The recent proscription by the Northern Zhou of both Buddhism and Daoism was reversed, while all of that dynasty's archaic introductions were unceremoniously junked. Confucian as well as Daoist stalwarts were artfully placated. The Buddhist community was deluged as never before with favours and patronage. Signifying the new dynasty's ambitious intent, the city of Chang'an was dismantled and its place taken by a replanned and rebuilt capital of cyclopean proportions. Agriculture recovered, tax receipts improved and labour was abundant. Meanwhile the military build-up continued.

When it came in 589, the conquest of the south had an air of inevitablility about it. Weakened by the loss of territory along the north bank of the Yangzi and in Sichuan, the Chen, last of the southern 'Six Dynasties', planned its resistance with little hope and dwindling conviction. Ideologically as well as physically, the ground had been cut from under the southern empire. The Northern Zhou's reunification of the north, and the Sui adoption of Han administrative norms, had undermined the southern case for an exclusive legitimacy. Unlike previous southern dynasts, the Chen were not artistocratic northern émigrés who could pose as guardians of a cultural tradition reaching back through the dynastic pedigree to the Jin, the (Cao) Wei and the Later Han; rather were they local military leaders of no more illustrious descent than their counterparts in the north.

Cultural and commercial contacts between north and south had never ceased during the 'Period of Disunion', but the social distinctions that had struck the visitor in, say, the fifth century were no longer so clear cut. The stereotyping of northern rulers as bloodthirsty and uncultured 'barbarians' who lived on mutton-and-dumpling stews was as unsustainable as that of southerners as effete and indolent courtiers picking at fish-and-fried-rice delicacies. Non-Han steppe-men in the north increasingly conformed to Han Chinese norms; Han Chinese émigrés in the south were increasingly tainted by association and intermarriage with the indigenous Man and other southern ethnic groups. North and south shared more than they cared to admit. Both segments of the erstwhile empire accorded primacy to devotional Buddhism; both honoured Daoist, Buddhist and Confucian scholarship; both treasured their common linguistic and literary heritage; and both still subscribed to the ideal of the 'Middle Kingdom' (*zhongguo*) as a single integrated entity.

Like the Qin First Emperor, *Sui* Wendi planned his assault on the south as an affair of many prongs. From Sichuan to the sea, half a million troops massed along the Yangzi in eight strike forces. In recognition of the difficulties of combat in the south, they included contingents of Man boatmen, a large infantry component and vast fleets of warships and transports. These had been constructed as surreptitiously as possible at four strategic locations: on the coast, near the middle Yangzi, on the Han River, and at Fengjie just above the gorges in Sichuan. It had taken two years of meticulous preparation, but by the winter of 588/89 all was ready. In a well-coordinated movement, the amphibious advance got under way.

Down through the Yangzi gorges came the Sui's most feared commander at the head of an armada that included what must have been the largest vessels afloat in the sixth century. Each was a five-deck fortress from whose embrasured cladding 800 men could discharge their crossbows, while overhead, like gesticulating antennae, 15-metre (16-yard) derricks swung spiked iron weights to disable approaching vessels. Yet despite their superior weaponry, the northerners remained wary of river combat, especially amid the treacherous currents and commanding heights of the gorges above Yichang. To outflank and overpower the assortment of fleets, fortified obstructions and chain barriers strung across the stream, they relied more on landward excursions, often under cover of darkness. Progress was steady and occasionally sanguinary but was soon overtaken by events downstream.

There the main Chen forces were concentrated around Jiankang. But because much of the Chen fleet was engaged upstream and cut off by the intervening Sui flotillas, the river itself was here poorly defended. Two Sui columns crossed it unopposed, and after just one battle of note, both entered the city of Jiankang. It was all over in a matter of days. Some Chen units fled rather than fight; others readily surrendered when the Chen emperor so ordered. (An early captive, he had been extricated from his place of refuge at the bottom of a well, where he was found in the clammy embrace of two favoured concubines.) In proportion to the number of combatants, the casualties of the campaign had not been heavy; and the clemency now shown to the vanquished was exemplary. Jiankang was not sacked, the ex-emperor and his officials were spared, and a rumour of mass transplantations proved to be exaggerated.

Though a heavy death toll resulted from the suppression of a series of subsequent rebellions, by the end of 590 the south was pacified. Demobilisation throughout the empire was then declared, if not universally effected. Weapons were supposedly collected, their private manufacture banned and, setting a precedent that would have long-term consequences, all boats of more than 10 metres (33 feet) were confiscated. As well as outlawing local navies, this had the effect of containing mercantile enterprise and ensuring that water transport served the interests of the state. From his new capital at Chang'an, *Sui* Wendi ruled a realm that, long divided, was now to be physically united.

SUI-CIDE

The emperor had been raised a devout Buddhist. 'With the armed might of a Cakravartin [a world-ruling 'turner-of-the-wheel' in Indian Buddhism], We spread the ideals of the Ultimately Enlightened One,' declared *Sui* Wendi's first edict. 'With a hundred victories in a hundred battles We promote the practice of the Ten Virtues. The weapons of war We regard as incense and flowers offered to the Buddha . . .'[7]

Nearly four thousand temples, pagodas, nunneries and monasteries were founded during *Sui* Wendi's reign, many of them in his rebuilt Chang'an, where one pagoda reportedly measured 100 metres (109 yards) in height and 120 metres (131 yards) in girth. The number of new Buddha images erected ran to over a hundred thousand, while those repaired following the Northern Zhou's iconoclasm exceeded 1.5 million.[8] In China there was no nobler exemplar of the Buddhist sovereign as *maha-danapati* (supreme donor) than *Sui* Wendi. Towards the end of his reign he organised a ceremonial distribution of Buddha relics to thirty specially built reliquary sites dotted throughout the land. Packed and sealed in jars by the emperor himself, the relics were distributed by an army of monks and were all enshrined on the same day. Offices everywhere were closed for a week. It was an act of empire-wide dedication consciously modelled on a distribution of the Buddha's remains by the Indian emperor Ashoka, Buddhism's first imperial patron. Ashoka's action had been intended not just as a demonstration of piety but as a celebration of sovereign power over a sprawling empire. So it was with *Sui* Wendi. The distribution twice repeated, the number of Sui-sponsored reliquary shrines, which also served as places of congregation and pilgrimage, rose to 114.

But if the emperor's actions stemmed from a concern to expiate his sins and improve his karma (rather than from a complete misunderstanding of the Buddha's non-violent doctrines), his munificence needed to be on the grand scale. All too easily roused, *Sui* Wendi sent many to the executioner, readily awarded 'the privilege of suicide' to others, penalised even his sons, and himself caned to death those whom he considered not chastised vigorously enough by his officials. His justice was stern, his energy prodigious. Yet, for an emperor, his tastes were modest and his personal life exemplary. With his non-Han wife, he shared the burdens of state in what was tantamount to a joint sovereignty. She bore him seven children, and by mutual consent he had no others. The imperial couple were 'inseparable and . . . in the palace they were referred to as "the two sages"'.[9]

Something similar might well have been said of *Sui* Yangdi (r. 604–18), Wendi's son and successor. Also a Buddhist benefactor, he too combined personal brutality with operational clemency, while his marriage to a southern princess seems to have been equally harmonious. But the Standard History of the Sui was written under the direction of their nemesis, the Tang; and while *Sui* Wendi, as the reunifier, could scarcely be denied his share of praise, *Sui* Yangdi, as the last of his line, could conveniently be credited with more than his share of opprobrium. *Sui* Yangdi brought the empire to the brink of ruin; therefore rumours of his having murdered his father (the most heinous crime in an ultra-filial society) and having ravaged his father's consorts (which was deemed incest) must be true. V. C. Xiong, his recent biographer, observes that even the name by which he is remembered, Yang (plus the imperial signifier ' -*di*'), was in fact a posthumous pejorative reserved exclusively for those who 'lust after beautiful women ... abandon ritual ... defy Heaven and abuse the people'. Summarising *Sui* Yangdi's many-sided persona as revealed in the traditional histories, Xiong notes 'a hedonistic philanderer, a prodigal spendthrift, an oppressive ruler, a cold-blooded murderer, an impulsive aggressor, a hater of remonstrance, a lover of sycophancy, and above all, a tyrant ...'[10] Yet Yangdi's achievements were far from mean and his crimes not dramatically worse than his father's – or than those of his immediate Tang successors. As commander-in-chief of his father's southern invasion and then a sympathetic governor of the south, he had played a leading role in his father's reunification; and when the apprentice became the autocrat, he pursued almost identical policies with equal, if eventually disastrous, zest.

Sui Wendi's declared preference for the Han dynasty and the Cao family's Wei dynasty had been intended to signify dynastic ambition and imperial resurgence. The Cao family's Wei dynasty provided an acceptable blueprint for a legitimised usurpation and the Han an unassailable example of Confucian rectitude. Wendi's new Chang'an was called Daxiangcheng, meaning 'Great Revival City', and of the Five Phases or Elements, he chose fire and its colour red, they being the same as those adopted by Han *Wudi*. No scholar himself, *Sui* Wendi had little interest in the niceties of Confucian morality but saw its value as a basis for social order and bureaucratic centralisation.

Over the previous centuries the proliferation of provincial units and semi-autonomous fiefs had run unchecked. It has been calculated that, since the Later Han, the number of commanderies had increased by six and a half times and the number of prefectures by twenty-two times. There were so many mini-entities, so many parallel administrations, so many tiers of government and so many salaried officials that they absorbed most of the revenue; according to one adviser, it was like having nine shepherds for every ten sheep. *Sui* Wendi abolished nearly all of them and substituted ministerial offices, departmental hierarchies, graded ranks and parallel inspectorates as favoured by the Han. Grist to the mill of China's bureaucratically inclined historians, the restored titles, portfolios and pecking orders had a certain rationality but would be subject to constant change. Adjustments by Yangdi further centralised, streamlined and, where convenient, sidelined the system, which would then be thoroughly overhauled by the Tang.

Much the same could be said of the legal codes introduced by *Sui* Wendi and *Sui* Yangdi and famously reworked for export throughout east Asia by the Tang. Both of the Sui codes professed superior logic and greater leniency; yet they were regularly flouted by emperors exasperated as much by the corruptibility of the judicial process as by the growing prevalence of crime. Wendi's 'Ten Abominations' – crimes unpardonable even by imperial amnesties – were reduced by Yangdi to eight, 'incest' and 'discord' (or 'plotting to kill or sell relatives who are of the fifth or closer degree of mourning') being omitted, presumably because they were misdemeanours of which the emperor himself might be guilty. But given that for petty crimes like the theft of a copper cash, the purloining of a roof joist or even the picking of a melon offenders were routinely executed, penal severity seems not to have been significantly restrained by legal codification. Suffice it to say that in opting for Han precedent in matters of ritual, administration and justice, the Sui launched China's 'Second Empire' as a fair approximation to the highly regulated, bureaucratised and draconian despotism that had characterised its First – and which would remain until its last.

Ferocious punishment, although probably no more revolting or, per head of population, more commonly administered in seventh-century China than in seventh-century anywhere, served as a deterrent in a society riven by conflicting loyalties. These were not simply the ethnic, political and regional residue of four centuries of strife. A downside of the Confucian emphasis on family ties was that it encouraged office-holders, for instance, to aim at perpetuating a monopoly of office within the circle of their kinsmen and dependants. Nepotism being respectable, corruption flourished, competence declined and the gap between statutory intent and actual practice widened. If the frequency and tenor of imperial appeals are anything to go by, discovering candidates for office whose ability was uncompromised by hereditary loyalties had challenged every emperor since the First. An efficient bureaucracy, and indeed the whole legitimacy of the regime, depended on its ability to attract men of calibre; yet this had to be done without antagonising existing magnates and, in the case of empire-builders like the Sui, while enlisting the loyalties of powerful new constituents in the south, the east and along the northern frontiers.

The Sui solution to expanding the base of civil service recruitment was to set up a Board of Civil Office to centralise all appointments and scrutinise the selection process. They also revived and developed the Han system whereby each commandery had to identify and recommend a certain number of outstanding candidates for future office; the chosen few were then dispatched to the capital, assigned to one of three academies and there tutored and examined. Though still rudimentary, the examination system was refined by the introduction of degrees in different subjects.

Among them was one with a literary bias, known as *jinshi*, that would eventually become the acme of social and scholastic achievement. Though it would be left to the Tang, and more especially the Song, to elevate the examination system into one of imperial China's most distinctive features, the Sui may be credited with having promoted the idea, and laid down the framework, for a genuinely meritocratic civil service.

As with the penal system, it is not clear how closely practice conformed to principle. But if one may judge by documentation relating to the early Tang period and recovered from Dunhuang and Turfan in the twentieth century, the imperial writ carried far and wide. Registration for the purposes of taxation and labour service is seen to have been remarkably thorough. Each household submitted detailed returns of its family members, servants, livestock, cultivable land (and whether hereditary or not), other property and crops. These were then checked, entered, assessed, and the assessments levied. On such meticulous record-keeping depended the revenue and manpower at the Tang's disposal; and it is reasonable to suppose that the system worked just as smoothly under the Sui since their programme of public works, military expansion and ostentatious expenditure was second to none.

Not content with his father's replanning of Chang'an, *Sui* Yangdi founded an alternative capital, more centrally located for a reunited empire, by rebuilding Luoyang. It was not as extensive as Chang'an/Daxiangcheng, being a mere 47 square kilometres (18 square miles) instead of the latter's 80 square kilometres (30 square miles); and as usual, building materials from the previous city were recycled. Timbers could be rehung and roof tiles relaid; bricks baked easily in the hot dry summers and *hangtu* foundations required only the tireless tamping of an abundant labour force. The almost stone-free nature of most Chinese architecture goes a long way towards explaining the rapidity with which city after city rose and fell. Completed in 606, *Sui* Yangdi's Luoyang had taken little over a year. Yet by all accounts the result was something special.

> It was unrivalled in its extraordinary splendour [says the Standard History of the Sui]. Since the emperor, as imperial prince, had pacified the south in person, he assimilated the curvilinear and angular [forms] of Liang and Chen [architecture] . . . Its walls rose higher than the Mang mountains. Floating bridges spanned the Luo River. Above the golden gate and ivory watchtower were erected winged belvederes. Precipices were collapsed and rivers cut off to make way for pillars [or perhaps mounds] shaped like multi-coloured clouds . . .[11]

The main palace hall stood on a 2-metre-high (6.5-feet) pedestal. It was about the length of a football pitch and as tall as a stadium. Its roofline commanded the city; and between its pillars probably hung the mother-of-pearl blinds that had adorned its predecessor and which 'at sunset flashed with a dazzling radiance'.[12] Yuwen Kai, the architect who laid out the city as well as designing the main buildings, seems to have been preserved for just such work, he being one of the few members of the Northern Zhou's Yuwen clan not to have perished in *Sui* Wendi's purge. His Luoyang creation delighted Yangdi, and his abilities as a civil engineer would be further tested. Among several other palaces commissioned by Yangdi in the course of his extensive travels was one on wheels. In 607 it accompanied the imperial entourage on a grand tour of the northern frontier. Carried there in kit form by cart – a palace-on-wheels on wheels – it was assembled *in situ* and then trundled into an auspicious alignment. It was used for the reception of tribute missions and, in addition to the dignitaries, could apparently accommodate 'several hundred' imperial guardsmen.

Sui Yangdi's 607 northern excursion took him beyond the Ordos, where, like his father, he sought to emulate the Qin and Han in respect

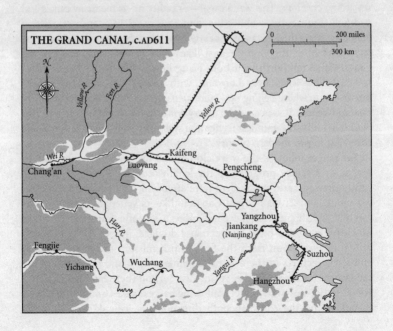

THE GRAND CANAL, c.AD611

of frontier management and wall-building. The strategic value of a walled or fortified northern frontier had been somewhat discredited over the preceding four centuries. In fact, as wave after wave of steppe-people poured into China, it was hard to think of any incursion that had been inconvenienced by it. *Sui* Wendi, and then Yangdi, ascribed this to the lamentable state of the surviving earthworks; and while Wendi had built westward, Yangdi set a workforce doubtfully put at 1 million, of whom half were said never to have returned, to construct a new wall east from Yulin to the Taihang mountains. But the new walls proved just as provocative, ineffective and ruinously expensive as their predecessors. Disowning Sui precedent for once, the Tang would make little attempt to maintain them. Across the Gobi desert in Inner Mongolia those parts of *Sui* Yangdi's wall that survive may therefore be genuine examples of seventh-century workmanship. A recent visitor noted 'a massy stretch of earthen rampart, perhaps 2.5 metres [8 feet] tall, running between solid towers rising twice as high out of archetypal Gobi vistas . . . it looks more like a termite-infested bank than a man-made defence'.[13]

Decidedly less redundant are the still-churning thoroughfares of what was *Sui* Yangdi's, and indeed one of imperial China's, most ambitious and rewarding creations. This was a canal – or rather it was the many canals and hydraulic features that, connecting numerous rivers, lakes and pre-existing conduits over a total distance of nearly 2,500 kilometres (1,550 miles), came to be known as the Grand Canal. Excavated between 605 and 611, the Grand Canal ran north-west from Hangzhou (south of the Yangzi delta) to the Yellow River near Luoyang, with a long extension from there north-east to where Beijing now stands. In effect it linked north and south, east and centre. It was an axial artery for a reunited empire. It was also 'without doubt, the grandest navigation system ever undertaken by a single sovereign in pre-modern history'.[14]

Sui Yangdi followed the work closely, and by way of inauguration, in 611, made a stately progress up the length of it; his flotilla of extravagantly dressed craft was said to have stretched for over 100 kilometres (62 miles). But China's Grand Canal, unlike its Venetian namesake, was rarely a stylish processional path, more a gigantic transport corridor. Much rerouted and often widened and dredged, in 1793 it would wring grudging admiration from the first British mission to imperial China; and some sections of the original alignment must still today be among the busiest waterways in the world. Past Suzhou (between Shanghai and Nanjing) tug-towed strings of wallowing barges snake continuously, head to tail, round the clock, in both directions, at a bank-sloshing pace;

gondolas would be swamped, vaporettos vaporised. Nor is the canal's utility exhausted. Twenty-first-century plans envisage its conversion into a giant aqueduct to divert the Yangzi's flood waters to the now parched and polluted aquifers of Beijing and the north.

To the pre-motorised economy, bulk transport had posed a logistical problem that was nigh insuperable. It frustrated trade in all but high-value commodities, inhibited urbanisation, impeded the development of industry and undermined efforts at major state-formation. This was especially so in Sui China, where roads were subject to annual inundation and coastal shipping was deemed precarious. Yet coinage being scarce and paper money still to be invented, the entire tax yield came in kind – usually grain and silk – and so in bulk. Moreover, the movement and storage of this agricultural surplus was the only insurance against the ever-present threat of famine and was a strategic necessity for provisioning frontier garrisons and supporting military ventures beyond.

The Grand Canal, linking the Yangzi region with its rice surplus to the heavily populated and famine-prone northern plains, thus had a similar effect to the first transcontinental railroads in North America. It made China's economic integration feasible. Disparities of climate, terrain, produce and demographic distribution were suddenly converted into assets. Granaries – which were less mud-built silos than vast installations, walled and guarded, like oil-storage depots – were strategically located along the canal. Big government-owned grain barges, hauled by manpower wherever sluice and current required, constituted the bulk of the water traffic; a burgeoning private trade in salt, fish, vegetables and manufactured goods made up the rest. Along the route, irrigation schemes fed off the canal to increase crop yields, so boosting population figures, tax yields and corvée numbers; and below the Yangzi in 'Nanjiang' (all 'south of the Yangzi River') more land was brought into cultivation courtesy of the canal, so accelerating the pace of the population drift from north to south. Great cities – the future Hangzhou, Suzhou, Zhenjiang, Yangzhou and Kaifeng – grew up along the towpath. Existing metropolises, such as Chang'an, to which *Sui* Wendi had constructed a short canal from the Yellow River, and Luoyang, which *Sui* Yangdi similarly integrated into his system, could now outgrow the alimentary limitations of their immediate hinterlands.

But the cost was colossal and the human suffering incalculable as corvée demands took their toll of agriculture. Millions, or rather 'tens of hundreds of thousands', are said to have dug the channels and distributed the spoil of *Sui* Yangdi's waterways, though whether such figures refer to the total labour force involved or the total number of corvée periods worked is unclear. They used spades and picks, plus wicker baskets balanced at either end of a pole to maximise carrying capacity and absorb jolts. Wheeled transport was provided more by barrows than ox-carts. The man-drawn wheelbarrow, a Chinese invention, had made its first appearance some time in the previous three centuries. By transferring the weight from the human frame to an axle, it more than quadrupled average loads. Men – and then women when the corvée pool began to dry up – graduated from being beasts of burden to serving as draught animals.

Ultimately it was all too much. The canal system could distribute only what the farmer could produce. But serious flooding of the Yellow River in 610/11 had reduced yields, while military requirements drained the labour pool and emptied the granaries. As the demand for manpower for both the army and public works raced ahead of supply, truancy increased and soon turned to popular revolt. Critics at court were ruthlessly silenced: powerful challengers began to mobilise within the provinces and the army. The final straw came when the last of three disastrous expeditions against Koguryo, a reluctant tributary state occupying much of Manchuria and northern Korea, was in 614 recalled in the face of minimal gains and escalating mutinies. Leaving the north in turmoil, in 616 Yangdi retired to the south. It had earlier been his adoptive homeland; now it became his last refuge. With Yangdi isolated from events as much by his tremulous courtiers as by distance, his megalomania subsided into melancholia. In 618, at his southern capital in what is now Yangzhou, he was murdered. The assassin was the son of one of his generals and a member of the once-purged Yuwen clan; but it could have been anyone.

According to the traditional histories, his fate was no less than he deserved. The sufferings *Sui* Yangdi had inflicted on his people had been intolerable and the strains he had imposed on the just-reunited empire unforgivable. Seldom had the Mandate been so obviously forfeited. Yet the products of so much distress would be acknowledged even by critics as an inestimable boon, 'enormous indeed' and 'monumental'. Better still, according to a writer of the later Tang period, they came at no cost to posterity. The canal, for instance, 'did not require a single [Tang] labourer to carry a basket of soil nor a single [Tang] soldier to hack through an obstruction'. 'Is it not true', concluded this observer with a smug flourish, 'that Heaven has greatly benefited us with the help of the despotic Sui?'[15] Such was the function, and such the fate, of an intercalary dynasty.

SONS OF THE SUNSET AND THE SUNRISE

As the just-reunited empire dissolved into chaos again, the chances of *Sui* Yangdi's successor inaugurating the most glorious era in the whole of China's history looked remote. The empire seemed to be relapsing into the anarchy of 400 years earlier, when the knights-errant of the emerging 'Three Kingdoms' had confronted the likes of 'Poison Yu' and 'Yang of the Eighty-foot Moustache'. Between 614 and 624 some two hundred mutinies and rebellions reportedly affected practically every province and army unit. More non-Chinese from beyond the frontier were enticed south as auxiliaries, allies and predators. The Chang'an bureaucracy ground to a halt – as bureaucracies do – when the supply of paper ran out. Meanwhile emperors galore were being proclaimed, some of them Sui minors, some supposed descendants of earlier dynasties, and some redemptionist hopefuls in the Yellow Turbans' tradition of Daoist millenarianism.

Many of the contenders were called Li, there being current at the time a catchy verse that credited someone of that name with an imperial destiny. The language seemed innocuous enough:

> Peach-plum Li
> Be reserved in speech.
> As a yellow heron, fly round the hill
> And turn about within the flower garden.

Yet in the context of the time, and to an audience attuned to the subtleties of poetic allusion, it was dynamite. 'As intended, the seditious character of this refrain emerges only on close examination,' explains a recent authority. The first two lines identify the subject as a certain Li, whose utterances give nothing away; the third line signifies Li's high-flying ambition in relation to 'yang' (literally 'the hill' but sounding like the emperor); and the fourth promises him the freedom of herbaceous precincts, presumably the empire. Whoever composed it – and it could have been *Sui* Yangdi himself in search of a pretext for eliminating some troublesome Li – 'it encouraged the idea of rebellion in any outstanding person of the Li name . . . [and] caused the emperor to suspect such a person'.[16]

Then, as now, Li was about the commonest name in China. A purge of all who bore it would have been a demographic disaster. Yangdi had had to content himself with executing only the more obvious candidates while sparing those of proven loyalty. Those spared included one of his most dependable commanders, the fifty-one-year-old Li Yuan, duke of Tang. Like the Northern Zhou and the Sui, to whom he was related by marriage,

Li Yuan was from the frontier region of northern Shanxi, of martial background and mixed ethnicity (though genealogists would later present him with the noblest of pedigrees going back to one of *Han* Wudi's generals and even Laozi). He belonged to the same horse-loving, conjugally loyal, open-minded and culturally eclectic social milieu as the Sui, and despite promptings from his own family, he continued to protest loyalty to the Sui until after Yangdi's departure for the south.

Sui rule succumbed spontaneously, a victim less of the assassin's sword or the rebel's challenge than of its own ambitions. Only in 617, when the emperor had practically retired and his empire was being torn apart by others, did Li Yuan endorse the Peach-plum prophecy about a Li succession, summon forces and supporters, enter the fray, and march on Chang'an. The city fell after a stout resistance. Li Yuan then went through the motions of installing one of Yangdi's sons as emperor, all the while resisting appeals that he assume the Mandate himself. Heaven, of course, was not to be denied. Heeding the portents and prognostications cited by his supporters, within a year Li Yuan had had himself installed as emperor and had named his dynasty after his dukedom of Tang. During the short reign that followed (618–26), most of which was devoted to quelling opposition, the first of the Tang reinstated all but the most recalcitrant of Sui generals and officials. He and his successor would then adopt, with only minor adjustments, the entire Sui fiscal, military, administrative and legal framework.

As the Tang founder, Li Yuan would come to be known by his posthumous title of *Tang* Gaozu ('Great Progenitor'), while his more illustrious son and successor is remembered by his temple-name of *Tang* Taizong ('Supreme Ancestor'). The dynastic emphasis was justified. The Tang would last, at a generous estimate, for nearly three centuries. But the empire that the Tang inherited had come ready made, albeit battered; like the stately boulevards of *Sui* Wendi's temple-studded Chang'an, or like *Sui* Yangdi's Luoyang palaces with their winged belvederes, or indeed the Grand Canal, it required only restoration. This called initially for patient campaigning and strict financial restraint, policies alien to the Sui. But once peace had been established and the economy resuscitated, *Tang* Taizong and his heirs would find themselves masters – and mistresses – of the most productive and effective empire in the world.

The wider world figures prominently in the history of the Tang. Contact with maritime Asia through the seaports of the south, which were now restored to the empire, was about to be complemented by throwing wide the western 'Jade Gate' into central Asia. Turkestan, Tibet and Persia, no less than Vietnam, Korea and Japan, would fall within the Tang perspective and loom large in imperial policy-making. Still farther afield in India and the Byzantine empire, the political, cultural and productive pre-eminence of Tang China gained widespread acceptance. Its tolerance of alien belief systems and its enthusiasm for foreign craftsmanship and performances brought a cosmopolitan dimension to urban life. Society savoured the exotic; artists showed a willingness to experiment. There was now substance to the conceit of 'All-under-Heaven' looking up to the Celestial Emperor. It was as if the world had so tilted on its axis as to leave the 'Middle Kingdom' at last in the middle. The period from *c.* 650 to *c.* 750 would be the first and most convincing 'China century'.

But this wider world beyond *zhongguo*'s traditional frontiers was not that into which explorer Zhang and the armies of Han had ventured eight centuries earlier, nor was it that from which had emerged the Tabgach Northern Wei and the forebears of the Northern Zhou and Sui. As adversaries, the Xiongnu, Xianbei, Qiang and others had faded from the records. Some of those so identified had been incorporated into the ethnic mix of north China; others had been absorbed by new confederations and kingdoms outside it.

Their place along the northern and north-western frontiers had been taken by peoples whom the Chinese histories call 'Tujue'. Turkic inscriptions of the eighth century in the Orkhon region of Mongolia support the identification of these 'Tujue' as Turks, although the inscriptions provide little help with the origins of the Turkic-speaking peoples. Like so many inner Asian peoples, their early trajectory remains 'wrapped in obscurity'.[17] Under the leadership of a qaghan (kakhan, khan), the equivalent of the Xiongnu *shanyu*, the Tujue/Turks had emerged rapidly in the mid-sixth century and at the expense of peoples who had previously replaced the Xiongnu and Xianbei.

By the 570s the Northern Zhou had been obliged to buy off the Turks with 100,000 silk pieces a year; in return Chang'an received horses of lesser value; both sides regarded the trade as tribute, though differing as to who was the tributary. In the standard history of the Sui, the Turks are described as their own worst enemies, 'preferring to destroy one another rather than live side by side'. Certainly a succession dispute in the 580s divided the Turk qaghanate into western and eastern branches. The former's authority extended beyond the Tian Shan into what is now Kazakhstan and the latter's throughout Mongolia and into western Manchuria. One contender for the qaghanate sought support, and then refuge, from *Sui* Wendi, who by dexterous intrigue promoted and exploited the divisions among the

Turkic clans. But it would be left to *Tang* Taizong to perfect this policy and reap the dividends.

In foreign relations, as in domestic policy, the Sui had emulated the Han. That meant establishing concentric rings of subordinate territories, allied dependants and tributary states that rippled to the horizons of the sinocentric world in all directions. *Sui* Wendi's conquest of the southern Chen dynasty had been followed by an expedition to re-establish Chinese authority in northern Vietnam. This succeeded in 602, though further expeditions down the Vietnamese panhandle to Champa, a Hindu-Buddhist kingdom located near Danang, amounted to little more than raids. 'All the Chinese had to show [for them] were the stolen ancestral tablets [of the Chams], some cases of Buddhist scripture, and a troupe of captured musicians.'[18] Thereafter Champa, along with its great rival, the proto-Khmer kingdom on the lower Mekong, would send and receive occasional missions which, though gratifying Chinese sensibilities, in no way prejudiced south-east Asian sovereignties.

Into the same wishful category fall Sui relations with the island world of the Yellow and East China Seas. *Sui* Yangdi is said to have launched two naval expeditions against somewhere called 'Liuqiu'; it could have been Taiwan/Formosa or possibly Luzon in the Philippines, but was probably the Ryukyu Islands. The first expedition was repelled and the second, though more successful, withdrew. Both ventures, being Yangdi's, are represented as ill conceived and ruinously expensive. Of 'Liuqiu' all that can be said for certain is that it was hot and sticky and that it was not Japan.

For from Japan, or from its self-styled 'Sunrise Son of Heaven', there had come to Chang'an in 607 a large embassy, plus monks, conveying congratulations on the efforts made by the 'Sunset Son of Heaven' to promote Buddhist precepts. *Sui* Yangdi heartily deplored all this fraternal terminology; at best it implied equality of status between Heaven's twin sons, at worst a dawn precedence for the Japanese emperor. But with a view to setting the record straight, the religio-diplomatic intercourse continued with more missions in both directions. Uniquely they are chronicled not only in Chinese sources but also in the *Nihon Shoki*, an eighth-century text that is Japan's first comprehensive history. The slant put on diplomatic protocol for the benefit of the 'Sunset Son' may thus be compared with that put on it for the the 'Sunrise Son' (actually a daughter, the Yamato ruler of the time being a lady emperor). Yangdi was reassured that the Yamato acknowledged Sui suzerainty, revered its Buddhist scholarship and emulated its culture. The Japanese, on the other hand, while conceding their need for further religious, literary and bureaucratic novelties, seem never to have accepted that their diplomatic presentations amounted to tribute or that their ruler was other than a counterpart of the Sui and Tang.

Official contacts between Japan and China would continue sporadically throughout the next two centuries. But they were conducted in the face of great difficulty. Nearly half of the traffic was lost at sea, and this despite the route usually involving a landward crossing of the Korean peninsula, so halving the sailing distance, and despite such Chinese maritime inventions as the magnetic compass, the sternpost rudder and watertight bulkheads. In 838, a Japanese mission would fare better on the high seas and would yield the first account of life and travel in China to be penned by a foreigner. But the mission would also prove to be 'the last to be dispatched abroad by the Imperial court of Japan until the nineteenth century'.[19] Though cultural, commercial and piratical contacts flourished, authority in Japan fell a prey to feudalism and its diplomacy slipped into a milliennium-long hibernation.

Korea served as both a conduit and an obstacle in this Sino-Japanese intercourse. The Sui and then the Tang generally kept on good terms with the southernmost Korean kingdom of Silla, whose mariners' intimate knowledge of the treacherous Tsushima strait was invaluable. But from the north Korean kingdom of Koguryo (whence derives the name 'Korea'), Chang'an failed dismally to win other than token acknowledgements of suzerainty. *Sui* Yangdi's three disastrous invasions had been preceded by an equally unrewarding intervention under *Sui* Wendi and they were followed by worse under the Tang.

Relations had briefly improved when the advent of the Tang coincided with a change of ruler in the Koguryo capital of Pyongyang. *Tang* Gaozu at the time was too busy pacifying the empire, and then *Tang* Taizong too busy with the Turks, to launch assaults in the north-east. But the temptation to upstage *Sui* Yangdi eventually proved too great. Buoyed by success elsewhere and ignoring the almost unanimous advice of his ministers, in 645 Taizong launched a massive assault across the Liao River supported by a naval attack from Shandong. Unusually the emperor led his forces in person, such was the importance he attached to the campaign. Not unusually, 'the whole expedition ended in disaster'.[20] The imperial forces got bogged down trying to reduce the fortified cities of Liaodong and were then overtaken by the Manchurian winter. They scarcely entered the Korean peninsula.

Taizong tried again in 647, but with little success; and he planned yet

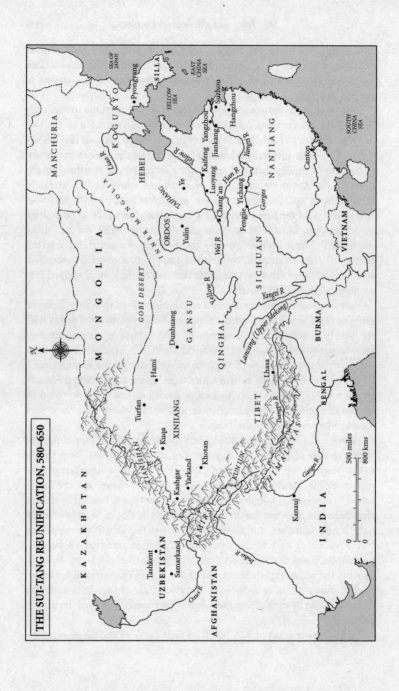

THE SUI-TANG REUNIFICATION, 580–650

a third invasion that was cancelled on his deathbed in 649. Not until twenty years later would Tang troops finally enter Pyongyang and complete the reassembly of the Former Han's territorial behemoth by appending its Korean tail. But the triumph would be short-lived; and in the eyes of the annalists, it would be vitiated by its being less that of Taizong's successor than of the latter's formidable consort, the Empress Wu.

BEYOND THE JADE GATE

Born in 599, the great *Tang* Taizong, constructor if not architect of the Tang empire, belonged to a generation of Asian empire-builders. From the Tsangpo basin of southern Tibet, Srong-brtsan-sgam-po, his exact contemporary, was masterminding the first unification of the scattered peoples of Asia's high plateau to lay the foundations of a formidable Tibetan empire. Across the Himalayas in the Gangetic plain, Harsha-vardhana of Kanauj was performing a similar feat in establishing his imperial sway over the Hindu-Buddhist kingdoms of north India. Simultaneously the Sassanid ruler Chosroes (Khosrau) II was overrunning the Levant and Asia Minor to recreate a Persian empire that stretched from Xinjiang to Egypt. And in the far south-west, along the caravan routes of Arabia, another contemporary took rejection in Mecca as cause for flight (*hegira* or *hijra*) to Medina, where, acknowledged as the Prophet, he found a following and launched a crescentade that in less than a century would obliterate the Sassanids and buffet the frontiers of both India and China.

Asia was being reconfigured. For anyone keen on amateur exploration or individual travel it was a difficult time. The fast-changing scene could frustrate departure, impede progress and provide a homecoming full of surprises. So it was for Xuanzang, an exact contemporary of *Tang* Taizong, who in 622 – the year of the Prophet's flight from Mecca – set off for Chang'an as a just-ordained Buddhist monk. There, like Muhammad in Medina, Xuanzang felt the call to action. He must go, as he put it, 'in

THE SUI / TANG SUCCESSION, 580–650

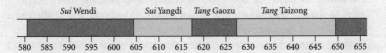

Sui Wendi					*Sui* Yangdi	*Tang* Gaozu		*Tang* Taizong				

580   585   590   595   600   605   610   615   620   625   630   635   640   645   650   655

search of the truth', 'to seek the Law'. Though he was the product of a Confucian upbringing, Xuanzang's conspicuous Buddhist devotion was rivalled only by his passion for Buddhist scholarship. Both could best be served by undertaking a journey of pilgrimage-cum-research to the Buddhist 'Holy Land' of India.

There was nothing new in this. Religious traffic along the Silk Road had been two-way since at least the fourth century. In the early fifth another Chinese monk, Faxian, had gone west overland and returned home by sea. He had then written a brief account of his travels. Monk Xuanzang had read it and noted the horrors of the sea voyage: the ship had been blown off course, there had been weeks without drinking-water, and Faxian had narrowly escaped being sacrificed by his superstitious shipmates. Xuanzang opted for the overland route. But this too posed problems. With the Turks pressing from the north and the Sassanids from the south-west, anyone attempting to squeeze between them by one of the silk-and-sutra routes through Xinjiang could no longer count on the residual loyalty to Chang'an of the oasis-states. All were now under some form of duress or obligation, mostly to the Turks.

To complicate matters further, *Tang* Taizong's web of intrigues and incentives designed to exploit divisions within the leadership of the Turks was at a delicate stage. Neither the Sui nor the Tang had enjoyed much success in their efforts to control the Eastern Turks on their northern frontier. *Sui* Yangdi had been surrounded and nearly captured by them during a northern excursion in 614, a disgrace that would be overshadowed only by his defeats in Koguryo. Li Yuan (before becoming *Tang* Gaozu), in return for their neutrality and some support in his march on Chang'an in 617, had been obliged to employ language that effectively declared him a vassal of the eastern qaghan. And *Tang* Taizong, in the early days of his own reign, had been similarly humiliated when, having deposed his father and killed two of his brothers, he had had to buy off a Turk army of retribution within a day's march of Chang'an.

In the 620s, while Taizong schemed, monk Xuanzang waited and prayed, all the while adding to his reputation as the foremost exegetist of his age. Then in 628 the eastern Turk qaghanate, assailed from without by other Turkic peoples and from within by famine, was reported on the verge of collapse. Throwing caution to the winds, Taizong abandoned appeasement for active intervention; new candidates for the qaghanate were encouraged to declare themselves, and a Tang army of 100,000 was readied to march. It was now or, very possibly, never for Xuanzang's great design. Defying an imperial embargo on non-essential foreign travel, the monk slipped out of Gaozhou in Gansu and, with an old horse and a crazed guide, headed west for the frontier and Xinjiang.

His horse died, the guide tried to murder him, a warrant was issued for his arrest, and, becoming lost in the desert, he spilled his water-sack and would have perished but for a Bodhisattva's intervention. This all happened before Xuanzang had reached Dunhuang and the Jade Gate frontier. Thereafter, when things should have got worse, they improved. His unshakeable faith in supernatural protection was not misplaced; word of his distinction invariably preceded him, and his credentials as the devoutest of Buddhist scholars proved more valuable than any official documentation. Thus the ruler of Turfan (Turpan), a vassal of the Western Turks who was particularly anxious to add such a luminary to his court, undertook to provide the transport and funds necessary to secure the monk's safe return.

Rewarding detours and miraculous interventions, no less than mishaps and encounters with monsters, would ever be the pilgrim's lot. Xuanzang's peregrinations across northern Xinjiang, through the Tian Shan to Tashkent and Samarkand, and then south to the Oxus (Amu Darya), Afghanistan and India, were only the beginning. He was gone for sixteen years, some of them passed in study at the great centres of Buddhism, most of them on the road. In all he covered a distance of perhaps 15,000 kilometres (9,320 miles), half of it during extensive wanderings in the Indian subcontinent that took him as far south as Tamil Nadu. He learnt new languages, explored new doctrines, won countless debates, went everywhere, met everyone, and kept a detailed record of it all. The qaghan of the Western Turks took a liking to him, the king of Samarkand let him conduct an ordination, and Emperor Harsha-vardhana became one of his keenest supporters. Indeed, most of what is known of Harsha and his empire, and of India in the seventh century, derives from Xuanzang's *Record of the Western Regions*.

Well before any foreign traveller had explored Chinese culture, a Chinese scholar had explored a foreign culture. The repercussions would be surprising. In the mid-nineteenth century, armed with a French translation of Xuanzang's itinerary (the first to appear in any European language), Alexander Cunningham, a Scots general in British India, devoted his retirement to rediscovering the long-forgotten sites associated with the Buddha's life and early Buddhism; from this exercise there grew the Archaeological Survey of India, whose responsibilities now probably exceed those of any other heritage body and of which Cunningham was both founder and director. Half a century later it was the memory of Xuanzang as invoked by Aurel Stein, another archaeological traveller, which would be the key to gaining access to the treasures of Dunhuang. Stein's claim to be retracing the monk's footsteps would so impress Dunhuang's local curator that he was persuaded to reveal the greatest trove of Buddhist texts and paintings ever discovered. Arguably no book played a greater part than Xuanzang's in relaying to an international posterity the achievements of early Buddhism.

In China the impact of Xuanzang's travels would take a different turn. This was partly due to his own success but more substantially to *Tang* Taizong's. Having left a fugitive in 629, Xuanzang returned a hero in 645. At the head of a caravan laden with over five hundred trunks of statuary and texts, bearing letters of congratulation from numerous Asian potentates, with a hundred monks in tow and minus only the elephant provided by Harsha (it had fallen off a precipice), Xuanzang led home something more like a tribute mission. Not even Stein and his rivals for the wealth of Dunhuang would secure a greater archival haul. Choosing a southern variant of the Silk Road through the Pamirs, the pilgrim formally announced his approach to the emperor and, receiving a favourable reply, continued east along the skirts of the Kun Lun.

No less encouraging was the warm reception received at the oasis-states of western Xinjiang. It was as if the empire were stretching out to greet him – and in a sense it was. During the monk's sixteen-year absence, *Tang* Taizong had not only triumphed over the Eastern Turks, but with his northern border secure had then directed the same mix of intrigue and force at the Western Turks. Shule (Kashgar), Yutian (Khotan) and Suche (Yarkand), all cities on Xuanzang's return route through Xinjiang, had submitted to Tang suzerainty during the 630s; and the northern states, including Kuqa and Turfan, were even now (645) being either annexed or bullied into submission – which was doubtless why Xuanzang preferred the southern route. Victorious at last over the Turks, the Son of Heaven *Tang* Taizong now bore the added title of 'Heavenly Qaghan'. In effect, he had restored the elephantine proportions of the Han empire in respect of its long western proboscis. Only with the Korean tail would he fail.

Though Xuanzang's *Record* stops short of his re-entry into Chang'an, it was evidently a triumphant affair. Painted silk scrolls and wall frescoes from Dunhuang depict the event. Though the emperor was absent, commanding his first assault on Koguryo, on his return he forgave the traveller his original disobedience and insisted on his writing an account of his wanderings. He also tried to persuade him to accept office as an expert on foreign relations. Xuanzang declined. But his journey was not without diplomatic repercussions.

Harsha-vardhana of India had earlier sent emissaries to Chang'an and in 643, around the time of Xuanzang's departure from India, a Tang mission under a military official called Wang Xuance had repaid the compliment. Five years later, in 648, Wang Xuance was back in India at the head of a more impressive embassy that was doubtless influenced by Xuanzang's reports on Harsha. But this time ambassador Wang Xuance received a very different reception. Harsha had died the previous year, his empire was already crumbling, and a Brahminical reaction had set in against the Buddhist community. Evidently Xuanzang's long sojourn and his influence on Harsha had encouraged the idea that Chinese support was enabling Indian Buddhists to subvert the political primacy claimed by India's priestly caste. Wang Xuance's 648 mission was therefore waylaid. Its valuables were stolen, its personnel detained and Wang Xuance himself barely escaped with his life. He withdrew to Tibet.

There he took advantage of a rare moment of amity in Sino-Tibetan relations. In the 630s the great Srong-brtsan-sgam-po had been engaged in sporadic warfare with Tang forces in both Sichuan and Qinghai. Unusually the Tibetans fought not to keep the Chinese out of Tibet but to secure closer relations with them, or rather to secure parity of treatment with that extended by Chang'an to their local rivals. These were the Tuyuhun, a Xianbei clan established in Qinghai between Gansu and Srong-brtsan-sgam-po's swelling territories. The Tuyuhun eventually forfeited their favoured status; they were first incorporated into the Tang empire and then, in 667, into the Tibetan. Meanwhile the Tibetans had renewed their solicitations to Chang'an, and in 641, with a view to ending their raids, *Tang* Taizong had granted the Tibetans what was in effect a 'peace-through-kinship' treaty. It was sealed as usual with the dispatch of an imperial princess. Further exchanges followed, the Tibetans regarding them as evidence of Tang vassalage and the Tang as evidence of Tibetan vassalage.[21]

Into this happy state of mutual misunderstanding straggled Wang Xuance on his way back from his rebuff in India. The rout of an embassy from the Son of Heaven, not to mention the Heavenly Qaghan, could not go unavenged. Wang Xuance demanded troops for a retaliatory attack on India and the Tibetans obliged. It was thus a joint Sino-Tibetan force that in 649, probably by way of the Chumbi pass between Sikkim and Nepal, crossed the Great Himalaya and inflicted a heavy defeat on Harsha's successors. 'Thereupon', says the standard Tang history, 'India was overawed.' Elsewhere it is recorded that Wang Xuance brought back as a prisoner to Chang'an the man who had supposedly usurped Harsha's throne. A statue of 'this contumacious Indian' was erected among the many in front of

Tang Taizong's tomb and 'so [the Indian] found lasting fame – but as a trophy and an emblem'.[22] Needless to say, Indian tradition is blissfully ignorant of all this. The Sino-Tibetan incursion probably affected only a corner of Bengal and had no known repercussions. Though a Chinese assault on Indian territory had been shown to be feasible, it would not be repeated until the 1960s.

In the same year as this obscure affair (649), both *Tang* Taizong and Srong-brtsan-sgam-po died. Monk Xuanzang was still alive – he lived till 664 – but took no account of the Indian incursion. He was otherwise engaged. Instead of imperial office, he had asked for a monastic base where he could devote the rest of his life to translating and expounding his textual hoard. He asked that it be built of stone like the monasteries of India, but this proved difficult. Brick was seen as a compromise and, though much restored, the monastery's brick-built 'Great Pagoda of the Wild Goose' still stands in what is now Xi'an. Its proportions, if not its size, are reminiscent of the pyramidal tower of the great temple at Boddh Gaya that marks the spot of the Buddha's enlightenment.

During his final years, Xuanzang remained in imperial favour. *Tang* Taizong, whose reign had been marked by indifference to Buddhism, is supposed to have adopted Xuanzang as his spiritual adviser; he may even have undergone some form of deathbed conversion. His successor, *Tang* Gaozong (r. 649–83), declared Xuanzang 'the jewel of the empire' and continued to support his work with generous endowments. The results were almost as important as his journey. 'In his influence on later Buddhist thought, Xuanzang is second only to Kumarajiva; he translated more Buddhist scriptures than anyone else ... [and] produced over seventy-three works, totalling more than a thousand scrolls,' writes a latter-day admirer. The emperor himself penned a foreword to Xuanzang's treatise on yogic practices. His works on Buddhist logic and epistemology added a new dimension to the intellectual life of China.[23]

Yet for none of these is Xuanzang best remembered in China today. Rather is he known almost exclusively in connection with a novel. The novel is called *The Journey to the West* (or sometimes *Monkey* or *The Monkey King*); and a clearly recognisable Xuanzang actually features in it. Written in the sixteenth century but incorporating a variety of earlier narratives, it is a work not just of fiction but of the wildest fantasy, of fable and allegory, humour, tragedy, spectacular nonsense and such profundity that no two commentators can agree about it. *Tang* Taizong features in it too (he visits the Underworld), as do many other historical figures, including the Buddha. But by Chapter 13, with eighty-seven to follow, the celebrities make way for a small band of human and animal wayfarers. Among them, the eponymous monkey Sun Wugong is prominent and is thought somehow to be related to the monkey-god Hanuman in the Indian *Ramayana*. 'Courage and prowess in battle, ability to fly, and the tendency to attack their enemies through their bellies' have been noted as characteristics common to both.[24]

Some readers have interpreted the book, which freely incorporates Confucian, Daoist and Buddhist concepts, as an allegory on the convergence of these 'three schools' of learning. Others, especially Marxists, have read the wayfarers' endless encounters with gods and monsters as evidence of class struggle and the triumph of the proletariat. The martial as well as the magical arts are well represented, providing scope for illustrators, a challenge to film-makers and a gift to animators. Today, as ever, this comic derivative from Xuanzang's often taxing *Record of the Western Regions* remains perhaps the best-loved work in all Chinese fiction. It is as if, confronted by a wider world beyond its comprehension, the pre-modern mind sought reassurance in exaggeration and fictionalisation. Europeans would do the same. The mysterious John de Mandeville would peddle exotic nonsense that was acceptable as travel literature; and Marco Polo would peddle facts so apparently 'outlandish' they were taken as fiction.

9

HIGH TANG
650–755

THOUGH EMPERORS WERE NEITHER SUBJECT TO any form of law nor accountable to anything in the nature of a representative body, they were not therefore beyond all restraint. The Mandate might be forfeited if they abused it; more immediately, ministers could offer objections and criticism. 'If it is not right, remonstrate,' Confucius had told one of his office-seeking disciples. In the Confucian scheme of things, strict obedience to one's betters by no means precluded constructive protest. On the contrary, confronted by injustice, 'the son cannot but remonstrate with his father', said the Master, 'and the minister cannot but remonstrate with his prince'. [1]

The exercise of absolute power being peculiarly liable to abuse, Confucian tradition required ministers and advisers to be vigilant and to give voice to their misgivings, albeit in allusive language larded with respectful sentiments and laced with historical references. It was not just their right to do so but their moral duty. Serving the emperor meant dissuading him from conduct that might alienate his subjects or otherwise jeopardise his enjoyment of the Mandate. Corrective advice was thus a moral obligation enshrined in the responsibilities of office. Whatever the risks – and they could be fatal – those charged with the role of remonstrance were expected to exercise it. And just as fearless reproof distinguished the greatest ministers, so a receptive disposition was the mark of a truly great emperor.

Tang Taizong's thirty-two-year reign was notable for the establishment of one of the empire's longest-lasting dynasties and for a dramatic extension of its frontiers, but no less important – in fact the clearest evidence of the moral rectitude that made these achievements possible – was the forbearance initially shown by the emperor towards his badgering

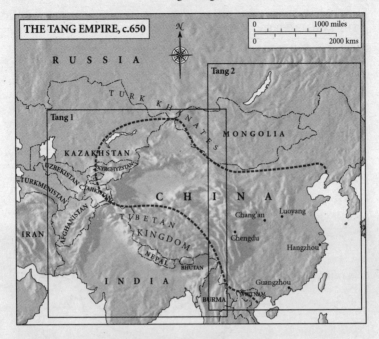

THE TANG EMPIRE, c.650

ministers. Of these, not the most powerful but certainly the most persistent was a cantankerous old office-holder with a chequered history called Wei Zheng. Twenty years the emperor's senior, abstemious, humourless, ultra-cautious, partially blind and infuriatingly doctrinaire, Wei Zheng typified the Confucian bureaucrat. In an age more notable for entrenched privilege, he represented the ideal of high moral and intellectual worth triumphing over hereditary influence; and as such, as a beacon of rectitude, a barrier to indulgence, a stickler for etiquette, and the doughtiest of remonstrants, he would become a model to future generations.

After Wei Zheng's death in 643, the emperor revered him as 'a sturdy bamboo touched by frost', the reference being to his crusty temperament as much as his age. In *Monkey*, the sixteenth-century novel based on Xuanzang's travels, Wei Zheng is portrayed as a vigilant martinet who gets to guard the door of Taizong's bedchamber. Indeed, his effigy is said to play this role still at the entrances to some Taiwanese temples.[2] But in the People's Republic of China there would be no place for a figure so closely associated with legitimate protest. Ostensibly for republishing a standard eleventh-century biography of Wei Zheng, in 1966 Lu Dingyi, the then

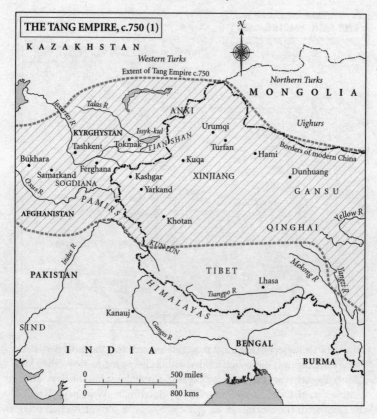

THE TANG EMPIRE, c.750 (1)

minister of culture, member of the Communist Party's Central Committee and director of its Propaganda Department, was disgraced and removed from office. 'It is now clear', intoned the *People's Daily*, 'that Lu Dingyi's concoction "The Biography of Wei Zheng" was a poisonous shaft directed at Chairman Mao, the red sun in our hearts; it was a manifesto for stirring up a counter-revolutionary restoration.'[3] According to the newspaper, the relationship between Wei Zheng and *Tang* Taizong had been a sham; both ruthlessly exploited the peasants; they differed only as to the means; their altercations were therefore irrelevant, and publicising them could only be mischievous.

This was a bit unfair on Wei Zheng, who had often cited the welfare of the people when endeavouring to restrain his headstrong emperor. But

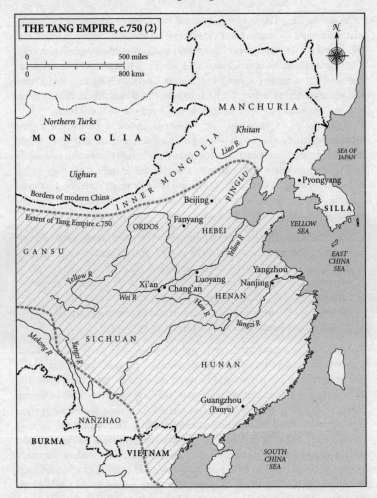

THE TANG EMPIRE, c.750 (2)

N

0 — 500 miles
0 — 800 kms

MANCHURIA

Northern Turks

MONGOLIA

Khitan

Uighurs

Liao R

INNER MONGOLIA

Borders of modern China

PINGLU

Beijing

Pyongyang

SEA OF JAPAN

SILLA

Extent of Tang Empire c.750

ORDOS

Fanyang

HEBEI

Yellow R

YELLOW SEA

GANSU

Yellow R

Xi'an

Chang'an

Wei R

Luoyang

Han R

HENAN

Yangzhou

Nanjing

EAST CHINA SEA

Yangzi R

SICHUAN

Mekong R

Yangzi R

HUNAN

NANZHAO

Guangzhou
(Panyu)

BURMA

VIETNAM

SOUTH CHINA SEA

such niceties went unnoticed in the Great Proletarian Cultural Revolution. The perils that attended the reissue of an eleventh-century text typified the constraints under which historical scholarship in the twentieth century long laboured. Criticism, admonition and reproof, though obligatory in a minister of the emperor's 'feudal regime', could be revisionist heresy in a minister of the People's Republic.

In reality *Tang* Taizong often ignored Wei Zheng's criticisms. He particularly resented the bureaucrat's insistence on frugality, fiscal restraint and the avoidance of war; *wuwei* ('inaction') was not in his nature. Their relationship eventually deteriorated and in the late 630s, as the emperor assumed the offensive against the Eastern Turks in Xinjiang, Wei Zheng lost some of his influence. Yet he kept his official rank, most of his offices and the emperor's avowed esteem. It was a tribute to them both.

It also helps explain why *Tang* Taizong, despite deposing his father, murdering his brothers and waging a disastrous war on Koguryo, would receive highly favourable treatment from Wei Zheng's Confucian colleagues and successors when they came to compile the Standard History of his reign. According to one of them, *Tang* Taizong's reign rated as a halcyon age. His subjects basked amid plenty in as peaceful a realm as the conventional hyperbole reserved for such eulogies could depict.

> Merchants travelling in the wilderness were never again robbed by bandits. The prisons were usually empty. Horses and cows roamed the open country. Gates went unlocked. Repeatedly there were abundant harvests and the price of grain fell to three or four copper cash per peck. Travelling [even to the extremities of the country] . . . no one had to carry provisions but could obtain them on the way . . . There has been nothing like this since antiquity.[4]

Nor was this generous assessment without substance. *Tang* Taizong faced less opposition and therefore had less need of prisons than either of the Sui emperors or his father; and harvests do seem to have been plentiful. The granaries filled, famine relief was available, and destitution-driven banditry declined, making travel less hazardous. While the economy was recovering, labour-intensive projects were shelved. Like *Sui* Wendi, Taizong pruned back the root and branch of the administration, reorganised the provinces and took special care in the selection of office-holders; for ready reference, he claimed to have had the names and records of all candidates for office painted on sheets of paper that were pasted to the walls of his chambers, like Post-its. He reorganised the *fubing* militias, embarked on a new legal codification that was again supposed to be more lenient and rational than its predecessors, and endeavoured to curb the social influence exercised by a coterie of powerful clans whose pedigrees eclipsed that of the Tang's Li clan.

Acutely conscious of his place in history as well as society, he also turned his attention to the historiographical process. Over the previous centuries of the 'Period of Disunion', dynasties had come and gone so quickly that the work of compiling Standard Histories for each had fallen behind. To eliminate this backlog, Taizong set up the first Bureau of Historiography with Wei Zheng as one of those at the helm. Dynastic histories – of the Northern Qi, Northern Zhou and Sui, and of the Jin, Liang and Chen from the Six (southern) Dynasties – were soon pouring from the bureau's massed brushes. Earlier works, such as the *Shiji* and the *Hanshu*, had been compiled privately by individuals or families who had received imperial endorsement only in the course of compilation or afterwards. But the new bureau made history-writing an official and ongoing undertaking. Culled from whatever records were available, cross-checked and counter-checked, the work became more formulaic and, as is the way with collaborative endeavours, less revealing.

Simultaneously, the bureau began the collection and editing of materials that could be used as a basis for the history of the Tang. Again the procedure was carefully regulated, with court circulars and reports being distilled into yearly calendars, the calendars into the reign-by-reign 'veritable records', and the veritable records into the dynasty's 'Standard History'. Theoretically the emperor had no say in the process; objectivity was supposedly paramount. Yet, over the howls of bureaucratic protest, Taizong demanded sight of early drafts and, confounding precedent, bullied his scribes into rewriting the murky events surrounding his accession.

Whether the favourable gloss put on the rest of his reign owes anything to imperial interference is less clear. Extrapolating from the Standard Histories, one twentieth-century admirer would be moved to describe *Tang* Taizong as 'the man of destiny to whom no task seemed impossible, the saviour of society, the restorer of unity and peace' whose personality was 'so dynamic . . . that he became a legend with posterity [and] has had no equal on the throne of China'.[5] Taizong would have settled for this; but he can scarcely have formulated it. The Standard History of his reign was not completed until seven years after his death and that of his dynasty not till very much later. Other reasons prompted the Bureau of Historiography to portray him as a towering figure, most notably the need to diminish the stature of his de facto successor.

Designating *Tang* Taizong's successor had run into trouble in the 630s when the bureaucratic establishment had been scandalised by his eldest son and presumed heir rejecting Han etiquette and adopting the ways of his steppe ancestors. The young prince cast aside his girdled gown and clogs in favour of the nomad's tunic and boots, would speak (and be spoken to) only in a Turkic dialect, and took to living in a tent, cooking on a campfire and 'slicing himself gobbets of boiled mutton with a sword'.[6]

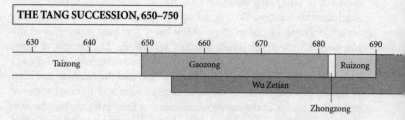

No doubt the details were much exaggerated, but it would seem that the heir apparent disdained scholarship, hankered after the outdoor life and took his succession to the Heavenly Qaghanate more seriously than his succession to the Heavenly Mandate.

The situation erupted in 643 when the emperor had some of the prince's less savoury companions executed. Other sons were then emboldened to enter the fray, and in a series of doubtful plots and counter-plots, the heir apparent was accused of planning fratricide. He was banished to Guizhou, where he died. An alternative candidate was also driven into exile; apparently he was rather too confident a scholar and so less likely to be amenable to remonstrating ministers. The succession was then settled on the ninth of Taizong's fourteen sons, a compromise candidate who was young enough to be malleable and delicate enough to encourage doubts about his permanence. And there it remained, not without further challenges, nor deep misgivings on the part of Taizong, until the emperor's death and the elevation of this unlikely contender as *Tang* Gaozong (r. 649–83).

Tang Gaozong reigned without much impact or conviction. For a weakling who soon became an invalid, his thirty-four-year occupation of the throne was an achievement in itself. He was followed by his sons, Zhongzong and Ruizong, both of whom were enthroned twice, though never for long; their comings and goings are of merely chronological interest and their influence was even less than their father's. For throughout the half-century from 655 till 705 real power resided elsewhere, in fact in the capable if bloodstained hands of one who might have ranked among China's most outstanding rulers but for the handicap of gender. This was Wu Zetian, the consort of Gaozong, mother of Zhongzong and Ruizong, and so empress, dowager empress and then, uniquely, for fifteen years (690–705) emperor (*sic*) in her own right.

In truth, more than her sex told against Wu Zetian. Being preceded by the revered *Tang* Taizong would have put any ruler at a disadvantage.

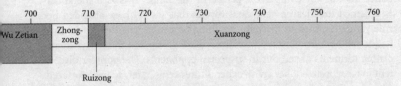

Wu Zetian | Zhong-zong | Xuanzong

Ruizong

Preserving his record of internal peace, maintaining his vastly increased empire and matching his example of responsive government were formidable challenges. Worse still for Wu Zetian's prospects of posthumous applause, she would be followed – after Zhongzong and Ruizong had made their second curtain calls – by *Tang* Xuanzong, the dynasty's *roi soleil*. Another colossus whose long and mostly glorious reign (715–56) would gild the heights of Tang civilisation, Xuanzong (not to be confused with the pilgrim Xuanzang) would set a dazzling example of humane government, exit the throne as a romantic hero, and be remembered as that rarity among China's rulers, a popular emperor.

Sandwiched between a legendary paragon and a national treasure, a third contender for best-ever emperor would have been an embarrassment. In comparison with such giants, even a legitimately chosen, Heaven-favoured and decently whiskered descendant of Li Yuan (*Tang* Gaozu) would have struggled for historical recognition. Indeed *Tang* Gaozong's pitiful showing rather proves the point. But Wu Zetian (or Wu Zhao, as she started off in life) enjoyed none of these advantages. As a usurper who eliminated more people called Li (in this case Tang family members) than had *Sui* Yangdi in response to the Peach-plum prophecy, she could expect no favours from compilers of the Tang dynastic histories. As a woman, a member of that half of humanity relegated to domestic subservience by Confucian orthodoxy and deeply distrusted by every history-conscious bureaucrat, she could count on neither contemporary support nor posterity's sympathy. And as one who not only manipulated the succession but commandeered the throne and ruled in the most arbitrary and unreceptive of fashions, she was simply beyond the pale of dispassionate scholarship.

The result is a career chronicled exclusively by detractors. With policies excoriated and every disaster magnified, this could still be revealing. But in fact the histories credit the empress with little more than a catalogue of atrocities, scandalous liaisons and diabolical intrigues. 'From the very first the historical record of her reign has been hostile, biased and curiously fragmentary and incomplete,' note the contributors to *The Cambridge History of China*. 'Less is known of her half century of dominance than of any comparable period of the Tang.'[7] It is as if the annalists, denied the Heaven-sent catastrophes that should have attended her rule yet determined to discredit anything of a more positive nature, had had to fall back on personal invective, palace gossip and the always excruciating torments meted out to suspected opponents. The popular discontent to be expected of her lavish expenditure seems barely to have surfaced. Tang loyalists failed to muster other than a spluttering and ineffective resistance. For those bureaucrats who were eliminated or declined to serve, others just as capable were found. And external foes seeking to take advantage of a supposedly gender-impaired empire would be bitterly disappointed.

That Wu Zetian nursed ambitions and skills beyond the ordinary was conceded even by her detractors. *Tang* Taizong had taken her into his household as a thirteen-year-old concubine of junior rank, probably to honour her deceased father, who had been ennobled by *Tang* Gaozu. Her mother, a devout Buddhist, was related to the Sui but commanded no great following. She herself is said to have been 'beautiful and enticing'.[8] Whether or not Taizong was enticed, the future *Tang* Gaozong was. Their teenage affair may have begun before Taizong's death and certainly blossomed soon after it, for by 654 she had given birth to at least one son by the now *Tang* Gaozong. Either way, because of her original selection by Taizong, their relationship counted as incest, a crime that Taizong's legal code had reinstated as one of 'the Ten Abominations'. Moreover Gaozong already had an empress, albeit without issue.

But obstacles that would have thwarted most power-seeking maids were as nothing to the ingenious and unscrupulous Wu Zhao. In 654, having given birth to a daughter, she is said to have encouraged Gaozong's Empress Wang to play with the baby, and then, having suffocated it, to have convinced Gaozong that the empress, as the last in attendance, must be the murderess. Such, at least, is the explanation offered for the demotion and detention of Empress Wang and for the wholesale purge of all who had supported her, including many of the most respected ministers inherited from *Tang* Taizong's reign. Within a year Wu Zhao herself was installed as empress with the title Wu Zetian and with her son as heir apparent. *Tang* Gaozong, possibly fooled but quite likely complicit, seems to have rejoiced in the outcome; the old guard of senior bureaucrats had been removed and replaced by more amenable and less well-connected figures who owed their positions entirely to the new dispensation.

More accurately, it was the new empress's dispensation; and perhaps to ensure against any backsliding among her supporters, she reportedly consummated her coup by having the ex-empress surgically dismembered limb by limb and then drowned in a vat of wine. This revolting procedure would be more credible were it not for the fate, 850 years earlier, of Lady Chi, alias the 'human pig'. Falling foul of the Empress Lü – she being the lifetime consort and effective successor of *Han* Gaozu ('Great Progenitor' of the Han dynasty) – this Lady Chi, according to the *Shiji*, had also been disjointed, her limbless torso being left to rootle to death in a dung-heap. Quite aside from whether dismemberment would not in itself have been fatal, the resemblance between the two cases prompts suspicion. Possibly empresses bent on revenge looked to precedent for inspiration; more probably historians bent on traducing them lacked imagination.

Comparisons with the Empress Lü were drawn throughout Wu Zetian's life and would give rise to much subsequent moralising on the venomous character of female rulers. C. P. Fitzgerald, Wu's English biographer, cites a saying that might be loosely rendered as:

> Wayward, not wanton, was Empress Lü;
> Wanton, not wayward, the Empress Wu.[9]

Lü, in other words, had been erratic and disorderly though not particularly promiscuous; Wu was capable and efficient but insatiably promiscuous. Her ability was actually conceded in what could have been a slip of the pen by one of the Tang histories: 'She was perspicacious, and rapid and sure in decision. Therefore all the brave and eminent of the epoch were glad to serve her and found opportunity to do so.'[10] Repeatedly she outwitted opponents, stymied rebellion, defended and extended the frontiers, and launched grand dynastic initiatives. Gaozong, the emperor, while he lasted, 'sat with folded hands', says Sima Guang; it was she who exercised supreme power; 'promotion or demotion, life or death, were settled by her word'.[11]

Needing all the legitimacy she could muster, she was drawn to the revival of the ultra-orthodox practices and terminology of the Zhou, much like Wang Mang; and to mark her assumption of the emperorship in 690 she would actually adopt the dynastic name of Zhou, like Yuwen Tai of the Northern Zhou. Luoyang, the Zhou eastern capital, was reconstituted as the Tang eastern capital, and at great expense the court and most of the administration shuttled to and fro from Chang'an. In 666 she accompanied Gaozong to Shandong, where, for the first time since

Han Guang Wudi in AD 56, the emperor appraised Heaven of the dynasty's achievements by performing the great ritual sacrifices at Mount Tai. Not to appear a mere onlooker, Wu Zetian devised a parallel ceremony involving the imperial womenfolk. She evidently took her feminist responsibilities seriously. A ceiling was imposed on the value of marriage dowries, the mourning period for deceased mothers was made the same as that for deceased fathers, and among her various literary commissions was a collection of biographies of eminent women. Latterly her daughter (the Taiping Princess) and an eminent lady scholar (Shangguan Wan'er) would constitute something of a petticoat government.

Reigns of terror, during which informants were rewarded and the innocent convicted, were more than matched by amnesties, remissions and grand proclamations promising economies and tax cuts. Remonstrators were invited to remonstrate; the kangaroo courts were quickly dismantled. To Tang historians these were just amateurish attempts to curry favour; but to Marxists they would appear humane, even revolutionary, concessions; and since they seem to have served their conciliatory purpose, they may at least be considered statesman-like.

In reconciling all sections of society to the novelty of her rule, no ideological stone was left unturned. Besides wooing Confucian opinion, Wu Zetian dallied with Daoist sages and showered the Buddhist *sangha* with favours. How much of this ecumenism was dictated by statecraft, how much by devotional caprice and how much by sexual convenience is unclear. Her Daoist phase does seem to have dovetailed with the ascendancy at court of a potent Daoist practitioner, while her Buddhist fervour peaked during a long and passionate liaison with an abbot. He was originally a cosmetics salesman who, for easy access to the female quarters of the palace, had taken vows, none of which he kept. Outside his duties in the empress's apartments, he distinguished himself by discovering a text that was interpreted as foretelling the advent in China of a female Maitreya, the Future Buddha. The empress was delighted – it could only refer to her – and adopted 'Peerless Maitreya' as one of her titles. She was less delighted by the abbot's monks running riot in Luoyang and by his presumption and all-consuming jealousy. In 695 he apparently took leave of his senses and burned down the empress's newly built Mingtang (a colossal ceremonial hall). Days later, he was found murdered. Liabilities, like enemies, could expect no mercy from Wu Zetian.

'With his death, the attitude of the empress towards Buddhism seems to have changed,' notes Richard Guisso in *The Cambridge History of China*.[12] So did her attitude towards the succession. In 697 she abandoned the pretence of founding her own Zhou dynasty and recalled *Tang* Zhongzong (one of her bit-part sons by *Tang* Gaozong) as heir apparent. The risk of her reputation being relegated to an intercalary dynasty was eliminated, and a Tang restoration looked certain. But it was not this which finally undermined the authority of the now eighty-something empress, rather a deadly mix of vanity and senescence. The sources insist that she was well preserved for her age and that a heavy dependence on aphrodisiacs had resulted in her sprouting fashionably bushy eyebrows and a fine new set of teeth. These doubtful achievements are offered by way of explanation for her welcoming into her confidence, and very possibly her bed (for by now she rarely left it), two young and feckless dandies, both called Zhang (they were half-brothers); she indulged their every whim and would have no word said against them.

The Zhangs, like the abbot, took full advantage of her favour. Bureaucrats and Buddhists alike were scandalised by their orgies. Wu supporters joined Tang supporters, their deadly enemies, in detestation of the pair. But the empress stood by her protégés and mustered all her failing energies in repeatedly rescuing them from the courts. No one thought to mention that equally dissolute conduct in a besotted old emperor would have passed unnoticed. Then, in early 705, one too many imperial pardons for Zhang crimes tipped the scales. With the empress clearly ailing, a group of outraged senior statesmen rallied troops, coaxed the heir apparent Zhongzong from his chambers and entered the Chang'an palace. The Zhangs were confronted and executed on the spot. Only a dishevelled and unsteady empress barred the path. 'Rapidly comprehending the situation,' writes Guisso, 'she addressed her trembling son [Zhongzong] and the other plotters in terms of contempt. Then, her half century of power at an end, she returned to bed.'[13]

She died later the same year. In the words used of *Tang* Taizong's golden age, there had been 'nothing quite like her since antiquity'.

As noted, the histories gloss over Wu Zetian's personal role in directing the wider business of the empire. Yet, on their own admission, and despite *Tang* Gaozong's delaying his death until 683, it would seem that as of 655 'government proceeded from her alone' and as of 664 'all the great powers of the empire devolved on the empress'.[14] With or without her ailing and possibly epileptic husband, therefore, and despite the historians' reticence, the empress must be held ultimately responsible for all transactions during her five decades of ascendancy.

Economics were evidently her weakest suit; they were for most emperors. The tax base had mysteriously contracted from *Sui* Wendi's

606 figure of nearly 9 million registered households to *Tang* Taizong's 640s figure of under 3 million. It is presumed that this was the result of laxity in registration, further population movement and widespread exemptions, rather than some demographic catastrophe. Tax receipts were therefore inadequate for the lavish expenditure dictated by the empress's penchant for bureaucratic proliferation, dynastic extravaganzas and devotional endowments, let alone the defence of the empire. Yet the normal expedient of tinkering with the currency seemed only to make things worse. Minting less coin, then devaluing the existing stock and reducing its copper content, encouraged counterfeiting, which was easy to outlaw but hard to eliminate. The Han salt monopoly had long since ceased to be dependable; other sources of revenue were barely explored, the one exception being a patently desperate scheme to sell manure from the imperial stables.

Inflation became a feature of the period. Grain prices on the open market reportedly rose by a hundredfold from 'the three or four cash per peck' of *Tang* Taizong's halcyon days. On the other hand, the great granaries and the canal system seem to have served their purpose of subsidising the needy in such times of stress and relieving the worst cases of famine. Agrarian protest was notably muted; indeed, 'among the people, the empress may even have been popular', suggests Guisso.[15]

Perhaps of necessity given the short shrift shown to intransigent officials, she was more successful in increasing the supply of scholars qualified for office. A few outsiders – sharp-witted women as well as plausible young men – found rapid advancement courtesy of her personal favour. Otherwise she followed the example of her Sui and Tang predecessors by opening up the education system, increasing the number of examinees and refining the actual examinations. She also established a group of scholars within the palace which eventually became the famous Hanlin academy. Recruits from hereditary office-holding families still dominated the bureaucratic intake, though more of them now sat the examinations and brought to their work a level of intellectual proficiency. Examination candidates from outside these charmed circles, and especially from the minor aristocracy in the provinces, had less chance of office. But their gravitation towards court and capital furthered the cause of national integration and would add to the intellectual lustre of the age. From this pool of aspiring but often frustrated talent would rise some of the best-loved Tang poets, musicians and artists.

THE GREATEST POWER IN ASIA

To one so necessarily preoccupied with maintaining her own position, tributary relations and military deployments could have been a distraction. Yet Wu Zetian was conscious of their importance to her legitimacy and far from neglectful; indeed, her half-century of managing the Chinese empire at its greatest but most vulnerable extent may constitute one of her most neglected achievements. In earlier times *Han* Wudi's inner Asian empire had vanished into the desert within a matter of decades; but thanks in no small part to the empress, *Tang* Taizong's would flourish for well over a century, opening up new perspectives for both the Middle Kingdom and its tribute-bearing satellites, while setting a benchmark against which subsequent Chinese dynasties, and then republics, would measure their success.

Heaven's Sons – and Daughters – needed to look no further than the Mandate for the moral right to regulate the affairs of 'All-under-Heaven'. The reverential relationships and tributary terms of such an imperium were by now well rehearsed and its structure generally understood as a concentric arrangement in which close subordination shaded into distant dependency. Like cartographic contours, the levels of submission rippled outwards from the emperor through the tightly controlled inner rings of the palace, the capital and the metropolitan hinterland, to the provinces, the frontier command areas, the vassal chiefs and tribes beyond, and so to the farthest-flung states on Heaven's tribute-tendering horizon.

Only the methodology and the means for enforcing this ambitious arrangement left something to be desired. Confucian doctrine, formulated during the 'Warring States' era and partly in reaction to it, was adamant about civilian control over military affairs. It was one of the features that distinguished China's culture from that of its nomadic neighbours. Though expansive and often downright aggressive, at few moments in history could the Chinese empire be characterised as militaristic. Military matters were traditionally treated as a subordinate function of the bureaucracy; under no circumstances should the bureaucracy become a subordinate function of the military. Theoretically, standing armies were anathema, professional soldiers parasites. Troops, whether conscripts or *fubing* (territorial militias), should be farmers-on-horseback and peasants-with-crossbows; generals should be, and usually were, bureaucrats-in-uniform. They were commissioned for a single campaign and, unless reappointed, reverted to civilian life after it. With military success offering a short cut to the highest office, a term disparaging an upstart as one who 'went out a general and came in a chancellor' (*chu jiang ru xiang*) gained wide currency.[16]

Military manoeuvres were ideally held during the slack season of the agricultural year, campaigns were kept to a matter of months, and expeditions were launched on a there-and-back basis with objectives clearly specified and minimal discretion allowed to the commander in the field. According to the *Sunzi*, the classic text on warfare of perhaps the fourth century BC, armies constituted 'a way of deception'. Their well-drilled presence should serve to coerce and deter, but their actual use was to be discouraged. Far better to inveigle others into a multi-partite alliance and get them to do any fighting; hence the cliché, as old as China's history, of 'using barbarians to control barbarians'. For just as war, being notoriously unpredictable, was to be considered a last resort, so battle was to be offered only when victory was guaranteed. Indeed, if war represented a failure of diplomacy, then deployment represented a failure of strategy, and battle a failure of tactics.

It was not a question of 'Confucian passivity', nor, though the peoples of the steppe often interpreted it that way, of a sedentary and agrarian lifestyle being inimical to martial prowess. In his youth, the future *Tang* Taizong had been the very model of a warrior-prince and, latterly against Koguryo, one of the few emperors to accompany his troops into battle. Military discipline was strict, and when action was deemed necessary, vast imperial armies took the field and often inflicted colossal casualties. Given the 'All-under-Heaven' nature of the Mandate, any peoples in breach or ignorance of their obligations to the emperor were considered miscreants who must be induced to submit or be punished. In this sense, war was a corrective, an extension of the penal code from the recalcitrant individual (and his supposedly complicit family) to all those who dared defy the Heaven-ordained ruler, whether from within the frontier as 'bandits' (that is rebels) or from outside it as 'barbarians' (that is aliens).

In ancient times the carrot-and-stick of conventional strategy had worked well in cowing indigenous peoples like the Di, the Rong and the Man. Likewise the tribute-for-trade and peace-through-kinship compromises with the Xiongnu, Xianbei and Qiang had blunted the threat posed by the nomadic and generally unstable tribal confederations of the steppe. But as of the seventh century, the empire found itself confronted by more formidable foes – Turkic, Tibetan, Korean and Khitan – with their own cultural identities and political institutions, and with sedentary or semi-sedentarised populations at some remove from the Middle Kingdom.

Following the seven disastrous invasions of Korea by the Sui emperors and *Tang* Taizong, Wu Zetian's 668 conquest of Koguryo smacked somewhat of face-saving. The Han empire's Korean appendage had finally been reclaimed; protectorates were established in the peninsula; and of its three kingdoms, only that of Silla was left standing. But from an ally, Silla soon turned into a focus for resistance and then, with some Japanese assistance, into a determined enemy. As one imperial official had anticipated, '[The] dilemma was that, if the number of troops [sent to Korea] was small, China would be unable to exert enough force to retain control, but if the number was large, China would be exhausted trying to supply that force.'[17] Korea was not a steppe-land from which the enemy could simply be driven off. Its proud and bounteous kingdoms proved as costly to hold as they had been to take. Some Koreans found service in the imperial forces, while large numbers of Koguryo's farmers were transplanted west of the Yalu River into Manchuria and Hebei. But by 672 a process of Chinese retraction from the peninsula (Korean sources imply expulsion) was already under way. It culminated in the evacuation of Pyongyang in 676. Korea was not destined to form an integral part of the Chinese empire. Substantially reunited by Silla, it would acknowledge Tang suzerainty but retain full autonomy until, like China itself, it was overrun by the Mongols in the thirteenth century.

The empress had to console herself with a short-lived victory and a net territorial gain in what is now Liaoning province. As the protectorate of Andong (later Pinglu), this foothold in Manchuria with its residual claims on Korean allegiance and that of various Manchurian peoples would be echoed in the extreme south, where a protectorate based on what is now northern Vietnam continued to exercise tenuous claims over the adjacent kingdoms of south-east Asia. Both typified the adjustments, military and administrative, that characterised the organisation of the vastly extended Tang empire under Wu Zetian.

Of India in the eighteenth century it would be said that it 'fell into Britannia's lap while she was sleeping'. Less dozy, *Tang* Taizong had patiently positioned himself beneath the Turk qaghanates and then in the late 630s shaken their easternmost branch with a lunge into Mongolia and well-directed prods at the oasis-cities along the silk routes. But ultimately in Turkic Asia, as in Mughal India, the plums had fallen ripely, one dislodging others, with no laborious picking. Known as the On Oq (the 'Ten Arrows', or tribes), the various Turkic-speaking peoples who had comprised the Western Turk qaghanate succumbed in similar fashion during the 640s to fratricidal strife exacerbated by what one of their inscriptions describes as 'the cunning and deceitfulness of the Chinese'; 'the sons of the nobles became slaves of the Chinese', it bemoans, 'and their lady-like daughters became servants'.[18] While the On Oq squabbled, their subject territories

– rich city-states and any intervening pasturelands – had been gathered in and their allegiance transferred to the Heavenly qaghanate.

As witnessed by monk Xuanzang on his return journey through Xinjiang in 645, the harvest was substantial. All inner Asia was opened to Chinese penetration, and the so-called 'Western Regions' – an elastic term at the best of times – were stretched to their utmost. Under *Tang* Gaozong and Wu Zetian new protectorates were established over these frontier regions whose dependent territories sprawled in a great arc from Manchurian Andong on the Yellow Sea through what are now Outer Mongolia and eastern Kazakhstan to the deserts of Khorasan in north-eastern Persia/Iran. China's empire would never again be so vast. On paper – itself a commodity symbolising both the novelty and fragility of the new imperium – Tang China was indeed 'the greatest power in Asia at this time'.[19]

But it would be wrong to suppose that the frontier protectorates were subject to a level of control comparable to that in China's domestic provinces and prefectures. Protectors-general exercised a theoretical command over vast areas, parts of which, such as those beyond the Pamirs or the Tian Shan, could be reached only by months of travel and might be quite inaccessible for long periods of the year. The protector-general was responsible for their pacification, but his role was as much supervisory as punitive, diplomatic as bureaucratic.

The term used for a protectorate's far-flung components, whether prefectures or military commands, was *jimi*, meaning 'control by loose rein'. Subordinate but autonomous, *jimi* territories were designated to fit within a military and administrative framework that satisfied imperial criteria, yet they were otherwise barely distinguishable from the political entities they replaced. The *jimi* prefects and commandants were themselves often non-Han, typically former rulers of the regions they controlled who had tendered their submission in return for recognition; their staff and military establishments were also substantially non-Han. They could be called on to assist in frontier defence, to dispatch or accompany tribute missions to the capital annually, and to lodge their sons there as security for their loyalty. The tribute might include some element of tax revenue, especially in respect of the settled and easily assessable oasis-states of Xinjiang. In return the *jimi* prefects enjoyed hereditary tenure and might receive titles, brides, revenue grants and food subventions from the imperial government, plus presents of greater value than those tendered as tribute.

The 'loose rein' chafed little, and least of all in peripheral regions like northern (i.e. Outer) Mongolia, Ferghana, Sogdiana and the trans-Pamir region, whose submission could only be described as nominal. Such tracts, so impressive on the map, would prove a liability. Conservatives like Wei Zheng, *Tang* Taizong's crusty old adviser, had remonstrated vehemently against their inclusion and would not have been surprised at the ease with which some were about to be detached. As in Korea, Chinese ambivalence in military matters, and the ad hoc forces available for deployment, were woefully inadequate for maintaining an imperial colossus when challenged by other empire-builders.

The first of these challengers was Tibet. The amicable relations reached between Srong-brtsan-sgam-po and *Tang* Taizong had broken down around 660, the bone of contention being again the status of the Tuyuhun people in the treeless and boggy no man's land that was Qinghai. By now, after various missions and a long stand-off over a Chinese envoy's refusal to kowtow to the Tibetan king, the Tang should have realised that the Tibetans were not a mere confederation of nomadic tribes. An ambitious kingdom and would-be empire, Tibet had developed an integrated military, an effective administration and a literate culture based on its own grammar and script (an alphabetic one derived from a form of Sanskrit). The adoption of a distinctive and largely indigenous form of Buddhism (Vajrayana) was under way, metallurgical skills were highly developed, and Tibet's mixed economy included artisans and traders as well as farmers and pastoralists.

Through the 660s the Tibetans pushed outwards, reclaiming the Tuyuhun lands in Qinghai and penetrating into both Sichuan and Xinjiang. In the last, they joined forces with disaffected local kingdoms and remnants of the Western Turk qaghanate to sever the southern Silk Road as used by monk Xuanzang. Then with the capture of Kuqa in 670 they virtually eliminated the Chinese presence throughout western Xinjiang and the Pamirs. The Tang retained control of the northern Silk Road from Turfan over the Tian Shan via what is now Urumqi to Ferghana, where a military base was established at Tokmak on the Issyk-kul. They also mounted a determined defence of the Gansu corridor against the Tibetans with a major expedition of 670 into Qinghai. This was heavily defeated, as was a repeat performance in 678. 'I am afraid that the pacification of Tibet is not something that you can expect to accomplish between dawn and dusk,' concluded an all-too-prescient submission to the imperial court of about this time.[20]

China's two decades of domination in Qinghai and southern Xinjiang gave way to what has been called the first Tibetan empire. But Wu Zetian was far from reconciled to the situation. Though urged to write off what were called the 'Four Garrisons' (Tokmak, Kuqa, Kashgar and Khotan) of Anxi, the protectorate that corresponded to the Western Regions, she bided her time and in 692 in fact recovered them. Then she reinforced them. Thirty thousand troops were now permanently stationed in Anxi, with similar build-ups in other frontier protectorates. Against sustained and organised opposition, the traditional one-off, out-and-back 'punitive' expedition could no longer guarantee the security of the empire. Instead the frontier regions were to be policed by large permanent troop concentrations; and these, because of the difficulty of rotating soldiers so far from home, increasingly consisted of long-service recruits, both Han and non-Han, with a decidedly professional, even mercenary, approach to soldiering.

The empress had effectively buttressed *Tang* Taizong's imperial construct but at some damage to both Confucian principles and centralised authority. For supplying and remunerating such garrisons would strain the economy and deplete the resources, military as well as financial, available at the centre. Worse, in the longer term these heavily militarised protectorates and provinces would prove as fractious as the peoples they were supposed to be controlling. In upgrading the defences of its extended frontiers against external attack, the dynasty exposed itself to attack from within its traditional frontiers. Even the great *Tang* Xuanzong would fail to resolve this dilemma and would eventually pay the price.

Nonetheless, Xinjiang and Ferghana had been safely restored to the fold. Not without interruption, they would continue under Tang supervision for another fifty years. Tibet, though, remained an enigma. When offering allegiance it often confused matters by demanding reciprocity, and when offering battle it often cheerfully proclaimed that it did so out of loyalty. As the seventh century drew to a close, succession disputes within the Tibetan leadership led to a lull in hostilities. It ended in 700 with resounding Chinese victories and a peace settlement that was thrashed out in the dying days of Wu Zetian's reign. Sealed with a Chinese bride in 707, the terms of the settlement were vague but again implied an equality of status that future emperors would find intolerable.

Attacks and counter-attacks would continue along the length of the Tibeto-Tang frontier. Interminable and indeterminate, this zone ran all the way from the tousled hillsides beside the Mekong in Yunnan to the glacial gravel-beds of the upper Oxus in Afghanistan and the upper Jaxartes in Kyrghyzstan. The flashpoints were ever in the middle, where it brushed the Gansu corridor in Qinghai and veered towards Chang'an. But at its extremities the Tibetans were no less active and there found strange foes who quickly became staunch allies. In Yunnan these were the peoples of the emergent kingdom of Nanzhao, whose subsequent defiance of the Tang would destabilise the whole of south-west China including Vietnam. And in far Ferghana, the Tibetans' new ally was even more formidable, he being Qutaiba bin Muslim, military governor of the now Ummayad province of Persian Khorasan.

Islam had arrived in central Asia within decades of the Prophet's death. After rolling back Persia's Sassanid empire much as Alexander of Macedon had its Achaemenid empire, the Arabs first briefly took the Sogdian city-states of Bukhara and Samarkand in 708/9. At about the same time, Qutaiba bin Muslim's counterpart in south Asia established an Arab bridgehead in India with the conquest of Sind in what is now Pakistan. Both initiatives were directed from Baghdad, headquarters of the Ummayad caliphate's western viceroy.

The Chinese responded to the new presence by affording sanctuary to Pheroz (Firuz), a son of the last Sassanid ruler of Persia, and by encouraging their Western Turk *jimi* to resist the newcomers. But anything approaching a head-on clash between the two imperial juggernauts, the one triumphant throughout west Asia and the other throughout east Asia, failed to materialise. The Tang no more halted the Arab advance than did the Arabs the Tang advance. Both ground to a standstill in the political dust-storm stirred up by the Turks and Tibetans. When in 751 Arab and Tang forces did finally come face to face on the Talas River in Ferghana, the battle proved less bang than whimper. The victorious Arab and Tibetan forces failed to follow up their triumph, and the defeated Chinese had already written off Ferghana. World history was the only loser.

For the Tang, the Tibetan menace, though barely contained, had in fact been decisively overshadowed since as early as the 680s, when a greater threat emerged, or re-emerged, in the north. Though *Tang* Taizong had picked off the Eastern Turks of Mongolia in the 630s, in the early 680s they reformed under dynamic new leadership, repudiated their Tang protectoral status and, like a swarm returning to the hive, set up a Second Turk Qaghanate along the Orkhon River near what is now Ulan Bator in Outer Mongolia. From there they spilled across the Gobi, and with scant regard for either garrisons or walls, harried the Chinese provinces of Shanxi, Shaanxi and Ningxia. The new Eastern Turks demanded tribute-cum-trade plus the return of Turks who had been resettled within the empire; they undermined Wu Zetian's authority by insisting their relationship was exclusively with the Tang emperor, not a Zhou empress; and like the Xiongnu of old, they commanded the supply of bloodstock on which the horse-loving Tang court, no less than its cavalry, had come to depend. They could not be ignored.

Exchanges, largely hostile but also commercial and diplomatic, dragged on for a quarter of a century. Under the great Qapaghan (Bag Chor, Mochuo, r. 695–716), the new qaghanate rivalled any of its predecessors, including that of *Shanyu* Maodun in Han times, and exacted enormous sums from the imperial exchequer as blood money. But any Turk plans for territorial enrichment at the expense of core China were held in check, partly by bolstered defence arrangements such as those introduced in Anxi and partly by the relentless pressure being experienced by the Turk qaghanate along its farther frontiers.

This pressure, though poorly understood by historians, would have been familiar enough to the Turks; it had powered their own eruption two centuries earlier. North-east Asia's capacity for demographic upheaval was again making itself felt. As if spewing from ethnic geysers somewhere in the vicinity of where Siberia, Manchuria and Mongolia meet, a whole new generation of peripatetic peoples had begun herding its way into history.

Their names enter the records in the mid-seventh century, among the more familiar being Kyrgyz, Uighur and Khitan. They in turn would be followed by Jurchen, Mongol and Manchu. Like the Xiongnu and Xianbei, each attracted support from other ethnic groups to become composite peoples whose identity was dictated by the language group to which the leading clans belonged. And poorly differentiated at first, they would assume these distinct identities only as they entered the Chinese arena and steadily hijacked its history. Their impact can scarcely be exaggerated. By the thirteenth century a traveller like Marco Polo could genuinely suppose that 'Cathay', a name derived from 'Khitan' hegemony, was the appropriate designation for the Middle Kingdom, that its renaissance was down to Mongol rule, and that 'khan' (that is 'qaghan') as in 'Kublai Khan' was the normal title of its emperor. Fatimid Egypt as sampled by, say, a Frankish spice merchant would have been just as misleading, its Islamic present and Graeco-Roman past obscuring its pharaonic heritage.

Of the newcomers, the Kyrgyz, a Turkic-speaking people, would be the most peripheral; gravitating westward through and round Mongolia, they would play only a cameo role in the affairs of the Middle Kingdom. The Uighur, who also spoke a Turkic dialect, might have followed a similar trajectory; but as ferocious horsemen, they were sidetracked into contention for supremacy on the Mongolian steppe. Their presence attracted over-tures from Wu Zetian in her tussle with the revived Eastern Turk qaghanate and began the long association between the Uighur and the Tang. As allies the Uighur would be of special assistance to *Tang* Xuanzong in his own tortuous dealings with the Eastern Turk qaghanate; and in 745, when the Turk qaghanate fell, it was the Uighurs who would succeed it in Mongolia with an essentially Uighur 'Third Turk Qaghanate'. This would render even more crucial service to the Tang in their greatest hour of need, rescuing the dynasty while ravaging the empire on at least two occasions. The Third Qaghanate lasted nearly a century (745–840) before the Uighurs were finally dispersed, many of them resuming their westward drift to Xinjiang, where they would remain.

Rather different were the Khitan (Qidan). Their language has been called 'proto-Mongol with Turkic borrowings', and their cultural identity 'Turko-Mongol'. How and where they acquired this pedigree, and what other than some vocabulary they shared with the later Mongols, is uncertain; but they had been known to the Chinese since the third century and by the seventh were established along the Manchuria–Mongolia border. In 648 *Tang* Taizong, pursuant to his abortive invasion of Korea, had secured their nominal allegiance. But in 695, when Wu Zetian had her hands full with the Tibetans and Qapaghan of the new Eastern Turks, they rose in unexpected revolt. Two imperial armies, one commanded by an impressive twenty-eight generals and the other reportedly consisting of 200,000 men, were rushed to the rescue only to be routed near where Beijing now stands. The Khitan then halted their advance and pitched camp in northern Hebei. In a reign replete with crises, this was possibly the greatest. Yet the empress, despite her years, handled it 'with a calm and decision that were wholly admirable'.[21] Qapaghan was bought off, in fact persuaded to lend his assistance against the Khitan; a determined effort was made to recruit more troops; and in 697/8 the Khitan were at last defeated. Though they withdrew, and after a dalliance as Turk allies accepted imperial suzerainty under *Tang* Xuanzong in 714, it was not the last that would be heard of them. The Khitan would remain an irritant for more than a century and then become major contenders for power in China itself in the tenth century.

LIKE A BREATH OF SPRING

They swore to wipe out the nomads, no thought for themselves,
Five thousand in sable and brocade, gone to barbarian dust.
Pity them – these bones by the shores of the Uncertain River –
to those who dream in spring chambers, they are still men![22]

In his 'Song of Longxi' (Longxi being a remote outpost in western Gansu) Chen Dao, a ninth-century poet, highlighted the human cost of an extended empire by juxtaposing the frontier's cruel oblivion and the homeland's fond recollections. Poetry, like remonstration, could be a form of protest;

and since poets were products of the Confucian education system, extravagant military adventures often came in for criticism in their verses.

No dynasty was graced by so many poets, or such famous ones, as the Tang. Around 50,000 poems survive from the Tang period, and of its over 1,400 known poets at least two – Li Bo (701–62) and Dou Fu (712–70) – are generally considered to be, in their different ways, without peer. Li Bo, 'a Mozart of words' and 'the Chinese Byron', was the more versatile.[23] Probably in 751, the year in which Tang armies were defeated by both the Nanzhao kingdom in Yunnan and the Arabs and Tibetans on the Talas River in Ferghana, he composed a lament called 'Fighting South of the Ramparts'. In it, an old campaigner describes how he and his comrades crossed the Tian Shan and watered their horses in 'Parthian seas', how they fought on the northern border last year and are fighting in Xinjiang this. The enemy never has anything to lose, 'the fighting and marching never stop'; swords clash, riderless horses 'neigh piteously', and men die; crows peck at their guts and festoon the withered trees with their entrails;

> Captains and soldiers are smeared on the bushes and grass:
> The General schemed in vain.
> Know therefore that the sword is a cursed thing
> Which the wise man uses only if he must.[24]

Poetry exposes contemporary sentiments and activities that elude the plodding official histories. But it travels badly. Apart from the difficulties of translation and the challenge of conveying things like rhyme, tonal rhythm and wordplay, China's poetry expects more of the reader than that of most other traditions. Poets wrote to engage one another, not to reach out across the land and down the ages to a vague and indeterminate general public. Since composition was a vital part of the Confucian curriculum and especially of the *jinshi* examination, all well-educated persons aspiring to high office were poets of a sort and could appreciate virtuosity among their peers. It was 'a companionable art for private and social use' by an initiated, discerning and allusion-conscious elite. Moreover, its speciality lay in conveying not just the imagery that survives the rough handling of translation but the poet's state of mind and the subtle flickering of his emotions. According to one authority, 'learning to be a good reader of Chinese poetry is an art as fine as being a good poet' (a dictum that has sometimes been supposed valid when applied to Chinese history and the historian).[25]

Tang Xuanzong, whose forty-five-year reign (712–57) witnessed the

Inland waterways provided imperial China with its main arteries of trade and communication. The Grand Canal, a series of channels linking the Yangzi delta with the Yellow River and Beijing, is still very much in use. It was cut by the Sui emperor Yangdi (604–17) but has been constantly realigned and widened. Paddle-powered shipping (with anything from two to twenty paddle-wheels) was developed during the Song dynasty in the twelfth century. And from this period dates the great Qingming scroll depicting frantic riverside commerce.

Nanjing on the Yangzi was first adopted as the capital of an all-China empire by the founding *Ming* Hongwu emperor (r. 1368–98). Its massive walls and monumental gateways long remained the most extensive urban fortifications in China.

The Great Wall as seen today in the vicinity of Beijing (below) was constructed under the Ming dynasty (1368–1644). Earlier walls of pounded earth (*hangtu*) had anticipated sections of it. But the familiar curtain of stone and brick, liberally dotted with towers, dates from the sixteenth century when, under the Wanli emperor, plans like the above were produced to record the deployment of troops along it.

It was probably blue-white glazed *qingbai* ware that Marco Polo called porcelain in the thirteenth century. It was 'exported all over the world', he reported. By the seventeenth century the kilns of the porcelain capital of Jingdezhen (Jiangxi) had discovered an even greater foreign demand for decorated blue-and-white china, like this Ming (c.1630) vase.

Silk scroll entitled 'Bird's-Eye View of the Capital' by Xu Yang, 1767. First adopted as the capital of all China by the Mongol Yuan dynasty, Beijing retained its primacy thoughout most of the Ming period and all of the Qing. The painting was designed to illustrate a poem of the same name written by the *Qing* Qianlong emperor (r. 1735-96).

This c.1755 oil painting of Dawaci, a Mongol dignitary, has been attributed to the Jesuit priest Jean-Denis Attiret. Jesuits attained considerable influence at the Qing court, whose artists readily adopted European ideas of perspective and shading.

Engraving of Mongol army with artillery mounted on camels. In their war (c.1688–97) for control of western Mongolia and Tibet, both the *Qing* Kangxi emperor and Galdan, his Zunghar Mongol opponent, deployed cannon on camel-back.

The First (Qin) Emperor undertook tours of inspection, a custom revived by all subsequent dynasts whenever conditions permitted. The last (Qing) emperors memorialised their tours in narrative scroll paintings, some of them fifty metres long. Here subjects tender submission in a scene from the 1689 southward tour of the Kangxi emperor (beneath the parasol).

The *Qing* Qianlong emperor is borne aloft to his ceremonial tent at Jehol for a reception of tribute-bearing envoys in 1794. Among them is a mission from George III led by Lord Macartney (all lace and feathers on the extreme right). Although his was the most elaborate mission ever despatched by the Court of St James, Macartney's overtures were rebuffed.

Near-lifesize portraits of the Qing emperors in ceremonial dress (this is the Qianlong emperor) betray a high sense of imperial self-awareness. Painted by teams of court artists, they were designed to project an image of imperturbable dignity and unassailable authority.

greatest flowering of Tang poetry, was not therefore unusual in being himself a noted poet. He was also a musician, an actor and a connoisseur of most other arts. His patronage was lavish, poet Li Bo being among the many who benefited from it. 'High Tang', a phrase synonymous with Xuanzong's reign, was as much a 'golden age' because of its artistic and cosmopolitan flamboyance as because of the empire's comparative tranquillity and vast extent. *Tang* Xuanzong set the tone. But poetry was also indebted to him in another sense. Unusually his reign, and especially its denouement, would provide Chinese culture with perhaps the richest of the many tragic themes derived from history.

All went well at first. For a decade the new reign rivalled *Tang* Taizong's utopian early years, and for three more decades it continued to fulfil its promise. An accomplished and likeable twenty-seven-year-old, in 712 Xuanzong had ascended the throne after a chaotic interlude under *Tang* Zhongzong and Ruizong (the bit-part sons of Gaozong and Wu Zetian) and amid a bloodbath that was mercifully shallow by the standards of the age. Wu Zetian's generally capable ministers, many of whom had been dispersed in the interim, were recalled to office. The most influential of them, Yao Chong, virtually dictated his own terms of employment with a ten-point programme that included all that was dearest to a Confucian bureaucrat and most conducive to ensuring a *wuwei* emperor. There were to be no reigns of terror, no military adventures, no legal immunity for imperial favourites, no interference by consorts and their families, nor by eunuchs, no imperial princes in central government office, no expenditure on Buddhist and Daoist endowments, and of course no retribution for remonstrating ministers.

The emperor concurred and, until Yao Chong's death in 721, he more or less kept to his promise. The administrative irregularities and the bureaucratic proliferation that had characterised Wu Zetian's rule were reversed; monastery-building was banned and some thirty thousand Buddhist clergy were defrocked as tax-dodgers; court, consorts and eunuchs were kept out of politics; and on the frontier the emperor continued the build-up of Wu Zetian's garrisons. Reorganised among nine command areas under permanently appointed military governors, and increasingly manned by *jian'er* (literally 'sturdy lads' but in fact long-serving and substantially non-Han career veterans), these garrisons began to resemble professional armies. Meanwhile the emperor pursued a generally conciliatory policy towards his restless neighbours, which was much helped by the death of Qapaghan in 716 and subsequent instability in his Eastern Turk qaghanate.

Imperial revenue returns failed to recover, however; instead expenditure raced ahead, and coinage counterfeiters continued to enjoy a field day. Like Wu Zetian, Xuanzong made a habit of moving between Chang'an and Luoyang. Prior to 736 he changed capital ten times, an average of nearly once every two years. The expense and labour of maintaining twin capitals and shuttling the entire court and government between them was colossal, yet it has been argued that economics actually dictated this erratic behaviour. Evidently *Sui* Yangdi's canal system was not performing well enough to keep either of the capitals supplied for long. The court was having to move because its conspicuous consumption rapidly exhausted the sustenance and luxuries available in any one place. A 300-kilometre (185-mile) trail of destitution was worn between the two capitals, and when the emperor processed farther afield, as to Shandong in 725 to perform the ritual sacrifices at Mount Tai, his vast entourage devoured its way across the countryside like a cloud of locusts.

The revenue deficit could be redressed by ensuring that all taxable households were actually taxed. This meant re-registering those families that had decamped, sold out, been exempted or had otherwise disappeared from the rolls, while discouraging any more of the same. Incentives for re-registering were offered (for instance, a six-year moratorium in return for a modest upfront payment), penalties for not registering were promulgated, inspections were conducted, and by 726 the number of registered households had increased significantly to over 7 million. It continued to rise, reaching 8.5 million by 742. At the standard five inmates to a household, this gave an overall population of 42.5 million, but there were undoubtedly many more who remained unregistered. Tax receipts improved, so relieving the strain on the exchequer and encouraging *Tang* Xuanzong to forsake his early restraint and embark on an ambitious programme of frontier stabilisation at the expense of the Khitan, Tibetans and the nascent kingdom of Nanzhao in Yunnan.

But the reforms were all highly controversial. Resentment came not so much from those who were now officially re-entered in the registers (judging by the uptake, they may actually have been better off) as from those local interests that had been exploiting the previous situation to tax the unregistered on their own account, buy them out or otherwise deprive them of their holdings and the fruits of their labour. Substantial estates had been built up in this way, and naturally the main estate-holders were often the very officials who were supposed to be enforcing registration. When around the year 740 registration was relaxed and, in a new departure, tax quotas were set for each prefecture rather than each household, the bad old ways returned. Estates grew larger and heralded the end of the 'equal-field' system – that legacy of the Northern Wei whereby each household had been entitled to a lifetime's tenancy of a fixed area of land. The system had long been open to exploitation. Provisions like that for mulberry plantations to be held as heritable property (otherwise the trees on which silkworms fed would hardly have been worth planting) had been abused. Ever more fields, with or without mulberries, had become heritable, especially on large estates, so reducing the pool of land available for re-allocation. Evidence from Dunhuang suggests that 'equal-field' allocations had shrunk to a fraction of the area intended; in a place of such limited cultivable potential, they may never have been large enough to support a numerous household. In effect the system was collapsing and the state was withdrawing from the direct allocation of land just as it was from the direct collection of taxes.

The transport problem was less controversial. Proposals for redressing it were adopted in the 730s, when the canal system was overhauled with new channels being dug and some much-needed maintenance undertaken. Because navigation depended on the rise and fall of water levels in the intervening rivers, convoys of tax grain from the Yangzi could take a year to reach the Yellow River; and the long stopovers en route left cargoes so depleted by pilferage, deterioration and running costs that barges might arrive empty. To rectify this, a relay system was tried with shorter sailings between intermediary holding points. There was also some reorganisation of granaries and some contracting out of barge management. These and other measures had the desired effect. Suppplies reaching Chang'an rocketed; 'indeed, the reform was so successful that it was not necessary to continue it in full force'.[26]

As of 736, therefore, the court ceased its Luoyang shuttling and stayed put in Chang'an. The city duly became the undisputed Tang capital. Its grand dimensions as laid out under *Sui* Wendi had promised the most extensive city in the world; now, as its inhabitants surged towards 2 million, it became much the most populous city in the world. But a greater distinction lay in its cosmopolitanism. Port cities such as Guangzhou in the deep south and Yangzhou in the Yangzi delta hosted large merchant and seafaring communites from Arabia, Persia, India and south-east Asia. But for exoticism nothing could match the great markets and court spectacles of Chang'an. The flow of foreigners was continuous. Traders and tributaries, fugitives and diplomats, hostages and prisoners, missionaries and miracle-workers, performance artists and pleasure-seekers – they poured through the gates from everywhere in Asia. Siberian pelts of sable and ermine sold alongside cloves and nutmeg from eastern Indonesia; pepper and peacock plumes from India were displayed with frankincense and myrrh from the Hadhramaut and coral and glassware from the Mediterranean.

A literary diversion of the time, somewhat like the parlour game of 'subjects', involved listing examples, preferably witty ones, under categories such as 'ambiguities', 'irritations', 'social clangers' and so on. One such category included in a composition attributed to a Tang poet called Li Shangyin was 'anomalies', or 'contradictions in terms'. Here one finds the predictable ('an illiterate teacher', 'a sick doctor') alongside the contentious ('a grandfather frequenting courtesans', for instance). More revealing is 'a teetotal *chela*', a *chela* being the attendant-cum-disciple of a Buddhist monk; boozing and Buddhism were evidently no strangers. But topping the list at number one, the most convincing example of an anomaly in early ninth-century China was 'a poor Persian'.[27] Chang'an's Persians, like their Sogdian colleagues, were never poor. They dealt in money. Come Turk, Tibetan or Arab, the overland trade flourished, and it was Persians who financed it while Sogdians managed it. Indeed, in the markets, Persia's silver coinage was preferred to the often debased copper cash; it was the dollar of its day.

Rivalled only by poetry and its associated arts of calligraphy and painting, what most interested a Tang connoisseur like *Tang* Xuanzong were items of alien provenance. In a categorised listing of 'exotics', had there been one, horses would probably have come first, followed by heterodoxy. *Tang* Taizong is said to have been the finest horseman of his generation and Xuanzong a great hunter in his youth. With forebears fresh from the steppe, the Li (Tang) and other northern aristocratic families retained their passion for bloodstock as for archery and hawking. Annually some tens of thousands of mounts had to be supplied for military and ceremonial use from the imperial breeding stations and – or exclusively when these outlying stud farms fell into hostile hands – by purchase at inflated prices from the Turks. At court, the game of polo, another Persian import, won converts, found favour with artists and encouraged a trade in ponies; but more sought after were the famed mounts of Ferghana and central Asia. Swifter and more fiery, they could yet be trained by their exotically attired grooms to perform and amuse. Imitating the tavern temptresses from central Asia who 'danced in a dress of gauze' and beguiled the poet Li Bo with laughter 'like a breath of spring', the prancing horses might conclude their performance by accepting a drink. Unassisted, the soft equine noses nuzzled brimming goblets of wine, delicately raised them and then drained them in one.

From Sogdiana, Persia and beyond, the flow of novelties never ceased. Cuisine and fabrics, clothing styles and make-up, song and dance were all influenced by the new craze for the exotic. Quaint fauna stalked the imperial menageries. In the bazaars long noses and bushy beards, some fair to auburn, were commonplace. Strange scents and plaintive sounds, especially that of the lute of Kuqa, were savoured for the first time. But nowhere was there as much variety as in the cornucopia of belief systems. Just as Islam was making its first appearance in China, so were Nestorian Christianity, Manichaeism, Zoroastrianism (Mazdaism) and even Judaism. Steles commemorate some of these introductions, and adherents of each had their own place of worship granted by the emperor. Conversions were not unknown. Nestorian Christianity would still be flourishing when Franciscans and Dominicans introduced its Latin counterpart in the sixteenth century. The Uighurs in Mongolia, after flirting with Buddhism, adopted the doctrines of Manes en masse; only after settling in Xinjiang as enthusiastic Manichaeans would they convert to Islam and so complete a doctrinal odyssey to rival their geographical drift.

Nor were contacts with India neglected. Monks as well as merchants continued to pass back and forth, bringing new texts, new disciplines and new metaphysical and scientific challenges. Both Tantric Buddhism and the more esoteric doctrines from which developed Chan (or Zen) Buddhism gained adherents under the Tang; Indian mathematics and ayurvedic medicine were closely studied; and the Indian game of chess proved such a success that it was included in the curriculum of the Hanlin academy. Chinese artists delighted in depicting Indian deities and did so in a style that was itself decidedly hybrid. A cross-cultural extreme cited by Edward Schafer, the great connoisseur of Tang connoisseurship, has a Chinese painter using a geisha girl to model a Hindu goddess in a scene illustrating a Buddhist narrative.[28]

A TURNING POINT

Foreigners were closely monitored. They required a licence to trade and were separately domiciled. Tang fascination with all things foreign did not exclude ridiculing them and was often tinged with contempt. Nor could familiarity dull a sense of apprehension. Though constituting an insignificant fraction of the population, non-Han people enjoyed a disproportionate prominence. The danger of the empire capitulating to the foreigners within it sometimes seemed greater than the chances of capitulation to the foreigners without it, and indeed it was. For all these attitudes would play a part in the great cataclysm of the mid-eighth century known as the An Lushan rebellion. The never-to-be-equalled magnificence of *Tang* Xuanzong's reign was about to be terminated, and the dynasty plunged into protracted decline, in one of the great upheavals of China's imperial history.

Much has been written on the An Lushan rebellion yet as much remains unexplained. Xuanzong's long reign can be seen as building towards the crisis, with different groups within the ruling elite – examination graduates, traditional office-holding families, landholding aristocrats and disgruntled regional interests – vying for ministerial office while advocating policies of sectional convenience. Alternatively the rebellion can be seen as evidence of an ageing emperor losing interest in government and succumbing to faddish delusions and romantic fantasies while still cherishing unrealistic ambitions. Economic historians cite numerous contributory causes; and the Standard Histories offer their usual catalogue of unverifiable natural disasters. But insofar as the rebellion was essentially factional and military, with neither the credentials of a peasants' revolt nor the dynamic of a messianic movement, its immediate causes may be sought within the mutinous armies of the north-east and the troubled mind of their commander, the redoubtable An Lushan.

An Lushan was a half-Sogdian and half-Turk general in the Tang army who rose to prominence in the 740s. Since the late 730s Li Linfu, an aristocrat with an imperious manner and a genius for organisation, had been acting as virtual dictator while the increasingly *wuwei* emperor dabbled in Daoism and mystical Buddhism. Bringing his tidy mind to bear on the military, Li Linfu had strengthened the frontier armies still further. Some 85 per cent of the empire's now nearly 600,000 troops were stationed on its borders. Resounding victories over the Tibetans in Qinghai and the Pamirs, and over the Khitan in Manchuria, seemed to justify the vast expense of this mostly professional establishment. But to nullify the challenge to his own ascendancy from those who 'went out generals and came in chancellors', Li Linfu began replacing the senior military commanders with generals of non-Han origin. He argued that they made better fighters, and being unacquainted with court intrigue, posed less of a threat to the government. This was especially true of a rough-and-ready soldier like An Lushan, who, though speaking several non-Han languages, was illiterate in Chinese and so theoretically ineligible for civil office.

By 750 all but one of the major commands were held by foreigners. Most of these men were Turks or part-Turk, though it was under a Korean general that the Tang forces were defeated by the Arabs at the Talas River in 751. Conversely, at the other end of the empire, on the borders of Korea and Manchuria, it was as military governor of Pinglu that the Sogdian An Lushan rose to high command. To Pinglu (in Liaoning province) was added the neighbouring command of Fanyang (northern Hebei province) in 745 and of Hedong (northern Shanxi province) in 751. As of 752 one of An Lushan's relatives held the next two frontier commands, so that 'the whole northern border from the Ordos to Manchuria was controlled by the Ans'.[29]

Despite a military record of mixed achievement, An Lushan seems to have enjoyed the devotion of his troops. They were better supplied than their counterparts farther west thanks to the Grand Canal's north-eastern extension, and they may even have brought a measure of prosperity to the otherwise neglected north-east. He also enjoyed exceptionally close relations with Chang'an. Li Linfu's imperious manner could be alarming; but An Lushan was careful not to antagonise him while endearing himself to the emperor as a loyal and simple soldier. The histories accuse him of pretence. All courtiers dissimulated, and in playing the bumpkin, An Lushan seems to have been appealing to a new and more playful constituency at court.

For in 745 the sixty-year-old *Tang* Xuanzong had allowed his attention to stray from contemplation of the Daoist ineffable to admire the porcelain perfection and fashionably fulsome figure of one whose beauty was rivalled only by her vivacity. This was the famous Yang Guifei, and the emperor was instantly smitten. She had previously been the consort of one of his sons, so was probably no more than half his age, and through her influence over the emperor, she soon came to dominate the court. Under her patronage, a distant cousin, Yang Guozhong, emerged as Li Linfu's main rival, and on the latter's death in 752 as his ministerial successor. The Yangs were now all-powerful.

At first An Lushan ingratiated himself with them. Though the records for the period would be largely destroyed in subsequent upheavals, and though the portrayal of An Lushan in the Standard Histories is highly suspect, he seemingly basked in imperial favour. Yang Guifei reportedly adopted him as her son, and in a grotesque performance consecrated this move by having the now portly and fifty-something general dressed in baby clothes and given a bath. This might appear preposterous but for the fact that the emperor went one better, designating An Lushan a duke and then a prince, a title never previously accorded to any but imperial progeny. Had *Tang* Xuanzong not already fathered fifty-nine sons, one might suspect that An Lushan was being groomed for the succession. Lands, offices and exemptions were showered upon him and he could do no wrong. In 754, and despite his illiteracy, a chief ministership looked likely. Instead, he was given an additional command as commissioner for the imperial stables and the great stud farms in Gansu. As well as more manpower than anyone else in the empire, An Lushan now controlled the vital supply of cavalry mounts.

The sources hint at an incestuous liaison between the general and his adoptive mother, the lovely Yang Guifei; it was probably just another attempt to smear his memory. But as between the general and the other Yang – chief minister Yang Guozhong – relations plummeted. Each saw the other as the only serious threat to his supremacy and intrigued against him. When in 754 An Lushan returned to his command in Hebei, Yang Guofang purged the general's agents at court, dismissed potential supporters and floated rumours of rebellion. An Lushan, fearing for his safety, travelled east by boat and never once stepped ashore.

Yet his sudden metamorphosis from palace pet to avenging pariah remains hard to explain. His actions of 755 can be construed either as careful preparation for revolt or as desperate responses to the increasingly ominous reports coming from Chang'an. Spies from the capital sent to investigate him were stalled or bribed, requests for his attendance at court rebuffed or ignored. When in late 755 he declined even to perform obeisance before an imperial envoy, it was tantamount to a declaration of war. In similar circumstances, a Han general imbued with the Confucian ethos would either have answered the summons and accepted the consequences or have availed himself of the privilege of suicide. An Lushan, the son of a Sogdian, did neither. Claiming that he had been ordered to rid the empire of the far-from-popular Yang Guozhong, he marched forth at the head of his formidable army.

Luoyang fell to the rebels before the year 755 was out. Hastily summoned armies were defeated while new recruits proved no match for the general's veteran *jian'er* and his Manchurian – largely Khitan – auxiliaries. But Chang'an and the Wei valley behind their screening mountains remained under imperial control. In fact they were reinforced by the recall of the frontier armies in Gansu, Xinjiang and Sichuan. Turks, Tibetans, Arabs and others would take advantage of this retraction to dismantle the empire's entire western extension. Still more ominous was the introduction into core China of these frontier armies under their non-Han commanders, and the concurrent appointment of military governors and defence supremos in the heartland provinces. An Lushan's challenge to the authority of the central government had set a precedent. It betrayed the weakness of the dynasty, condemned it to invoking the support of military contingents as dangerous as the rebels, and hastened the devolution of power from the capital to the provinces.

The year 756 brought An Lushan's first reverses. Loyalist forces behind his line of advance nearly regained Hebei and others barred any progress south towards the Yangzi. The general responded by proclaiming his own dynasty. It was to be called the Great Yan, Yan being the age-old name for the north-east, where the rebels enjoyed the widest support. Greatly provoked by this move, in mid-756 the emperor and the impatient Yang Guozhong overruled their commanders to launch a massive counter-attack. It was ambushed and routed. Defeat left the capital undefended. As An Lushan advanced to claim the prize, all who could vacated the great city.

> I remember when we first fled the rebels,
> Hurrying north over dangerous trails;
> Night deepened on Pengya Road,
> the moon shone over White-water Hills.
> A whole family endlessly trudging,
> begging without shame from the people we met:
> valley birds sang, a jangle of soft voices;
> we didn't see a single traveller returning . . .[30]

The poet Dou Fu, along with the heir apparent, the future *Tang* Suzong, fled north. A Robert Burns to Li Bo's Byron, Dou Fu was no stranger to disappointment. 'Caught involuntarily in the machinery of history', he explored its impact on the common man and showed a greater awareness of life's intimate tragedies than any contemporary writer. This empathy, along with a daring use of language and compositional techniques, won him little fame in his lifetime but would come to be revered as the essence of a later and more humanitarian Confucianism. Like Burns, Dou Fu drew on his own circumstances to mirror the history of his times. In universalising the apparently inconsequential, both poets furnished an image of the cultural hero as social conscience that posterity would savour.[31]

Meanwhile the emperor, the lovely Yang Guifei and the dictatorial Yang Guozhong, accompanied by attendants and a cavalry escort, fled towards Sichuan. The Yangs originated from there; the mountain trail through the Qinling, a successor of 'Stone Cattle Road', would discourage pursuit; and preparations had already been made for receiving the imperial entourage in Chengdu. Two weeks out, at a place called Mawei, they ran into a party of Tibetan envoys. The Tibetans wanted food, but Yang Guozhong's dealings with them roused the suspicions of the imperial escort. Accused of treachery, Yang Guozhong was manhandled and murdered on the spot along with members of his family.

The emperor was unharmed in the fracas, as was Yang Guifei. But presumably to eradicate all hated Yangs, the troops now demanded that the emperor have her executed too. Powerless to protect his beloved, the emperor, it is said, concurred. Yang Guifei herself requested only that, instead of execution, she be strangled with a length of silk, whereupon the emperor's trusted eunuch performed the deed. Thus did Yang Guifei pass to the spirit world with her beauty intact, there to be eventually reunited, in countless verses, plays, paintings, songs and novellas, with the emperor who so loved her. Romance transcends history. To ask why she had to die, or why the emperor, however old and powerless, failed the basic test of a hero in not dying with her, not even defending her, is beside the point. The emperor's loss and his lover's devotion were tragedy enough.

Broken-hearted, the great *Tang* Xuanzong continued on to Chengdu, to exile and to imminent abdication. He lived another five years, so outlasting An Lushan and witnessing the Tang restoration. In neither is he said to have taken the remotest interest.

10

RECONFIGURING THE EMPIRE
755–1005

LOW TANG

SEEN IN THE ESSENTIALLY DYNASTIC TERMS preferred by the traditional histories, little was changed by the An Lushan rebellion of late 755. An Lushan himself was murdered by his son in early 757. Later in the same year, with Uighur help, Chang'an was recaptured by *Tang* Suzong, Xuanzong's designated heir (r. 756–62). Although An Lushan's Great Yan dynasty soldiered on through four would-be emperors – himself, his son, a general and the general's son – none lasted more than a couple of years and all bar one were murdered by their successors. The exception was the last who, though probably murdered, had no successor; for when in 763 this man's severed head was presented to the Tang emperor in Chang'an, the Great Yan dynasty petered out; a record of four assassinations in eight years invited no further candidates; evidently the Great Yan were not great enough for the Mandate. Instead of imperial supremacy, An Lushan's still-rebellious generals and governors set their sights on provincial autonomy.

Meanwhile the Tang, having reclaimed their capital, steadily clawed back the core of their empire. Under a succession of mostly competent emperors the dynasty would continue to occupy the throne as the sovereign power and source of all legitimacy for another 150 years. Just five generations of Tang 'ancestors' (the shared '-zong' element in their posthumous names means 'ancestor') had reigned before the rebellion; seven would reign after it. Unlike the Former to Later Han succession, the Tang succession was unbroken, comparatively orderly and rarely challenged. In terms of scholars, poets and artists, the second half of the dynasty was as illustrious as the first. Jikaku Daishi, the Japanese pilgrim better known as Ennin, who travelled widely in China in the early 840s, found the roads secure, government effective and Buddhist devotion ubiquitous. The level of economic activity was especially impressive, with barge convoys laden with grain, salt, charcoal, coal and timber plying the rivers and canals. Commercial and cultural contacts with central Asia were maintained via the Uighurs, whose fluctuating domains fingered west from Mongolia to Xinjiang and Ferghana. Nor did losing control of the Western Regions eliminate a Chinese presence there; in Turfan and Hami, garrison colonists stayed on to farm and serve under non-Han rulers as influential minorities. Meanwhile tribute-bearing missions continued to beat a path to Chang'an, and the empire's maritime trade flourished as never before.

But change there was, indeed a transformation, not just in terms of the empire's size but of the exercise of power within it. Despite some military successes, the Tang were unable either to extinguish the rebellion or to reassert firm control over their own hastily summoned forces. When in 763 hostilities were suspended, it was the result of a stalemate brought on by mutual exhaustion and compromise. The rebels were mollified by generous amnesties in which they were confirmed in the provincial and prefectural commands they had usurped, while some loyalist generals who had marched against the rebels expected, and exacted, similar recognition. In either case, the beneficiaries would often ignore imperial directives, contest attempts to unify the command of their forces, and show other signs of independence. The Tang restoration was thus offset by a much-diminished authority throughout the remaining empire. Supremacy had become contingent on concessions to the provinces and exploiting the rivalries of their mostly military governors.

Allies proved an equally mixed blessing. Assorted Turks and even an Arab contingent had joined the Tang forces against the rebels. But it was the Uighurs whose expert cavalry enabled the Tang to stem the tide of defeat, and Uighurs did not come cheap. A painful equality of status as well as massive subventions in cash and trade goods, plus an imperial

LATER TANG SUCCESSION, 750–907

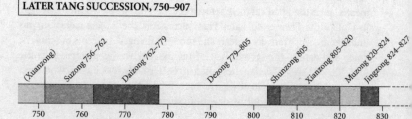

bride, had to be extended to their qaghan, whose horsemen might still, as in Luoyang in 762, sack an imperial capital when so inclined. In his *Zizhi Tongjian* Sima Guang puts the dead in Luoyang at tens of thousands and says the fires burned for several weeks. Elsewhere it was an army from Pinglu province (Shandong and part of Liaoning) which ran riot. Sent south to put down one of many unrelated rebellions and mutinies along the Yangzi, the supposedly loyalist forces from Pinglu plundered Yangzhou, the great commercial centre that had been *Sui* Yangdi's southern capital; among those reportedly massacred were several thousand foreign merchants.

More predictably, old adversaries from outside the frontier weighed in as challengers within it. In the extreme south-west the kingdom of Nanzhao, a composite state of indigenous non-Han peoples that had adopted Han principles of government while fiercely resisting Han intervention, expanded rapidly. From its lakeside capital at Dali, Nanzhao occupied most of modern Yunnan and in 763 established a second capital at what would become the city of Kunming. The site, well protected by more lakes and Yunnan's deep riverine gorges, was chosen 'both for its strategic location and its ability to support a large population'.[1] As Tang weakness became apparent, Nanzhao's forces penetrated north of the Yangzi into southern Sichuan, south-west into the Burmese states and south-east to the present-day Lao and Vietnamese borders.

Throughout the remainder of the eighth century Nanzhao accepted Tibetan rather than Chinese suzerainty. Its forces may even have fought with the Tibetans in their sustained offensive against the Tang. The ninth century brought a return to Tang suzerainty, but in the 860s Nanzhao broke away again and resumed its offensive, first in Sichuan and then in the south-east. Pushing down the Red River (Songkhoi), it made common cause with Tang's ever-rebellious subjects in Vietnam and briefly overran

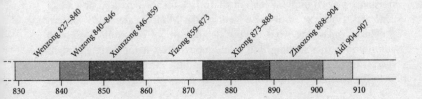

that province. A Tang general restored Chinese rule in Vietnam in 864, but with the empire then disintegrating, the Vietnamese were emboldened to launch another bid for independence. This time it succeeded. By 939 northern Vietnam had set up the first of its own imperial dynasties and the province was lost to China. Though, like Korea, the now-named 'Annam' would acknowledge nominal Chinese suzerainty when hard pressed (as, for instance, by the French in the nineteenth century), only in the direst of times (as, for instance, under Mongol rule) would it form part of the Celestial Empire. Nanzhao, likewise, would retain its hard-won identity until overrun by the Mongols and would reassert it thereafter whenever opportunity offered.

Nanzhao had merely nibbled at the Tang frontiers. The Tibetans bit deep. Thrusting into Xinjiang, Gansu and Shaanxi as rapidly as the Tang armies were withdrawn to oppose An Lushan, Tibetan forces were soon within striking distance of Chang'an itself. In 763 they actually took the city and ransacked it. *Tang* Daizong's reign (762–79) thus began with another ignominious flight from the capital. Though regained in 764, Chang'an continued under constant threat from the Tibetans until the end of the eighth century. The Gansu corridor and the imperial horse-breeding pastures in Shaanxi and Ningxia were in Tibetan hands; and in 791, despite Uighur support, the last remaining Chinese garrisons in the Western Regions surrendered to the Tibetans. Though the new 'Tibetan empire' proved short-lived, it was troubles within Tibet itself and pressure from the Uighurs and the Arabs which terminated it rather than any Tang resurgence. The aftermath of the An Lushan rebellion thus marked 'the end of Chinese administration in Eastern Turkestan [Xinjiang] for almost a thousand years'.[2] Though it scarcely deprived the Tang of much in the way of population or revenue, it severed nearly half of its erstwhile territory and put a stop to Chinese intervention in central Asia.

In the north, the defence of the long Mongolian frontier against Kyrgyz and Khitan encroachment was effectively subcontracted to the expensive Uighurs and, in the north-east, to the unruly successors of An Lushan's Great Yan dynasty. The rebellion had started in northern Hebei, and there, as in neighbouring parts of Shanxi, Henan and Shandong, the spirit of resistance proved impossible to quell. In fact, for the next four and a half centuries, from 755 until the advent of the Mongols, the north-eastern provinces (including what is now Beijing) would constitute a zone of autonomous rule shading into rival empire. Over it the Tang and their successors might claim suzerainty but had little effective control.

In the aftermath of the rebellion, An Lushan's generals in the north-east had been confirmed as provincial governors; this implied legitimacy but scarcely restrained their independent tendencies. They would remit no taxes to Chang'an except when Tang recognition was deemed desirable and then only in the form of tribute; they would usually nominate or select their own successors; and they would rarely respond to imperial appeals for military support. There is evidence that separatism here accorded with regional grievances nursed since the defeat of the north-east's Northern Qi by the north-west's Northern Zhou in the late sixth century. Military rule may even have been popular insofar as the withholding of central revenues may have reduced the tax burden on the cultivator.

With a fine sense of history, these military rulers in the north-east harked back to the pre-imperial 'Warring States' period. They favoured the loose vassalage that had then been on offer from the Later (Eastern) Zhou kings in Luoyang; and as of old, they vied for the conjectural status of the sovereign power's *ba* ('hegemon' or 'protector'). The north-east's then name of Yan had been revived by An Lushan; in a similar spirit, his successors would compare Tang demands for their submission with those of the Qin First Emperor when conducting China's first unification. As one anxious ruler put it in 782, 'martial, autocratic and possessing the same gifts that enabled *Qin* Shihuangdi and *Han* Wudi to exterminate figures of any independence, the Tang emperor intends to sweep clear Hebei and deny to its provinces the hereditary succession of command'.[3]

The emperor in question was *Tang* Dezong (Daizong's successor, r. 779–805); and he did indeed attempt to 'sweep clear Hebei'. But he succeeded no better than his predecessors. In fact this second Tang assault on the north-east in the 780s merely confirmed the feudatory tendency there. The military governors now declared themselves 'kings' and named their dynasties Qi, Zhao, Wei and Jin in accordance with 'Warring States' practice. In 805 an imperial emissary to Youzhou in the north of Hebei found its governor-king suitably deferential but otherwise the antithesis of a bureaucratic official. He wore 'a red turban round his head [and was dressed] in black boots and pantaloons, with a sword hanging from his belt to his left and a bow and a quiver of arrows to his right'.[4] Court formalities were curtailed in the north-east; martial values held sway.

Tang loyalists in Chang'an may also have endorsed the example of the 'Warring States' period. For a dynasty as reduced as the later Tang, the long-lasting suzerainty of the enfeebled Later (Eastern) Zhou (*c.* 770–250 BC) provided a face-saving precedent, plus the prospect of a nigh-indefinite tenure. Certainly, if one may judge by the frequency with which it was rejected, 'the idea that China had passed into an age of fragmented sovereignty like the feudalism of the Later Zhou was commonplace in the late eighth century'.[5] Du You, a neo-legalist much enamoured of Shang Yang's 'totalitarian' reorganisation of the Qin state in the fourth century BC, compiled a compendious history of government institutions in which he argued strongly against any abrogation of central power: feudal kingdoms might suit their feudal superiors, he noted, but directly ruled commanderies benefited the people. Similarly, in the early ninth century, Han Yü, an immodest and outspoken reformer whose polemics and literary revivalism anticipated the neo-Confucianism of the Song dynasty (960–1226), rejected both military rule and feudal fragmentation; they were undesirable expedients, alien to Han tradition (in both its ethnic and dynastic sense) and symptomatic of a creeping 'barbarisation'.

With the north-east virtually lost and the loyalties of Sichuan's governors far from certain, the axis of the empire slewed on to a north-west to south-east bearing that roughly followed the line of the Grand Canal or, farther west, the Han River. At one end, the Chang'an metropolitan area behind the hills that hemmed in the Wei valley in Shaanxi provided the Tang with a strong and hallowed base; but it was not self-supporting and, being vulnerable to attack from outside (as by the Tibetans), required a concentration of forces, plus Uighur amity. At the other end of the axis the lower Yangzi yielded the bumper crops and revenues on which the regime would depend. Tang survival therefore rested on control of this critical axis. By force of arms the separatist spirit was here ruthlessly stifled, while carefully positioned garrisons along the canal kept the north-eastern governor-kings at bay.

For all of which, reliable troops and dependable revenues were essential. To reduce the danger of military governors creating their own fiefs, the Tang endeavoured to replace them with civilian administrators or regulate them through supervision by palace eunuchs. The civilian administrators were not an immediate success. Steeped in the tactics of the Confucian 'Spring and Autumn' Annals, one bookish bureaucrat resurrected the ancient bullock-drawn chariot as a deterrent against An Lushan's veteran cavalry; it was like sending triremes against dreadnoughts. As late as 821 another civilian governor caused consternation in northern Hebei by arriving in a sedan chair and then desecrating An Lushan's tomb, pocketing military funds and allowing his followers to ridicule the pantalooned troopers as illiterate rebels. 'He did not understand the customs of the country,' says the Standard History of the Tang. In the end 'the people of Qi [this being the "kingdom's" assumed name] could restrain their anger no more ... They rebelled *en masse*, and imprisoned [Governor] Zhang Hongjing.[6]

But the policy of restoring civilian rule did enjoy some success, especially when backed by a credible military threat. In a third and last Tang offensive against the rebels, the forceful *Tang* Xianzong (r. 805–20) came nearest to re-establishing central authority with a series of military interventions in Sichuan, Zhejiang, Hebei and Shandong. As a result, by 820 all except three north-eastern provinces were under governors appointed or endorsed by Chang'an. Yet Xianzong's success was deceptive. Governors might renege or, as in the case of the tactless Zhang Hongjing, be removed by their own troops. Despite valiant attempts at recentralisation, the effect of *Tang* Xianzong's interventions was merely to regularise decentralisation.

In Confucian eyes, even this achievement was tainted by his resorting to eunuch support. To the emperor, eunuchs were indispensable as confidants, emissaries and informants. Their loyalties lay exclusively with their imperial master, and through them he could personally conduct policies of which his ministerial advisers might disapprove. A eunuch-led palace army had stood by the Tang in their dark days of exile in 756 and 763 and constituted the backbone of the imperial troops. Subsequently eunuch overseers were used to spy on military governors, restrain them and, where possible, supersede them as commanders in the field. Some eunuchs had acquired an education; others demonstrated military aptitude; all were credited with a genius for intrigue. But to the exam-empowered bureaucrat as to the office-accustomed aristocrat, eunuchs remained despicable parvenus and whining parasites. Since most were the product of slave-raiding expeditions in the wilder parts of Fujian and Guangxi, to a cultural purist like Han Yü they represented another 'barbarising' element as insidious as the unruly Uighurs and the never-poor Persians.

The rivalries within the administration itself were as acute as those within the empire at large – between civilians and the military, aristocrats and bureaucrats, the palace and the court, Buddhists and Confucianists. Han Yü is perhaps best known for an 819 diatribe against Buddhism and Daoism; it was censured at the time, but in 843 *Tang* Wuzong (r. 840–46) introduced a draconian proscription of Buddhism from which the Buddhist establishment never entirely recovered. The visit of the Japanese monk Ennin happened to coincide with this episode, and he suspected it had been triggered by a Confucianist vendetta against a pro-Buddhist eunuch. No rivalry was more intense than that between the palace eunuchs and all those who, on whatever grounds, deemed themselves courtiers as of right.

Though soon reversed, the 843–48 crackdown on the Buddhist estab-lishment may have occasioned as much misery as the Cultural Revolution. Thousands of monasteries are said to have been destroyed and as many as 250,000 monks and nuns defrocked, some being injured or killed in the process. Ennin portrays *Tang* Wuzong as a Daoist fanatic and notes that the Buddhists were not the only ones to suffer; Manichaeans, Nestorian Christians and Zoroastrians were also subject to censure. But as he admits, the motivation was as much economic as ideological. The dissolution of the monasteries brought the confiscation of their buildings, the reposses-sion of their extensive landed estates, the return of their inmates and dependants to the tax and labour pool and, most important of all, the melting down of their vast accumulations of gold, silver and copper stat-uary to underpin the fragile currency.[7]

Raising and provisioning armies, maintaining garrisons and paying off the Uighurs – or deflecting their exodus when in 840 the Uighur qaghanate was expelled from Mongolia by the Kyrgyz – placed a heavy strain on the imperial exchequer. In later Tang's interminable struggle to reclaim the empire, revenue was both a requisite and an objective. At the height of the An Lushan rebellion, when practically no tax receipts were reaching Chang'an, a proposal had been adopted for reintroducing the defunct salt and iron monopoly. Iron's inclusion was a nod to the Han dynasty prece-dent and was only spasmodically regulated; but salt was commandeered. A hefty tax was imposed on it and a special commission set up to collect the tax and enforce the monopoly. Since the salt panning and mining areas were comparatively easy to oversee, it proved an instant success. By the 770s half of the empire's revenue was coming from salt. The monopoly principle was extended to other commodities, most notably liquor and then tea, a crop grown largely in hilly areas like Fujian and Sichuan. It had been popular since the mid-seventh century and was now much in demand by Uighurs and Tibetans as well. Based in Yangzhou in the south, the Monopolies Commission was staffed by a new class of commercial experts and grew into a financial agency that rivalled the regular bureaucracy as an avenue for professional advancement. It also spawned a thriving nexus of licensed merchant-distributors, plus another of unlicensed merchant-smugglers.

The catastrophic decline in the registration of households as a result of the An Lushan rebellion boded ill for the restoration of the old system of taxation based on population and landholdings. By way of replacement, therefore, in 780 a 'two-tax system' was introduced. 'Generally considered one of the major events in Chinese economic history', its 'two-tax' dimen-sion was in fact incidental; it simply meant that, to spread receipts, it was levied in some areas at one time of the year, in others at another, and in most at both, in effect splitting the levy between late spring and harvest time. Not revolutionary either was the quota system whereby central government negotiated each province's tax liability with the local authorities and took no further part in its collection. The novelty lay in its assessment, which was to be graduated according to wealth and assets rather than the number of household members, calculated partly in cash (though collected mainly in kind), and apportioned in accordance with prevailing local practice. In other words it recognised the inconsistencies that had developed before and since the rebellion, and 'in giving up any pretence at uniformity . . . tacitly accepted existing tax inequalities'.[8]

The inequalities were between one district and another and between the tax-collector and the taxpayer. Since grain prices plummeted in the early ninth century, all who were assessed in cash but paid in grain found their liability soaring by the year; unable to meet the demand, peasants either deserted, leaving their peers to make good their contributions, or gravitated into paid labour; either way, their holdings were swallowed up by large estates. Meanwhile the system afforded the provincial authorities numerous opportunities to reapportion, manipulate or simply withhold receipts due to the central government. *Tang* Xianzong attempted to redress this situation, breaking up existing provinces and negotiating quotas direct with the smaller prefectures. But the cost of his military adventures was never covered, and any reduction in the military establishment by his successors invited mutiny.

Resistance mounted as soon as *Tang* Xianzong died in 820. Agrarian and military uprisings, mysterious acts of terrorism and organised smuggling by large gangs were commonplace by mid-century. The smugglers, waterborne as well as land-based, were heavily armed and infested those very regions on which the government was most dependent – the Yangzi and the south. In 856, in a sudden spate of disturbances, the south 'was transformed almost overnight from one of the most stable regions into one of the most volatile'.[9] Three years later a bandit group in Zhejiang beat off attempts at suppression – the region had been starved of troops to preclude the provincial intransigence that characterised the north-east – and, attracting support from other gangs, vagrant peasants and aggrieved officials, soon fielded a well-organised army of some thirty thousand. To defeat it, a crack general had to be summoned back from Vietnam, and forces sent from the north, including the first Uighur cavalry ever to serve south of the Yangzi.

This was followed in the 860s by a succession of army mutinies

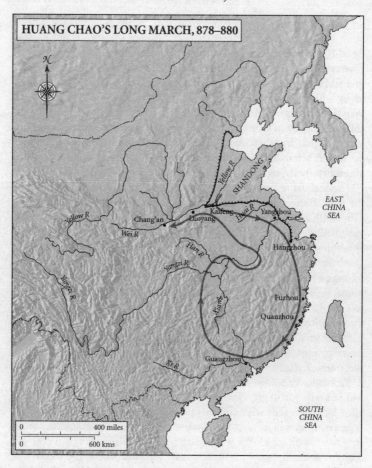

HUANG CHAO'S LONG MARCH, 878–880

triggered by the demand for troops to oppose the Nanzhao forces in Vietnam. In 868 a battalion stationed in Guizhou broke ranks and marched north, heading for home in Henan. Again the revolt snowballed and was put down only after the dispatch of more troops from the north, many of them this time Turks. Their commander, himself a Turk, was rewarded with the Tang family name of Li; his son, Li Keyong, would emerge as a major contender during the last days of the Tang, and his grandson would found one of the many post-Tang dynasties.

The great all-China upheaval that finally undermined Tang authority owed something to both these prior insurgencies. It began in the 870s among bandit gangs on the western borders of Shandong. Joined by its eventual leader, a minor official from Shandong called Huang Chao, the revolt spread west to threaten Luoyang and then south to the middle Yangzi. Mutinies among the imperial troops and dissension among their commanders played into the rebels' hands; provincial capitals were sacked; the administration collapsed throughout much of central China. A major Tang victory in 878 only spurred Huang Chao into one of the most outrageous peregrinations in history. Back in Shandong at the time, he led his men south to the Yangzi delta, crossed Zhejiang into the mountains of Fujian, and then trekked through some of the most difficult terrain in the country to Fuzhou and Guangzhou (Canton), both of which port cities he sacked. It was said that 120,000 were massacred in Guangzhou, over half the city's population. Reports reaching the Persian Gulf told of Arab, Persian and Indian merchants suffering disproportionately.

In 879 Huang Chao turned north again. Anticipating the long marches of the Taiping rebels in 1851–53 and of the communists in 1934–35, he looped west through Guizhou before regaining the middle Yangzi. There was method in these meanderings: like Mao Zedong, Huang Chao was turning tactical retreat into political triumph. The government had interpreted his southern excursion as a retreat; indeed, in the course of his thirty months on the move (as against Mao's thirteen), Huang Chao repeatedly sought a favourable amnesty. But the failure of these negotiations obliged and emboldened him to raise his sights. Once he was back across the Yangzi, Chang'an became the goal; court, eunuchs and the dynasty itself were now the target. Dissidents of some calibre began to flock to his standard and disillusioned Tang commanders to stand aside. Effecting an almost miraculous escape from the rich Yangzi delta, in 880 the footsore rebels homed in on Luoyang. They took it almost unopposed, such was the imperial disarray. Then, after nearly three years and 4,800 kilometres (3,000 miles) on the march, they stormed into the Wei valley to capture Chang'an.

Tang Xizong (r. 873–88), like most of the last Tang emperors, owed his throne to the eunuchs. Emulating his great ancestor *Tang* Xuanzong, he and they fled into Sichuan. In early 881 Huang Chao entered the city in triumph and at first put on a brave display of founding his own dynasty. But his troops proved uncontrollable. Not for the first time the world's greatest city was sacked and its palaces torched. *Citoyens* joined in the carnage, streets ran with blood. 'The Lament of Lady Chin', a long poem by Wei Zhuang, who himself fell foul of the rebels but later rose to prominence in Sichuan, paints a Goya-esque scene of devastation, rape, butchery and cannibalism. Suppressed by the poet himself, the poem in question was thought lost until no less then fourteen copies of it were found among Aurel Stein's treasure trove from Dunhuang in the early twentieth century. Evidently it had struck a chord at the time.

The last Tang emperors, their names in Pinyin sounding an alphabetic cadenza (Yizong, Xizong, Zhaozong, Zhaoxuan), were paraded as puppets and died as pawns in the war games of their would-be successors. It was a repeat of the last days of Han; the imperial entourage was carted from one place of exile to the next; Chang'an changed hands half a dozen times, its spoils depreciating with each takeover; the eunuchs were massacred; the tenth century dawned on another period of chronic disunion.

FIVE DYNASTIES OR TEN KINGDOMS

The Tang theoretically staggered on until 907, from which date the Standard Histories grudgingly recognise a Later Liang dynasty. Later Liang (907–23) was the creation of one of rebel Huang Chao's erstwhile lieutenants. A scruple-free tyrant, he disciplined his troops by having them tattooed (it made defectors easier to identify) and by executing any who survived defeat or whose commanders were killed in battle. Despite such incentives to victory, the Later Liang managed only sixteen sanguinary years before being toppled by the Turk general Li Keyong, he whose father had helped the Tang in the 860s.

Trading on the legitimacy implied by the Tang emperor having awarded them his Li surname, this new dynasty (923–37) also called themselves Tang and claimed to be restoring Tang rule; they did resume the Tang struggle with its north-eastern governor-kings in Hebei and enjoyed some success there. But they too soon succumbed and were followed in quick succession by three other dynastic founders, the first two Turk and all

THE FIVE (NORTHERN) DYNASTIES, 907–959

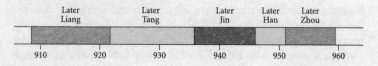

| Later Liang | Later Tang | Later Jin | Later Han | Later Zhou |

| 910 | 920 | 930 | 940 | 950 | 960 |

three in fact successors of the Hebei governor-kings. Each adopted a dynastic name (Jin, Han, Zhou) that will be familiar. To avoid confusion, all the houses in this cluster of post-Tang northern dynasties are generally prefixed with a 'Later'; and the resulting sequence of 'Five Dynasties' (Later Liang, Later Tang, Later Jin, Later Han, Later Zhou) gives its name to the whole period.

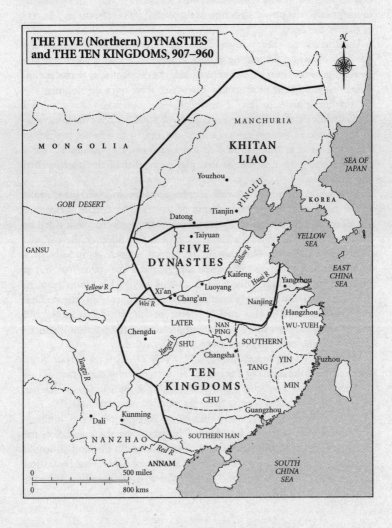

THE FIVE (Northern) DYNASTIES and THE TEN KINGDOMS, 907–960

Traditionally dated 907–60, the 'Five Dynasties' period ended when the last of the five gave way to a sixth, the long-lasting Song. The Song would reunite most of the empire, and their accession is usually taken to mark the beginning of a dazzling new age. But reunification was not completed till 979. Until then the Song conformed to patterns of rule set during the Five Dynasties period. The early, or Northern, Song dynasts are therefore best considered in that context, any other 'making it very difficult for us to understand the power structure of the Wudai ["Five Dynasties"] as well as that of the Song'.[10]

But there is another problem. Since the Five Dynasties rose and fell – 'controlled' would be putting it too strongly – within a comparatively small, if growing, part of northern China, the conventional periodisation may exaggerate their prominence. Elsewhere there were developments of no less importance. In the far north powerful new states that straddled the erstwhile frontier began to emerge, most notably under the leadership of the Khitan in the north-east and of the Tangut (a Tibetan people) in the north-west; as the Liao and Xi Xia kingdoms, they would achieve a cohesion and pose a challenge that prefigured that of the later Jurchen and Mongols.

Meanwhile, within the erstwhile empire, provinces followed the example of the north-east before the collapse of the Tang to declare themselves kingdoms and form rival and sometimes stabler states than that ruled by the Five Dynasties. Almost without exception, they adopted the regional identities of antiquity. There was a Shu (and then another) in Sichuan, a Chu in Hunan, a Wu on the middle Yangzi, and a Yue (later Wu-Yue) at the mouth of the Yangzi. Collectively known as the 'Ten Kingdoms' (though there were sometimes more, sometimes fewer) they have been little studied. But 'Ten Kingdoms' is also used as a term for the period as a whole, and it does perhaps give a more accurate impression of the political fragmentation than the exclusively northern 'Five Dynasties'.

Ouyang Xiu's *Historical Records of the Five Dynasties*, a private work later accorded the status of a Standard History, portrays the period as one of such unrelieved treachery and bloodshed that the Chinese preference for a single centralised empire becomes readily understandable. The rash of regional sovereignties proves disastrous. Foreign incursions multiply and justice is nowhere to be found. Disasters come thick and fast, the virtuous suffer with the vicious, and destitution stalks the land. 'It would be wrong to assume a total absence of loyal men in the Five Dynasties,' says Ouyang Xiu, 'I have found three.' 'Woe it is', he elsewhere laments, 'that for a total of fifty-three years, in a world ruled by five houses, so few

THE TEN KINGDOMS OF THE FIVE DYNASTIES PERIOD

KINGDOM	ERA	RULERS	CAPITAL
Wu	35 years (902–937)	4 rulers	Yangzhou/Nanjing
Southern Tang	38 years (937–975)	3 rulers	Nanjing
Former Shu	18 years (907–925)	2 rulers	Chengdu
Later Shu	30 years (935–965)	2 rulers	Chengdu
Southern Han	54 years (917–971)	4 rulers	Guangzhou
Chu	24 years (927–951)	6 rulers	Changsha
Wu-Yueh	71 years (907–978)	5 rulers	Hangzhou
Min	36 years (905–945)	5 rulers	Fuzhou
Nanping	39 years (924–963)	5 rulers	Jiangling
Northern Han	28 years (951–979)	4 rulers	Taiyuan

of the officials with the misfortune to live then insisted on total integrity and undivided loyalty.'[11]

As with accounts of the 'Warring States' and the post-Han 'Period of Disunion', Ouyang Xiu's magisterial history of the Five Dynasties focuses on the northern plains and features marches and countermarches ad nauseam, bewildering intrigues and brutal encounters. Often unedifying, it sometimes verges on the unreadable with more places and persons per page than a directory. No doubt the period was indeed a troubled one. But as always, allowance needs to be made for the circumstances under which such histories were compiled and for the preferences of their writers and editors.

Historians, official and otherwise, belonged to that class of scholarly bureaucrats whose status and livelihood depended on the authority of the emperor and the stability of the state. They were seen as the empire's adornment and they acted as its propagandists. Ouyang Xiu wrote under the Song, when the empire had been substantially reunited. If his account of the Five Dynasties is unduly depressing, it is in part because it was meant to be. By disparaging a fragmented past, he glorified a more integrated present. Described by his translator as 'a giant among giants on the eleventh century intellectual landscape', Ouyang Xiu may have been above ingratiating himself with the Song emperor. But he was dependent on materials compiled by men who, keen to do just that, used history to emphasise the singularity of Heaven's Son and the indivisibility of 'All-under-Heaven'. The historiographical tradition invariably talks up empire while playing down regional variables.

This makes it difficult to answer some fundamental questions. How long has China been united? For how much of its history has it been ruled by Chinese? How continuous is its record of political integration? It all depends on how one defines the Chinese and where one starts the history. A timeline of empire based on the traditional dates of each all-China dynasty suggests that 'the political coherence of [the] Chinese population . . . has been maintained for almost three-quarters of the time that has elapsed since the First Emperor of Qin'.[12] So says the excellent *Cultural Atlas of China*, though *The Cambridge History of China* suggests 'around half' rather than 'almost three-quarters'. Both assume that the Chinese population is synonymous with those considered ethnically and culturally Han, so excluding all those non-Han peoples prominent in the country's history plus all those Tibetans, Uighurs and other minorities whom the government of today regards as Chinese. Moreover, both estimates raise the question of why earlier periods, like that of the pre-imperial Zhou and the 'Warring States' – periods more seminal to Chinese civilisation than the Greek and Roman republics to Mediterranean civilisation – should be left out of the equation. Include them, and the three-quarters-to-a-half of recorded history during which China has been 'politically coherent' shrinks to no more than a quarter.

Ouyang Xiu himself conceded the point. Looking back, admittedly from an eleventh-century vantage point, he could detect little in the way of political coherence.

> Since antiquity, times of good governance have been the aberration and tumult the norm. Kings of the the Three Dynasties [Xia, Shang and Zhou] ruled for hundreds of years, yet a mere handful of rulers merit much attention. More, then, can hardly be expected of later times, let alone the Five Dynasties![13]

But all the above estimates may be further flawed. The tendency has already been noted for official histories to exaggerate – or elasticate – the duration of favoured dynasties and credit them with exercising a universal authority that was not actually effective for anything like as long. For instance, the empire of the Tang, though traditionally coterminous with the dynasty (618–907), can hardly be described as politically coherent after

Huang Chao's capture of Chang'an in 881; it had in fact been in turmoil throughout the three decades previous to that, and had been seriously compromised ever since An Lushan's rebellion in 755. Similar reservations apply to the last century of the Later Han. Add the imminent Song (who lost half the empire for 150 years), the Mongol Yuan (whose decentralised dominion became basically 'a conglomeration of regions under strong regional governments'[14]), the Manchu Qing (whose last century was also one of ill-disguised chaos) and the twentieth-century republic (beset by warlords and Japanese invaders until 1949), and China's record of political integration, whether under Han rulers or non-Han, becomes still less impressive. As in the case of the 'Great Wall' or the 'Grand Canal', episodic segments of monumental achievement have been exaggerated and conflated to convey a misleading impression of near-continuity.

This is not to deny a remarkable continuity of political culture. The Mandate, the supremacy of Heaven's Son, the concept of *zhongguo* (whether as 'the central states' or 'the Middle Kingdom'), reverence for a political hierarchy grounded in Confucian morality, and the superiority of this shared culture over the uncultured 'barbarism' of non-Han peoples – these were universally acknowledged. Political integration was invariably applauded, inter-dynastic disorder invariably disparaged; the one was synonymous with 'good governance', according to Ouyang Xiu, the other with 'tumult'. Any possibility of things being the other way round, of empire being a burden and regional autonomy a boon, is not so much as scouted in any surviving text.

Yet latter-day historians, especially non-Chinese ones accustomed to Europe's record of political fragmentation, have indeed queried this equation. They note the periodic resurgence throughout Chinese history of regional entities such as Shu, Chu and Wu, potential states that were as populous and distinctive as any European kingdom; they observe the search for power-balancing constructs based on them; they deplore the dearth of regional historical studies; and though quite unacceptable to most of China's historians, they sometimes interpret a phrase like 'imperial inter-dynastic disorder' as 'only a derogatory term for multi-state order'.[15] Centralised rule is seen as a recipe for ossification, while state-on-state 'tumult' is recast as a competitive dynamic, productive of social renewal, commercial enterprise and great outbursts of creativity and invention.

Thus the 'Warring States' period spawned the 'hundred schools of philosophy', and the 'Period of Disunion' hosted the transformation of Daoism and the consummation of the great affair with Buddhism. The Five Dynasties/Ten Kingdoms looks to have been too brief and chaotic for anything comparable. Yet if it is taken to cover the whole period of imperial eclipse between the collapse of Tang authority in, say, 850 and the final triumph of Song authority *c.* 980, then it too was by no means barren of distinction.

From the archival treasure trove of Dunhuang, Aurel Stein's 1907 haul would include numerous fragments of a Buddhist doctrinal text called the *Diamond Sutra.* It had first been translated by Kumarajiva around AD 400 and was so called because it held the promise, for those who mastered it, of cutting away all worldly illusions 'like a diamond'. One complete version, comprising seven sheets of paper printed with the Chinese text, pasted together to form a scroll, and now in the British Library, carries a Chinese date equivalent to 11 May 868. Contrary to popular opinion, it is probably not 'the world's first printed book'. Replicating images and written characters using inked blocks carved in relief, a process not much removed from that used for making moulds for ceramics and metals, had been practised in China since at least the eighth century. But it is the oldest complete printed text with a date. The development of printing, seven centuries before Gutenberg, and eleven before any of India's scripts was printed, was undoubtedly the most momentous of all Chinese inventions; as a result, Europe and India still have dozens of languages and literatures but China only one. And this 'infotech' revolution substantially took place during the extended Five Dynasties/Ten Kingdoms period. The first use of movable type may also be datable to the period, though 'the earliest authoritative account of its use' comes a few decades later in the early eleventh century.[16]

These were not mere technical landmarks. Under the Five Dynasties there appeared the first complete printed edition of all the Confucianist classics. It ran to 130 volumes, took twenty-one years and was completed in 953. Arguably the ability to replicate and disseminate the classical corpus ad lib did more to permanently enshrine both Confucian values and the Chinese system of writing than the edicts of any emperor or the injunctions of any scholar. An eccentric character called Feng Dao is generally credited with overseeing this first printing, and one might expect his name to be held in awe by his fellow literati. Yet historian Ouyang Xiu does no such thing. In his Five Dynasties history, his biographical sketch of Feng Dao is to be found neither among the 'Martyrs to Virtue' nor the 'Martyrs in Service' but tucked away, between a Tuyuhun leader who jumped down a well and a man who was 'perpetually busy without achieving anything', in a section entitled 'Miscellaneous Biographies'. Ouyang Xiu disapproved of Feng Dao.

It was not because he was 'frugal to the point of self-deprivation'. For a long time Feng Dao lived in a hut, slept on straw rather than a mattress, and 'found quiet contentment' in passing his salary on to his servants. Captured damsels that came his way as chief minister he lodged separately until he could ascertain their origins and discreetly send them home. He alleviated a famine, slipped out at night to till the fields of those who neglected them, and mourned the death of his father with full honours. He was a Confucian paragon in everything – except, that is, his professional career.

Ouyang Xiu explains this with a story of the period about a woman called Li. Lately widowed, Li set off with her young son and her husband's corpse to return to her parents' home. An innkeeper, suspicious of her travelling unaccompanied by servants, refused her a bed; she refused to leave; he took her by the arm to evict her. For a chaste gentlewoman this was too much. She grabbed an axe and, letting out a long wail, 'lopped off her own arm'. As she later explained, the stranger's touch had defiled her; and since she 'had failed to protect her chastity', it was her duty to remove the arm rather than let it pollute her whole body. The story was cited as a classic example of Confucian piety; Ouyang Xiu prefers terms that translate as 'integrity' or 'regard for one's moral repute'; and it was these that Feng Dao, for all his learning, so conspicuously lacked. In the Confucian system of interlocking relationships, the minister should be as exclusively jealous of the dynasty he served as the emperor of the Heaven he served or the wife of the husband she served. Yet instead of being shamed into retirement by the failure of his chosen dynasty (it was the Turk Later Tang, second of the Five Dynasties), Feng Dao had taken pride in ingratiating himself with the next, then the next, then the next.

He had in fact served under all Five Dynasties except the first – plus, briefly, a Khitan ruler. No doubt the supervision of his great publishing venture required that he cling to office. But for Ouyang Xiu, as for Sima Guang, who tells the same story in his slightly later *Zizhi Tongjian*, Feng Dao's complacency was unforgivable. 'In a world beleaguered by universal chaos and alien invasions that gravely imperilled the fate of all living souls', Feng Dao seemed to have rejoiced in his infidelity. He was actually proud to have cohabited with so many emperors. 'I have always found contentment with the times,' Feng had written in his autobiography. 'And with age, I find contentment within. Whay joy could be greater?' Almost any, Ouyang Xiu might have snorted. A man unembarrassed by prospering in an age of such self-evident depravity had forfeited all claim to virtue. In effect, the times reflected the calibre of the man and the man the calibre of the times. Since an empire in disarray could expect little in the way of righteous achievement, Feng Dao's publishing programme is not so much as mentioned by Ouyang Xiu.[17]

Another complete set of the Confucian classics was produced a decade later in the Shu (Sichuan) capital of Chengdu. 'It was intended by its sponsor to be sold inexpensively to poor scholars.'[18] In general, Tang literary and artistic traditions fared better under the Ten Kingdoms than under the war-torn Five Dynasties in the north. In Hangzhou (the Wu-Yue, and nowadays Zhejiang, capital) and Nanjing (the capital of a 'Southern Tang' state), the poems of the great Tang masters appeared in print for the first time. Chengdu saw the publication in 940 of an important anthology of the lyric verses known as *ci* that were originally composed for a musical accompaniment. The title of the collection, 'Amidst the Flowers', refers to the company of courtesans. Love poems of a dreamy and erotic nature, they must have seemed to Ouyang Xiu, as they did to later Confucianists, typical products of a degenerate age. Instead of extolling the integrity of noble ladies like the armless widow Li, they explored the charms of sated harlots and inebriated sirens. Analogies have been drawn between this anthology with 'its comfort sex in a curtained feminine space' (as one modern critic puts it) and the failure of its contributors, who might otherwise have found useful employment in the bureaucracy, 'to confront the crisis of a divided and war-torn nation'.[19]

At around the same time, and also in progressive Sichuan, printing facilitated the first-known appearance of paper money when merchants began issuing promissory notes in lieu of the often scarce and always burdensome strings of iron or copper cash. Officially certified and standardised under the Song, the practice gave birth to the banknote. Marco Polo's description, three centuries later, of money 'made out of the bark of trees', while not entirely accurate, well conveys a foreigner's utter incredulity at this momentous development: in converting arboreal pulp into a universally accepted medium of exchange with a value far in excess of its intrinsic worth, 'you might say that the Great [Khubilai] Khan . . . has mastered the art of alchemy', notes Polo. 'He has such a quantity made that with it he could buy all the treasure of the world.'[20]

Helped by such innovations, much of the world's treasure had been circulating more freely in China than anywhere else. As of the tenth century what has been called 'a commercial revolution' was under way. With Chang'an in ruins, its thoroughfares already choked by weeds, the Five Dynasties in the north sometimes located their main capital at Luoyang but more commonly farther east at Kaifeng. The subsequent Song adoption of Kaifeng would confirm this significant eastward shift in the empire's political fulcrum, away from the now impoverished and vulnerable Wei valley to a more strategically useful point from which to oppose Khitan encroachment in the north-east. Ironically the process would be completed, three centuries later, with relocation to what had been the Khitan capital – but had by then become the Mongol metropolis – of Dadu, a city later known as Beijing.

But commanding the crucial junction between the Grand Canal and the Yellow River, Kaifeng's importance was also economic. As the northern capital, it grew to a city of over a million with sumptuary and revenue requirements to match. Its vulnerability to flooding (368 inundations would be recorded over the next 750 years) was the price to be paid for hosting the riverine entrepôt of the north. Fields and crops, together with the old system of taxation and service grounded on them, were being matched by money and trade as the basis of the economy. Higher-yielding grains, greater specialisation in manufacturing (ceramics and ironmongery as well as paper and printing), cheap and efficient transport, larger, freer markets and burgeoning financial and brokerage services made commerce sufficiently attractive to lull Confucian reservations about profiting from the product of others. Markets and ferry ports generated towns, local merchants became local magnates. The salt and tea monopolies, whether as officially operated or informally circumvented, had shown the way, creating both public revenue and private wealth.

Urbanisation was especially notable along the Yangzi and in the south, from whose great port cities a wind of adventurous endeavour blew inland. As of the tenth century, maritime trade for the first time exceeded that conducted overland. Locally built shipping was increasingly prominent, and Chinese vessels began to make regular sailings to mainland south-east Asia, the Indonesian archipelago and possibly Sri Lanka and south India. Financed by local investors, the trade generated something like the commercial fever that would seize the Italian city-ports in the thirteenth century, and later Lisbon and London. Past estuary and anchorage, from Yangzhou to Guangzhou, the tide of liquidity spread up river and canal. In China seaboard zones of economic enterprise, though as yet informal, were not invented in the nineteenth century by foreigners – let alone in the late twentieth century by bespoke communists. Nor should official participation in a market free-for-all that was frowned on by conventional ideology cause any surprise.

Whether or not the political fragmentation of the tenth century encouraged these developments, the wars and disturbances reported by Ouyang

Xiu prompted a new wave of migration to the south. Yet there is no sign of an overall decline in population like that in the 'Period of Disunion'. Quite the opposite. In the mid-eighth century, the total population is thought to have been around 60 million, of whom 60 per cent were living in the Yellow River basin. By the end of the tenth century, it was nearing 100 million, of whom less than 40 per cent resided in the Yellow River basin; over 60 per cent now lived in the Yangzi basin and the south. Accelerated by territorial losses in the north, the long-drawn-out shift to the more productive south had finally tipped the demographic scales. As of the Five Dynasties/Ten Kingdoms period, more Chinese grew rice than millet and wheat; their winters were warmer and their summers wetter; their acquaintance with the Inner Asian steppes was slight; and they lived not under the turbulent Five Dynasties but among the opulent but historically neglected Ten Kingdoms.

SONG AND LIAO

An insistence on 'dynasties' in the north but mere 'kingdoms' or 'states' elsewhere betrays the need, born of the historians' insistence on the pre-eminence of empire, for an unbroken pedigree of imperial validation, or 'legitimacy'. This was usually expressed in terms of the Mandate, which, descending from dynasty to dynasty, could neither be shared nor suspended. Though many might claim it, only one at a time could actually enjoy it. But a difficulty lay in deciding which one. In the case of the third-century division of the Han empire into 'Three Kingdoms' (Cao Wei, Han-Shu and Sun Wu), the problem was never satisfactorily resolved. But when in the eleventh century historians such as Ouyang Xiu and Sima Guang addressed the same problem in respect of the Five Dynasties/Ten Kingdoms, they had an advantage. The longevity and distinction of the Song dynasty under which they lived made it indisputably a 'legitimate' holder of the Mandate, and this in turn provided a reassuring perspective from which to assess the status of its predecessors.

Like the long narrative scroll-paintings that became fashionable under the Song and were so rolled that, on unfurling them, the concluding scene came into view first, the historians spooled backwards. The Song had superseded the Later Zhou, who must therefore have been legitimate; the Later Zhou had succeeded the Later Han, who must be likewise; the Later Han the Later Jin, ditto; and so on back to the Later Liang, who had overthrown the indisputably legitimate Tang. The legitimate line must follow this northern succession of 'Five Dynasties'. It mattered not that more Chinese in fact lived under the other, stabler dispensations of the Ten Kingdoms. Empire had traditionally emanated from the north, successful dynasties had almost invariably hailed from there, and the record allowed no other interpretation. Not until the Ming (1368–1644) would the entire empire be governed from the south, and then only briefly.

For Ouyang Xiu, a minor problem remained: the scheme meant recognising as legitimate the detestable rebel regime of the Later Liang. Besides tattooing its troops, a stigma as demeaning as torture in that it would stay to disfigure them into the afterlife, the Later Liang had murdered two Tang emperors and in general 'represented an horrific evil that deserves eradication from history'. Earlier accounts of the period had done just that – eradicate them – hence in effect reducing the Five Dynasties to four. Ouyang Xiu considered doing the same but was dissuaded by an estimable regard for the facts, backed by Confucius's insistence on rectifying names – or in this case calling a spade a spade. 'Acknowledging vice' would serve as a warning to posterity, he thought; and it could only enhance the general credibility of his account.[21]

The other four of the Five Dynasties posed no problem. Three were non-Han, but that was nothing unusual; and though all were usurpers, so had been the founders of most previous dynasties. All being descended from military governors of the Tang, it was their mutual jealousies which made for instability rather than their ethnicity. To gain power, any dynastic contender needed the support of his peers, which meant placating other governor-commanders with promises of titles and territories. But to rule he needed to rein in these same magnates and reduce their forces – which could all too easily provoke another challenge. The cycle was hard to break; and the troops themselves had a habit of propelling their commanders towards the throne. What mattered was that a new dynasty provide tangible evidence of its having inherited the Mandate, and this, in tumultuous times, meant enlarging its empire.

In alliance with the resurgent Khitan, the Later Tang (923–36), second of the Five Dynasties, had overcome the unspeakable Later Liang, so doubling the size of their territories. They had also briefly grabbed the state of Shu (Sichuan). The Later Jin (936–46), another Turk family, had fared less well. Puppets of the Khitan from the start, they were obliged to cede to them sixteen crucial prefectures lying in an arc from what is now Beijing to Datong in northern Shanxi. They also had to recognise the Khitan leader as their 'father' and overlord; thus 'for the first time a Chinese regime openly acknowledged the suzerainty of an alien dynasty'.[22] Heaven duly showed its disgust with a spate of natural disasters. In 946–47 the Khitan actually occupied Kaifeng. This ended the Later Jin's wretched decade; assuming they had in fact possessed the Mandate, they clearly did so no longer. The Later Han (947–50), who were also Turks, reclaimed Kaifeng and might perhaps have regained the prefectures lost to the Khitan. But within a matter of months they were ousted by the Later Zhou (951–60), the fifth of the Five Dynasties.

The founder of the Later Zhou was ethnically Han Chinese, well educated and in every respect a worthy precursor of the mighty Song; so was his adopted son and heir. As is the way in the Standard Histories, their attributes foreshadow their success. Most of China north of the Huai River (but excluding the north-east and the sixteen ceded prefectures) was consolidated; and under the founder's son (*Later Zhou* Shizong, r. 954–59) expeditions regained two of the lost prefectures and probed south as far as the Yangzi. There one of the largest of the Ten Kingdoms was forced to acknowledge Later Zhou sovereignty. In 955 *Later Zhou* Shizong felt strong enough to emulate *Tang* Wuzong and pillage the resurgent Buddhist establishment. '*Zhongguo* [i.e. the Middle Kingdom of the Five Dynasties] faced a shortage of cash at the time,' explains Ouyang Xiu, 'so the confiscation of all Buddhist bronze statuary was mandated for recasting as coin.' In the process, some '3,336 monasteries were eliminated'. Yet Shizong himself made light of the affair. Since the Buddha, as he understood it, had attached no importance to physical existence and had resumed his bodily form only so that mankind might benefit from his teaching, 'how', enquired the emperor, 'could he possibly begrudge us a bunch of his bronze statues?'[23] Muffled by deference and often marred by translation, an imperial sense of humour can never be discounted.

The Later Zhou's one great misfortune was the premature death of this Shizong, aged thirty-eight, in 959. His seven-year-old son succeeded him, but within months the dynasty was challenged by its most trusted general. A certain Zhao Kuangyin, fearless in battle and consummate in statecraft, this was the man who, as the next dynastic founder, would be posthumously known as *Song* Taizu (r. 960–76). At the time he appeared just another usurper. His background was identical to other contenders'. His prospects seemed no better than those of the five ephemeral dynasties to which he was about to add a sixth. Sure enough, move for move, his usurpation mirrored that of the Later Zhou. Other potential contenders were won over, while in public he proclaimed himself utterly unworthy of the throne; but his troops and their commanders clamoured for his elevation; the portents were adamant; and the matter was settled when, acknowledging his superior merit, the mother of the last of the Later Zhou insisted on her son abdicating in his favour.

The whole procedure was suspiciously predictable, yet the results were far from expected. Defying precedent, *Song* Taizu, and then his brother and successor, *Song* Taizong (r. 976–97), not only quelled all opposition within their northern empire but accelerated the programme of southern conquest begun by the Later Zhou. One by one, most of the Ten Kingdoms were brought to heel so that within thirty years the empire was substantially reunited. To their still greater credit, the Song achieved this with a minimum of violence and some conspicuous gestures of magnanimity. The new dynasty had a measured feel to it, evincing intent without provoking antagonism. Song rule was revealed as more formal and much more restrained than that of the Tang. Executions and floggings would be comparatively rare, vendettas and purges comparatively few. Though the founding brothers campaigned vigorously, and though the forces under their direct control were massively augmented to nearly a million men, both they and their successors emphasised civilian rule. Instead of declaring a grandiloquent new beginning, they discreetly manipulated or bypassed existing offices to create a centralised and responsive system of control that was largely proof against the breakaway forces that had shattered the Tang empire. They cultivated the arts of peace, surrounded themselves with scholars, and encouraged a lofty imperial mystique that proved more effective in deterring internal challengers than the threat of punitive expeditions.

But what made all this possible, and what in posterity's eyes seriously tarnished the early Song achievement, was a painful accommodation with the Khitan in the north-east. The abject capitulation of the Later Jin (third of the Five Dynasties) to the Khitan would not be repeated; 'the suzerainty of an alien dynasty' was repudiated and the son-to-father relationship with the Khitan qaghan was firmly terminated – but only to be replaced by that of brother to brother. The Khitan qaghan's claim to be an emperor and an equal of the Song would be grudgingly recognised. The honours paid by him were reciprocated by those paid to him; and the subsidies disbursed to him were acknowledged as tribute in all but name. Thus China under the early Song presented an anomaly: though most of what was left of the Tang empire was reunited, imperial sovereignty remained divided.

Like a Damoclean sword, the Khitan menace had dangled over the Five Dynasties throughout their five fraught decades. Those who defied it, it felled; those who embraced it, it scarred. Either way, it took a hefty cut of state revenues in the form of indemnities and tribute. None of the Five

Dynasties had found a satisfactory way of dealing with the Khitan presence in Hebei and it was a contributory factor to their instability. Meanwhile, under Abaoji (r. 907–47), a charismatic figure whose career has been likened to that of Chinggis Khan, the Khitan had spread their wings in other directions, overrunning much of Mongolia and various northern peoples beyond, dispossessing a sinicised kingdom called Bohai (Parhae) to the east in north Korea, subduing most of Manchuria, and so creating an empire that in its territorial reach dwarfed all others in east Asia, including the *zhongguo* of the Five Dynasties.

This Khitan empire is known as Liao after the dynastic name adopted by Abaoji's successor, itself culled from a state of the 'Warring States' period that roughly corresponded to the Khitan heartland and which originally took its name from the Manchurian river that watered it. About Chinese culture in general, the Khitan of Liao were ambivalent. They considered themselves both superior to it and participants in it. Instead of extending steppe rule to the plains, let alone plains rule to the steppes, Abaoji introduced the novelty of a two-government system. A northern chancellery administered the clan-based society of the Liao's nomadic subjects in accordance with traditional steppe norms, while a southern chancellery administered the empire's settled subjects, principally Han, in accordance with Chinese bureaucratic practice. The former, based at a supreme capital in what is now eastern Inner Mongolia, was organised on military lines for tribute collection and offensive operations; the latter, based at what is now Beijing, was run by Han civilians in order to maximise tax and labour receipts. Over both, in the dual role of qaghan in the north and emperor in the south, presided a Liao dynast who, at moments of crisis, was not infrequently a woman.

Women in migratory societies probably shouldered more responsibility than their settled sisters. Raiding and herding kept the men from their hearths for long periods, while betrothals were more informal, and strict seclusion was precluded by the exigencies of steppe domesticity. But the Khitan, unlike many of their subject peoples, were at most only semi-nomadic. Their mainly Manchurian homeland was not open steppe but a configuration of forested hills and arable flood plains that limited pastoralism and localised transhumance. Fearless horsemen, they neither lived in the saddle nor slept in encampments. As among their Tangut neighbours in central Shaanxi, the tendency towards matriarchal rule seems to have been less a steppe legacy and more the result of the ruling clan attempting to impose a regular system of succession. Instead of the tribal councils and the trials of strength that traditionally decided the succession in steppe confederations, the Liao sought to impose a father-to-son system of primogeniture more in keeping with their imperial status and the concept of the heritable Mandate. This was frequently contested by their nomadic subjects, especially when, Liao longevity being far from guaranteed, the throne passed to a minor. But such minorities also afforded an opportunity for empresses and dowagers to exercise a de facto sovereignty that might continue after the emperor came of age.

Such was the situation in the critical years at the turn of the tenth to eleventh centuries when the Song, having mopped up the Ten Kingdoms of the south, switched their attention to the Khitan Liao in a bid to reclaim the north-east and so complete their reunification of the empire. Fresh to the throne, in 979 *Song* Taizong overran a part of Shanxi to which the Later Han (fourth of the Five Dynasties) had retired, and in the process inflicted a heavy defeat on a Khitan Liao army sent to assist this time-warped enclave. Success then encouraged *Song* Taizong to defy all advice to the contrary and invade Liao itself. His exhausted troops reached the Liao capital at what is now Beijing ill prepared and short of supplies. They were routed. Vast quantities of booty and weaponry were lost. Taizong himself was reduced to fleeing the field of battle in a cart, ever the most ignominious of imperial fates.

Two years later the Liao emperor died in a hunting accident and was succeeded by the eleven-year-old *Liao* Shenzong (r. 982–1031). Sensing an opportunity for revenge, *Song* Taizong resumed the offensive. But he reckoned without the military skills and formidable resolve of a Khitan dowager empress. In 986 Dowager Empress Chengtian took the field in person at the head of the Khitan forces and thrice defeated the Song armies. A ten-year lull, broken only by border clashes, ensued, at the end of which *Song* Taizong died. His successor, *Song* Zhenzong (r. 997–1022), was handicapped less by youth than by a superstitious disposition that bordered on the timid. It was the turn of the Liao to take the offensive.

As of 999 Khitan armies poured into the Song territories north of the Yellow River annually. Though *Liao* Shenzong had now come of age, his mother continued to direct policy and in 1004 again commanded one of the Khitan armies that, in a full-scale invasion, marched on the Song capital of Kaifeng. They struck the Yellow River below Kaifeng at a place called Shanyuan. A decisive armageddon seemed inevitable. But behind the Khitan's line of advance lay still-strong and uncaptured cities, while before them massed an enormous Song army. Both sides had reason to avoid a battle whose outcome was far from certain; and both sides enjoyed the services of Han intermediaries whom they trusted. The outcome, all too rare in Han-to-non-Han relations, was a frankly negotiated treaty, unmarred by trickery, that would stabilise Song–Liao relations for a century.

The Liao had demanded the concession of some strategic territories, while the Song sought recognition of their overall suzerainty. Both had to compromise. Instead of territory, the Liao were bought off with cash – a yearly payment of 200,000 lengths of silk and 2.8 million grams (100,000 ounces) of silver, plus gifts of comparable value on special occasions such as New Year and the Liao emperor's birthday. The Song would interpret this as a triumph, arguing that the cost was trifling in terms of their empire's revenue, far less than they feared, and certainly less than further military operations would have occasioned. Critics were not so sure, frequently citing the payouts to the Khitan Liao, and similar subsidies to the Tangut kingdom in the north-west, as an unacceptable drain on the Song economy. Latterly it has been suggested that the value of Song–Liao trade as regularised by the treaty far exceeded the cost of the subsidies and that, since the Khitan bonanza was used to purchase Song exports, most of it found its way back into the Song economy.

But while ceding no territory, the Song did suffer a major loss of face. In the double-speak beloved of diplomacy, they dismissed the payments to the Khitan as 'contributions to military expenses'; the Khitan nevertheless regarded them as tribute, and so – since they were unreciprocated, ongoing and in 1042 substantially increased – they surely were. Using the kinship terminology familiar to both sides, the Liao were recognised as brothers of the Song, albeit 'younger brothers'; thus Dowager Empress Chengtian was to be addressed by the Song emperor as 'aunt'. Perhaps in analogy with the Liao system of dual government, it also became conventional to refer to the 'Great Khitan state' as the 'Northern Court', and the 'Northern Song' as the 'Southern Court', of an otherwise entirely fictitious imperial entity. That the object was peaceful partition rather than contentious aggregation is clear from other provisions. Both sides bound themselves to avoid further hostilities and to respect and demarcate their mutual frontier. The demarcation was conducted throughout the frontier's 600-kilometre (370-mile) length from the westernmost reaches of the Yellow Sea near modern Tianjin to the northernmost reaches of the Yellow River west of Datong. 'Constituting a genuine international frontier in the modern sense' – and so quite unlike the often provocative and ineffectual fortifications known as the Great Wall – it was 'something unprecedented in Chinese history'.[24]

In essence the Shanyuan treaty of 1005 amounted to a damaging acknowledgement that empire was divisible and that non-Han rulers like the Khitan might also enjoy some pedigree of legitimacy – a Mandate, as it were, for 'All-*not*-under-Heaven'. Though never dignified with formal recognition by China's historians, this non-Han Mandate would also pass from ruler to ruler and might be transferred from dynasty to dynasty. Its holders, well versed in Han sovereignty, fully understood its implications; and had their history been written by their own historians rather than by Han scholars, it would surely have mapped the sometimes contested progress of this non-Han Mandate from Khitan to Jurchen, from Jurchen to Mongol, and from Mongol to Manchu (Qing) – by when, it might reasonably be claimed, the clash of the Mandates had been resolved in favour of the non-Han pedigree.

If the Khitan and the Jurchen had been exclusively nomadic herdsmen from Mongolia rather than substantially settled peoples from Manchuria, it would be tempting to call it 'a steppe Mandate'. One might even trace it back through the Uighurs and the other Turkic peoples to the Xianbei and Xiongnu. But that would be to ignore another cardinal feature of these hybrid new empires of the north. Though enjoying the mobility, the consensual traditions of succession and the militant ethic of the tribal confederations of old, they now boasted institutions, accomplishments and ideologies that made for states as strong and stable as that of the Song. All, for instance, possessed or developed their own written scripts, recorded their own laws and minted their own coins. And most promoted the devotional practices of Buddhism, a universal faith rich in concepts of sovereignty and sources of prestige untainted by Han Confucianism.

It may, then, be helpful to think of China's history post-950 as following a two-track narrative. The tracks diverge and converge with much interchange between them. China's historians traditionally present the crossover as essentially one sided, with the non-Han northern rulers gradually adopting the superior cultural norms of the indigenous Han southerners. But evidence that Khitan, Jurchen, Mongol and Manchu were fully alert to what they saw as the dangers of creeping sinification might suggest otherwise. Certainly, non-Han regimes whose subjects were overwhelmingly Han had perforce to compromise, even conform. But so too, if careers were to prosper, did their Han adjutants and subordinates. While qaghans embraced imperial protocol, emperors adopted the more dictatorial attitudes of the qaghans. Bureaucrats took one step sideways, military men one step forwards. Empire itself would undergo a sea-change.

11

CAVING IN

1005–1235

THE GREAT STATE OF WHITE AND HIGH

UNTIL COMPARATIVELY RECENTLY, international excitement over the discoveries made along the Silk Road by foreign archaeological explorers – Japanese as well as Europeans such as Aurel Stein and the brilliant French scholar Paul Pelliot – somewhat obscured China's own archaeological tradition. In such a historically conscious culture, the physical reclamation of the past had almost miraculous properties. Deciphering an ancient script or recovering some antique artefact linked present rulers to the illustrious dynasties of the past and enhanced their credibility. A Shang bronze unearthed by a mudslide turned the ill omen of flooding into a manifestation of heavenly approval; and the find of a Buddha statue conferred numinous prestige while emphasising that faith's Chinese credentials. In similar vein the discovery of the First Emperor's terracotta army so soon after the Cultural Revolution would be seen by some as sanctioning the reassertion of Party control by that professed admirer of the First Emperor's authoritarianism, Mao Zedong. Throughout China's history reverence for the antique has also inspired the imitation of ancient styles in verse, prose and painting, the concern with textual authenticity, the frequent readoption of archaic design elements, and not a little counterfeiting.

A less partisan approach to archaeology first emerged during the Song period. Ouyang Xiu, a noted reformer and cultural impresario as well as the author of the *Five Dynasties History*, encouraged archaeological study in the eleventh century; and in the early twelfth the husband-and-wife team of Zhao Mingcheng and Li Qingzhao collected and classified a vast range of antiquities that they then catalogued in a work on inscriptions in stone and bronze published in the 1120s. Until their intellectual idyll was brought to an abrupt end by the Jurchen capture of Kaifeng in 1127, scholar-bureaucrat Zhao provided the funds and scholarship, with Li, an outstanding poet and critic, acting as his muse and collaborator. Working 300 years before the Renaissance lent impetus to such pursuits in Europe, this devoted couple have been 'credited with anticipating modern standards in the handling of archaeologically recovered objects'.[1]

Since discoveries forwarded to court were an excellent way of advancing one's career, officials in the provinces made a point of tracking down antiquities; and so did local antiquarians, both lay and clerical. The philistine ignorance attributed, for instance, by Aurel Stein to Wang Yuanlu, the Daoist monk who had first discovered the great hoard at Dunhuang and was endeavouring to conserve it when Stein appeared, was probably disingenuous. Wang knew what he was parting with when he finally agreed to sell some of Dunhuang's treasures; and he did so only because he needed cash for his restoration programme and perhaps believed Stein's story about returning the archive to India, the supposed land of its provenance. Despite many instances of both casual and wilful destruction, indifference to the antique has seldom been a Chinese failing.

A century before Stein, in 1804 a carefree young official called Zhang Shu heard tell of an ancient stele in his native town of Wuwei. Then known as Liangzhou, Wuwei had been a Han, and subsequently Tang, garrison-town-cum-caravanserai on the Silk Road; it lies, in what was then good pastureland, about 250 kilometres (155 miles) north of Gansu's now capital of Lanzhou. Home on sick leave at the time, Zhang Shu was 'enjoying my leisure with a group of friends' when it occurred to him that they might investigate the stele. It stood within the precincts of one of the town's Buddhist monasteries and had been bricked up for as long as anyone could remember. According to the monk in charge, unbricking it would trigger a catastrophic hailstorm. Zhang and his friends promised to take full responsibility for any such mishap, and the monk at last agreed to the stele's exposure. Some nearby labourers were summoned to demolish the brick casing. The grey stone slab emerged covered in more than an inch of dust.

> We wiped it away and suddenly characters appeared and could all be recognised. Looking closer, however, we could not read a single character . . . I said that the back side must certainly have the translation, and so ordered that [the bricks at] the back side be cracked open, revealing its substance to be indeed a [Chinese] translation . . . My discovery of this stele has now made it available to the world for the first time.[2]

Yet the world paid scant attention to Zhang Shu's discovery. Not until a century later did the same stele attract the notice of Baron Carl Gustav Mannerheim. A Finn who in old age would famously lead his country's futile resistance to Stalin's 1940 invasion, Mannerheim was in 1908 a colonel in the imperial Russian army with a choice assignment combining archaeology and espionage on the fringes of what was still, just, the Qing (Manchu) empire. The Russians were latecomers in the exploration of the Silk Road sites. 'The Liangzhou steles' (there were others with purely Chinese inscriptions) had in fact already been studied by French orientalists, who had concluded that the strange script, which to Zhang Shu had looked so much like Chinese yet wasn't, was in fact 'in the Sisia [Xi Xia] language'. But the only Frenchman actually to visit Liangzhou had failed to obtain a facsimile of it. Mannerheim planned to rectify this using wetted muslin to take an impression.

Again the attempt was a failure. Being January, 'it was so cold that everything froze before we could get the cloth into the hollows', he explains. Instead, he had the lettering painted white and then photographed it. The work for some reason had to be done by candlelight and Mannerheim thought it 'possible that mistakes may have occurred'.[3] Nevertheless, using his photos and other materials, scholars would eventually unravel some of the mystery surrounding the stele's not-quite-Chinese and decidedly code-like script, then tease meaning from it. Of the many revelations that have resulted, perhaps the most surprising has come from the characters forming the inscription's first column, which had been partially obliterated in the Chinese 'translation' on the back. For from them it emerged that, although the people thought to have been responsible for the stele were called Tangut in the Turkic languages, and although the Tangut state was known in the Chinese histories as Xi Xia ('West Xia'), this was not what the people themselves called it. They had a much grander name for their dominion. As per what was in effect the inscription's heading, the stele belonged to the Gantong temple in Liangzhou 'in the Great State of White and High'.

Later in 1908 another Russian expedition under Major Pyotr Kuzmich Koslov made an even more dramatic discovery – no less than a lost city. It stood on the edge of the Gobi desert, about 500 kilometres (310 miles) north-east of Wuwei/Liangzhou in what is now the province of Ningxia (meaning 'Pacified Xia'). Sand had drifted up against its crumbling walls, but within the gateways Koslov found 'a quadrangular space whereon were scattered high and low, broad and narrow, ruins of buildings with rubbish of all kinds at their feet'.[4] The place was known as Karakhoto and is now thought to have been the Etsina or Edsina 'in the [Mongol] province of Tangut' noted by Marco Polo; according to Polo, it was where you laid in 'stores for forty days' if you were heading across the Gobi. Koslov thought a nearby stupa worth excavating. He returned for further digging in 1909 and eventually left for Russia with mainly Buddhist paintings, statuary and texts to rival the hauls made by Stein at Dunhuang. Housed in St Petersburg as the Koslov Collection, these materials gave Russian scholars a head start, not to mention a proprietary interest, in the study of this 'forgotten empire' which, according to the Chinese histories, had lasted for two centuries and had challenged the Khitan Liao and the Song for control of northern China. Many of the texts Koslov had garnered proved to be in the same challenging script as the Liangzhou stele; and from them Karakhoto was identified as indeed an outpost, and later capital, of this same empire, otherwise the 'Great State of White and High'.

Much about this enigmatic polity still remains uncertain. No Standard History in Chinese was devoted exclusively to Xi Xia, as it was to the empires of Liao and Song, and extant texts in the Tangut language have yet to yield anything so helpful. The ethnic origins of the Tangut remain a mystery. They are thought to have been descended from the Qiang or Chiang of earlier centuries and to be related to the Tibetans. Yet they themselves claimed descent from the Tabgach or Tuoba people of the Northern Wei dynasty (386–534), which had reunited the north towards the end of the 'Period of Disunion'. Certainly their language had affinities to Tibetan. Yet their script was quite unconnected to the alphabetic script used in Tibet. Developed in the eleventh century, it was indeed derived from the Chinese as Zhang Shu had supposed, though more complex if not wilfully obscure.

The people often called themselves Mi and their country Minia. Turks and Mongols preferred 'Tangut' or some such; and the Chinese used 'Xia', 'Xiaguo', 'Xi Xia' or more generic terms for non-Han peoples such as *fan*, *rong* and *hu*. No satisfactory explanation has been found for the grandiloquent title of 'White and High'. 'White' could refer to salt, one of the state's main exports, or to the winter snows; and 'high' to Xia's location on the upper Yellow River as opposed to Song's on its lower reaches. Alternatively the phrase could refer back to some earlier Tangut sojourn among mountains. Combining arable skills with stock-rearing, the Tangut, like the Tuyuhun, had spread from Qinghai in Tang times and been settled within the empire on land south of the Ordos in northern Shaanxi, a traditional dumping ground for incoming pastoralists. There, in the ninth century, one of their leaders had been appointed as the Tang military governor of a local prefecture called Xia and then given the title 'duke of Xia'. In the post-An Lushan period (after 755) and on into that of the Five Dynasties/Ten Kingdoms (907–60), the duke, and then prince, of Xia garnered more honours, disposed of rivals both Tangut and non-Tangut, and cultivated autonomy like other military governors of the period.

Early in the eleventh century, when the Khitan Liao and the Song were resolving their differences by the treaty of Shanyuan, the Tangut ruler Li Deming (r. 1004–32) obtained recognition from both these powerful neighbours – from the Song as an autonomous tributary and from the Liao as 'king' of Xia. In effect he was playing one off against the other, a tactic that would amount to a guiding principle for Tangut Xia. Meanwhile Li Deming's son, Yuanhao Weiming, began expanding the kingdom westwards into Gansu at the expense of that region's Uighur and Tibetan occupants. The capital of the Tangut's Xia state ('Xia' being used here for 'the Great State of White and High' simply for brevity) was moved to the Yellow River in Ningxia; Wuwei/Liangzhou, where the stele was erected, was first captured in 1032. Twenty years later Tangut Xia forces reached Dunhuang, so adding the whole of Gansu to Ningxia and northern Shaanxi to form the Xia empire. Stretching over 1,200 kilometres (745 miles) from east to west, it was of near-imperial proportions; and that it was indeed an empire was signified when in 1034 Yuanhao Weiming 'assumed the title of *wu tsu*, the Tangut equivalent of emperor or qaghan'.[5]

Yuanhao Weiming (r. 1032–48) introduced all the usual trappings of an imperial newcomer – new dynastic name, new reign title, new calendar, new dress code – and he added another, new hairstyle. According to Song sources, the Tangut emperor himself was the first under the scissors, quickly followed by a stampede of his countrymen; for by decree, anyone whose hair was uncut three days later might have his throat cut. The new look helped to distinguish the Tangut from their Song and Tibetan neighbours and may have owed something to Tabgach traditions of hairstyling. 'The top part of the skull was shaved, leaving a fringe across the forehead and down the sides, framing the face.'[6] It was not quite a tonsure but, as shown in Tangut paintings such as those discovered by Koslov, it did tend towards the monkish. This was appropriate in that what distinguished the Tangut's Xia empire, especially from the reign of Yuanhao Weiming onwards, was that it employed almost exclusively Buddhist terminology and Buddhist devotional patronage to validate its authority. In effect Tangut Buddhism was a state religion and Xia a Buddhist state.

Athough the Liangzhou stele dates from somewhat later (1094), a comparison of its Tangut and Chinese texts made by Ruth Dunnell, the leading expert on early Xia, may serve to illustrate the point. Each of the two inscriptions offers much the same information but does so in terms carefully tailored to its particular readership. The Chinese text, designed to appeal to the substantial Han component in Tangut Xia society, is strong on history, extolls 'the Southern Court' (i.e. the Song), and regards Liangzhou as one of its prefectures, and its ruler as one of its subjects. On the other side, the Tangut text glosses over the history to digress at length on the origins and redeeming qualities of Buddhism and the miraculous powers of the state-supported temple complex at Liangzhou. It stresses the legitimacy of Xia and the imperial status of its rulers, and it treats what it calls 'the eastern Han' (a demeaning term for the Song) as little more than an interested party. The inscriptions are not in fact translations of one another but opposed versions, though of a similar import.

Under Yuanhao Weiming, the composition of the Tangut script was finalised, and it was officially adopted for all administrative, educational and religious purposes. Translations of the *tripitaka* (the Buddhist scriptures) into Tangut were made from printed Chinese versions obtained from the Song, who rather hopefully threw in copies of the Confucian classics as well. Other translations were made from Tibetan texts. A legal code like that used by the Song, itself based on that of the Tang, was also promulgated in Tangut, and a hybrid administration, less formalised than that in Liao, established. Xia now fielded a loosely organised army of around 200,000 and controlled not only the overland trade through the Gansu corridor but also the vital supply of horses from the steppe to the Song empire via Shaanxi. It was not therefore in Song interests to provoke a direct confrontation with its upstart neighbour. Instead the Song encouraged others, especially the Tibetans, to harry Xia.

In 1038 Yuanhao Weiming felt strong enough to throw down the gauntlet. After staging a formal enthronement of himself as emperor, he dispatched an embassy to the Song capital of Kaifeng bearing a letter designed to elicit recognition of his sovereign status. It was 'something for which its author clearly expected to have to do battle'.[7] *Song* Renzong (r. 1022–63, grandson of *Song* Taizong) rejected both the embassy and its gift of horses and camels. Yuanhao Weiming did the same to a reciprocal Song embassy. The Song then revoked all Yuanhao's titles, closed the frontier and shut down the border markets on which Xia depended quite as much as Song. The expected battle was now inevitable.

There ensued five years of intermittent war (1039–44), punctuated by negotiation and sabotage and greatly complicated by the interventions of the Khitan Liao, sometimes as go-betweens, more often as adroit opportunists. Xia scored notable victories but was incapable of making inroads into Song territory. The Song remained adamant that Xia accept their suzerainty, although as with Khitan Liao, they were prepared to sweeten the pill; they offered generous annual subsidies and would turn a blind eye to whatever airs and honorifics the Xia ruler arrogated to himself among his subjects. Eventually the compromise evident in the bilingualism of the Liangzhou stele emerged. To the Song, the Xia ruler remained a subject, in kinship terms 'a son' not 'a brother', but he was also accepted as a quasi-emperor whose use of imperial regalia and protocol within his own domain would not be contested. Like Liao, Xia became the recipient of an annual subsidy from the Song; it included several tonnes of brick tea as well as copious quantities of silver and silk. And the all-important border markets were reopened, so giving the Song access to Tangut bloodstock and the Tangut somewhere to spend their tribute.

Xia's further history would be less than tranquil. But the state would outlast both the Khitan empire of Liao and its twelfth-century successor in the north, the Jurchen empire of Jin. For all of 200 years Xia shared control of northern China with one or other of these alien dynasties, plus the Song. The tripartite arrangement proved workable and, however distasteful to Song Confucianists and later historians, may be seen as an example of a sustainable multi-state system. Even the terrible fate that awaited Xia when in 1226–27 it became the object of Chinggis Khan's last and bloodiest campaign may not have completely extinguished it. Evidence from Koslov's excavations strongly suggests that, in the sands of Ningxia, 'the Great State of White and High' lived on, ghost-like and abuzz with devotion, for another half-century.

REFORM AND REAPPRAISAL

The challenge thrown down by Yuanhao Weiming's imperial enthrone-ment in 1038 had long-term consequences for the Song too. It was bad enough that the Song had had to make concessions to the Khitan Liao in the 1005 treaty of Shanyuan. Now it was worse: in 1038 they faced the defi-ance of the long-subject Xia in a far corner of the empire, plus the likelihood of the Khitan making common cause with this upstart. The Khitan Liao would eventually have to be bought off with a 50 per cent increase in the annual tribute paid them. Yet Xia, even without their support, proved strong enough to withstand a long Song offensive combining deployment and diplomacy.

In the Song capital of Kaifeng the resulting loss of face was bitterly felt and occasioned serious heart-searching. Clearly there was something wrong in the great empire of the Song. Like the Han and Tang empires of old, Song China was more prosperous, more advanced, more populous, more organised, probably more urbanised and certainly more culturally refined than any contemporary power in the world. Yet regional supremacy eluded it. It exercised no substantive authority in central or south-east Asia, had lost the north-west, failed to regain the north-east, was liable for heavy subsidies to both, and could scarcely defend its own constricted frontiers. The prestige of Heaven's Son, now replicated by the Khitan Liao and aped by the Tangut Xia, seemed notably impaired.

Military failure could be put down to the Song dynasty's early preference for civilian control of the provinces and a reluctance to maintain large frontier armies like those that had turned on the Tang and competed as the Five Dynasties. Officials who urged the reversal of this policy as the only way of avoiding further embarrassment from Khitan Liao and Tangut Xia could all too easily be accused of favouring military deployment for ulterior reasons, such as building a power base of their own from which to overthrow the dynasty. But a way round this objection was found by linking the case for frontier militarisation with the more acceptable cause of moral regeneration and political reform.

To this end Ouyang Xiu, in the 1030s a rising star at the Song court with a reputation for formidable learning, aligned himself with a Confucian idealist called Fan Zhongyang, who was the prefect of Kaifeng. They were an unlikely pairing, the young Ouyang being a notorious womaniser and partygoer while Fan aspired 'to be the first in worrying about the world's troubles and the last in enjoying its pleasures' (his definition of a good Confucian official). But both looked to the idealised past for inspiration in reforming the dysfunctional present – a normal default position for Confucianists. And both identified Buddhism as the latter-day source of all corruption. It was 'an opiate of the people' even, and all the more so now that it was central to the pretensions of both Tangut Xia and Khitan Liao. 'Trumpeting abroad its grand, fantastic doctrines', as Ouyang Xiu put it, this evil could best be defeated by a return to Confucian 'rites and rightness, . . . the fundamental things whereby Buddhism may be defeated'.[8]

Fan Zhongyang's first proposed reforms were quickly rejected; both he and Ouyang suffered criticism and were demoted. But in 1040, as the threat to the Song empire from Xia and Liao worsened, they were recalled to favour. Ouyang Xiu anticipated a frontier command where he could put into practice his ideas on military strategy; instead he was directed to catalogue the imperial library, all 80,000 volumes of it, an important assignment with access to the emperor but no military responsibilities. Meanwhile it was Fan Zhongyang who was sent to the frontier. More plenipotentiary than general, Fan corresponded at length with Yuanhao Weiming and persuaded him to consider moderating his demands. Back in Kaifeng and now painfully aware of Song's military weakness, in 1042 Fan proposed a new ten-point programme of reforms. As the confrontation with Xia dragged on, Ouyang Xiu urged the programme at court and *Song* Renzong endorsed it. By 1043 Fan had a free hand to implement his ten points.

They included improving the quality of the administration by weeding out the incompetent, rewarding the able and outlawing favouritism. There was to be more emphasis on problem-solving and less on literary skills in the examinations. Schools were to be set up throughout the empire to ensure a wider base for civil service recruitment. Local government was to be upgraded with better salaries and more investment in local projects to benefit agriculture. And of course military recruitment was to be boosted, especially in frontier areas. It was an ambitious programme and, encountering vigorous opposition from entrenched bureaucrats, it got nowhere. By 1045 the crisis with Xia had been resolved, Fan Zhongyang was out of favour and his measures were repealed.

Known as 'the Minor Reforms' (major ones would follow), the episode is chiefly notable for Ouyang Xiu's reaction to the downfall of Fan and his associates. It took the form of a written submission 'in defence of parties' – in this case the political kind rather than the alcoholic. Fan had been accused of organising his supporters into what amounted to a faction, and to which his critics imputed subversive intent. Ouyang contended that factions, parties and the like were perfectly natural and even beneficial. Those formed by inferior men in search of profit would soon disintegrate, but those formed by like-minded 'gentlemen who abide by the Way [of Confucius] and rightness, who practise loyalty and good faith, and care only for honour and integrity' were an asset. United in principle, their members could only improve one another. If the emperor would make use of them, 'then the state may be ordered'.[9]

But this ran contrary to long-standing opinion and could be refuted from Confucian texts; nor was it clear how groupings of high-minded gentlemen were to be distinguished from those of self-seeking place-men. Parties, factions, cliques and 'gangs' – no distinction was made between informal association and organised lobbying – were a feature of political life. Yet they were not recognised as such. Rather were such groupings condemned as insidious and inherently prejudicial to the authority of the emperor, even when their purpose was to bring order to the state and uphold imperial authority. From the quasi-Daoist associations of Red Eyebrows, Yellow Turbans and Five Pecks in Han times right through to the Triad organisations of the later empire, associations with a political agenda thus found themselves obliged to adopt a code of secrecy, which of course made them all the more suspect.

Ouyang Xiu's submission was rejected. For his temerity he was again banished to the provinces, and under any but the comparatively indulgent Song might well have been granted 'the privilege' of suicide. Although the issue was far from dead, subsequent reformers, and counter-reformers, would repeatedly fall foul of this embargo on political association. At a time when, in Europe, barons were about to mobilise, estates to organise, diets and parliaments to convene and qualified representation to be accorded a legitimacy of its own, in China no concept of legitimate political organisation was permitted to ruffle the stern surface of absolutism. One man's worth as defined in purely moral terms remained the basic unit of political and administrative society. Opinions might be canvassed and remonstrations invited from individuals so qualified, but any aggregation of like-minded officials remained suspect. Reform would repeatedly falter because, on losing the emperor's favour, it must languish for want of concerted support; Ouyang Xiu's plea for the recognition of parties had merely elicited their proscription; and as F. W. Mote puts it in his *Imperial China*, 'China still struggles with the heritage of this eleventh-century political failure'.[10]

If anything, reform initiatives tended to promote still greater central control and further entrench the imperial prerogative. In 1069 the twenty-year-old *Song* Shenzong (r. 1068–85), having just succeeded as emperor, called to court Wang Anshi, an unkempt, combative but highly regarded Confucianist who was governor of Nanjing. Wang had earlier submitted a long memorandum urging a return to the principles, if not the practices, to be found in the *Zhouli*, 'the rites' or 'institutes' of the Zhou, that 'fundamentalist' text which had so entranced Wang Mang a thousand years earlier and to which countless other reformers had since turned. Wang Anshi outlined how, applied to the education system, these principles might work to improve the calibre of recruits to the civil service; he produced his own masterly version of the *Zhouli*; and from his time in Nanjing he was known to have effective ideas on taxation and agricultural improvement. Now, under a conscientious new emperor, when further trouble was looming with Xia, and following a spate of reformist pleas from other intellectuals, his time had come. Wang Anshi was about to introduce what amounted to the most ambitious scheme of reorganisation ever attempted during the two millennia between the reign of the First Emperor and the triumph of the Chinese Communist Party.

'The Major Reforms' or 'New Policies' of Wang Anshi included economic and social provisions of which any responsible government could be proud. A system of designedly low-interest loans to tide the cultivator over until harvest time was introduced; and the principle of state granaries buying at above-market rates when prices were depressed, and selling below when they were buoyant, was reactivated. With such measures Wang could genuinely claim – and did – to be serving the interests of the people. New irrigation and canal schemes were undertaken, state intervention in the regulation of market prices was introduced, and the corvée was made subject to commutation so that those liable for it would either be paid for their labour or pay to be exempted from it. These were far-sighted enactments that, in making the well-being of the people a prerequisite for strengthening the state – or in generating the wealth that would enable the taxpayer to meet new and more efficiently collected taxes – won for Wang Anshi the accolade of 'China's greatest statesman'.

But whether they were part of a humane and socially responsible master plan is doubtful. Ad hoc enactment, piecemeal implementation and a mixed reception seem to have characterised the whole programme. Moreover the dramatic increase in tax receipts that resulted, though notable and needful, can hardly have eased the taxpayer's burden. Ouyang Xiu, no longer a rabid reformer and by 1070 in semi-retirement, disapproved; and Sima Guang, the other great historian-statesman of the period, who succeeded Wang Anshi as chief minister, was even more critical. He thought Wang 'self-satisfied and opinionated, considering himself without equal'; and he condemned his measures as having been 'aimed at the accumulation of wealth' and as having 'pressed the people mercilessly . . . as if they had been cast into hot water and fire'.[11]

Especially onerous was a new system of militia based on the old legalist idea of grouped households (ten to a group in this case) with collective responsibility for local recruitment, law and order and one another's good behaviour; the scheme was expensive, claimed Ouyang Xiu, the recruits were useless, and it left frontier commanderies unsusceptible to civilian control. Not much better was a novel idea to 'adopt a horse'. This was designed to reduce Song's dependence on its neighbours for cavalry mounts. People could either foster a government horse (it came with its own supply of fodder) or buy their own (with a guaranteed sale to the state when it was full-grown); in either case, the keeper's responsibility was one of care and he was liable for a replacement if it died. Since little more is heard of the scheme, the take-up was probably as disappointing as the product. Though Song forces briefly penetrated into Xia territory in southern Gansu in the 1080s, neither of these reforms would redeem the dynasty's dismal military record. Reverting to the expedient of 'employing barbarians to control barbarians', by the early twelfth century the Song were looking for allies beyond their frontiers. With catastrophic results, they would find them among the Jurchen, a Manchurian people who were rising against the sovereignty of Khitan Liao.

As was to be expected, Wang Anshi also tinkered with the central government's administrative machinery, restoring some departments, re-allocating responsibilities among others and reintroducing structures and nomenclatures sidelined by the first Song emperors in their haste to wrest control from the military. Dignified as a Confucian 'rectification of names', such manipulation was also a good way of rationalising procedures while ridding oneself of opponents. As for local government, its clerks and other junior ancilliaries were to be integrated into the administration, paid a salary (raised by local taxation) to reduce their dependence on perks and bribes, and encouraged to seek promotion into the ranks of minor officialdom.

Equally predictable, but of much more enduring significance, were Wang Anshi's numerous educational reforms. Aimed, as ever, at broadening the base of civil service recruitment by attracting men of talent and probity and preparing them for office, Wang's programme affected all levels of the educational system. At the bottom, school boards nominally established in every district and prefecture to evaluate students from private teaching establishments were themselves to teach. A quota of students, teachers and classrooms was allocated to each; exams were to be held at the prefectural level, leaving the central examining body free to judge and rank only those who had passed; and the criteria for success were adjusted with more emphasis on practical solutions and less on literary composition and rote learning of the Confucianist classics. At the very top, the National Academy, where graduates studied for the highest degrees, including that of *jinshi* (roughly equivalent to a Doctorate of Letters), was reorganised into a more effective teaching establishment with a wider syllabus; and separate schools were set up in the capital for medicine, law and military science.

How effective all these changes were is hard to judge, for like Fan Zhongyang before him, Wang Anshi fell from favour before fully implementing his programme. The emperor had become impatient for tangible results in the form of military success; opposition from all manner of landowning and bureaucratic interests had mounted; and popular discontent, once directed at moneylenders and merchants, had increasingly attached itself to the state in its new role as agrarian creditor and trade regulator. As of 1076 Wang's programme became the plaything of others, reversed by counter-reformers, diluted by post-reformers and finally distorted and discredited by Cai Jing, a member by marriage of Wang's family, who presided over the fall of the Song empire in the north and would subsequently be vilified for it in works of both history and fiction.

Despite that cataclysm, Wang's reputation would live on. Under the Southern Song (as the dynasty would be known after losing the north, the prior period being known as that of Northern Song), Wang would be revered as an early political exponent of a new and pervasive orthodoxy for which the term 'Neo-Confucianism' was eventually coined. But at the time his reforms had only limited success and may actually have been counterproductive. The strong executive powers needed to push them through had the unfortunate effect of 'making powerful centralisation . . . a permanent feature of the government structure'. Additionally, Wang's doctrinaire attitude produced the very conformity that his curricular reforms were supposed to frustrate; examination candidates, instead of regurgitating the classics, now simply regurgitated his own interpretation of the *Zhouli*. And ultimately, in a misguided attempt to protect Wang's reputation, Cai Jing went so far as to ban all works by anti-reformers and order the re-education of those tainted by them.

This late-eleventh-century crackdown on deviance prompted some mid-twentieth-century writing about the past by way of comment on the present. In the late 1950s the eminent professor J. T. C. Liu dubbed Cai Jing's re-education programme 'political persecution' and, while conceding that 'no detail of this [Song] measure has been recorded', drew clear parallels between it and the denunciations and corrective techniques being employed by the Chinese Communist Party. Song students 'assigned to self-indicting study rooms', wrote Liu, 'were to do further reading and thinking in order to correct their allegedly mistaken opinions'.[12] Since Cai Jing is traditionally regarded as a monster and his administration as a disaster, this evidence of his having resorted to 'study sessions' could only be taken as a direct criticism of the party. The professor, needless to say, was writing from afar at the time, namely the United States.

Few historians can forgo selecting and emphasising features of the historical record that appear to have relevance to current affairs. But Chinese historiography takes this a stage farther by introducing an admonitory element. As Sima Guang put it, history should 'include all that a prince needs to know – everything pertaining to the rise and fall of dynasties and the good and ill fortune of the common people, all good and bad examples that can furnish models and warnings'.[13] Consulting more than three hundred works and employing the highest critical standards, in his *Zizhi Tongjian* ('Comprehensive Mirror for Aid in Government') Sima Guang was himself well aware that history was habitually written, and read, as a subtle commentary on current personalities and policies. All texts, even his own, had their agendas. This does not mean that they are therefore less reliable, only that they may reveal as much about the times in which they were written, or rewritten, as about those they actually describe. The 'mirror' in the title of Sima Guang's great work reflected both the then and the now. Completed in the 1070s, it can be read as a blast from the past against Wang Anshi's disruptive reforms and the demand for military action against the Khitan, as well as a superb chronicle of China's history up to the year 959.

IN SINGING-GIRL TOWERS

Wang Anshi's reforms, while revolutionary in scope and of abiding significance, were not quite as dangerous as they seemed to conservatives like Sima Guang. Indeed, much about Song China was not quite as it seemed. The examinations as rejigged under the Song would become the defining institution of elite society for the next seven centuries; yet at the time they may have had little impact on the social base from which office-holders were recruited and certainly did not open up the administration to all-comers. Talent was recognised, higher standards required, but neither was a guarantee of advancement. The upwardly mobile still found the going tough and the professional gradient vertiginous. Not until the Ming would the examinations system spawn a genuine meritocracy.

More statesmen hailing from the Yangzi and the south – Ouyang Xiu, Fan Zhongyang and Wang Anshi among them – secured high office, but this may simply reflect the changing demography. Very few of them were from families with no previous record of government service, and though printed books and new schools made education more widely available, most of those who sat the higher examinations and aspired to office still relied on the influence of patrons and family networks. Moreover they were still heavily outnumbered by those who, with or without a degree, attained office courtesy of a system of privileged induction that no reform had yet successfully addressed.

On the other hand, just sitting for the highest degrees conferred a recognised intellectual status and could become something of a profession in itself. Hundreds prepared for the exams every year, although the preset quota of passes rarely exceeded a handful – some years there were none at all – and by the 1090s only one candidate in ten could expect to pass. The rate fell even farther thereafter. Luckily the failed could always resit; there was no limit to the number of times nor, within reason, to the age of the candidate. Fifty-year-old students were not unknown, though by that age most had settled for another avenue of advancement. On the well-known principle that 'those who can, do, while those who can't, teach', many set up as tutors, started schools or joined monasteries. Under the Jurchen Jin dynasty (and very probably under the Northern Song since the Jurchen simply took over their educational procedures) every state school would reportedly be staffed with 'one professor who had taken the civil service examinations five times (without passing) or who held a *jinshi* degree but was over fifty years of age (and therefore too old to embark on an official career)'.[14]

As is the way with dynasties facing disaster, the last decades of the Northern Song were troubled. Famine ravaged the north in 1074–76, and a 1077 Song naval attack on Annam, considered a softer option than invading Xia or Liao, proved disappointingly inconclusive. The Northern Song had initiated a build-up of warlike shipping and, as a result of the expedition's failure, would devote resources to constructing a formidable navy. But for the attack on Annam in 1077 merchant vessels had been hired as transports, their owners being assured of compensation for any losses in the novel form of what were called 'monk certificates'.

Evidence as to the state of the economy as well as the status of Buddhism, these certificates were transferable titles that empowered the holder, whether lay or monastic, to nominate a number of candidates for the Buddhist monkhood. No vocation was necessary, residence was optional and the required vows were not to be taken seriously. The attraction of ordination now lay almost entirely in the exemption from taxation and service that a monastic attachment conferred. Buddhist schools of study, especially the esoteric Chan (Zen) school, continued to flourish despite the decline in contacts with central Asia and India (where Islamic encroachment had already severed the 'Sutra route' via Afghanistan). But the Song were not notable Buddhist patrons like the Sui and Tang; ordination was strictly regulated, with the sale of monk certificates affording the state a useful source of revenue; and in the face of the Confucianist revival, Buddhist establishments were undergoing a slow secularisation that marginalised their doctrinal heterodoxy while emphasising their social role in teaching, caring for the sick and elderly, managing their large estates and, as here, affording an economic sanctuary to those to whom the state was indebted. Buddhism, in effect, was slowly buckling under regulatory pressure from above and subsidence from below as popular practice became permeated by indigenous superstitions and local spirit cults. The Middle Way was becoming one of many – Daoist, Confucianist and animist – and barely distinguishable from them. As for the economy, unprecedented issues of coin and paper money were fuelling a rampant inflation that made certificated privilege more valuable than depreciating cash.

The reformer Wang Anshi had deplored foreign adventures like that against Annam; but in another attempt to redeem Song honour overtures were made towards the Korean kingdom with a mission by sea across the Gulf of Bohai from Shandong. The idea seems to have been to outflank the Khitan Liao empire on Asia's eastern seaboard; and when the Korean initiative came to nothing, in 1211–15 attention turned farther north to the Jurchen of Manchuria as potential allies in a common front against Khitan Liao. The old and generally satisfactory arrangement with Liao was about to be jettisoned, and two centuries of multi-state order repudiated. Neither ambitious reform within, nor salutary reverses without, had reconciled the Song to partial sovereignty. Such was the burden of empire.

And yet, by all accounts, the period of the Song was 'China's greatest age'.[15] Revolts broke out in Shandong and Zhejiang during the dynasty's dying days in the early 1120s, but for the most part it had been an era of internal tranquillity, booming trade, technological innovation and cultural sophistication. Around 5 per cent of the population lived in cities, not a spectacularly high proportion but still about 6 million people, a figure 'probably equal to the urban population of the rest of the world at that time'.[16] Kaifeng, the capital and much the largest conurbation, was smaller than Chang'an under the Tang yet accounted for about a million, 'which is not far short of the total population of England under William the Conqueror, the exact contemporary of [*Song*] Shenzong'.[17] There were thirty cities with populations of 40,000–100,000; Europe had perhaps six. As centres of commerce and overseas trade Yangzhou (in Jiangsu), Hangzhou (in Zhejiang), Fuzhou and Quanzhou (in Fujian) and Guangzhou (Canton, in Guangdong) all rivalled Venice.

Marco Polo, himself a Venetian, would award Suzhou (in Jiangsu) 6,000 stone bridges (the so-called 'Venice of the East' has about the same today) and a circumference of 65 kilometres (40 miles). But Hangzhou, which would be the Southern Song's capital and which Polo called 'Kinsai', was 'undoubtedly the finest and most splendid city in the world'. Polo's '1.6 million houses' must have been a wildly exaggerated guess, the sort that back in Italy would win him notoriety as *il Milione*, 'Mr Millions'. But guesswork apart, his wonderment at the industry, order and invention – in the countryside as well as the cities – rings true enough. The bustling vignettes of road and riverside life depicted in contemporary paintings such as the twelfth-century Qingming scroll confirm the impression. To the medieval European visitor, China afforded a glimpse of a futuristic utopia in which industry and abundance were complemented by just and effective government.

To printed books and paper money might be added a host of contemporary developments in medicine, mechanics, mathematics, chemistry and metallurgy. Of the three inventions credited by Francis Bacon with having changed his sixteenth-century European world – printing, the magnetic compass and gunpowder – all had been anticipated by the Chinese and all had entered everyday use under the Song, so distinguishing that age of innovation from the Tang age of importation. The printed book dealt a telling blow to ignorance, the compass discovered its vocation as a navigational instrument, and gunpowder graduated from fireworks to warfare (mainly for the mining of fortifications and as an explosive projectile rather than as a propellant). Coal began to replace charcoal in furnace, forge and kiln as tree cover in the north was depleted, steel to replace iron for weapons, implements and in construction. Surveying and map-making achieved a high degree of accuracy; so did astronomy, ever a strong suit in the Celestial Empire. A calculation of the world's circumference proved accurate to within a matter of metres; the fall of the Grand Canal over a 420-kilometre (260-mile) section was measured to within millimetres.

Song Huizong, the last Northern Song emperor (r. 1101–25), took little interest in government but delighted in these achievements, maintained his own academy of scholars and artists, and extended unrivalled patronage to all the arts. He was himself a fine painter and outstanding calligrapher, and his imperial collection of paintings and antiques is thought to have been the largest ever amassed in China. Aware as he was of no limit to the largesse at his disposal, his expert connoisseurship encouraged the production of exquisite ceramics, while his fascination with Daoism, the most nature-loving of speculative philosophies, resulted in elaborate gardens and grottoes flanked by palaces and pavilions.

Meanwhile agriculture, still the base of the economy, underwent 'a green revolution' with the eleventh-century introduction and development of quick-growing high-yield rice varieties obtained from Champa in central Vietnam. Two crops per year became standard in the Yangzi basin, three in its delta and farther south. Farm implements of iron and steel made the heavier soils of the south easier to work and extended the area of cultivation. The resulting surplus enabled farmers near the big cities to concentrate on cash crops of fruit and vegetables, fish and fowl. Local traders clogged the roads and waterways; markets and eating-houses proliferated. Seaworthy shipping and the expansion of maritime trade turned an exotic luxury such as India's black pepper into a culinary commonplace. Merchants had never had it so good.

> In singing-girl towers to play at dice, a million [cash] on one throw;
> By flag-flown pavilions calling for wine, ten thousand a cask;
> the Mayor? the Governor? we don't even know their names;
> what's it to us who wields power in the palace?[18]

In 'The Merchant's Joy' Lu You, the most prolific of Song poets and a great admirer of the compassionate Tang poet Dou Fu, contrasted the louche lifestyle of Yangzi traders with that of the impoverished Confucian scholar, 'belly crammed with classical texts and body lean with care', whose 'teeth rot, hair falls out [and] no one looks your way'. 'Merchants are the happiest of men,' he concludes, although officials and landowners must have run them a close second. Courtiers were in a league of their own. As to their dress, imported cottons and furs vied with silks and brocades; for their attentions, prostitutes and courtesans competed with concubines and wives. The exquisite met the gross in an endless round of banquets and bacchanalia, of poetasting and whoring.

No doubt it was a great age in which to live. Had early medieval man been invited to pick his country of birth, he would surely have opted for China. Not so, though, early medieval woman. Of those who made up the distaff half of society, most faced a perilous infancy leading to an agonised childhood followed by an exploited adolescence and an often sad maturity. The frequency of infanticide – which as elsewhere was predominantly female infanticide – so distressed Lu You that he urged the establishment of a maternity fund; he thought it would encourage families not to jettison the newborn before the bonds of nurture and affection had reconciled them to the burden of having another mouth to feed.

Whether survival was always in the best interests of the infant, though, is questionable. Female toddlers of pleasing potential might still be sold; and if not, no sooner had they learned to walk than they were reduced to toddling again. For according to one of Lu You's contemporaries, 'little [female] children when not yet four or five, who have done nothing wrong, are nevertheless made to suffer unlimited pain from foot-binding'.[19] Cosmetic therapy this foot-binding was not. The bandages used were 10 metres (33 feet) long and were so tightly strung back and forth – over toes, round heels – as in time to foreshorten the whole foot, winching the toes inwards, compressing and distorting them until, with bones bent and flesh taut, they caved in to form a pungent little maw nestled into a now high-arched instep. The moment the pain became bearable, or the subject became mobile, the bandages were tightened; shoe sizes slowly shrank by half. The whole process took several years, but 'if it was done skillfully, after the foot healed in [a further] two years, the young woman could walk short distances in no pain'.[20]

The custom came into widespread use under the Song, being report-edly rare prior to 1086 but widely practised by 1100; and it would remain in force until the late nineteenth century. Non-Han women shunned it; their revulsion provides a good example of resistance to Han accultura-tion, and as a result the practice never caught on in the north among Khitan, Tangut, Jurchen or Mongol. Nor, for obvious reasons, was it wide-spread among peasant families whose children had a hard life's work in the fields ahead of them. But for perhaps a third of all China's small girls, for all of 800 years, foot-binding was de rigueur. Though pain can hardly be quantified, given the numbers and the time-span it probably added more to the sum of human misery than male castration, female circum-cision, mutilation for mendicancy and all other custom-endorsed outrages combined.

Xu Ji (d. 1101), another Song poet, celebrated the results in a verse in which he 'found tiny feet an object of wonder and wanted to hold them in his hands to get a better look'.[21] Pleasingly rounded and never publicly exposed, they added to the female form two soft and intimate new zones of male arousal. Courtesans, performers, dancers (slow-footed ones pre-sumably) and other commodified womenfolk are thought to have pioneered the custom. Its adoption in wider society probably had some-thing to do with the Confucian reassertion of proprietary male attitudes. Insistence on the subordination of wife to husband, and strictures against the remarriage of widows, however burdened they might be with children, were promoted by exemplars such as the 'disarmed' widow Li cited by both Ouyang Xiu and Sima Guang. Hobbled women constituted a domestic convenience, ever available to their masters and not easily removed by others without a sedan chair or cart. Yet the women too were not blame-less. The actual enforcement of foot-binding was entrusted to mothers and grandmothers, themselves teetering on hoof-like stumps and strangely unmindful of the tearful adolescence that had condemned them to crippledom.

JIN AND SONG

Lu You, the Song poet who wanted to do something about infanticide, was born in 1125, just as Jurchen invaders began toppling the Northern Song, and he died in 1210, just as Mongol invaders began toppling the Jurchen. Compared with the imperial sway of the other non-Han dynasties of the period – Khitan Liao, Tangut Xia and eventually Mongol Yuan – that of the Jurchen Jin dynasty was comparatively short, just the eighty-five years of Lu You's life (though courtesy of the historians' penchant for dynastic extension, Jin's standard dates are usually given as 1115–1234). The Jurchen nevertheless had a greater impact on northern China than any of the others except the Mongols. Their onslaught was of a devastating suddenness, and by wresting from Song rule the central northern plain, the very heart of *zhongguo*, and then penetrating south to the Yangzi, they shook the empire to its core. The Khitan and Tangut had merely challenged Song sovereignty; the Jurchen challenged Song survival.

No one felt the psychological blow more than Lu You himself. All his life he railed against the shame of losing the north and was so outspoken in his condemnation of those who appeased the enemy that his professional career got nowhere. 'Border Mountain Moon', written in the 1150s, said it all.

> Fifteen years ago the edict came: peace with the invader:
> our generals fight no more but idly guard the border.
> Vermilion gates [of officialdom] still and silent; inside they sing
>   and dance;
> Stabled horses fatten and die, bows come unstrung . . .
> Spear-clashes on the central plain – these we've known from old.
> But since when have traitorous barbarians lived to see their heirs?
> Our captive people, forbearing death, pine for release,
> Even tonight how many places stained with their tears?[22]

Such sentiments would strike a chord through the ensuing centuries of humiliation by Mongol and Manchu, so ensuring Lu You's eventual fame as one of China's outstanding patriot-poets. Yet the enemy, those 'traitorous barbarians' – Jurchen, Khitan, Tangut or Mongol – would themselves come to comprise substantial elements in the ethnic mix that later subscribed to this Chinese patriotism.

Ethnic labelling is helpful in handling all these non-Han regimes, but it can be misleading as to their composition. Based on confederal arrangements with other clans, the non-Han regimes were never exclusively of one ethnicity. All included other peoples, and all rapidly attached still more as their fame spread. Tangut clansmen fought both with and against Khitan, Khitan both with and against Jurchen, and Han Chinese both with and against all of them. Whether defined by lifestyle, leadership, language or myth, ethnicity became more diluted at every stage of conquest. Like the contemporary Norsemen (Vikings) in Europe, the steppe and forest peoples who swept down from the north, swift-borne on horses rather than in longships, tended to settle, intermarry, adjust to existing society and co-opt its peoples and institutions.

Khitan Liao and Tangut Xia had set up dualistic states, their rulers being both emperors and qaghans; there was one administration for their steppe subjects, another for their Han subjects. The Jurchen went further. Taking over the Khitan Liao empire and the northern half of the Song, their Jin empire (not to be confused with that of the Western/Eastern Jin of the third and fourth centuries AD) would claim to be Song's successor. While retaining its native military structure, it would so embrace all the Confucian trappings of a Han-type administration as to be widely adjudged the legitimate Celestial Empire. Like those Vikings who, having settled in France and become thoroughly acculturated, were currently resuming their far-ranging exploits as the French 'Normans' (a mere variant of 'Norsemen'), the Jurchen Jin provided an object lesson in what might be called ethnic overlay.

The Jurchen's origins are as obscure as those of the Turks or Khitan. But unlike the proto-Mongol-speaking Khitan or the proto-Tibetan-speaking Tangut, the Jurchen (sometimes Jurchid, Juche, Ruzhen, etc.) spoke a language belonging to the Tungusic family, so named after a people called the Tungus, who are now, and were perhaps then, associated with eastern Siberia. By the time they made their documented debut in the eighth century, the Jurchen were established along the Heilongjiang (Amur), Wusuli (Ussuri) and Songhua (Sungari) rivers in the far north-east of Manchuria. They lived simply, hunted in the forests, fished in the rivers, raised oxen and horses, grew crops where feasible, fought hard, drank heavily, and endured the bitter winters in felts and furs. Their clans were many, but their common language and their custom of frequent assembly for open decision-making conferred a strong sense of common identity

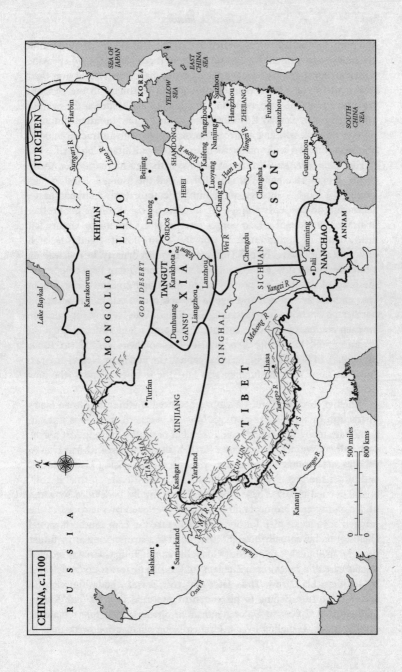

CHINA, c.1100

and purpose. Partially incorporated within the Khitan Liao condominium of Chinese-speaking cultivators and far-flung Turkic- and Mongol-speaking nomads, they may have felt themselves an anomaly. Resentment over their treatment by the Khitan fuelled autonomous sentiment in the eleventh century; and in the early twelfth a dynamic Jurchen leader at the head of a powerful clan fanned this sentiment, rallied a few hundred mounted supporters and, winning a succession of engagements, attracted enough followers, Jurchen and non-Jurchen, to challenge Khitan Liao itself.

His name was Aguda (r. 1113–23), and as with the Khitan founder Abaoji or the Tangut Yuanhao Weiming – or indeed the Mongol Temujin (aka Chinggis Khan) – success swept him to empire with indecent haste. Succeeding to the leadership of the Jurchen on the death of his brother in 1113, Aguda fought a Liao border force in 1114. Convincing victory left little chance of accommodation and less desire for it; Aguda declared himself a serious rival by proclaiming his own Jin dynasty. In 1115, leading a force reckoned now at 100,000, he defeated the Khitan Liao emperor at the head of an army supposedly seven times as numerous. The Khitan Liao empire lay exposed and Aguda pressed south, out of the wastes of northern Manchuria into Liaoning. The Khitan Liao had five capitals, one for each compass point plus another at the centre. The eastern capital (in Liaoning) fell to the Jurchen in 1116, the northern capital (in Inner Mongolia) in 1120, and the central capital (in northern Hebei) in 1122. Later the same year the Jurchen also took the southern capital (the now Beijing).

Whether these dramatic developments owed anything to Khitan Liao's distraction by Song sabre-rattling along its southern frontier is unclear. Song statesmen like Cai Jing, ever hopeful of regaining the long-lost north-east, had entertained the idea of a Jurchen alliance against Khitan Liao as early as 1115. Contacts were made by sea to avoid crossing Liao territory, and under the pretext of buying horses from the Jurchen, formal negotiations opened in 1117. These progressed only fitfully, bedevilled by issues of suzerainty and protocol and constantly overtaken by the speed of the Jurchen advance. A plan for Song forces to take the Liao southern capital (Beijing) had eventually brought into the field a strong Song army under the veteran eunuch-general Tong Guan. But in 1121 Tong Guan was recalled to take care of a rebellion in Zhejiang and in 1122 he was soundly defeated by a Khitan Liao army. Thus, later that year, it was Aguda himself who added the future Beijing to his clutch of captured capitals. The Khitan Liao court fled west to Datong (northern Shanxi), their one remaining capital. More wrangling over a Jurchen–Song alliance followed, then in

1123 brought a new treaty. Its ill-defined terms merely served as a basis for further acrimony between the would-be allies, which eventually turned to war.

In the same year, 1123, Aguda died. Inside a decade, he had created out of nothing an empire that covered all of what is now north-east China. He had commissioned a Jurchen script which, based on that of the Khitan, evinced dynastic and administrative intent, though it was never as widely used as the Khitan and Tangut scripts. He had established an extremely effective system of mobilising and controlling subject peoples by grouping them into units, each headed by one of his trusted kinsmen, who was made responsible for raising 1,000 fighting men; the kinsmen in turn appointed members of their own kin over units each of 100 families and 100 fighting men. Standardised yet capable of indefinite expansion, the system cleverly rewarded tribal loyalty, ensured the submission of conquered peoples and brought their instant mobilisation. As a result Aguda also left an apparently irresistible fighting force now numbering nearly a million.

In accordance with Tang and Song dynastic practice, Aguda would be posthumously entitled *Jin* Taizu, and his younger brother, who succeeded him, would be *Jin* Taizong (r. 1123–35). The latter resumed the Jurchen

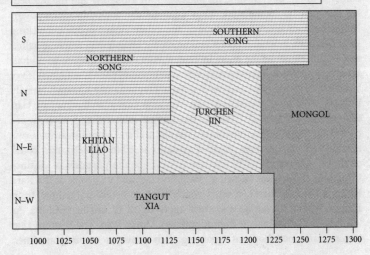

THE SUCCESSION OF REGIONAL DYNASTIES, 1000–1300

advance with scarcely abated urgency. By way of preparation for an onslaught on the Song, in 1124 the 'Great State of White and High', or Tangut Xia, was bullied into rejecting its nominal allegiance to the Song and acknowledging itself an 'outer vassal' of the Jurchen Jin. Meanwhile the remaining Khitan Liao forces were driven off into the Gobi desert and their last emperor was captured. By 1125 the Jurchen Jin had supplanted the Liao and dispersed the Khitan, secured the neutrality of Xia, and were ready to take on the Song.

At this point it is worth noting that the Khitan Liao, though soundly defeated, were by no means finished. Another century of dominion elsewhere in Asia awaited this most persistent of peoples. While often treated as an inconsequential postscript to two centuries of China-based empire, the second Khitan imperium deserves better. It would, if anything, be even more extensive than the first. And by exposing the vulnerability of cities and peoples far beyond the steppe to fast-riding armies that had mastered the logistics of long-range warfare, it would set a telling example. Assuming the future Chinggis Khan took note of recent history, the Khitan achievement in central Asia may well have provided more inspiration than the sudden Jurchen success in China.

By the time of Aguda's death in 1123 some Khitan had already defected to the Jurchen. Others had headed off into Mongolia as fugitives and there re-formed, along with the Liao garrisons in Mongolia, under a surviving member of the ruling Khitan Liao family. This Yelü Dashi declared himself emperor in 1131 and, turning his back on both Mongolia and the Jurchen, led his men far to the west. They followed the trail through northern Mongolia once taken by the Kyrgyz and other Turkic peoples. Reaching Lake Balkhash in what is now Kazakhstan, the empire-less emperor halted and began constructing anew in central Asia the lost empire of Khitan Liao. It would soon extend over a vast area north of the Oxus (Amu) River and include all the great cities of Sogdiana, Ferghana and Xinjiang. Heavily influenced by long association with northern China, well served by Han followers and fluent in Chinese, the Khitan rulers of this new empire contributed to the dissemination of the cultural and administrative norms encountered during their previous existence in China; indeed, they could easily be mistaken for Chinese themselves. For the purposes of distinction, their empire was known as 'Western Liao' and its people as the Kara Khitai ('Black Khitan'), a term which thirteenth-century visitors from Europe would transcribe and then apply to all of northern China. As 'Cathai' or 'Cathay', it was duly adopted by Marco Polo. The Western Liao never abandoned hope of regaining their previous empire, but when pushing back eastwards, they came up against the Xia in Gansu and got no farther. The 'Great State of White and High', long accustomed to Khitan threats emanating from the direction of the sunrise, may have been surprised to find the same menace mysteriously translated to the sunset; but they held firm. For the rest of the twelfth century, says one authority, 'the [Kara Khitai] Western Liao, the [Tangut] Xia, the Jin empire of the Jurchens, and the Southern Song dynasty in [southern] China were the four great mainland powers of eastern Asia'.[23]

Northern Song had abruptly become Southern Song when the Jurchen, continuing their inexorable southern advance, crossed the Yellow River and, at their second attempt, captured the Song capital of Kaifeng in early 1127. The Song's great eunuch-general Tong Guan had been disgraced after the first attack; and Cai Jing, the ministerial reformer who had anticipated modern methods of self-corrrection, corrected himself by committing suicide. Experience, like troops, deserted the Song in their hour of need, and stout resistance proved hopeless. When Kaifeng fell, two emperors were taken prisoner; the dilettante *Song* Huizong plus the irrelevant *Song* Qinzong (r. 1126–27), in whose favour Huizong had just abdicated. They were dispatched to the Jurchen capital near Harbin in far-off Manchuria and there held as hostages. Huizong was ignominiously enfeoffed with the title of Hunde, meaning 'Muddled Virtue', Qinzong with that of Chonghun, meaning 'Doubly Muddled'. The Jurchen treated them not unreasonably; but neither would ever see their homeland again.

Forewarned, a younger son of 'Muddled Virtue' had evaded capture at Kaifeng and, rallying resistance, was declared the next Song emperor. It was he who would be posthumously titled *Song* Gaozong (r. 1127–62), or 'founding ancestor' of the revered Southern Song dynasty (1127–1279). His first years were inauspicious. Jurchen armies advanced from Hubei and Sichuan, driving the Song forces before them. Several times they even crossed the Yangzi. In 1129 they stormed what would be the Southern Song's 'temporary capital' of Hangzhou on the coast of Zhejiang. This time *Song* Gaozong managed to escape courtesy of the Song navy. No emperor had ever fled out to sea before, and though he was swiftly landed, the implications of this move would be profound. Rarely had the coast-line featured in Chinese strategic calculations as a frontier, or the sea in cosmic theory as an 'All-under-Heaven' element. Their utility lay almost entirely in the fish, salt and tributary bounty (otherwise trade) that they yielded. But under the Song, and especially the Southern Song, attitudes changed. Naval fleets began to nose forth from the rivers, mercantile ship-ping to wing across the high seas. Mongol ambitions beyond China would accelerate this maritime initiative, and under the Ming dynasty in the fifteenth century China would, albeit briefly, rule the world's waves.

None of which would have been much consolation to *Song* Gaozong, the founder of the Southern Song, as the Jurchen Jin continued to heap humiliation on defeat. In the 1130s Jin policy veered away from the Khitan precedent of a part-steppe, part-sown empire to swing decisively towards a sino-centric dominion. The Xia in Gansu, the Kara Khitai of Western Liao and the peoples of Mongolia would never be more than remote, occasional and decidedly nominal vassals of the Jin. The records mention an expedition against 'the Meng', an early reference to the Mongols, but it 'could not subdue them'. Instead, in 1146, a treaty was signed with the Meng chief, probably Khabul Khan, grandfather of Chinggis, which effectively wrote off Mongolia as a Jin dependency. Even the Jin homeland in Manchuria was downgraded when a great migration of the Jurchen clans was ordered southwards to Hebei, Henan and Shanxi. The move was consummated in 1151 when the northern capital near Harbin in Manchuria was largely abandoned in favour of what had been the southern capital. This was the future Beijing; the Jurchen Jin were the first to rule *zhongguo* exclusively from it. They had clearly come to stay. Theirs would not be an overlap empire of the frontier but as near a 'Middle Kingdom' as any, with the Yellow River plain as its heartland.

Yet such was the extent of Jin conquest, and such the overstretch of its Jurchen manpower (2–4 million amid a northern Han population of 30–60 million), that for a decade the Jin toyed with subcontracting the task of pacification to an artificially constituted buffer state. South of the Yellow River there thus arose yet another Chu, then another longer-lasting Qi (1130–37). Only a new treaty with the now Southern Song, concluded in 1142, ended this experiment in indirect rule. The Jin sought a more permanent arrangement along their southern frontier. Their armies had not had it all their own way in the south. Like many before them, they had found the malarial climate debilitating and the terrain unsuitable for horses; additionally the Song navy made river crossings hazardous. On the whole it was better to let the Song retain what the Jin could not comfortably subdue. A Jin–Song frontier along the Huai River about 150 kilometres (93 miles) north of the Yangzi was mutually agreed; and the Song were to pay the Jin an annual tribute roughly equivalent to that paid to Khitan Liao by the Northern Song.

The actual sum was less important than Song's acceptance that it was indeed 'tribute'. Imperial blushes were not this time to be spared by the usual euphemisms. In the treaty oath, the Song were obliged to refer to their empire as 'our insignificant state' and to Jin as 'your superior state'. For these embarrassing concessions, all the Song received in return were a pledge of coexistence and the corpse of the lately deceased hostage, *Song* Huizong, he of 'muddled virtue' who was the father of the Southern Song's founder. The Song were now vassals of the Jin, and their emperor 'must have regarded the extorted documents [of the treaty] as the nadir of his career'. He was not even awarded kinship status as the 'younger brother', 'son' or 'nephew' of the Jin emperor. Instead he must call himself 'Servant Gou', Gou being *Song* Gaozong's personal name (and, doubly degrading, imperial personal names being normally taboo). '[This] must have taxed to the extreme his gift for self-denial.'[24]

The peace lasted nearly twenty years; it was this 'edict' to which Lu You, representing Song irredentism, so poignantly objected in the poem 'Border Mountain Moon'. Meanwhile the 'traitorous barbarians', that is the Jurchen Jin, were indeed 'living to see their heirs' – though not especially liking what they saw. Organising their new empire meant, for the Jin, not just accommodating themselves to Han norms but coming to grips with their own tribal heritage. Consensual institutions like the Jurchen chiefs' periodic councils had already been abolished as incompatible with the dignity of an emperor; and in a further rebuff to Jurchen supremacism, Han subjects had been excused from adopting the Jurchen hairstyle. (This should not be seen as a dynastic innovation, like the Xia tonsure, but as a standard token of submission; it involved shaving the front of the crown, a style which, with the addition of a queue, would be reimposed in the seventeenth century by the latter-day Jurchens who called themselves Manchu.) Now, in a further move to regularise the empire, the independent tendencies of the Jurchen nobles at court and of the clan leaders in the provinces were severely curtailed and their authority restricted to military recruitment.

A Han-type bureaucracy, partly recruited through examination and wholly dependent on the emperor, took over their administrative responsibilities. Tax rolls were revised, censuses conducted, scholars encouraged, degrees awarded and Buddhism esteemed, if still closely regulated. Literature flourished; new literary forms including musical dramas proved especially popular. The court rituals and etiquette of imperial China were adopted wholesale. Only the constraints of Confucian morality and ministerial remonstrance were neglected. The authority of the emperor was more absolute than ever, with the rough-and-ready justice of tribal leadership adding a sharper, bloodier edge to the unimpeded exercise of power.

Responsible for these changes were two tyrannical emperors: the alcoholic *Jin* Xizong (r. 1135–49), and his cousin and murderer, the lecherous Prince Hailing. (Too tyrannical to qualify for a posthumous title, Hailing nevertheless reigned, 1149–61). Xizong is portrayed as an incompetent wastrel, Hailing as a butchering monster. 'In the rogues' gallery of Chinese history, Hailing Wang occupies a place of honour,' writes a sarcastic Herbert Franke in *The Cambridge History of China*; 'he even became an anti-hero in popular pornography, where his exploits are embellished with gusto.'[25] Both emperors had no compunction in murdering enemies, executing supposed opponents and abusing their womenfolk in defiance of custom. They were violent and dangerous autocrats. Yet they were by no means tribal ruffians, and their victims were more often Jurchen chiefs than Han subjects. Both spoke Chinese and had received an upbringing in the Confucian classics. Hailing reputedly composed elegant verse. His intelligence was formidable, and if he inspired universal fear, he did so in the conviction that terror had its place in the authoritarian tradition of Han-type emperorship.

With territory and prestige beyond the dreams of any previous conqueror, the Jin should have been content after the 1142 treaty; likewise the Song, who, despite Lu You's plaint, had not only survived but retained control of what was now much the most productive region of China. Trade between the two empires revived and diplomatic niceties were respected. Yet in 1161 Prince Hailing of Jin, possibly to counter his extreme unpopularity, revived Jin designs on Song with a massive new invasion. Song hit back in 1206–08. Neither advance achieved its objectives or significantly altered the political geography; rather were both counterproductive.

The Jin attack of 1161 was quickly aborted. Never popular, it did, however, provoke the murder of the unspeakable Prince Hailing and bring to the throne his antithesis. A cousin, this *Jin* Shizong (r. 1161–89) restored the good name of Jurchen rule and is highly praised by the official historians for his moderation and good sense. Revolts among the Jin's Khitan subjects were put down. Jurchen sensibilities were appeased with new responsibilities and the promotion of things dear to Jurchen tradition, such as hunting, archery and the Jurchen language and script. Meanwhile Han opinion was mollified by Shizong's high regard for the Duke of Zhou and his remote utopian age; like every good Confucianist, Shizong urged its adoption as a model to which Jin China should aspire. Peace with the Song was restored at little cost. From a 'servant' the Song emperor was promoted to 'nephew' and his annual 'tribute' downgraded to a simple 'payment'. The amount stayed unchanged, and Jin supremacy remained intact, though now avuncular rather than magisterial.

The lopsided nature of the relationship was conceded by the Song when in 1206 they ended four and a half decades of mostly peaceful coexistence by issuing a declaration of war. By way of justification, and in the hope of attracting defectors, they offered the view that the Jin 'through their evil actions and incompetence, had lost the Mandate of Heaven and thus the legitimate claim to rule their country'.[26] Clearly, to lose the Mandate, they must once have held it; thus either the Song had long been ruling in defiance of the Mandate – an unlikely admission – or there were indeed two legitimate rulers under Heaven. Ironically it would take yet a third, who in this same year, 1206, on the banks of the Onon River in central Mongolia, was acclaimed khan of all the Mongols, to resolve this clash of the mandates.

The Song's claim that the Jin had forfeited the Mandate may not have seemed unreasonable at the time. Troubles had lately assailed the Jin from all directions. In the north, Mongol raids were already obliging the Jin to spend heavily on fortifications and punitive expeditions. The additional taxation required to meet this expense bore heavily on farmers in the central plain, who were already struggling with that bane of the period, inflation fuelled by a shortage of coin, plus the usual end-of-dynasty cycle of drought, disease, locust attack and, increasingly, floods. Ever since the 1160s the Yellow River had been behaving erratically. There were serious inundations in the Kaifeng area in the 1170s and farther downstream in Shandong in the 1180s. Siltation was evidently raising the river to spate levels that the levees could not contain and which the Jin lacked the experience to deal with.

The disaster struck in 1194. The river burst it banks in several places. It not only turned its normally productive flood-plain into plain unproductive flood, but completely changed its course, shunning the channels that had previously conducted it to estuaries north of the Shandong peninsula in favour of a new cross-country route (later incorporated into the Grand Canal) to the mouth of the Huai River south of the Shandong peninsula. It was almost an exact reversal of the great change that had taken place in AD 11/12; and just as that cataclysm, by undermining Wang Mang's fundamentalist reform programme, had clearly demonstrated that his one-man dynasty had forfeited the Mandate, so Heaven, it seemed, had now withdrawn its favour from the Jin.

The disruption to communciations and grain shipments may have been as serious as the loss of crops and property. Famine and unrest ensued. Economically crippled as well as dynastically delegitimised, the Jin now looked an easy target to the Song. No doubt the irredentist poet Lu You,

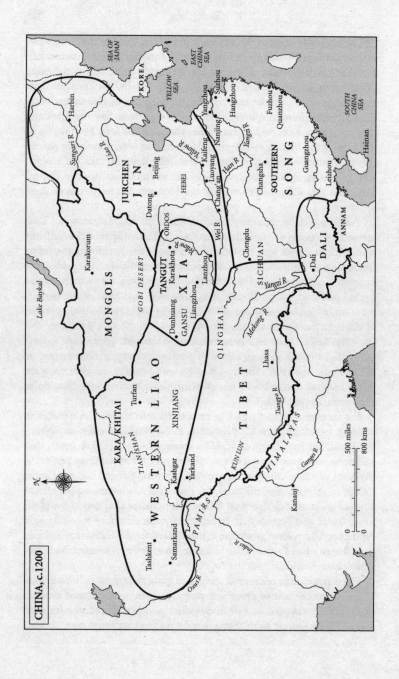

CHINA, c.1200

already into his seventies, lent what support he could to the emerging warmongers in the Song capital of Hangzhou. The Jin then made things worse for themselves by an ostentatious attempt to reassert their legitimacy. After several years of heated debate, in 1202 *Jin* Zhangzhong (r. 1189–1208) ceremonially adopted from among the 'Five Phases' (or 'Elements') that of Earth (colour: yellow, etc.) as the one appropriate to the Jin. The move clearly signified that the Jin considered themselves the sole Mandatees with the Southern Song as their vassals. The long debate had simply been over which Phase/Element to plump for; it depended on which dynasty – Northern Song, Khitan Liao or Tang – the Mandate had supposedly been inherited from; when the decision went in favour of the Northern Song, whose Phase/Element had been Fire (colour: red, etc.), the sequence of Phases as then understood dictated that Earth come next.

Undeterred by Earth having sustained long-lasting dynasties like the Han and Tang, the Song hastened to invade. In 1208 their forces pushed north across the Huai River. They met unexpectedly stiff resistance and found surprisingly few defectors. Instead Sichuan, part of their own empire, chose to revolt. Like the Jin attack of 1161, the campaign achieved next to nothing beyond discrediting the belligerent party. Lu You lived to see its failure and die a disappointed man.

That was in 1210. A year later, the Mongols ceased their sporadic raiding of Jin territory to launch a full-scale invasion. Chinggis Khan in person led one of the two armies, each of about 50,000 well-mounted archers, that began systematically plundering the Jin empire. Datong in Shanxi was captured, Beijing besieged. In 1213/14 the invaders were back for more triumphs, more booty and a truce that thoroughly humiliated the Jin. It lasted a year. When, for security, the Jin moved their capital to Kaifeng, Chinggis Khan took it to be an infringement of the treaty. The Mongols returned and in 1215 took Beijing.

Submission and loot, rather than thrones and territory, were the Mongol objectives at the time; conquest and government would come later. Thus for the next two decades, while Chinggis terrorised the rest of Eurasia, the Jin were left to the tender mercies of his lieutenants. Manchuria was soon lost, although Jin territory south of the Yellow River remained intact and elsewhere some of the devastation was repaired and the scattered population resettled. Rebuilding the military proved more difficult. Many Jurchen and Khitan had deserted to the Mongols; and appeals for help to Xia and Southern Song met with contempt. When in 1228 the Mongols returned in force, the by now largely Han forces of the Jin nevertheless offered a fierce resistance. It continued until 1233, in which year Kaifeng finally fell to the enemy. The last Jin emperor committed suicide a year later. A dynasty that, for all its faults, had set an example, substantially followed by both Mongols and Manchus, of how non-Han rule could be made acceptable to an overwhelmingly Han population had finally proved itself worthy of the Mandate; extinction with honour had been preferred to the shame of a mock abdication. The Southern Song, come their turn, would know what was expected of them.

12

BY LAND AND SEA
1235–1405

SUNSET OF THE SONG

AFTER THE SONG THERE WOULD BE just three more imperial dynasties: the Mongol Yuan (1279–1368), the Ming (1368–1644) and the Manchu Qing (1644–1911). Although definitely legitimate, in Chinese eyes all would in some way be compromised. The first and last would often be portrayed as alien regimes indifferent to the plight of their Chinese subjects, and the Ming, though indigenous and in many ways admirable, as culpable for a decline in China's international standing relative to that of the European powers that began frequenting China's ports towards the end of the Ming period. That left the Song at the apex of the dynastic trajectory. The Song, and more especially the sunset blaze of the Southern Song (1127–1279), would come to be seen as a halcyon age of imperial China.

Talent and industry, along with fugitives and colonists, had gravitated south with every incursion into the north. The demand for ink and pigments was never so high as among the artists and calligraphers, poets, philosophers, playwrights and diarists who plied their brushes in the benign climate of Southern Song. Block-printed books of reasonable price now circulated widely, connoisseurs and collectors drooled over landscape paintings of exquisite delicacy, and the production of fine lacquerware reached industrial proportions. Above all, it was 'the classic period of Chinese ceramics'.[1] Technical mastery combined with a revival of interest in archaic forms to produce stonewares of elegance and restraint for a rich and discerning domestic market. Meanwhile the booming export demand was increasingly supplied from southern kilns within waterborne reach of the coast, most notably those at Jingdezhen in Jiangxi province. Here, high-quality deposits of a clay enriched with kaolin made possible the production of a shell-like ware whose transparent glaze gave a 'blue-white' (*qingbai*)

THE SONG AND JIN SUCCESSIONS

	NORTHERN SONG	KHITAN LIAO	JURCHEN JIN	MONGOL
960	Taizu (960–976)			
980	Taizong (976–97)			
1000	Zhenzong (998–1022)			
1020				
1040	Renzong (1022–63)	907–1125		
1060	Yingzong			
	Shenzong (1068–85)			
1080	Zhezong (1086–1101)			
1100	Huizong (1101–25)			
1120	Qinzong (1126)		(Aguda) Taizu (1115–23)	
	SOUTHERN SONG		(Wuqimai) Taizong (1123–35)	
1140	Gaozong (1127–62)		Xizong (1135–49)	
1160			Prince Hailing (1149–61)	
1180	Xiaozong (1163–94)		Shizong (1161–89)	Chinggis Khan (1167–1227)
	Guanzong (1190–94)		Zhangzong (1189–1208)	
1200	Ningzhong (1195–1224)		Weishao (1209–13)	
1220			Xuanzong (1213–24)	
			Aizong (1224–34)	Ogodei (1229–41)
1240	Lizong (1225–1264)			
1260				Mongke (1251–9)
	Duzong (1265–74)			Khubilai (1260–94)
1280	Gongzong/Duanzong/Bing Di		Gongzong (1275) Duanzong (1276–8) Bing Di (1279)	
1300				

tinge. It was probably this *qingbai* ware that Marco Polo termed porcelain and ascribed to a place called 'Tyunju', which could be Jingdezhen. 'They make it nowhere but in that city, and thence it is exported all over the world.'[2] Along with other ceramic wares, Jingdezhen's porcelain found its way to ports throughout east and south-east Asia and farther afield to India, Egypt, Europe and east Africa. When around 1340 Jingdezhen began producing a decorated blue-and-white porcelain, it too was almost entirely for export. A prime candidate for the doubtful honour of being 'the first truly global "brand"', this Jingdezhen blue-and-white ware would come to be known in English as 'China-ware' or just 'china'.[3]

The logic behind the provenance of this 'China/china' terminology is indicated by Polo. When his Mongol hosts used the word *Chin* (which was Polo's rendering of 'Jin'), ''tis Manzi they mean', he reports. Evidently the Jurchen dynastic title 'Jin' had been extended by the Mongols to all parts of China that they had still to conquer, while 'Manzi' was Polo's transcription of two characters signifying the land of the aboriginal 'Man peoples', a derogatory northerners' term for the subjects of the Southern Song.[4] With the Southern Song still flourishing when Polo claims to have arrived on the scene some time in the 1270s, *Chin* and Manzi were indeed the same. The East China Sea was known as the Sea of Chin, and the porcelain exported from its ports was known to foreigners as 'Chin ware', hence 'china-ware'. There seems no compelling reason for launching an etymological grappling iron across centuries of silence to establish some tenuous link with Ptolemy's 'Sinae', the Graeco-Roman 'Sinai'/'Thinai', India's 'Cina'/'Chitan', the First Emperor's 'Qin', or the warring state of 'Jin'.

The seaports and rivers of Southern Song bristled with shipping, but as yet no impertinent visitors from beyond the seas questioned the superiority of China's culture. Foreign trade offered some compensation for the loss of the north and was officially encouraged. Just as local bureaucrats and landed gentry invested in commerce, so financiers and merchants participated in government, especially in the operation of the official monopolies. Meanwhile famines were few and prosperity the norm. Emperors were attentive to the advice of councillors; the bureaucracy was seldom bypassed. Like ceramics and brushwork, the values and institutions dear to China seemed transcendent throughout East Asia – eagerly adopted in Japan, Korea and Vietnam, resilient and indispensable to alien regimes in the north, and acknowledged as of surpassing prestige far beyond. Chinese was the lingua franca of the whole region, its characters written and read by a discernng few from Almaty (Alma Ata) to Angkhor. Dazzling as had been the achievements of the Han and Tang dynasties, the legacy of the Song would seem still brighter and, following the dynasty's extinction, be bathed in a nostalgic afterglow.

But this elevation of the Song presupposes that eminence lay more in intellectual distinction and cultural sophistication than in territorial dominion and military clout. Neither the humiliations suffered at the hands of the Khitan and Jurchen under the Northern Song, nor the loss of northern China and the eventual capitulation to the Mongols under the Southern Song, would be allowed to tarnish the glittering image. Even the person of the emperor proved largely immune to these catastrophes, blame being reserved for a succession of powerful ministers, such as Cai Jing, whose prominence remained a feature of the period. The six emperors of the Southern Song who actually reigned (three end-of-the-line emperors were infants) merit scant mention. Neither saints nor monsters, some, like the founder *Song* Gaozong, took a keen interest in government; all showed restraint in dealing with critics; none was especially forceful. Of the six, three abdicated or retired prematurely, one being deranged, the others simply keen to indulge their prurient interests without interruption from ministers and wordy didacts.

Yet with the Mandate itself in dispute during much of the period, a sense of crisis remained palpable. Across the placid surface of Hangzhou's West Lake – a watery wonderland and pleasure park adjoining the Southern Song capital – beyond its bristling pagodas and behind its bosky hills, the storm clouds massed and the threat of conflict flickered like summer lightning along the northern horizon. War and peace dominated the period. They dictated the rhythms of political life, determined reputations, sharpened perceptions and concentrated great minds wonderfully.

After the 1127 loss of Kaifeng, their northern capital, the Song had found a doughty champion in Yue Fei, a professional soldier of little education but heroic stature. From Nanjing and then Wuchang – near where southern forces had defeated those of the north at the battle of the Red Cliffs some nine centuries earlier – Yue Fei led his men across the Yangzi and up the Han River. Raids deep into Jurchen Jin territory during the 1130s somewhat redeemed the reputation of Song arms. No less memorably, Yue Fei also suppressed a local uprising and commandeered its formidable river flotilla, including several ships propelled by paddle-wheels. The technology was not unlike that of the waterwheel used in irrigation, and had long since been adapted for boats. But the novelty of these vessels lay in their size and the number of their paddle-wheels. The biggest were armed with derricks, from which swung wrecking irons, and deck-mounted trebuchets (cannon-size catapults used in siege warfare) that fired both smoke bombs and incendiary shells. Behind armoured screens, the multiple decks could accommodate hundreds of men; and with up to twenty-four paddle-wheels – twelve per side – the riverine giants must have churned through the water like juggernauts on a flooded highway. 'A truly remarkable piece of technology', the paddle-boat was unrivalled elsewhere in the world and would remain so. 'No other civilisation produced anything like them,' says Joseph Needham.[5] The numerous crew was essential for propulsion, and since this depended on a pedalled treadmill mechanism, they were not paddle-steamers but steamer-size pedaloes. They nevertheless proved a conspicuous addition both to the mythic reputation of Yue Fei and to his now amphibious forces, which grew with every daring escapade.

Unfortunately for Yue Fei, by 1140 this martial spirit had ceased to be to the court's liking. His success was seen as a threat and his devotion to the Song as an embarrassment; his undoubted fame had revived Song paranoia about powerful generals defying civilian rule, while his belligerent utterances ran counter to the peace feelers that were already being extended to the Jin (and would produce the settlement of 1141/42). Yue Fei was therefore recalled, deprived of his command, imprisoned for insubordination, poisoned on the orders of the chief minister, and erased from official memory. Not until 1161, twenty years later, when a Jin invasion (it was the one mounted by the unpopular Prince Hailing) again threatened the Southern Song, was Yue Fei's memory partially rehabilitated. Military role models were suddenly back in vogue; the minister responsible for Yue Fei's disgrace and death was labelled a detested appeaser.

Later still a grandson of Yue Fei took it upon himself to ferret out documentary evidence of his grandfather's achievements, embellish them and, early in the thirteenth century, publish an adulatory biography. This coincided with another bout of Song bellicosity when in 1206–08, with the Jin reeling from Yellow River floods, the Song armies moved north to take advantage. The attack soon petered out, but such were the enduring properties of the printed word that the grandson's biography established Yue Fei and his ill-requited exploits as a model for all time. Much mythologised in reaction to Mongol rule, under the Ming dynasty Yue Fei would be elevated to the position of 'number two military hero of all Chinese history' (as F. W. Mote puts it), second only to Guan Yu, the most warlike of the three swashbuckling companions in the *Romance of the Three Kingdoms*. Both Guan Yu and Yue Fei featured in countless other novels and plays and had temples dedicated to their memory. 'Recover our Rivers and Mountains', a slogan adopted against the Japanese invader in the 1940s, was culled from lyrics supposedly composed by the now immortalised Yue

Fei and subsequently set to music. With lines like 'My hair bristles in my helmet, ... My fierce ambition is to feed on the flesh of the Huns' (literally 'Xiongnu flesh' but figuratively that of Jurchen, Mongol, Japanese or any other non-Han invader), Yue Fei symbolised the spirit of a nation's resistance. Communist cadres rallying to the homeland's liberation must, though, have choked on the last line in which recovering the mountains and the rivers was to be but a prelude to 'paying our respects once more to the emperor'.[6]

The warmongers of 1206–08 were discredited when Song forces again failed to reclaim much in the way of territory. Peace was restored, and another militaristic minister paid the price; his head, gift-wrapped and forwarded to the Jin, formed part of the indemnity settlement. In Hangzhou pacific counsels reasserted themselves, as well they might, for the Jin, now facing the full force of Chinggis Khan's rough-riding armies, posed a much-reduced threat. When in 1233–34 the Mongols finally eliminated the Jin altogether, Hangzhou drew a long sigh of relief. Not until two decades later, when the Mongols resumed their advance on the Yangzi, would West Lake's rhapsodising patrons realise that a similar fate might yet be awaiting them.

The lull in hostilities and the triumph of Southern Song's peace-loving bureaucrats over its war-waging militarists reopened the question of reform. While at the height of his power, Han Tuozhou, the general whose head had since been detached and gift-wrapped, had taken against the scholarly elite and in particular against a school of what he called 'false learning'. Its exponents had been denounced and dismissed from office, among them the man who is now generally considered as (to ape Mote's phrasing) the number-two philosopher-moralist of all Chinese history, second, that is, only to Confucius himself. This was Zhu Xi (1130–1200), an intellectual colossus responsible for a new orientation, 'a new culture' even, which, becoming the dominant ideology during the empire's seven remaining centuries, would come to be known as Neo-Confucianism. The 'Confucian persuasion' was about to become more intellectually persuasive.

Perhaps mischievously, Confucianism prior to the Song has been characterised as 'more a curriculum than a philosophy'.[7] Lacking a bedrock in natural law or divine revelation, all Chinese scholarship probed the past for structural validation. Pile-driving into the depths of documented antiquity, it sought an acceptable purchase much as construction engineers building on China's soft alluvial soils must today drill deep to secure their skyscrapers. Writing of any sort had a bibliographical flavour and involved copious citation; the compilation of anthologies, historical encyclopedias, geographical gazetteers, biographical collections and all manner of other compendia constituted a veritable industry. It was by selecting, editing, interpreting, listing and reproducing the extant works of other ages – curriculum-building in effect – that scholarship progressed. Such constant revision could be a sterile process, which was how it had seemed to Han Tuozhou when he labelled it 'false learning'. But it also possessed its own dynamic. In the 1170s Wang Anshi's reinterpretation of the contentious *Zhouli* had triggered the most revolutionary of reform programmes. Likewise the number of works enjoying canonical status as 'the Confucian classics' had varied over the centuries between five and thirteen, additions and subtractions providing the stimulus for new trends in thought and government as well as affording a barometer of these trends.

Under the Song, concern over the marginalisation of Heaven's Son within the cosmic and geographical schema of 'All-under-Heaven' set thinkers to thinking and writers to writing as never before. It generated the candid historical scholarship of Ouyang Xiu and Sima Guang, the furore over the reformist programmes of Fan Zhongyang and Wang Anshi, endless debate about the merits of peace versus the risks of war, and urgent scrutiny of the entire Confucian legacy. Neo-Confucianism in its broadest sense embraced all these activities. Like the Renaissance in Europe, the term came to be used to sum up the spirit of an age and highlight its defining characteristic. This was not the rediscovery of a classical past but the re-evaluation of an intellectual and ethical heritage that, though always cherished, was thought to have long been imperfectly understood.

The parameters of scholarly reference remained tight. Education and tradition kept speculation on the straight-and-narrow of what could be sourced in the Confucian classics and illustrated from the historical record. On the other hand, these repositories of wisdom were sufficiently capacious and enigmatic to accommodate challenging and often contradictory new thinking about the dynamics of the universe, the composition of human nature and the social and political conduct appropriate to both. In this ferment of ideas, the formation of pressure groups and parties remained taboo. Confucian tradition urged self-cultivation; virtue was to be sought within, through arduous study and such vigilant examination of one's motives that doing the right thing became second nature. Exceptional scholars like Zhu Xi, though encouraged to teach and publish, tended therefore to stress their association not with contemporary thinkers but with past sages and to construct a pedigree for their ideas. Sometimes dignified as a 'Way' or a 'Great Tradition', it linked them to key figures, concepts and phrases from the textual tradition.

Bearded and twinkly-eyed (if one may trust his portrait) and apparently indifferent to career advancement, Zhu Xi chose his textual pedigree rather sparingly. His curricular contribution was to pare down the Confucian classics to just 'Four Books' (*Sishu*). Two were from the same text, the perhaps fourth-century BC *Liji* or 'Book of Rites'; he selected extracts, reorganised them as two works entitled the *Great Learning* and the *Doctrine of the Mean*, reinterpreted them, and then repositioned them within his own 'Four Books' sequence. The other two of the four, also heavily abbreviated and glossed, were the *Analects* of Confucius and the *Mengzi* of Mencius, the Master's acknowledged successor. Forming 'a coherent humanistic vision' and stressing the humane and socially responsible side of Confucianism, the Four Books would soon take priority over all the other classics and as of the fourteenth century become the foundation texts for both primary and civil service examinations. Memorised by millions, they 'exerted far greater influence on Chinese life and thought over the next six hundred years than any other works'.[8]

Surveying the historical record, Zhu Xi was equally sparing. The mythical Five Emperors of prehistoric times were unassailably virtuous, likewise the pre-imperial Xia and Shang dynasties and of course the grand old Duke of Zhou. Then things had gone downhill. Confucius had managed to 'transmit' the accumulated wisdom of this sage past, and Mencius had refined and humanised this 'transmission'; but the principles and the rationale underlying it had been too often ignored in public life. The nadir was reached in the tenth century under fly-by-night dynasties like that of Later Liang, the most unspeakable of Ouyang Xiu's Five Dynasties.

Only under the Northern Song in the eleventh to twelfth centuries had the great 'Way of Learning' (*Daoxue*) at last resurfaced. Prompted by the Song's political embarrassments, and goaded by the mystical and metaphysical subtleties of Daoist and especially Buddhist doctrine, Confucian studies had revived. At the core of this new, or Neo-, Confucian thinking lay a host of different ideas about how the cosmos worked and how the individual, as part of it and in accordance with its workings, might discover his own parallel path to moral perfection. The society and government composed of such enlightened individuals would then automatically be realigned in harmony with the cosmos. Man had the potential for good, or 'humaneness', within him; but to realise it, he needed to understand what human nature consisted of and how the mind functioned. Ancient concepts such as the 'Mean' (a state of lofty impartiality) and the 'Supreme Ultimate' held the key. According to Zhu Xi, the 'Supreme Ultimate' was 'merely the principle [or the polarity] of Heaven and Earth and the myriad things'; it resided in each and every one; and its 'movement generates *yang* and ... its tranquillity generates *yin*'.[9] Rationally reinterpreted, reformulated and, of course, exhaustively sourced, these and other such key ideas generated several schools of philosophy and so, for the first time, gave to Confucianism a metaphysical root-structure that was every bit as philosophically respectable, not to say mentally testing, as for instance Buddhist notions of non-being. Indeed, whether in reaction to Buddhism and Daoism or in imitation of them, Neo-Confucianism owed to both a considerable debt.

Finally, in its narrowest possible sense the term Neo-Confucianism is sometimes reserved exclusively for the immensely influential synthesis of ideas distilled from this cauldron of speculation by Zhu Xi himself. His synthesis is called *Lixue*, the 'doctrine of principle', the 'principle' in question somewhat resembling a metaphysical gene, inherent in all things but not uniform, basically good, and decisive in determining a human being's moral nature. Zhu supposed it dormant until activated by 'material-force', which in the case of man meant the 'investigation of all things'. His achievement lay not just in synthesising and organising what one writer calls these 'fruitfully ambiguous concepts' but in their cogent presentation and practical application.[10] As a teacher with his own academy he disseminated them, and as a provincial official he endeavoured to practise them.

A handbook on family rituals – marriages, funerals, ancestor reverence, etc. – prepared under his direction was probably as influential as the 'Four Books', though it did his later reputation no favours. As a stickler for the Confucian submission of young to old and female to male, Zhu Xi ordered girls to cover their faces in public; wives were to be denied either financial or intellectual independence; and in those regions 'notorious for their frequent cases of abduction', he advised the women to 'attach wooden blocks to their shoes so that they made a noise in walking'. Assuming they could actually walk, as opposed to shuffling on stumps, this scarcely amounted to protection; the clatter may have been more advertisement than safeguard. The Japanese scholar responsible for unearthing such strictures has suggested that they instilled a deep conservatism. The standardisation of Confucian family rites, in Japan (where Zhu Xi's writings were equally influential) as in China, reinforced a stifling degree of social conformity by adding the weight of canonical sanction to the burden of convention. 'If Christianity ... attaches importance to the sense of guilt, and Buddhism to the sense of pain [or suffering],' says the same scholar, 'Confucianism stresses the sense of shame.'[11]

Come reaction, let alone eventual revolution, Zhu Xi would be an easy target. His 'Four Books', instead of encouraging 'the investigation of all things', stressing the obligation to think for oneself, and so ending the set-piece tyranny of the examinations, came in time to comprise that tyranny; and in encapsulating Neo-Confucianism, Zhu Xi would be roundly condemned for it. For ignoring political realities and obsessing about abstract theories of human nature, he invited contempt, while 'the no doubt unintended consequence of his social thought was to harden the status quo, close minds to unconventional views, and discourage those in government from taking any disruptive actions'.[12] The more he became the central figure in the ideology of the later empire, the more exposed he would be to the criticisms of those who would overthrow it.

Ironically the official adoption of Zhu Xi's Neo-Confucianism would come not under the Song but under the supposedly uncultured Mongols. In 1259 Mongol forces reached the Yangzi, so bringing the prospect of confrontation between the mannered lifestyle of Southern Song and the raw fury of the steppe uncomfortably close. Visions of Mongol cavalry watering their horses in Hangzhou's West Lake before carrying rape and pillage into the heart of Polo's 'finest city in the world' were too horrible to contemplate. Rote-learning students in lakeside bowers must have shivered in their chest-gaping gowns, carousing grandees aboard pedalled pleasure-craft have choked on their kumquats. 'The people of this land [i.e. Manzi] were anything but warriors,' says Polo, 'all their delight was in women, and nought but women.' Their 'king', too, 'thought of nothing but women, unless it were charity to the poor'. Though his kingdom 'had no horses', the lakes and rivers provided a natural defence; he could have held out if the people had been a little more martial, thought Polo; 'but that is just what they were not, and so it was lost'.[13]

MONGOL REUNIFICATION

Seldom can more mismatched adversaries have squared up to one another. The Song, with a massive army but a wretched military record, had been retreating, on and off, for nearly three hundred years; the Mongols, though fewer and occasionally repelled, had been advancing for fifty years, had never lost a war, and had conquered most of the known world. Their onslaught, more sudden than that of the Arabs, more widespread than that of Alexander, and more traumatic than either, was like nothing that history had ever known – or would again. According to both Christian and Muslim sources, bleached bones and charred timbers marked their trail; the slaughter of those who offered resistance was generally as comprehensive as steel and muscle could manage. Urbanisation in much of Asia was halted in its tracks, fragile agricultural systems never recovered, and population figures are thought to have nosedived. Like the plague, which they may unintentionally have spread, the Mongols came from nowhere and were suddenly everywhere.

It had all begun in north-east Mongolia in 1206 when a resourceful and audacious twenty-year-old called Temujin, scion of a junior branch of the neither numerous nor powerful Meng people of that region, having united the Meng and overrun more formidable neighbours, was acclaimed their 'Chinggis Khan' ('Oceanic Qaghan' or 'Universal Ruler'). A great white banner was unfurled at the windswept gathering near the source of the Onon River where this ceremony took place, a basic military-cum-administrative organisation was set up, and plans laid for further triumphs. The unity of the peoples of the Mongolian steppe, no less than the authority of their new ruler, depended on maintaining the momentum of success. Only by more raids, more proof of invincibility and more redistributed plunder – livestock, gold, furs, textiles, foodstuffs, craftsmen, presentable women and enslaveable children – could loyalty be rewarded and the allegiance of others attracted.

Though 'Meng' or 'Meng-wu' was just the Chinese rendering of 'Mongol', 'Mongolian' better describes the composition of Chinggis's following. Turkic-speaking neighbours, some of whom had adopted Nestorian Christianity, were already more numerous than native Mongols. Included, too, were the Tatars, another Mongolian people whose name both Chinese and European writers would often prefer to that of 'Mongol' – much as the Mongols would prefer 'Jin' (or 'Chin') for Song China. Other early adherents included numerous Uighurs from the northern city-states of Xinjiang. They would play a major part in Mongol administration. Their script was adapted for Mongol use, and their confessional odyssey – through Buddhism to Manichaeism and Islam – lent an ecumenical diversity to the profile of the Mongol court. While much of contemporary Eurasia counted professing the wrong faith a greater incitement to war than the possession of conspicuous wealth or irresistible women, the Mongols begged to differ. Their demands, though exhorbitant, rarely extended beyond the portable and the serviceable; freedom of worship, for those who lived to enjoy it, was officially guaranteed.

First among their prosperous southern neighbours to feel the impact of Mongol power was Tangut Xia, or the 'Great State of White and High'.

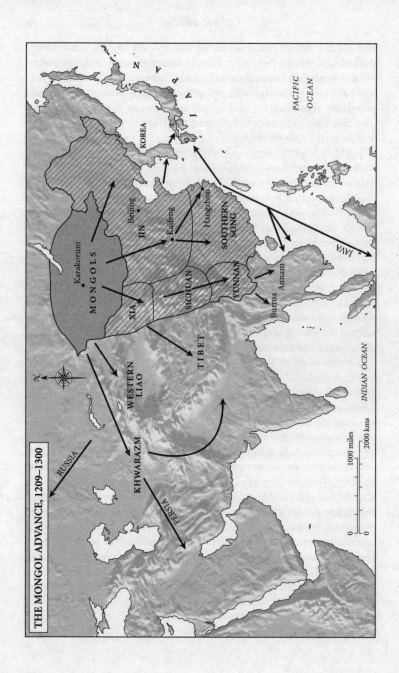

THE MONGOL ADVANCE, 1209–1300

PACIFIC
OCEAN

INDIAN OCEAN

JAPAN

KOREA

Beijing
JIN
Kaifeng
Hangzhou
SOUTHERN
SONG

Karakorum
MONGOLS

XIA
SICHUAN
YUNNAN
Burma Annam

TIBET

JAVA

WESTERN
LIAO

KHWARAZM

PERSIA

RUSSIA

N

0   1000 miles
0   2000 kms

Mongol armies rode in from the Gobi in 1209 and laid siege to the Tangut capital beside the upper Yellow River in Ningxia. It was the first Mongol assault on a sedentary people with a fortified city and it fared indifferently. A Mongol attempt to flush out the defendants by destroying their irrigation system flooded the Xia defences but also swept through their own positions. The Mongols withdrew, wet, undefeated and yet not exactly victorious. They had secured Xia's submission, plus a Tangut bride for Chinggis, but left the state intact. This would turn out to be a mistake.

The Xia campaign served as a trial run and strategic prelude to the more rewarding task of raiding the northern territories of the Jurchen Jin. Begun in 1211, the raids had climaxed with the capture of the Jin capital (the later Beijing) in 1215 and the attachment of much of Manchuria, whose remaining Khitans transferred their allegiance to the Mongols. Chinggis then turned west. The submission of the Kara Khitai (or Western Liao) of Turkestan in 1218 was easily won, though not so that of their more powerful neighbour, the Muslim kingdom of Khwarazm (roughly Uzbekistan). While its shah took refuge on an island in the Caspian Sea, where he died in 1221, his son went on the run and led the Mongols a none-too-merry dance through what are now northern Iran, Afghanistan, Pakistan and then back again. This bloodiest of campaigns ended in 1223 with Khwarazm's collapse and the dispersal of its forces. Many entered India, where they swelled the ranks of the Muslim conquistadors under the Delhi sultanate; others gravitated towards Syria and there carved for themselves 'a small niche in history as the Muslim force that (more or less incidentally) finally evicted the Crusaders from Jerusalem in 1244'.[14]

Further Mongol probes in the 1220s into Azerbaijan, Georgia and Russia presaged the great advance into Europe of 1241. Meanwhile Chinggis Khan ended his foreign adventures as he had begun them, with an attack on Tangut Xia. From end to end the 'Great State of White and High' was blackened and brought low before its capital was again besieged. It was still holding out when in 1227 Chinggis died, apparently from complications resulting from a fall from his horse. (Mongols were forever falling off horses, according to Brother William of Rubruck, a missionising Franciscan who, with encouragement from Louis IX of France, reached the Mongol capital in 1253; for men who lived and often slept in the saddle, it was an occupational hazard.) Days later, Xia surrendered and the khan's corpse could be taken home to be interred on a mountain in eastern Mongolia. As for the 'Great State of White and High', within a couple of decades it too had disappeared under the sands of history.

The Tanguts of Xia had brought all this upon themselves by failing to support ongoing Mongol operations against the Jin and then signing a unilateral peace treaty with them. From 1216 to 1223, while the main Mongol forces were subduing Khwarazm in the west, one of Chinggis's generals had rampaged up and down the Yellow River from Shandong to Shaanxi at the head of an army composed principally of Khitan and other ex-Jin subjects, including many Han Chinese. Experience in siegecraft was gained and sophisticated weaponry amassed; but the Tangut absence, and then defection, had limited its territorial gains.

Once the succession to Chinggis had been resolved with the elevation of his third son, Ögödei, as Great Khan (and with the installation of other sons as subordinate khans elsewhere in Eurasia), offensive operations in China were resumed. In 1230 Ögödei himself campaigned in Sichuan, ever the strategic key to an all-China dominion. Then in 1233–34, with some gleeful assistance from the Southern Song, he completed the conquest of the last Jin redoubts in Henan. All northern China down to the Huai River was now under the Mongols' control and at the mercy of their military commanders. A sinicised Khitan official favoured by Ögödei remonstrated against indiscriminate pillage and supposedly convinced his master that

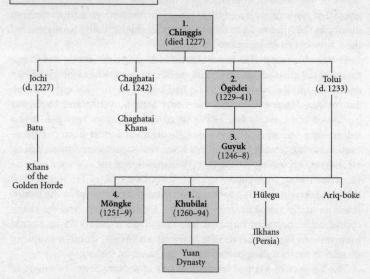

THE MONGOL SUCCESSION

```
                        1.
                     Chinggis
                   (died 1227)
    ┌──────────────┬──────────────┬──────────────┐
  Jochi        Chaghatai          2.            Tolui
 (d. 1227)     (d. 1242)        Ögödei        (d. 1233)
                               (1229–41)
                 Chaghatai
  Batu            Khans
                                   3.
                                 Guyuk
  Khans                         (1246–8)
   of the
 Golden Horde   ┌──────────────┬──────────────┬──────────────┐
               4.             1.           Hülegu      Ariq-boke
             Möngke        Khubilai
            (1251–9)       (1260–94)
                                           Ilkhans
                                           (Persia)
                            Yuan
                          Dynasty
```

depriving China of its people in order to turn it into pasturage would be less rewarding than sparing the population in order to tax their labours and enjoy their produce. He set up a basic administration, reinstated the examination system (though practically no successful candidates were entrusted with office) and briefly curbed the excesses of military rule. But with Ögödei's death in late 1241, this first Mongol experiment in Chinese-style government ended. The examinations lapsed and tax collection was farmed out among a coterie of central Asian merchants and moneylenders who had attached themselves to the Mongol leadership. Their extortionate demands and brutal enforcement methods laid waste the countryside. The northern Chinese, though spared annihilation to make way for grass, thus got an early taste of a most pernicious form of colonial oppression. 'It is difficult to imagine a more ruinous or exploitative economic system,' says a contributor to *The Cambridge History of China*.[15]

Succession crises occurring on and off through the 1240s brought a lull in Mongol operations in China. They ended with the elevation of Möngke, a grandson of Chinggis, as Great Khan in 1251. Like Ögödei, Möngke apportioned responsibilities for the wider Mongol empire among his kin. A cousin headed the Kipchak khanate in Russia, otherwise the Golden Horde ('horde' being derived from the Mongol *ordos* or *ordu*, meaning an 'encampment', like 'Urdu', the 'language of the camp', as spoken by those Mongols, or 'Mughals', who would one day set their sights on India). A brother of Möngke, Hülegu, was dispatched to Iran, where he would found the Persian Il-khanate, capture Baghdad and overthrow the Abbasid caliphate. And another brother, Khubilai, was given responsibility for operations in China.

Khubilai resumed Ögödei's offensive in Sichuan and continued south through its steep ravines into still-little-known Yunnan. There in 1253 he defeated the proud kingdom of Dali, which had succeeded that of Nanzhao in the tenth century. 'Thus it was the Mongols who first made Yunnan a directly administered province of China.'[16] In the course of these operations, contact was established with Tibet, or rather with its dominant lama-hood. Mongol–Tibetan relations were thereafter close, though their nature is obscure and controversial. Chinese sources imply a conventional subordination with military and administrative arrangements that provoked much Tibetan 'banditry' and necessitated several punitive invasions. Tibetan sources take little account of political relations and stress the influence of Tibetan Buddhism within the Mongol court. In neither case is it clear which of Tibet's several peoples was involved or what part of the Tibetan region was affected. After careful research, Herbert Franke has concluded that no Mongol incursion reached central Tibet, that 'most of

Tibet proper remained outside the direct control of the Sino-Mongol bureaucracy and that even the border regions were throughout the [Mongol] Yuan dynasty an unruly and troubled region'.[17]

Since he had hitherto been supposed the least martial of Mongol princes, Khubilai's success in Yunnan caused some surprise, while his willingness to spare lives and reinstate the king of Dali looked like a repeat of Chinggis's mistake in dealing with Xia. From Yunnan an expeditionary force descended the Red River into Vietnam, whose Tran dynasty took fright and formally recognised Mongol suzerainty. The landward encirclement of the Southern Song was now complete. It remained only to cut off any seaborne assistance from the Korean kingdom, an objective that was attained, after numerous bloody incursions, when the Koreans submitted in 1259.

Meanwhile Möngke had come south in person in order to deliver the *coup de grâce* to the Southern Song. In time-honoured fashion a many-pronged attack was planned with the main thrust coming from Sichuan in the west. Möngke advanced there in 1258, Khubilai pushed down to the Yangzi through Hubei in 1259, and in the same year another Mongol prong prodded into Anhui. Southern Song resistance proved unexpectedly resolute; yet it was already crumbling when another Mongol succession crisis brought an unexpected reprieve. For in 1259, either from dysentery or a direct hit from a Song missile, Möngke died. Operations were immediately suspended. Khubilai, who was poised to cross the Yangzi to Wuchang, did so, but then reluctantly headed north to contest the succession. Before he got there, one of his brothers mobilised against him, whereupon Khubilai declared himself Great Khan. There then ensued a many-sided war fought largely in Mongolia between the contending Mongol princes (1260–64).

The war effectively ended Mongol unity. Khubilai emerged as the Great Khan with direct control of the Mongolian homeland, northern China, Manchuria and Korea, plus nominal authority over the entire empire as successor to Chinggis; but his khanate was just one of four, all vast Eurasian powers that now acted more like fraternal states than constituent parts of a single empire. The so-called *pax Mongolica* was deceptive. Travellers with information to share, merchandise to sell or expertise for hire passed freely through the Mongol lands; in what would prove to be the swansong of the Silk Road, east and west engaged in a fruitful exchange of technologies and ideas as well as luxury goods. But familial ties among the khanates were no longer sustained by a common purpose, and the overarching claims of the Great Khan provoked more dissension than collaboration. Thus Khubilai and his successors in China, though the one celestial dynasty to rule something approximating 'All-under-Heaven', would do so only in theory.

Nearly fifty when in 1264 he emerged triumphant from the Mongol war of succession, Khubilai Khan is traditionally portrayed by Chinese historians as an example of a 'barbarian' ruler who responded well to Chinese acculturation. He had already located his capital south of the steppe within what had been Jin territory at a place called Shangdu, about 300 kilometres (185 miles) north-west of Beijing near the Hebei/Inner Mongolia border. Marco Polo would wax lyrical about Shangdu's palace and hunting park; and Samuel Taylor Coleridge would make it sound even more exotic, not least by spelling Shangdu as 'Xanadu'. In Yunnan and then in Mongolia, Khubilai's success had owed much to the manpower, revenue and advice available from his Chinese subjects. His fellow Mongols despised such indulgence of a conquered people, decried his adoption of a settled lifestyle and ridiculed him for preferring Chinese forms of sovereignty over the cut-and-thrust charisma of traditional steppe dominion. Indeed, the war of succession between the Mongol princes had been seen as a conflict between opposing styles of rulership as much as contending personalities. But whether willing convert or wily statesman, Khubilai seemed enthralled by his Chinese dominion at the expense of his Mongol heritage.

Traditionally his imperial reign is dated 1279–94, so prolonging to the maximum the Song's exclusive claim on the Mandate and foreshortening the duration of Mongol rule. In reality Khubilai had been active in China from the early 1250s and supreme throughout all but the south from 1260. In that year he adopted a Chinese reign-name and calendar; it was evidence of imperial intent. In 1264, victorious over his Mongol rivals and acknowledged as Great Khan, he moved his capital still farther south into core China. Shangdu was retained as a summer capital, but for most of the year court and government would now operate from what had been the Khitan Liao and Jurchen Jin capital in the heart of Hebei. Renamed Dadu ('Great Capital'), and later incorporated into the Ming city known as Beijing, its construction began in 1266/67 and took eight years. The layout was painstakingly Chinese. Based on an idealised city as outlined in that repository of ultra-traditionalism, the *Zhouli* ('Rites of Zhou'), it advertised Khubilai's assumption of the Mandate. Within high rectangular walls aligned with the compass points and pierced with towered gateways, the grid of Dadu's wide thoroughfares radiated from an inner walled city wherein stood the south-facing palace. Though commissioned by a Mongol emperor and then realised by a Muslim architect, its remains constitute the earliest surviving example of a quintessentially Chinese imperial capital. As emperor, Khubilai would be the first to rule all China from the future Beijing; and as Great Khan he was the first to preside over Mongol Eurasia from China.

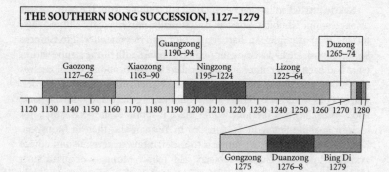

THE SOUTHERN SONG SUCCESSION, 1127–1279

Guangzong 1190–94 · Duzong 1265–74 · Gaozong 1127–62 · Xiaozong 1163–90 · Ningzong 1195–1224 · Lizong 1225–64

1120 1130 1140 1150 1160 1170 1180 1190 1200 1210 1220 1230 1240 1250 1260 1270 1280

Gongzong 1275 · Duanzong 1276–8 · Bing Di 1279

In 1272, while the Southern Song yet reigned in the south, Khubilai clearly signified acceptance of the Mandate. He did so in a formal announcement declaring that his dynasty was to be known by the unusual title of (Da) Yuan, '(Great) Originator'. Historians ought to be eternally grateful. The tiresomely confusing habit of recycling old dynastic names had finally been broken. As he proudly explained, 'Yuan' derived neither from his state of origin, like Qin and Han, nor from some feudal dukedom, like Sui and Tang. 'In all these cases, they [the dynasties] fell prey to the ingrained habits of common people . . . [and] adopted momentary measures of expediency for the sake of control,' he declared.[18] Clearly they were doomed. Khubilai, successor to the 'sage-like' Chinggis Khan and now ruler of the largest empire Heaven had ever seen, was above such parochialism. On the best possible advice, he had sourced his dynastic title in the 'Book of Changes' (*Yi-jing*, *I-Ching*), perhaps the most venerable of all the ancient classics. This transcended previous practice; and such was the exalted provenance of the new title that there could be no question of sharing the Mandate with someone else or conceding its duplication. The Southern Song were, by implication, delegitimised and must bow in submission.

To that end, military, and more especially naval, operations were again under way. Abandoning the idea of an advance from Sichuan, Khubilai had resolved on a frontal attack across the Yangzi. The prerequisite for this was gaining control of the great river's Han tributary, on which the twin cities of Xiangyang and Fancheng (now amalgamated as Xiangfan) constituted Song's formidable northern bastion. Facing one another across the Han River, both were heavily fortified and well supplied with the shipping with which to intercept any Mongol armada or bring in reinforcements and provisions if besieged.

They were indeed besieged. Invested in 1267/68, the twin cities held out until 1273. In one of the most protracted and celebrated actions in China's history, the Mongols soon discovered that cavalry were useless against ships and unhappy under firebomb attack. Summoning shipwrights and sailors from Korea and Shandong, experts in siege engines and ballistics from the Muslim west, engineers experienced in the use of gunpowder from the north, and vast contingents of Han infantry, the Mongols pressed the blockade in most un-Mongol fashion.

Heroic endeavours are recorded on both sides, none being more desperate than that of two Song colonels, both called Chang. When in 1272 Fancheng's outer defences were breached, the Changs assembled a supply convoy of a hundred giant paddle-boats and, churning their way to the relief, tried to run the Mongol blockade. They succeeded, though at a heavy cost in men, ships and supplies. One of the Colonels Chang was lost on the approach, the other while trying to escape downriver under cover of darkness. Later in the same year, Song engineers built a pontoon bridge of timbers across the river to connect the two cities. The Mongol commander reportedly met this challenge with craft equipped to cut through the bridge with specially designed 'mechanical saws'. Needham interprets this to mean that the boats were again paddle-powered and that the, presumably, circular saws were so mounted as to be run by the river's current turning the paddle-wheels, and so the saws, when the boats were stationary against the bridge.[19] More prosaically the pedalling crew could have been linked directly to the saws in an arrangement like that of a treadle grindstone.

In Marco Polo's 'Description of the World', it is claimed that Polo himself was present towards the end of the Xiangfan siege. In fact, he supposedly introduced the Mongol command to the two catapult experts – 'a German and a Nestorian Christian' – who devised the trebuchets, each capable of launching rocks weighing over 100 kilograms (220 pounds) that eventually battered the defenders into surrender. This is almost certainly a fabrication. Other sources say the experts were Muslims, and modern scholars doubt whether Polo had yet reached China. But whether Polo himself was responsible for making the claim is uncertain. It could just as well have been inserted by others, either by the far from reliable writer who allegedly wrote down Polo's word-of-mouth narration or by one of the many who further elaborated on his story over the following centuries.

So problematic is the provenance of the various versions of this cele-brated text, and so apparently minimal Polo's authorial control, that revisionists have had a field day. Some question whether Polo ever got to

China at all. The fact that he never notices the Great Wall is offered as evidence that he didn't, though since 'long walls' are little mentioned after the Sui, and since the Great Wall, as we now know it, was a creation of the Ming, this could be taken as evidence that he did. Other omissions – tea-drinking, foot-binding and the Chinese system of writing – deserve consideration. Yet, while in travel-writing the commonplace is notoriously easy to forget, incidental description is hard to invent. It has been suggested that he could have plagiarised some now lost, possibly Persian, source. The process of transcription must then have been one of elaborate collusion, a feat that its slapdash composition argues strongly against. In the end, trying to disprove his narrative proves as inconclusive as trying to substantiate his itinerary. And whatever Polo did, or wherever he went, the text itself retains an immediacy that it would be perverse to ignore.

When at last the twin cities fell in 1273, there was a year's delay before the Mongol advance to the Yangzi, and on down that river towards Hangzhou, could begin in earnest. Again it met stiff resistance. A seasoned official called Bayan was given command of the Mongol armies; Polo calls him 'Hundred Eyes'. Khubilai himself took no part in the campaign other than to urge clemency wherever possible. Bayan did just that, enticing defections, conciliating opponents, massacring the population of only one or two major cities, and winning a series of great battles. In Hangzhou, the weak young Southern Song emperor (*Song* Duzong, r. 1265–74) chose this moment to die. It was no great loss. His place was taken by a five-year-old and his powers by a dowager empress. Meanwhile Jia Sidao, the last in a long line of disposable Song ministers, took the blame. For the widespread disaffection and the military defeats, he also paid the price and was quietly murdered. Though savaged by later commentators, Jia Sidao was probably no more culpable than Cai Jing or Han Tuozhou. Not even a correct understanding of the Supreme Ultimate could by now have saved the Song. In late 1275 'Hundred Eyes' Bayan was approaching Hangzhou.

Happily the surrender and occupation of the great city early in the following year belied the Mongols' fearsome reputation. The city was spared, the imperial tombs protected (though later plundered), officials pardoned, and the dowager empress treated with respect. Taken north to Dadu, she would be befriended by Khubilai's empress, while the last Song emperor would opt for a monastic life and was eventually exiled to Tibet. Even the discovery that courtiers had smuggled two of his brothers out of Hangzhou and down the coast by sea brought no reprisals.

It did, though, prolong resistance. Leapfrogging from port to port ahead of the Mongol advance, the young Song princes and their court-in-exile remained on the run for three years. Each prince in turn was acknowledged as emperor, one succeeding when the other died. From the Leizhou peninsula in the extreme south (near Hainan island), an escape was contemplated to Champa (in southern Vietnam), then abandoned in favour of a return to the offshore islands at the mouth of the Pearl River. There, somewhere in the archipelago that includes Hong Kong island, the Song flotilla was finally surrounded and the young emperor's ship sunk. It is said that a loyal follower took the seven-year-old emperor in his arms and leapt overboard as the vessel went down. The year was 1279.

With the incorporation of the south into Yuan China, four centuries of division came to an end. Not since the disintegration of the Tang empire had all China been united under one ruler. The conquest of the Southern Song was Khubilai's supreme achievement, 'and it was indeed a mighty conquest', says Polo, 'for in all the world there was no kingdom worth half as much'.[20] The population of southern China, no less than its wealth, was probably double the north's and may have exceeded that of all the rest of the Mongols' domains put together. With such assets the Yuan dynasty might well have asserted its authority over the other Mongol khanates and so added a reunited Mongol empire to that of China. World dominion beckoned, and Khubilai seems to have been tempted. Yet within less than a century the Mongols would be bundled out of China back to the windswept steppe from which they had come. For the Yuan, as for the Qin and the Sui, assembling an empire was one thing, consolidating it quite another.

MONGOL MISADVENTURES

If traditionally 1279 marks the beginning of Mongol rule in China, realistically it marks the end of Mongol achievement there. The story of the Yuan dynasty reads as one of protracted decline, and since Khubilai occupied the throne for another fifteen years – longer than any of his nine dynastic successors bar the last – he must bear much of the responsibility. He failed to override the chaotic system of succession that threw up all these quickfire emperors. His administrative arrangements, far from centralising authority, seem to have dispersed it. His attempts to improve agricultural production did little to improve revenue receipts and nothing to reverse the decline in population, itself the result of plague and famine as well as incessant war. And his foreign adventures brought still less in the way of returns and were seldom short of catastrophic. All these failures could be attributed to advancing years and declining health. In his mid-sixties and, as of 1281, deprived by death of the wise counsel of his empress, Khubilai was already succumbing to overindulgence. By the time of his own death aged nearly eighty in 1294, he was crippled with gout, often insensate from alcohol and quite grotesquely obese. His consequent neglect of business, punctuated by whimsical obsessions, was not congenial to effective government.

On the other hand these shortcomings could equally well be attributed to his Mongol heritage. Informal succession procedures, for instance, were as typical of the steppe-lands as the imperial addiction to greasy meat and fermented mares' milk. Among the Mongolian clans, leadership had always depended more on peer approval than primogeniture, seniority or prior nomination. A contender for the throne was expected to secure the approbation of rivals by demonstrating his fitness to rule; and this meant either worsting them or placating them, usually with gifts and subordinate appanages. Khubilai did in fact designate one of his sons as his successor and prepared him accordingly. But when in 1285 the son died, leaving three sons of his own, Khubilai prevaricated and the succession was thrown wide open. Winning support from the Mongol elite, the third of these grandsons succeeded; but it was descendants of the other two sons who soon followed him on to the throne. The pool of Yuan princes quickly grew and thereafter guaranteed fraught and often bloody successions interspersed by short reigns and marked by erratic swings of policy in which Mongolia-based military leaders and China-based bureaucrats often found themselves at loggerheads. The one exception to this staccato tale was

THE MONGOL YUAN SUCCESSION, 1279–1368

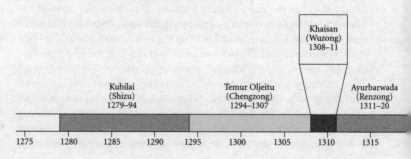

Toghon Temur or *Yuan* Shundi (r. 1333–68). Possibly illegitimate and much maligned as a typically 'bad last emperor', he would cut a sorry figure while what remained of the empire disintegrated around him. Yet he was no monster, and in his youth, when enjoying the services of some excellent ministers, might just have reversed the situation.

Many of the troubles confronting *Yuan* Shundi stemmed from another feature of steppe rule that Khubilai had unwisely applied to China. For administrative and military purposes he famously divided the country into a dozen large provinces; somewhat fragmented and with their borders often redrawn, they remain the basis of today's provincial structure. But instead of then integrating these provinces into the central administration and subordinating them to its agencies, he tended to endow each province with a replica of the central administration. Each acquired a secretariat and civil and military bureaux, while the activities of the central government were largely restricted to Zhongshu, its own metropolitan province comprising Hebei and neighbouring areas of Shanxi, Henan and Liaoning. Thus '[the imperial government's] engagement in empire-wide administration was at best transitory or limited to very restricted activities'. The provincial secretariats, on the other hand, 'were not organs of local government like the circuit bureaus of Song times, but governments of external territories, separate vassal states surrounding a nuclear state – the emperor's metropolitan domain'.[21] In effect China had no sooner been reunited than it was being parcelled up into the equivalent of the steppe's interdependent khanates, each with considerable potential for autonomy.

Various safeguards enabled a strong central government to fend off this danger. The emperor retained the right to appoint all officials; a parallel

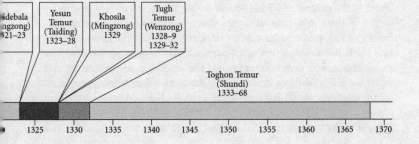

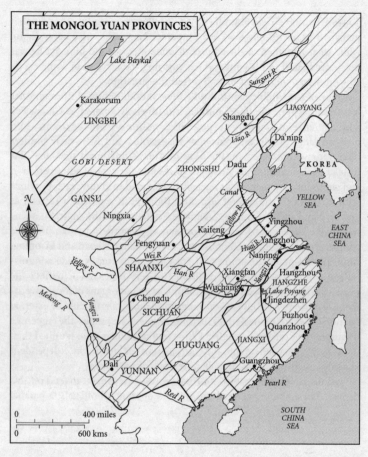

THE MONGOL YUAN PROVINCES

Lake Baykal

Sungari R.

Karakorum

LINGBEI

LIAOYANG

Shangdu

Liao R.   Da'ning

GOBI DESERT   ZHONGSHU Dadu

KOREA

N

Canal   YELLOW
SEA

GANSU   Yellow R.

Ningxia

Yingzhou   EAST
CHINA
Kaifeng   SEA

Huai R. Yangzhou

Fengyuan   Nanjing

Wei R.

Yellow R.   SHAANXI   Han R.   Xiangfan   Hangzhou

Mekong R.   Wuchang   Yangzi R. JIANGZHE
Lake Poyang
Jingdezhen

Yangzi R.   Chengdu

SICHUAN   Fuzhou

Quanzhou

HUGUANG   JIANGXI

Dali   Guangzhou

YUNNAN

Red R.   Pearl R.

0   400 miles   SOUTH
CHINA
0   600 kms   SEA

censorate kept a close watch on all aspects of government and reported direct to the centre; and what was probably the most efficient post-relay service in the world ensured rapid communication (350 kilometres – 215 miles – a day seems to have been standard) between the court and the provinces. But under a weakened administration, when senior positions and fiefdoms were doled out as favours and could become hereditary, and when local disturbances demanded a prompt local response, provincial administrations would have no compunction about taking independent action.

Containing the two imperial capitals (Dadu and Shangdu), acting as a conduit to the Mongolian fatherland and yet boasting no agricultural surplus, the metropolitan area undoubtedly required special consideration. Yuan attempts to increase agricultural production were concentrated there and may have had some effect. But the region remained heavily dependent on rice imports from the south via a canal system badly disrupted by the flood-prone Yellow River. Khubilai, after witnessing the utility of coastal shipping in the pursuit of the last Song emperors, was persuaded to try maritime transport. This meant accepting the services of two notorious pirates who were well supplied with vessels and familiar with the treacherous navigation round the Shandong peninsula. The first shipments were a success; but when a convoy was wiped out by a storm, the court turned again to inland waterways.

A scheme was adopted to augment the Grand Canal with a new section connecting the Yellow River to another river that debouched into the sea near Dadu. 'About three million labourers took part in its construction, for which the government expended vast sums of money.'[22] It was completed in 1289, though like the Sui sections of the canal, it still required expensive maintenance. Nor did it put the pirates out of business. The sea route remained in use and, by occasionally holding the court to ransom, the pirates accrued a fortune. Repeatedly frustrating government efforts to control the coast, they were still all-powerful in the 1350s and happily contributed to the then general subversion of Yuan authority.

If the maritime route continued in use, it was because the Grand Canal was still more often inoperable than not. Come the 1340s this was because the Yellow River was on the move again. Having veered south in the 1290s, it was now inclined to head back north, flooding part of the Grand Canal and debouching into the Gulf of Bohai. In 'one of the greatest hydraulic projects ever undertaken in China in pre-modern times', 200,000 local labourers were dragooned into digging and dredging a new channel to the south. Completed in late 1351, the scheme was a success, though, as predicted, the coercive methods used to get it dug were not. Spontaneous uprisings marked its progress, and in mid-1351 'the first action in a rebellion soon to involve almost all of China' saw the seizure of Yingzhou in Anhui.[23] The trouble quickly engulfed sections of the Grand Canal, spread far beyond the Yellow River basin and, becoming vastly complicated by all manner of other revolts, threatened to overwhelm the dynasty. Meanwhile traffic on the canal, while no longer impeded by flooding and siltation, was blocked by the insurgents. In a final bid to outwit both canal 'bandits' and maritime 'pirates', a novel attempt was made to introduce the cultivation of rice in the north. Two thousand paddy farmers from the south were brought to the region north of Dadu/Beijing as instructors, and the cost of acquiring and terracing the land is said to have exceeded that of taming the Yellow River. But though well intentioned, the scheme seems not to have realised its expected potential and was overtaken by other events when, as of 1354, localised defiance flared into all-out war.

No less disastrous for the economy, and perhaps more damaging for Mongol repute, had been Khubilai's foreign adventures. Unable to construe success in other than the expansionist terms of his Mongol antecedents, between 1274 and 1294 Khubilai had mounted an almost continuous series of assaults by land and sea on his neighbours. Some of these exploits may best be described as quixotic, nearly all ended in failure, and only a long-fought struggle with Mongol rivals in and around Mongolia can be accounted necessary. Elsewhere, Burma was invaded repeatedly: Marco Polo describes an epic encounter with an elephant corps in 1279; eight years later Pagan, the capital, was taken and its king overthrown; and in 1301–03 further expeditions were vainly mounted in support of the Yuan candidate there. It was a similar story with Annam and Champa in what is now Vietnam. By sea and then land, Annam was cowed in 1281 and the Cham kingdom assailed in 1285. But the Mongol forces, though mostly Chinese, fared poorly in the heat and were no match for the Chams in jungle warfare. They eventually withdrew with little more than a token acknowledgement of Yuan suzerainty.

Meanwhile further Mongol demands for submission had been lodged with the Khmer kingdom of Angkhor and the expanding Javanese kingdom of Singosari (later Majapahit). Both repudiated the Mongol envoys. Angkhor was spared invasion, thanks no doubt to the stiff resistance offered by its Cham neighbours; but in 1292 Khubilai excelled himself by unleashing an armada of 1,000 ships and 20,000 men on east Java. By now such was the Chinese familiarity with the south seas that these reached their destination at Kediri on the north coast of the island without difficulty. Adopting the cause of the lately overthrown Singosari dynasty in return for its vassalage, the Mongol forces duly defeated the incumbent usurper but were then, in the hour of victory, themselves treacherously assaulted by their supposed ally. Three thousand men were lost; the Mongol commander barely made it back to his fleet; and the fleet, after much deliberation, sailed home to China.

A pattern was by now discernible, and it was identical to that pursued by Chinggis and his immediate successors in Inner Asia. The Mongols opened relations by dispatching envoys to demand submission in the form of tribute plus a personal attendance at the imperial court by the king so targeted. He, the king, perhaps assuming this was just another pro forma approach typical of traditional Chinese diplomacy, prevaricated. The Mongols then sent a second mission whose insistence and insults usually provoked their hosts into retaliation (the Burmese beheaded a Mongol mission, the Javanese 'defaced' its leader). And since to a universal emperor such affronts were totally unacceptable, war followed.

The prelude to Khubilai's two most celebrated invasions, both of Japan and both catastrophic, ran true to form. Apart from occasional trouble between Korean shipping and Japanese 'pirates', the only justification for intervention in Japan lay in the aggressive diplomacy that preceded it. The first assault force sailed from a reluctant Korea in 1274 and reached the coast of Kyushu. Too small for the task in hand, it would probably have been annihilated anyway. Instead a storm sent the Mongol forces rushing back to their ships, and while riding out the tempest, 13,000 lives were lost and the bulk of the fleet was sunk. In 1275 and 1279 follow-up diplomatic missions to the Japanese emperor – Khubilai insisted on designating him 'the king of a little country' – got the reception they deserved; the staffs of both were executed. The second invasion of 1281 was by way of response.

This time Khubilai did not underestimate his foe, sending two fleets, one from Korea and the other from Zhejiang, with a total complement of perhaps 140,000 men. The Japanese were prepared. A wall had been built on the Kyushu coast that prevented the forces from southern China joining up with those from Korea. But as in 1274 it was the intervention of the gods which proved decisive. Another storm, this time a typhoon, bore down on Kyushu. Again there was a rush for the boats and again there was panic in the Sino-Mongol ranks. 'One-third of the 40,000 Northern soldiers perished,' says Khubilai's modern biographer, 'and more than half of the 100,000 Southern troops died while trying to escape.' This certainly 'shattered the mantle of Mongol invincibility'; in terms of fatalities and expenditure, it was probably the costliest defeat in Mongol history.[24] In seeking to validate Mongol rule with a string of easy victories, Khubilai had merely discredited it, leaving his sucessors with a legacy of tarnished valour and chronic insolvency.

Thus his reputation as a ruler who abandoned steppe traditions to accommodate himself to Chinese norms of imperial conduct and bureaucratic government may need revision. Despite concessions such as building a traditional capital, indulging Confucian scholarship and observing (if not often personally performing) the imperial rites, he never learned to read and write Chinese. Nor did many of his successors. The laborious transcription of official papers from Chinese to Mongol and back again, though it provided employment for an army of clerks, must have distanced the Yuan emperors from the minutiae of government.

Nor was the employment of Chinese advisers and officials any indication of imperial preference. Grading the population into a four-tier hierarchy ensured that Mongols and other non-Chinese enjoyed positive discrimination in respect of office and privilege. Under this system, first came those of Mongol birth, then the 'coloured-eye people' (mainly Uighurs, central Asian Muslims and oddities like the Polo family, who might or might not have eyes that were other than brown), then, well behind in terms of privileges, the 'Han people' (northern Chinese plus Khitans, Jurchen and Koreans), and finally the 'Southern people' (ex-subjects of the Song). Directives were issued against Mongols adopting Chinese dress or marrying Chinese girls, though these were little honoured, and against Chinese wearing Mongol dress or learning the Mongol language. When in 1313–15 the examination system was reintroduced by the scholarship-loving Ayurbarwada or *Yuan* Renzong (r. 1311–20), it was effectively 'dumbed down' to give the less-educated Mongols and their 'coloured-eyed' henchmen a better chance. Literary composition was excluded altogether; Zhu Xi's Neo-Confucian 'Four Books' distillation became the basic syllabus; degrees were awarded in accordance with preset ethnic quotas; and lest Han scholars still outshine their non-Han competitors, the latter were encouraged with simplified papers and lower pass marks.

Since far more official appointments were made on the basis of hereditary privilege and recommendation than scholarly attainment, this weighting may not have made much difference to the composition of the bureaucracy. But it did reflect social and political realities under the Yuan. Mongolians, Uighurs, Tibetan lamas, Nestorian Christians and central Asian Muslims enjoyed an influence at court, in government and in the armed forces that was quite disproportionate to their numbers. Religious and ethnic diversity was not just tolerated but positively encouraged as a counterweight to Chinese numerical and educational preponderance.

Ever on the lookout for knowledgeable foreigners, in the 1260s Khubilai had asked the Venetian merchants Maffeo and Niccolo Polo to bring 'a hundred Christian men of learning' back to China on their next visit; instead they had brought young Marco. But there were already Latin as well as Orthodox Christians enjoying Mongol hospitality. In 1307 John of Monte Corvino, long resident in Dadu, was appointed its first archbishop, while 'Zayton's last bishop' was reportedly among those massacred by anti-Yuan forces in 1362.[25] ('Zayton' was the great port of Quanzhou in Fujian.) Muslims, mostly from central Asia, were much more prominent. It was under Mongol patronage that close-knit Islamic communities became established in most of the cities and formed settled colonies in some outlying areas. As merchants and moneylenders, then as tax farmers, monopoly contractors and financial administrators, Muslims were particularly associated with the economy. They may, too, have been useful to the Yuan emperors as a foil for Chinese wrath over new fiscal impositions and the inflation that resulted from the irresponsible issue of ever more paper money. Certainly, if Polo is to be believed, they were unpopular and occasionally suffered reprisals. The only province actually run by a Muslim was Yunnan. There, under several governors of the same Bukharan family, overt proselytisation was rare, though many of the indigenous people were attracted to the faith and several waves of Muslim colonists were settled in Yunnan. From among the descendants of its ruling clan, in this backward and largely non-Han province as remote from the sea as anywhere in the empire, would come the greatest of all China's maritime commanders.

TRIUMPH OF THE MING

It has sometimes been suggested that in China death, even premature and violent death, was not viewed with the awesome finality accorded it by other societies. From early times, dying is said to have been 'unproblematic' and 'simply not the issue it was for the Mesopotamians or the ancient Greeks'; the trappings of tragedy and extreme regret did not attend it.[26] Ideally the Confucian emphasis on social harmony and the subordinate relationships proper to this harmony overrode personality and its selfish concerns. Group identity with family, clan, locality or trade was supposedly dearer than individual identity. With the living located in a continuum of deceased ancestors and extant family, the transition from one to the other was simply a biological inevitability. The survival of the group transcended that of its individual members, and thus death was denied something of its awful dominion.

Such observations are found mainly in non-Chinese writings and no doubt derive from revulsion over the extreme violence and disregard for life that punctuates the Standard Histories and is taken as typical of China's historical record. The last decades of the Yuan and the first of the Ming furnish particularly compelling evidence. But whether, after allowing for its size and density, China's society was really more violent, or its rulers more bloodthirsty, than, say, ancient Rome's or Reformation England's is doubtful. One might wonder, too, whether that sense of group identity was any more consoling to an about-to-be-deceased Confucian than the promise of resurrection to a dying Christian.

It could, though, make matters worse. Instead of the individual being held solely responsible for his actions, it was presumed that his entire group shared responsibility and was therefore equally liable. 'Execution to the fifth degree' as stipulated for a variety of heinous offences in the much-copied Tang Legal Code meant not a cocktail of slow-death experiences, such as hanging, drawing and quartering, but the extension of the individual's sentence to all his relatives as far as the fifth degree of consanguinity. Associates, dependants and exhumed ancestors might also be included, so turning an execution into a purge, even a pogrom. Under the first Ming emperor one such case involving a disgraced minister famously resulted in the deaths of an estimated 30,000–40,000 persons. Admittedly this was exceptional, the circumstances being as peculiar as the emperor's temperament. Tumultuous times called for draconian deterrents, and none were more tumultuous than the transition from Yuan to Ming. China in the mid- to late-fourteenth century was again teetering on the brink of disunion. Another long period of multi-state fragmentation like those which followed the collapse of the Han and of the Tang looked a real possibility.

The troubles had built up slowly as the hardships and shortcomings of Mongol rule became more apparent. From the 1340s a higher than usual level of rural distress and populist resentment had acquired added militancy from an upsurge in sectarian activity. Miracles and apparitions were reported, an imminent new age of universal redemption was preached, and in cells and secret societies adherents armed and organised themselves for action. Various strands of belief were involved – Manichaean ideas of a purificatory transformation, traditional Buddhist expectations associated with the Maitreya or 'Future Buddha', Tibetan Tantric practices supposedly affording instant enlightenment, various Daoist disciplines and predictions, and the usual credulous response to freakish weather patterns, epidemics and other natural visitations. A 'White Lotus Society' provided direction, plus a certain cohesion, and its followers' adoption of red headgear afforded easy recognition. As the 'Red Turbans' (not to be confused with the 'Red Eyebrows' or 'Yellow Turbans' of the Later Han period) the movement spread in both the south and the north, attracting the disaffected, succouring the afflicted, providing cover for the downright criminal, and exciting expectations of a new social order that specifically excluded Mongol rule.

On to this agrarian and millenarian rootstock in the 1350s were grafted other elements of righteous protest and opportunist aspiration. In the north the discovery of a supposed descendant of the Southern Song provided a focus for legitimist sentiment; in Sichuan and the south, regional warlords reasserted local autonomy and adopted the usual nomenclature – Chu, Wu, Shu and even Xia, Zhou and Han; rural distress and the demand for forced labour triggered uprisings like those of 1351/52 over the rechannelling of the Yellow River; and in response to this growing lawlessness, local interests everywhere – provincial administrations, landed gentry and regional commanders, some of them Mongol – mobilised their own militias and, while declaring loyalty to the Yuan government, often acted unilaterally. Only in the north, within and around the great metropolitan province, could imperial troops be counted on. Military contingents stationed elsewhere were notoriously lax, ill paid and open to offers.

From this mêlée of conflicting local movements there emerged along the Yangzi in the early 1360s three or four contenders for a much wider dominion. Zhu Yuanzhang was not untypical. A penniless orphan from Anhui who had barely survived famine, plague and the grimmest of childhoods to acquire some basic literacy as a Buddhist monk, Zhu had joined the Red Turbans in 1352. Gathering a growing band of followers that included a few scholars as well as ever more troops, he moved south, crossed the Yangzi in 1355, and in the following year captured Nanjing. Nestling between the river and the wooded slopes of Mount Zijin, the city would remain Zhu Yuanzhang's base and, massively rewalled, his stronghold for the rest of his career; much of the 33-kilometre (20-mile) wall he built is still the most impressive city fortification in China. Ten years later Nanjing would become his imperial capital and, thirty years after that, his resting place when he was interred in a great tomb on Mount Zijin. In adopting Nanjing, Zhu Yuanzhang, the Ming founder, would be the first to rule all China from a southern city.

By nature a firm disciplinarian and fearless leader, the young Zhu Yuanzhang possessed few other imperial attributes. He was ugly to behold, woefully ignorant and without that most basic unit of support, a family. But he was a good listener and a quick learner. Literary proficiency plus a knowledge of history, strategy and governance were acquired along the way; the steep curve of his learning experience mirrored that of his rise to power and seemed to validate it. So did the example of the founding emperor of the Han dynasty. Liu Bang (*Han* Gaozu) had risen from among the ranks of the 'black-haired commoners' to become emperor of all China; it was a noble precedent, and comparisons with the Han founder were encouraged. But whereas Liu Bang's upbringing had been remarkable for frequent signs of heavenly favour, Zhu Yuanzhang's had been about as unpropitious as possible. Self-made emperors were rare, and none had more ground to make up than Zhu.

Following an epic four-day battle with a neighbouring warlord in 1363, ground in the form of territory was quickly won, while ever more armies and navies transferred to his victorious banner. The battle itself had been waged on Lake Boyang, one of the vast Yangzi spillover reservoirs, in northern Jiangxi; if Zhu Yuanzhang really deployed 'a thousand ships and 100,000 men' – and his opponent still more men and still taller ships – it may have been the greatest lake-battle ever fought. Hunan and Hubei then fell to the Nanjing regime, followed by Zhejiang and Jiangsu. By 1366 Zhu Yuanzhang controlled the entire Yangzi basin below the Gorges and 'had emerged as the obvious heir to the Yuan empire'.[27]

Increasingly conscious of his destiny, Zhu now withdrew from active campaigning. Heaven seemed to be taking his side; and his generals, some being companions of many years and others erstwhile opponents who had been allowed to retain the services of their own troops, were genuinely attached to him. Moreover, the army he sent north by way of Shandong and Henan in 1367 scarcely needed him. During the early 1360s most of the Yuan forces in the north had been siphoned off by rival warlords who preferred war among themselves for the privilege of defending the emperor – it was still Toghon Temur or *Yuan* Shundi – to actually defending the emperor. As Zhu Yuanzhang's 1367 proclamation put it, the Yuan, though initially legitimate, had 'deserted the norms of conduct' and 'the time had come when Heaven despised them and no longer sustained their rule'.[28] In January 1368 Zhu followed this up with a formal declaration of his own dynasty. It was to be called 'the Great Ming', 'Ming' meaning 'brilliant' or 'effulgent'. Nine months later Ming forces entered Dadu (Beijing) almost unopposed. *Yuan* Shundi had fled north into Inner Mongolia. For the first time in centuries China had a Chinese emperor, and for only the seond time ever, he was a man of the people.

Zhu renamed the great city 'Beiping' – not a misprint of its current name but a Pinyin rendering of the two characters signifying 'North Pacified' or 'Northern Pacification'. Meanwhile the deep south had also been pacifiied, Fujian being taken by land, Guangdong by sea and Guangxi by river. In the north-west, Shanxi, Shaanxi and most of Gansu were cleared of Yuan loyalists over the next two years. Sichuan was reclaimed in 1371, and only Yunnan held out under a Mongol commander. When it was finally overrun by the Ming in 1381/82, among those captured was an intelligent eleven-year-old Muslim called Ma He. Castrated, dispatched to Beiping and taken on to the household staff of one of the first Ming emperor's sons, Ma He would be renamed Zheng He. As such, he grew to become the most trusted confidant of the prince; the prince eventually became emperor; and thus would a Yunnanese Muslim eunuch find himself entrusted with the command of China's greatest maritime enterprise.

After a century of Mongol rule, all of what was regarded as China had now been reconquered. It was back under the rule of a dynasty whose indigenous origins were beyond dispute; and for the first time the initiative for reunification had welled up from the south, not been imposed from the north. The credentials of the Ming dynasty (r. 1368–1644) were so impressive that later nationalists would hail Zhu Yuanzhang's achievement as a triumphant reassertion of Han Chinese identity after centuries of 'alien rule'. In the process the south had come into its own, with the empire being officially realigned in accordance with demographic and economic realities. In effect, the Yangzi had supplanted the Yellow River as its lifeblood, and Nanjing, the river's northernmost city, had ousted Dadu/Beiping as the centre of power. At the heart of this reconfigured and re-sinified China, Nanjing would hold a strong appeal as the spiritual home of later Chinese nationalism. In 1925 Dr Sun Yat-sen, the first president of the republic, would be buried hard by the first Ming emperor on Mount Zijin. Soon after, General Jiang Jieshi (Chiang Kai-shek) would make the city the capital of the Nationalist republic.

But the triumph of indigenous culture and identity was not so obvious at the time. For one thing, the Mongol menace, though removed, was far from eliminated. Following their triumphs in the north, in the 1370s Ming armies struck deep into Mongolia, but with dwindling success. Mongol cavalry still enjoyed supremacy on the steppe. The Yuan and their adherents soon reclaimed what is now Inner Mongolia and would show themselves more than capable of striking back into northern China. The Mongol threat would dangle over the Ming for another two centuries, to be nullified only when the Jurchen, reincarnated as the Manchu, replaced it with a still greater menace.

Nor were the Ming quick to learn from the misadventures of the Mongols while ruling China. Though piously claiming to be restoring the institutions and rituals of the Tang and the Song, in practice Zhu Yuanzhang seemed bent on reconstituting the empire he had just toppled. Khubilai's division of the country into provinces was retained, with modifications; and both in the provinces and in Nanjing 'the formal structure of governmental institutions ... began by imitating the Yuan almost exactly'. It was the same with the military. Zhu's genuine determination to improve the lot of the cultivator, a legacy of his dreadful childhood, meant holding down taxation and giving a high priority to agricultural development, including military colonies. But with this proviso, the challenge of demobilising and resettling his armies was not dissimilar to that faced by the Yuan. Thus, like the Yuan, 'the emperor made his army into a distinct occupational caste within the population, created a hereditary officer class to govern it, [and] gave the military officers a clearly superior status compared to their civil equivalents'. Edward Dreyer actually calls them 'a new conquering horde, but this time Chinese in origin'. Generals became nobles with hereditary titles and fiefs; and imperial offspring became princes with supervisory responsibilities at the apex of this great military structure.[29]

Such change as there was revealed itself most clearly in the tone of government and the increasingly paranoid conduct of the emperor. Compared to the Song, the Mongol Yuan emperors had seemed beyond Confucian remonstrance, autocratic in their exercise of power and arbitrary in their judgements. But compared to the Mongol Yuan, Zhu Yuanzhang was even worse. Courtiers and ministers were beaten in his presence, sometimes to death, and as of the great purge of 1380 that accounted for those 30,000–40,000 lives, scarcely a day passed without mass executions. No reign of terror in Chinese history can compare with it. Obsessed with controlling every aspect of government and deeply suspicious of any who might ridicule his deficiencies of birth and education, the emperor dispensed with the office of chancellor and himself took on the executive role in government. The examination system was eventually reinstated but only with a view to improving the supply of bureaucrats, not to restoring their influence. In the 1390s it was the military hierarchy, the emperor's own creation, which became the target of his suspicions. A word of complaint from a long-serving general in 1393 brought his immediate execution, followed by that of his supposed associates to the tune of four marquises, an earl, a minister, ten other nobles, sixteen chief commissioners and an unspecified number of junior officials, plus the extended families of all of them, giving a grand total of over fifteen thousand.

When in 1398 the emperor himself died, the empire heaved an almighty sigh of relief. The enthronement of his eldest grandson (the son of his designated, but lately deceased, heir) seemed to represent a return to Chinese norms of succession and to herald an era of civilian government. In fact, the empire was almost immediately plunged into a bloody civil war (1399–1402). By the end of it the young emperor had disappeared, his civilian policies had been rejected and his bellicose uncle, the prince of Yan, had swept to power. In retrospect the struggle thus closely resembled that which accompanied most Mongol successions. As if to reinforce the point, the new emperor's forces had pushed down from his power base in the north, conquering the south and capturing its capital, just like Khubilai.

Nanjing never entirely recovered. The imperial palace had caught fire in the fighting and the new emperor would spend little time there. He preferred Beiping, which he immediately renamed Beijing ('Northern Capital'), and which in 1424 he would adopt as the supreme Ming capital. Nanjing meanwhile acquired a different distinction. In 1403 the new emperor announced his intention of dispatching a fleet to 'the countries of the Western Ocean'. The largest vessels in this fleet, indeed in the world at that time, were constructed on the Qinhuai river where it meets the Yangzi at Nanjing. Others would follow, making Nanjing, for the next three decades, the shipbuilding capital of the world's greatest maritime power. For with the 1405 departure of Admiral Zheng He in command of China's first world armada, the Ming were poised not just to emulate Khubilai Khan's overseas adventures but sensationally to upstage them.

13

THE RITES OF MING

1405–1620

FROM THE EDGE OF THE SKY TO THE ENDS OF THE EARTH

THE PIVOTAL POSITION OF AN EMPEROR, as the Son of Heaven, in the all-transcending operation of the cosmos entailed heavy responsiblities. Assisted by a Ministry of Rites, he must perform frequent ceremonies and sacrifices to win the collaboration of gods and ancestors in warding off disasters and ensuring bounteous harvests. Shrines and tombs must be lavishly maintained, seasonal and familial rituals meticulously observed. Other related responsibilities extended to the conduct and interpretation of astronomical observations and portents, the regulation of protocol, titles and rankings, and the management of time (clocks, calendar, festivals) and space (territorial organisation and the geometry of the capital, the palace, the audience chamber). Adjusting the workings of 'All-under-Heaven' to harmonise with the ruling principles of the wider universe, the emperor himself partook of the supra-terrestrial. No mere mortal, he was not so much a deity as a constellation; and as such, the question of how to identify him was problematic.

THE MING REIGN PERIODS, 1368–1644

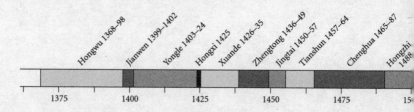

An emperor's personal name was rarely mentioned. Its use could only be defamatory and was therefore taboo. So were all those words that happened either to require the same written character(s) or to sound like them when pronounced; inadvertently or otherwise, they might be used to criticise or disparage the emperor. Thus every new reign began with a lexicographical purge. Whole word families were rounded up and temporarily removed from circulation. Scholars and scribes had to be especially alert; lives could be lost by a slip of the brush.

In history-writing, the safest way to distinguish one emperor from another was to use either their posthumous titles or their temple-names. The former are standard for dynasties until the Sui, the latter from the Tang till the Yuan. But there existed yet another method of identifying an emperor, and this was to invoke the officially named era, or eras, during which he reigned. In effect he was referred to not by name but as 'the emperor of such-and-such an era'. These era, or reign-period, names, usually proclaimed to mark a triumph, launch an initiative or celebrate some other pressing aspect of sovereignty, could be confusing – there might be several new eras in the course of one reign. Year-on-year names, an adaptation of the same principle by impatient revolutionaries such as President Sukarno of Indonesia (e.g. 'The Year of Living Dangerously'), mercifully never caught on in China. But the named eras could be quite short, typically four or six years, with the result that 'altogether some 800 era names were used in Chinese history'.[1] Inevitably duplication resulted, and since all dates were expressed in terms of these named periods (counting up from the year in which each was adopted), a tabulated listing of them with their BC/AD equivalents forms an essential tool for scholars of Chinese history, much as log tables do for mathematicians.

When claiming the Mandate in 1368, Zhu Yuanzhang had introduced a

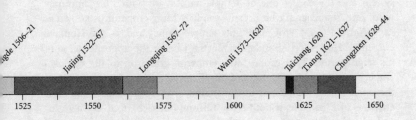

PROFILE OF AN EMPEROR

The Yongle Emperor
(1360–1424)
reigned 1403–1424

Father:
The Hongwu Emperor

Succeeded:
The Jianwen Emperor
(his nephew)

Married:
Empress Xu (d. 1407)

Buried:
Changling, Hebei

Personal Name:
Zhu Di

Pre-Imperial Title:
Prince of Yan

Reign Period Name:
Yongle ('Perpetual Happiness')

Temple Name:
Taizong ('Supreme Ancestor')

Changed to:
Chengzu ('Accomplished Progenitor')

great improvement on this system. Besides designating his dynasty the 'Ming' ('Brilliant', 'Effulgent'), and so following the Yuan precedent of showing some welcome originality in the choice of dynastic name, he adopted an era-name that was to last for his entire reign. Other Ming emperors followed suit, and so would those of the subsequent Qing dynasty. Henceforth era-names are therefore reign-names; the dating based on them corresponds to regnal years; and the emperors concerned can be confidently identified in terms of these reign periods. The first all-China emperor of the Manchu Qing dynasty, for example, is almost never called *Qing* Shengzu, his temple-name, but invariably 'the Kangxi emperor' (that is 'the Kangxi *period* emperor').

Yet for some unfathomable reason, in the case of the Ming this new system and the earlier one of 'temple-names' are both still commonly used. Zhu Yuanzhang, who became the first Ming emperor, is known as *Ming* Taizu ('Great Progenitor', his temple-name) and as 'the Hongwu emperor', 'Hongwu' ('Abundantly Martial') being the apposite name of his reign period. The second Ming emperor, grandson of the Hongwu emperor, is both *Ming* Huidi and 'the Jianwen emperor'; and the third, the uncle and early usurper of the second, who would launch the great armadas of Zheng He, is both *Ming* Taizong (later changed to Chengzu) and 'the Yongle emperor'. Some books not only interchange these two types of name but, when so inclined, throw in a posthumous title as well. Here, for the Ming as for the Qing, only reign-period names are used. Each emperor gets the definite article, followed by his reign period, and no inverted commas.

The Yongle emperor, then (r. 1403–24), third son of the rags-to-rulership Hongwu emperor, was the former prince of Yan who successfully challenged the young Jianwen emperor (r. 1399–1402), captured Nanjing and eventually moved the capital back north to the site of the Mongols' Dadu. There, having renamed it Beijing, the Yongle emperor began constructing a spacious new metropolis. It took most of his reign, and its innermost 'Forbidden City' is substantially that which remains to this day. Presiding over an age of comparative plenty, the Yongle emperor, unlike his father, had no conception of frugality. Further enormous sums were spent on restoring the Grand Canal and increasing its capacity so that the new capital could be assured of grain supplies from the south. Long and largely abortive campaigning in Mongolia and Vietnam would also weigh heavily on the public purse. But according to the Standard Histories, there was no greater example of wanton extravagance than the series of voyages that the Yongle emperor ordered Zheng He, his trusty Yunnanese Muslim eunuch, to conduct into 'the Western [or Indian] Ocean'.

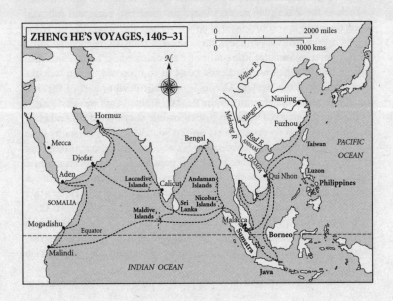

There were seven such voyages, six of them ordered by the Yongle emperor himself between 1405 and 1421, plus one of 1431 that was an after-thought by an admiring successor. All were commanded by Zheng He; each included between 100 and 300 ships carrying in total up to 27,000 men; and of these ships, around fifty were usually 'treasure ships', colossal constructions about five times the size of any wooden vessel built else-where in the world at the time and ten times the capacity. In the most considered of several recent interpretations of the textual and archaeolog-ical evidence, the Ming scholar Edward Dreyer concludes that the largest vessels stretched to over 130 metres (425 feet), and with a beam of around 50 metres (164 feet) could have displaced 20,000–30,000 tonnes. They were the size of small cruise liners. (By way of comparison, later in the century the pioneering voyages commanded by Christopher Columbus and Vasco da Gama involved only three or four ships, none longer than 20 metres (65 feet) and whose capacity barely amounted to one twentieth that of a Ming treasure ship.) Rectangular in cross-section and of comparatively shallow draught for estuarial sailing, the treasure ships were constructed with watertight bulkheads, fitted with retractable sternpost rudders and centreboards, and had six to nine masts, each up to 60 metres (195 feet) tall, with collapsible rattan sails. 'In the language of a later era of navalism,' says Dreyer, 'China had the ships, had the men, and had the money, too.'[2]

Each of the Zheng He voyages lasted just over two years and followed much the same monsoon-dictated course – from the Yangzi to Qui Nhon in Champa (southern Vietnam), Java, Malacca (Melaka, near Singapore), various ports in Sumatra, the south or west coasts of Sri Lanka, and then Calicut (Koshikodse) on the Kerala coast of south India, which was 'the great country of the Western Ocean'. From Calicut, all or part of the fleet sometimes sailed on. Hormuz in the Persian/Arabian Gulf was first visited by the fourth voyage, Djofar and Aden on the south coast of Arabia by the fifth voyage, and various ports on the Somali coast of Africa by both that and the sixth voyage. Chinese envoys also reached Mecca, though not in Chinese ships, and Malindi in what is now Kenya, possibly in Chinese ships. Various island stopovers – in Borneo, the Philippines, Andamans, Maldives and Laccadives – have also been identified, and numerous other parts of coastal mainland Asia seem to have been occasionally frequented, including Bengal and Thailand. Just seventy years before Vasco da Gama's cockleshell craft ventured round the Cape of Good Hope, Zheng He's stately armadas had demonstrated maritime mastery of the entire Indian Ocean.

For an empire that had previously taken little official cognisance of overseas trade and had never played a political role west of Java, it was a sensational achievement. The superiority of China's shipbuilding techniques, navigational expertise and organisational skills was incontrovertible. Like a space-launch programme, or the great airship boom of the 1920s and 1930s, the voyages of the majestic treasure ships seemed to herald a new age of commodious travel, bulk transport and unchallenged maritime security under the wave-ruling Ming. Overland travellers like Polo and the great fourteenth-century Moroccan adventurer Ibn Battuta could scarcely believe their eyes when they first encountered such ships. Though wary of Indo-Arab craft, they embarked on the great junks without hesitation. Aboard a Chinese merchantman even traders had their own cabins; you could sail for weeks in comfort and privacy without ever being aware of your fellow passengers; and all the while, in the words of Zheng He's diarist, 'by day and night the lofty sails, unfurled like clouds, continued their star-like course, traversing the savage waves as if they were a public thoroughfare'.[3]

Wherever it had a coastline, 'All-under-Heaven' was comfortably within reach of the Ming armadas. China looked poised to command the seas and engross that trade on which, within a century, European states would construct empires and claim world dominion. But in China's case nothing of the sort happened. Rather did the Yongle initiative discredit the whole idea of overseas enterprise. The great ships were allowed to rot; the construction of replacements was specifically forbidden; and so, for over a century, were all but coastal sailings. Subsequent mention of the voyages is so rare that some scholars would come to doubt whether they ever took place; others, going to the opposite extreme, have exploited the paucity of records to postulate preposterous theories of polar endeavour and world circumnavigation; nearly all have wondered why so ambitious a scheme was suddenly adopted and then, just as suddenly, abandoned.

An explanation may lie in reconsidering the motivation for the voyages, which was quite different from that which informed European expansion. For domestic consumption, it was also wilfully obscured. Thus the main reason for scouring the Indian Ocean as given in Zheng He's biography in the Ming dynastic history was to track down the Jianwen emperor, the nephew whom the Yongle emperor had overthrown. This was partly a red herring, partly a convenient fabrication, the intent being to rally support for the voyages from a Confucian bureaucracy that disliked their expense, resented eunuchs commanding them and yet could ill afford to appear other than zealous in eliminating any threat to the Yongle emperor's legitimacy.

For in 1402–04 residual loyalties to the previous (Jianwen) emperor had unleashed another purge that was 'among the most brutal and barbarous political acts in Chinese history' – no mean distinction given the recent excesses of the Hongwu emperor. Tens, perhaps hundreds, of thousands perished in agony for being connected with someone who had served the previous regime or who might be sympathetic to it. Famously one suspect official, already beaten to near-death and bleeding profusely from the extraction of his tongue, still managed a defiant retort. Using a finger as brush, his blood as ink and the floor as paper, he drew the characters for 'And where is King Cheng?' The reference was to the Yongle emperor's claim that he, like the Duke of Zhou, had come to the aid of his nephew and to rescue the dynasty at a time of crisis. So where, then, was King Cheng, the legitimate emperor in whose name the grand old duke had acted? demanded the blood-red characters.[4]

The Yongle emperor's response, if any, may be inferred from the instructions given to eunuch Zheng He: the missing emperor had taken flight; even if it meant going to the ends of the earth, he would be found; and thus would the Yongle emperor's conduct be vindicated. Needless to say, this exchange did nothing for the tongueless official, who was then dismembered limb by limb. But his challenge lived on, and not just in the minds of the faithful; for his bloody calligraphy defied the palace scrubbing brushes and was said ever after to have glowed in the dark. This luminosity was too much for the Yongle emperor. Tradition has it that his decision to move the capital north to Beijing sprang from revulsion over the floor that would not come clean.

Another greatly respected Confucian scholar had his already tongueless mouth surgically extended so that it stretched from ear to ear. A week later, grinning hideously, he too died from limb-by-limb subtraction, to be followed by 873 relatives and an untold number of those whom he happened to have taught or examined. Yet in reality, as everyone knew, the Jianwen emperor was already dead. His corpse had almost certainly been among the charred cadavers hauled from the burnt-out ruins of the Nanjing palace when the Yongle emperor's forces first took the city. Even if he had miraculously escaped, such public exhibitions of vengeance were more likely to inflame loyalties than extinguish them. Sure enough, two and half centuries later someone claiming descent from the Jianwen emperor would indeed topple the Ming. As for the ex-emperor having somehow reached India, say, or Africa, and having there elected to await recovery by Zheng He's armadas, it was a Peking canard.

Likewise one may doubt the 'world history' thesis that supposes the Yongle emperor to have been casting about for Afro-Asian allies against Timur Leng (Tamerlane, r. 1369–1405), the all-conquering khan of Samarkand. As of 1398 Timur, a Muslim as well as a Mongol remotely descended from Chinggis Khan, had indeed been planning to round off his Asian acquisitions, already extending from Anatolia to India, by invading Ming China. The Hongwu emperor had offended him by sending envoys who treated him as a vassal – he detained them – and by nursing designs on the Hami oasis which conflicted with Timur's claims over Xinjiang. In 1404/05 Timur actually set off for China leading an army of 200,000. But he died within a matter of weeks, whereupon the campaign was aborted amid the usual Mongol succession struggle. Timur's troops never reached the limits of Ming rule in Gansu; the Yongle emperor seems not to have taken the danger very seriously; anyway, it was over by the time Zheng He first set sail; and there is absolutely no mention of Timur in connection with the voyages.

Much better relations were established between the Yongle emperor and Shahrukh, Timur's eventual successor (r. 1407–47). In fact, they provide an altogether more convincing context for the voyages. Once Shahrukh had disowned Timur's Chinese ambitions, missions of a size, opulence and frequency never before witnessed began to ply back and forth between Ming China and Timurid central Asia. The issue of protocol was shelved; an equality of status was implied in address and accepted in Shahrukh's capital, though tributary obeisance remained compulsory at Beijing. During the Yongle reign, the Ming court 'received 20 missions from Samarkand and Herat [Shahrukh's new capital], 32 from the various oasis states of central Asia, 13 from Turfan and 44 from Hami'.[5] Nearly all were reciprocated, usually on a still-grander scale. As had commonly been reported at the height of the Han and Tang empires, such was the traffic through the Gansu corridor that missions were rarely out of sight of one another, and traders posing as tributaries were commonplace.

A Ming mission of 1414 that visited seventeen states, including Herat and Samarkand, compiled the century's most exhaustive report on every aspect of the central Asian economy. Never was China better informed about its overland neighbours, nor more particular about the products required from them. Incoming tribute featured 'precious metals, jade, horses, camels, sheep, lions and leopards'.[6] In return the Yongle emperor gave silks, silver and paper money, all of which could be exchanged for Chinese products of a more utilitarian nature before the foreigners departed. Manufacturers and merchants thereby profited. Though the private importation of foreign produce was officially outlawed, the tribute system encouraged trade in general, albeit at imperial discretion.

With a lesser volume of tribute-bearing missions arriving at the Ming court from potentates elsewhere – in Burma, Tibet, Mongolia, Manchuria, Korea and Japan – scarcely a week passed without one or more grand receptions. These were the responsibility of the Ministry of Rites and were so choreographed as to emphasise the emperor's cosmic ascendancy and the envoys' utter abasement; for instance, the prostrations ('kowtow') that Europeans would find so objectionable were performed to barked orders and acclaimed with musical fanfares. All foreign relations, however politically or commercially important, came within the compass of the emperor's ritual responsibilities; and every official reception was therefore an affirmation that all those under Heaven acknowledged their subordination to Heaven's Son. Yet in other respects emissaries fared well. They were transported, fed and housed at government expense and they invariably left both richer and wiser. In 1407 the emperor set up the first College of Translators to handle correspondence in connection with all these foreign contacts, plus another of interpreters to handle and impress the visiting tributaries.

The contribution of Zheng He's voyages to this diplomatic traffic is especially notable. During the twenty-two years of the Yongle period some ninety-five missions from the states of south-east Asia and the Indian Ocean reached the Ming court, many of them aboard Zheng He's ships. The emperor 'wanted to display his soldiers in strange lands in order to make manifest the wealth and power of the Middle Kingdom', explains the Ming dynastic history. Zheng He was commissioned, says a stele erected by him at the port of Changle (near Fuzhou), 'to go to the [foreigners'] countries and confer presents on them so as to transform them by displaying our power while treating distant peoples with kindness'. As a result, adds the same inscription:

> From the edge of the sky to the ends of the earth there are none who have not become subjects and slaves. To the most western of the Western Region and the most northern of the northern extremities, the length of a voyage may be calculated, and thus the barbarians from beyond the seas, even those who are truly distant [and whose speech requires] double translation [through an intermediary language], all have come to court bearing precious objects and presents.[7]

The great voyages of the Yongle period, like its shuttle missions overland, were designed to demonstrate and affirm the peculiarly Chinese concept of universal subordination under Heaven's Son. The envoys that were received, the tribute they delivered, the gifts of greater value with which they were presented, and the trade that undoubtedly accompanied these exchanges – all were primarily indicators of imperial centrality and supremacy rather than objectives in their own right. This was in marked contrast to how Europeans construed their own maritime endeavours. For them, exploration led to trade and trade led on to empire. It was the other way round in the case of China. Putative empire preceded actual contact; informal trade had been established long before the great voyages; and scientific exploration in the sense of distance measurements and navigational star charts came last, being just a further confirmation of terrestrial mastery.

Naturally the emperor took delight in the more exotic items that came his way as a result of the voyages. Unfamiliar spices and incenses conferred an aroma of otherworldly distinction. Precious gems and metals provided a dazzling visual confirmation. Lions, camels, ostriches and elephants advertised the all-terrain nature of his dominion. And giraffes and rhinos, especially, bore a welcome resemblance to the mythical creature known as the *qirin* whose rare sightings had always proved extraordinarily propitious. In short, tribute brought trophies that made manifest Heaven's favour and the emperor's incontestable supremacy.

Naturally, too, the fleets were well supplied with troops. No conquests were contemplated and no colonies planned; Khubilai Khan's mistakes in Java and Japan were not be repeated. But parades and demonstrations of weaponry were an essential part of educating unenlightened peoples in Chinese superiority and so 'transforming' them into loyal tributaries. Dreyer likens such exercises to 'showing the flag' and emphasises the further need for the fleet's self-defence and the suppression of piracy. In the course of the seven voyages, the fleet's offensive capacity was tested on just three occasions, twice in Sumatra and once in Sri Lanka. The Sri Lankan affair resulted from native hostility, much complicated by a civil war. But the Sumatran actions were undertaken on behalf of two local rulers; one faced a pretender, the other pirates; and the pirates, at least, were Chinese.

Along the coasts of what are now western Indonesia and Malaysia, a basic tributary system already existed. In fact it probably predated Khubilai Khan's disastrous invasion of Java over a century earlier. Additionally, small Chinese communities, mostly from Guangdong, had established themselves in the main ports of the region. Maritime equivalents of the cross-border outposts in, say, Tibet or Mongolia, they were influential in trade and amenable to closer supervision at a time when the Ming were actively engaged in nearby Vietnam. Large-scale Chinese settlement in south-east Asia came later in the Ming period but may owe something to these contacts.

Here, then, Zheng He's voyages served some practical purpose in upholding the established order, ensuring the safety of the vital straits of Malacca, and deterring any interference with Champa, a Ming ally. At Malacca itself Zheng He established a landward depot, erected a commemorative stele (only in Calicut and Sri Lanka was this repeated), and supported as ruler an émigré prince from Sumatra. This man's descendants, after adopting Islam, would become the sultans of Malacca; and Malacca itself would develop into the trade hub of the region. Perceived as a heavily fortified portal to the China and Java seas, by the turn of the century it would be a prime target of Portugal's maritime drive to engross the spice trade.

But in the early fifteenth century it was the dire situation in Vietnam which compelled Zheng He's fleets to play a more active part hereabouts than anywhere else in the Western Ocean. Champa, the main Ming ally on the mainland, was 'shown the flag' by every voyage. So were most of the Sumatran maritime states; and Malacca was the nearest thing to a colony that Zheng He ever established. Moreover, if the friendly relations with Timurid central Asia suggest a context for the launching of Zheng He's great voyages, the decidedly unfriendly relations with Vietnam suggest a context for abandoning them.

MISADVENTURES AND MISFORTUNES

Like the Zheng He voyages, the early Ming misadventure in Vietnam is something of a mystery. While in the far north of China there were pressing reasons for intervening in Mongolia, in the far south the mainland kingdoms of south-east Asia neither posed a threat nor offered much advantage. Historically the Red River region had served China as a place of exile and a source of fragrances, iridescent feathers and incessant revolt. Its climate was reckoned lethal and its people ungovernable. With a dangling configuration like that of a seine net, Vietnam already seemed to exist for the sole purpose of ensnaring great powers.

Sensibly the Hongwu emperor (Zhu Yuanzhang) had declared it off-limits to the Ming. In a set of 'ancestral injunctions' designed to govern the conduct of his successors – and often discomfit them – the Ming founder had included a list of countries that were not to be invaded. Annam, as most of Vietnam was then known, was the first on the list, followed by Champa and eventually Cambodia, which together shared the Mekong delta and its adjacent coastline. But the Yongle emperor chose to ignore this injunction. As proclaimed in Zheng He's Changle inscription, he aspired to 'surpass the Han and the Tang'. To an emperor who, by ousting his Jianwen nephew, had effectively usurped the imperial throne, there could be no clearer proof of Heaven's approval and his own legitimacy than successfully recreating the greatest empires of the past; and since those of Han and Tang had embraced the Red River flood plain and extended down Annam's coastal panhandle, so must his.

But by now Annam had been independent under its native Tran dynasty for around four hundred years. It had acknowledged Song suzerainty at its own convenience and Yuan supremacy only under duress. During the *Ming* Hongwu and Jianwen reigns it had been largely ignored; and it could have been by the Yongle emperor. When in 1404 he was misled into recognising a rebellious pretender as the ruler of Annam, when in 1405 he corrected his mistake by recognising a supposed Tran descendant, and when in 1406 this claimant and his Ming escort were slaughtered the moment they set foot in Annam, the emperor might still have cited his father's injunction and backed off. Instead he sent an army of 215,000 to invade. Worse still, in 1407, after a comprehensive victory, he annexed Annam, renaming it the Ming province of Jiaozhi. This is what it had been called under the Han, and now as then the Annamese proved anything but agreeable. Drawing on cherished memories of the Trung sisters, those indomitable Boadiceas who had defied the armies of the Later Han, they found inspirational leadership in members of the Tran and Le clans, plus a spirit of unquenchable resistance that freedom fighters of a later age would recognise as pristine nationalism.

The hostilities that followed lasted twenty years. Thrice the country was thought pacified and thrice revolt broke out anew. The Ming forces seldom lost a battle; the Vietnamese never gave up the fight. By land and sea, more and more troops and supplies went south, but it made no difference. Terrain and climate weakened the invader and favoured the guerrilla tactics of the invaded. By the mid-1420s the Vietnamese resistance enjoyed almost universal support under the great Le Loi, a patriot who would one day inspire the young Nguyen Ai Quoc, otherwise Ho Chi Minh. (But the twentieth-century parallels are too numerous for mention.) Ming forces won no hearts and Ming administrators eased no minds. Champa, the Ming support base and ally in the south, became thoroughly disillusioned. And by 1423 a face-saving disengagement was already under consideration in Beijing. It had been the most comprehensive military failure in the history of the early Ming.

Disengagement was not completed until 1427, four years and two emperors after the Yongle emperor's death; and relations were not formally regularised until ten years, and two more emperors, later. Thereafter, though threatened with another invasion in the 1530s, Vietnam went its own way, overrunning Champa and part of Cambodia to assume its current dimensions, and evading conquest even by the expansionist Qing. But the Chinese cause had effectively been lost back in 1423. In that year the sixth of Zheng He's voyages returned to China, a moratorium was announced on further sailings, and the Yongle emperor died. Failure in Vietnam had ended the need for propping up Champa and for policing the maritime states of the Malay and Indonesian coastlines. Without this strategic justification, the enormous expense of voyaging farther afield and maintaining the fleet necessary for such prestige exercises could no longer be justified. Confucian opinion had long opposed the voyages. The emperor's eunuchs, the main supporters and beneficiaries of the whole maritime initiative, fell from favour with the Yongle emperor's death.

Perhaps ultimately, as the Hong Kong academic Wang Gungwu has noted, the Yongle emperor's interventionist experiments were allowed to lapse because 'the traditional tribute system was never meant to support active international politics'. The emperor might appear to have anticipated a European form of power projection, but without adjusting the concepts and conventions on which imperial China's foreign relations had always been based, it was a wasted exercise. 'More money, power, and ceremony applied in the same old way was simply bound to fail.'[8] From a modern perspective, the whole exercise looks like one of China's great lost opportunities. Pursued to a logical conclusion, the Zheng He voyages would have made European mastery of the sea lanes problematic and so forestalled that westward tilt in the global equilibrium that is only now, in the twenty-first century, being corrected. But at the time, for a dynasty unsure of its destiny and an emperor in need of legitimacy, it was precisely the ritual nature of traditional diplomacy and its cosmological context which recommended the voyages. Having served that purpose, having exhausted their utility in respect of the Vietnam war, and having failed to discover any other rationale that might justify their expense, they could be terminated.

This tension between tributary tradition and interventionist potential was evident elsewhere. Another reason for abandoning both Vietnam and the voyages was that by 1420 the empire had shouldered heavier commitments in the far north. The expense of constructing the new capital of Beijing, its proximity to Mongolia and a revived Mongol threat relegated south-east Asia and the Western Ocean to the status of distractions.

Significantly, Mongolia (which term now comprehended all the peoples of the northern steppe) had not been included in the list of countries that the Hongwu emperor had enjoined his successors on no account to invade. The steppe remained a dangerously open frontier and all the more so now that court and capital had been relocated within easy reach of it. No doubt the Yongle emperor appreciated this. Indeed, the move to Beijing would appear to indicate that the early Ming nursed ambitions of following the example of the Yuan, imposing their authority throughout Mongolia and Manchuria, and so re-creating a dual empire combining the steppe and the sown.

In return for envoys and tribute, the Hongwu and Yongle emperors had extended titles and trading privileges to distant Mongolian, Manchurian and Siberian peoples with a view to neutralising them. Meanwhile diplomatic and military offensives were directed at a nearby confederation of eastern Mongols and the increasingly formidable Oyirat Mongols in the west, both of whom aspired to re-establish the empire of Chinggis Khan. The Ming emperors played one off against the other and either sent or led large expeditions against them. They established supposedly self-sufficient military colonies on the fringes of the steppe and constructed lines of fortified positions and observation posts at strategic locations. Some scholars read these 'lines' as 'walls'. 'It would probably be incorrect, however, to think of these walls at the passes as constituting either an ancient, or a prototype, "Great Wall",' writes the great Wall authority Arthur Waldron. 'The first mention of the phrase *changcheng*, "long walls", in the Ming *Veritable Records* does not appear until the year 1429.'[9] Nor, even then, did the new *changcheng* resemble the great bastioned and crenellated curtains of brick and stone that had lately been built round cities like Nanjing and the new Beijing. Judging by complaints over the damage caused by rain, frontier walls were still being constructed of *hangtu*, that compound achieved by tamping earth between timber shutterings; indeed, *hangtu*'s durable and compacted nature, the product of uncounted blows, might serve as an analogy for the steppe-hammered civilisation that championed it.

As in Vietnam, so in Mongolia – the last years of the Yongle emperor brought a scaling down of operations and a retraction of the outermost defences. Their maintenance had proved a more crippling expense than their establishment; and the emperor, now rheumy-eyed and sixty-something, must have been as exhausted as his treasury. The frontier retrenchment continued under his immediate successors. By 1430 even places within a few days' march of the capital had been abandoned, among them Kaiping, the renamed city that had been Khubilai's Shangdu and would live on as Coleridge's Xanadu. At court the merits of a harder, more manageable and less expensive frontier were championed by Confucian civilians, and there was much to be said for such a policy; but only if the nomadic peoples outside could be mollified by trade-as-tribute arrangements whereby they might dispose of their annual livestock surplus and obtain the Chinese supplies and manufactures on which they had come to rely. Yet markets set up for this purpose were strictly controlled, trade remained an imperial monopoly, and the number and frequency of Mongolian tributary missions, typically two thousand strong, so drained the empire's hospitality fund that they often had to be turned away.

As in the past, consolidating the frontier had an uncanny way of consolidating those whom it excluded. In the west, as of the 1430s, the Oyirat Mongols under a leader called Esen raided settled regions from Hami in Xinjiang to Gansu and Shaanxi. By conquest and alliance Esen secured the support of the Eastern Mongols and the Jurchen of northern Manchuria. When in 1448 a horde of his swaggering tribute-bearers was rebuffed by the Ming, he launched simultaneous invasions into Liaodong, Hebei and Shanxi. Beijing responded by fielding an army hopefully estimated at half a million men. It marched forth in early August 1449; and thus the scene was set for the 'Tumu Incident', a catastrophe so unincidental as to blight the Ming dynasty's reputation for the next two centuries.

The *Ming* Zhengtong emperor (r. 1436–49), great-grandson of the Yongle emperor, was of a mind to emulate his forebear's example and lead his troops in person. He had succeeded to the throne at the age of eight, had liked playing with soldiers and, now twenty-one, eagerly embraced the chance to do so for real. His advisers were aghast; but Wang Zhen, a eunuch who had been his tutor and was now his all-powerful head of security, dismissed their doubts and personally undertook to accompany the emperor and oversee operations.

The twenty-eight-day campaign that followed has been described as 'totally frivolous and irresponsible', which is a fair reflection of the official account.[10] Nothing went to plan – if indeed there was a plan. It rained incessantly, the minister of war kept falling off his horse, and eunuch Wang Zhen, inspiring nothing but hatred, was lucky not to be murdered in the first week. Amid reports of Mongol successes right along the frontier, and despite growing disaffection in the ranks, the army trundled west to Datong. Whenever the rain stopped, ominous black clouds kept materialising out of nowhere. Unease spread. After just two days in Datong, and still without sight of the enemy, Wang Zhen abandoned the idea of invading Mongol territory and agreed to the withdrawal for which all had been clamouring. By 30 August the Ming forces, now more a rabble than an army, were back in Hebei and just three days from Beijing. It was then that Esen's rough-riding bowmen, their horses at their strongest after the summer grazing, caught up with the Ming rearguard.

The rearguard was instantly overwhelmed. So were the 30,000 cavalry sent to take its place – they rode straight into an ambush. Next day the main army reached a post-station called Tumu. The rain had stopped, the wells were already dry, and men and horses were now suffering from thirst. Rations also seem to have run out. A violent debate between eunuch Wang Zhen and the horse-allergic war minister sent the latter limping off to his tent, where he wept all night. He had wanted to send the emperor straight to Beijing for safety; Wang Zhen opposed the idea, supposedly because his personal baggage-train of 1,000 wagons had not yet caught up with them. Next morning was the first of September and the Mid-Autumn Festival, a day of feasting and family reunions. The army awoke parched, hungry and surrounded on all sides. More altercations scuppered any chance of a truce; and when the order to advance was given, the Mongols took it as their signal to attack. Seemingly quite unprepared for this turn of events, the Ming ranks broke at the first onslaught. Thousands reportedly defected; thousands more presumably did not; either way, about half perished.

Meanwhile the emperor, still ringed by his imperial guards, dismounted from his horse and sat on the ground. Arrows rained down around him; the guards were all killed; the emperor somehow survived. He was still sitting there when a Mongol prince, suspecting he was someone special, led him off into captivity. Not until the following day was his identity established. Esen, as surprised as anyone at such an unlikely prize, considered executing him, but was then persuaded to use him as a bargaining counter. In Beijing the court and government were equally at a loss. History offered plenty of precedents for Heaven's Son being a Mongol but none at all for his being a Mongol hostage. The fallout of the 1449 Tumu Incident would be as instructive as the affair itself.

So much, though, for the details of the battle as extrapolated from the Ming dynastic history. It goes without saying that Wang Zhen was a godsend to the historians. As a eunuch by choice (he had fathered a family before sacrificing sex to advance his career prospects), he was beneath male Confucian contempt; as a notorious oppressor of ministerial remonstrants, he could expect no posthumous favours from the career bureaucrats who doubled as historians; and as a thoroughly incompetent commander, he was the perfect scapegoat for the whole affair. On the other hand, good

Confucians, such as the war minister, came out of it well and even got their revenge. Wang Zhen had died on the battlefield, probably at the hands of his own officers; but there remained the need for some exemplary posthumous punishment, including the eradication of his five degrees of relatives.

Accordingly, a week after Tumu, a mass gathering of officials in Beijing attended the palace to demand action from the acting regent. There, in open court, they found themselves opposed by a group of eunuchs – which raises doubts about the extent of Wang Zhen's unpopularity. Bravely if most unwisely, the eunuchs defended Wang Zhen and argued for clemency. This proved too much for normally deferential bureaucrats. The cream of Ming officialdom rose as one and transformed itself into a lynch mob. Baying for the blood of Wang Zhen's relatives, male or female, child or crone, whose only crime may have been a claim on his largesse or patronage, these dignitaries and degree-holders, the flower of the Neo-Confucian academies and the pick of the hereditary office-holding families, proceeded to gouge, kick, bite and beat – they were armed with nothing more lethal than their footwear – to such injurious effect that three eunuchs were killed outright, more were seriously wounded, and another palace floor was steeped in blood. Clearly emperors and their eunuch henchmen did not have a monopoly on violence.

Citing this mini-massacre as a triumph for the righteous, the histories, while strangely indifferent to the plight of the hostage emperor, put the best possible gloss on the closing of ranks that followed the Tumu Incident. A brother of the captive Zhengtong emperor was elevated to the throne as the Jingtai emperor (r. 1450–57). The court firmly refused to treat with the Mongol leader Esen. The ranks of the army were rapidly replenished from military reserves elsewhere in the empire. And the city of Beijing, against all expectations, was heroically defended. The Mongols, being unable either to enter the capital or offload the emperor, withdrew within weeks. Esen's Mongolian confederation then began to unravel, and within the year the Zhengtong ex-emperor was simply returned to China as surplus to requirements. It was as if he had been absent in Mongolia on legitimate business. Handed over with all the ceremony accorded a still-reigning monarch, he re-entered Ming territory unharmed, unransomed and, it has to be said, largely unwanted. For there were now two Sons of Heaven, each legitimately enthroned, which was almost worse than none at all. To the empire, the Tumu Incident had proved no more than a misfortune, but to the dynasty it still had the potential for disaster.

Luckily, after such a shock to the system, neither of the emperors was overconfident. Rather were they conscious of their debt to, and so receptive to the opinions of, a ministerial establishment that had managed the recent crisis so effectively. The Zhengtong emperor was installed in the southern palace and there kept in reserve, as it were, while the Jingtai emperor reigned on for another eight years. Then in 1457, when the latter prevaricated over nominating a successor and appeared to be ailing, the former was simply reinstalled in his stead. In an incident known as the 'forcing of the palace gate', a cabal of officials, after securing the support of the Imperial Guard, entered the southern palace, thrust its occupant into a sedan chair, 'forced the gate' of the main (northern) palace, and plonked the surprised ex-emperor back on the throne. 'The coup d'état par excellence of Ming history', as the *Cambridge History* has it, this was the gravest possible violation of ritual propriety and one motivated almost entirely by self-seeking opportunism.[11] The deposed Jingtai emperor died soon afterwards – suspiciously soon afterwards – and it remained only to think up a name for the new reign period of the reinstated Zhengtong emperor. The title chosen by his ritual advisers, tongues in cheeks surely, was 'Tianshun', 'Obedient to Heaven'; celestial subservience and bureaucratic advantage were showing a remarkable convergence. Uniquely among the Ming, then, this emperor had two reign periods; or to put it another way, the Zhengtong emperor (r. 1436–49) and the Tianshun emperor (r. 1457–64) in the Ming succession tables are one and the same man.

THE GREAT RITES CONTROVERSY

Most Chinese dynasties conformed to a pattern: they peaked quickly and declined slowly. Vigorous emperors deserving of respectful names (Gaozu, Taizu, Taizong) came early on in the succession; less effective ones with condescending names (Aidi, Pingdi, Shundi) came towards the end. A similar top-heaviness had characterised the Mongol succession and was about to find classic expression in the Mongols' Indian offshoot, the first of whose six 'Great Mughals', Babur (1483–1530), was a fifth-generation descendant of Timur Leng. This is in marked contrast to the ruling houses that were emerging in Europe at around this time. The Habsburgs and Bourbons, Tudors and Stuarts, all took some time to produce their best-known rulers – Maria Theresa, Louis XIV, Elizabeth I, Charles II. European dynasties peaked later and subsided more rapidly. Since both East and West endorsed the principle of succession by primogeniture, it does not appear that genetics can explain these trends; and since exceptions are not too hard to find, it could all be coincidence. But just as the 755 An Lushan rebellion seems to form a dynastic watershed in terms of the calibre of the Tang emperors, so with the 1449 Tumu Incident and the Ming emperors.

After Tumu, the Ming empire did not in fact fragment like the Tang; if anything it stabilised. But the initiative displayed by its later dynasts and the influence they chose to wield would never rival that of the Hongwu and Yongle emperors. On the other hand, for a time the bureaucracy grew in confidence and on occasion relieved emperors of their ruling responsibilities. This did not preclude tension between the two. On the contrary, throne and executive were interminably at cross-purposes, and their disagreements had a way of escalating alarmingly. The executive could usually rely on the support of its bureaucratic cohorts, and the throne on that of its eunuch henchmen, whose numbers grew so vast as to constitute a parallel bureaucracy. Although not always the obvious bone of contention, ritual matters provided an especially fertile field of dispute, and in the 1520s precipitated a head-on collision. Known as the Great Rites Controversy, this would be an affair of titanic proportions that was in no way diminished by the apparently molecular insignificance of the ritual issues themselves.

The bureaucracy at the time was unusually assertive because it had undergone something of a sea-change. In their reports on China, one of the first things noted by Europeans (who began reaching the China coast in the early sixteenth century) was the enormous respect shown to scholar-bureaucrats. As a class, they were unmistakable. They wore 'cap and girdle ... conferred by the king', travelled everywhere in 'seats of beaten gold' (gilded sedan chairs) shaded by umbrellas, and were always accompanied by servants who cleared a path for them and by banners proclaiming their rank.[12] The Portuguese sometimes called them 'louteas', a respectful form of greeting used in Fujian; but borrowing a term commonly in use for officials of Chinese extraction in south-east Asia, they had also begun using the word 'mandarin' almost as soon as they took Malacca in 1511.

The word had no Chinese currency and may in fact derive from an Indic language. But as 'mandarins' it would become the stock term for China's scholar-bureaucrats among Europeans, and hence for the language they spoke, which was typically that of the court in Beijing. In other words, the bureaucratically eligible, whether called *shi* or *guan* in Chinese and whether translated as 'gentlemen', 'officials', 'literati', 'louteas' or 'mandarins', now constituted an elite whose distinctive language hinted at its salient feature: access to this elite depended on education, not birth. After centuries of slow encroachment, examination candidates were at last coming into their own as office-holders. Indeed, 'at no time in China's premodern history was government in all its aspects more dominated by civil servants recruited and promoted on the basis of merit than in Ming times'.[13]

The founding Hongwu emperor deserves much of the credit. When, from the humblest origins, he had seized power in 1368 he showed no fondness for scholars but soon discovered a need for civil servants. To improve the lot of the cultivator through an empire-wide system of re-registration and fairer tax assessment, and to entrench his dynasty through a recodified body of law plus his numerous and much-revised 'ancestral injunctions', he sought bureaucratic recruits from the widest spectrum of society and of a standard that only the examination system could guarantee. To this end, government-funded Confucian schools were set up in every prefecture, sub-prefecture and county to augment those institutions privately maintained by monasteries, individual tutors and ambitious clans. Four thousand teachers were employed and, though pupil entry depended on adequate means and some prior tuition, the school system was theoretically open to almost anyone.

It was the same with the various exams, all of which required a thorough understanding of Zhu Xi's 'Four Books', and by means of which the successful student might progress up the academic ladder and from locality to provincial capital and eventually the metropolis. There he might continue his studies in one of the unversities and/or try his luck in the three-day-long ordeal – as much an academic endurance test as an exam – that could bring a *jinshi*, or doctoral, degree and automatic qualification for office. Such at least was the theory, and although there were supplementary streams of privileged advancement and many run-offs for the less ambitious, practice seems to have matched it. By the late sixteenth century, 'there were between one million and ten million men who had been educated to [the basic examinations] level', a remarkable figure for a time when elsewhere even basic literacy barely registered. It represented 10–20 per cent of the adult male population, with 1 per cent proceeding to exam-certificated status and 0.01 per cent to *jinshi* rank.[14] For the first time ever, 'as of the 1440s success in the examinations was the only means to assure the possibility of a first-class civil service career'.[15] Entry into the bureaucracy being now based on a rigorous assessment of ability and application, the calibre of officials improved and their sense of self-esteem advanced.

Social as well as professional status was at stake. Successful exam candidates are said to have enjoyed the acclaim nowadays accorded to style gurus and raddled entertainers. The exams were state occasions. Held triennially, the *jinshi* event constituted a high point in the capital's calendar with thousands participating, thousands more providing tutorial support, sustenance and encouragement, and yet more working as invigilators, scrutineers and assessors. To preclude cheating, each candidate was installed in his own wooden cubicle. His desk by day served as his couch by night, and for better supervision the lines of cubicles lay open along one side, like a row of latrines. Responsibility for the exam rested not with the Ministry of Personnel but the Ministry of Rites, and *jinshi* literally meaning 'presented *shi*', it included a final viva in the presence of the emperor himself. Once again, ritual underlay the whole system. Scholars, just like tribute-bearers, supposedly conformed to the cosmic pattern of attraction, being drawn into the imperial orbit by its sheer centrality. Their attendance affirmed its legitimacy and their distinction added lustre to its brilliance.

The Great Rites Controversy of the early 1520s, like the previous 'forcing of the palace gate' affair, resulted from an irregularity in the succession. In good order, the son, grandson and great-grandson of the twice-ruling Zhengtong/Tianshun emperor had occupied the throne from 1465 until 1521. None had shown too much ambition, the first being a nonentity, the second a well-meaning scholar and the third a thuggish buffoon. But despite his gargantuan philandering, this last (the Zhengde emperor, r. 1506–21) left no issue. Moreover he had long since consigned the affairs of the realm to senior officials. These dignitaries were therefore in an excellent position to settle the matter of his successor, and in doing so assert their authority to determine ritual issues of the utmost delicacy.

There was no difficulty in deciding who should succeed. Contrary opinions were silenced, and a dictum was invoked that dated back to the pre-imperial Shang and which had recently been reinforced by inclusion among the Hongwu emperor's 'ancestral injunctions'. This declared that, assuming there was no direct heir, 'when the elder brother dies, the younger brother succeeds'. 'Brother' being taken to signify all male collaterals directly descended from the same ancestor, it thus endorsed what is called agnatic succession. The way was clear for the accession of the fifteen-year-old prince of Xing, senior grandson of the nonentity emperor and cousin of the thuggish and just-deceased Zhengde emperor. Said to be sober and well educated, the prince was summoned from provincial obscurity and would reign as the Jiajing emperor (r. 1521–66). But even before he reached the capital, unexpected difficulties began to emerge.

The young man evidently had a mind of his own. Instead of entering Beijing by one of the eastern gates as stipulated by the Ministry of Rites, and then residing outside the palace until summoned for the ceremonies of accession, he insisted on entry by the south-facing main gate and immediate assumption of his imperial powers. He was emperor as of right, he protested, 'and not just an heir apparent'. He also took exception to the reign-period name that was being proposed. It would have made him the Shaozhi emperor, the 'Carry on Governing' emperor, a title implying continuity and not much else. Jiajing, his own suggestion, meant 'Prosperity and Peace', a less grudging and much more aspirational moniker.[16]

On both these issues he more or less got his way. But they proved only the opening salvoes in a battle of wills that steadily escalated over the next three years. The points in dispute – changing the colour of the tiles on the roof of his father's tomb, for instance, or dropping a couple of written characters from the wordy titles awarded to both his parents – might seem insignificant, even mind-numbingly obscurantist. So, to many, do the arguments over clerical attire, devotional formulae and ecclesiastical furnishings that were racking European Christendom at the time. In both cases, lurking within the niceties of ritual wording and liturgical performance lay claims to an authority of transcendent consequence. As with Zheng He's voyages and the traffic in tribute missions, rites were of the essence for a Celestial Empire. 'In traditional China', notes Carney Fisher, an authority on the Great Rites Controversy, 'ritual was power and the knowledge of ritual brought power.'[17] Without overmuch licence, the ritual arena in imperial China might be compared to the constitutional arena in, say, contemporary England. Crises, ritual or constitutional, were emphatically not just about forms and formulae. Arguably the outcome of the rites 'power struggle' of 1521–24 would determine the nature of Ming rule during its remaining century and consign both dynasty and bureaucracy to their dismal latter-day showings.

The fundamental issue still concerned the nature of the emperor's succession. Ritual experts, expressing the views of the Confucian bureaucracy, insisted that the Jiajing emperor's legitimacy depended on his undergoing posthumous adoption as the son of the deceased Zhengde emperor. That would make him his direct heir, ensure that the lineage remained unbroken, and permit him to reverence all the imperial Ming ancestors as his forebears. But it also meant demoting his real parents. His father must henceforth be acknowledged as his 'uncle' or, at best, as merely his 'natural' parent.

Precedents for imperial adoption and for these other adjustments to his paternity were not hard to find. Historians and ritualists explored them in mind-boggling detail and memorialised the throne about them remorsely. The Jiajing emperor was unmoved. His objection was based not on historical precedent but on moral principle. If filial piety was the linchpin of Confucian morality, no power on earth could persuade a dutiful son to deprive his natural father of the honours due to him. Heaven, rather than history, was the Jiajing emperor's judge. In fact as emperor his first duty must be to organise not the demotion of his parents but their promotion to imperial status, with temple-shrines of suitable magnificence and all the honorifics and reverential rituals to which an imperial ancestor was entitled. Agnatic succession was clearly sanctioned in respect of both the emperorship and the dynasty. Adoption was therefore quite unnecessary. He had been emperor from the moment the Zhengde emperor died; he would be beholden to no one for the legitimacy of his accession.

This was spirited talk from a young man who was practically unknown in the capital and as yet lacked either powerful palace support or any constituency in the bureaucracy. He looked sure to be overwhelmed, if not by the sheer weight of scholarship deployed against him then certainly by the machinations of ministers genuinely concerned about ritual propriety and united in their resolve to rein him in. Nor was it easy to dilute this opposition by installing supporters of his own in positions of power. Emperors, 'fixed and constant as the Northern star' in their state of *wuwei* suspension, were expected to read memorials and listen to remonstrants; they could approve or disapprove policy proposals; but they could not appear to initiate them. 'Emperors disposed only when ministers proposed' was the age-old custom, and this applied as much to appointments as enactments.[18] Naturally, those ambitious of imperial favour or fearful of imperial retribution would somehow divine the emperor's wishes and memorialise or remonstrate accordingly. That was how autocratic authority operated. But without such promptings, and in the face of unanimous disapproval, the inexperienced Jiajing emperor was vulnerable.

It so happened, though, that in the middle ranks of the administration, and especially in distant Nanjing ('the southern capital'), there were those who sympathised with his stance. To what extent they did so with a view to advancing their personal careers is hard to say. When their well-argued memorials, expanding on the principles involved and refuting the historical examples offered, began to trickle through to the emperor, he pounced on them gleefully. The missives were relayed to the Ministry of Rites, and their authors would eventually be summoned to Beijing. But as well as ambition, these comparative outsiders shared a common intellectual legacy. Nearly all had either studied under, or been influenced by, Wang Yangming (1472–1529, also known as Wang Shouren), the outstanding philosopher of the Ming period and successor to the great Neo-Confucianist Zhu Xi.

Wang Yangming thought highly of Zhu Xi but was no slave to the orthodoxy of his *lixue* ('doctrine of principle'). Taking his cue from Mencius, he taught that man was born with an already fully developed sense of what was right and good rather than with Zhu Xi's dormant gene waiting to be activated by the bookish 'investigation of all things'. 'The sense of right and wrong requires no deliberation to know, nor does it depend on learning to function,' insisted Wang. 'It is my nature as endowed by Heaven, the original substance of my mind, naturally intelligent, shining, clear, and understanding.'[19] Protestant reformers in Europe might have supposed he was talking about what they called 'conscience'; and some of his followers would indeed develop this idea to challenge many of the basic tenets of Neo-Confucianism, claim moral equality for all (including women) and espouse radical social agendas. But more than just a moral faculty, Wang Yangming's 'innate sense' had a functional capacity, like that of a muscle; too much study and it would atrophy; it needed to be exercised by living an active public life and helping others. Wang himself set a fine example in this. An admired administrator and military comander as well as a thinker and teacher, he practised what he taught and so demonstrated the unity of thought and action.

Reflecting Wang Yangming's doctrine of this 'innate sense' of what was right, the memorials reaching the Jiajing emperor from Nanjing in late 1521 'stressed that human feeling alone provided a guide to the natural order and urged the emperor to follow its lead'.[20] Historical precedents were not relevant; each was of its time, and times changed. Only the natural order, discoverable within oneself, was permanent; and if this enjoined reverence for one's parents above all else, then so be it. The ritual usage and terminology that indicated otherwise must be at fault. Another 'rectification of names' was called for.

None of this made any impression on the Ministry of Rites. The first Nanjing official to have broken ranks was simply censured and then removed from office. In 1522 the emperor himself appeared to cave in. Three small palace buildings had caught fire; though not a disaster, it could be a portent of worse to come and a sign of Heaven's mounting displeasure; clearly the emperor must quickly regularise his position by undergoing adoption. Anxious as well as isolated, the Jiajing ruler now did so. In return for being adopted by a dead emperor, he wrung from the ritualists a few minor concessions in respect of the titles proposed for his natural parents. The crisis seemed to have blown over. But a year later, it was back. Two more disciples of Wang Yangming, both of them highly respected scholars, had circulated memorials in support of the emperor. It is possible even that they were speaking for Wang Yangming himself, he being temporarily in retirement while he observed the customary three years' mourning following the death of his father.

In 1523 the emperor, reinvigorated by this evidence of influential support, proposed upgrading the status of his natural father's ancestral shrine so that it was on a par with that of his now adopted father's shrine. The roof was to have imperial yellow tiles and the number of dancers retained there for ceremonial purposes was to be increased. Howls of protest came from the Ministry of Rites, but they were ignored; the re-roofing and the dancers went ahead regardless. Eighteen years old in 1524, the Jiajing emperor was clearly gaining in confidence as the struggle moved rapidly to its climax. In that year the senior Grand Secretary retired; one of three such dignitaries who, ever since the Hongwu emperor had issued one of his ancestral injunctions against the office of chancellor, had headed the executive, it was he who had been largely responsible for organising the opposition to the emperor. At around the same time, more memorials came from Nanjing where support for the emperor's stance was evidently widespread. A compromise that would elevate the emperor's real father to 'Natural Deceased Father Esteemed and Majestic Emperor' looked possible; but it broke down when the Jiajing emperor took the title to mean parity between his two fathers and the Ministry of Rites took it to mean nothing of the sort.

As if inviting a showdown, the emperor now summoned his supporters from Nanjing. This was construed as a sign that they would soon be given positions of power, and indeed they were; one was nominated to head the Ministry of Rites, others to tenures at the prestigious Hanlin academy. Matters were getting personal. Each side accused the other of misleading the emperor and forming factions, both crimes being tantamount to treason. Threats of impeachment flew back and forth; talk of violence filled the air. The decisive move came from the emperor. In August 1524 he approved a suggestion from the now amenable Ministry of Rites that his mother be awarded an imperial title that did not include the term 'natural'; she was, in other words, to be acknowledged as the supreme dowager empress and his adopted mother as merely the dowager empress-aunt. Since a similar move in respect of his two fathers looked to be only a matter of time, this announcement was greeted with a new storm of protest.

Dissenting memorials from thirteen of the government's leading agencies bearing 250 influential signatures, plus entreaties from two of the three Grand Secretaries, left no doubt as to the continuing strength of opposition. It was given tangible expression next day when, after pledging solidarity, a crowd of some two hundred dignitaries converged on the gate giving access to the throne room. There they went down on their knees and began chanting the names of the most respected Ming emperors by way of a pointed reminder to the unworthy incumbent. Orders to disperse were ignored, and arresting the ringleaders failed to quell the tumult. The protesters now pounded on the throne-room door. They kept it up for much of the day until the emperor, his patience exhausted, ordered his fearsome Embroidered Guard to clear the area by force.

No deaths resulted from this operation, but 134 men were taken into custody. All were then heavily sentenced, and of the thirty-seven who were awarded floggings, nineteen died under the lash. It was actually a rod. The offenders were stripped and made to lie on the ground, and the strokes were administered on their bare buttocks, the indignity being exceeded only by the pain, as blood flowed copiously. Officialdom was horrified. Emperors were supposedly too concerned for their future reputations to risk alienating the bureaucratic majority. The Jiajing outrage was considered worse than any of the early Ming purges, and the historians would indeed eventually take their revenge. On the other hand, the young emperor had got his way: his real parents took their place among the imperial ancestors with titles undemeaned by the inclusion of the word 'natural'; filial piety had triumphed over ritual precedent; agnatic succession was accepted; over-assertive bureaucrats cowed; Wang Yangming's ideas disseminated; and the seeds sown for a more critical approach to history.

But the casualties were ritual propriety and moral certitude, those twin ideals on whose conjunction depended the dynasty's right to rule and the government's ability to govern. If the Tumu Incident had disgraced the dynasty in the eyes of the empire, the Great Rites Controversy disgraced it in the eyes of its own officials. The Jiajing emperor reigned for another twenty-three years – and the dynasty for nine decades after that – but such was the legacy of mistrust and uncertainty engendered by the controversy that little could be expected of the period. The official histories report much unrest, many setbacks, still more ill omens and few successes. Following their lead, a recent writer has diagnosed 'sclerosis at the heart of the bureaucracy' under the late Ming. Another, swayed by the official histories, calls the Jiajing emperor 'one of the most perverse and unpleasant men ever to occupy the Chinese throne' and an exemplar of 'the long procession of delinquent Ming emperors'.[21]

LANDMARKS AND INROADS

Despite such verdicts, and for the most part despite the absence of forceful direction, the sixteenth and early seventeenth centuries witnessed great change. It was during the Ming that China's population growth seems to have taken off; the reasons are obscure, and the percentage rate of growth would tail off in the eighteenth to twentieth centuries, though the net gain would not be significantly slowed until the 1980s. Under the Ming, too, education and publishing broadened the market for cultural productions, prompting a passion for connoisseurship and ensuring the success of new literary forms, most notably the novel. In the far north, new frontier defences were constructed, linked and battlemented to create what, some time before 1610, the Jesuit missionary Matteo Ricci called 'an unbroken line of defence with a tremendous wall 405 miles [650 kilometres] long'. The 'Great Wall' as we know it today had finally arrived. In the south, ships armed with guns brought Europeans armed with ideas, no less devastating in their way, about the community of nations, the conduct of diplomacy and their own God-given right to dictate the terms of trade and further the spread of Christianity. Throughout the empire, silver superseded paper money as the standard currency, with the domestic economy growing increasingly dependent on the importation of silver, mainly from Japan and mostly by foreigners. Other importations, principally from the New World, such as maize, cassava, groundnuts, tobacco and sweet potatoes, but also cotton and sugar cane, rendered marginal lands much more productive. And in the extensive hilly areas of the south and south-west, where such land was most abundant, Han settlement and the empire's social and administrative structures made substantial inroads. In short, a China with a more familiar profile was emerging and being slowly integrated into the world economy.

The philosopher Wang Yangming had gained his great insight into man's 'innate sense' of right and wrong as a result of a near-mystical experience while serving in Guizhou in 1508. The posting was only slightly better than exile. Wang had fallen foul of the imperial eunuchs, been jailed and flogged, and had narrowly escaped liquidation. A hardship assignment was the best he could hope for, and the malarial badlands of Guizhou were certainly that. Not one of the original provinces created by the Yuan, Guizhou had been officially constituted in 1413 after an expedition dispatched there by the Yongle emperor had suppressed an uprising. A century later, when Wang Yangming arrived, the region was still far from tranquil following major revolts in neighbouring Guangxi in the 1460s and western Guizhou in 1500–02. In the latter case the insurgents were led by a woman. The latest in a succession of formidable southern matriarchs to challenge Ming supremacy, she belonged to a tribe called the Yi.

At the time, northern Guangdong and all Guangxi, Guizhou and Yunnan were still overwhelmingly populated by non-Han peoples. Though within the empire's frontiers, these were yet frontier lands, intersected by secure rivers and trails and dotted with administrative centres and military outposts but for the most part suspicious of outsiders, if not downright hostile to them. The forested hills and deep valleys had an ethnic ecology of their own, with many quite different peoples pursuing highly specialised lifestyles. Some, such as the Yao and Miao (Meo, Hmong), practised swidden cultivation in the high hills; they have since spread, or migrated, south to swell the minorities of Laos, Vietnam and northern Thailand. Others, such as the Dai of Yunnan and the Zhuang of Guangxi, belonged to the same ethnolinguistic family as those lowland peoples known elsewhere as Lao, Shan or Thai and, like them, practised wet rice cultivation. Yet others, including the Yi (Lolo), Tujia and Bai of Guizhou and Yunnan, can only be categorised as *sui generis*. Though numerically insignificant compared with the Han, none of these peoples was subject to registration for tax and service purposes and so they do not figure in estimates of China's population.

Wang Yangming's appointment coincided with a renewed effort to pacify and settle these regions. It was a gradual process, sometimes consequent to hostilities, sometimes provocative of them. 'The Ming used force, appeasement and guile' – in roughly equal measures. At first a self-governing administration might be encouraged, 'much as "autonomous status" is given to ethnic minorities in China today'.[22] The more amenable clan chiefs and local headmen were organised into a hereditary hierarchy of command with impressive titles – 'soothing minister', 'pacification minister', 'conciliation minister' – plus some unpaid responsibilities. Alongside these *tusi* ('native office') arrangements a basic administrative structure might be set up with the establishment of districts, prefectures and provincial headquarters, the last staffed by officials who were either Han or had, as the term puts it, 'entered the current [of Chinese acculturation]'. As areas of Han settlement spread, and as, by attraction and intermarriage, more of the native population were deemed to have 'entered the current', the full panoply of Ming administrative arrangements inched outwards. Taxation replaced occasional tribute, households were registered, and the needs of defence and labour service came to be supplied from the local population.

The whole process was notoriously open to abuse. Though Wang Yangming proved a model settlement officer and established good relations with the non-Han peoples, others exploited the differences between the various ethnic groups, extorted resources from them and grossly exaggerated their own achievements. The most infamous case was that of a 'pacification minister' in the *tusi* of Bozhou in what is now north-western Guizhou. This Yang Yinglong, who was evidently of mixed descent, was the subject of repeated complaints yet somehow retained the government's support for twenty years, during which he built up his own power base among the local Miao and Tujia. Eventually his depredations and vendettas endangered the stability of the whole region. In 1599 it took the best of Ming generals and an expedition of 250,000 men, 70 per cent of them drawn from other *tusi*, to end his reign of terror and bring Bozhou within the standard system of directly administered prefectures.

Demographic pressures, internal migration and the insatiable demand for cultivable land undoubtedly added urgency to the settlement of such regions, though the statistics afford insufficient corroboration. Extrapolating overall population figures from the Ming registers has taxed great minds without producing much consensus, mainly because the registers themselves show negligible growth; either they could not keep up with the growth or it suited those responsible to under-report, so reducing the tax yield expected by the central government and maximising their own take of it. It seems likely, however, that during the Ming period China's population grew at 0.3–0.5 per cent per annum and that by the year 1600 the total may have stood at around 275 million. This was from a base of perhaps 85–100 million at the dynasty's founding in 1368. Having for nearly two and a half millennia hovered within the 40–100 million bracket, during the two and half centuries of the Ming the number of the empire's subjects nearly trebled. Thereafter, as if having passed some critical threshold, the rate of growth might slow, but such was the base total that the year-on year increment remained astronomical. Staggering natural disasters and catastrophic wars in the eighteenth to twentieth centuries would barely break its stride. By 1800 the total would be around 300 million and by 2000 around 1.3 billion.

This had all sorts of repercussions. According to some, it set China on a trajectory of labour-intensive growth rather than the West's capital-intensive growth; with no incentive to save on manpower, mechanisation had limited appeal and industrialisation was delayed; mass production came to mean production by the masses rather than the production of a mass of standardised items using minimal labour. Conversely the bureaucracy, which in earlier times had expanded much faster than the population, now failed to respond. Stretched ever thinner, bureaucrats in the provinces, however well educated, fell behind in updating tax assessments and so deprived government of the tax yield from the growth in population.

The area of cultivable land increased, yet the number of cultivable land-holdings may actually have fallen, the result of ever more of them being consolidated into large estates. In this respect, the Ming's two and a half centuries of internal peace had a downside. The dispossessions and repossessions inherent in wars of conquest did not materialise; land for redistribution was therefore scarce; and to make matters worse, much of what there was went to providing imperial cadets with estates. Since several members of the Ming lineage managed fifty or so children, by the seventeenth century the number of imperial dependants ran to tens of thousands. The stipends they received (in addition to tax revenue from their estates) actually overtook the military budget as the most expensive of the empire's fixed charges. Exiled to Guangxi province in 1549, Galeote Pereira, one of several Portuguese who had been convicted of smuggling, reported that Guilin, the province's modest capital, possessed 'a thousand of the emperor's kin lodged in great palaces in various parts of the city'. None was entrusted with any responsibility, and they were forbidden to leave the city lest they stir up rebellion. But they lived well enough behind their red-painted walls (red being the dynasty's colour, since fire was its Phase/Element) and were excellent company; 'neither did we find, all the time we were in that city, so much honour and good entertainment anywhere as at their hands', recalled Pereira.

Migration of a more traditional nature took many forms: to the northern frontier regions to form military colonies, to the south and south-west to take up marginal lands, to underpopulated sections of the rugged Jiangsu, Zhejiang and Fujian coastlines, and from there and Guangdong to places overseas. As well as the ports of mainland and island south-east Asia, Chinese commercial interests became established in Taiwan, the Ryukyu Islands between there and Japan, and Luzon in the Philippines, where there was a substantial Chinese community by the 1570s, when, by way of Mexico, the Spanish arrived. But then as now, perhaps the greatest migration was that from the countryside to the cities. Pereira likened the empire's thirteen provinces – or 'shires' in his English translation – to European countries, and on the basis of a brief acquaintance with Fujian, Jiangxi and Guangxi, reckoned each had some seven major cities, 'all well walled . . . and very gallant, specially near unto the gates, which are marvellously great and covered in iron'.[23] A contemporary gazetteer lists sixteen of the empire's cities as being of the first or second rank, only two of which (Guangzhou and Fuzhou) were in the provinces visited by Pereira. To these sixteen great cities, there might then be added fifty or more of lesser but still 'gallant' proportions.

Social historians have noticed how in Ming times the cultural life of the empire was less concentrated in the imperial capital than under previous dynasties. Nanjing, the southern capital with its own metropolitan province, hosted as many scholars and writers as Beijing; Suzhou, the canal city famous for its silk manufacture, and Hangzhou, the capital of the Southern Song, attracted artists and poets; and if Guilin is anything to go by, even lesser cities could provide the court patronage and civilised comforts to make them foci of cultural activity.

Under the Mongol Yuan dynasty, literature had descended from its ivory tower. Dramas written in the vernacular rather than in the classical and often incorporating risqué material had enjoyed both courtly and popular currency. Prose fiction written in the vernacular came with the Ming. Sometimes called 'unofficial history', it mostly explored historical themes and is best represented by the swashbuckling *Romance of the Three Kingdoms*. Several versions of the *Romance* were in circulation during the Ming period, although the best known today looks to have been composed or revised after the dynasty's fall. *Water Margin*, another historically based narrative, this time set among bandits under the Song, had a similar provenance, and like the *Romance* had been anticipated in Yuan drama. The earliest extant edition of *Journey to the West*, or *Monkey*, that fantastic allegory loosely derived from pilgrim Xuanzang's seventh-century journey to India, dates from 1592; and with *Gold Vase Plum* (or *Plum in a Golden Vase*), a domestic saga of sex and power, it completes 'the four master-works of Ming fiction'.

While to most non-Chinese 'Ming' means a vase, it would be wrong to attribute this association entirely to the great porcelain exports of Jingdezhen's kilns. Drawing heavily on the novel *Gold Vase Plum*, the art historian Craig Clunas has stressed the visual and material nature of all Ming culture. Things, just like words in the literary tradition, exercised a fascination that transcended their obvious function or aesthetic appeal. Each had its own repertoire of allusion and its own etymology. The Ming connoisseur observed the creative and manufacturing processes closely; artists and craftsmen responded by endowing their creations with contextual clues – dates, signatures, inscriptions, seasonal motifs, suggestive colours, archaic resonances. Objects had something of the instructive potential of portents. 'It is not surprising that a work like *Jing Ping Mei*

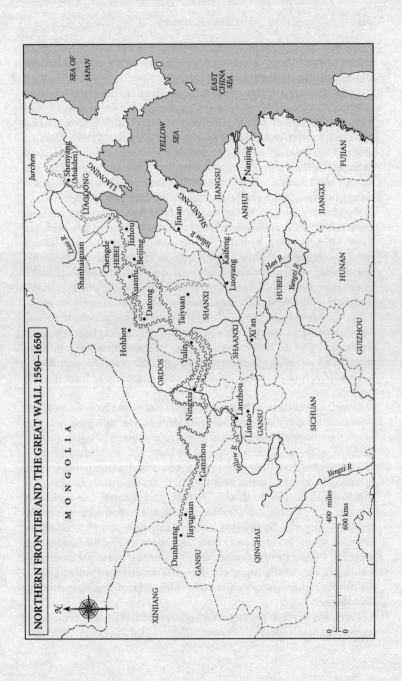

NORTHERN FRONTIER AND THE GREAT WALL 1550–1650

[*Gold Vase Plum*] should include so many descriptions of looking at things,' writes Clunas; objects were seen 'as one of the central pleasures and anxieties of the period'.[24]

Sadly, in respect of the greatest of all Ming artefacts, the countless millions who created it were not as conscientious as the historian would wish. The 'Great Wall' was unquestionably a Ming creation, both in terms of its construction and of its later repute. But plaques recording different stages of its construction are rare and only a few bricks bear an incised indication of their provenance. Moreover, archaeologists, faced with a site 6,000–7,000 kilometres (3,700–4,350 miles) long, remain more concerned about conserving what can be seen than exhuming what cannot.

Disjointed references in the standard Ming history provide the best guide to the wall's construction. They indicate that most of what remains today was undertaken between the mid-sixteenth and mid-seventeenth centuries. Before that, some earthen walls in Liaoning have been identified as Ming work of the 1420s; they may represent a diversion of funds by the Yongle emperor following his suspension of the Zheng He expeditions to the Western Ocean. The defeat and capture of the emperor at the Tumu Incident of 1449 provided a new stimulus. After prolonged debate, and in response to Mongol settlement in the Ordos area within the great northern loop of the Yellow River, in the 1470s walls, often of two or three strands, and still of *hangtu* construction, were built across the neck of this 'peninsula' between Ningxia and Yulin. Only fragments of them are still visible.

Ongoing Mongol raids and the establishment of the Mongol capital at Hohhot in what is now Inner Mongolia exposed the vulnerability of the frontier farther east, especially between Datong and the Beijing area. In the 1540s, as Mongol incursions multiplied, an elaborate system of fortifications, towers and walls was thrown across and around this area of northern Shanxi and Hebei in what the authorities invariably call 'a lozenge'. Some structures were faced with brick or stone, though not many and probably not till later. The complex nevertheless withstood a major raid in 1550 – or rather, it diverted it. For Altan Khan, another would-be Chinggis, simply led his forces round the eastern edge of the lozenge and straight to Beijing, there to ravage the capital's farmlands and fire its suburbs within full view of the Jiajing emperor and his dismayed subjects. Only the heavily fortified gates and massive stone walls of Beijing itself went unchallenged.

There was a lesson here, and throughout the rest of the century and on into the next, sections of frontier wall were clad in brick or stone and elaborated with crenellated battlements and towers. In the same period, the wall was extended east over the hills north of Beijing and on to the coast in Liaoning. Enormous gateways combining defensive potential with palatial effect were constructed at the main points of ingress. Signal towers, guard posts and subsidiary walls covered the flanks and ranged far afield wherever the terrain required. The work was still going on when in 1619 Ming forces were driven out of most of Manchuria. A new horde, not Mongol but Manchu (as the Jurchen now called themselves), was pressing south, intent on giving the wall its baptism of fire.

In the following year the Wanli emperor (r. 1573–1620), grandson of the rites-obsessed Jiajing emperor, died. The longest reigning of all the Ming emperors, he had been the least effectual. After an early flurry of activity, for thirty years he had ignored the needs of the empire and withdrawn from public life, the better to cultivate extravagance and put on weight. Memorials went unread, posts unfilled, troops unpaid, taxes uncollected. A long war against Japanese invaders in Korea in the 1590s had taken a heavy toll in casualties and strained the exchequer; likewise the assault on Guizhou's upstart 'pacification minister', Yang Yinglong. In the west the Mongols had forged unwelcome links with the Tibetans. Banditry and rebellion were rife all over the empire. Japanese, Portuguese and now Spanish and Dutch mariners were monopolising the trade of the southern ports. If it was ironic that wall-building had been preferred to the Zheng He voyages in the first place, it was still more ironic that the construction of the Great Wall itself had been given priority just as Japanese pirates were terrorising the coast and the Portuguese were ensconcing themselves at Macao. But the Ming empire was wilting more from neglect than insult. As of 1591, the Wanli emperor had ceased even to observe the ancestral rites. His Jiajing grandfather had risked all to honour his natural parents; he, on the other hand, could not even be bothered to attend his mother's funeral. Such dereliction of ritual duty bespoke a moral bankruptcy more fatal than the empty treasury and invited a censure more certain than maritime embarrassment. In quick succession the Ming empire would succumb to rebellion and then foreign conquest.

14

THE MANCHU CONQUEST
1620–1760

OVERWHELMING MING

THERE WERE FEW CLEANER BREAKS IN imperial China's long history than that between its last two dynasties. The switch was so abrupt as to leave the historians with little scope for dynastic elastication and so dramatic as to appear almost staged. Some time after midnight on 25 April 1644, accompanied only by an old eunuch, the *Ming* Chongzhen emperor, grandson of the Wanli emperor, ascended Coal Hill, an eminence within the Forbidden City, surveyed Beijing's unmanned walls and the fires that raged in the still-dark suburbs beyond, and then, retiring into a nearby pavilion – it was the headquarters of the Imperial Hat and Girdle Department – hanged himself from a cross-beam. On 5 June Manchu forces entered the city, quickly occupied the palace and, declaring the Mandate forfeit, arrogated it to their own pre-declared Qing dynasty. The deer had been loose, as the saying had it, for just six weeks. In the same decade, around six hundred weeks of godly ferment followed the removal of the crowned head of Charles I of England and Scotland. But in China, so short was the interregnum between Ming and Qing that it served only to betray the capital and precipitate the conquest of the empire. Resistance, though sometimes heroic, would prove marginal. For once there would be no enduring north–south split, no long multi-state 'Period of Disunion', and no excruciating free-for-all among incoming warlords and competing regional dynasties.

After a six-week bloodbath an indigenous lineage was again being displaced by an alien one. High-cheeked warriors on horseback clattered through the Beijing streets, their Inner Asian origins ferociously advertised by incomprehensible languages, soft-soled boots and the shaven fore-crowns and long greasy queues of Geronimo lookalikes. Besides the Jurchen, who called themselves Manchu, there rode in the ranks of the incomers large contingents of 'Mongols', a term now denoting language, lifestyle and attachment to the memory of Chinggis Khan and which comprehended peoples once identified as Turkic and Khitan as well as Mongol. The steppe and the forest were reinvading the sown; it was as if all those who had previously savoured Chinese dominion were back for a banquet of lasting empire.

The Ming's nearly twenty-seven decades were up, the Qing's nearly twenty-eight just beginning; a tired and now ineffectual regime looked to have succumbed to a fresh and still-dynamic one. The eclectic society of the later Ming would soon be superseded by a more rigid social and cultural conformity. Likewise, the Ming flirtation with the wider maritime world would appear repudiated in favour of a typically Inner Asian obsession with territorial conquest. Zheng He's voyages, the 1557 accommodation of the Portuguese at Macao, the interest taken at court in well-primed foreigners like the Jesuit Matteo Ricci, and the economy's growing dependence on the exchange of silk and ceramic exports for bullion from Japan and the New World – these things could not be reversed. But their aftermath might have been better managed had priority not been given to territorial expansion into the unproductive wastes of Mongolia, Tibet and Xinjiang. By the late eighteenth century, thanks to the Qing, China would have acquired the subcontinental girth that it rejoices in to this day. On the other hand the price for neglecting its seaboard and underestimating the foreigners who increasingly frequented it would be national humiliation, and not just by trading companies, upstart empires and 'great powers' but by domestic revolutionaries, opportunistic neighbours and itinerant ideologues.

Not surprisingly, then, the year 1644 – or less explicitly, the first half of the seventeenth century – is taken to mark an important milestone in China's historical marathon. Hereabouts period-conscious histories flag the end of one era, or 'world cycle', and the beginning of another, though whether 'late feudal' is superseded by 'proto-capitalist', 'late imperial' by 'post-imperial' or 'pre-modern' by 'early modern' is a matter of mouth-watering debate. Many recent works carry their narratives up to the 1600s, after which others take over for the homeward stretch. In the changeover from Ming to Qing, the tradition, hallowed by China's historiography, of chopping the past into dynasty-size lengths looks for once to have been justified. And yet change is seldom so sharp, transition never so tidy. Arguably a chronology inflexibly based on dynasties and reign periods imposes artificial divisions, or 'conceptual barriers', that truncate and obscure more deep-rooted trends in society, culture and government.[1] The thematic continuities, within Jurchen-Manchu society as well as Chinese, though they play havoc with a date-dependent narrative, may be more rewarding than the comings and goings of dynasts.

Travelling from Nanjing to Beijing in 1598, the Italian Father Matteo Ricci had opted for the Grand Canal. He was no stranger to the country. He had been in Guangdong for sixteen years, had mastered the language and was now superior of the small Jesuit mission based on Portuguese Macao. He was nevertheless amazed by the volume of shipping on the canal. It was said that 10,000 vessels were engaged in transporting the tax produce of Shandong and the Yangzi provinces to Beijing, and Ricci saw no reason to doubt it. He was equally impressed by the 'great number of well known cities' he passed. As for the banks of the canal, they were lined by 'so many towns, villages and scattered houses that one might say the entire route is inhabited'. Throughout a distance of around 1,700 kilometres (1,060 miles), the commercial activity never ceased.

Later, returning south by land because in winter there was insufficient water and too much ice for the canal to function, Ricci stayed in Suzhou. Like Polo he was reminded of Venice; 'the city is all bridges', he wrote in his journal, 'very old but beautifully built ... [and] the water fresh and clear, unlike that of Venice'. As a location for a Christian mission, though, Suzhou had a major disadvantage: it was subject to 'a tremendous tax'. Reportedly an indemnity dating back to the Ming conquest, it meant that fully half of what was grown in and around the city passed to the imperial treasury. 'Hence it may happen in China that one province pays twice as much as another in taxes.'[2]

There was nothing new in all this. The size and ubiquity of towns and cities, the commercialisation of agriculture as farmers concentrated on specialised crops for market rather than food grains for subsistence, the consequent development of local networks of commercial, manufacturing and socio-political activity, and the extremely uneven nature of tax liabilities are all discernible in earlier accounts like those of Ennin, Polo and Ibn Battuta. But in no small part thanks to the survival of more in the way of documentation – tax registers, local gazetteers, genealogies, unofficial histories – provincial conditions during the Ming and Qing periods have attracted greater scholarly scrutiny.

The main conclusion of this scrutiny is predictable, if disconcerting: generalising about the empire is shown to be a dangerous exercise. Not only taxation but crops, productivity, patterns of landownership, standards of law and order, and levels of social well-being varied enormously from province to province, prefecture to prefecture, and county to county. Yet communications being excellent, social as well as commercial linkages between the cities, towns and countryside were highly developed. Government officials were forever returning to their rural roots to attend ancestral festivals, observe the long mourning periods for a deceased parent, nurse the wounds of censure and demotion, or simply retire for good. Nor were they starved of appreciative company once they got there. Since the supply of graduates now greatly exceeded official demand, and since living with kin in a village was cheaper than keeping up appearances in a city, local society had acquired a whole new tier of cultivated office-seekers and opinionated mentors. Genealogical researches by such underemployed scholars contributed to the formation of local clan associations that might own land, offer social and educational support to their members, actively engage in local affairs, and disconcert official bureaucrats. The urban exiles, mixing more freely with landowning, military and mercantile families now that they too included degree-holders, augmented a gentrified local elite that, in an age of bureaucratic 'sclerosis', could exercise considerable influence.

This influence was far from consistent, however, and local society anything but coherent. Differences convulsing the late Ming court would be exposed by the Qing conquest as common throughout the empire. Mostly they were couched in the high moral terms of a controversy that pitched latter-day disciples of the hands-on, 'thought as action' Wang Yangming and his 'innate sense' of what was right (which all too easily became what was convenient or permissive) against those who, true to Zhu Xi's emphasis on 'the investigation of all things', insisted on the cultivation of moral integrity as the prerequisite for office entitlement and for the empire's salvation. The latter, at first overwhelmingly disappointed junior officials, were vociferous, even suicidal, in challenging the Grand Secretariat and bombarding the emperor with remonstrances; as the Donglin faction (named after an academy in Wuxi near Suzhou) they suffered persecution in the 1620s; as the Fu She ('Restoration Society') they fared slightly better in the 1630s; but as a component in Ming resistance to the Qing conquest in the 1640s they failed dismally. Many other shades of opinion were represented; some brave spirits would wonder whether abstract speculation of any sort was appropriate at a time of growing crisis. But all schools of thought were tainted by deep personal and professional animosities, were exercised by the age-old rivalry between the palace and the bureaucracy, and were susceptible to competing opinions about the post-Wanli succession.

As for the bureaucracy itself, its plight had little to do with the calibre of its personnel. Loyal and devoted public servants were no rarer in the early seventeenth century than formerly; indeed, the Qing conquest revealed some quite exceptional officials. But because of the rivalries and suspicion engulfing the government in Beijing, central direction was lacking. Instead the provinces were bombarded with ever more demands for revenue. Partly these impositions and levies were needed to defray the expense of war against the Japanese in Korea in the 1590s, against Jurchen advances in Manchuria after 1615, and increasingly against rebellious subjects in China itself, who were often driven to take up arms by the severity of the very same impositions. But new taxes were also needed because the existing ones, and the liabilities on which they were assessed, had come to bear little relationship to actual landownership, population totals or theoretical liability. The later Ming had bartered such extensive exemptions to the imperial clan, the Buddhist clergy, the military, office-holders, degree-holders and anyone else with influence that the tax burden now fell overwhelmingly on small landholders and sharecroppers who were least able to support it.

This placed local officials in an unenviable position. Should they side with those powerful interests accustomed to exemption or evasion, or with downtrodden cultivators not unreasonably inclined to violence? Worse still, as of the late 1590s the local administration had become increasingly sidelined; poor returns from the new taxes had led the emperor to entrust the collection of the most detested levies – or more accurately, their extortion – to that alternative bureaucracy of palace officials that constituted the 'eunuchracy'.

Ricci observed this phenomenon with dismay. As he understood it, in the past emperors had obtained sufficient in the way of precious metals – principally copper and silver – from mines within the empire. But these mines had long been officially closed because 'thieves and robbers' had taken to despoiling them. Now the Wanli emperor, out of dire necessity, had ordered their reopening, had imposed a 2 per cent tax on 'all merchandise sold in every [mineral-yielding?] province' and, bypassing the regular officials 'who always administer the laws with moderation', had dispatched eunuchs to enforce compliance. These 'semi-men', of whom Ricci was as scathing as any unemasculated Confucianist, had then gone berserk, 'their greed turning them into savages'.

> The tax collectors found gold mines, not in the mountains, but in the rich cities. If they were told that a rich man lived here or there,

they said he had a silver mine in his house, and immediately decided to ransack and undermine his home ... Sometimes, in order to secure an exemption from being robbed, the cities and even the provinces bartered with the eunuchs, and paid them a large sum of silver, which they said was taken from the mines for the royal treasury. The result of this unusual spoliation was an increase in the price of all commodities, with a corresponding growth in the general spread of poverty.[3]

Regular officials protested, even resisted, but to no avail; they were either dismissed or imprisoned. The eunuchcrats had the emperor's full backing and grew ever 'more insolent in their attitude and more daring in their depredations'. In the eyes of the inarticulate masses the entire government apparatus was at risk of being discredited by the scandal.

All of which, while attested elsewhere, overlooked the underlying problem: besides inadequate revenue receipts, the Ming faced a serious monetary crisis. Paper money had first run into problems under the Yuan dynasty. Insufficiently backed by silver, copper or even silk, new issues of notes had been declared non-convertible by the Mongol regime. As a result they rapidly lost their face value and were generally shunned; those who could preferred to hoard metals. The Hongwu emperor, founder of the Ming, had persisted with paper and shut down mining operations to cut off the supply of metals. But this merely boosted their value, especially that of silver. By 1400 the purchasing power of silver was higher in China than anywhere else in the world, and would remain so. The country 'had entered a new monetary age in which unminted silver traded by weight, and copper coins both legal and counterfeit, were the dominant forms of currency'.[4]

The *Ming* Yongle emperor – he who championed the Zheng He voyages – continued issuing notes. Salaries were paid in them, and all those foreign tribute missions were plied with them; since they were worthless outside China – and soon worthless within China – recipients did well to spend them quickly. The Yongle emperor also reopened the mines. For a time the supply of precious metals had improved, and in 1436 some taxes became payable in silver, others in copper. This trend away from paper money accelerated in the sixteenth century so that by the 1550s most taxes were payable in silver. Meanwhile, judging by government receipts from mined silver, the yield from domestic sources had either dramatically declined or was being wilfully misrepresented. As of the sixteenth century by far the largest source of silver, and so of China's money supply, was foreign trade. Against exports, the silver initially came from eastern Europe by way of

Indo-Muslim and then Portuguese merchants; as of mid-century, it came from Japan and was shipped mainly by the Portuguese; and after the 1570s, it came substantially from the Americas, carried across the Pacific by Spanish galleon to Manila and thence to the coast of China in Chinese vessels, a development made possible by the 1567 lifting of that ban on Chinese participation in maritime ventures imposed after the Zheng He voyages.

Curiously, though silver was mined in China, it was never minted in China. The only coins in circulation remained copper cash that were strung together through their central hole into 'strings'. As late as the 1870s overland explorers, such as those of France's Mekong Exploration Commission, having bartered their way to some remote Chinese frontier with a variety of trade goods and currencies, were amazed to learn that on entering the Celestial Empire they must convert their resources into silver ingots. From these ingots, as from a cheese, chunks were cut or slivers pared, then weighed and essayed, for every substantial cash transaction. Though silver, its weight expressed in terms of *liang* or taels (37.6 grams, 1.3 ounces), was the standard unit of currency, there were no silver coins and no units of guaranteed weight and purity. In theory the metal retained its original function as a reserve and tax currency, handier to transport and store than copper, silk or grain. It was meant as the medium of the state, of its servants and the financial community, not of the black-haired commoner.

So long as silver was abundant worldwide, its high purchasing power in China acted as a magnet. (An embarrassingly favourable balance of payments is no novelty in China.) But from about 1600 to 1620, and again post-1630, the silver supply was interrupted by a combination of factors – declining production in the New World, ructions in Manila and hiccups on the high seas as Dutch and English shipping challenged the Iberian powers. This seems to have determined the Wanli emperor and his successors to maximise the revenue from domestic mines by imposing the new tax mentioned by Ricci and by entrusting its collection to eunuchcrats, many of whom were already in the provinces as tax overseers in connection with the salt monopoly. 'Mines' soon became just a generic euphemism for any enterprise or individual suspected of having large silver reserves. Since local administrations were notoriously ambivalent about this wealth, it could reasonably be assumed that little or no tax had already been levied on it; an equitable redistribution of the fiscal burden was indeed highly desirable and long overdue. But this was not it; and Ricci was right to highlight the abuses and hardships that resulted. Hoodlums were hired to terrorise those targeted; commercial life was interrupted;

casual labourers were laid off; with silver in short supply, the silver-to-copper ratio rose in silver's favour; so did prices; and hardest hit were those who sold their produce for copper but must pay their taxes in silver.

Urban unrest and tensions within the provincial elite were soon widespread. The death of the Wanli emperor in 1620 brought a respite in respect of the mining tax but not of the eunuchcrats, who continued to harry the rich and antagonise the righteous. Resentment was most evident in prosperous Jiangnan, a term denoting the region of 'the Yangzi south' and principally applied to the booming Nanjing–Suzhou–Hangzhou corridor. But it was more obvious upheavals within the heavily militarised society along the Great Wall in the far north which heightened these tensions and finally overwhelmed the Ming.

Throughout the empire in the 1620s and '30s a succession of unusually cold summers brought crop failures and famines. Smallpox and possibly some form of plague were also rampant. As so often, dynastic change would take place against a background of widespread dislocation and hardship that was no less ominous than it was catastrophic. Simultaneously Mongol and Jurchen incursions into Liaodong (now Liaoning), the Ming province in southern Manchuria, necessitated the dispatch of ever more troops beyond the wall's easternmost extremity. This weakened the garrisons to the west, creaming off their manpower, supplies and even wages. Here, and especially in Shaanxi, goaded by hunger and neglect, deserters formed gangs of roving 'bandits' that by 1630 were snowballing into rebellious armies. They coordinated their movements to avoid clashing with one another and roamed ever farther east, west and south (so panicking Jiangnan) to commandeer supplies and recruits. Though amenable to amnesties and occasionally defeated by imperial troops, they displayed remarkable resilience, in part because the imperial forces hastily raised to oppose them often proved no more disciplined – and rather less fair-minded when it came to sharing their spoils with the oppressed.

By 1641 these rebels had gelled into two main armies, one operating principally in Hubei and Sichuan, the other in Shanxi and Henan under a self-styled 'Prince of Shun'. The 'dashing prince', as he was popularly known, was otherwise Li Zicheng, a man in his mid-thirties with little education or military experience but a commanding personality and soaring expectations. In 1642 Li Zicheng captured Luoyang and then, after flooding it, Kaifeng; millions are said to have drowned, including 10,000 of his own men. He could afford the loss; his forces now supposedly numbered in the hundreds of thousands. Late in 1643 he added to his bag of ancient imperial capitals the city of Xi'an, renaming it Chang'an as in

Tang times. In the same year he took Xiangyang, one of the twin cities from which the Southern Song had once defied the advancing Mongols by running their blockade with paddle-boats. There, like the *Ming* Hongwu emperor at Nanjing in his own pre-imperial days, Li Zicheng began setting up a rudimentary administration with the help of assorted officials attracted as much by his success as by his populist sentiments.

The extent of his ambitions was as yet unclear. The rebels had generally executed members of the extended Ming family along with senior Ming officials; indeed, rumour consistently had it that, in doing so, Li Zicheng was merely asserting his legitimacy, he being none other than the direct descendant of the *Ming* Jianwen emperor (the grandson of the founding Hongwu emperor who had either disappeared into the Western Ocean, where Zheng He had failed to find him, or been burnt to death when the Yongle emperor stormed Nanjing and usurped the throne). Yet Li Zicheng's personal propaganda, like that of insurgents in the past, tirelessly stressed his loyalty to the present emperor; he was supposedly intent only on liberating him from self-seeking officials and dependants who abused his authority and frustrated his efforts to deal with the Jurchen-Manchu threat. There was something in this. Not mere rhetoric for once, it tallied with the views of many, including the Jurchen-Manchu themselves, who proclaimed equally loyalist sentiments to justify their own advance from the east, though of course they would rescue the emperor from his rebellious subjects. On the other hand, the weight of unmistakably imperial precedent building up behind Li Zicheng can hardly have gone unnoticed. As with the *Qin* First Emperor and *Han* Gaozu, his trail of conquest began in Shaanxi; like *Han* Gaozu and the *Ming* Hongwu emperor he had overcome the handicaps of humble birth; and as with the Tang emperors his surname was the auspicious Li. In conscious imitation of the Tang, he had reinstated Chang'an and awarded his officials Tang-style titles. All options were being kept open.

The year 1644 had begun with Li Zicheng's elevation as 'Great King of the West', another ambiguous move, followed by his immediate departure for the east. After storming Taiyuan, the Shanxi capital, half his army had made straight for Beijing, the other half going via Datong to pre-empt attack in the rear from the Great Wall garrisons. Neither encountered much resistance; Manchu incursions into Liaodong had siphoned off the bulk of the imperial troops. By 22 April Li Zicheng was bivouacking among the imperial Ming tombs, singeing their architecture but not actually ransacking them. He was two days' march from the capital. A Beijing Spring beckoned.

What precisely followed – or which of the several accounts deserves the greater credibility – is uncertain. As the rebel army entered the suburbs, the defenders melted away and the Ming simply bowed to the inevitable. The granaries were bare, the treasury empty, the depleted garrison unpaid and unfed. The government, riven by factional struggles, was as impotent as ever; senior ministers who could well afford to contribute to the defence of the realm turned a deaf ear to appeals for donations; and as for the Chongzhen emperor himself (r. 1628–44) he seemed more cut out for tragedy than heroics. In his early thirties at the time, he was neither an idiot nor an invalid; he worked hard and worried incessantly. But distrustful – he had got through fifty Grand Secretaries in seventeen years – and chronically indecisive – for months he had been havering over a possible retreat to Nanjing – he inspired neither confidence nor respect.

Some accounts have him summoning his ministers to a last-minute audience; no one turned up. Did he then get drunk? Order his empress to commit suicide? And stab to death his other womenfolk to save them from dishonour? Or did he simply put on his ceremonial robes, tramp up Coal Hill and hang himself? Was it in fact called 'Coal Hill'? Or was it 'Prospect Hill', otherwise the 'Hill of Ten Thousand Years'? And was it really from a beam in the Hat and Girdle pavilion that he hanged himself, or was it from a tree outside? No two accounts agree. 'For this set of events', writes Jonathan Spence, the most candid of Ming-Qing chroniclers, 'the historian can usually decide for himself which are the likeliest versions.'[5]

Either later that day or the next Li Zicheng's forces entered the Forbidden City. They were practically unopposed; someone had even left the gates unlocked for them. Over the next few weeks, as the blossom fell and the trees put out new leaf, Li Zicheng could conceivably have made good his usurpation. A horrific purge of officialdom was eventually scaled down, the torture sessions to extract confessions and reveal treasure were stopped, and some senior officials were re-employed. Looting continued, but when, a month after the capture of the city, there came news of a loyalist army preparing to attack from the east, Li Zicheng was still able to extricate the bulk of his forces for a pre-emptive strike against this new threat.

The decisive battle took place on 26 May (1644) near Shanhaiguan. About 300 kilometres (185 miles) from Beijing, Shanhaiguan is the massive gateway in the Great Wall nearest to the sea and commanding the eastward approaches from Liaodong. Before the fall of Beijing, Wu Sangui, Liaodong's senior Ming general, had been withdrawn there to keep the Jurchen-Manchu forces out; but so dire was the news now coming from Beijing, including word of his own family's detention by Li Zicheng's rebels, that General Wu invited the Jurchen-Manchu in; they were to fight along-side his Ming forces to disperse the rebels, reclaim the capital, restore order and bury the deceased emperor.

It was to pre-empt such a hostile conjunction that Li Zicheng had hurriedly marched out of Beijing; and he did indeed reach Shanhaiguan before the arrival of the main Jurchen army. But he had underestimated General Wu Sangui. At the head of his Ming troops, and with or without decisive help from the first Jurchen contingents – this is another set of events about which the historian 'can decide for himself' – General Wu prevailed. Thus the first major battle in defence of the Great Wall was fought not against alien attackers from without but against Chinese attackers from within. And when the Manchu-Jurchen arrived in force, they passed through the Shanhaiguan unopposed, in fact keenly welcomed.

Li Zicheng, after defeat at Shanhaiguan, fell back on Beijing. In what was almost an afterthought, he stayed there just long enough to declare himself emperor and torch the palace; then he fled west with what remained of his army. Wu Sangui went after him. As a native of Liaodong himself, General Wu knew and respected the Jurchen; with the death of the Ming emperor and with an imperial heir nowhere to be found, he was ready to serve the newcomers as loyally as were other senior figures, including some of his own family, who had already changed sides – and as countless more soon would. Hence his departure from the scene with orders to pursue and annihilate the rebels; and hence, on 5 June, the Jurchen-Manchu host rode alone and unannounced into the still-smouldering Forbidden City. When their leader announced that they had come to avenge the Ming, a mystified crowd listened in fear and silence. Some supposed the speaker must be the descendant of a child fathered by the *Ming* Zhengtong emperor while he was in Mongol captivity following the Tumu Incident; few realised they were witnessing a transfer of the Mandate. Though all Chinese dynasties might reasonably be described as conquest dynasties, none had conquered less of China before gaining the throne than the Manchus.

FROM JURCHEN TO MANCHU

Beijing's new rulers pose something of an enigma. In terms of numbers, economic resources, military technology and governmental experience, the Jurchen of the early seventeenth century appear so disadvantaged as to make their chances of conquering all China seem quixotic. Yet much the same might have been said of the Khitan and Mongols when first they

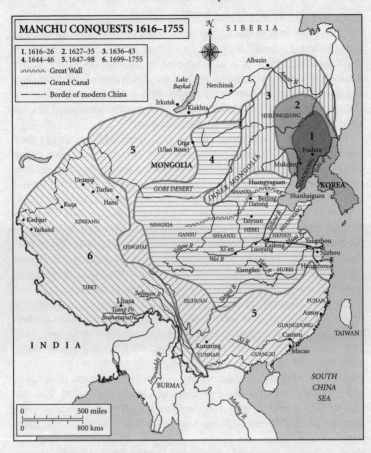

MANCHU CONQUESTS 1616–1755

1. 1616–26   2. 1627–35   3. 1636–43
4. 1644–46   5. 1647–98   6. 1699–1755

~~~~~ Great Wall
········ Grand Canal
— · — Border of modern China

SIBERIA

N

Albazin

Lake Baykal   Nerchinsk

Irkutsk   Kiakhta

Urga (Ulan Bator)

MONGOLIA

Urumqi   Turfan
Kuqa   Hami

Kashgar   XINJIANG
Yarkand

GOBI DESERT

INNER MONGOLIA

HEILONGJIANG

Fushan
Mukden

KOREA

Huangyaguan
SHANXI   Beijing   Shanhaiguan
Datong

SHANDONG

NINGXIA   Taiyuan
HEBEI

GANSU   SHAANXI   HENAN
Kaifeng
QINGHAI   Xi'an   Luoyang
Wei R   Yangzhou
Xiangfan   HUBEI   Suzhou
Hangzhou

TIBET

Lhasa
Tsang Po
Brahmaputra

SICHUAN

FUJIAN
Amoy

GUANGDONG
Canton   TAIWAN

Kunming   GUANGXI   Macao
YUNNAN

INDIA

BURMA

Irrawaddy R
Salween R
Mekong R
Xi R

SOUTH CHINA SEA

0   500 miles
0   800 kms

invaded. Under their own Jin dynasty, the Jurchen had already had one
bite at the cherry, evicting the Khitan Liao and then the Northern Song
from northern China in the twelfth century before themselves succumbing
to Mongol conquest in the thirteenth. Some Jurchen had then served under
the Mongols, others had trickled back to their homeland, yet others had
never left it. They had remained a restless presence in the far north-east,
whether within the Yuan empire or later as tributaries of the Ming.

Sin Chung-il, a Korean emissary who in 1595 had visited the Jurchen
living north-west of the Yalu River, found a people heavily influenced by
their exposure to both Han and Mongol culture. The educated spoke some

Chinese as well as their native Tungusic tongue. They used the Mongol script in preference to the Khitan-based script developed by the Jin, and they combined a regard for Confucian values with respect for the devotional Buddhism of Tibet as lately adopted by the Mongols. Above all they retained an abiding attachment to their own traditions of divination and sacrifice; ancestors and deities were regularly consulted through a male or female 'shaman', the term itself being 'the only commonly used English word that is a loan from [the Jurchen] language'.[6]

Yet they lived in a manner that was little removed from that of their pre-Jin ancestors. Dispersed, along with their livestock, in fortified village settlements, they were grouped under hereditary leaders called *beile*. These chiefs lorded it over their dependants, distributed land, slaves, brides and arms among them, and often fought with one another. Defensive walls were of mud and wattle with stone foundations; houses were of timber or brick and might be half buried in the ground, a Jurchen concession to the harsh climate of the north-east. It could indeed be cold. The visit of the Korean Sin Chung-il coincided with midwinter, which might explain his taking notice of the Jurchen propensity for strong liquor, impromptu wrestling and vigorous dances. The fields, fallow at the time, produced wheat and millet, the stables were well stocked with horses, and from the forests and uplands came pelts, pine nuts and ginseng root. The Jurchen of the Yalu and Liao basins harvested, herded, hunted and foraged. They were not even semi-nomadic, though other 'wild' Jurchen farther north were, and likewise the Mongols of the region.

It was a surprisingly cosmopolitan society with immigrants from Korea and especially from the Ming province of Liaodong mingling with the various Jurchen and Mongol clans. Sin Chung-il's Jurchen host, an impressive figure called Nurhaci (Nurgaci, r. 1616–26) who held court in robes trimmed with sable, was already engaged in welding these disparate elements into an organised and effective fighting force. All were encouraged to wear leather tunics and adopt the shaven fore-crown and long queue of the Jurchen (the resemblance to indigenous Americans being not perhaps incidental in that the peoples of the Aleutian islands and Alaska also spoke a Tungusic language). Moreover Nurhaci's forces rode beneath distinctive flags described by Sin Chung-il as being either yellow, white, red, blue or black. Denoting the troops enrolled under each colour, these 'Banners', reduced to four, then expanded to eight, and eventually, identified with specific ethno-social groups, formed the basic military units into which the people of the north-east, whether Jurchen, Mongol or Han, were being steadily absorbed as Nurhaci extended his sway. As Bannermen

they would constitute the Manchu striking force in China and the privileged backbone of Manchu society throughout the seventeenth and eighteenth centuries.

Nurhaci attracted adherents by the judicious distribution of lands,
women, slaves and prestigious merchandise, while forcefully overcoming
potential rivals in order to obtain these assets. In 1606 a local Mongol
confederation acknowledged him as their leader, and in 1616 he had himself
enthroned as the Jurchen emperor, reviving for this purpose the dynastic
title of Jin. He and his successor are thus sometimes known as the 'Latter
Jin' – a rather feeble attempt to distinguish them from the 'Later Jin' of
the Five Dynasties period. Meanwhile Nurhaci advanced his capital steadily
westward, taking the town of Fushun in 1618 and the city of Shenyang
(renamed Mukden), capital of the Ming province of Liaodong, in 1621. As
the Jurchen pushed west, hostilities with the Ming developed spontaneously over matters of migration and trade; but they took on a new
dimension when in Shenyang Nurhaci began laying out a palace complex
of unmistakably imperial proportions and referring to the Ming as 'the
southern dynasty', his own Latter Jin being 'the northern dynasty'. This
recalled the thirteenth-century controversy between the Jin and the Song
about the duplication of the Mandate and was ill received in Beijing. Yet
the Ming 'did not deny the historical link . . .; on the contrary they dese-
crated the imperial Jin tombs at Fangshan, near Beijing, "to celebrate it"'.[7]

Nurhaci died in 1626. He was succeeded by a son, Hong Taiji (or
Abahai/Abatai, r. 1626–43), who so transformed Jurchen prospects as to
deserve recognition as co-founder of the dynasty. Campaigning in Mongolia
and Korea, as well as north to the Amur in what is now Heilongjiang
province and west to the outskirts of Beijing, the Banners under Hong
Taiji's direction became acquainted with other modes of warfare, including
artillery and siegecraft. Large cities such as Datong were invested, and in
repeatedly passing back and forth through the undermanned Great Wall,
the Banners exposed the futility of a static, if monumental, defence. In
Mongolia a descendant of Khubilai Khan's Yuan dynasty was overthrown,
allowing Hong Taiji to claim the title of the Mongols' Great Khan, plus a
Mongol bride, a vast Mongol following and much of what is now Inner
Mongolia. More Banner recruits came from among the 'wild Jurchen' of
the far north, from Korea and from Ming China; as the number of
Bannermen grew to six figures, their purely Jurchen component shrank
from a half to a quarter.

Hong Taiji also began employing Han bureaucrats, selected by examination, to staff an administrative service. An external affairs bureau was

set up, too; initially concerned with Jurchen–Mongol relations, the bureau was soon reorganised and renamed to handle all 'colonial' relations, including the close ties lately established between the Mongols and the Tibetan religious establishment, especially its Dalai Lama (of whom more later). In 1636 Hong Taiji put the seal on all these developments by discarding the terms 'Jurchen' and 'Jin'. Both were too freighted with contentious baggage and irredentist sentiment. In the past neither Jurchen nor Jin had achieved the universal dominion to which their descendants were now aspiring; in Chinese eyes, 'Jurchen' remained a term of disparagement and 'Jin' a dynasty of questionable legitimacy. A newer, more inclusive orientation was needed: the Bannermen, and by extension the regime, were henceforth to be known as 'Manchu', and the dynasty as 'Qing'.

'Qing', meaning 'pure', was extracted from the same textual pool of prestigious aspirational titles as Yuan ('original') and Ming ('brilliant'). It transcended the regional associations of most other dynastic names and positioned its claimants in line to the succession of legitimate all-China dynasties. 'Manchu' is more problematic. Freely used, and by foreigners often confused with Tatar/Tartar and Mongol, the word was soon applied to the dynasty as well as the people and then to the northeastern region from which both originated: hence the word *manchuguo/manchu-kuo/* 'Manchuria', a term that the Chinese have since found objectionable, partly because the Japanese adopted it as the name for their twentieth-century puppet state in that region and partly because it implies a distinct status for somewhere that the Chinese now consider as just north-east China and no more distinct than, say, south-east China. The origin of the word is not clear. Like Aisin Gioro, the lineage to which the Manchu imperial clan was supposed to belong, it seems to have been extracted from Jurchen genealogy. Equipping an imperial dynasty with an illustrious and Heaven-favoured pedigree was standard procedure for the Ministry of Rites and would be championed by the Qing themselves when they became hostages to the conceits of their own imperial mythology in the eighteenth century.

Laden with universalist claims – as Han emperor, Mongol Great Khan and, thanks to the Dalai Lama, Buddhist *cakravartin* and Bodhisattva – Hong Taiji dispensed with a Jurchen tradition whereby rulership was sometimes shared with brothers or sons; such collegial habits obviously had no place in an autocrat's arsenal. In the event of the ruler being a minor, however, this collaborative tradition could be advantageous. While not precluding factional struggles, it encouraged a cohesion and continuity of purpose that had eluded the eunuch-run administrations and dowager-led cliques of imperial regencies in the past. In fact, just such a test had arisen in 1643; for on the eve of the 'great enterprise' – as the Manchu termed their move into China proper – Hong Taiji had died, leaving as successor a five-year-old son known as the Shunzhi emperor (r. 1644–61).

Thus in June 1644 the Manchu leader whose identity so mystified the Beijing populace, and who then confidently moved into the imperial palace, was not in fact an imperial claimant but Prince Dorgon, one of deceased Hong Taiji's many brothers who was acting as regent. The Shunzhi emperor would not assume the reins of government until 1652, when he was fourteen, and would die eight years later, leaving the succession to yet another minor. There then followed a second regency before this new minor came of age in 1669 as the long-lasting Kangxi emperor (r. 1661–1722). By then the 'great enterprise' had been substantially realised and resistance to Qing rule lingered on only in out-of-the-way places such as Yunnan and Taiwan. In effect the Manchu/Qing conquest of China was largely realised without the benefit of an active emperor and by a coterie of Jurchen-Manchu commanders, mostly sons and grandsons of Nurhaci, assisted – and often hampered – by various ex-Ming generals and ex-rebel warlords.

But if the Qing advance was therefore occasionally uncoordinated, this was as nothing compared to the chaotic state of those who would resist it, whether Ming loyalists, rebels or any of a host of other special interest groups. As already noted, conditions in the Jiangnan region at the time could hardly have been less conducive to concerted resistance, with intellectual ferment, natural disasters, economic meltdown, industrial unrest, widespread brigandage and piracy, unruly militias and rabid tax-collectors all conspiring to shatter the social fabric. The same was true of the northwest, to where the rebel Li Zicheng had withdrawn, of Sichuan, where another rebel army was causing havoc, of Henan/Anhui/Jiangsu, where the Grand Canal was out of action, and of the far south, where trade was at a standstill.

Basically the Manchu Banners and their ex-Ming affiliates, like General Wu Sangui, made good progress in the first year (1644/45). They drove Li Zicheng's rebel forces out of the north-west, secured Shandong and the Yellow River basin, and pushed south along the line of the Grand Canal to the city of Yangzhou (near the canal's junction with the Yangzi). There the conciliatory policy of the Manchus – amnesties, reinstatements in office, abolition of the most extortionate taxes, remissions of others – won over some local power-brokers but failed to entice defenders professing loyalty to a makeshift Ming regime that had just been set up in Nanjing.

This Nanjing administration, the first of four short-lived regimes under 'Southern Ming' pretenders, was as cash-strapped and faction-ridden as its Beijing predecessor; but in Shi Kefa, who commanded at Yangzhou, it boasted a military leader of unimpeachable character and the loftiest principles. Such attributes should have guaranteed success as well as immortality, yet they availed the Ming defence not at all. Undermined by Nanjing's dithering and more desertions, Yangzhou soon fell to the Manchus. Shi Kefa died in the carnage, the most elegant of port cities was comprehensively sacked, and the entire populace massacred or enslaved. Three weeks later, without a fight, Nanjing itself surrendered, and the first of the four 'Southern Ming' regimes promptly collapsed. From a Manchu point of view, Yangzhou's salutary fate had served its purpose of deterring opposition. On the other hand, the ten-day slaughter, 'one of the most infamous massacres in Chinese history', and especially the fate of Yangzhou's womenfolk, all of which was chronicled in explicit detail, would top every subsequent indictment of Manchu excesses; and in the heroic figure of Shi Kefa, the Ming resistance – not to mention a patriotic posterity transfixed by the fate of China's last indigenous dynasty – would recognise its first great martyr.[8]

The fall of Yangzhou, and then Nanjing, in June 1645 seemed to bode well for a speedy conclusion to the Manchu conquest. Unfortunately, just days later, Regent Dorgon and his associates issued a directive so gratuitously provocative that it would prolong hostilities for decades. Included in a package of otherwise welcome pronouncements, this directive ordered all males to demonstrate their allegiance to the Qing dynasty by adopting the Manchu dress and hairstyle. They had ten days to comply, after which any head with an unshaven pate (costume could too easily be improvised and the queue would obviously take time to grow) would be forfeited.

An identical directive had been issued after the capture of Beijing, then swiftly retracted in the face of bitter protest; the Manchus can have been in no doubt as to the probable reaction. But like other non-Han peoples, they set great store by physical conformity. A sign of submission and a useful means of distinguishing friend from foe in chaotic times, the shaven pate and the uncut queue were also seen as a concesssion: ex-subjects of the Ming were being invited to identify with the new regime and join it as participants in the 'great enterprise'. Much stress had already been laid on this collaborative aspect of Manchu rule. The Banners by now included far more Han Chinese, both long-serving farmer-soldiers from Liaodong and more recent recruits from south of the Great Wall, than native Jurchen and Mongols. Schools were being re-established, examinations rescheduled, and the whole paraphernalia of Han bureaucracy reinstated. The Kangxi emperor would make accommodation with his Han subjects the keystone of his long reign. 'We are of one family,' declared the 'clothes and hair' directive. 'The emperor is like the father, the people like his sons. Father and sons being of the same body, how can they be different?'[9]

But to a proud people whose sense of cultural distinction vis-à-vis their neighbours was indebted to just such differences, and who were anyway allergic to all forms of disfigurement that might prejudice posthumous acceptance by their ancestors, the haircutting order was anathema. Compliance was a matter of the most abject shame, and for a Confucianist shame remained the ineluctable sanction. Many preferred suicide; others chose a life of exile in the hills or seclusion in a monastery (Buddhist monks, shaven-headed anyway, were excused the queue); still others were driven to gestures of defiance that were demonstrably futile. The directive did not inspire greater unity of purpose, only a wider spectrum of resistance. Those social elements that now entered the fray have been usefully listed by one scholar as:

> ... incumbent or retired Ming civil and military officials, members of the district yamen [administrative offices] or constabulary staffs, Ming imperial clansmen, local landowners and merchants, leaders of political and literary societies, regular Ming military units, local sea and land militia, freelance military experts, armed guards from private estates, peasant self-defense corps, martial monks, underground gangs, secret societies, tenant and 'slave' insurrectionary forces, and pirate and bandit groups.[10]

The fighting flared again and dragged on. More cities shared the fate of Yangzhou, more makeshift Ming regimes that of Nanjing. Pacified areas broke out into revolt a second time, unpacified areas aspired to forms of local autonomy. Both sides were repeatedly betrayed by supposed allies. Many Ming loyalists, appalled by the chaos or revolted by their supporters, construed endorsement of the Qing as the ultimate act of sacrifice. Instances of spectacular defiance would be cherished and celebrated; but they were vitiated by a brutality that was by no means the monopoly of the Manchu Banners.

A more intriguing feature of the fighting was the widespread use of firearms. The war, in fact, was the first on Chinese soil in which guns look to have played a decisive part. Cannon bombardments feature in nearly all contemporary accounts of the fighting, and muskets receive frequent mention, though the crossbow remained commoner. A survivor of

Yangzhou – one of the very few – recalled that the defence of the city had been prejudiced by the discovery that the top of the city walls was too narrow for ordnance. 'To provide more room for mounting the cannons', therefore, the admirable Shi Kefa had ordered the construction of supplementary platforms supported in part by the wall, in part by the roofs of the houses abutting the wall from behind. Unfortunately the carpentry was still incomplete when the Bannermen stormed the defences. Advancing under cover of heavy fire, plus the screening afforded by roofed and wheeled siege engines (like aircraft boarding steps), the Bannermen came pouring over the parapets. The defenders had no choice but to flee by way of the nearly-ready gun platforms, which collapsed under their weight. 'People fell like leaves, eight or nine of every ten being killed.' Others reached the rooftops, only to crash through them too, 'startling the inhabitants out of their wits; [and] soon every room in those homes, from the outer reception halls to the inner apartments, was totally filled with soldiers and people who'd been on the wall'.[11]

Though Yangzhou's walls were clearly not designed for it, artillery was no novelty. Joseph Needham dates the first Chinese ordnance to around 1250, and there is a cannon of sorts in Beijing's National History Museum with a date equivalent to 1332. Yet according to the Standard History of the Ming, the first serviceable guns were acquired in 1410 in the course of the *Ming* Yongle emperor's long and otherwise unrewarding vendetta against the Vietnamese; probably they were transported back to Nanjing aboard one of Zheng He's great ships. In China, as in the contemporary Middle East and Europe, developments in the casting and boring of barrels and in formulation of the explosive charge took time. China's use of gunpowder from at least the ninth century had provided the wider world with the key component; but the Ottomans and Europeans had since been more successful in harnessing saltpetre's explosive potential for ballistic purposes. As Matteo Ricci noted, in 1600 the Chinese still favoured gunpowder, 'not so much for their arquebuses, of which they have few, nor for bombards and artillery which are also in short supply, but for their firework displays . . . that none of us ever saw without amazement'.[12]

Arquebuses (long-barrelled matchlocks supported on a swivelling tripod), bombards (basic muzzle-loading cannon) and culverins (which could be either) had comprised the arsenal of the first Portuguese vessels to reach east Asia in 1517–20. The 'breech-loading culverins presented at the Ming court in 1522' were a gift from the Portuguese; and Portuguese arquebuses were acquired in the 1540s by the Japanese, who copied and greatly improved them.[13] The China coast acquired them from Japanese pirates, and they were being manufactured in Zhejiang by the 1560s. To defeat the pirates, some of whom had reached Nanjing in 1555/56, Yu Dayou, one of the Wanli emperor's commanders, had urged equipping all ships with cannon, declaring: 'In sea battle, there is no trick: the side that has more ships defeats the side that has fewer, the side that has more guns defeats the side that has less.'[14] In respect of firearms – as in other scientific fields such as astronomy, cartography, mathematics and medicine – Chinese interest in foreign technology stemmed from long familiarity with the basic principles, not ignorance of them; and if adoption was sometimes slow and ineffectual, the blame lay in official ambivalence rather than with military men like Yu Dayou.

From pirate patrol in Zhejiang, a protégé of Yu Dayou's called Qi Jiguang had been transferred to the Great Wall north of Beijing. There, from 1568 to 1582, he had pioneered field artillery using the guns known as *folangji* (i.e. *farangji*, 'Frankish' or 'foreign'). 'More large calibre rifles than cannon', they were mounted on mule carts, usually two to a cart. The carts had side-screens with apertures; and minus their mules, they could be arranged end to end to form a continuous stockade. Like the chariots of the 'Warring States' period, each gun-cart was accompanied by infantry – ten men to work the guns and another ten, four of them equipped with muskets, to 'form an assault team round the wagon'.[15] Clearly Qi Jiguang had given these arrangements much thought, though to what extent they were actually tested he does not say.

Nor is he very informative about the puzzling relationship between artillery and the wall itself. He does mention some colossal cannon that might have been used on the wall; one such piece, cast in bronze and inscribed as 'made by the Armaments Bureau in [1574]', has since been unearthed near Huangyaguan, a gateway on the Beijing–Chengde road. Certainly Qi Jiguang's period of service coincided with what Waldron calls 'the hey-day of wall-building'; indeed, literary sources, supported by inscriptions, credit Qi Jiguang with building 1,200 watchtowers and undertaking 'a major reconstruction' of the whole section from Beijing to Shanhaiguan.[16] But this rebuilding of the Great Wall (as it survives today) is nowhere specifically linked to the new ordnance. Nor is it clear whether the wall would have been intended primarily as a platform and highway on which to deploy guns, or as a more solid defence against them – or both. An illustration of the defence of Liaoyang (in Liaodong) in the 1620s shows *folangji* ranged outside the walls. Assuming the scale is accurate, the wall-top walkway there, as at Yangzhou, was clearly too narrow for them. The rebuilding of the Great Wall and the addition of so many towers may well have been prompted by the proportions of the new guns and their field-of-fire requirements.

Beyond the wall the Jurchen-Manchu had also been quick to latch on to the importance of guns. Ming cannon and *folangji* had been captured by Nurhaci, who had then stipulated that half of all new Banner recruits from Liaodong be equipped with muskets or trained in cannon use. These Han troops from Liaodong, whether defectors or captives, were further encouraged by Hong Taiji to specialise in the manufacture and management of artillery. Meanwhile the Ming court had acquired, through Ricci's associates, both Portuguese armourers and some of the large-bore cannon, 6 metres (20 feet) long and weighing 1,800 kilograms (1.76 tons), known as *hongyi*, which were being cast in Macao. Again the Manchus responded, with Hong Taiji establishing a manufactory for *hongyi* and other large cannon at Jinzhou (west of the Liao river). In what was becoming an arms race, both Ming and Manchu were producing guns in quantity by the 1630s. The Manchu became adept at siegecraft and learned to coordinate the mobility of cavalry with the firepower of artillery. The Ming obtained the services of the Jesuit Father Adam Schall von Bell, whose foundry in Beijing is said to have produced some five hundred cannon of a lighter, more manageable design during the months immediately preceding the city's capitulation to Li Zicheng and then Regent Dorgon.

This trend towards lighter guns that were easier to transport, quicker to load and probably more accurate looks to have been crucial to the success of the Manchu Banners in suppressing Ming resistance, especially in waterlogged Jiangnan and Sichuan and throughout the hilly regions of the south and south-west. In such terrain the range and firepower of artillery offset that disadvantage under which cavalry-based armies from the north had traditionally laboured. Hilltop redoubts that no horse could reach could be reduced by field guns, and likewise towns and villages islanded in flooded rice paddies. Major cities being almost invariably sited on rivers, they were no less vulnerable to naval bombardment.

Just as the Ming had obtained the cannon-casting services of Father Schall, so, when Schall died in 1665, the Manchus retained in Beijing another Jesuit, the Belgian Father Ferdinand Verbiest. Verbiest, like Schall, first won fame as an astronomer and instrument-maker and became one of the Kangxi emperor's closest advisers. Accompanying him on several imperial tours, he was one of the first Europeans to see something of the reconstructed sections of the Great Wall. They exceeded his wildest expectations, and accepting the idea that the wall was a continuous construction thousands of kilometres long and all of it equally well appointed, Verbiest pronounced it 'prodigious'. 'The seven wonders of the world put together are not comparable to this work,' he ventured, so drawing an anachronistic comparison that has been echoed by just about every wall-visiting foreigner ever since.[17]

Verbiest's first cannon were produced in the 1670s specifically for hill warfare. They were deployed in the final stage of the Manchu conquest and were soon followed by others. 'Over 500 out of a total of about 900 artillery pieces made during the Kangxi reign (1661–1722) were cast under [Verbiest's] direction or on the basis of his designs.'[18] Besides field guns effective over a range of 300 metres (330 yards), they included cannon weighing up to 3.5 tonnes (3.43 tons) that fired cannonballs as heavy as 10 kilograms (22 pounds). With such a formidable arsenal, as well as the best cavalry in Asia and almost unlimited infantry, the Qing commanded a military machine capable of suppressing more than internal opposition.

MUCH IN DEMAND

The Qing dynasty's famous 'Three Emperors' – those of the Kangxi (1661–1722), Yongzhen (1723–35) and Qianlong (1723–95) reign periods – monopolised the throne until the dawn of the nineteenth century. Capable, generally conscientious and occasionally capricious, they gave the empire unprecedented continuity and comparative stability. During the same period, monarchies elsewhere fared indifferently: thirteen Mughal emperors came and went as India succumbed to foreign conquest; seven British sovereigns, three being Georges, fretted over the constraints of constitutional monarchy; and five French kings, all called Louis, eked out their *ancien régime* until overwhelmed by the revolution. Qing China, like Romanov Russia, bucked the trend. Once established, its 'Three Emperors' ruled virtually unchallenged over much the most populous and sophisticated society in the world. Its culture, insofar as foreigners understood it, was almost universally admired and its products proudly displayed. A craze for chinoiserie was sweeping the salons of Europe; 'Shantung' (Shandong) was best known as a silk, 'Nankeen' (Nanjing) as a cotton; blue-and-white 'chin-ware' from Jingdezhen might share a shelf – in Limoges, say, or Limerick – with a caddy of the loose tea from Fujian in which it had originally been packed for shipping.

In Europe an Age of Enlightenment that could have scorned Neo-Confucian navel-gazing celebrated it. The philosopher Leibniz pored over the *Book of Changes* and 'had no trouble construing a theist's sense of divinity in Zhu Xi's concept of *li*.[19] Voltaire, likewise, exulted over a society that, innocent of church or clergy, yet cherished moral values. China's 'constitution' he ranked 'the best in the world'; and he wrote poems in honour of the Qianlong emperor. Dr Johnson merely urged a doubtful Boswell to visit the Great Wall; even if he never came back, future Boswells would be famed as 'the children of a man who had gone to view the wall of China', declared the doctor.[20]

Those who did actually visit the country marvelled at the empire's prosperity and invariably praised its orderly government and its industrious and law-abiding people. Some, with relief, even noted its official reluctance to compete for overseas trade and a share of the world's natural resources. Only its landlocked neighbours quailed at the prospect of such a productive society being at the disposal of what was still an Inner Asian regime with continental ambitions.

Ironically, no sooner had the Great Wall (as we know it) been built than it appeared redundant. Instead of defining and defending the empire, which was presumed to have been the Ming intention, it now bisected it. Long before 1644, when the Manchu-Jurchen had ridden through Shanhaiguan at Wu Sangui's invitation, the extramural lands of Manchuria and Inner Mongolia had been integral to the Manchu empire. They remained so after the conquest of China, increasing the Celestial Empire's stature by about ten degrees of latitude, or 1,000 kilometres (620 miles). The wall, straggling across what was now the Qing midriff, already had the look more of an internal folly than a frontier fortification.

Conversely, though, and no less plausibly, the wall could be seen as poised to come into its own. Even Ming territory had not stopped at the wall; the Ming province of Liaodong, for instance, had stretched for hundreds of kilometres beyond the wall – until, that is, Nurhaci began nibbling away at it. The wall provided a means of communication and supply, and like earlier walls had a purpose other than defence. It may not, then, as widely proposed, furnish overwhelming testimony to the pacific intentions of China's rulers or the reclusive tendencies of China's culture. It may in fact have been designed for precisely the far-flung operations that the Qing, taking advantage of its armouries and granaries and its nexus of interlinked roads and signal towers, were about to launch into the Asian interior.

But first the Qing had to douse the fires of Ming resistance in southern China. In 1651 the last of the four 'Southern Ming' regimes had been flushed from its retreat close to the Vietnamese border in Guangxi. Its Ming pretender, a grandson of the Wanli emperor, fled west to Kunming in

Yunnan, where support was promised from a doubly rebellious army (having first rebelled against the Ming, it now challenged the Qing). To eliminate this pocket of defiance, three Qing expeditions converged on Yunnan in 1658, whereupon the Ming pretender and his allies fought a fierce rearguard action as they withdrew over the Shan hills from the Mekong to the Salween and the Irrawaddy in Burmese territory. In this they traced a trail that neatly anticipated that taken, nearly three centuries later, by General Chiang Kai-shek's Nationalist Kuomintang or KMT (in Pinyin, General Jiang Jieshi's Guomindang or GMD) as they fled before the communists' People's Liberation Army. Half the KMT would hole up in Burma and neighbouring Laos, there to discover a new vocation in narcotics; the other half would descend on the island of Taiwan for an, as yet, indefinite sojourn. In doing so, they too followed a Ming trail; for in 1661 those loyalists who baulked at a Burmese exile had also taken ship across the Taiwan Strait.

Taiwan at the time was as much Dutch as anyone's. Having deprived the Portuguese of their Indonesian spice empire, plus the great port citadel of Malacca, the Vereenigde Oost-Indische Compagnie (the Dutch 'United East Indian Company') was by the 1640s the best represented of the European powers in Eastern waters. But the Compagnie had failed to persuade the Ming of its need for a permanent trading base on the China coast, and it had failed, in 1622, to winkle the Portuguese out of theirs at Macao. Instead Dutch traders had had to make do with an offshore facility, first in the Pescadores Islands between Fujian and Taiwan, and as of 1624 on the south-west coast of Taiwan itself. Taiwan, or Formosa, as the Portuguese had called it, was not at the time a province of China. Sparsely populated by a non-Han and implacably hostile people, and with a climate of equally evil repute, the island had tendered tribute to the Ming but had attracted no more settlement than the neighbouring Ryukyu Islands. This, however, was changing. The enterprising Zheng family of Xiamen (Amoy) in Fujian – part privateers, part Mandarin traders, latterly Ming officials and increasingly coastal overlords – had used the island as an occasional naval base and had encouraged the Dutch settlement there.

The Dutch company had a near-monopoly of the carrying trade of south-east Asia and Japan (from which, for different reasons, both Chinese and Japanese shippers were currently barred). It was a valuable trading partner. But if the Zheng family owed part of its fortune to the Dutch, it owed its status to the Ming. Zheng Chenggong (1624–62), a second-generation scion of the family and better known to many as 'Coxinga' (Koxinga), had been born of a Japanese mother at Hirado, near Nagasaki, where the

Zheng family had maintained an establishment; but he was educated in Nanjing and was there adopted by the first of the 'Southern Ming' pretenders and showered with titles and favours. Meanwhile his father, having held high office under the Ming, had been won over by the Qing. The Zheng clan was worth cultivating; by the 1640s it could call on ships by the thousand and followers by the tens, if not hundreds, of thousands.

When Nanjing fell to the Qing in 1645, Zheng Chenggong returned to Fujian. Taking command of the family navy, he dedicated it to the Ming cause and for a decade lorded it over all the coastal settlements and islands of Guangdong, Fujian and Zhejiang. At sea he proved more than a match for anything the Qing could launch against him; from Hong Kong to Shanghai (in modern terms) the inshore waters constituted a Zheng thalassocracy. Heady with success, in 1659 he sailed into the Yangzi as part of a bold plan to recapture Nanjing for the Ming. It meant confronting the Qing Banners and their cannon on dry land. Zheng Chenggong welcomed the prospect. He allowed the Qing all the time they needed to assemble a formidable army; one great battle was to settle the fate of southern China once and for all. And so it did. Heavily defeated, Zheng Chenggong slipped back downriver, and with his navy still largely intact, sailed home to Fujian.

In 1660 the Qing emperor – it was the short-lived Shunzhi emperor whose coming of age had interrupted the succession of regents – sent a naval force after him. It fared no better than others; Zheng was still invincible at sea. But a new Qing directive designed to cut off Zheng's source of supplies made a greater impact. The entire coastline was declared a no-go zone; all fields and fishing ports, villages and settlements within 50 kilometres (30 miles) of the shore were to be evacuated, the entire population resettled, and all coastal shipping outlawed. The prohibition would lapse within a couple of decades, and whether it really applied to the whole coast 'from Canton [Guangzhou] in the south to the northern coastal region near Beijing' seems doubtful. But as the typically inward-looking ploy of an alien and continental regime, it would be blamed for blunting China's maritime potential as well as causing extensive social disruption. Certainly it affected Fujian; there the coastal strip reportedly reverted to wilderness; all habitations were abandoned; 'even the swallows' nests were empty'.[21]

It was this measure, plus an overland approach by Qing forces, which in 1661 triggered the first great wave of mainland migration to Taiwan. It also determined Zheng Chenggong himself to relocate there. Only the Dutch in their fort on Taiwan stood in the way. Still angling for a Macao-like concession on the mainland, the Dutch company had now allied itself with the Qing; it was therefore obliged to contest the approach of Zheng's armada. There followed an epic battle in the Taiwan Strait which spread to the island itself, then a long siege of Fort Zeelandia, the Dutch citadel. Zheng's forces ultimately triumphed and the Dutch sailed away. To Zheng Chenggong's considerable reputation as the most daring of sea-dogs and the most loyal of Ming supporters was added the accolade, later upgraded to semi-divine status, of being the first patriot to inflict defeat on a European intruder and expel its representatives from what he proudly claimed as Chinese territory.

Zheng Chenggong died the following year. Still in his thirties, he seems to have suffered from a psychological disorder that was exacerbated by disappointment. Withdrawing to Taiwan had been retrograde enough, but it was the news from distant Yunnan which is supposed to have finally shattered his peace of mind. For from there came word that Wu Sangui, the general who fourteen years earlier had routed Li Zicheng at Shanhaiguan and welcomed in the Manchus, had led a Qing expedition into Burma, reached the capital of Ava (near Mandalay), secured the person of the last Ming pretender, and on orders from Beijing had had him strangled. Zheng Chenggong was so convulsed with grief that he could barely dig out a cherished memorial addressed to one of his forebears by the Hongwu emperor. Clasping this keepsake from the first of the Ming, he collapsed, 'and with that the last defender of Brightness [i.e. "Ming"] stopped breathing'.[22]

It was not quite the end of the Zheng saga. Zheng Chenggong's son succeeded to the Taiwanese patrimony and, more merchant prince than Ming loyalist, let alone Chinese patriot, would befriend early traders of England's East India Company. When in 1683 his navy was finally sunk by a Qing armada, the latter was commanded by one of his father's old comrades-in-arms. The defeat of the Zheng meant that Taiwan could at last be incorporated into the empire. With its Han population augmented by further waves of migration following a revolt in 1721, it remained a prefecture attached to Fujian province for a couple of centuries. By the time it was wrested from the Qing in 1898 by the Japanese, temples to Zheng Chenggong abounded there; in fact even the Qing had eventually recognised Zheng as 'a Paragon of Loyalty'. The Japanese had no problem with this. Zheng, after all, had been born near Nagasaki of a Japanese mother; they too revered his memory. Naturally, the KMT Nationalists would hail him as their Taiwan pioneer; naturally the communists would celebrate his achievement in making Taiwan an inalienable part of China; and naturally both would applaud his triumph over the encroaching

Westerners. In death as in life, the rebellious Zheng Chenggong, alias Coxinga, would be much in demand.

The same cannot be said of General Wu Sangui. Though his devotion to the Qing deserved generous recognition, he was ultimately disgraced. The hero of the hour after his Burmese elimination of the last Ming pretender, General Wu had initially been rewarded with almost unlimited authority in Yunnan and Guizhou plus considerable influence in adjacent provinces. Just as Zheng Chenggong had controlled the south-east fringes of the empire on behalf of the Ming, Wu Sangui controlled the south-west fringes for the Qing. He monopolised tax receipts and appointments, maintained a formidable army, opened trade relations with Tibet, developed Yunnan's considerable mineral wealth (especially its copper deposits) and lived in regal style. He, and two other so-called 'feudatories' in Guangdong and Fujian, were effectively draining the empire while they carved out hereditary fiefs for themselves. Yet any attempt to topple them could be expected to re-ignite resistance to the Qing throughout the south.

The Kangxi emperor inherited this dilemma when in 1669 he took over the reins of power. Four years later, overriding the advice of several ministers, he graciously accepted pleas from Wu Sangui and one of the other feudatories that they be allowed to retire from active service. Though an apparently genial response, this was in fact dynamite; for far from actually wishing to retire, the plaintiffs expected the young emperor to refuse their requests and reconfirm their powers, preferably with the option of transferring them to their heirs. Instead they were being dismissed, even disgraced. All three southern 'feudatories' accordingly rose in revolt. By 1674 their armies were converging on the Yangzi; cities were being stormed, pigtails cut; had the feudatories managed to coordinate their movements they might even have severed the south from the north as in the days of the Song. But since all three feudatories had originally defected to the Qing, their calls to now evict the Qing were greeted with suspicion even by Ming loyalists. Wu Sangui declared his own dynasty – it was to be another Zhou – and sustained his defiance until his death in 1678. His rebellious colleagues had by then given up. Only Yunnan held out under the command of his grandson. When in 1683, trapped in Kunming by Qing forces, the grandson took his own life, the revolt was over.

Vastly encouraged by this success and abrim with youthful energy, the Kangxi emperor further strengthened his position among his conquered subjects by reversing some of the blatantly pro-Manchu measures taken by his regent predecessors. Through example and patronage, he also sought to tempt into official employ those scholarly celebrities, mostly from the south, who were still scornful of the Manchus and nostalgic for the Ming. Some were assigned to work on anthologies, dictionaries, gazetteers and other mammoth digests. Their labours foreshadowed the twin pillars of later Qing scholarship – one an enormous encylopedia, 'surely one of the largest books in the history of the world', commissioned by the Kangxi emperor, and the other a comprehensive anthology of all the historical, literary and philosophical works ever written in Chinese that was commissioned by the Qianlong emperor; running to 36,000 manuscript volumes, this last was too vast ever to be printed.[23] Other luminaries were seduced by an invitation-only exam to select a group of scholars to work on the official history of the Ming dynasty. Though some scholars preferred to compile their own histories of the Ming (and especially of its ill-fated 'Southern Ming' successors), and though any scholarship that could be construed as remotely seditious brought draconian punishments, these measures, plus regular recruitment to the civil service, did reassure many in the Han Chinese elite.

ZUNGHARIA, XINJIANG AND TIBET

Meanwhile the Kangxi emperor played to his non-Han constituency of Manchus and Mongols with a personal regimen of archery, hunting and travel, and by addressing far-flung political challenges. The greatest of these was that presented by the rising star of a new confederation of Oyirat (Oirat, Oyirod, etc.) whom the Qing designated as 'Mongols'. Located in the north-west of what is now Outer Mongolia and in neighbouring northern Xinjiang, but with a catchment area for grazing and cereals that was still wider, a section of this confederation, the Zunghar (Dzungar, Junghar), threatened to destabilise and detach those central and eastern Mongols who had thrown in their lot, or might yet, with the Manchus. The Zunghars had emerged as a force to be reckoned with by combining claims to the pan-Mongol legacy of Chinggis Khan with the divinely sanctioned sovereignty and legitimacy extended to them as devotees and patrons by Tibet's spiritual leadership. In fact Galdan, the inspirational khan of the Zunghars (r. 1671–97), had himself studied as a novice in one of Tibet's monasteries. The threat, therefore, though it emanated from the north-west, also affected relations with Tibet and the frontier provinces of Gansu, Qinghai, Sichuan and Yunnan. The Dalai Lama had been implicated in Zunghar expansion from the start. Tibet's relations with Wu Sangui had aroused Qing suspicions in the 1670s; and a Tibetan refusal to cooperate in the suppression of Wu Sangui's Yunnan regime had been deplored. But before engaging this formidable combination, the Kangxi emperor thought it well to secure his north-eastern flank; and that meant addressing the little matter of the Russian empire.

Driven by hopes of gold and, more realistically, by the profits to be made from furs, Russian expansion in Siberia had been as rapacious and rewarding as that of Europe's maritime powers in the Americas and the East. After crossing the Urals in 1579 and disposing of the only organised opposition in Siberia, Muscovite traders with Cossack escorts had pushed east, founding as they went the forts of Tobolsk (1587), Tomsk (1604), Yakutsk (1632), Okhotsk on the Pacific seaboard (1647) and Irkutsk (1651). Mostly the trader-settlers kept north of the steppe. As in North America, the fur trail followed frigid latitudes where the great river systems provided easy paddling, or sledging, interspersed with short portages. But Irkutsk is next to Lake Baykal on the northern edge of Mongolia. Already the Mongols were alert to the Russian newcomers; and so were the Manchus when in the mid-seventeenth century Russian expeditions began appearing in the basin of the Amur River (Heilongjiang) in northern Manchuria. The first clash between Qing and tsarist forces had occurred near the Amur in 1652 at a time when the Qing were disposing of the last of the four 'Southern Ming' regimes. Six years later a Russian force was ejected with heavy losses from Albazin, a settlement north of the Amur. The Russians nevertheless returned and remained thereabouts throughout the 1670s while the Kangxi emperor was distracted by the rebellion of Wu Sangui and the other 'feudatories'.

Misapprehensions on both sides dogged these early Manchu-Russian contacts. The Russians may not have appreciated that Jurchen tribesmen encountered on the Amur were the 'wild' brethren of Beijing's Manchu emperors; and the Manchus seem not at first to have realised that their adversaries in the far north-east were subjects of an empire from which several merchant-diplomats had reached China via more conventional trade routes. A Russian mission of 1618 to the Ming court had in fact pipped the Portuguese and the Dutch to become the first ever from a European power to reach Beijing and return safely. Unfortunately it took no Chinese interpreter back with it; a letter from the Wanli emperor inviting further 'tribute' missions thus languished unread for nearly sixty years. Other Russian missions of a more commercial character in the 1650s and '60s had established that China offered an excellent market for furs. The potential of trading furs for silks, silver and especially food grains (in which Siberia was chronically deficient) excited the Russians.

The Manchu Qing, while exercised over Russian encroachment on their north-eastern border, were increasingly concerned about Russian support, supplies and sanctuary being extended to Galdan's Zunghar Mongols. Once the Qing grasped that trade was the Russian priority, the basis for an agreement began to emerge. Another scuffle over the remote outpost of Albazin in the mid-1680s brought matters to a head, and in 1689 drew delegations from both sides to Nerchinsk on the Shilka tributary of the Amur. The Qing delegation included two Jesuits, Verbiest's successors in Beijing, and the Russian delegation a classically educated Pole. Latin thus served as the common language for the negotiations and for the definitive version of the Nerchinsk Treaty. Its use may, though, have had as much to do with protocol as comprehension. Manchu, Mongol, Chinese and Russian versions of the treaty, each agreeable to those who could read them, were also produced; but the priority given to Latin, a neutral and, to most of the delegates, incomprehensible language, meant that the Russian insistence on equality of status and the Qing refusal to concede it could be buried in devices like the ablative absolute. If, as sometimes contended, the Treaty of Nerchinsk should be regarded as the first of imperial China's 'unequal treaties', that was not how the signatories read it, nor were the Chinese disadvantaged by it.

For China the treaty was nevertheless an important first. Since it implicitly acknowledged the existence of another sovereign state – so contradicting the traditional concept of the universal Mandate that underlay all those peace-through-kinship and trade-as-tribute agreements – the act of signature certainly constituted 'the most significant Qing concession'.[24] Other provisions concerning trade missions, boundary demarcation, the surrender of one another's fugitives and an implied neutrality in respect of one another's internal affairs benefited both parties. The Russians relinquished claims to the Amur in return for commercial access to the Qing empire; the Qing got a secure frontier and a neutral neighbour. Further adjustments, especially to the size and frequency of Russian trade missions and the alignment of the Russo-Mongolian border, necessitated subsequent protocols and then a new treaty, signed at Kiakhta in 1727/28. Additionally a Russian Orthodox church was to be built in Beijing and a language school established there for Russians to learn Chinese. It says much for the pragmatic approach of both sides that potentially explosive issues, such as obeisance to the emperor and diplomatic gifts being construed as tributary offerings, were never allowed to torpedo negotiations. This was in marked contrast to the acrimony and hostility these things generated among the powers seeking maritime trade with China. When in the 1950s fraternal relations between the USSR and the

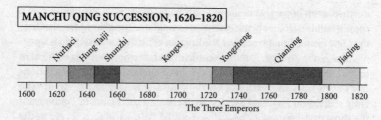

MANCHU QING SUCCESSION, 1620–1820

Nurhaci · Hung Taiji · Shunzhi · Kangxi · Yongzheng · Qianlong · Jiaqing

1600 1620 1640 1660 1680 1700 1720 1740 1760 1780 1800 1820

The Three Emperors

People's Republic of China were at their closest, references to the harmonious accords of this earlier era of Sino-Russian intercourse were not misplaced.

With the northern border secured, the Kangxi emperor could pursue his vendetta against Galdan and the Zunghar Mongols. It brought out both the best and the worst in him. Thanks mainly to the survival of his letters, many of them written in the course of operations against the Zunghars, more is known about the character of the Kangxi emperor than any previous ruler of China. He is revealed as a sympathetic figure who would surely have enjoyed a favourable press without the later official eulogies to his all-conquering exploits. Spirited, decisive, insatiably inquisitive and devoted to his growing family, he was also genuinely concerned for the welfare of his troops. He took a lively interest in practically everything that came to his attention. He was especially passionate about hunting, some letters reading more like entries in a game-book. Indeed, Galdan is identified as his personal prey, his prize quarry; he would track him, it seemed, to the ends of the earth. Hunting him and his successors became an obsession, pursued regardless of cost, sometimes of reason, and to the detriment of regional stability. Like *Han* Wudi or *Tang* Taizong, the Kangxi emperor knew not when to stop; and since he was mostly successful, he set standards of intervention in Inner Asia that his Qing successors would feel obliged to follow.

From 1690 to 1760 the 'Three Emperors' conducted against the Zunghar Mongols a devastatingly long, if intermittent, war of attrition. It was a conflict of many phases and highly complex relationships involving not only numerous Mongol confederations but most of Inner Asia's other peoples. The size of Qing territory would be doubled as a result, and something approximating the configuration of China today would emerge. Invading western Mongolia and northern Xinjiang, then Tibet, Qinghai, eastern Kazakhstan and southern Xinjiang – all of them more than once – was a logistical triumph in itself. It meant coordinating and supplying, over several thousand kilometres of the harshest terrain imaginable, a host of irregular allies as well as large armies composed of the polyglot Banners. Some armies marched directly from Hebei and Shanxi through Inner Mongolia, others were launched across the Gobi from the opposite end of the Great Wall in Ningxia and Gansu and from beyond it in Hami. Forts had to be built, garrisons established where no imperial troops had been since the days of the Tang and the Empress Wu, and interminable caravans of supplies and feedstuffs organised.

The object was ever to ensnare the Zunghars, bring them to battle, and so capture their elusive leaders and transport them, dead or alive, to Beijing. They would be ceremonially executed by slicing, followed by the pulverisation of their bones – a punishment designed less to fit the crime than to serve the purpose of imperial ritual by eradicating all trace of the criminal's existence. 'Exterminate' was the constant Qing refrain, at first in respect of the Zunghar leaders, then of the entire people when in the 1750s the Qianlong emperor sought what one authority does not hesitate to call 'the final solution'.

'Gunpowder is the key to exterminating Galdan,' declared the Kangxi emperor in the course of the great campaign of 1696/97 that he himself accompanied. He encumbered his troops with a corps of cannon-bearing camels – useful against recalcitrant cities but of largely psychological value against nomadic pastoralists. The steppe was set ablaze to deprive the Zunghars of grazing, livestock by the million were sequestered; imported diseases, especially smallpox to which the Inner Asian peoples had little resistance, proved the most lethal allies; overkill became official Qing policy. When in late 1759 the Qianlong emperor finally declared victory, Zungharia (western Mongolia, the northern Urumqi area of Xinjiang and the neighbouring district of Kazakhstan) was almost deserted. Of the 600,000 Zunghars, it was reported that 40 per cent had died of smallpox, 30 per cent had been killed by the Qing armies and 20 per cent had fled across the Russian, Kazakh and Kyrghyz frontiers. 'Zungharia was left as a blank social space, to be filled by a state-sponsored settlement movement of millions of Han Chinese peasants, Manchu Bannermen, Turkestani oasis settlers, Hui [Chinese Muslims] and others.'[25]

Tibet and southern Xinjiang (comprising the oasis-cities south of the Tian Shan) were undoubtedly destabilised by the conflict. Whether they were dragged into it, or whether they actively sought advantage from it, is a matter of opinion. In respect of Xinjiang the Qianlong emperor became acutely conscious of the costs involved and of the criticism that such far-flung adventures attracted. On the other hand, he was ever hopeful of an easily defensible frontier and mindful of the exploits not only of the Han and Tang dynasties but of Chinggis Khan and his successors. For a Manchu, as for a Mongol, distance was no deterrent.

Southern Xinjiang's conquest came last and was a direct result of the Qing victory in Zungharia. In fact it was conducted by the same Qing general fresh from his Zungharian triumphs. The Zunghar Mongols had depended on Xinjiang's oasis-cities, by now with a substantial Muslim Uighur population, for supplies and taxes, and had exercised a loose supervision over them. The Qing elimination of the Zunghars left a power vacuum that members of a formerly prominent and still greatly revered Muslim family sought to fill. These were the Khojas of the Naqshbandi sect of Sufis, whose authority in the region spread even to Kashmir and Afghanistan and had occasionally been endorsed by the Zunghars. Exploiting this connection, the Qing demanded submission and tribute. The Khojas, counting on their remoteness, declined, recruited a sizeable army, and fortified Kuqa (Kucha), the Silk Road city that commanded access to the region. In 1758 they were there defeated by a Qing force, and in 1759 were driven back to Kashgar, Yarkand and finally across the Pamirs to Badakshan in northern Afghanistan. Despite latter-day opinion, as yet 'there was no unified "Uighur" nationality either fighting against the Qing state or yearning to be incorporated within it'.[26] The region was indeed incorporated within the empire, but not as a regular province. 'Xinjiang's overall administration [under the Qing] was in essence nothing more than a huge garrison under the command of the military governor.' Officials there 'neither respected nor learned much about the languages and customs of the people whom they ruled'. They learned even less about the nominally *jimi* ('loose rein') lands beyond, including Tashkent, Bukhara, Afghanistan and Hunza in what is now northern Pakistan, over all of which the Qing inherited a vague suzerainty.[27]

Tibet's involvement in the Qing–Zunghar conflict was very different. It preceded that of Xinjiang and was much more influential, though the outcome was less conclusive. Like Taiwan, and despite vague claims by the Yuan dynasty, Tibet had never been administratively part of any Chinese empire. But the Mongols had become intimately involved in Tibet's religious politics, mostly as champions of the Yellow-hatted order of monks (Gelugpa), whose spiritual leader was the Dalai Lama of Lhasa. Khubilai Khan had patronised visiting lamas for their learning and occult powers, and by the late sixteenth century Mongol khans, like the Manchu leaders, were accustomed to seek confirmation and legitimacy from the Tibetan religious establishment. Tibetan Buddhist monasteries founded in

Mongolia, such as that at Urga (Ulan Bator), became nuclei of Mongol settlement and later cities. In a mutually rewarding arrangement, Mongol leaders provided Tibet's competing religious leaders with temporal clout in the form of recognition, donations and troops, while the lamas provided the competing Mongol leaders with titles, divinely sanctioned authority and monastic power bases. It was Altan Khan, a Mongol leader claiming descent from Chinggis Khan, who in 1578, in return for recognition as 'Protector of the Faith', had first acknowledged the leader of the Yellow-hatted order as 'Dalai' ('Oceanic', 'Universal') lama. (He was later known as the Third Dalai Lama when his father and grandfather were retrospectively recognised as the Second and First; the Fourth was in fact one of Altan Khan's descendants, and so a Mongol.) Mongol contacts with Tibet, for educational and commercial as well as religio-political purposes, were frequent. But this rich seam of legitimacy was also worked by the Qing, who in 1652 had feted the 'Great Fifth' Dalai Lama (r. 1617–82) in Beijing and confirmed his title. Whether as ally, opponent or umpire, Lhasa's Dalai Lama could not but play a pivotal part in the Qing–Zunghar struggle.

Matters were vastly complicated by two further factors: the first was the rival claims of other senior lamas, both Mongol and Tibetan, whether Yellow-hatted (like the Panchen Lamas of Tashilunpo) or not (like those of other orders); and the second was the dilemmas arising from a firm belief in the principle, and much latitude in the practice, of reincarnate succession. As a manifestation of the Bodhisattva Avalokiteswara, the Dalai Lama did not die; but when relinquishing one incarnation, he left it to others to determine the next, so creating great potential for controversy and uninvited interference.

To avoid this, the Great Fifth's 'non-death' in 1682 was kept secret from the Kangxi emperor for sixteen years. The emperor blamed Galdan and his Zunghars for contributing to the deception and endorsed intervention by a loyal (to the Qing) Mongol confederation from Qinghai. These Qinghai Mongols, keen to unseat the Zunghar-backed administration in Tibet and its Sixth Dalai Lama, reached Lhasa, but were in turn evicted by their Zunghar brethren. Imperial troops were then sent to the rescue, and in 1720, for the first time, entered Lhasa. The Zunghars evacuated the city ahead of their arrival, the Qing Banners occupied it, and a Seventh Dalai Lama was installed. A precedent for Qing protection in central Tibet had finally been established; civil power was now entrusted to a council of ministers who would be advised by two Beijing-appointed ambans ('commissioners' from the Qing Colonial Office, they 'were basically political informants') and a few troops were left to support them.[28] This did not accord with the expectations of the emperor's Qinghai Mongol allies, who rose in revolt. On orders from the Yongzhen emperor (the Kangxi emperor having finally died) the revolt was suppressed. Then Qinghai (north-eastern Tibet) and Kham (eastern Tibet) were effectively detached from the rest of Tibet (Xizang) to become 'inner' parts of the empire under more direct rule. They have never since been officially regarded as part of Tibet.

All these arrangements have, of course, subsequently been minutely scrutinised as bearing on the later status of Tibet. But any temptation to draw analogies between them and the events of the 1950s should be resisted. Qing intervention in Tibet in the eighteenth century was designed to uphold the religious establishment and the spiritual authority of the Dalai Lama, not to undermine them. The Manchu emperors were as sincere in their regard for the reincarnate lamas as were the Mongol khans, and just as jealous of Tibetan endorsement. Arguably Tibetan Buddhism gained more from imperial patronage than did the Qing from political intervention. By the 1750s over a third of all Mongols were monks settled in monasteries. 'There were nearly 2000 monasteries and temples in Mongolia', with more in the neighbouring provinces of Gansu, Sichuan and Xinjiang. In Beijing the 'Three Emperors' erected or renovated some thirty-two Tibetan temples; one within the inner city became a major centre of scholarship with over five hundred Mongol, Manchu and Tibetan monks.[29] Translation of the Tibetan texts into Chinese, Mongol and Manchu was officially funded, and the emperors themselves participated in Tibetan Buddhist rituals. Encouraging a proliferation of incarnate lamas, especially in Qinghai and Mongolia, may have been designed to dilute the influence of the Dalai Lama; but it was also evidence of the vitality of Tibeto-Mongol Buddhism within the empire.

So ended one of history's great continuums of conquest. Other Qing interventions in Burma, Vietnam and Nepal during the Qianlong period would prove unproductive, even disastrous. The expansionist onslaught launched by Nurhaci and his Jurchen Banners in Manchuria a century and half earlier ended at the Himalayas and in the deserts of Xinjiang. Chinese historians often see it as a restoration of the Han and Tang empires. The empire had reacquired a territorial extent, a capacity even, that was commensurate with the size of its population; a 'manifest destiny' had finally awarded China the proportions of a subcontinent; *zhongguo* had reached its 'natural' frontiers. Non-Chinese historians are more inclined to equate Qing expansion into the steppe and the desert with

China-ware being packed in crates for export, as depicted by a Chinese artist in gouache on paper. Loose tea was crammed between the pots to prevent breakages. By the nineteenth century tea far exceeded the value of all other Chinese exports, including the porcelain it once protected.

An oil painting of the Cantonese school shows the waterfront of Shamian Island (Guangzhou) in the eighteenth century. Otherwise known as Canton, Guangzhou was the multi-national hub of the tea trade and subsequently of the traffic in opium.

While under intense pressure from the foreign powers in the late nineteenth century, the Chinese empire was further destabilised by two massive rebellions. In 1851–65 Taiping armies swept north as far as Tianjin, where a Taiping encampment is shown in a contemporary scroll painting. And in 1900 Beijing itself succumbed to what foreigners called the Boxer Rebellion. Qing ambivalence towards the Boxers failed to save their leaders from the public executions demanded by the foreign powers by way of reprisal.

Cixi (1835–1908), empress dowager of the *Qing* Xianfeng emperor and regent for both of his successors, presided over the fate of the dynasty for forty-five years. A controversial figure who antagonised the foreign powers and stifled the 1898 'Hundred Days' reforms, she yet supported the self-strengthening movement and outlawed the practice of foot-binding. (Portrait of 1905 by Hubert Vos.)

Pu-yi (1906–67), also known as Henry, was 'the Last Emperor', though he scarcely reigned. Reared in the Forbidden City, he was obliged to abdicate following the 1911 revolution. Restored for a few weeks in 1917 (and given a British tutor), he was forced to flee into Japanese custody in 1924 and made titular emperor of Japanese Manchuria in 1934. After the Second World War he underwent re-education and ended his days working for the Beijing parks department.

Left In 1930 the Nationalist leader Chiang Kai-shek (right) and the young Manchurian warlord Zhang Xueliang (left) formed a joint front against the Japanese and the communists. Six years later Zhang took Chiang Kai-shek hostage in a bid to end the Nationalist vendetta against the communists and unite all China against the Japanese.

Below Shanghai's waterfront of hotels, banks and shipping companies was more cosmopolitan than anywhere else in China. In 1937 Chiang Kai-shek's Nationalist government chose to open a new front against the Japanese. No enemy vessels were sunk but the erratic Chinese bombing killed 2,000 Chinese civilians in a single day.

From Shanghai, Japanese troops pushed west up the Yangzi. Nanjing, the Nationalist capital, fell in December 1937. Suspecting Chinese troops of having donned civlian clothes, the Japanese then conducted a horrific massacre that included using prisoners for bayonet practice.

After the fall of Nanjing, it was Chongqing, above the Yangzi gorges in Sichuan, that became the Nationalists' last redoubt. Though heavily bombed (as here), the city held out and with Allied support remained the Nationalist capital throughout the Second World War.

Above left A youthful Mao Zedong (1893–1976) addressing troops at Yan'an in Shaanxi, to where the communist forces had withdrawn in the Long March of 1934–35.

Above right 'Rivers and Mountains are Charming' is the title of this 1980s poster celebrating the four-man leadership of the 1949 communist revolution – Xu De, Mao Zedong, Liu Shaoqi and Zhou Enlai. All had died in 1976 except Liu, who, though a victim of the Cultural Revolution, had been posthumously rehabilitated. Not so the conspicuously absent Lin Biao.

Security became an obsession following the Sino-Soviet rupture of c.1960. By 1970, when this poster appeared, strategic industries were being relocated inland for fear of a US assault. Entitled in English 'Survey the Enemy', the poster urges vigilance and surveillance (rather than surveys) even in the lotus beds.

A 1980s poster promotes the one-child-per-family policy, while the Yangzi's Three Gorges Dam (with its staircases of shipping locks) provides the world's largest output of hydro-electricity. Both projects have their critics; but the stabilisation of China's population and the provision of green energy may be accounted sensational sucesses for any regime.

The *gelugpa* monastery of Labrang Tashikyil in Amdo (Gansu) was one of many that, nearly half a century after the Dalai Lama's 1959 flight to India, was still staging protests against Beijing's interference in Tibetan affairs and against Han settlement in Tibet itself.

other contemporary colonialisations in Siberia and the Americas. China does not like to be considered a colonial power; but in Beijing's prompt efforts to demarcate, map and regulate these new regions, to settle their existing populations, to encourage or condone inward migration, and to realise their resources, the criteria of colonialism are discernible. Perhaps, though, what actually motivated Nurhaci and his successors was the legacy of Chinggis Khan and his successors. As the Qing, the Jurchen-Manchus had inherited the universalist claims of Heaven's Son, as Manchus they had secured Buddhist recognition as the 'wheel-turning' *cakravartin*, but as the Jurchen, a people whose Jin empire had been an early casualty of Mongol expansion, they had assumed the 'world ruling' rights of the Great Khan.

15

DEATH THROES OF EMPIRE
1760–1880

SELF-EVIDENT TRUTHS

ON THE MORNING OF 14 SEPTEMBER 1793, the Qianlong emperor, third of the Manchu Qing dynasty's long-reigning 'Three Emperors', received tribute-tendering deputations from some of 'All-under-Heaven's' farthest extremities. One came from the Kalmuck (Kalmyk) Mongols on the north-western borders of Xinjiang; closely related to the Zunghars, the Kalmucks had famously migrated from one end of Asia to the other, from Mongolia to the Volga, and then, falling out with the Russians, back again, an odyssey that the opium-eating Thomas de Quincey would recount in his 'Revolt of the Tartars'. The second deputation supposedly hailed from Pegu, the erstwhile capital of Burma, though it more probably originated in Ava, the seat of the Burmese monarchy. And the third came from London. George Viscount Macartney of Dervock, ambassador and leader of this first ever embassy from a British sovereign to a Chinese emperor, was at pains to emphasise that his mission had nothing to do with tribute. Rather was it an exchange between equals, between 'the greatest Sovereign of the West and . . . the greatest Sovereign of the East'; and when describing the occasion he somehow managed to overlook the presence of the Kalmucks and the Burmese. 'I forgot to mention it,' he politely explains in his journal. A slip of the pen, perhaps, it could have been corrected. But he left it as it was, apparently because 'their [the Kalmuck and Burmese deputations'] appearance was not very impressive' when compared to that of the English.

The formal reception was held in a vast marquee within the imperial park at Jehol, the Manchus' summer retreat north of Beijing and just beyond the Great Wall. Macartney, who had risen at 4 a.m. to dress, chose pink for the occasion. Over a suit of embroidered white velvet, he wrapped himself in the technically 'crimson' mantle of satin, lined with white taffeta, that was proper to a Knight of the Bath. An enormous diamond brooch, more starfish than star, was clamped to his breast, further diamonds festooned the badge that secured his lace jabot, a chain (or 'collar') of gold medallions weighing a kilogram was strung across his chest, and from his cocked hat, which was also pink, reared a spray of nodding egret plumes. 'I mention these little particulars', he explained, 'to show the attention I always paid, where a proper opportunity offered, to oriental customs and ideas.'[1]

The Kalmucks, the Burmese, even the emperor, were outdazzled by this apparition. Macartney was doing things in style. His official entourage ran to ninety-five persons, and as presents he brought enough choice British productions to stock a trade exhibition – fine woollens, clocks of exquisite manufacture, guns of every shape and size, glassware, chinaware even, swords, astronomical and musical instruments, oil paintings, a complete planetarium and a hot-air balloon. Two ships, one a sixty-four-gun warship, the other the largest and fastest vessel in the English East India Company's fleet, had taken a year to convey the mission to the northern port of Tianjin. From there, after a short river journey, the whole circus had been hauled to Beijing in 85 wagons and 39 handcarts, requiring 209 horses and 2,495 porters. Macartney had counted them. It was not excessive for the 'tribute mission' that the Qing flags announced it to be; but for an embassy, it was enormous. In fact it was possibly the grandest ever dispatched from Britain.

In keeping with the scale of the thing, Macartney's diplomatic wish-list was also ambitious. China and Britain were to establish amicable and reciprocal relations. He was to persuade the emperor to agree to his staying on as a permanent British ambassaor in Beijing and to encourage the dispatch of a complementary Chinese embassy to London. Three new ports on the China coast were to be opened to British trade; the numerous exactions to which the existing trade at Guangzhou (Canton) was subject were to be either rescinded or clarified and frozen; a couple of small islands, one within striking distance of Guangzhou and the other at Zhoushan (Chusan) near the mouth of the Yangzi, were to be secured as 'magazines for unsold goods' and 'places of residence'; and the potential of China's vast market for British manufactures was to be explored.

Macartney did his best. An experienced diplomat and an appreciative guest who went out of his way to cultivate good relations with the Qing officials, he even negotiated the tricky issue of the kowtow; he says he merely genuflected, as he would to his own king. But otherwise he failed dismally. In a parting edict addressed by the emperor to George III and entrusted to the mission for delivery, the British king was congratulated on his 'sincere humility and obedience'. Any permanent embassy, however, was contrary to ritual practice 'and definitely cannot be done'. Trade required no such level of representation; there were already channels for redress in the event of disputes; as for island 'magazines' and additional ports, they were not so much as mentioned. Knick-knacks such as guns and instruments the emperor did not value, 'nor do we have the slightest need of your country's manufactures'. In effect, reciprocity with the Celestial Empire remained an impertinent notion as well as a contradiction in terms: 'You, O King, should simply act in conformity with our wishes by strengthening your loyalty and swearing perpetual obedience so as to ensure that your country may share the blessings of peace.'[2]

At enormous expense, most of it borne by the East India Company, the Macartney mission achieved nothing; but it was not therefore insignificant. Allowed to withdraw to Guangzhou via the Grand Canal and the Yangzi before sailing home, Macartney and his colleagues observed something of the Qing empire at the height of its power. His journal, and other publications and paintings arising from the mission, offered English readers a new overview of China and rivalled in their influence the earlier works of Ricci and his Jesuit successors. Even the emperor's edict, though unbending in its assumption of imperial supremacy and sino-centric ascendancy, has been called 'the most important single Chinese document for the study of Sino-Western relations between 1700 and 1860' – no mean claim for a period during which China's international reputation would plummet as the Western powers presumed to extract concessions and the empire itself started to unravel.[3] Macartney anticipated this, his careful observations on the political, social and economic climate being both acute and prescient. Himself humiliated, his visit would come to be seen as the harbinger of China's humiliation.

Of the three major themes of the Qing period – the successful expansion into Inner Asia, a mixed record in managing the empire and its vastly increased population, and the disastrous handling of the insistent Western demand for commercial penetration – it is the last which has usually received the greatest attention. But as the eighteenth century drew to a close, and with it the long Qianlong reign, intervention by the Western powers still looked remote. As yet, what Macartney called 'the illegal and contraband trade of opium' constituted only a quarter of the total value of China's imports from the British-ruled parts of India; sales of Indian raw cotton were worth more, and though both commodities 'are now become in great measure necessaries in China', the trade in neither would be served by hostilities. Macartney noted the shortage of flintlocks and the antiquated nature of China's ordnance; he foresaw that 'half a dozen broadsides' would level the forts that protected Guangzhou, that 'a few frigates' could destroy the coastal shipping of the entire country, and that Indo-British forces 'might vulnerate them [the Chinese] as sensibly in other quarters', such as along Tibet's Himalayan frontier. But the cost in terms of lost trade would be disastrous. 'Our present interests, our reason, and our humanity equally forbid the thoughts of any offensive action,' he concluded.[4]

He worried more about the empire's internal stability, about 'the breaking up of the power of China'. This too would throw international commerce into confusion while heralding a free-for-all among the trading powers on the China coast. And it was a distinct possibility, indeed 'no very improbable event'. The Manchu rulers would not 'be able much longer to stifle the energies of their Chinese subjects'; 'insurrections' in outlying provinces were already commonplace; 'the tyranny of a handful of Tartars [i.e. Manchus] over more than three hunded millions of Chinese' could not long endure. The empire in the late eighteenth century could best be described as an impressive hulk, 'an old, crazy, First-rate man-of-war', that had been kept afloat only by a fortunate succession of able commanders. But in less skilled hands, discipline would collapse and the barque would flounder. 'She may not sink outright,' wrote Macartney, 'she may drift sometime as a wreck, and will then be dashed to pieces on the shore; but she can never be rebuilt on the same bottom.'[5]

The ship's commanders whom Macartney so admired were the 'Three Emperors' of the Kangxi, Yongzheng and Qianlong reigns. But in September 1793, when Macartney met him at Jehol, the last of these was just three days short of his eighty-fourth birthday. He looked younger and was still healthy; but he had already declared his intention of abdicating so that his reign would not outlast and so, in most unfilial fashion, eclipse that of his Kangxi grandfather. The end of an era was clearly nigh. Though clinging to the reins of power beyond his 1796 abdication, the Qianlong emperor would die in 1799; and as Macartney feared, none of his successors would last anything like as long or command a fraction of his authority.

Personal authority was important, although Macartney – better informed about the emperor than about his administration's shortcomings – may have exaggerated it. In a bold initiative to short-circuit the formalities, and expand the reach, of ministerial remonstration, the Kangxi emperor had encouraged officials all over the empire to send to him personally, without prejudice to themselves, private memorials on the state of affairs under their oversight. The hard-working Yongzheng emperor had standardised and extended this practice, and the Qianlong emperor had continued it. Both the Kangxi and Qianlong emperors had also undertaken long and sometimes arduous tours by road and river throughout the empire. Recorded in a series of great scroll paintings (twelve to a journey, each scroll being 10–30 metres long for a grand total of 120–360 metres of painted narrative per journey), the tours were no more just ceremonial exercises in seeing and being seen than the scrolls were just pictorial mementoes of the tours. Both celebrated the centrality of the Manchu emperors in respect of their empire and both proclaimed a rather un-Confucian legitimacy based on active rulership.

On tour, petitions were received, impromptu information recorded and on-the-spot inspections conducted. The 'Three Emperors' were better informed about conditions in their vast territories than most of their predecessors; and they strove valiantly to improve them. In a Valedictory Edict that carried something of the authority of the *Ming* Hongwu emperor's 'Ancestral Injunctions', the Kangxi emperor had taken issue with the ideal of the *wuwei* ('non-action') emperor. Far from being immovable icons, the greatest emperors had never rested from their labours. Even Shun, the fourth of the dawn-of-history 'Five Emperors', and he who was supposed to have insisted that 'through non-action one governs', had died while out on tour. 'To work as hard at government as [such paragons], to travel on inspection, to have never an idle moment – how can this be called valuing *wuwei* or tranquilly looking after oneself?' demanded the Kangxi emperor.[6]

On the basis of these tours and memorials, vigorous efforts had been made to hold down the burden of taxation on those least able to support it and to grapple with the consequences of the growth in population. At the same time the imperial finances had to be replenished and the efficacy of expenditure on public works improved, both of which had suffered from the disruptive campaigns that had followed the dynastic changeover. One way to increase revenues was to update the tax registers. The Kangxi emperor tried this; but he was not the first and he met with little success. The campaigns in Mongolia and a period of laxity towards the end of his reign left the imperial finances as much in deficit as he had found them.

A more successful approach, adopted by the Yongzheng emperor, was to stem the haemorrhaging of such revenues as were actually collected by clamping down on local ad hoc surcharges and embezzlement. This too had been tried before, but not as aggressively as by the Yongzheng emperor. A central Board of Audit was set up and provincial governors were ordered to investigate the revenue shortfalls and report to the emperor via the confidential system of memorials. When it emerged that without surcharges and other fees the county and district administrations could scarcely operate, a whole new system of apportioning revenues between the central and local government, and of remunerating officials realistically, was introduced. A healthy surplus accrued to the exchequer and 'for the first time in Chinese history, the state took account of both the administrative needs of officials and the duty of local government to provide ... public services and infrastructural improvements'.[7] The Yongzheng emperor simultaneously pressed ahead with a hoary proposal to incorporate the labour tax (in most areas the duty of corvée had been replaced by a tax payable in silver) with the land and poll taxes. Implementation of all these measures was left to the discretion of provincial governors; they were not draconian exercises in centralised standardisation and the results remained patchy. But they did challenge traditional ideas of gentry-led and community-based self-regulation as championed by degree-holding families, whose fiscal privileges and exemptions were specifically targeted. The tax burden was being more equitably distributed, granaries better stocked, canals, roads and irrigation schemes better maintained, and the imperial finances vastly improved; but all at some cost in anti-Manchu sentiment.

Another source of revenue was trade. Under the Qing, encouraging wealth creation was acknowledged as a function of the state, and the Confucian disparagement of merchants and credit agencies became largely rhetorical. With domestic stability, an expanding economy and an improved supply of silver thanks to buoyant exports, internal trade grew rapidly throughout the eighteenth century, encouraging the formation of complex kin-based networks and bringing in substantial revenue in the form of local dues and from the sale of licences and brokerage rights. The state created a favourable economic environment, invested in specific projects such as land reclamation, and creamed off fees and taxes. But it was more a hybrid economy than a command economy. The distinction, for instance, was blurred between, on the one hand, private manufacturers and traders organised into guilds licensed by the state and, on the other, their public sector equivalents engaged under licence in operating state monopolies like those of copper or salt – still a major contributor to the imperial revenues. Even the lucrative collection of maritime customs on overseas trade at Guangzhou (Canton) had been delegated to the private sector. As of a 1707 decree from the Kangxi emperor, several merchant guilds were licensed to deal exclusively with the cargoes of specific ships or nations in return for collecting and remitting the duties payable on them. In respect of the English East India Company, this exclusive privilege belonged to the famous Co-hong group of merchants. Other guild groupings handled Chinese-owned shipping, one for the coastal trade, another for overseas trade.

Meanwhile new industries were established – cotton-spinning and weaving in and around Suzhou, Hangzhou and up-and-coming Shanghai became as important as silk production – and the population went on growing. The statistics remain controversial. A figure of around 300 million by the year 1800, about twice that of all Europe at the time, is generally accepted, though what rate of growth this represents is uncertain. More people meant more productivity but also a greater demand for cultivable land. Swamps were laboriously drained, lake-beds reclaimed and hilly forests cleared and terraced for cultivation, all at growing cost to the environment, both natural and human. For now heavy rains leached and eroded the deforested hillsides, so adding to the downstream problems of siltation and flooding, while reducing the water-retentive properties of the upstream terrain. Though the state was better equipped to meet the needs of disaster victims, the incidence of local droughts and floods increased. Accessible timber became scarce. In the south, as long since in the north, coal began to replace wood as fuel; beams of iron or steel were increasingly used in construction. But the new lands were never enough and the pool of wage-earners always too many. Seasonal migrations and the pull of the cities wrenched ever more from their village roots. 'Most evidence seems to suggest that the empire's rapidly expanding population was geographically mobile on a scale . . . unprecedented in Chinese history.'[8]

Since most of the new territories in the far north and west ('Xinjiang' translates as 'new territories') were as yet reserved for military settlement, were closed to Han migration and were separately administered as a Manchu-Mongol preserve, the obvious regions for agricultural expansion were in the south and south-west. Here, in the great arc of rugged and often wooded or mountainous country that stretched from western Guangdong right round to Sichuan, both Han and non-Han settlement made substantial progress. But it was preceded by ruthless campaigns against the indigenous non-Han peoples that rumbled on throughout the Yongzheng and Qianlong reigns. The *tusi* ('native officer') system of indirect control once favoured by the Ming was largely superseded by standard administrative units; and amnesties, land grants and subsidies were offered as incentives to settlement. But non-Han chiefs were removed from their territories, and their clansmen – Zhuang, Miao, Yao, Lolo, etc. – were expected to adopt Chinese names, grow queues and submit to registration for the purposes of taxation, labour service and military recruitment. Of those who refused, some migrated south to Laos and Vietnam; others retreated farther and higher into the hills.

No longer much of a threat, it was the latter's fate to furnish the Manchu Qing, and later the (overwhelmingly Han) People's Republic of China, with the material for catalogued inventories of the empire's exoticised ethnic minorities, each with its colourful and carefully coded costumes, its musical and choreographic traditions, its professional specialisations, and its supposedly casual grasp of morality, especially female chastity. In another late-eighteenth-century collection of colossal scroll paintings, this time of Qing tributaries, one entire series of scrolls was devoted to 'Minorities from Yunnan, Guizhou and Guangxi'. Each of the seventy-eight featured peoples was represented by a male and female of the species engaged in some characteristic activity. 'A commentary in both Chinese and Manchu was written above each pair, describing them, their religion, national dress, customs, local products, the taxes and tribute they paid and their relationship with the Qing court.'9 Thus in China's empire, as in other colonial empires, marginalised minorities were already being portrayed in a context calculated to advertise the distinction and the all-embracing dominion of the ruling power. Replicated in print and paraded on the podium, such attitudes to China's 'human sub-species' would be adopted by later regimes, whether chauvinistically Nationalist, patronisingly Maoist or tourism-minded market-socialist.

Despite the size, stability and apparent prosperity of their empire, the Qing remained uneasy rulers. Elsewhere in the world of the late eighteenth century self-evident truths and inalienable rights were being loudly asserted. Across the Atlantic 'Life, Liberty and the Pursuit of Happiness' vied with *Liberté, Égalité, Fraternité* in uniting peoples and galvanising governments. Social contracts and the rights of man were eating into privilege; votes had begun to count. China, by contrast, was still what Macartney called 'a tyranny'. To a Qing emperor, consultation was optional, representation suspect, and any talk of accountability treason. Imperial pronouncements savoured heavily of indoctrination, and given the moral authority of the emperor, that was indeed their purpose.

Theoretically, and to a wide extent in practice, all subjects of the empire were still enrolled in a system of 'mutual security' that was actually more about shared liability and mutual surveillance. Known under its Song dynasty variant of *baojia*, it grouped households into decimal units of a thousand (*bao-*) and a hundred (*-jia*), the latter being composed of ten groupings of ten households, and each unit having its own headman. Chosen by rotation, the headman was responsible for the good order and prompt compliance of his unit, rarely for the expression of its grievances; it was not a desirable post. The penal code made the headman and his unit liable not only for the conduct of its constituents but also for any crimes committed by them. Ideally the *baojia* grouping cut across the bonds of kinship, clan or professional association, and instilled a sense of equal and responsible participation in the machinery of government. But while in practice it might cement existing bonds, it did little to stem the exodus of the landless, and it often atrophied for want of support. Admirable as had been the attempts of the 'Three Emperors' to address the needs of their realm and placate their various constituents – Manchu, Mongol and Chinese – neither they nor their subjects had any concept of popular legitimacy. Government still relied on the penal code and the force of arms; Heaven's judgement was the ultimate sanction, and the dynastic cycle the only guarantee of change.

The regime at the height of its power revealed something of its paranoia in the Qianlong emperor's 'Four Treasuries' – the second of the Qing's monumental compendia and the one which, containing all that had ever been written in the way of literature, history and philosophy, was too vast ever to be published. For despite the project's avowed purpose of rescuing and preserving for posterity the entire corpus of Chinese scholarship, it soon transpired that the great work was also expected to 'serve some of the functions of a literary inquisition'. Compilation meant discovering and assembling all relevant extant works, weeding out and destroying any that slighted the Jurchen-Jin/Manchu-Qing or contained other unwelcome material, and punishing the individuals responsible for harbouring them. 'So thorough was this campaign that over 2000 works that we know were scheduled for destruction by Qianlong's cultural advisers have never been rediscovered.'[10] The project attracted a host of underemployed and potentially disaffected degree-holders; editorial standards were high, and the classics and histories were subjected to some much-needed forensic philology; the Qianlong emperor, an indefatigable collector, connoisseur and practitioner of all the arts, took a genuine delight in the work. But in his censorship, as in institutions like the *baojia* and massive Qing building projects like the Jesuit-designed Summer Palace (Yuan Ming Yuan), this last of the great emperors could not but remind anti-Manchu scholars of the dictatorial extravagance and heavy-handed legalism of the first great emperor, the book-burning *Qin* Shihuangdi.

INSULTS AND OPIUM

Like most dynasties, that of the Qing would succumb to internal disturbance, not foreign assault; and like the Tang dynasty after the An Lushan
revolt, the Qing would stage a recovery from the great rebellions and
foreign encroachments of the mid-nineteenth century to linger on into
the twentieth century. But the foreign presence remained, undermining
imperial authority, discrediting the Confucian ideology on which it was
based, and inciting a tumult of protest. All dynasties were doomed; the
Qing would have fallen without foreign intervention; indeed, it lingered
as long as it did only because of foreign intervention. But not perhaps the
empire. While indigenous causes would topple the dynasty, it was extraneous forces which would cripple the empire.

When in the late 1830s, forty years after Macartney's mission, the hostilities known as the Opium War broke out, European shipping had been
trading on the China coast for more than three hundred years. For most
of that time the Portuguese enclave of Macao had afforded the foreigners
a sanctuary and an agreeable home on Chinese soil. The volume of trade
had steadily increased; and over time the main foreign participants had
changed, as had the commodities most in demand. Guangzhou, the port
nearest to Macao and that to which the trade had been restricted since
the mid-1700s, had grown into a major financial and intellectual centre.
Foreign merchants, minus wives, were allowed to reside there only during
the trading season and were restricted to Shamian Island, today a leafy
river frontage beneath the flyovers but then a mudbank lined with 'colonial' buildings flying the flags of their respective nations.

There was nothing inherently destabilising about these commercial
contacts between West and East. Geographically and ideologically they
were peripheral to a still-agrarian empire beset by the problems of
managing an explosive population while distributing and taxing the fruits
of its labour. Overseas imports were advantageous to the economy, especially in respect of liquidity (silver) and some raw materials (ores, spices,
furs and latterly cotton). The trade provided the state with revenue and
the emperor himself with a rich source of ready cash in the form of sweet-
eners remitted directly to Beijing by Guangzhou's merchant groupings;
and it was of course profitable for all those directly engaged in it, both
Chinese and foreigners. As Macartney had stressed, neither they, their
respective governments nor the emperor had anything to gain by disrupting
intercourse. Disputes had arisen, mostly over unpaid debts and alcohol-
fuelled affrays; everyone found much to complain of; but moneymaking

good sense generally prevailed. Many nations were involved, including the Spanish in the early days and latterly the French and the Americans. But the Portuguese had enjoyed a near-monopoly for most of the sixteenth century, in the seventeenth the Dutch had been pre-eminent, and as of the early eighteenth it was the English who accounted for by far the most ships.

Chartered in 1600 to compete for the Asia–Europe spice trade, the London (or English) East India Company, after being ousted from Indonesia's Spice Islands by the Dutch, had found compensation in favourable trading conditions and substantial 'factory' bases on the coast of India. With its chartered monopoly of the 'out-and-back' trade between London and the East, the company imported from India to Britain mostly finished cotton fabrics, while both it and its servants, acting in a private capacity, competed for freight in the unmonopolised inter-port carrying trade of the East. From the company's factory-cum-fort of Madras (Chennai) a group of these freelancing company employees led by the brothers Elihu and Thomas Yale (later of Connecticut) had dispatched the first company ship to Guangzhou in 1691. For hospitality at nearby Macao they trusted to the amicable relations that had subsisted between England and Portugal ever since Charles II's marriage to Catherine of Braganza; and for trading rights at Guangzhou they depended on the Qing authorities not penalising them for earlier contacts with the Taiwan of Zheng Chenggong (Coxinga) and his son. Despite early misunderstandings, they were not disappointed. As of 1699 company ships sailed annually for the place they called 'Canton' (a word supposedly derived from 'Guangdong' but applied to that province's capital of Guangzhou).

A mere sideline in 1700, China soon proved a bonanza for the company. By 1770 the Guangzhou trade was the most important and lucrative in its considerable portfolio. This was thanks to massive dealing in a single and much-sought-after sedative – which was not opium but tea. The Englishman's thirst for the beverage knew no bounds. 'The 200,000 pounds sold [in London] by the Company in 1720 was up to a million pounds a year by the end of the decade . . . In 1760 it was just under three million and by 1770 nine million.'[11] It would double and double again in the nineteenth century. Porcelain, once packed in tea to prevent breakages, was now carried largely as 'kintledge', or ballast to stabilise sailing ships too lightly laden just with dried leaf. Taxation levels of over 100 per cent on imports entering Britain did nothing to stem demand. British colonists were equally taken by the brew. Famously it was protests over the re-export from Britain of a commodity that, by the time it reached Boston, was more tax than tea which triggered the war that cost the British their North American territories.

Although a Commutation Act of 1784 reduced the duty on British imports to 12.5 per cent, the taxes soon rose anew. By the 1830s tea was contributing nearly 10 per cent of the British government's entire revenue receipts. Nor was this the full story; for the Commutation Act (so called because it 'commuted' most of the tax on tea into one on windows) had been prompted by the knowledge that similar quantities of tea were reaching Britain's high streets untaxed. To circumvent both the company's monopoly and the British exchequer's demands, private adventurers and interlopers, many of them British, had taken to operating under flags of convenience provided by the rival East India companies of Ostend, Sweden, Denmark and Austria-Hungary. They too purchased in Guangzhou but shipped mainly to the Low Countries, from where the tea was smuggled across the North Sea. Nocturnal flurries and occasional firefights in Britain's inshore waters in the eighteenth century nicely anticipated similar scenes in China's inshore waters in the nineteenth century. The British attitude to tea and the Chinese attitude to opium would be radically different; tea enlivened society and was welcome, opium destroyed it and was banned. But in purely economic terms they posed a not dissimilar challenge.

The tea, mostly black bohea not from Guangdong but from farther north, was purchased with silver. Barter would have been preferred by the company, but other British exports enjoyed little demand in China; woollens were generally unwelcome in steamy Guangdong, and as the emperor had told Macartney, China had as yet 'not the slightest need of British manufactures'. The balance of trade throughout the eighteenth century was thus overwhelmingly in China's favour. The Celestial Empire came to rely on this abundant source of silver, while British manufacturers and economists deplored the disregard of the national interest and what they called the 'drain of specie'. Indian produce sometimes supplemented silver, notably raw cotton shipped direct from Bombay (Mumbai) to Guangzhou; so did a roundabout trade involving the shipment of Indian textiles to south-east Asian markets, then of south-east Asian spices and culinary exotica to China. It was in this three-way trade, conducted mainly by non-company adventurers and agencies, and involving the mercantile communities of the Malay and Indonesian ports, among whom Chinese emigrants were now prominent, that the potential of Indian-grown opium first became apparent.

In China home-grown opium, mainly for medicinal use, had been consumed, as it had in Europe, for at least a thousand years. But smoking it – rather than infusing or eating it – for the greater 'hit' nowadays classed as 'recreational' seems to have originated in Taiwan in the seventeenth century. It may have been the result of novices experimenting in tobacco smoking, itself then a novelty. The habit spread to the mainland, where the *Qing* Yongzheng emperor made opium dens and opium dealing illegal but did not actually proscribe the drug. It also spread to south-east Asia, where Indian-grown opium was already circulating and from where both Chinese and Europeans began shipping some on to China from the 1720s.

When in 1773 the East India Company assumed monopoly control over poppy-growing and opium production in Bengal, about a thousand chests (60,000 kilograms, 60 tons) a year were reaching China. This figure had quadrupled by 1796, the year of the Qianlong emperor's abdication and from which date, on orders from the Guangzhou authorities, the company stopped exporting its opium to China; ignoring the Chinese ban would have meant risking an embargo of its tea purchases, which was unthinkable. Instead the company's Indian opium crop was auctioned in Calcutta, purchased by private syndicates organised as 'agency houses', and then shipped by them to Guangzhou in still greater quantities. As prices fell, demand increased; so did the profits of shippers and dealers; and so did official concern in Beijing. The Jiaqing emperor (successor of the Qianlong emperor; r. 1796–1821) introduced heftier penalties for smokers. He also banned opium imports altogether, which meant that it was now the turn of Guangzhou's Co-hong merchants to forgo any overt involvement in the trade. The consequences were much the same as with the company: dealing moved offshore and out of control. Singapore, acquired by the British in 1819 and developed as a free port, had attracted Chinese émigrés and a vast concourse of shipping; the opium trade there found the perfect entrepôt. From Singapore, vessels, not all British, carried the chests to Lintin island at the mouth of the Pearl River, to hulks moored in its vicinity and to fast clippers cruising up the coast. From headlands and inlets, smaller craft, well oared and armed, put out to meet them. They were usually expected, terms and timing having been prearranged at Guangzhou. The chests were trans-shipped, then landed.

Echoing the exponential growth in Britain's tea imports, China's imports of Indian opium topped 13,000 chests in 1828 and had doubled again by 1836. By then, 'total imports came to $18 million, making it the world's most valuable single commodity trade of the nineteenth century'.[12] The syndicates and agency houses that handled the shipments – mainly British but also American – looked to the company's influence at Guangzhou for protection and made the proceeds of their trade available to the company for its tea purchases; it was the ideal way to convert – or launder – opium profits (and other perks of Eastern empire) into London stocks, country estates and parliamentary seats. As of the late 1820s, therefore, foreign tea purchases no longer required an outlay of bullion; opium credits more than sufficed. Silver no longer flowed into China; it flowed out. By the 1830s it was flowing out at the rate of 9 million taels a year. The balance of trade had reversed. It was now imperial officials in Beijing who worried about the national interest and complained of 'the drain of specie'. Within China, and especially in the south, the demand for silver pushed up its value against copper cash, causing the same distress as in Ming times among the cash-earning but silver-taxed classes. 'Reduced growth, unemployment and urban unrest (another of the clusters of problems associated with dynastic decline) are directly attributable . . . to the sudden impact of this dramatic and disastrous shift in the balance of payments.'[13]

Under the Daoguang emperor (r. 1821–50) official concern about opium and its consequences mounted. Opinion was canvassed, memorials submitted and debates held. Many officials argued for legalisation, for a state monopoly and licensed dealers. As they saw it, prohibition had failed; penal deterrents were hard to enforce, and enforcers were too readily corrupted; both consumption and corruption could be better contained by punitive tariffs; these would also bring in substantial revenues; and state control would make the foreign traders more amenable to regulation.

The last was especially relevant because in 1833 the British government, under pressure from British manufacturers keen for access to China's markets, had seen fit to end the East India Company's monopoly of the China–London trade. The out-and-back trade with India had been opened to all twenty years earlier; both deregulations were part of a protracted assault on the company that left it a mere scapegoat for official policy. In China the move meant the replacement of the company's supervision of Guangzhou's foreign trading community by that of the British government. His Majesty's first superintendent arrived at Macao in 1834 in the person of Lord Napier. Representing a sovereign power rather than a trading company, Napier had been instructed to deal only with mandarins of equivalent status, like the Qing governor-general of the southern provinces, not with Co-hong merchants or customs officials. The change had not, though, been notified to Beijing, let alone authorised there, nor was it remotely acceptable. Napier, who had advanced from Macao to Guangzhou, stood his ground. Ordered to depart, he refused and was blockaded; he summoned a couple of warships and sent to India for troops. But trade had been halted, and the merchant community grew restless.

On their insistence, after a couple of weeks Napier withdrew in disgust back to Macao and there died of dysentery. Both sides then misread the incident. The British took it to be a national affront that cried out for redress; the Chinese took it as proof that state intervention in the form of blockades and embargoes could bring the foreigners to heel.

Relishing this triumph, in the debates of 1836–38 other senior Qing officials argued against the legalisation of opium and in favour of stronger measures to suppress both the trade and the habit. Lin Zexu, an able scholar and experienced administrator, stressed the moral aspect: opium addiction undermined the social relationships so essential to Confucian society. He accepted that addicts could not simply be executed. They must be encouraged to reform; treatment as well as penalties must be offered. But above all it was imperative to staunch the flow of the 'poison' by clamping down on dens, dealers, suppliers and shippers. As governor-general of Hubei and Hunan provinces, Lin had successfully pursued such a policy. 'Glow[ing] with the confidence of a man who had never made a serious mistake in his life', in early 1839 he headed for Guangzhou as Imperial Commissioner for Frontier Defence with a special responsibility 'to sever the trunk from the roots' in respect of opium smuggling.[14]

Commissioner Lin wasted no time. As well as propagandising, rounding up dealers and confiscating all opium pipes, he boldly targeted the foreign importers. Ordered to surrender all existing stocks of opium with no offer of compensation, they refused. A contemptuous 1,000 chests were offered, whereupon Commissioner Lin demanded that Lancelot Dent, a leading offender and head of one of the agency houses, must stand trial. If he was not handed over, Lin threatened to execute two Chinese merchants in his stead. Down at Macao Captain Charles Elliot, the new British super-intendent, took this as 'the immediate and inevitable' prelude to war. Just like Napier, he called for reinforcements, sailed hastily up to Guangzhou, and was there blockaded. Meanwhile Dent had not been surrendered and Lin had therefore embargoed all trade. The commissioner still hoped to avoid war; but to the British it was seeming more desirable by the day.

In early 1839 it failed to materialise. Superintendent Elliot lacked the authority, as well as the means, to prosecute hostilities; and the agency houses, with heavy opium stocks on their hands in anticipation of possible legalisation, badly needed unfettered access to their Guangzhou buyers. After six weeks of being cooped up on Shamian Island, Elliot, like Napier, backed down and was allowed to withdraw to Macao. Lin's gamble had paid off. Twenty thousand chests (over 1,000 tonnes, 980 tons) were duly surrendered and, under tight security, were destroyed in lime pits, like infected livestock. Lin himself looked on and afterwards apologised to the spirit of the Southern Ocean for defiling her waters with the 'poisonous' effluent. He kept the emperor apprised of his triumphs; and more famously, employing a mix of reasoned argument, paternal exhortation, provocative bombast and bureaucratic rectitude, he wrote to Queen Victoria.

There were two letters; one was never sent, the other never arrived; but their tone and content were similar. 'The Way of Heaven holds good for you as for us,' Lin told the queen; all peoples are aware of what is good for them and what not; the Celestial Empire shares with others only its good things, such as rhubarb, tea and silk; but 'a poisonous article is manufactured by certain devilish persons subject to your rule' who 'tempt the people of China to buy it'; Your Majesty, though surely in ignorance of your subjects' involvement, must be aware of the drug's harmful effects.

> Our Heavenly Court's resounding might ... could at any moment control their [the opium traders'] fate; but in its compassion and generosity it gives due warning before it strikes. Your Majesty has not before been thus officially notified ... but I now give my assurance that we mean to cut off this harmful drug forever ... Do not say that you have not been warned in time. On receiving this, Your Majesty will be so good as to report to me immediately on the steps that have been taken at each of your ports.[15]

The translation here paraphrased and abbreviated comes from that made by Arthur Waley (1889–1966) in a work based on Commissioner Lin's writings which is devoted to presenting the Opium War 'through Chinese Eyes'. The finest translator of his generation, Waley never visited China; and its history interested him less than its literature – either of which may explain a significant difference between his translation of the letter and that offered in most other works of Western scholarship. For Waley, whose knowledge of written Chinese was unrivalled, translated the Chinese character rendered by the Pinyin word *yi* as 'foreigner', not as the pejorative 'barbarian'. The equation of *yi* with 'barbarian' seems to have originated with a Pomeranian missionary who was serving the British as a translator at the time; it is not evident in earlier works, such as Macartney's or Ricci's journals. A small mistake perhaps, it surfaced in the run-up to the Opium War and gained a wide and notorious currency. The Chinese insisted that *yi* had always signified merely those non-Chinese peoples who were 'easterners' (the British frequented the east coast) – just as *man* did those who were 'southerners', *rong* 'northerners' and *di* 'westerners'. They were directional, not objectionable, terms. But the British declined to find *yi* as other than highly insulting, indeed indicative of a wider, deeper contempt for themselves and for all the norms of international discourse.

The ramifications of the mistake, if that is what it was, were enormous. More even than opium, this tiny monosyllable poisoned diplomatic exchanges, and would require an article of its own – number 51 – in the 1858 Anglo-Chinese Treaty of Tianjin. It infected the translation of other Chinese characters and slewed the interpretation of whole passages, invariably rendering them more reprehensible to foreign readers. It fouled Anglo-Chinese social relations; it permeated racial stereotyping; and it corrupted – and still does – most non-Chinese writing on the entire course of China's history. A British equivalent would be substituting 'wog' for every mention of 'foreign' or 'foreigners' in the archives of the Public Record Office. 'Never has a lone word among the myriad languages of humanity made so much history as the Chinese character *yi*,' writes Lydia Liu. Indeed, in a fine study of the subject, she does not overstate the case by entitling her book *The Clash of Empires*.[16]

Behind the arguments over opium, over trading rights and commercial access, over protocol, diplomatic representation and extraterritorial jurisdiction, there yawned throughout a chasm of linguistic misapprehension and mutual suspicion. Napier and Elliot were decent men, more often perplexed than apoplectic. And the British, of all people, should not have been surprised by another nation's presumption of moral superiority and international centrality. But in supposing such attitudes to be more contemptuous and adversarial than they were, in making them an excuse for aggression and in reciprocating in kind (the phrase 'half-civilised governments such as China' featured in one Palmerstonian pronouncement), they were being woefully provocative.

Commissioner Lin, another honourable and conscientious man, tried to understand his adversaries. When asking an American doctor for information about the treatment of opium addicts, he is known to have requested a translation of a Western work on international law (though what he made of it is not known). The Qing government could be surprisingly pragmatic. In Lin's first letter to Queen Victoria, it was hinted that the opium issue might be resolved by an offer to replace the drug with British or Indian imports of a less pernicious nature. As for protocol, the problem had already been resolved in respect of the Russians; equal status had been conceded in the treaties of Nerchinsk and Kiakhta, and trading arrangements, including regular Russian commercial missions to Beijing, had since been established. More surprisingly, when in the 1830s Napier and Elliot in Guangzhou were demanding official recognition and the extraterritorial right of administering justice to their own subjects, far away at the other end of the empire in Xinjiang precisely these rights were in fact being extended to nationals of another foreign government.

Xinjiang had been racked by incursions and rebellion throughout the 1820s. The trouble stemmed from neighbouring Kokand, an independent Muslim khanate west of Kashgar and astride the old Silk Roads. There, leading members of the Khoja fraternity, the ex-rulers of Xinjiang, had taken refuge when the Qianlong emperor first conquered Xinjiang. Muslim solidarity and a major interest in Xinjiang's commerce later led Kokand to support Khoja rebellions in Xinjiang and claim control of its trade. The Qing responded harshly; but the administrative and military costs of holding down the remote oasis-cities proved exorbitant. Instead, in 1835 an agreement – sometimes billed, like Nerchinsk, as 'China's first "unequal treaty" settlement' – was signed in Beijing with a Kokandi ambassador. Kokand got the right to station a 'resident political representative' at Kashgar and commercial representatives at five other cities, including Yarkand (Suche), Aksu and Turfan (Turpan). And all these officials enjoyed full consular, judicial and police powers over foreigners in their jurisdiction, plus the right to levy duties on their trade. Napier or Elliot might have settled for less.

Accommodation was possible, then; indeed, following the transfer of several military and administrative officials between Xinjiang and Guangdong, the Qing government would eventually 'apply the lessons of [Xinjiang] to its difficulties with the British on the China coast'.[17] But Kokand, unlike London, was not oversolicitous of its international image; nor were its treaties subject to parliamentary scrutiny. To obtain the treaty, the khan's representatives had accepted China's idiosyncratic attitude to foreign relations and conformed to tributary tradition. For the British, this was impossible – as impossible as it was for Commissioner Lin to disavow 2,000 years of managing neighbours, most of them predatory nomads, on the understanding that dialogue signified submission and that trade counted as tribute.

By mid-1839 the die was cast; events now assumed a momentum of their own. In Guangzhou, Commissioner Lin followed up his success in extracting opium from the foreigners by demanding that they sign bonds never again to carry the drug. On Elliot's advice the British, as usual, refused. Lin then pressured the Portuguese into expelling them from Macao. Now baseless, Elliot and his countrymen sailed across the Pearl River estuary to a high and largely uninhabited island composed of uncultivable rock but with a sheltered anchorage. Its name they understood as 'Hong Kong'.

From there, in late 1839 while requisitioning provisions on the neigh-bouring mainland and in several encounters at sea, gunfire was exchanged. Lin reported victories and fortified the approaches to Guangzhou; the British logged the junks they had sunk and bided their time. In London, Elliot's request for troops had been rejected by foreign secretary Lord Palmerston. But then, under pressure from opium barons and manufac-turing interests, it was granted. A large naval and military force set sail from India in early 1840.

The fleet carried a letter from Palmerston to the Qing court that 'demand[ed] from the Emperor satisfaction and redress for injuries inflicted by Chinese Authorities upon British subjects . . . and for insults offered by those same authorities to the British Crown'. To this end, there were to be no negotiations. The fleet was to blockade Chinese ports, detain Chinese vessels and take possession 'of some convenient part of the Chinese terri-tory' until such time as satisfaction was forthcoming in a signed treaty and an agreed reparation for the expenses incurred.[18] Opium was mentioned in the letter; Palmerston conceded that Beijing had every right to ban it; but he contended that, since the ban was not rigorously enforced by Chinese officials, who were often complicit in breaking it, it was unfair to expect foreign suppliers to respect it – a logic from which smugglers the world over may have taken comfort.

The British fleet arrived off the Pearl River in June 1840 but did not test Lin's new defences by sailing up to Guangzhou. Nor was Palmerston's letter delivered. Instead the fleet sailed out to sea again, leaving only a token force to blockade the mouth of the river. Lin thought his defences had done the trick. But ten days later the fleet reappeared, this time off Zhoushan in Zhejiang. The city was heavily bombarded, forced to surrender and occupied. The fleet then continued north, round the Shandong pen-insula and towards the mouth of the Beihe, the river on which Beijing lies. Palmerston's letter was now handed over; but it was concern for the capital's safety which persuaded the Daoguang emperor to dispatch an envoy to treat with the British. Meanwhile Commissioner Lin, who had totally misrepresented the strength of the enemy and had now exposed the capital to attack, was disgraced and sacked pending disposal.

The new Qing envoy and plenipotentiary, a provincial governor general called Qishan, talked the British into sailing back to Guangzhou on the understanding that he would there address their grievances in full. This he did to the extent that, with Guangzhou now at the mercy of Britain's naval gunnery, an agreement was reached in January 1841: British superintend-ents at Guangzhou were to have access to Qing officials, Hong Kong was to be handed over, a $6 million indemnity paid, and trade to be reopened. In return the British were to leave Zhoushan. But though the terms were immediately effective, the agreement was swiftly repudiated. The emperor was so horrified by the severity of the concessions, especially the cession of Hong Kong, that he now sacked Qishan, while Palmerston was so appalled by their leniency (no reimbursement for the destroyed opium, no new ports, only 'a barren island') that he too suspended his plenipotentiary.

By the time a replacement arrived in August 1841, the war had resumed. The British fleet had twice sailed up to Guangzhou, demolishing shore batteries, sinking junks and landing troops. An iron-built, steam-driven paddle-steamer proved especially effective, defying wind and tide and greatly embarrassing its still pedal-powered Chinese equivalents. In guns as in ships, the technological gap was not that great; Chinese yards and foundries would soon be turning out serviceable copies of anything the British could deploy. But the gulf between what pre-industrial China and post-industrial Europe made of the technology, and the confidence with which it was handled, was painful to contemplate. The only Qing seaborne counter-attack was a disaster; in a matter of days, seventy-one junks were destroyed and Guangzhou's waterfront razed.

Naval superiority was conceded; but on land the Chinese still supposed that their forces would be more effective. Troops had already been sent to Guangzhou and local militias raised there. Additionally, large bodies of incensed Guangdong villagers and 'braves', some under the command of local gentry or popular leaders, had been encouraged to arm themselves and repel the invader. At Sanyuanli, a village north of Guangzhou, in May 1839 these irregulars gathered en masse after some of their women were violated by the invading troops; then, amid heavy rainstorms, they engaged and briefly repelled a force of Indo-British infantry, inflicting minor casualties. Wildly exaggerated – and swiftly disowned by the Guangzhou authorities who had just agreed an armistice – the 'battle' of Sanyuanli would assume mythic proportions and come to be seen as the first triumph of popular resistance against the foreigner. 'A Bunker Hill and an Alamo rolled into one,' as Frederic Wakeman, an American authority on southern China's insurgent movements, puts it, Sanyuanli stimulated a bewildering upsurge of other irregular bands and secret societies operating independently of the Qing authorities and often in defiance of them.[19] The Qing were seen as incapable of dealing with the foreigners, and even as acting in collusion with them. From this eruption of anti-Manchu sentiment would originate, within no great distance of Sanyuanli, the cataclysmic Taiping Rebellion.

The new British plenipotentiary arrived off Hong Kong in August 1841 along with a vastly increased task force and a heftier list of unnegotiable demands. From there the force proceeded to capture Xiamen (Amoy), recapture Zhoushan (Chusan) and then take nearby Ningbo. After wintering and receiving more reinforcements, in 1842 the fleet proceeded up the Yangzi. Manchu Bannermen offered fierce resistance, the British bombardments were often indiscriminate, and there was much looting by both sides. But Shanghai was found undefended; Zhenjiang's fall meant that the Grand Canal was severed; and Nanjing was saved only by a last-minute offer of negotiations.

The Daoguang emperor still hoped to buy off the British; but his negotiators found they could do little to avert capitulation. The Nanjing Treaty of 1842, while it left much for further discussion and recrimination, met the British demands and was ratified by both parties. The indemnity, now raised to $21 million and payable (plus interest) in instalments, would be a crippling burden on the empire's shattered finances. Five ports, including Guangzhou and Shanghai (where a large 'concession' area was rapidly developed by, and exclusively for, the foreigners), were to be opened to both British trade and residency under the supervision of British consuls; Hong Kong stayed British; derogatory language as detected by Britain's interpreters was outlawed; and opium was nowhere mentioned. In that the Chinese ban had been acknowledged by the British, the drug remained contraband; but in that the British had not forsworn the trade, the smuggling continued; indeed, it prospered greatly under the paternal gaze of the British navy.

The Nanjing Treaty of 1842 was swiftly followed by others. With the mistaken idea that only by winning the support of competing nations could China hold the British in check, the Qing government signed treaties with the Americans and the French (and later other nations). Both these treaties included provision for missionary activity in China – Protestant Evangelical in the case of the Americans, Roman Catholic in the case of the French. They also elaborated on the practice of extraterritorial justice and, in the American case, allowed for a revision of the treaty after twelve years. Additionally both contained a 'most favoured nation' clause under which any concessions extended to others might also be claimed by the signatory nation. Since the British, in an 1843 supplement to the Nanjing Treaty, obtained an identical provision, the foreign powers, far from quarrelling among themselves, had a vested interest in supporting one another's ever more outrageous demands.

It was the American provision for treaty 'modification' after twelve years which would be invoked by the British in 1854 to ratchet up their requirements, including access to the Chinese interior and an ambassador in Beijing. Another war would back up these demands, and the inevitable concessions would follow. The so-called 'Treaty System' was thus a collaborative and progressive exercise in the diminution of China's sovereignty through the appropriation of large sectors of its economy, its foreign relations, its society (in 'the Treaty ports' and concession areas) and its territory (in Hong Kong and later Manchuria and Xinjiang). Nanjing was just stage one.

TAIPING AND TIANJIN

The series of defeats suffered by the Qing in the 1839–42 Opium War, though the worst in the dynasty's two centuries of rule, did not long go unchallenged. Exposed by the outsiders, in less than a decade the empire faced rebellions within on a quite staggering scale. The two catastrophes were of course related. Had the Qing not just been humiliated, their forces trounced and their economy fractured, the insurgencies might not have arisen. On the other hand, without foreign forbearance and eventual support, the Qing could scarcely have hoped to suppress them. Relations with the foreigners were becoming more complicated. Having crippled Macartney's 'old, crazy, First-rate Man of War', the Western powers now opted to keep it afloat; rather than tangle with the wreckage, they would make it safe in the name of salvage.

Nearly all of China was affected by the rebellions. 'Red Turban' armies fighting for a Ming restoration (Ming pretenders were never in short supply) terrorised Guangdong in the mid-1850s. Muslim separatists took over Yunnan from 1855; other Muslim revolts plagued Shaanxi and Gansu from 1862. A host of heavily armed peasant bands known collectively as the Nian rampaged across Anhui and Jiangsu north of the Huai River from at least 1851. On cue, the Yellow River, capricious as ever, burst its dykes, causing devastating floods that climaxed in 1855 when it opted for an old estuary north of Shandong. Meanwhile Triad fraternities flexed their muscles in the ports, taking over Xiamen and then Shanghai in 1853–55; they and other secret societies also mobilised among the rural masses; ethnic minorities rebelled in the hills; pirates infested the coast. And there were more. But all these outbreaks were localised and little coordinated. They paled into insignificance beside the Taiping upheaval, 'one of the great pivotal events of Chinese history', or, as contemporary writers in both *The Times* and the *North American Review* had it, 'the greatest revolution the world has yet seen'.[20]

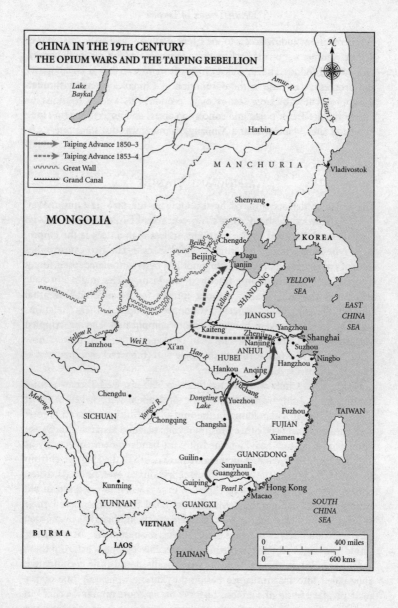

Whether revolution, civil war or mere uprising, the Taiping movement spans the insurrectionist watershed between the dynastic challengers of the past and the ideological engineers of the future. It was both a nativist throwback and a radical new departure, a people's revolution masterminded by ideological simpletons, an Asian peasants' revolt flavoured by Judaeo-Christian messianism. In all its fury it raged for more than a decade (1850–64). From Guangdong and Guangxi in the far south it extended to within a few days' march of Beijing, affecting sixteen out of the eighteen provinces and turning the heart of the country along the Yangzi into an extended battlefield. Its magnitude seemed at the time, and possibly remains, unprecedented. Sober analysts have tried to quantify the death toll: 'twenty million people lost their lives' (Reilly), 'twenty million or more' (Spence), 'between 20 and 40 million people' (Teng). Not all died in battle; the famines, retributive feuds and casual massacres that dislocation engendered took a heavy toll; so did power struggles and purges within the Taiping leadership. Thousands died simply from exposure, despite having burned whole libraries to warm themselves (including three of the four manuscript copies of the Qianlong emperor's 'Four Treasuries'). As ever, the greater the loss, the less certain the body count. Suffice it to say that, if the figures are even remotely accurate, more of the human race perished in the Taiping convulsion than in the First World War.

Throughout its few turbulent decades the man at the heart of this phenomenon was Hong Xiuquan (1814–64), a member of Guangdong's large Hakka community. The Hakkas claimed descent from one of the early waves of Han migration into the south – that which had accompanied the Eastern Jin dynasty when in 311 Luoyang fell to the Xiongnu as reported in that miraculously preserved letter of the Sogdian merchant Nanai Vandak. Hardworking and opinionated, some Hakkas had since migrated to south-east Asia; more would follow. But mostly they were marginal farmers subject to the fiscal, environmental and demographic pressures of the times. Of Hong Xiuquan, a good-looking youth and promising scholar, much was expected by his impoverished family and rural clansmen. But like countless other aspiring examinees, he found this weight of expectation insupportable when failure greeted his attempts to pass the district examinations. He tried four times, and on one of them, when entering the Guangzhou examination compound, he was handed a loosely bound collection of tracts containing translated extracts from the Bible, a production of the London Missionary Society's Singapore branch. Hong took it and put it aside for later reference.

Unlike the Jesuits in the seventeenth century – those polymath padres who had directed their talents and their proselytising towards the court and officialdom – the Protestant missions operated at a lower social level. Rather than pursuing a doctrinal accommodation with Confucian tradition and pinning their hopes on the top-down conversion of an empire, they looked to the saving of individual souls and the refutation of heresy. The Word of God, carefully translated, widely disseminated and selflessly advertised by their own example, was deemed sufficient unto the task; and in the case of Hong Xiuquan, it did indeed work in mysterious ways. Hong, now a village schoolmaster, started having hallucinations and dreams. When later he thought to peruse the mission's 'Good Words for Exhorting the Age', as the tracts were entitled, he realised that his dreams were in fact visions. The bearded gentleman with fair hair who had given him a sword was God himself; and the younger man who had taught him how to use it against evil demons, and who had then accepted him as a sibling, was Jesus Christ. Hong must therefore be the next son of God, China's son of God; and clearly the sword meant that he had been entrusted with a weighty mission – to root out idolatry and so perform for China the redemptive miracle that his elder brother Jesus had worked in the Western world.

Openly proclaiming his task, and proving an inspirational preacher, Hong converted Hakka friends and family in rural Guangdong and began destroying local shrines dedicated to Buddhist or Confucian worship. This proved controversial. He was obliged to flit between Guangdong and neighbouring Guangxi, where an early adherent had successfuly formed a satellite community of 'God-worshippers'. In 1847 Hong was back in Guangzhou city, extending his acquaintance with the Bible through instruction from a Baptist minister from Tennessee. The Reverend Isaacher Jacox (*sic*) Roberts was the first to take advantage of the tolerance extended to missionaries under the Sino-American treaty. A difficult man, he would later report that Hong, though prepared for baptism, never actually received it; he, Roberts, had not been 'fully satisfied of his fitness'.[21]

Repairing to the 'God-worshippers' in the gorges of Guangxi, Hong resumed his recruitment of followers. His mission began to assume a more political and military character. Arms and gunpowder were hoarded, signals practised, troops drilled and plans laid. As well as proclaiming his visions and destroying more shrines, Hong and others in his hierarchy who were possessed of a basic education began to integrate their revelatory faith with their knowledge of China's historical past. Their starting point, and the inspiration for their military organisation, seems to have been the *Zhouli*, or 'Rites of Zhou' – the 'fundamentalist' text describing a utopian society in which names corresponded to realities that had supposedly been composed by the Duke of Zhou and had inspired reformers ever since. In those far-off times, according to the 'God-worshippers', China had been the recipient of 'the original doctrine of the Heavenly Father'. It had then shared it with the wider world, and there it had survived and been renewed. But in China, Heaven's first home, it had been turned on its head by a succession of 'devilish' invaders after the fall of the Han dynasty. *Zhongguo*'s road had thus diverged from the true path. The Manchus – 'imps' or 'demons', the Taipings called them – were the latest manifestation of these 'devilish' usurpers and, like shrines and idols, they must be destroyed. Only then could there be re-established the *taiping tianguo*, the 'Heavenly Kingdom of Great Peace'. A tag by which the movement would be known, this phrase neatly combined the Christian *tianguo*, 'Kingdom of Heaven'/ 'Heavenly Kingdom', with the Zhouist or Daoist *taiping*, 'Great Peace'.

Other contemporary movements, such as the Red Turbans and the Triads, also opposed the Manchu Qing as alien usurpers; they wanted to set the clock back to 1644 and restore the Ming. But the Taipings opposed the Qing as the last in a long line of heretical alien dynasties; the clock should go back to AD 221. This chimed, as it were, with important strands in recent thought. Eighteenth-century scholars equally unreconciled to the Qing had blamed the failure of the indigenous Ming on the Neo-Confucianism of Zhu Xi (he of the 'Four Books' and the text-bound 'investigation of all things') or Wang Yangming (and his dangerously malleable 'innate sense' of what was right and humane). They too, therefore, had looked back to an earlier tradition and especially to the Han dynasty when the classic texts still retained a pristine quality uncorrupted by later editing. Practising what they called 'evidential research', these scholars brought to bear on the classics a more scientific approach in linguistics, geography and astronomy, and so restored a certain vitality to Confucian studies.

Earlier another Ming loyalist, Wang Fuzhi (d. 1692), had pursued a similar line of anti-Manchu argument but with quite different results. Questioning the cherished belief that alien invaders always succumbed to *zhongguo*'s superior culture and were assimilated by it, Wang Fuzhi had proposed that Han and non-Han values were in fact incompatible; alien regimes had warped Chinese civilisation rather than being absorbed by it, and Confucius himself had foreseen as much. Therefore, wrote Wang, 'destroying the [aliens] to save our people may be called humane, deceiving and treating them as they hate to be treated may be called loyal, and occupying their territory . . . confiscating their property . . . may be called righteous'.[22] Wang Fuzhi sought only a rationale for opposing the Manchu Qing; but in such sentiments later writers have discovered 'the first hesitant gropings towards the discovery of a "national" tradition'. Ethnocentric and exclusive, these gropings did not as yet amount to 'a new organic tradition' of Han assertiveness. But as an experiment to this end, the contribution of Hong Xiuquan and the Taipings would be significant, 'albeit fantastic, visionary, and intellectually distasteful to upper-class Chinese of the time'.[23] Whether by chance or design, the Taipings tapped into some of the sources of later Chinese nationalism – antipathy to Qing imperialism on the grounds of its alien origin, authenticity through alignment with an impeccably organised agrarian society, insistence on China's centrality (even within Christianity's universal 'All-under-Heaven'), a yearning for social justice and gender equality, and the espousal of a common Han Chinese identity based on place, race and culture rather than dynastic mandates and historiographic sanction.

After three years in and around Guiping in Guangxi, Hong and his associates had gathered disciples and recruits to the tune of about twenty thousand. Some had useful experience, having belonged to pirate and other insurgent groups or worked in the local mines. Many were Hakkas, both men and women. A few had a genuine flair for military tactics and organisation. Discipline was strict, with opium, alcohol, tobacco, gambling and sex outlawed on both religious and practical grounds. Money and possessions were pooled, foot-binding banned, pigtails cut and the hair allowed to grow. There were frequent prayer and instruction sessions; on the Seventh Day they rested and worshipped. Such practices could scarcely fail to attract attention, and in late 1849 the 'God-worshippers' narrowly repelled an assault by the authorities. Soon after, Hong officially declared himself 'the Heavenly King', and the whole community moved out of the Guiping area, heading north through the hills to the Yangzi watershed.

What began as a migration turned into a crusade. The Taipings' 'Long March' lasted over two years (1851–53) and took them from the obscurity of Guiping to centre stage in Nanjing. Sometimes compared to Moses' Exodus or the Prophet's hegira (*hijra*), in its military aspect the advance more obviously resembled the Arabs' post-hegira jihad. Closer to home, the most remarked precedent was Huang Chao's marathon progress of 879–80, when he led his rebel army north along much the same route to exterminate the Tang dynasty. Like Huang Chao, the Taipings had mixed fortunes. Despite fanatical onslaughts, they were forced to fall back before the well-defended cities of Guilin and Changsha. They gathered adherents and defectors by the thousand, but the larger the heavenly host, the greater the need for supplies and munitions. In this respect, while the capture of Yuezhou on Lake Dongting proved a breakthrough, that of Wuchang and Hankou, the twin cities of the Middle Yangzi, was the turning point. Now with guns, money, supplies and above all boats, the Taiping armies took to the river. Downstream, Anqing fell in early 1853, then – amid the slaughter of every Manchu they could lay their hands on – the high-walled metropolis of Nanjing. Zhenjiang at the river's confluence with the Grand Canal followed. In March 1853 the 'Heavenly King' entered Nanjing in style, borne aloft in a golden palanquin and wearing the dragon robe of a Chinese emperor plus the tinsel crown of a Christian king.

Arrived in 'the southern capital', from where the Ming founder had proclaimed his rule, the Taiping commanders seem to have opted to follow his example. Instead of continuing their barnstorming advance to Beijing, they held back to institute the new Jerusalem and savour the fruits of victory. Momentum and surprise – not to say panic – were lost. When two months later the advance was at last resumed, smaller expeditionary armies, minus their Heavenly King, headed north to Beijing and west up the Yangzi, where Anqing and Wuchang had already been retaken by Qing forces. But the northern thrust was by now expected. Boats had been removed from the Yellow River to prevent a crossing and Banner troops massed to oppose the insurgents. The Taipings veered west to Kaifeng and received some assistance from the Nian rebels. By the time they approached Beijing, their lack of cavalry was telling. Worse still, the northern winter, a novel experience for Guangxi Hakkas, was setting in. They halted outside Tianjin and would get no farther. Reinforcements arrived in 1854 and the campaign resumed, only to peter out in a series of irrelevant sieges. It was abandoned in 1855.

The western thrust fared better. Anqing was secured and Wuchang retaken – though later lost again to a provincial army from Hunan. With forces reckoned in the hundreds of thousands, plus control of the vital Yangzi corridor over a distance of around 500 kilometres (310 miles), the Taiping kingdom now bestrode the empire. Suzhou, Shanghai and the other teeming cities of the delta were threatened. Trade in the region was at a standstill; the wider world took notice. Anglo-American missionaries, sensing a triumph beyond their wildest dreams, urged support of the rebels. The Reverend W. A. P. Martin expected them to 'revolutionise the empire, rendering all its vast provinces open to the preachers of the Gospel'.[24] But the French were sceptical; Catholic images were as liable to be vandalised as Buddhist or Confucian ones. And the other foreign powers, though initially sanguine, grew more cautious when the northen expedition failed and a Qing army held steady around the *Ming* Hongwu emperor's tomb in the hills behind Nanjing. All observers, too, had deep reservations about the Taipings' inexperience, the more so when their literary productions were scrutinised and first-hand reports of the Heavenly Kingdom began to filter out.

Most foreigners who reached Nanjing could not fault Taiping discipline and dedication. They were impressed by an idealism and a puritanical abstinence unknown among contemporary militias, by the important role assigned to women (including military deployment), by the pervading spirit of fraternity, and by the common ownership of resources. On paper, and to an unascertainable extent in practice, the *taiping tianguo* was as much commonwealth as kingdom. The sexes were segregated, equal rights were enjoyed by each, and land was made available to all. But there was a naivety and presumption in it all. Even the missionaries were taken aback by Taiping ignorance; they baulked at the sight of animal sacrifices in Taiping chapels, were riled by patronising comments about 'Our Lord' (meaning Hong) being 'Your Lord too', and were embarrassed by Taiping questionnaires asking for God's personal details ('How tall is God? And how broad? How large his abdomen? Does he write verse? How rapidly?', etc.).[25]

This questionnaire came in response to one of a more political nature submitted by a British mission to Nanjing in 1854. The attitude of the British was crucial and, though initially ambivalent, was already souring. The Taiping kings – Hong's seniormost commanders had just been crowned as subkings of the Heavenly Kingdom's four compass points – were as disrespectful of foreigners as any Qing official. They, and Hong himself, had already embraced a life of luxury, surrounded by concubines, that was at odds with both their emphasis on the Ten Commandments and the austerities expected of their hard-working subjects. There were also deep divisions within the leadership. In 1856 a horrific bloodbath took the lives of tens of thousands when two overbearing kings were toppled and their supporters massacred. The 'Heavenly Kingdom of Great Peace' was looking more like a hellish kingdom of great purges. It was this, as well as the movement's military setbacks, which slewed international opinion against the Taipings and in favour of the Qing.

For the Qing, too, the attitude of the British was crucial. The British had the largest fleet and the only one capable of reopening the Yangzi. The young Xianfeng emperor (r. 1851–61), though deeply suspicious of Anglo-Taiping contacts and distrustful of foreigners in general, had already asked the British for naval assistance in attacking the Taipings. It had been declined on the grounds that the British were neutral. The other powers took a similar line, happily advertising their contacts with the rebels if only to cow the Qing. In the case of the British, this was more like holding the Qing to ransom; for they had just tabled a demand for the revision of the 1842 treaty confident that the Taiping menace would find the Qing court at its most amenable.

Revision of the treaty meant rewriting it. Backed by the French and Americans, the British were now demanding more treaty ports, commercial access to the interior of China, a permanent ambassador in Beijing, the legalisation of the opium trade, the suppression of piracy and the lifting of internal transit dues. That was the first list; but as with the earlier treaty, cause was soon found to extend it. The interplay of negotiation and bombardment that ensued also closely resembled that which preceded the first treaty. Talks got under way but were suspended when in late 1856 a Chinese-owned but Hong Kong-based lorcha (small freighter) was suspected of piracy and seized by the Guangzhou authorities. The ship was called the *Arrow* and its legal status was highly debatable. But the incident was enough to ruffle British feathers and precipitate the 'Arrow War' (1856–60).

Despite the demands of other wars in the Crimea and then India (the Great Rebellion or Mutiny), sufficient shipping was found for an Anglo-French task force. It stormed Guangzhou, captured and deported its governor, took over the city and then sailed north. In April/May 1858 the Anglo-French force took the Dagu forts at the mouth of the Beihe and reached Tianjin. Beijing was again at the foreigners' mercy; and again the Qing capitulated. The result was the punitive Treaty of Tianjin. With more insults to redress and more expenses to recoup, the British and French now imposed terms so heavy that one of their own negotiators considered them unreasonable. 'We asked or rather dictated what . . . the Chinese could neither safely promise nor be fairly expected to perform.'[26] Expanding and adding to the earlier list, the British and French demanded the opening of six new treaty ports, four in the hitherto closely guarded areas of Taiwan, Shandong and Manchuria. The Yangzi, and with it the richest provinces of the empire, was also to be opened to foreign trade as soon as the Taiping occupation permitted; and there were to be four treaty ports on the river, including Nanjing and Hankou. Travel in and around the treaty ports was to be unrestricted, and passports afforded to those who wished to go farther afield. Christian preachers were to be protected (it was attacks on Catholic missionaries which had provoked the French into participating in the task force); the new British ambassador in Beijing was to be accompanied by family and retainers and suitably accommodated; the noxious word *yi* was never again to be used of foreigners; and the import of opium, though its use was still banned, was legalised subject to a not unreasonable rate of duty.

Of all these concessions, that for a resident British ambassador in Beijing proved the least palatable – as it had when Macartney came calling sixty-five years earlier. Mainly because of it, the court prevaricated over ratification. In 1859, in the course of pressing for ratification, an Anglo-French detachment was repulsed at the Dagu forts. This all-too-rare triumph led the Qing court to repudiate the treaty and led the foreigners to plan drastic action. Within a year some twenty thousand British and French troops stormed Dagu, took Tianjin and, when fired up by news of the execution of some of their captured colleagues, sacked the Qing emperors' summer retreat at Jehol. In the process the Summer Palace, a fanciful Louvre designed for the Qianlong emperor by the Jesuits, was looted and burned. Though no great loss to architecture, it was a body blow to Qing prestige. Despite the emperor's absence – he had fled Jehol for Manchuria just in time – the court sued for peace on the same day.

The negotiations that produced the 1860 'Convention of Peking' were less notable for their terms – ratification of the 1858 treaty, another massive indemnity, a bit of the Kowloon peninsula to be added to Hong Kong, and Tianjin made a treaty port – than for the negotiators. On behalf of the court, Prince Gong, a brother of the Xianfeng emperor, emerged as a realistic and resourceful representative. He would preside over the empire's foreign relations for the next thirty years, winning the respect of his adversaries and the reputation of a reformer. When the Xianfeng emperor died, aged thirty, a year after the Peking Convention, his mother, the Dowager Empress Cixi, engineered a succession of minors. It ensured her ascendancy but introduced an element of uncertainty to the succession. Prince Gong was one of those who provided the stability, continuity and realism that would lead to the period being acclaimed one of *zhongxing*, 'restoration'.

The other newcomer to the negotiations was Russia. Taking advantage of the Qing's embarrassments at the hands of the Western powers and the Taipings, the tsarist government had again taken up the question of Manchuria's north-eastern borders. Russian expeditions had re-explored the Heilongjiang (Amur River) and could find little sign of Manchu administration either north of it or in the long coastal region east of its Wusuli (Ussuri) tributary. The Qing claimed the whole vast area as part of their Manchu patrimony but had forbidden Han settlement there, or anywhere else in Manchuria. The Russians claimed it mainly for the potential, at its southernmost tip, of a warm-water port on the Pacific.

Sino-Russian negotiations to resolve the matter coincided with those between the Anglo-French forces and the Qing over the Tianjin Treaty.

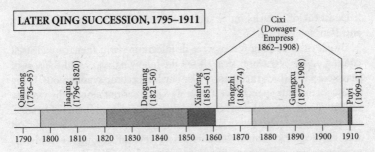

LATER QING SUCCESSION, 1795–1911

Cixi (Dowager Empress 1862–1908)

Qianlong (1736–95)
Jiaqing (1796–1820)
Daoguang (1821–50)
Xianfeng (1851–61)
Tongzhi (1862–74)
Guangxu (1875–1908)
Puyi (1909–11)

1790 1800 1810 1820 1830 1840 1850 1860 1870 1880 1890 1900 1910

Skilfully interposing themselves as intermediaries while promising secret support to the Qing, and taking every advantage of Qing weakness, the Russian delegates secured a treaty 'that opened the entire northern frontier of the Qing empire, from Manchuria to Xinjiang, to Russia's political and commercial influence'; moreover the subsequent demarcation of the Manchurian frontier awarded them all the territory north of the Heilongjiang and east of the Wusuli border.[27] There, in due course, would be constructed Vladivostok, Russia's only year-round Pacific port.

Back in Nanjing, the God-worshippers of the Taiping kingdom followed all these developments with interest. Little attempt was made, however, to take advantage of them until 1861, by when it was too late. In that year Taiping forces thrust east into the Yangzi delta, taking Suzhou, then Hangzhou and Ningbo, and threatening Shanghai. Reassurances were given to the foreigners about their concessions and their trade; and in Ningbo, a treaty port, the Taiping occupation proved exemplary. But the Westerners had by now secured all their demands from Beijing and were anxious only to enjoy them in peace, especially in respect of access to the Yangzi ports. They were therefore as keen as the Qing to see the rebellion ended. Guns and gunboats, transport, munitions and loans were made available to the Qing. More famously, volunteer units composed mainly of Chinese irregulars but equipped, drilled and officered by French, Americans and British fought alongside the Qing troops. The French-officered unit was called the 'Unvanquished Army', while its Anglo-American equivalent was the 'Ever-Victorious Army'. The names were translations of those given them by the Chinese for recruitment purposes, not hard-earned accolades; both in fact suffered their share of reverses. But with modern rifles, howitzers, horse-drawn field guns and inspirational commanders – initially the American buccaneer Frederick T. Ward, latterly the God-fearing British hero Charles Gordon – they helped beat off attacks on Shanghai and reclaim the cities of Zhejiang and Jiangsu.

By 1863 the Taiping forces were disintegrating and their capital itself coming under ever closer siege. It fell the following year amid the sort of massacre with which the name of Nanjing has become synonymous. Hong Xiuquan, the latterly reclusive 'Heavenly King', was not among the victims. He had died a few weeks earlier of supernatural causes; a surfeit of 'manna' was diagnosed by his physicians. The martyrdom to which a Son of God was entitled was denied him. Heaven's revenge, though confidently predicted, also failed to manifest itself. Harried and dispersed to the four corners of the empire, the remnants of his forces were absorbed by other rebel groups and by 1870 the movement was extinct.

In Nanjing today, a Ming garden complex houses the little 'Taiping Heavenly Kingdom Historical Museum'. Integration being the modern message, the exhibits and photographs tell less about the Taipings and more about those who suppressed them. Prominence goes to the dashing exploits of the Ever-Victorious and Unvanquished armies. But well represented too are armies from Hunan and Anhui under their provincial generals Zeng Guofan and Li Hongzhang. Zeng, his protégé Li (both of whom would also be involved in ending the Nian revolts) and Zuo Zongtang (who finally extinguished the Muslim revolts in the west in the 1870s), represented the real legacy of two decades of rebellion.

With the Manchu Banners proving too moribund to check the rebels, provincial governors and governors-general led by Zeng Guofan's example in Hunan had been encouraged to raise and train their own forces. To pay for them, they were granted fiscal rights that included the sale of degrees and imposts on internal trade. Known as *likin*, the latter in particular brought in large revenues destined exclusively for the provincial administrations at a time when imperial revenues from conventional taxation were declining owing to the disturbances. The new armies, better paid and equipped, gave a good account of themselves and had largely contained the Taipings throughout the late 1850s. But the situation was potentially as explosive as that at the end of the Tang dynasty when over-militarised governors of the frontier provinces had exacted a heavy price for coming to the aid of the dynasty.

In the late nineteenth century it was the empire rather than the dynasty which suffered. With military and financial resources of their own, the provincial administrations assumed a prominence and displayed a dynamism that helped shore up the dynasty and stabilise the economy. But this reprise, or 'restoration', was attained at a price. To foreign observers in particular it looked as if the empire itself was ripe for fragmentation. The Russians debated plans for detaching Mongolia, Manchuria and Xinjiang; the British began to take an interest in Tibet; the French, lately established in what they called 'Indo-Chine', showed a proprietary interest in Guangxi and Yunnan; and a Japan transformed by the Meiji reforms staked a claim to the Ryukyu Islands and an interest in Korea that would soon extend to Manchuria.

16

REPUBLICANS AND NATIONALISTS
1880–1950

BRUSH TO PEN

WHEN REVIEWING CHINA'S RECORD DURING THE twentieth century, historians of the future may see things differently. The wars and the revolutions that loomed so large to contemporaries, the men who led them and the ideologies that polarised them are likely to be set alongside less conspicuous developments that seemed at the time secondary or intermittent. Already all those revolutions – republican, Nationalist, communist, cultural – may be bracketed within a finite sequence, a sixty-year continuum of turbulence whose horrors are mercifully diminished by a longer perspective and a more pragmatic present. The ideologies have been declawed, the revolutionaries cut down to size, the wars consigned to museums and monuments. Attention is switching to other, longer-term agents of change.

One of these is the integration into public life of the half-billion Chinese formerly condemned to subservience on the grounds of gender. Female emancipation is ongoing and not, of course, unique to China. But as visitors often noted, women in Qing China had farther to go than most. Not just irrelevant, they were largely invisible. Literacy was denied to all but a determined handful; for the rest, drudgery lasted a lifetime and strict confinement was reckoned a privilege. This struck late-nineteenth-century observers as ironical given that China was effectively ruled by a woman. But Cixi, the diminutive dowager empress who presided over the empire as either regent or power-broker throughout its last half-century (1862–1908), did so in silence from behind a large silken screen. A presence rather than a person, as dread and devious as her Victorian counterpart was dumpy and reassuring, she betrayed none of the spirited allegiance to her sex shown by the Tang empress Wu Zetian.

In an edict of 1902 she did, though, eventually ban foot-binding.

Protestant missionaries, some of them women, had been railing against female infanticide ever since the 1850s. Chinese reformers had anticipated them; so had the Catholic missions. But the Protestants, often American, were more numerous and better at organising; and while both infanticide and arranged marriages drew their fire, it was foot-binding which concentrated it. The first of many anti-foot-binding societies had been formed in the treaty port of Xiamen in 1874. As of 1895 a high-profile 'Natural Foot Society' based in Shanghai lobbied hard for official action. Reform-minded activists took up the cry and duly persuaded the dowager empress – who as an unbound Manchu probably disapproved of the custom anyway – to ban it. Christian schools, which unlike Confucian academies and local crammers had been admitting girls since a Miss Aldersley opened the first in Ningbo shortly after the Opium War, generally made admission dependent on the pupils' feet being unbound. But the link thus established between big feet and a foreign education seems to have cut both ways, for as late as 1909 'only around 13,000 girls were enrolled in schools [all run by missions] in the whole of China, and a few hundred more overseas'.[1]

Despite the efforts of missionaries, of social mavericks such as the Taipings and a few pioneering reformers who had been exposed to Western thought, dramatic change had to await all those wars and revolutions. When mobilising the masses, it helped to magnify them by including women; realising the nation's potential meant extending educational opportunity to everyone, regardless of gender; discipline, deprivation and the other burdens of resurgence must also be shared. Yet nowhere in the world would so many emerge from such abject inconsequence, or overcome such hobbling handicaps, as the women of China in the twentieth century.

Another theme, common to many reform programmes and also designed to equalise opportunity, concerned the Chinese language in both its spoken and written form. The matter was of the essence. What distinguished China's ruling elite and preserved its monopoly of office was familiarity with a demanding body of literature written in a refined and archaic medium (called *wenyan*). Government was conducted exclusively in this medium, as was scholarship and literary composition. The examination system with its formulaic 'eight-legged' essays was designed to assess not a candidate's intelligence or ability but his mastery of this higher culture and his moral eligibility to be inducted into it. It has been estimated that male literacy in late Qing times was as high as 30–45 per cent (and female as low as 2–10 per cent), but for the most part this was literacy of a different kind, informal and basic in that it embraced the limited number of written characters needed to express vernacular speech. It afforded little understanding of the classical language and less of the ancient texts that gave that language its rich resonances and satisfying allusions. Popular works had long been written in the vernacular, including famous novels such as *The Dream of the Red Chamber* (or *Story of the Stone*) in the eighteenth century; but all that pertained to higher culture and government, the essence of Chinese identity, was beyond the reach of the majority of Chinese.

Bringing culture to the masses, let alone acquainting them with those sciences and humanities on which the foreigners' superiority seemed to be grounded, meant going back to basics. In 1859 Yung Wing, the product of a missionary education and the first Chinese to have acquired an American degree (at Yale), had been invited to Nanjing. There the Taiping leaders were interested in acquiring foreign firepower. Although the programme of reforms that he drew up proved too ambitious for them, four years later Yung Wing was summoned by Zeng Guofan, the scholarly general and governor of Hunan whose provincially raised army was then closing in on the Taipings. As a leading advocate of modernisation, Zeng Guofan was planning China's first munitions factory and arsenal (at Shanghai) and wanted Yung Wing's advice on equipping it. Yung, instead of recommending machine tools specifically designed for 'making guns, engines, agricultural implements, clocks etc', advised buying machinery that could make the machines to make such things. 'A machine shop that would be able to create . . . other machine shops' was what was needed, one equipped with 'lathes of all sizes, planers and drills'. 'I should say that a machine shop in the present state of China should be of a general and fundamental character and not one for specific purposes,' he declared.[2] The governor agreed; Yung was packed off back to America, found the machinery he wanted, and by 1868 the Shanghai arsenal was turning out not only ordnance but ships and boilers.

An approach no less 'general and fundamental' was required in addressing the language problem, though in this case the answer was found nearer to home. It lay in universalising the use of the vernacular – or rather, of the written form of the northern vernacular known as *baihua*, and by foreigners as Mandarin. Pronunciation continued to vary in different regions and among different communities (Cantonese, for example). Moreover the name of the language changed in line with the political climate, the Nationalists calling it *guoyu*, the 'National Language', and the communists *putonghua*, the 'Common Speech'. And the language itself underwent extensive adaptation with the incorporation of new grammatical structures and a vast vocabulary of foreign loan-words. Nevertheless it remained recognisably Chinese and so preserved the 3,000-year continuity of the oldest of the world's still widely used tongues. Agitation for the adoption of *baihua* followed the abolition of the examination system in 1905 and is closely associated with a second generation of reformers, among them Hu Shi and Chen Duxiu. Both these men had travelled and studied abroad before joining the faculty of Beijing University, and both championed the vernacular as part of their assault on a Confucian value system that they saw as irreconcilable with a modern state. In 1920 Chen Duxiu became a founder member of the Chinese Communist Party, and it was under the party's aegis that the classical language would be completely eclipsed.

The script posed similar problems. Missionaries and interpreters such as Thomas Wade, a prime negotiator in the 1858 Tianjin Treaty and later the first professor of Chinese at Cambridge, explored the possibilities of rendering Chinese characters in the alphabetic Roman lettering of most Western languages; this led to the still-common 'Wade-Giles' system of transliteration, Herbert Giles being Wade's successor at Cambridge. In Vietnam, where Chinese characters had been the only script for 2,000 years, an equivalent system of Romanisation was adopted in the schools in 1906 and nationally in the 1920s. Partly thanks to French encouragement, partly to Vietnamese enthusiasm for distancing their culture from China's, this *quoc ngu* completely replaced the Chinese characters.

But in China reformers were chary of so fundamental a change. It would mean debasing their whole written heritage as well as adding immeasurably to the work of the Qing translation bureau, already burdened with having to render official business in Manchu and Mongol as well as Chinese. Unexpectedly the solution – though by no means a perfect one – to making the script more accessible lay ultimately in technology. As the soft brush and the inkstone, those cherished accoutrements of the scholar, made way for the steel nib and the lead pencil, then the biro, typewriter and keypad, the written characters were necessarily simplified and standardised and their components dissected. Writing was liberated from the lofty constraints of calligraphy, and the unadorned characters could attain popular currency as a vernacular script. Like the spoken language, they still retain a recognisable relationship to the earliest written characters as found on the oracle bones and turtle plastrons of the Shang.

Simultaneously printing and publishing underwent a revolution of their own. Though movable type had been familiar to the Chinese for centuries, its use had been limited, largely because of a preference for woodblock fonts. The 1859 introduction of metal typecasting using an electrotype process was the brainchild of William Gamble, an Irish-American missionary keen to leaflet China's masses with the Christian message. 'Thanks to Gamble's invention, the American Presbyterian Mission Press was able to supply complete Chinese fonts to printers in other parts of China (including to the leading Shanghai newspaper *Shenbao*) and, indeed, all over the world.' [3] Gamble's process remained in use for over a century 'until the advent of computer generated fonts in the 1970s'. Shanghai became the centre of the printing industry, as of most other industries. And *Shenbao*, founded by the Englishman Ernest Major in 1872, established itself as both the leading Chinese-medium newspaper and the pioneer in photolithography and then rotary printing. Among the numerous other publications and periodicals produced by the *Shenbao* press was the first journal in the vernacular. It started publication in 1876 – and ceased in 1876. Ahead of its time, it was yet the forerunner of several hundred such publications by the 1920s.

The first period of modernisation from which all these long-term developments date – roughly from 1860 when Anglo-French forces had stormed the Summer Palace until the 1880s when another catastrophic series of defeats provoked more radical change – is generally characterised by the then current slogan of 'Self-Strengthening' (*ziqiang*). The term had first appeared in a series of essays submitted by a concerned scholar in 1860. These stressed the need to learn from the foreigners by studying their languages and sciences and by emulating their example in the exploitation of their nations' resources and manpower. The object was thereby to re-establish the ascendancy of the empire and reprise the authority of the Qing, not to overthrow them. As in Japan, where a parallel transformation was under way, the initiative came more from within than from the strangers without, and more from above than from the degree-less masses below.

The Self-Strengthening movement is particularly associated with that group of provincial governors-general who, by raising revenues and armies of their own rather than relying on the decrepit Banners or the gentry-led militias, had defeated the mid-century rebellions. Zeng Guofan, the Hunan governor-general who had harried the Taipings, was the classic example. A distinguished Confucian scholar, Zeng accepted the need for some foreign technology (as in his Shanghai arsenal) and guidance (he had endorsed the services of the Ever Victorious Army), yet he still emphasised traditional panacea, such as recruiting only officials of the highest principles. Of a similar bent was Zuo Zongtang, who as governor-general of Shaanxi and Gansu doggedly suppressed the Muslim revolts there and in Xinjiang. Before taking up his north-western assignment, Zuo too had established an arsenal and dockyard, this time in Fuzhou. Like Zeng Guofan's Shanghai foundation, it would spawn a naval base and an officer-training academy.

Li Hongzhang, Zeng Guofan's imposing protégé, was younger and more pragmatic. As governor of Anhui he had assisted in the suppression of the Taipings and had then wiped out the Nian bands. Transferred to Tianjin as governor-general of the important capital province around Beijing, and as commissioner of trade for all its ports, Li Hongzhang occupied a pivotal position until his death in 1901. Under a joint initiative involving 'official supervision, merchant management', Li started a shipping line that took over the coastal transport of grain from the Yangzi to the north, then a coal mine to supply his ships with a return cargo, a railway line to get the coal to the ships, and a telegraph line to get the orders to the mine. The telegraph and the railway were among the first in China. At Tianjin he set up another naval and munitions facility and in Shanghai a cotton mill. All involved foreign expertise and some offshore capital. In the 1870s Li was responsible for a programme that sent more than a hundred students to the United States for further education. The exercise was aborted when the US government refused them access to the Annapolis and West Point academies; instead students were sent to Europe and then Japan.

As a Self-Strengthener, Li Hongzhang was not above strengthening himself. But his personal fortune seems to have come less from business than from international diplomacy. His influence in this sphere was second to none thanks to his rapport with the Dowager Empress Cixi, the respect he commanded among the foreign community, and the strategic and commercial importance of his Tianjin power base. Not even Prince Gong, Cixi's nephew, who was nominally in charge of foreign relations, was inclined to overrule Li Hongzhang. As for the Zongli Yamen, a newly created agency for foreign affairs, according to the foreigners it was but a run-down office full of experts in the art of frustration. Through the devastating crises that were about to expose China's international weakness, Li Hongzhang's most useful associate would prove to be an Irishman, the estimable Robert Hart, who served as the Beijing-based Inspector General of Maritime Customs.

The collection of China's maritime dues had first passed to the safekeeping of British officials when in 1854 the court's customs receipts were threatened by the anti-Manchu Triads' occupation of Shanghai. The Triads in fact behaved quite responsibly, but British supervision of customs collection was reconfirmed when the city was then menaced by the Taipings.

Indeed, foreign regulation and supervision were being revealed as rather advantageous. They guaranteed a substantially increased yield; and since this revenue proved dependable and was remitted directly to the imperial exchequer, the court could raise loans for the construction of the new shipyards and academies on the strength of it. The system was therefore retained and extended to the other treaty Ports, and the headquarters of the service was moved to Beijing. What looked like a massive infringement of China's sovereignty was, for once, an amicable and profitable collaboration – indeed, a fine example of the Self-Strengthening slogan about 'offical supervision, merchant management'. Hart, a Chinese scholar himself and a model of discretion, proved the ideal Qing employee; his service acquired a reputation for exceptional probity; and its customs receipts, amounting to 20 per cent of the empire's total revenue but over 50 per cent of its disposable revenue, 'must be regarded as a principal underpinning of the Qing government's finances'.[4]

The international crises that taxed the self-strengthening Li Hongzhang (assisted by the discreet Hart, the affable Prince Gong and the bumbling Zongli Yamen) began obscurely enough. In 1871 tsarist Russia unexpectedly occupied the Ili region west of Urumqi in northern Xinjiang. The occupation was supposedly a temporary arrangement to protect Russian trade through the area; in this respect it could be likened to the 1841 British seizure of Hong Kong; foreign encroachment across China's interminable land borders often bore an uncanny resemblance to that on the coast. But more obviously the occupation was a Russian retort to British feelers in the southern part of Xinjiang. There Yaqub Beg, a Kokand-backed adventurer and Islamic zealot, had in 1865 seized Kashgar, Yarkand and the other oasis-cities, and had then been courted by several British expeditions from across the mountains in India. Briefly the British saw Yaqub Beg as a potential Timur who would reunite the Muslim khanates of central Asia and so interpose a barrier against the supposed Russian advance towards India. Zuo Zongtang put paid to this pipe-dream. Having quelled the Muslim revolts in Shaanxi and Gansu, he reclaimed Xinjiang for the Qing in 1876–78. But the Russians stayed put in Ili. Although their trade was no longer endangered, they demanded an indemnity and concessions as the price of withdrawal. The Zongli Yamen responded by sending an ill-informed Manchu to St Petersburg. He caved in to Russian demands in the 1879 Treaty of Livadia; the treaty caused such a furore in Beijing that it was immediately repudiated; and Li Hongzhang had to rescue what he could in a second treaty, that of St Petersburg, in 1881. Advised by Hart and backed by the British, he got the return of most of Ili, a reduction in the indemnity and the retraction of many of the concessions. Xinjiang was then constituted as a regular province of the empire and opened to Han immigration.

Neither side had wanted a war so far from home, but bellicose Qing officials took comfort in the belief 'that by their forcefulness they had induced the Tsarist court to accept many of their demands'.[5] This was a dangerous delusion; in reality the Russians had backed down in the face of international disapproval and domestic instability. Meanwhile, on the opposite side of the empire, an assertive Japan was registering a strong interest in Korea and had seized the Ryukyu archipelago, the chain of islands (including Okinawa) strung between Japan and Taiwan.

Both the Koreans and the Ryukyu islanders customarily sent tribute missions to Beijing. The status of tributary relationships was, however, unclear in terms of contemporary international law, itself a consensus unilaterally devised by the Western powers and only recently divulged to the Qing court in a translation into Chinese of Henry Wheaton's *Elements of International Law*. The translation had been made by an American missionary, W. A. P. Martin – and not without prejudice or difficulty since it meant devising new compounds of Chinese characters to convey even the approximate sense of basic concepts like 'human rights' and 'jurisdiction'. Li Hongzhang and his colleagues had nevertheless accepted Martin's work, having already spotted encouraging inconsistencies between Wheaton's precepts and Western practice. Prince Gong declined to write a preface for it – the language was too inelegant and China had her own traditions in such matters – but he saw international law as offering some hope to a government keen to renegotiate one-sided treaties and expose the iniquities of extraterritoriality.

The French had been especially suspicious of the Reverend Martin's work. Their chargé d'affaires had urged his American counterpart in Shanghai to 'kill him – choke him off; he'll make us endless trouble'.[6] The trouble expected by the French was more in relation to Vietnam than China. From Saigon, taken in 1859, France had been acting in flagrant disregard of Wheaton's precepts by launching a series of forays into northern Vietnam. They were not always successful. Fierce resistance came not only from the Vietnamese themselves but from a bewildering array of other adversaries, including the multicoloured 'flags' (bands of Red Turbans and other Chinese rebel armies from Guangxi and Yunnan who had sought refuge in the Vietnam hills) as well as the sizeable Qing contingents sent south to assist the Vietnamese in suppressing them.

When in 1882 the French seized Hanoi, for a third time, and bombarded the approaches to the ancient capital of Hué, the Vietnamese court wearily conceded defeat. The subsequent Franco-Vietnamese treaty gave the French virtual control of Tonkin (Haiphong, Hanoi and the Red River basin) and was immediately contested by the more bellicose of the dowager empress's counsellors in Beijing. Not only was Vietnam a Chinese tributary, they stated, but there were Chinese troops there to prove it. Precisely, retorted the French, the Chinese must therefore be the invaders. Both Beijing and Paris then boosted troop levels, and by 1883 they were at war. Li Hongzhang hastened to soothe matters by agreeing to a withdrawal of Chinese troops in return for French recognition of China's southern border. But events on the ground overtook this agreement when in 1884 a French expeditionary force was routed by Qing forces at Bac-le. Such a defeat was so embarrassing to French pride that one observer could think of 'no greater since Waterloo'.[7] A worse followed at Langson, just south of today's border, in March 1885; it brought down the French government. But by then France's navy was wreaking a savage revenge on the coast of China itself.

Steaming north, Admiral Courbet bombarded the great port of Fuzhou, pulverised the shipping that constituted China's southern fleet, and seized the port of Chilung (Keelung) in northern Taiwan, plus the Pescadores Islands. In Tianjin, Li Hongzhang again hastily convened a meeting with the French minister in Beijing (ambassadors at the time were called 'ministers' and their embassies, however permanent, 'legations'). A new treaty, dated June 1885, ended the hostilities, if not the rancour. 'Ironically enough the agreement . . . was almost identical to the one reached a year earlier.'[8] France got a free hand in Vietnam in return for relinquishing Taiwan and the Pescadores and recognising the Sino-Vietnamese frontier.

Throughout these troubles in the south Li Hongzhang and Hart had managed to keep the empire's northern fleet, based at Tianjin, well out of range of the foreigners' guns; in fact they strengthened it. Not for long, though; for in 1894 events in Korea precipitated China into another war, this time with a resurgent Japan. Like Vietnam, Korea had sent regular tribute missions to Beijing and had been otherwise independent. But in 1876 the Japanese, tearing a leaf from the Westerners' book, had secured a handful of Korean treaty ports and insisted on extraterritorial rights for their residents there. The Western powers followed suit with encouragement from Li Hongzhang, who saw internationalising the Korean situation as the best way to advertise China's special relationship with the country and offset Japanese influence. This worked to the extent that in 1885 Beijing and Tokyo signed an agreement not to send troops into Korea unless the other did, and then only in equal numbers. For the first time since its conquest by the Mongols, the Korean court accepted the presence and oversight of a resident Chinese commissioner (it was the young Yuan Shikai, Li's protégé and later republican China's first president). But all these careful arrangements came to nothing when in 1894 a sectarian rebellion in Korea, not unlike that of the Taipings in its size and fervour, threatened the throne. The king asked for and, despite Li's protests, received Chinese troops; the Japanese sent larger forces of their own and rapidly overran the country; and an intervention supposedly designed to shore up the Korean monarchy turned into all-out war between Qing China and Japan.

For the Qing and Li Hongzhang it was an unmitigated disaster. While in thirty years of Self-Strengthening, China had yet to find a firearm for every conscript, a field gun for every detachment, or sufficient ships – bought, built, reconditioned – for a couple of fleets, the Japanese had constructed a large modern navy and trained up the only professional army east of India. Defeat followed defeat as the Chinese were quickly driven out of Korea. Within a couple of months the Japanese were at the Chinese border and not inclined to stop there. Crossing the Yalu River, they occupied Liaodong to within easy reach of the Great Wall. Meanwhile at Weihaiwei, a naval base on the tip of the Shandong peninsula, they found the Chinese fleet sheltering beneath coastal defences. Japanese marines promptly took the defences from the land and then emptied the base's big guns into the Chinese fleet. One of the Qing's two battleships was sunk, plus four of its ten cruisers. Coupled with the earlier losses at Fuzhou, China's coastline lay almost as undefended as it had in the 1840s.

Prince Gong, who had lately been in disgrace, and Li Hongzhang, who soon would be, were sent to Tokyo to sue for peace. In the 1895 Treaty of Shimonoseki, the most humiliating in modern Chinese history, they had to accept an indemnity about five times that exacted by the Western allies in 1860, concede to Japan the whole of Taiwan, the Pescadores and Liaodong (the last later commuted for a further indemnity), open four new treaty ports, including Chongqing above the Yangzi gorges in Sichuan, and of course recognise Korea's 'full and complete' independence – 'which, under the circumstances, effectively made Korea a Japanese protectorate'.[9] Li Hongzhang's reputation never entirely recovered. Given no credit for his pre-war moderation, he was vilified for the treaty and blamed for having diverted funds from the navy to pay for the dowager empress's new Summer Palace and its defiantly eloquent folly. This was a lakeside marble pavilion in the form of a two-deck pleasure barge, with paddle-wheels, which still graces the palace's Kunming Lake; unserviceable, it was at least unsinkable. With Shimonoseki and the fall from favour of Li Hongzhang, Self-Strengthening seemed to be getting nowhere; more radical solutions were being canvassed.

FROM EMPIRE TO REPUBLIC

In the dying years of the nineteenth century the scramble for concessions among the foreign powers reached fever pitch. Anxiously eyeing one another's gains, the British, French, Russians and Americans (not to mention the Spanish, Belgians, Austrians and Italians) strove to restrain Japan's appetite for Chinese territory while accommodating another voracious latecomer in the shape of Bismarck's new Germany. With missionaries to protect and munitions to sell, Germany's China interests were no more questionable or tenuous than those of its European rivals; but lagging well behind them in the acquisition of foreign markets, it could ill afford scruples in dealing with what the Kaiser was the first to call *die gelbe Gefahr* – 'the yellow peril'.

The concessions now in demand were commercial as well as territorial and included mining rights, transport systems and industrial ventures, any of which might become a nucleus of extraterritoriality as well as a source of income. Affording the Chinese a foretaste of the game of Monopoly, the competitors – the warship, the corporate top-hat, etc. – chased each other round the empire's perimeter snapping up properties, utilities, railways and investment funds, while scooping a share of the indemnities in lieu of passing 'Go'. The Russians concentrated on Manchuria – or what was left of it after their earlier infringements. In return for their help in persuading the Japanese to relinquish Liaodong, in 1896 the Qing government grudgingly awarded them the right to construct, across what is now the Chinese province of Heilongjiang, that part of the trans-Siberia railway that would connect up Vladivostok. The agreement embodying this concession was negotiated by Li Hongzhang, who, while out of favour, found his services still in demand, and pocketed 3 million roubles for them. Though the railway was technically a joint venture, most of the shares in it were bought by the Russian government, which reserved the right to move troops along it and to police it. A year later, when the Germans were granted the Shandong port of Qingdao in reparation for the murder of some of their more zealous missionaries ('a splendid opportunity', the Kaiser called it), the Russians secured a balancing concession. It took the form of a lease of Liaodong (the just-restored southern portion of

Manchuria) plus the right to construct another railway to Dalian (Dairen, Dalny), a port on the Lushun peninsula in water still warmer than that at Vladivostok.

By 1898, such was the competition between the foreign powers, and such internally the centrifugal drift of authority to the provinces, that there was a real danger of China sharing Africa's fate and being scrambled over and partitioned. Russian railway tracks were ensnaring the whole of Manchuria; the Japanese had already detached Taiwan; the Germans were expanding their presence in Shandong; the British and the Americans controlled traffic into the productive interior via the Yangzi; and the French were eyeing up the commercial potential of the Red River into Yunnan. No one wanted to be left out. On the other hand, fragmentation was clearly not in the interests of those with the most investments at risk, such as the British. Yet to prevent it, they saw no alternative to matching the other powers move for move, thus raising the stakes.

To counter the Russians in Lushun and the Germans at Qingdao, in 1898 the naval base at Weihaiwei, more or less midway between the two, was snapped up by the British. They also leased more of the Kowloon peninsula – Hong Kong's so-called New Territories – to supply and secure that colony; and as of Lord Curzon's 1899 appointment as Viceroy of India, they opened a new front by asserting commercial interests in Tibet and demanding a frontier demarcation there; much like the Russian manoeuvres in Manchuria thirty years earlier, these Himalayan moves were the prelude to armed intervention in Tibet by the Younghusband expedition in 1904. Not to be outdone, the French leased a port west of Hong Kong and obtained mineral rights in Guangxi and Yunnan. Meanwhile the United States again led the way in levelling the playing field by demanding that any concessions extended to one be open to all.

All of which brought a vigorous if varied Chinese response. It came from students attending the 1895 *jinshi* examinations in Beijing, who submitted a memorial urging renewed resistance to the Japanese and an inordinately long programme of economic and administrative reforms. It came from émigrés like the young Dr Sun Yat-sen, born in Guangdong but more often overseas in the 1890s as he orchestrated clandestine support for replacing the Qing with a representative government. It came too from senior scholars in the Zeng Guofan tradition who rubbished the hotheads' talk of a republic ('Where did they find this word that savours so much of rebellion?' asked one) and argued that the West's undoubted expertise could be comfortably accommodated within an ever evolving and progressive Confucian tradition.[10] A response came, too, from Chinese 'compradors' (commercial intermediaries) in and around the treaty ports who had imbibed the spirit of venture capitalism and begun setting up their own commercial enterprises, competing for industrial concessions, and bitterly resenting those handed on a plate to the foreigner. And it came, finally, from the unenlightened masses who, thanks to the widely dispersed missionaries, could now put a face to the foreign presence; big-nosed and often condescending, the missionaries challenged traditional values, antagonised the local gentry, fanned latent xenophobia, and furnished a handy scapegoat for every fiscal surcharge and crop failure.

Only from the Imperial Palace in Beijing came there no response at all. The Guangxu emperor (r. 1889–1908), an effete young man with a voice that reminded people of the whine of a mosquito, seemed a cipher in the hands of his aunt, the redoubtable Cixi. It was known that he had been reading widely, even studying English. Now in his mid-twenties, it was high time he packed off the dowager empress into retirement and assumed the reins of power. But when, in June 1898, he did just that, it came as a scarcely credible surprise. While Cixi was enjoying a summer retreat in one of her new palaces, the emperor held long consultations with Kang Youwei, a renowned scholar who had been behind the students' 1895 memorial, and then dramatically issued a whole string of modernising edicts. Known as the 'Hundred Days' reforms', they were comprehensive enough. A vast range of educational, military, administrative and economic innovations were announced, designed to overhaul the entire state apparatus and turn Confucian bureaucrats into Confucian technocrats.

But constitutional reform was notably absent; representation was not mentioned, nor was any limitation of the imperial prerogatives. Whether such initiatives would have followed is uncertain, for three months later Cixi staged a comeback. A hundred days having been just long enough for a bureaucratic reaction to set in and military indifference to be evident, she drew up an edict in the emperor's name that requested the dowager empress to resume her duties immediately. This she then dutifully did, having the emperor cast into palace detention and having six of his leading advisers executed. The reforms died with them, though Kang Youwei escaped to Japan from where Sun Yat-sen was now extending his web of intrigue to mainland China. As so often in the coming years, the great breakthrough had proved deceptive. Instead of advancing the cause of the reform, it had retarded it, provoking the removal of its leadership and cowing moderate opinion.

Two years later, Cixi's undoubted genius for weathering any crisis was even more in evidence. In late 1899 what history calls the Boxer Rebellion broke out in Shandong. The trouble rapidly spread through Hebei, Shanxi and part of Henan, where many foreigners, mostly missionaries, were massacred. In the summer of 1900, it engulfed Tianjin and Beijing, and resulted in their expatriate communities (including women and children), along with several thousand mainly Christian Chinese, being besieged, often under heavy fire, in their legations and in the grounds of one of Beijing's Catholic cathedrals. Highly coloured reports that the Beijing contingent had all been massacred provoked an international outcry; and though the reports proved to be incorrect, the besieged did suffer about seventy fatalities, some deprivation and much trauma. The Beijing siege lasted fifty-five days. It was lifted when a 20,000-strong multinational force retook Tianjin and fought its way up to the capital; both cities were then comprehensively pillaged by the foreigners. Among the besieged in the Beijing legations had been the American sinologist Dr W. A. P. Martin and Sir (as he now was) Robert Hart of the Imperial Customs. Each wrote an account of the affair, as did a substantial percentage of their 400 detained comrades. An immense literature was thus generated; in British imperial mythology 'the Siege of Peking' took its place alongside those of Lucknow and Ladysmith.

How all this looked from the Chinese side is less well documented. Certainly the Boxer Rebellion was better understood: it was accepted, for instance, that Boxers boxed only for gymnastic exercise and were not technically in rebellion. Born of rural distress plus a belief in the protection afforded by esoteric cults and personal fitness, their movement conformed to a tradition of secret societies that had simmered among the rural masses throughout China's history, from the Red Eyebrows and the Yellow Turbans to the White Lotus Society of Macartney's time and the Red Turbans of the Taiping era. In times of crisis, their members might take the lead in acts of defiance and violence which, if not quickly punished, could snowball into mass insurrection. This is what had happened in southern Shandong in late 1899. But instead of targeting Qing officialdom, and so inviting a speedy suppression, the fraternity of 'righteous and harmonious boxers' turned on Christians, killing isolated foreigners and destroying the symbols – especially railway tracks and telegraph lines – of what they deemed an insidious, socially disruptive and morally revolting creed. Leadership was noticeably lacking among them, but not organisation. Colourful sashes and bandanas distinguished different troupes; an all-girl force called the Red Lanterns provided support and inspiration; discipline was strict and loot was shared. There was much to admire in such fearless patriots.

Cixi and her reactionary advisers bided their time. The Boxers posed no threat to the dynasty. Reform was not on their agenda; rather would they 'Support the Qing, Destroy the Foreigner'. Their entry into Beijing therefore went unopposed and their assaults on foreigners unpunished. When, however, Beijing's foreign diplomats refused an imperial request that, for their own safety, they evacuate the city and withdraw to the coast, Cixi began to view the Boxers as potential liberators from the alien presence. And when a precautionary allied capture of the Dagu forts protecting Tianjin provoked a Qing declaration of war, there could be no question that the Boxers had imperial backing. It struck observers as curious, though, that while the Boxers themselves attacked the Beijing cathedral with its teeming mass of Chinese Christians, they were seldom to be seen around the heavily invested legation quarter. There the assailants appeared to consist entirely of imperial troops.

It was curious, too, that despite overwhelming superiority in numbers and firepower, during eight long weeks these professional troops failed to overwhelm the garden walls and sandbagged barricades of the legations' makeshift defences. Guns and mortars that would have effectively demolished any but the Imperial City's gargantuan fortifications were never even deployed. On the contrary, whenever the extinction of the foreigners seemed imminent, the assailants withdrew or offered a truce. Clearly there were those at court who did not share the Boxers' desire to exterminate the enemy. Meanwhile the country's other fifteen provinces remained largely unaffected. Business in the treaty ports went on regardless; isolated missionaries outside the three northern provinces went unmolested; anti-foreign interests failed to support the Boxers; provincial governors, with a couple of exceptions, failed to support the court.

When the allied relief force finally reached Beijing, Cixi saw no alternative but to flee along with the imperial household – and not forgetting the emperor. Disguised as peasants, they left the city squatting in wooden carts, like the last of the Han when they slipped out of Luoyang in 189 BC. More like *Tang* Xuanzang and the delectable Yang Guifei fleeing Chang'an in AD 755, the imperial party was initially at the mercy of its own escort. But matters improved as they moved west into the loyal province of Shanxi and then, for safety's sake, farther west to Xi'an. There, on the site where imperial Chang'an had once stood, the court-in-exile awaited its fate at the hands of its last invaders.

Li Hongzhang, now in his late seventies, had been ordered back to Beijing as the only official capable of wringing acceptable terms from the eleven international powers that had taken part in the relief. It was his last such service, though by no means the most difficult. For as Robert Hart rightly saw it, the allies had little choice. They could opt for the partition of China, but that would be inviting disaster; for a change of dynasty, but there was no obvious alternative; or for 'patching up the Manchoo [Manchu] rule ... [and] in a word' – or five – 'making the best of it'.[11] Thus it was that under the terms of the Boxer Protocol, in return for the largest of all indemnities (payable over forty years from increased maritime customs), for the execution of ten officials deemed guilty of crimes and for various measures to secure the foreign legations in the future, Cixi and the court were permitted to reoccupy the capital and resume the government. They did so in style, turning what should have been a penitent procession into a triumphal progress. The chance of witnessing the imperial cavalcade making its grand re-entry into Beijing was a sight too good to miss even for the lately besieged; and when Cixi acknowledged them with a few short bows, 'there came an answering, spontaneous burst of applause' from the massed foreigners.[12]

The mystique of the Qing had survived, if not much else. Seven years later the Guangxu emperor made another bid to escape his aunt's tyranny, this time by dying. Natural causes were suspected; and they appeared confirmed when a few hours later, instead of taking advantage of the new situation, the dowager empress herself passed peacefully away after enjoying a compote of crab-apples. Not for a day, let alone a hundred, was the luckless emperor, even in the afterlife, to be rid of her baleful influence. In all but name it was she who had been the 'Last Emperor'; for the Guangxu emperor's designated successor was his nephew Pu-yi, then two years old and destined never to attain a reign title, only the faintly ridiculous forename of 'Henry'.

During her last years Cixi had emerged from her customary seclusion to host parties, pose for photos and present Qing rule as more receptive to change. Constitutional reform and curbing the powers of the provincial governors went hand in hand. As of 1909, the first provincial assemblies were elected, albeit on a very limited franchise; they would in turn elect members to a national assembly; both were essentially consultative bodies. At the grassroots level, attempts were made to graft some form of local representation on to the *baojia* groupings or replace them with self-governing units. But behind the constitutional window-dressing lay a determination to recentralise. A 'New Army' under Manchu control was strategically deployed to offset the forces raised by provincial governors, while the most powerful of these governors – such as Yuan Shikai, who had succeeded to Li Hongzhang's Tianjin power base – were eased from office. Simultaneously attempts to wrest from foreign investors the growing railway network, and especially the new north–south Beijing-to-Hankou line, led to a tug-of-war between Qing centralisers and provincial partisans.

The abolition of foot-binding in 1902 and of the examination system in 1905, though notable concessions to modernity, also served a political agenda; gatherings of revolutionaries could no longer pass themselves off as do-gooding 'natural foot' societies; and ending the exams, which had anyway been widely suspended under the terms of the Boxer Protocol, enhanced the credentials of those who had already secured degrees while swelling the ranks of the new naval and military academies. Additionally, there were now scholarships for students to pursue further education overseas. Japan proved especially popular; it was not just nearer than Europe or America but, thanks to its Confucian heritage and Chinese script, intellectually more accessible.

The Japanese model of modernisation also had much to recommend it. There the monarchy continued to be revered but had been reduced to constitutional status by the introduction of a parliamentary structure. Land tenure had been reformed, education redirected and heavy industries developed. 'Rich Country, Strong Army' being the slogan, a centralised government had forged national solidarity by giving the highest priority to the economy and the military. It had paid off in the Sino-Japanese war over Korea in 1894, and it was vindicated again when in 1904–5 a Russo-Japanese war broke out over concessions in both Korea and Manchuria. The Japanese navy destroyed the Russian fleet much as it had the Chinese ten years earlier; an Asian country thus notched up its first victory over a European empire; and Japan won recognition as one of the great powers. Dazzled by this Japanese model, Kang Youwei, the distinguished scholar who had advised the Guangxu emperor on his 'Hundred Days' reforms and was now in exile in Japan, headed a reform party that promoted the constitutionalising of the Qing monarchy as the best way to provide the sanction for an equally radical restructuring of China's social economy.

But there were other models to which students and activists could turn in their search for a solution to China's plight. Western-style democracy based on electoral representation also attracted interest. A Qing delegation seeking constitutional ideas visited the United States and Britain in 1905. Two years earlier Liang Qichao, one of Kang Youwei's associates, had preceded them and been received by President Teddy Roosevelt. But Liang Qichao came away disappointed. American democracy seemed to spawn 'mediocre politicans, corruption, disorder, racism, imperialism'. 'In short,' noted the late J. K. Fairbank, most prolific and influential of America's sinologists, 'he got our number, and it turned him off.' Since the Confucian ideal of government assumed a harmony of interest between the ruler and the ruled, in China, according to Fairbank, the individual was naturally more disposed to adhere than to confront, to conform than to contest. Democracy thus carried, and still carries 'right through to Mao and Deng' (Fairbank was writing in the 1970s), a collective connotation. The people are one – just as singular and plural are one, being the same written character. They, the people, are not a multiplicity; it, the people, is an entity. Says Fairbank, 'Nation came before individual,' adding, 'This was not a doctrine of human rights.'[13]

Nationalism was common to all schools of thought. The mere fact of exposure to the foreign, whether in and around the treaty ports and mission stations or through overseas travel, instilled a new sense of Chinese self-awareness. But the Chinese nation could be variously defined. While the geography of the empire lent support to the idea of a vast multi-ethnic community, culture suggested a narrower definition closely related to Han ethnicity. Nationalists might therefore uphold Manchu-Qing rule as the only basis for a super-nation of subcontinental proportions, or they might vehemently attack Manchu-Qing rule as an alien imperialism even more oppressive than that exercised by the other foreign powers. Not until communism trumped Nationalism with its supranational ideology would this dilemma be even semantically resolved.

Western theories such as socialism, social Darwinism – 'societies evolve, the fittest survive' – Marxism and anarchism also had their advocates. All took comfort from the evidence that dynastic despotisms had had their day. The Mughals were long gone, the Ottomans were succumbing to the Young Turks' revolution (1908), and the Romanov tsar had just (1905) narrowly avoided assassination. To historical determinists, the Manchus must be next for the chop. Marx's *Communist Manifesto* was available in Chinese by 1906, and an erstwhile adviser to Yuan Shikai made an appearance at the Second (Communist) International in Brussels in 1909. But as yet there was no Chinese socialist or Marxist party. Along with most other republicans and numerous social reformist and feminist groups, the radicals affiliated themselves to Dr Sun Yat-sen's Revolutionary Alliance.

Sun's genius lay in being all things to all men. A Guangdong peasant by birth but from a family some of whose members had already emigrated, he had acquired an education in Hawaii, a medical degree in Hong Kong, a moustache and natty suiting in Japan, and the contacts and profile to fund his operations in the course of extensive world tours. His reputation rested more on single-minded determination and organisational ability than flights of utopian fancy or fiery rhetoric. Propagandising, mobilising and, where possible, arming affiliated groups within China – the Triad societies, labour organisations, agrarian movements, trade boycotts, disaffected army units – he became the revolutionaries' great facilitator. Security was problematic, particularly for one who, with a price on his head, could not himself enter the country. One after another, his revolutionary initiatives, mostly in Guangdong, were betrayed or had to be aborted when the plot leaked out. But internationally his reputation was unaffected. It had eclipsed that of rivals ever since 1898 when, snatched from a London street by Qing agents, Sun had become a cause célèbre, his case taken up by British parliamentarians and his release eventually secured.

It was no surprise, then, that on 9 October 1911 ('9.10.11' by most foreign reckonings) Sun was fund-raising in America. In fact he was travelling by train from Denver to Kansas at the moment when, on the other side of the world, halfway up the Yangzi, a bomb went off within the Russian concession area of the treaty port of Hankou. More surprisingly, this dramatic start to the revolution owed little to the work of Sun's Revolutionary Alliance; the bomb, which was being assembled by an obscure cell of malcontents, had gone off by mistake. The injured bombmakers were rushed to hospital; and their colleagues were arrested when the Russians reported the matter to the Qing authorities.

It was the arrests, and the confessions that must then come out, which provoked the revolution; and it began not on the streets or behind the barricades but in the barracks of Wuchang just across the river (and now hard by the approach road to the high-level Wuhan bridge). There, revolutionary elements within the Qing 'New Army', anticipating exposure by their bomb-making associates, seized the local ammunition depot and were quickly joined by other army units. Wuchang fell to the mutineers on the tenth, Hanyang on the eleventh and Hankou on the twelfth. With the capture of these three adjacent cities, nowadays collectively forming the 'tri-city' of Wuhan, control of the middle Yangzi fell to the mutineers.

To suppress the trouble, the Qing court ordered south its northern army, and to bolster its support within the military, it recalled Yuan Shikai. Once Li Hongzhang's protégé, the stocky Yuan Shikai had proved himself a popular general and a loyal servant. He had supported Cixi in her termination of the Guangxu emperor's 'Hundred Days', represented the Qing in Korea, and accepted with reasonably good grace his removal as governor-general at Tianjin. The last had been justified on medical grounds; it was said there was something wrong with his foot. Yuan now turned this to account, pleading more foot trouble while he bided his time and dictated his terms. His position went from strength to strength as troops in the provinces of Hunan, Shaanxi, Shanxi, Yunnan and Jiangxi declared themselves against the Qing and for the mutineers. The provincial assemblies often supported them; the death toll rapidly escalated; and when part of the supposedly loyal northern army submitted its own ultimatum to the court, the Qing authorities caved in. A parliament was to draw up a constitution, review all foreign treaties and elect a premier; the Qing regency was to confirm the premier, forswear its right of execution, stay out of politics and offer an amnesty to political opponents. Just a month after the Wuchang rising, Yuan Shikai was confirmed by the court as the newly elected premier on 11 November 1911, '11.11.11'.

Suitably enough, when the new republic was officially declared on 1 January 1912, its first act was to adopt the West's solar calendar. A week now lasted seven days and numerologists could seek significance in the new dates. Because harmonising terrestrial and celestial time had always been one of the Son of Heaven's ritual responsibilities, the calendrical reform proclaimed more emphatically than bombs or parliaments the end of the Qing Mandate.

WAR AND MORE WAR

The first half of the twentieth century saw China submerged in a 'Period of Disunion' every bit as blood-soaked and confused – not to say narrative-testing – as the inter-dynastic free-for-alls of the past. If the plight of the Qing court after the Boxer Rebellion had recalled that of the last of the Later Han, the chaos that ensued mirrored that of the fourth-century Three Kingdoms. From 1911 to 1950 the fighting never really stopped; revolution became civil war, became revolution, became civil war, became foreign invasion, became freedom struggle, became civil war, became revolution. Kang Youwei, still in Japan, put the death toll at 20 million just for the two years 1911–12. How he reached this figure is anyone's guess. Jonathan Spence suspects it was a Japanese exaggeration, 'but even a figure one tenth as high is bleak enough, and in the context quite conceivable . . . [For] we are presented with cumulative evidence of violence and death that had moved beyond any rational justification, even in the grandiose terms of a final attainment of national order.'[14]

Throughout the period 1911–49, China remained a historico-cultural concept but was a coherent functioning state only during a brief interlude in the early 1930s. Diligent scholars trace a post-1911 pedigree of republican leadership stretching from Yuan Shikai's premiership to Sun Yat-sen's brief presidency in 1912, to Yuan Shikai's presidency (1912–16), followed by a succession of short-lived generals and warlords to Zhang Zuolin (1928), Chiang Kai-shek (1928–49) and Mao Zedong (1949–76). The ups and downs of the ideological seesaw may be followed, and the shifts of the nation's capital charted (from Beijing to Nanjing to Beijing to Nanjing to Wuhan to Chongqing to Beijing). But outside the big cities and the ports and away from the railway lines and the river traffic, power lay not with the republican strongmen or such constitutional devices as they tolerated but with those leaders who, by force or favour, controlled a particular locality and its resources. Under the empire these men with their regional bases and roving armies would have been called 'bandits' or 'rebels', but in an age when nationalism was dependent on accommodations with them, they were classified more ambiguously as 'warlords'. There were literally thousands of warlords, ranging from generals and officials who ruled whole provinces (successors, in effect, of Zeng Guofan and Li Hongzhang) to local toughs with a few hundred 'braves', or restive hill minorities with an assertive chief.

And beyond them – beyond the warlords – where the telegraph poles disappeared into the haze and the fields stopped, so did China. The steppe had reverted to a no-go area. Manchuria, which had attracted much Han settlement and industrial development in the early twentieth century, was already compromised. A bone of contention in the 1920s between the Russians in the north, the Japanese in the south (they had taken over the Russian concessions in Liaodong after the Russo-Japanese war of 1904–5) and a semi-independent Manchu warlord, the whole of Manchuria was finally overrun by Japanese forces in 1931 and so reduced to a colony in all but name. As Tokyo's satellite kingdom of Manchukuo – a 'kingdom' because the powerless 'Last Emperor' Henry Pu-yi was inveigled into lending legitimacy to this fiction – it provided Japan with the bridgehead and marshalling yard from which to launch its invasion of the rest of China in 1937. Not until 1946, after a post-war interlude under Soviet control, was Manchukuo reclaimed by Chiang Kai-shek's Nationalists. It was then promptly lost in heavy fighting to the communists in 1947–8; and by them it was reformulated as the three provinces constituting, not the now taboo 'Manchuria', but 'the North East' of the People's Republic.

Outer (i.e. northern) Mongolia fared better. Its autonomy was acknowledged by China as early as 1915; and with Soviet help, a Mongolian People's Republic was set up in Urga, the capital, in 1921. Despite recognition of a residual Chinese suzerainty, 'the Soviet Union now replaced China as the country which had the greatest influence on the [Mongolian] republic'. [15] This relationship would survive as long as the Soviet Union itself, China's claims to suzerainty having been finally retracted amid Sino-Soviet fraternising and following a 1946 Mongolian plebiscite in favour of independence. Urga was renamed Ulan Bator and the Mongolian People's Republic took its place in the UN.

Inner Mongolia (the arc of steppe south of the Gobi), by now with a substantial Han population, was more problematic. In the 1920s it was contested not by the Russians but by the Japanese, who entertained ideas of penetrating inner Asia from their Manchurian bridgehead by means of its steppe corridor. In the mid-1930s Tokyo therefore set up an 'Autonomous Government of Inner Mongolia'. A decade later, when the Japanese were finally defeated by the Second World War allies, it was China's communists from their base at Yan'an in northern Shaanxi who were best placed to fill the resulting vacuum. They duly did so, and the region became the Inner Mongolia (Nei Monggol) Autonomous Region of the People's Republic of China.

Xinjiang also enjoyed de facto autonomy from 1912 until 1949, but in this case under a succession of Chinese governors. Warlords in practice, they were 'governors' only by virtue of such recognition as they bothered to obtain from whoever headed the republic of China at the time. Muslim Uighurs and Kazakhs repeatedly rose against this local government. They were suppressed only with the help of Soviet Russia. Indeed, had it not been for the post-war strength of communism in China itself, and the Sino-Soviet front against central Asian Islam that resulted, the 'Eastern Turkestan Republic' set up by an alliance of Uighurs and Kazakhs in 1945 might still be standing. The Soviet Union became deeply involved in Xinjiang's development but returned the region to China following the communist triumph in 1949.

Finally there was Tibet. Press photos of Britain's 1904 Younghusband expedition mowing down Tibetans armed with nothing more lethal than hoes had gone down badly in London. Younghusband's one-sided Lhasa Convention with the Tibetans therefore proved highly unpopular. It was unacceptable to the other powers, including Russia, which saw it as an extension into central Asia of British influence; unacceptable to the XIIIth Dalai Lama, who had had no part in its terms since he had fled to China; unacceptable to London, which diluted it and censured Younghusband for having exceeded instructions; and totally unacceptable to the Qing government, which denied that the Tibetans had any right to negotiate with a foreign power. Beijing would, however, ratify the convention if the British would in return recognise China's sovereignty in Tibet. The British, splitting hairs in terms that must have taxed the translators no end, would acknowledge only China's suzerainty in Tibet, not its sovereignty. The matter being unresolved even in a 1906 Anglo-Chinese treaty on trade with Tibet, Qing forces began a slow advance through Qinghai. The Dalai Lama returned to Lhasa in late 1909, just ahead of the advancing Chinese. This did not stop them; and rather than face humiliation at the hands of more invaders, in early 1910 the Dalai Lama fled again, this time to India.

His Holiness's Indian exile was shorter than that which awaited his reincarnation in 1959. When in 1911 the revolutionaries' bomb went off in Hankou, Qing troops in Tibet found themselves besieged, first by their revolutionary colleagues, then by the Tibetans. Routes back to China being blocked, they had to be repatriated via the Himalayan passes and India. The same circuitous and humiliating route was used by Qing, and then republican, emissaries vainly trying to re-estabish contact with Lhasa. When in mid-1912 the Dalai Lama returned home, it was to an already liberated Tibet; 'the Chinese military occupation of the Dalai Lama's dominions, begun three years previously, had come to an end'.[16] Tibet was now effectively independent. Though this independence was never recognised by any Chinese government, in 1913 President Yuan Shikai did acknowledge Tibetan autonomy in return for British recognition of the Chinese republic.

Thirty years later, when the Second World War brought Britain and Nationalist China together as allies, the issue of Tibet's status resurfaced. The formula now favoured by the British was a swap: Tibet to accept China's suzerainty in return for China accepting Tibet's autonomy. This satisfied neither party and would have been difficult to implement. But the formula was maintained until 1949, when independent India's Jawaharlal Nehru indicated that he was not inclined to 'a legalistic view' of the matter. Mao Zedong took the hint and thereupon made the 'liberation' of Tibet a priority for the People's Liberation Army. It was invaded within the year and secured as an integral, if autonomous, region of the People's Republic. The XIVth Dalai Lama tolerated this situation until 1959. In that year the Tibetans rose against the Chinese presence, the army returned to suppress the revolt and His Holiness fled to India, this time indefinitely.

Shorn of these vast peripheral territories, riddled by warlord regimes within and hamstrung by infighting among their own leaders, the first republican governments of what remained of China were seldom in a position to take advantage of such international opportunities as came their way. In the First World War China had become an official combatant only when the war was nearly over, although around 100,000 Chinese recruits served as auxiliaries in northern Europe, suffering substantial casualties. On both counts, China was entitled to a place at the table when in 1919 the allied powers sat down to divide the spoils. A sixty-strong delegation duly made the trip to Paris with high expectations of at least regaining control of those treaty ports and concessions now forfeited by the vanquished Germans. Woodrow Wilson disapproved of all colonialisms and was preaching the doctrine of self-determination; there was just a chance that the Japanese would be ordered out of Manchuria and the British out of Hong Kong.

But the Chinese delegation would be disappointed. Ostensibly this was because its members were as disunited as the republic they represented. Sun Yat-sen's Revolutionary Alliance, now renamed the Guomindang (National People's Party) and with its strongest support in the south, had won China's first election in 1913. (About 40 million had the vote, although women were still not among them.) Yuan Shikai, his prior election as president doubtful after this Nationalist victory and his strongest support being in the north, then moved against the Guomindang and attacked provincial governors who supported it. Heavier fighting than usual followed, and the northern forces stormed and ransacked Nanjing. The parliament was dissolved, Sun fled back into exile and Yuan Shikai ruled as dictator, even attempting to set himself up as emperor, until his death in 1916. Meanwhile most of the southern provinces had seceded from the republic and declared themselves autonomous. For appearances' sake, the delegation sent to the Paris peace talks included some southerners. But its divisions proved hard to disguise and to Clemenceau, Lloyd George and Woodrow Wilson 'it was not clear whether [it] represented either a country or a government'. Moreover they assumed that it 'did not include either China's president or prime minister mainly because the political situation in China was so precarious that neither dared leave'.[17]

In reality, though, the composition of the Chinese delegation was irrelevant; for the republican government had already signed away the prized German concessions in Shandong. Qingdao, the nucleus of these concessions and by now a thriving port complete with German schools and an excellent brewery (the 'Tsingtao' of the still-popular label being the Wade-Giles form of 'Qingdao'), had in fact been taken from the Germans by the Japanese in 1914. Tokyo had then presented Yuan Shikai with an ultimatum known as the Twenty-one Demands. Since these would 'virtually have turned China into a Japanese protectorate', Yuan Shikai had chosen to buy off the Japanese by pledging China's support for Tokyo's claim to Qingdao.[18] The Chinese delegates, of course, claimed that this agreement had been signed under duress; but to the allies an agreement was an agreement. It clinched it. Qingdao went to Japan and Chinese hopes were dashed.

When the news of this sell-out reached Beijing, protesters massed in the square outside the Tiananmen, the 'Gate of Heavenly Peace' (a smaller space in those days, though no less symbolic). It was 4 May (1919), a date ever after identified with national outrage and reawakening. The lead was taken by students from Beijing's National University, itself founded in 1898 but reconstituted as the senior institution in a new system of modern tertiary education in 1912. Thousands were eventually arrested, in fact so many that they could not be contained and had to be released. Sun Yat-sen and Kang Youwei, though still constitutional sparring partners, both lent their support. Student unions were formed wherever there were students, workers' groups joined in, women mobilised as never before, and the 'May 4 Movement' spread throughout the country. In Shanghai 100,000 protested. Japanese goods were everywhere boycotted, while feeling against those powers whose liberal sentiments had been sacrificed to appease Japan ran high. But the political fall-out was modest. A couple of pro-Japanese ministers were dismissed, China refused to sign the peace accord, and then, three years later, as part of an international agreement on naval power in the western Pacific, Japan vacated Qingdao anyway.

The social and intellectual legacy of May 4 was a different matter. Born of outrage and impotence in the face of international betrayal, it intensified and radically redirected the whole future course of national resurgence. A new generation of leaders, among them the young Mao Zedong in his native Changsha (Hunan) and Zhou Enlai in Tianjin (Hebei), gained their first experience of political activism. Mass action took on new dimensions with labour unions and women's groups organising and mobilising as never before. 'Four hundred or more journals, written in the vernacular and devoted to culture and politics, were founded in this same period; hundreds of new schools, often with radical curricula, were set up';[19] textbooks also went vernacular; and a 'New Culture Movement' gained momentum with the publication of some of China's finest fiction. As ever, political chaos proved a stimulant to cultural activity. Qu Qiubai, a student in Beijing at the time and later a controversial figure in the Communist Party, recalled that it was like being 'sucked into the whirlwind'. 'Feelings

... ran so strong that restlessness could no more be contained.' For the first time 'the sharp pain of imperialistic oppression reached our bones, and it awakened us from the nightmares of impractical democratic reforms'.[20]

Throughout the early 1920s the strikes, protests and boycotts escalated, with organised labour – Hong Kong dockers, Shanghai mill workers, Guangzhou seamen, Wuhan railwaymen – increasingly setting the pace. Demonstrators were shot and sympathy strikes followed. Occasionally the strikers' demands were met, more often not. A growing awareness that the Beijing government's reliance on foreign loans made it an accomplice of the foreign-owned companies that were exploiting Chinese labour fuelled the idea of a nationalist revolution to overthrow the republic. This in turn called for unity between Sun's Guomindang Nationalists, who controlled Guangdong province, and a newer, much smaller but highly organised party of anti-imperialists with strong support in Shanghai – the Chinese Communist Party (CCP).

Inspired by the Bolshevik revolution in Russia and by Chinese students who had taken up Marxism-Leninism while on work-study programmes in Paris, the CCP had been formed in Shanghai in 1921. Mao Zedong attended this first convention as Hunan's representative, while Chen Duxiu, editor of the leftist journal *New Youth* and founder of several Marxist study groups, was chosen as secretary-general. Links with Lenin's Comintern (Communist International) had already been established, and they were cemented when the Russian leadership indicated a willingness to restore to a legitimate Chinese government all Russian concessions in China. Here clearly was a highly desirable ally in the struggle to liberate the country from the foreign imperialists. Comintern advisers, instructors, funds and munitions were therefore welcomed; and despite misgivings, the CCP accepted a Comintern directive that, rather than defer revolution until such time as the proletariat had been mobilised, the party should temporarily join forces with the Guomindang. Together they would then overthrow the 'feudal' warlords, by which time the country would be ready for a 'second stage' of struggle ending in the dictatorship of the proletariat.

Neither the Guomindang nor the CCP was entirely of one mind; but as of 1922 they were agreed on a joint programme to reunite the country and attain full independence. For the Guomindang, Sun Yat-sen and, following his death in 1925, Chiang Kai-shek set up a military government in Guangzhou. There Chiang, who had himself been trained in a Japanese military academy, established a nationalist naval academy that would provide a dependable corps and much of the leadership in the forthcoming struggle. Discipline and organisation were supplied by the Comintern agent known as Mikhail Borodin; funds came from local taxes and from landlords and industrialists who supported the Guomindang in return for its protection; and troops were drawn from among both parties' supporters and from the militias of various southern warlords. By July 1926 the so-called Northern Expedition of Nationalists and communists was ready to move out. One arm worked its way up the coast through Fujian to Hangzhou, another headed directly for Nanjing, and a third made for Changsha and the Wuhan 'tri-city'.

The last, following the route taken by the Taipings in 1851–53, made the most rapid progress thanks to the nearly completed Guangzhou–Wuhan rail link. Changsha fell in July and Wuchang, after heavy fighting and a desperate siege, in October. Chiang Kai-shek, as commander-in-chief, then faced the same decision as the Taipings in 1854 – whether to push on north straight to Beijing or whether first to veer east down the Yangzi to secure Shanghai and the agro-industrial heartland. Unlike the God-worshippers, Chiang favoured Shanghai. Nanjing was taken in March 1927 and Shanghai, already paralysed by a general strike organised by the CCP-dominated trade unions, welcomed the Nationalists later the same month.

The strikers, and the CCP, then became the victims of a flagrant and never-to-be forgotten betrayal. Chiang needed the recognition of the foreign powers, the forbearance of their navies and the loans and exactions available from Shanghai's banks and corporations. He did not need ardent supporters bent on ousting the foreign imperialists and reclaiming their concessions while using organised labour to smash the power of the corporate bourgeoisie. In short, the CCP was now an embarrassment. Moving all but his most reliable troops out of the city, and availing himself of the services of the Green Gang, an underworld organisation of well-armed thugs used by industrialists to intimidate strikers, Chiang Kai-shek launched an all-out assault on the labour unions. Hundreds of union leaders were gunned down, thousands arrested. Similar acts of repression followed in Wuhan and Guangzhou. The CCP's hopes of a Marxist revolution based on the seizure of the means of production by the industrial proletariat had always been a long shot in an overwhelmingly agrarian economy. Now those hopes were dashed. Likewise, the strategy of using the Guomindang to turbo-charge a communist grab for power had spectacularly backfired. As of 1928 Nationalists and communists were locked into a disastrous pattern of ideological detestation and military confrontation.

LONG MARCH, LONG WAR

In 1928, while the CCP withdrew to remote parts of Hubei, Hunan and Fujian to lick its wounds and regroup as best it could, Chiang Kai-shek went on to secure the northern provinces. The success of this second phase of the Northern Expedition was due, even more than the first, to concessions and alliances with existing warlords. In Shandong, Nationalist troops met their fiercest resistance not from Chinese opponents but from Japanese forces based there to protect Tokyo's concessions. To the now standard level of carnage was added a new venom as wanton atrocities were inflicted on civilians in the name of race.

Beijing, its latest warlord-master Zhang Zuolin having been blown up by a bomb in Mukden (Shengyang), was too vulnerable to Tokyo's zealots in nearby Manchuria and Shandong to serve as the Nationalist capital. Instead it was downgraded, as it had been by the *Ming* Hongwu emperor, from 'Beijing' ('Northern Capital') to 'Beiping' ('Northern Pacified [city]'). Nanjing was once again preferred as the national capital, and it

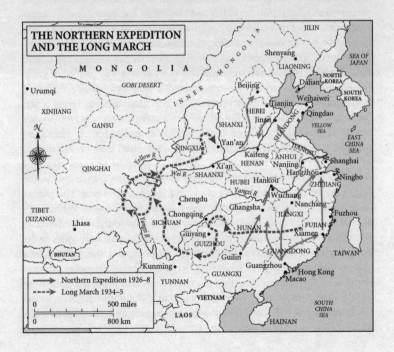

was effectively consecrated as such when Chiang Kai-shek had the remains of Dr Sun Yat-sen ceremonially reinterred there in a spectacular tomb. Again like the Hongwu emperor, whose own tomb was hard by on Mount Zijin, Sun was portrayed as the Guomindang's inspiration and his writings were accorded something of the authority of the Hongwu emperor's 'ancestral instructions'. In performing this pious act, Chiang sought to portray himself as Sun's protégé and delegated successor, an arrangement given quasi-dynastic substance by Chiang's new bride being the sister of Sun's widow. Legitimacy still lay with the past, not the people.

Since priority was being given to eradicating the CCP, extending Nationalist control into the warlord-ruled countryside and milking Shanghai for funds, 'there was little need for Chiang to worry about the trappings of democracy'.[21] A strongly centralist and bureaucratic form of administration was adopted by China's first Nationalist government, and an austere Confucianist ideology developed to underpin it. Known as the 'New Life' movement – supposedly a Chinese take on the American 'New Deal' – this stressed discipline, decorum and loyalty rather than righteousness or reverence for scholarship. When in the 1930s Chiang conceived an admiration for Hitler and Mussolini, it acquired fascist undertones. The now Generalissimo became the centre of a personal cult and launched his own morality police, the 'Blueshirts'.

Though Chiang's China was but a fraction of the Qing empire, and though within it warlords were still rife and fighting was continuous, the Nationalist revolution of 1926–28 attained a wider acceptance than had the republican revolution of 1911–12. This was nicely demonstrated when the British returned, or 'rendited', the 775 square kilometres (300 square miles) of mainland Chinese territory that comprised their Shandong concession at Weihaiwei. Technically Weihaiwei could have been returned in 1905 when, in the aftermath of the Russo-Japanese war, the Russians withdrew from Dalian. But the Japanese then took over Dalian and so the British stayed on as a counterweight to the Japanese presence. The matter came up again in 1915, at which point Reginald Johnston, Weihaiwei's district magistrate, was invited to summarise the reasons for its retention. He replied that he was 'aware of none'. Britain and Japan were allies at the time; the naval base served no strategic purpose, and the seafront was more noted for bathing machines than battleships, being a popular summer resort with foreign families. By 1920 the British had accepted Johnston's logic and were resolved to hand the place back. But a new problem arose: to whom to hand it. In Beijing warlords were coming and going too quickly, while the Guomindang were at the time far away in the south.

The difficulty was still unresolved when in 1926 Reginald Johnston returned to Weihaiwei as its commissioner. In the interim, he had occupied what he called 'the peculiar and rather interesting position' of tutor to Henry Pu-yi. The 'Last Emperor' had been allowed to stay on in the Imperial Palace after his 1912 deposition, and so Johnston, living with his young charge, probably enjoyed a closer acquaintance with palace life than any other foreigner during the 250 years of Qing rule. Since then, Pu-yi had been extracted from the palace for his own safety and was now living as a private citizen under Japanese protection in Tianjin. There could be no question of handing Weihaiwei to him; but when in 1929 the British recognised Chiang Kai-shek's Nationalist government, the problem was at last solved. With a legitimate and reasonably stable government in place, 'the first British surrender of crown territory since the American War of Independence' took place in October 1930. The ceremonial procedure adopted for the occasion – handshakes, flag-lowering, salutes, bagpipes, sombre seaward departure, ecstatic landward celebrations – would be repeated in outposts of Britain's empire at the rate of about one every two years over the next half-century. And a process, begun on the China coast, would culminate there. For in June 1997, when the ninety-nine-year lease of Hong Kong's 'New Territories' expired and the whole colony was 'rendited', Britain's empire was finally laid to rest. China regained the first of its alienated territories; and bar two (Macao, handed over in 1999, and Taiwan, still 'unrendited') it was the last.[22]

As well as reclaiming Weihaiwei, the Nationalist government opened the question of renegotiating the 'unequal' treaties of the nineteenth century, especially in respect of extraterritoriality and the treaty ports. Three Yangzi ports were duly handed back, including Hankou, where the bomb had gone off in 1911, while a system of power-sharing was introduced on Shanghai's municipal council. Negotiations with the foreign powers were still ongoing when in 1932 this brief window of opportunity was slammed shut. The Japanese had in the previous year contrived a pretext for occupying Shenyang (Mukden), the largest city in Manchuria, and then overrunning the rest of Manchuria. A year later in Shanghai, in response to anti-Japanese protests over this Manchurian grab and the killing of several Japanese nationals, the Japanese navy landed troops. Negotiations with the foreign powers were suspended as a fierce little war raged through the Chinese districts of the great city. By the time a truce was arranged in 1933, 14,000 had died.

These distractions, while affording a stay of execution to the treaty ports, proved the salvation of the communists in that they gave them time to

regroup. Since its betrayal by the Guomindang in 1928, the CCP had gone
back to the countryside. In several scattered enclaves, the party slowly re-
formed, usually following an accommodation with local warlords, and then
began establishing autonomous local soviets, still with Comintern guidance and support. Troops were recruited and trained; and the leadership
was viciously contested. Chen Duxiu and Qu Qiubai had been made scapegoats for the failure of the united front with the Guomindang, despite their
reservations about it in the first place. Other figures now contended for
high party office. They included: Zhou Enlai, a dedicated ideologue who
had studied in Paris, then headed the political department of the Guangdong
military academy, and now coordinated party activities; Lin Biao, one of
the Guangdong Academy's cadets who had distinguished himself as a
brilliant commander during the first phase of the Northern Expedition;
and Mao Zedong, a tall, slightly effete-looking maverick with little
military experience, an unreliable record, a ruthless reputation and an
unshakeable conviction that he alone understood the requirements of the
situation.

But attempts to extend the party's enclaves fared indifferently. By 1933
all of them were on the defensive as Chiang Kai-shek, relieved by the truce
with the Japanese, intensified his blockades and sent wave after wave of
Guomindang forces against them. The largest 'Red' enclave was located in
the hills of Jiangxi near the provincial border with Hunan. When, in 1934,
this Jiangxi soviet was faced with imminent extinction, the decision was
taken to evacuate it. About 28,000, including the wounded and nearly all
the women, were left behind to the none-too-tender mercies of the
Nationalists; equal status did not include equal opportunity of survival.
The rest, about 80,000, of whom perhaps half were combat troops, broke
out of the blockade under cover of darkness, heading west, on 16 October
1934. This was the start of the 'Ten-thousand Li [about 5,000 kilometres,
3,000 miles] March', otherwise the Long March.

'The most enduring myth in modern Chinese history, and one of the
biggest myths of the twentieth century', the Long March has since been
controversially exposed as just that, a myth.[23] According to Jung Chang
and Jon Halliday, Mao was very nearly left behind; he repeatedly led the
marchers astray; and like the rest of the leadership, he seldom actually
marched, being carried most of the way in a sedan chair. Moreover the
whole thing, far from being a saga of heroism and survival, was allegedly
a charade masterminded by, of all people, Chiang Kai-shek. Chiang's son
was at the time in Russia and supposedly being detained there as surety
for his father's collaboration. Were Chiang's forces to annihilate the

marchers, it would be as good as a death sentence for one on whom his father doted. Additionally Chiang could not afford to antagonise Moscow at a time when Tokyo posed the direr threat. And finally, while his Nationalist forces did indeed pursue the marchers through Guizhou and Sichuan, this supposedly served a different agenda, namely to wrest those territories from their warlords so that they would be available as a refuge for Chiang and his government in the event of a Japanese invasion.

The Comintern wanted the Jiangxi 'Reds' to relocate in the north-west, where they could supply and control them. Chiang's task, therefore, was to shepherd them there. Instead of decimating the communists, he was to deliver them. With air power and artillery, he could easily have annihilated them; but the planes buzzed without bombing, and the troops and guns were meant to overawe the local warlords. The battles of the march were invention, its year-long duration was due to quite unnecessary diversions, and the hardships encountered were the result of Mao's miscalculations and his power-thirsty manoeuvrings.

Much of which may be true – the details were always suspect – and none of which detracts from the central importance of the march. Removing from southern Jiangxi to northern Shaanxi, while saving the CCP from possible extinction and proving a strategic masterstroke, lent the party national credibility and set an example of improbable, even heaven-blest, survival. The sacrifices could not be gainsaid. Of the 80,000 who had marched out of Jiangxi, just 4,000 are said to have reached the new headquarters at Yan'an. Desertions accounted for some of these losses, perhaps most; deaths more often resulted from exhaustion and sickness than enemy fire; and since the Long Marchers were reshuffled with another 'Red' army en route, the exact number of survivors remains unclear. But disaster or triumph, the march came to be seen as bathed in glory, much like Gallipoli or Dunkirk, and was treated as a suitable subject for inspirational propaganda. Fairbank compared it to 'Moses leading his Chosen People through the Red Sea'; redemption through flight is something of an apostolic cliché.[24] In China, from the Han founder Liu Bang's repeated withdrawals before the fiery Xiang Yu to the long northward march of the Taipings, precedents aplenty demonstrated the genius of tactical relocation. And while to the average Chinese the doctrines of Marxism-Leninism may have seemed excessively abstract and alien, the march gave them a human dimension and a national relevance.

The march also gave birth to the Mao legend. A tendency to present mid-twentieth-century history in personal terms is not unique to China.

In a world dominated by wartime leaders and national heroes – Roosevelt, Stalin, Churchill, Gandhi, de Gaulle – China's redemption would readily lend itself to a Mao-centred narrative. Post-war reunification, mass indoctrination, implementation of the brand of communism labelled 'Maoism' and the cult of the Great Leader's personality – all ensured that Mao's story over the next four decades eclipsed China's. But it was not as simple as that. Without, for instance, the devastation caused by Japan's invasion and the Second World War, Mao and the CCP might have been a historical irrelevance.

In 1936, within a year of the party setting up its new soviet among the dusty canyons just south of the Great Wall in northern Shaanxi, another heaven-sent opportunity presented itself. Generalissimo Chiang Kai-shek was taken prisoner. While on a visit to Xi'an to meet Zhang Xueliang, playboy son of the warlord Zhang Zuolin and inheritor of his army, Chiang's bodyguard had been massacred and he himself held as a hostage. Zhang Xueliang's plan was the laudable one of acting as a go-between in bringing the Nationalists, communists and warlords together in united opposition to renewed Japanese incursions. In effect Chiang was to be forced into declaring a new united front and an end to anti-CCP hostilities on pain of being handed over to the CCP. Tortuous negotiations ensued in which the decisive move was made by the Comintern in Russia. For instead of encouraging the CCP to grab Chiang Kai-shek while it had the chance, it ordered the party to cooperate with the Nationalists, secure Chiang's release and even serve under his command in a united front against the Japanese. Zhou Enlai dutifully relayed this position and Chiang was freed. Not for several years would a united front result; the Nationalists were still too suspicious of the communists. But Nationalist offensives against the Shaanxi soviet were scaled down, Mao and the CCP gained the breathing space to embark on rural mobilisation, and all parties braced themselves for the Japanese onslaught.

Long anticipated, the fatal encounter took place at the so-called 'Marco Polo bridge', about 15 kilometres (9 miles) west of Beijing, on the night of 7 July 1937. In defence of their railway and industrial concessions, Japanese troops and Japanese-controlled Chinese forces were by now stationed all over Hebei and Shandong. The affair at the bridge, initially a misunderstanding over training manoeuvres, escalated rapidly because Tokyo was taking a more belligerent line and Chiang Kai-shek was under enormous pressure to stand firm. When the Japanese and their warlord allies swept all before them round Tianjin and Beijing, the same pressure saw Chiang risk opening a second front with a view to drawing off the enemy.

Chiang's new front was Shanghai, where Japanese troops were few and a Japanese naval fleet looked an inviting target. That it was also China's most populous city, its biggest port and richest financial centre seems not to have troubled the Generalissimo. Ordered to attack the Japanese fleet, in mid-August Chiang's Nationalist air force swept low over the city to drop their bombs. They failed to hit a single ship but sent three bombs into the heart of the international concession. One scored a direct hit on the Palace Hotel, a prestigious development on the corniche-like Bund, another just missed the nearby Cathay Hotel and landed in the crowds outside, and a third hit the Great World, an enormous pleasure-drome on Nanjing Road, the main shopping street. There alone 1,000 were killed, nearly all Chinese, and 1,000 more horribly mutilated. It was 13 August, a Friday.

Inauspiciously begun, the Nationalists' Shanghai front soon retracted to become a Yangzi front. Shanghai itself held out for a couple of months, during which the Japanese brought in aircraft carriers, heavy armour and several divisions of marines and infantry. 'As many as 250,000 Chinese troops were killed or wounded – almost 60% of Chiang's finest forces – while the Japanese took 40,000 or more casualties.'[25] The city never really recovered. Foreigners fled, business confidence collapsed, and it was in fact the Japanese who terminated the status of its international concession. The Nationalists then began their own Long March, retreating upriver to the capital, Nanjing, which fell in December (1937), to a new capital at Wuhan, which fell in mid-1938, and finally to Chongqing above the gorges in Sichuan, which, though heavily bombed, would serve as the last capital of what remained of Chiang's Nationalist China until 1945.

It was a similar story farther north, despite valiant resistance and the flooding – intentional for once – of the Yellow River. Meant as a way of slowing the enemy's advance, the blowing up of the dikes redirected the river for the umpteenth time and inundated an unrecorded number of Chinese civilians. By late 1938 the Japanese had reached Kaifeng. Meanwhile in the south Guangzhou had fallen and Hong Kong was effectively isolated. Worse by far, though, was the madness that had overtaken the Japanese when they entered Nanjing. That city, as fair as any with its graceful Ming palaces and massive walls beneath the wooded slopes of Mount Zijin, had known massacres before. Nothing, though, could compare with the butchery, rapes and other atrocities perpetrated over a seven-week reign of terror in the winter of 1937/38. As Japanese troops took their revenge on the capital, at least 50,000 Chinese – and possibly half a million – most of them civilians, were gratuitously slaughtered in one of the worst war crimes on record.

By 1939, when the Sino-Japanese war was subsumed within the Second World War, all the coastal provinces were under Tokyo's control, while its quisling regimes extended deep inland. China was fragmented; but *zhongguo*, in any meaningful sense, was subjugated. The Nationalists were penned up in Sichuan, desperately short of revenue and dependent for munitions and supplies on the newly built but only fitfully open Burma Road through semi-autonomous Yunnan. The communists were equally marginalised and equally cash-strapped in Shaanxi. There they cultivated self-sufficiency, harboured designs on Gansu and Ningxia, and accumulated manpower while experimentally re-allocating land and classifying and organising its cultivators. Meanwhile the fighting continued and the human tragedies multiplied. Despite massive Allied support for the Nationalists, especially after Pearl Harbor (December 1941) and American entry into the Pacific War, despite the eventual formation of a half-hearted Guomindang-CCP united front, and despite a major Japanese offensive in Hunan and Guizhou in 1944, the military situation remained basically unchanged until Japan surrendered following the August 1945 A-bombing of Hiroshima and Nagasaki.

China's contribution to victory had been in tying down vast numbers of Japanese aircraft, military vehicles and above all troops. In 1945 about two million, half of them in Manchuria, awaited surrender and repatriation. Both the Nationalists, with their promise of a 'Free China' now backed by the USA, and the communists, with their ambitions for a People's Republic backed by the Russians, swooped to secure the surrendered munitions and to claim the abandoned infrastructure, the mines, the factories and the teeming territories. In this race, Manchuria, now a heavily industrialised region thanks to Japanese investment and less devastated by the late war than the rest of China, constituted the greatest prize. It had been invaded by the Russians in the dying months of the war, which handed the advantage to the communists. When Nationalist and communist armies both converged on it, the Nationalists, while much the stronger, found their progress slowed by the Russians. The communists, joined by local partisans and some Koreans, were allowed to help themselves to the stockpiled Japanese weaponry and establish themselves in the far north. It was thus in Harbin, the first city run by the CCP, that Lin Biao reorganised his forces as the People's Liberation Army (PLA) and in late 1946 began to push south.

By then American attempts to get the two sides to accept a ceasefire and some form of power-sharing under Chiang Kai-shek's leadership had collapsed. 'The greatest obstacle to peace has been the complete, almost overwhelming suspicion with which the Chinese Communist Party and the Guomindang regard each other,' began General George Marshall's report on the failure of his mediating mission. 'They each sought only to take counsel of their fears.'[26] The fears proved real enough when in early 1947 the fighting flared into open war and each side assumed its true colours. The communists no longer disguised their revolutionary intent. Lands were confiscated and redistributed, landowners held to account, informants encouraged, and mass indoctrination campaigns organised. The Nationalists, on the other hand, betrayed their old preference for corporate croneyism, indifference to popular sentiment and economic incompetence. A collapse in morale as a result of rampant inflation (500 per cent a month in 1948), famines, rural unrest and student protests undermined the Nationalist regime more fatally than the communist victories. By 1948 the PLA had inflicted a series of disastrous defeats on the Nationalists in Manchuria, leading to mass desertions. All over northern China the CCP's peasant guerrillas were simultaneously making the countryside a no-go area. More victories and desertions meant that by the end of 1948 most of China north of the Yangzi was in communist hands.

Jonathan Spence likens Chiang Kai-shek's plight to that of the Ming pretenders after the Manchus had overrun the north in 1644–45. Chiang himself might have been more reassured by those earlier dynasties, stretching back through the Song and the Eastern Jin to the Wu of the Three Kingdoms period, which had made a greater success of their southern sojourn. He certainly considered standing firm south of the Yangzi, while he investigated the alternative possibility of again withdrawing to Sichuan and Yunnan. But in the end he opted for the greater safety of Taiwan, which had been restored to the republic after the defeat of Japan. Art treasures and texts from the Imperial Palace in Beijing, the nearest thing to regalia that he could lay his hands on, were removed there in 1948; and in early 1949, as the PLA overran the south in a series of lightning advances, Chiang himself fled across the Taiwan Strait with about a million of his troops. Other Nationalists were driven into Thailand, Laos and Burma. Many emigrated overseas.

As president of his rump 'Republic of China', Chiang ruled on in Taiwan until his death in 1975. In good dynastic tradition he was then succeeded by his son until Taiwan adopted a parliamentary form of government in the late 1980s. Mao, who would die in 1976, outlasted

Chiang by just a year. But his 'People's Republic of China', officially proclaimed from Tiananmen, the Heavenly Gate, in Beijing in October 1949, proved markedly more resistant to parliamentary representation.

EPILOGUE

THE QINGMING FESTIVAL, WHEN CHINESE FAMILIES honour their ancestors, generally falls around 5 April. Graves and shrines are swept clean, flowers are arranged, ribbons tied, and the deceased plied with food and token gifts – imitation banknotes, cut-out Toyotas, cardboard cellphones. Those unable to attend in person can access online catalogues of these make-believe modernities for virtual donation. A new generation is having to reconfigure the traditions of Qingming because for nearly half a century the festival was in abeyance. It fell foul of communist contempt for all superstitions and then of the Cultural Revolution's censure of 'old thinking'. In 1976 it acquired a positively insidious dimension when on 4–5 April a display of Qingming floral wreaths and poster poems brought crowds of mourners to Beijing's Tiananmen Square. They were protesting against official indifference to the recent death of Premier Zhou Enlai, which they saw as disparagement of a revered and long-serving revolutionary by the hard left leadership of the Cultural Revolution. Cars were overturned and a police post torched. But the main casualty was Vice-Premier Deng Xiaoping; accused of orchestrating the affair, he was dismissed from all his Party offices. Sometimes known as the Tiananmen incident, this 1976 protest is now more commonly called the Qingming Incident, so avoiding confusion with the more prolonged Tiananmen confrontation of 1989.

Deng, of course, soon rose again; and thirty years later, on 5 April 2006, Qingming itself was back in favour. Next day the papers were full of it. From Xi'an in Shaanxi came news of lavish ceremonies at a mausoleum lately built to commemorate Huangdi, the Yellow Emperor. First of the mythical Five Emperors, the Yellow Emperor was now credited by the *China Daily* with having fathered the Chinese people and invented the boat, the cart, the longbow and Chinese medicine, 'among other things'. Over $15 million had been subscribed for the emperor's new shrine, though Shaanxi's governor insisted that a more fitting memorial would be 'reunification of the motherland'. He was thinking of Taiwan, from where much of the money and many of the participants had come.

Meanwhile, in Shaoxing (Zhejiang province) the Qingming celebrations had focused not on the first of the Five Emperors but the last. This 'Great Yu' was he who, by making his son his heir, had founded the Xia dynasty, the earliest in China's long dynastic pedigree. Among the 3000 who had reportedly attended 'the ancient rituals' staged at Shaoxing were the city's Communist Party secretary, the Zhejiang Party's deputy secretary, the vice-chairman of the Standing Committee of the National People's Congress, and 115 people with the surname Si, all of whom claimed direct descent from Emperor Yu. A similar assembly, this time of Kongs, was reported at Confucius's birthplace of Qufu in Shandong. Out of his now 2–3 million descendants (there's a DNA test to prove it) luckily only a fraction had turned up; but more were expected for his birthday. Reviled as late as the 1970s, in the 1990s Confucius had been rehabilitated. Confucian injunctions were now eclipsing the slogans of both Marxism-Leninism and 'Mao Zedong thought' in official discourse. Pride in those 3000–6000 years of continuous civilisation, rather than the recent achievements of the proletariat, had been chosen as the theme of the Beijing Olympics. Emperors, no longer monsters of exploitation, were again being accorded national respect. And Qingming had been reinstated in the official calendar. In fact in 2008 it was made a public holiday. As the nation headed en masse for the ancestral burial grounds, thousands of extra bus and train services were laid on, incoming charter flights were taking off from Taiwan at the rate of one every fifteen minutes, and the traffic jams around Shanghai were said to be the worst ever recorded.

China has transformed itself – and is still doing so – more dramatically than any other region in the world. In fact the rate of change is so fast that it wrong-foots all but the most agile China-watchers. Up-to-the-minute histories written in the 1970s felt obliged to explore, in mind-numbing detail, the dialectics of Marxism-Leninism as adapted by Mao and adumbrated in the opaque pronouncements of plenums and praesidiums. Subjecting Asia's agrarian masses to an ideology devised for Europe's industrial proletariat seemed an experiment worth studying. The staggering statistics churned out by annual audits of output and successive five-year plans also proved irresistible. Faith in the efficacy of scientific socialism, planned economics and democratic centralism enforced the idea of progress as product: given the right machine and the right settings, it could be churned out like pig iron. To lubricate the leviathan, campaigns were launched and diktats promulgated – 'the Four Clean-ups', 'the Five Antis' (anti-corruption, etc.), 'the Ten Great Relationships', 'the Sixty Articles on Work Methods', and so on. China-watchers needed clear heads and a sceptical turn of mind.

They were not to know, writing in the 1970s, that within a generation many of the policies they had discerned would be considered mistaken and their studious analysis of them therefore excessive. With nose pressed against the present and eyes trained on the praesidium, it had been difficult to tell just what to make of it all. Isolating the significant needs patience and perspective, commodities not available in the heat of the moment, then or now. As history's stately march breaks into the trot of current affairs, then the stampede of news stories, scholars are expected to swivel from the reconstruction of a reticent past to the deconstruction of a clamorous present. Hammered by reality, the historian turns annalist, turns journalist.

Because so many Maoist achievements were quickly discredited, there then arose a tendency to gloss over all those initiatives that had loomed largest at the time – Soviet collaboration, agricultural collectivisation, industrialisation, the Great Leap and the Cultural Revolution – in favour of a narrative buoyed by the incidence of liberalising interludes. This ran from the 1956 'Hundred Flowers' movement to the 1972 détente with the United States, the 1978 'Democracy Wall' outburst, Deng Xiaoping's economic reforms, the 1989 Tiananmen Square challenge, and of course the end-of-century triumph of consumerism. But such a narrative has its drawbacks too. It supposes a progressive 'opening up' that was not self-evident at the time, and it foreshadows an ultimate liberalisation – including multiparty politics, electoral accountability, freedom of expression, and legal redress – that is far from assured.

It also misrepresents the Maoist era by downplaying some very real achievements. When on 1 October 1949 the People's Republic of China (PRC) was officially announced by Mao in Beijing, the People's Liberation Army had much liberating still to do. Guangdong had yet to be reached (it fell two weeks later); Tibet and Xinjiang, comprising nearly half of the erstwhile empire's landmass, aspired to qualified independence; the British were back in Hong Kong; and from Taiwan, alienated by the relocation there of Chiang Kai-shek's still internationally recognised Republic of China, a reinvasion of the mainland remained a distinct possibility. When the Korean War broke out in June 1950, the USA immediately moved its Seventh Fleet into the Taiwan Straits, so ratcheting up this threat; and when non-communist South Korea was quickly reduced to a tiny bridgehead around Pusan, Washington showed no hesitation in finding the land, air and naval forces for a massive counter-attack. Thus within a year of the inauguration of the PRC, most of the Korean peninsula had been retaken by the PRC's ideological opponents and US troops were nearing the Sino-Korean frontier. It was not unreasonable to suppose that, with

Taiwan as the bridgehead, an equally devastating assault might be launched into China itself. Indeed, it probably would have been, had Beijing not insisted that a Chinese counter-intervention in Korea was the work of a maverick 'People's Volunteer Army' rather than the official People's Liberation Army.

Regardless of such fine distinctions, China and the USA were effectively at war in Korea from 1950 until 1953. And though the Korean peninsula was eventually partitioned along the 38th parallel, China's ideological encirclement continued. 'The bamboo curtain', which looked from the inside more like an offensive blockade than defensive 'containment', extended down the length of China's seaboard from bisected Korea to the Taiwan Straits and on to an about-to-be-bisected Vietnam. Thus communist China was as firmly closed to the world's maritime trade as imperial China before the Opium Wars. The gargantuan task of reintegrating the nation, redistributing its assets, and reorganising and re-educating its society, all in accordance with principles of socialist revolution that were decidedly novel in Asia, had to be undertaken by a regime that was still embattled.

Ring-fenced to the east and south, China's communist leaders sought support from the north and west. The Soviet Union had inspired, funded, armed and often directed its revolutionary Chinese brethren throughout the war years. Both sides now had victories to celebrate and pledges to redeem. In December 1949, on his first ever trip outside China, Mao took the train to Moscow. There Stalin, basking in the cult of his own personality while tyrannising both people and Party, encouraged Mao's autocratic tendencies without overindulging his revolution. But in hammering out the terms of a treaty of 'Friendship, Alliance and Mutual Assistance', the principles of ideological fraternity and Sino-Soviet collaboration were established. In return for international solidarity, secret recognition of Moscow's strategic interests in Xinjiang and Manchuria, and various raw materials, Mao secured a promise of support in the event of war, a $300 million loan (half to be used for military purchases), and the know-how and personnel to set up fifty state-owned heavy industrial complexes. Additional armaments and aircraft were soon being supplied to aid the Chinese involvement in Korea. Assistance in the development of atomic weaponry was later promised, though soon withdrawn.

This Soviet support did nothing to advance Beijing's claims to Taiwan or Hong Kong; but it did facilitate the reintegration of regions once contested by Russia, notably the north-east (formerly Manchuria) and the far west (now Xinjiang). Thanks to Soviet links with India, it also silenced some of the international disquiet over the reclamation of Tibet. Thus within a year of its inauguration, the China of the People's Republic was territorially nearly as vast as the China of the mid-Qing empire. It was at last rid of foreign interference, master of its future, and more united than it had been for over a century. Given the appalling chaos that had overtaken republican China, this was no mean achievement. Order had been restored, inflation was being contained, national pride had been redeemed, self-belief had returned. To the Party and the PLA it all lent an impressive legitimacy, plus a certain latitude.

Since the PLA's success owed much to the discipline and dissemination of Marxist-Leninist precepts, it was to be expected that the new regime would give priority to extending the revolution to the whole country. This would involve sacrifices, but for many it was an exciting prospect. In the cities, families were organised into units based on places of work and residence (*danwei*); they encouraged a sense of local participation and purpose, as well as ensuring the surveillance associated with traditional systems of neighbourhood organisation like the Ming *baojia* and Qin's 'legalist' groupings. In the countryside, where 85 per cent of the population still lived, mobilising the masses was expected to take longer. Trained Party activists descended on village after village, identified and classified all households, incited the denunciation of those designated 'rich landlords', and, having dispossessed and disposed of these 'enemies of the people', redistributed their property among the landless. A million or more landowners and counter-revolutionaries may have been executed in this first phase of retributive justice; Mao himself would put the death toll at 700,000. But several hundred million peasants found themselves beneficiaries of the redistribution as, for the first time, they tilled their own fields and reaped the fruits of their labour.

Naturally the resultant proliferation of small subsistence holdings argued strongly for some collaborative work practices. Local cooperatives based on the sharing of draught animals and some pooling of labour were encouraged, although the results were disappointing. Newly landed peasants had a tendency to put personal profit before the common good; politicised cadres were often drawn into village vendettas; and the growth in output barely kept ahead of the growth in population. The generous surpluses needed to feed the expanding urban and industrial centres looked unlikely to materialise. This in turn would jeopardise the creation of an industrial base which, as per the Soviet model, was the prerequisite for a strong and self-sustaining socialism.

In 1955, rid of the Korean War and still on good terms with the Soviets, Mao addressed this problem personally by calling for an immediate acceleration in the pace of agrarian revolution. Cooperatives were now to be amalgamated into larger collectives. Land and implements would be collectively owned, the peasant's only input being labour and only reward a share of the collective's produce based on a complicated calculation of the 'work points' earned by each individual. Again, the scheme was not universally unpopular. Many of those with minuscule or marginal holdings welcomed the greater security on offer from collectivisation. Others were fired by the egalitarian ideals of the revolution. Women acquired some independence as a result of their individual entitlement to work points. Economies of scale promised a higher combined yield; small fields were amalgamated, dykes and pathways ploughed under, and the cultivable area expanded by deploying the larger labour force to terrace, clear and irrigate marginal lands. The state provided a market for the commune's surplus at guaranteed prices; and if these procurement quotas tended to escalate, they supposedly reflected the results of reclamation and irrigation.

With Party encouragement, by 1957 some districts were taking the process a stage farther. Just as cooperatives had been merged into the larger collectives, so now collectives were being merged into the still larger communes. Mao endorsed the move with an exhortation for all production to be 'larger, faster, better, cheaper'. Any privately owned plots that had survived collectivisation were now incorporated in the communised land area. With a work force of 20,000–100,000, a commune required an administrative infrastructure that, besides doling out work points and drumming in slogans, offered services likely to keep the existing workforce in good shape and augment it by freeing up women otherwise detained at home. Organised childcare, basic schooling, dispensaries, communal dining and competitive work teams were certainly a novelty. But while they undermined the traditional primacy of the household and the family, they also introduced some genuine social uplift. In return for better healthcare, wider literacy and several square meals a day, many saw neglecting the ancestors at Qingming and putting up with round-the-clock indoctrination as a small price to pay. The 1950s would later be remembered as Maoist China's 'golden age' – a comparative verdict, obviously – with the early phase of communisation being especially cherished as the 'eat it up' period. This was a reference not to the state's appetite for ever more unrealistic procurement quotas but to the workers' 'eat as much as you want' approach to the communal kitchens. 'Ah, in the beginning [of the communes] we were all so fat!' recalled a Guangdong peasant, 'We could eat anytime we liked at the canteens.'[1]

And it was all free. Free food and healthcare enhanced longevity, free education promised greater opportunity, and liberal new laws on inheritance and divorce ushered in more equality and association between the sexes. It sounded like bliss, a genuine liberation, in fact a lot like heaven. For these were precisely the celestial rewards that had been on offer from those millenarianist movements in the past. From the Yellow Turbans to the Taipings and Boxers, they too had promised a dazzling new utopia and inspired great idealism. But they had failed to deliver. Marxism-as-the-new-millenariarism was actually making good on its promises. Mao had conjured up visions of a socialist paradise with peace and plenty for all; sure enough, for a few months in early 1957, this 'great harmony' (*da tong* – he used the Confucian term) seemed imminent.

Even the barriers to freedom of expression were being lowered as dissidents and scholars were encouraged to speak their minds. This was another of Mao's ideas. In policy-making as in dialectics, he was fascinated by contradiction, by how friction sparked innovation, conflict generated endeavour, revolution validated authority. Order arose from chaos; but without more chaos, it would atrophy. Accordingly, and echoing the tag commonly applied to the 'Warring States' period of philosophical speculation, he urged 'a hundred schools of thought' to contend in the field of science and 'a hundred flowers' to bloom in the meadow of culture.

Both meadow and field were hastily ploughed under. Springtime's 'great harmony' lasted only weeks. 'The hundred flowers' bloomed in unacceptable shades of opinion and 'the hundred schools' contended much too contentiously; they even debated the defiance that had just been silenced in Hungary by Soviet tanks. By summer 1957 all those who had been rash enough to speak out were rounded up. Mao pretended that exposing and then purging these 'rightist' elements had been the plan all along. Whether true or not, it now seemed that nothing could be taken at its face value when viewed through the looking-glass of Maoism. A new unease permeated the Party and extended down through the ranks of the administration; to deluded ambitions born of extravagant idealism were added servile compliance and duplicity born of the terror of disapproval.

Ironically the 1958 harvest gave grounds for optimism. It was the best yet, though not as exceptional as the returns – or the procurement quotas based on them – suggested. Now heavy industry, especially steel production, was the sector lagging behind. Mobilising the masses to torment sparrows, mice and other grain-eating vermin had supposedly boosted the harvest; just so, mobilising the masses to turn pig iron into steel would boost industry. In *danwei* and communes the night sky flared as thousands of backyard blast furnaces spewed forth substandard metals. Fantastic production targets were set, and, if the quality was ignored and the returns believed, were nearly met. Thanks to a traditional technology – the blast furnace had probably been pioneered in Henan in the third century BC – China would become a world-class economy in one 'great leap forward'. This mass-action formula was emulated up and down the country as millions marched forth to undertake Herculean construction projects with no more in the way of equipment than the barrows and baskets used by the builders of the Great Wall and the Grand Canal. Caution was thrown to the wind; anything seemed possible in a climate of hysterical mass endeavour. Instead of grinding through the geared stages of growth laid down in the Marxist-Leninist manual – heavy industry first, then mechanisation, collectivisation, and eventually state ownership of all the means of production – Mao revved the engine and let fly the clutch.

But already there were rumours of famine; the reports were suppressed, the observers silenced. Instead of an investigation, the communes were favoured with a new wave of young urban ideologues intent on teaching the peasants how to grow corn, albeit 'larger, faster, better, cheaper'. Their innovations and naivety contributed to the impending disaster. Procurement quotas for 1959 had been set at hopelessly unrealistic levels; even without the drought of that year, the cold and rains of the next, and the inevitable Yellow River flood, the state's requisitions could be met only at the expense of the communal kitchens. There meals became fewer, weeds replaced vegetables, and muddy water was passed off as soup. The severity of the famine varied – from serious in the cities to acute in some provinces, absolute in others. Talk of cannibalism and of graziers eating their own grass was dismissed as mischievous; the bountiful reports still emanating from the local cadres belied it.

So wheat continued to be exported while those who grew it grazed on grass. And so, in an age when roads and railways should have made relief a formality, nothing was done. Alleviating conditions meant admitting the disaster; but since the leadership and its policies were beyond criticism, those responsible must be incompetent or reactionary elements within the communes. In effect, whistle-blowers merely denounced themselves. Prudence dictated signing off on the fictitious production figures and keeping quiet.

How many victims were claimed by the famine of 1958–61 will never be known. It was certainly the twentieth century's worst. From the pattern of population growth for the period, statisticians have extrapolated a catch-all figure of 20–30 million. Half may have actually starved to death; the rest were circumstantial victims. Minor diseases proved fatal to the enfeebled; the old died younger and the young failed to replace them. Aborted, still-born and short-lived babies were probably exceeded by the millions who were simply never conceived, abstinence and infertility being concomitants of malnutrition. Communes turned into death camps. The fields lay fallow because the new seed had been eaten or the people were too weak to sow it. Mao's impatient crashing of the gears had thrown the economy into reverse. The Great Leap Forward occasioned a catastrophic lurch backward.

A possible verdict on Mao's manic chairmanship might echo that applied to the Qin First Emperor, he whose great failing had been 'not changing with the times'. According to Grand Historian Sima Qian, the qualities essential for acquiring an empire were not the same as those needed for ruling it; or as an adviser had pointed out to Liu Bang, founder of the Han dynasty, an empire won from the saddle could not be run from the saddle. Violent and impulsive tactics were fine in the field but quite inappropriate in the council chamber. Thus, failing to adapt, or 'not changing with the times', was a flaw common to many dynastic founders. Mao was exceptional in just two respects: he lasted longer than most, so multiplying his potential for mischief, and he discovered a rationale for prolonging the mischief that masked his mere love of power. This lay in his belief that constant turmoil and class struggle were essential to the integrity of the revolution, which would otherwise be undermined by inertia, corruption and ideological backsliding. It did not occur to him that the revolution might also be undermined by histrionic efforts to perpetuate it.

Emperors were much on Mao's mind at the time of the Great Leap Forward. In 1958/59 he called for a re-evaluation of demonised autocrats like Cao Cao of the Three Kingdoms and the megalomaniac Qin First Emperor. He also praised Li Si, the latter's *éminence grise*, who had famously censured Confucian scholars and burnt their books. When the enormity of the Great Leap tragedy could no longer be concealed, Mao invoked a less hands-on imperial tradition, that of the *wuwei* (aloof or 'inactive') ruler. He withdrew from public view, surrendered the chairmanship of the PRC (though not of the Party), and secluded himself in various favoured retreats. 'The great helmsman' was thus below decks when the ship hit the rocks, although he surfaced for Party gatherings and would later accept that mistakes had been made during the Great Leap.

The task of relieving the famine, removing those held responsible and rescuing the economy was left to the politburo. From its ranks there emerged during the early 1960s a triumvirate whose considerable success entailed reversing recent policies and thus incurring Mao's suspicions. Liu Shaoqi, a fine-looking and capable bureaucrat whom Mao had installed as head of state and his preferred successor (dynastic preference trumped egalitarian principle in such matters), conducted a Socialist Education Campaign that found corruption and impropriety to be endemic in the Party, the provincial administrations and the state industries. The resultant arrests ran into the hundreds of thousands. The campaign was supported by Premier Zhou Enlai, Mao's bushy-browed and utterly dependable associate, and by Party secretary Deng Xioaping, a small and dynamic pragmatist whose devotion to the Party may have exceeded that to its Chairman.

Between them, Zhou and Deng presided over a stabilisation of the economy. The criterion for advancement was now to be technical and professional ability as much as political orthodoxy. A quip, later appropriated by Deng Xiaoping, about it being immaterial whether a cat is black or white 'so long as it catches the mouse' first surfaced in 1961.[2] 'Learning from the facts', another Deng-ism, inevitably meant skimping on the theory. The rural communes were downsized and their regimented ethic diluted. Communal kitchens were closed, some land was again made available for private cultivation, informal markets reappeared to handle this local output, and productivity began to shoot up. This was matched in the industrial sector, where incentives were introduced, innovation encouraged, and energy supplies improved when a major oilfield came online. Mass migration from the countryside to the cities was reversed, with restrictions on internal travel to prevent a further exodus from the fields. And the problem of an exponentially growing population was addressed in the first serious attempt to promote birth control. Mao had always insisted that the larger the proletariat the better. Not so, argued Deng Xiaoping; stabilising the population was essential to economic growth and social betterment. Nevertheless, and despite the famine, the 1957 population total of around 650 million had risen to around 950 million by 1977.

The gloom at the height of the famine had been compounded – and Mao's paranoia further excited – when in 1960 the Soviet Union withdrew its technical staff and cut off all aid. Ever since Moscow's posthumous denunciation of Stalin in 1956, the Sino-Soviet alliance had been slowly unravelling. Each side claimed to be the legitimate ideological heir of Marx and Lenin; but as their paths drifted apart, Moscow increasingly rested its case on its achievements (in weaponry, space exploration, the Middle East), leaving the high ground of ideological rectitude and unremitting class struggle to Beijing. Khrushchev's ridiculing of the Great Leap Forward provoked further resentment, and worse was his willingness to explore détente with the West. Not only did this leave China more internationally isolated than ever but to Mao it seemed the rankest apostasy. Moscow had betrayed the masses by taking 'the capitalist road'; a new generation of Soviet leaders was reversing the achievements of its predecessors; and given a shared ideological heritage, the same fate could all too easily overtake China.

There were other differences: over economic orthodoxy, China's nuclear ambitions, and Soviet support for India when a dispute over Tibet's Himalayan border flared into the short Sino-Indian war of 1962. But Khrushchev's overthrow in 1964 brought no thaw in Moscow's cold-shouldering. The backsliding 'revisionism' of its 'capitalist roaders' was more pronounced than ever. The only lesson to be drawn from the Soviet change of personnel was a personal one: 'in 1956 Mao had worried that he, like Stalin, might be denounced after his death; in 1964 he had reason to wonder if he, like Khrushchev, might be toppled *before* his death'.[3] Partly to forestall such a challenge from Liu Shaoqi and his reform-minded colleagues in the politburo, and partly to expose a younger generation to the rigours of revolutionary struggle and so inure them to the contagion of Soviet-style revisionism, in 1966 Mao unleashed the pandemonium of the Great Proletarian Cultural Revolution.

Whether Mao was right about Liu Shaoqi's treacherous intentions is doubtful. Liu would indeed be the Cultural Revolution's most high-profile victim, though Deng Xiaoping was also disgraced and even the faithful Zhou Enlai was obliged to offer self-criticism. But the unexciting Liu was no power-crazed gambler; nor, at the time, were accusations of revisionist treason sufficiently rare to carry much conviction. Lin Biao, the PLA zealot who replaced Liu Shaoqi as Mao's chosen successor, fared no better, for in 1971 he also replaced Liu as prime suspect in a supposed coup. He then perished in highly dubious circumstances when an aircraft supposedly carrying him to Soviet safety mysteriously crashed in Outer Mongolia. All of which was doubly ironic because Mao's place in the hearts of his countrymen had by then become unassailable largely thanks to the sycophantic Lin. It was Lin Biao who ensured the loyalty of the PLA throughout the most chaotic years of the Cultural Revolution, Lin who elevated the Chairman's personality cult into something approaching a religion, and Lin who compiled the Little Red Book of Mao's collected wisdom as brandished by several million Red Guards. The book carried as frontispiece a scrawled 'facsimile in his own handwriting' of Lin's injunction to study, follow and act solely in accord with the Chairman's teachings. So how could such an eminently suitable leader-to-be suddenly become a public enemy? If any single incident discredited the Cultural Revolution, it was this. Clearly Mao's vainglory and paranoia were contributing more to the chaos than any rational concern for his safety or the succession. Already in his seventies in 1966, but refreshed by a well-publicised wallow in the Yangzi, the Chairman had lost none of his old appetite for acting impulsively.

On the other hand, right or wrong about Liu Shaoqi, Mao had certainly read the threat of bourgeois revisionism correctly. Within little over a decade the Party would indeed follow the Soviet Union down the 'capitalist road' (albeit without relinquishing the wheel) and so betray its revolutionary principles. He was mistaken, though, in supposing that this danger could be averted by rekindling a spirit of mass radicalisation. Rather was it the Cultural Revolution's mass radicalisation, and the bitter reaction it occasioned, which propelled the Party down the rightist slope. The reaction came not only from the bloodied victims of 'struggle sessions' (at which 'counter-revolutionaries' were publicly humiliated, berated and beaten, sometimes to death) but also from the screaming ranks of their youthful tormentors, the Red Guards. For while in 1966 this new generation of dedicated idealists duly rose to the challenge of 'overthrowing those in authority who took the capitalist road', by 1968 their excesses were being condemned and they themselves shunted off into the provinces to learn from the peasants. As with the 'Hundred Flowers' episode, activism was encouraged and then disowned, though this time it was supposed rightists who were first pilloried and unruly leftists who were then reined in. Disgust extended across the political spectrum and led to a disillusionment with ideology itself.

There were other ironies. The Great Leap famine had hit the countryside hardest; with the domestic press muzzled and foreign correspondents restricted in their movements, its enormity had been appreciated only after the event. In contrast, the impact of the Cultural Revolution was limited to the cities, where it involved the more articulate classes and was instantly reported, extensively filmed and uncomfortably experienced by the foreign community. Spectacular rallies, wholesale vandalism and chaotic 'struggle sessions' sent shudders of horror coursing down international spines. The British embassy was ransacked and the Soviet embassy burnt. As children denounced their parents, and pupils their teachers, as temples and churches were vandalised, schools and colleges closed, libraries incinerated, museums pillaged and senior officials humiliated, it seemed that China was undergoing a collective brain haemorrhage. The most filial, literate, bureaucratic and history-loving of societies had imploded; civil war was widely predicted. Yet the PLA stood firm; workers played only a minor and belated role in the mayhem; and the rural majority of the population was barely affected. Agricultural and industrial growth remained steady, if unspectacular. The death toll was probably under a twentieth that of the Great Leap famine, most of it attributable not to the 'struggle sessions' but to fighting between different Red Guard groups and to the PLA's suppression of them.

If the Great Proletarian Cultural Revolution was not obviously proletarian, neither was it essentially cultural. On the contrary, according to a post-Mao aphorism, 'the Cultural Revolution was all about doing away with culture'.[4] This is not to gainsay the shrill role played by Jiang Qing, Mao's wife and sometimes mouthpiece, who was responsible for cultural affairs. But forays into literature and the theatre, as into history, seldom stopped at mere politicisation or proscription. The first salvo of the revolution saw a 'counter-revolutionary' clique in Beijing University being denounced for defending a play set during the Great Rites Controversy of the 1520s. The play's criticism of the *Ming* Jiajing emperor was interpreted as a criticism of Mao, while its sympathy for the honest bureaucrat who defied the emperor was taken as support for one of Mao's revisionist victims. The ramifications of this affair brought down the mayor of Beijing, among many others. A few months later, the propaganda chief Lu Dingyi was denounced on similar grounds, this time following republication of the biography of Wei Zheng, *Tang* Taizong's crusty old remonstrator. At about the same time, Zhou Enlai's detractors delighted in rubbishing his pretensions as an elder statesman by comparing him to his namesake, the now derided Duke of Zhou; and later, by way of an explanation for Lin Biao's fall from favour, someone dreamed up that most far-fetched of linkages with Confucius himself. Meanwhile Mao had invoked *Journey to the West*, the great compendium of fantasy and fable inspired by monk Xuanzang's travels in the seventh century. Red Guards were to model their exploits on Sun Wugong, its 'monkey king', and to regard his arsenal of wondrous powers and magical weapons as symbolic of their own potential for creating trouble. As ever, history and culture served as the currency of debate and suffered greatly in the process. But at stake was not a reading of the past but a correction of the present and a prescription for the future.

Perhaps the ultimate irony of the Cultural Revolution was that, even as 'capitalist roaders' were being hauled from their homes and publicly 'struggled', privately Mao and Zhou Enlai were exploring direct links with the Gomorrah of capitalism in Washington, DC. This tectonic shift, as decisive for modern China as the Cultural Revolution itself, would have few domestic repercussions until after Mao's death. At the time it reflected both sides' need to reposition themselves internationally. For in 1968 the

Tet offensive in Vietnam dealt a blow to American resolve, while suppression of the 'Prague Spring' in Czechoslovakia strengthened Soviet resolve. Washington began looking for a way out in South-East Asia, Moscow for a way forward in respect of its ideological satellites. The projected US retraction argued for some understanding with China as the best way to contain Soviet influence in the East, an appreciation shared by Beijing and heightened by the Brezhnev doctrine (Moscow's Monroe-like pledge to intervene in communist states contemplating disengagement from the Soviet bloc). In fact, Russian units had already been redeployed to disputed sections of the Sino-Russian frontier in 1966. Bombers followed, and in 1969 serious border clashes broke out along the Ussuri river and in Xinjiang. Washington and Beijing warmed to the urgency of an understanding.

It was delayed by outrage over the 1970 US bombing of Cambodia and probably by the machinations of Lin Biao. But in April 1971 an American team of table tennis players was invited to compete in China as a goodwill gesture; 'they may come to us, but we'll never go to them. The US is still an imperialist country!' exclaimed a Mao loyalist; disbelief was widespread.[5] But three months later Henry Kissinger accepted an invitation to secret talks. These were soon repeated, at which point the United Nations invited the People's Republic to replace the Republic (i.e. Taiwan) as China's repesentative. Then in February 1972 came 'the week that changed the world', as President Nixon would call it. His historic visit included a trip to the Great Wall and a meeting with the Chairman. Neither side gave much ground on Taiwan, but Beijing undertook to hustle Hanoi towards a settlement, and Washington gave assurances about no hostile collaboration with the Soviet Union. There was little discussion of trade, nor as yet was there much trade to discuss. But China's twenty-three years in international quarantine were over.

Meanwhile the Cultural Revolution rumbled on. With the disappearance in the early 1970s of Lin Biao and other leading figures, its more extreme views came to be associated with what Mao was the first to condemn as the 'Gang of Four'. Consisting of his wife Jiang Qing plus three 'Shanghai radicals', the Gang incurred his disapproval not because it robustly upheld the ideals of the Cultural Revolution – which demonstrated loyalty and suited his own divisive purposes – but because it constituted a gang; as ever, all forms of collusion were highly suspect, whether factions, cliques, gangs or parties (the Communist Party, as the essence of orthodoxy, excepted). Through the mid-1970s this radical grouping competed with a more pragmatic alignment headed by the reinstated Zhou Enlai and the rehabilitated Deng Xiaoping. Deng's return seemed to signify an unexpected spirit of reconciliation on the Chairman's part. Thousands of 'roaders' were pardoned, all too many of them posthumously; Liu Shaoqi, for instance, had died as a result of his ill-treatment. But the reconciliation also served to discomfort the Gang of Four and leave uncertain the direction of future policy and more especially the succession.

Mao, who turned eighty in 1973, was visibly fading, blinded by cataracts and barely able to speak; interpreting his mumbled utterances added a further uncertainty to the power struggle and kept both groups guessing. Each obliquely criticised the other, with the Gang extending the Lin Biao–Confucius linkage to include Zhou and Deng, while identifying itself with the anti-Confucian 'Legalist' school of the 'Warring State' of Qin. The Qin First Emperor was now portrayed as a progressive ruler whose mobilisation of the masses had united the country; the Chairman himself was happy to be identified with him. Historical revisionists obligingly recast Qin's autocratic totalitarianism as what one authority calls 'a kind of proto-proletarian dictatorship'.[6] The 1974 discovery of the first 'terracotta warriors' lent a heaven-sent sanction to this idea, though it is not known whether Mao was able to take a personal interest in the matter.

Zhou Enlai was also terminally ill. With terrible timing he died in January 1976 just when, thanks to another change of heart behind Mao's closed doors, Deng was out of favour and the Gang of Four in the ascendant. There was some official mourning for Zhou, though it was not enough for those millions who regarded him as the face (if not always the voice) of moderation, the architect of a less confrontational foreign policy, and the best chance for post-Mao stability. Unauthorised demonstrations of grief climaxed with the 4–5 April Qingming Incident in Tiananmen Square. Thousands laid wreaths, many of which were accompanied by verses that denounced the disrespectful Jiang Qing, her Gang, and even 'the Qin First Emperor' himself. The clean-up operation in the square was comparatively unbloody, although untold thousands were later hauled in for interrogation. It had been the first unofficial and apparently spontaneous demonstration of mass disapproval ever seen in the capital of the People's Republic.

With the Gang now in control, Deng Xiaoping was again denounced, deprived of all his offices and placed under surveillance. Five months later, in September 1976, the Great Helmsman himself passed away. This time mourners in their millions bade farewell. Their tears were genuine and there were no incidents. For all his faults, a China without 'the great red sun in our hearts' was unimaginable. Similarly, without its 'gang of one', the Gang of Four was rudderless. A doomed bid for power ended within the month when Jiang Qing and her associates were arrested. Ostensibly the work of Hua Guofeng, Mao's nominated successor (the fourth by most counts), this rejection of all that remained of the Cultural Revolution depended on PLA support as orchestrated by Deng Xiaoping.

For the third time, the diminutive Deng was bouncing back. In 1977 he was reinstated in the politburo and in 1978 he sidelined Hua Guofeng to launch the reform programme that would shape contemporary China. A year later he was in America being feted by Ronald Reagan and antici- pating China's becoming a superpower; a year after that, while authorising the creation of the first Special Economic Zone at Shenzhen (near Hong Kong), he lit on the formula that would turn China into 'the workshop of the world'.

The five years 1977–82 launched the country on a new trajectory as revo- lutionary in its way as any in its long history. The Cultural Revolution had attacked 'the Four Olds' (old ideas, culture, customs and habits); Deng's revolution promoted 'the Four News' (or 'Four Modernisations': agricul- ture, industry, defence and technology); the retrospective/negative made way for the forward-looking/positive. Rural collectives were gradually dismantled. Land was leased back to individual households or village group- ings and effectively privatised; provided it yielded a modest state procure- ment quota, it could be used as the lessees saw fit. Repair shops, brick kilns, cement works, fertiliser plants, timber mills and metal fabricators sprang up alongside fish farms, piggeries, poultry farms and market gardens. Official encouragement and easier credit meant that by the 1990s these non-urban industries employed a third of the total labour force. Meanwhile stricter enforcement of the one-child-one-family policy dramatically reduced the birth-rate. Population growth slowed, but still reached 1.3 billion early in the twenty-first century.

Neither population control nor rural employment was enough to coun- teract the drift to the cities. There, as controls were lifted and investment encouraged, entrepreneurial activity ran riot. The impetus came from the Special Economic Zones. Investment, mostly in foreign joint ventures producing for export, was attracted by a raft of incentives and preferences plus the availablity of a disciplined, low-cost and limitless labour pool. The model proved so successful that the three initial zones were quickly replicated, vastly extended to include whole regions, and then so copied by provincial administrations as to become almost universal. Capitalism was back, red in tooth and claw. Fortunes were made and brazenly flaunted; earnings rose; so did the skyline; and so did labour exploitation, environ- mental pollution, land appropriations, nepotism, crime, and a whole culture of corruption. 'To get rich is no sin,' argued Deng; pauperism tarnished socialism, prosperity vindicated it. But it was the people in general – and especially their Republic – who must benefit, not just individual tycoons. This meant wholesale restructuring of all the organs of the state, including the loss-making state industries, the overmanned PLA and militias, the faction-ridden administrations, the costly public services, and the corruption-riddled Party.

It was a massive undertaking and not without its setbacks. But GNP rose by about 8 per cent per annum through the 1980s, then soared into double digits. Sectoral imbalances, urban migration and the effects of inflation still troubled the leadership; a 1984 agreement with Britain about the rendition of Hong Kong in 1997 mollified it. The wider world, while profiting handsomely from commercial access, focused on what it saw as China's democratic deficit. Post-Mao, a more collective and consensual form of leadership had been adopted. Deng himself was never either chairman or premier; high office circulated more freely, and the demoted no longer disappeared. But within the high command this neither ended personal and ideological rifts nor ensured any popular accountability. Western observers, on doubtful evidence, predicted that a liberalised economy must in time induce a liberalised society. Even Deng talked of 'democracy'. But it was as a pot of gold at the end of the market-socialist rainbow. Elections, other than at the lowest village level where party cadres could influence them, would have to wait; strength and prosperity came first.

Not everyone agreed. The 'Fifth Modernisation', that is 'democracy', was first touted by the polemicist Wei Jingsheng in 1979. He was promptly imprisoned and the 'Democracy Wall', where he and others pasted their posters, was closed down. In the mid-1980s more specific demands for the redress of various grievances and greater tolerance of dissent resurfaced among students. This time some official sympathy was forthcoming, most notably from Party general secretary Hu Yaobang. But in 1986, as the protests threatened to get out of control, the students were dispersed and Hu forced to resign his office. He remained in the politburo, a focus for liberal sentiments and for restraint in handling them, until his sudden death in April 1989.

Events then closely mirrored those of the Qingming Incident of 1976, though on a very different scale. Student mourners poured into Tiananmen Square in their thousands, then from all over the country in their millions. Sympathy for the deceased Hu translated itself into censure of the regime and demands for a whole gamut of Western liberal reforms.

Beijing's citizens seemed to support the protesters, the local authorities seemed ambivalent, the politburo undecided. For six weeks the world looked on in amazement. As an alfresco spectacle, Tiananmen Square would defer only to the Berlin Wall later in the same year. The protesters in their jeans and T-shirts looked much like students anywhere; their music was familiar, their tactics standard, their cause universal. When a hundred or so went on hunger strike, amazement turned to admiration, then admiration turned to horror as the talks broke down and the tanks moved in.

The students had taken their cue from the May Fourth protests of 1919 and the Qingming Incident of 1976. But the leadership was more mindful of 1966 and the start of the Cultural Revolution. Then, too, radical youth had descended on the capital en masse, denounced the Party and its leadership, elected its own leaders and challenged the whole power structure. A repeat of the chaos that had ensued then would now derail the modernisation process, discredit the Party, endanger the government, and plunge the country back into chaos. Although the politburo remained divided, Deng secured sufficient support for the necessary crackdown from the old guard of the Party and the PLA. Crudely but literally, it was to be business as usual. Embalmed near by in his mausoleum, Mao was having the last laugh. The Cultural Revolution had finally borne fruit; 'bourgeois liberalisation' had been halted in its tracks; the fear of radical mayhem had succeeded where mayhem itself had failed.

In the 1960s the Western world had lost no sleep over the excesses of the Cultural Revolution; China was a global irrelevance; such things were to be expected of Marxist-Leninist fundamentalists in the Third World. But in the 1990s, with China a major trading partner and emerging world power, the televised defiance and the ruthless repression of a popular movement for democratic rights could hardly be ignored. The USA responded with economic sanctions and a suspension of weapon sales and high-level contacts; a few other Western countries followed suit; and Hong Kong, counting down the days till its 1997 handover, witnessed such large demonstrations of sympathy that its last British governor was emboldened to introduce some belated democracy of his own. But as Beijing had calculated, most of this was window-dressing. No nation broke off diplomatic relations, no multinational corporation withdrew, and there was no renegotiation of Hong Kong's future. For the world too, it was business as usual. Within a matter of months normal relations with the USA resumed, as did the rate of inward investment; in fact in 1991–93 it rose by a staggering 500 per cent. The collapse of the Soviet Union brought a

Sino-Russian rapprochement; but neither that, nor the bombing of China's Belgrade embassy, the downing of a US spy plane, the ongoing frictions in Tibet and Xinjiang, and the occasional outcries over human rights (especially in connection with the Falun Gong), were allowed to disrupt the passage of goods and the penetration of capital. In 1997/98 presidents Jiang Zemin and Bill Clinton exchanged visits that were rich in talk of 'strategic partnership' and 'complementary economies'. Three years later China was admitted to the World Trade Organisation and Beijing was awarded the 2008 Olympics. The leadership greeted both as international recognition of China's coming of age and vindication of its insistence on 'stability'. The global podium had a new contender.

Attracting foreign investment and technology had been a high priority ever since the 1970s; but as with the nineteenth-century swing in trade from tea to opium, the tide had now turned. Such had been the growth of China's economy, such the competitiveness of its exports, and such the restraints on domestic spending that surpluses now swamped deficits while outward investment powered ahead of inward. Globalisation had come at just the right moment. Deregulated, and supercharged by the new communications technology, the movement of goods and capital accelerated just when China had most to shift. The main beneficiaries were foreign consumers and foreign currency reserves, principally US Treasury bonds; and as of old, this largesse encouraged a dependency among the beneficiaries that in Chinese minds blurred the distinction between trade and tribute. Similar sentiments could be detected in China's dash to secure reliable sources of energy and raw materials, principally in Africa and central Asia. The concept of 'All under Heaven', now expanded and integrated to an extent unforeseen even by Clinton and Jiang Zemin, had acquired new substance. The 'Middle Kingdom' was closer to the middle, more pivotal and powerful, than at any time in its history.

NOTES

Abbreviations

CHAC: *Cambridge History of Ancient China*
CHC: *Cambridge History of China*
CHEIA: *Cambridge History of Early Inner Asia*

EPIGRAPHS

1 Confucius, *The Analects*, p.3.
2 Sima Qian, *Shiji*, quoted by Keightley in Ropp, *Heritage of China*, p.54.

INTRODUCTION

1 Waldron, *The Great Wall*, *passim*.
2 Di Cosmo, *Ancient China and Its Enemies*, pp.143–58.
3 See, for instance, Pulleyblank, *The Background to the Rebellion of An Lu-Shan*, pp.33, 128–9.
4 Jung Chang and Halliday, *Mao*, pp.135–73.
5 Spence, *The Search for Modern China*, pp.602–3.
6 See Twitchett, *The Writing of Official History*, pp.17ff.
7 Zurcher, *The Buddhist Conquest of China*, p.280.
8 Hunan Museum, *The Han Tombs of Mawangdui*, Hunan People's Publishing House, Changsha, 1978, pp.1–3; Chen Jianming (ed.), *The Exhibition of Mawangdui Han Tombs*, Hunan Provincial Museum, n.d., p.2.
9 For the etymologies of all provincial toponyms see Wilkinson, *Chinese History: A Manual*, p.137.
10 Fitzgerald, *The Empress Wu*, p.v.

CHAPTER 1: RITES TO WRITING, PRE-C. 1050 BC

1 *Huainanzi*, 3:1a, in de Bary and Bloom, *Sources of Chinese Tradition*, 1, p.347.
2 Kwang-chih Chang, 'China on the eve of the Historical Period', in CHAC, p.66.
3 Li Ling and Constance A. Cook, 'Translation of the Chu silk manuscript', in Cook and Major, *Defining Chu*, pp.171–3.
4 Kwang-chih Chang, 'China on the eve of the Historical Period', in CHAC, pp.66–7.
5 Pron. 'Shia'; Wade-Giles (W-G) 'Hsia'.
6 Pron. 'Joe'; W-G 'Chou'.
7 Robert Bagley, 'Shang Archaeology', in CHAC, p.125.
8 Ibid., p.137.
9 Ibid., p.165.
10 Ibid., p.197.
11 Chang, *Early Chinese Civilisation*, p.57.
12 'Exploring Chinese history' at www.ibiblio.org.
13 Mallory and Mair, *The Tarim Mummies*, p.8
14 A. P. Okladnikov, 'Inner Asia at the dawn of history', in CHEIA, p.79.

15 H. G. Creel, 'Dragon bones', *Asia*, 35, p. 182, cited in Keightley, *Sources of Shang History*, pp.140-1.

16 Keightley, *Sources of Shang History*, p.21.

17 Ibid., pp.154-5

18 William G. Boltz, 'Language and writing', in *CHAC*, p.88.

19 Oracle bone translations from de Bary and Bloom, *Sources of Chinese Tradition*, pp.7–19.

20 Keightley, *The Ancestral Landscape*, p.119.

21 Ibid., p.101.

22 Keightley, *Sources of Shang History*, pp.55ff.

23 David N. Keightley, 'The Shang', in *CHAC*, p.256.

CHAPTER 2: SAGES AND HEROES, C. 1050 BC–C. 250 BC

1 Fairbank and Goldman, *China: A New History*.

2 Quoted in Waley, *Three Ways of Thought in Ancient China*, p.35.

3 Creel, *The Origins of Statecraft in China*, vol. 1, pp.83, 93.

4 Edward L. Shaughnessy, 'Western Zhou history', in *CHAC*, pp.310–11.

5 *Shangshu zhengyi*, 13, 24a, quoted in Shaughnessy, *CHAC*, p.314.

6 Confucius, *The Analects*, vii, 5, in D. C. Lau translation.

7 Watson, *The Tso-chuan*, p.xvi.

8 *Shangshu zhengyi*, 18, 16a, quoted in Shaughnessy, *CHAC*, p.318.

9 Quoted in Shaughnessy, *CHAC*, p.337.

10 Quoted in Ebrey, *China: A Political, Cultural and Social History*, pp.174–5.

11 Jessica Rawson, 'Western Zhou archaeology', in *CHAC*, p.388.

12 Ibid., p.449.

13 Quoted in Shaughnessy, *CHAC*, p.149.

14 Hui, *War and State Formation in Ancient China*.

15 E.g. Frank A. Kierman, 'Phases and modes of combat in Early China', in *Chinese Ways in Warfare*, ed. Kierman and Fairbank, pp.52–3.

16 Watson, *The Tso-chuan*, p.62.

17 Ban Gu, *The History of the Former Han*, vol. 2, p.130.

18 See Michael Loewe, 'Introduction' to *CHC*, vol. 1, p.22.

19 Cho-yun Hsu, 'The Spring and Autumn period', in *CHAC*, pp.571–2.

20 Confucius, *The Analects*, ix, 2, trans. D. C. Lau, p.77.

21 Ibid., xi, 4, adapted from Lau trans., p.11, and de Bary and Bloom, *Sources of Chinese Tradition*, p.47.

22 Confucius, *The Analects*, vii, 20, trans. Lau, p.61.

23 Ibid., vii, 1, p.57.

24 David Shepherd Nivison, 'The classical philosophical writings', in *CHAC*, p.761.

25 Hubei Provincial Museum, *The High Appreciation of the Cultural Relics of the Zeng Hou Yi Tomb*, Fine Arts Publishing, Hubei, 1995, p.22.

26 Charles Tilly, 'Reflections on the history of European state-making', in *The Formation of the National States in Western Europe*, Princeton University Press, Princeton, NJ, 1975, p.73.

27 Sima Qian in Watson, *Records of the Grand Historian*, p.23.

28 Quoted in Hansen, *The Open Empire*, p.90.

29 Mark Edward Lewis, 'Warring States political history', in *CHAC*, pp.604, 622.

30 Sima Qian in Watson, *Records of the Grand Historian*, p.32.

CHAPTER 3: THE FIRST EMPIRE, C. 250–210 BC

1 Sage, *Ancient Sichuan and the Unification of China*, p.197.

2 Ibid., p.119.

3 Ibid., p.149.

4 Cook and Major, *Defining Chu*, *passim*.

5 Sima Qian in Watson, *Records of the Grand Historian*, pp.35–6.

6 Ibid., p.42.

7 Ibid., pp.42–3.

8 Ibid., p.163.

9 Ibid., p.164.

10 Jia Yi, quoted in ibid., pp.80–82.

11 Ibid., p.87.

12 Jenner, *The Tyranny of History*, pp.22–3.

13 Derk Bodde, 'The state and empire of Ch'in', in *CHC*, vol. 1, p.52.

14 Bodde, *China's First Unifier*.

15 *Han Feizi*, ch. 49, trans. Burton Watson, quoted in de Bary and Bloom, *Sources of Chinese Tradition*, vol. 1, pp.199–203.

16 Sima Qian in Watson, *Records of the Grand Historian*, pp.184–5.

17 E.g. Bodde, 'The state and empire of Ch'in', pp.69–71.

18 Sima Qian in Watson, *Records of the Grand Historian*, p.185.

19 Bodde, 'The state and empire of Ch'in', p.71.

20 Henry Yule and A. D. Burnell, *Hobson-Jobson: A Glossary of Colloquial Anglo-Indian Words etc.*, 2nd edn, Routledge & Kegan Paul, London, 1985, pp.196–8.

21 *Measure for Measure*, Act 2, scene 1.

22 Bodde, *China's First Unifier*, p.118.

23 Sima Qian in Watson, *Records of the Grand Historian*, p.213.

24 Ibid., pp.207–8.

25 Waldron, *The Great Wall of China*, pp.18–21.

26 De Crespigny, *Northern Frontier*, pp.455–7; Lovell, *The Great Wall*, pp.15–16.

27 Sima Qian in Watson, *Records of the Grand Historian*, p.63.

CHAPTER 4: HAN ASCENDANT, 210–141 BC

1 Sima Qian in Watson, *Records of the Grand Historian*, p.189.

2 Hardy, *Worlds of Bronze and Bamboo*, pp.49–50.

3 Sima Qian in Watson, *Records of the Grand Historian*, pp.192–3.

4 Ibid., p.204.

5 Ibid., pp.204–5.

6 Sima Qian in Watson, *Records of the Grand Historian*, vol. 1, 'The early years of the Han Dynasty 209 BC–141 BC', pp.19–22.

7 Ibid., pp.30–33.

8 Ibid., p.46.

9 Sage, *Ancient Sichuan*, p.160.

10 Sima Qian in Watson, *Records of the Grand Historian*, vol. 1, pp.70–71.

11 A catty being 16 taels, approximately half a kilogram (1lb 4oz).

12 Ibid., pp.72–3.

13 Ibid., pp.294–5.

14 Ibid., p.340.

15 Ibid., p.106.

16 Gao Zhixi in Hunan Museum, *The Han Tombs of Mawangdui*, Hunan People's Publishing House, Changsha, 1978, p.6.

17 Sima Qian in Watson, *Records of the Grand Historian*, vol. 2, 'The age of Emperor Wu, 140–c. 100 BC', pp.239–42.

18 Ibid., p.250.

CHAPTER 5: WITHIN AND BEYOND, 141 BC–AD 1

1 Compare Michael Loewe, in *CHC*, vol. 1, Sima Qian in Watson, *Records of the Grand Historian* and Homer Dubs, in Ban Gu, *The History of the Former Han*, vol. 2, p.13.

2 Laozi, *Daodejing*, quoted in de Bary and Bloom, *Sources of Chinese Tradition*, vol. 1, p.61.

3 Di Cosmo, *Ancient China and Its Enemies*, pp.270–72.

4 Sima Qian in Watson, *Records of the Grand Historian*, vol. 2, p.173.

5 Jagchid and Symons, *Peace, War and Trade*, pp.26–7.

6 Yu Ying-Shih, 'Han foreign relations', in *CHC*, vol. 1, p.390.

7 Sima Qian in Watson, *Records of the Grand Historian*, vol. 2, p.172.

8 J. K. Fairbank, 'Introduction; varieties of the Chinese military experience' in Kierman and Fairbank, *Chinese Ways in Warfare*, p.11.

9 Ban Gu, *Hanshu*, 96B, 2B, in Hulsewe, *China in Central Asia*, pp.146–7.

10 Sima Qian in Watson, *Records of the Grand Historian*, vol. 2, p.274.

11 Ban Gu, *Hanshu*, 96B, 3A, in Hulsewe, *China in Central Asia*, pp.148–9.

12 Ibid., 61, 12B, in Hulsewe, *China in Central Asia*, p.234.

13 Watson, *Ssu-ma Ch'ien: Grand Historian of China*, p.62.

14 Ibid., pp.60–70.

15 Bielenstein, *The Bureaucracy of Han Times*, p.157.

16 Ban Gu, *The History of the Former Han*, vol. 2, p.213.

17 Summarised in Michael Loewe, *Crisis and Conflict in Han China*, pp.179–80.

18 Bielenstein, *The Bureaucracy of Han Times*, p.19.

19 Ban Gu, *The History of the Former Han*, vol. 2, pp.265, 338.

20 See Michael Loewe, 'The former Han dynasty', in *CHC*, vol. 1, pp.187–90, and *Crisis and Conflict in Han China*, *passim*.

21 Ban Gu, *The History of the Former Han*, vol. 3, pp.38–9.

CHAPTER 6: WANG MANG AND THE HAN REPRISE, AD 1–189

1 Homer H. Dubs, in Ban Gu, *The History of the Former Han*, vol. 2, p.363.

2 Ban Gu, *The History of the Former Han*, vol. 3, pp.255–7.

3 Ibid., vol. 3, p.257, fn36.2.

4 Ch'en Ch'i-yün, 'Confucianist, legalist and taoist thought in Later Han', in *CHC*, vol. 1, p.773.

5 See Joseph R. Levenson, 'Ill wind in the well-field', in Wright, *The Confucian Persuasion*, pp.284–5.

6 Ban Gu, *The History of the Former Han*, vol. 3, pp.492, 394.

7 See James Legge, *The Religions of China*, Hodder & Stoughton, London, 1880, pp.147–8.

8 Ban Gu, *The History of the Former Han*, vol. 3, p.318.

9 Hans Bielenstein, 'Wang Mang, the restoration of the Han dynasty, and Later Han', in *CHC*, vol. 1, pp.241–3.

10 Ban Gu, *The History of the Former Han*, vol. 3, p.382.

11 Ibid., vol. 3, p.466.

12 Arthur F. Wright, 'Introduction', in Wright, *The Confucian Persuasion*, pp.3, 8,

13 Bielenstein, 'Wang Mang', pp.262–4.

14 De Crespigny, *The Northern Frontier*, p.218.

15 *Hou Hanshu*, quoted in *CHC*, vol. 1, pp.275–6.

16 De Crespigny, *The Northern Frontier*, p.380.

17 Ban Gu, *Hanshu*, 96A, 11B–12B, in Hulsewe, *China in Central Asia*, pp.107–12.

18 Yü Ying-shih, 'Han foreign relations', in *CHC*, vol. 1, pp.434–5.

19 Bielenstein, 'Wang Mang', p.262.

20 Quoted in Hansen, *The Open Empire*, p.140.

21 John K. Fairbank, various titles, *passim*

22 Sima Guang, *Zizhi Tongjian*, 1866, in De Crespigny, *The Last of the Han*, p.9.

23 C. J. Mansveldt Beck, 'The fall of Han', in *CHC*, vol. 1, p.341.

CHAPTER 7: FOUR HUNDRED YEARS
OF VICISSITUDE, 189–550

1 Sima Guang, *Zizhi Tongjian*, in De
 Crespigny, *The Last of the Han*, pp.25,
 59.
2 Ibid., p.13.
3 Ibid., p.83.
4 Lu Simian, quoted by Moss Roberts
 in Luo Guanzhong, *Three Kingdoms*,
 p.1049.
5 Ibid., p.378.
6 Goodman, *T'sao P'i Transcendent*,
 pp.99–100.
7 Robert Joe Cutter, 'Poetry from 200
 BCE to 500 CE', in Mair, *The Columbia
 History of Chinese Literature*, pp.253–7.
8 Wang Kan, 'Seven Sadnesses', quoted
 in ibid., p.256.
9 Cao Pi, *Lun Wen*, quoted in
 Goodman, *Ts'ao P'i Transcendent*,
 p.185.
10 Goodman, *Ts'ao P'i Transcendent*, p.86.
11 Nathan Sivin, 'Science and medicine
 in Chinese history', in Ropp, *Heritage
 of China*, p.174.
12 Russell Kirkland, *Taoism: The
 Enduring Tradition*, pp.75–6.
13 Richard B. Mather, 'K'ou Ch'ien-chih
 and the Taoist theocracy at the
 Northern Wei court, 425–451', in
 Seidell and Welch, *Facets of Taoism*,
 p.103.
14 Stephen Bokenkamp, 'Lu Xiujing,
 Buddhism, and the first Daoist canon',
 in Pearce et al., *Culture and Power*,
 p.183.
15 Quoted in Wright, *Buddhism in
 Chinese History*, p.21.
16 Quoted in Zurcher, *The Buddhist
 Conquest of China*, vol. 1, p.28.
17 Ibid., p.28.
18 Hansen, *The Open Empire*, pp.163–8.
19 Quoted in Zurcher, *The Buddhist
 Conquest of China*, p.66.
20 Quoted in ibid.; see also *Bulletin of
 the School of Oriental and African
 Studies*, XII(3), 1948, pp.600–615.

21 Wright, *Buddhism in Chinese History*,
 p.42.
22 Zurcher, *The Buddhist Conquest of
 China*, p.84.
23 *Jinshu*, quoted in Graff, *Medieval
 Chinese Warfare*, p.47.
24 *Jinshu*, ch. 101, pp.2645–6, quoted in
 ibid., p.48.
25 Zurcher, *The Buddhist Conquest of
 China*, p.181.
26 Wright, *Buddhism in Chinese History*,
 p.56.
27 Wright and Somers, *Studies in Chinese
 Buddhism*, p.37.
28 Ibid., p.16.
29 Graff, *Medieval Chinese Warfare*, p.65.
30 Ibid., p.69.
31 Ibid., p.50.
32 Jenner, *Memories of Loyang*, p.27.
33 Ibid., pp.27–8.
34 Holcombe, *In the Shadow of the Han*,
 p.64.

CHAPTER 8: SUI, TANG AND THE
SECOND EMPIRE, 550–650

1 Ssu-ma Kuang in Fang, *The Chronicle
 of the Three Kingdoms*, vol. 1, pp.45–7.
2 Scott Pearce, 'Form and matter', in
 Pearce et al., *Culture and Power in the
 Reconstitution of the Chinese Realm*,
 p.153.
3 Ibid., p.154.
4 Graff, *Medieval Chinese Warfare*, p.111.
5 Shufen Liu, 'Jiankang and the
 commercial empire of the Southern
 Dynasties', in Pearce et al., *Culture
 and Power in the Reconstitution of the
 Chinese Realm*, pp.35–9.
6 Wright, *The Sui Dynasty*, p.43.
7 Quoted in Paludan, *Chronicle of the
 Chinese Emperors*, p.82.
8 Figures as deduced in Xiong, *Emperor
 Yang of the Sui Dynasty*, p.160.
9 Wright, *The Sui Dynasty*, p.72.
10 Xiong, *Emperor Yang of the Sui
 Dynasty*, pp.226–8.

11 *Suishu*, 24.672, quoted in ibid., p.81.

12 Arthur Waley, 'The fall of Loyang', *History Today*, vol. 1, April 1951, p.7.

13 Lovell, *The Great Wall*, p.131.

14 Xiong, *Emperor Yang of the Sui Dynasty*, p.92.

15 Pi Rixiu, quoted in ibid., p.93.

16 Bingham, *The Founding of the T'ang Dynasty*, pp.51–4.

17 Pan Yihong, *Son of Heaven*, p.48.

18 Arthur F. Wright, 'The Sui Dynasty', in *CHC*, vol. 3, p.109.

19 Edwin O. Reischauer, *Ennin's Travels in T'ang China*, p.47.

20 Howard J. Wechsler, 'T'ai-tsung the Consolidator', in *CHC*, vol. 3, p.234.

21 Pan Yihong, *Son of Heaven*, p.238.

22 Schafer, *The Golden Peaches of Samarkand*, p.42.

23 Wriggins, *Xuanzang*, pp.191–3.

24 Wu Cheng'en, *The Monkey and the Monk*, p.xi.

CHAPTER 9: HIGH TANG, 650–755

1 *Songke Xiaojing* ('Classic of Filial Piety'), 5–31, quoted in de Bary and Bloom, *Sources of Chinese Tradition*, vol. 1, 'From earliest times to 1600', p.329.

2 Wechsler, *Mirror to the Son of Heaven*, p.206.

3 Quoted in ibid., pp.207–9.

4 *Chen-kuan cheng-yao*, ch. 1, pp.40b–41a, quoted in Arthur F. Wright, 'T'ang T'ai-tsung', in J. Perry and Smith, *Essays on T'ang Society*, pp.17–18.

5 Fitzgerald, *China: A Short Cultural History*, p.296.

6 Schafer, *The Golden Peaches of Samarkand*, p.29.

7 Denis Twitchett and Howard J. Wechsler, 'Kao-tsung and the empress Wu', in *CHC*, vol. 3, p.245.

8 Ibid., p.246.

9 Fitzgerald, *The Empress Wu*, p.76.

10 Ibid., p.146.

11 Zizhi Tongjian, 201, p.6343, quoted in Twitchett and Wechsler, 'Kao-tsung and the empress Wu', p.257.

12 Richard W. L. Guisso, 'The reigns of empress Wu, Chung-tsung and Jui-tsung', in *CHC*, vol. 3, p.312.

13 Ibid., p.321.

14 Twitchett and Wechsler, 'Kao-tsung and the empress Wu', p.257.

15 Guisso, 'The reigns of empress Wu . . .', p.331.

16 David McMullen, *State and Scholars in T'ang China*, pp.9, 265.

17 Pan Yihong, *Son of Heaven and Heavenly Qaghan*, p.225.

18 Orkhon inscription quoted in Denis Sinor, 'The establishment and dissolution of the Turk empire', in *CHEIA*, p.310.

19 Gernet, *A History of Chinese Civilisation*, pp.253–4.

20 Sima Guang, *Zizhi Tongjian*, 202, 6387–8, quoted in Beckwith, *The Tibetan Empire in Central Asia*, p.45.

21 Guisso, 'The reigns of empress Wu . . .', p.315.

22 Ch'en Tao, 'Song of Lung-hsi', in Watson, *The Columbia Book of Chinese Poetry*, p.29.

23 Mair, *The Columbia History of Chinese Literature*, p.296.

24 Li Bo, 'Fighting South of the Ramparts', adaptation of Arthur Waley trans. in de Bary and Bloom, *Sources of Chinese Tradition*, vol. 1, pp.565–6.

25 Stephen Owen, 'Poetry in the Chinese tradition', in Ropp, *Heritage of China*, pp.293–308.

26 Pulleyblank, *The Background to the Rebellion of An Lushan*, p.35.

27 Li Shangyin, quoted in E. D. Edwards, *Chinese Prose Literature of the T'ang Period*, AD 618–906, London, 1938, and reproduced in Ebrey, *China: A Cultural, Social and Political History*.

28 Schafer, *The Golden Peaches of Samarkand*, p.32.

29 Denis Twitchett, 'Huan-tsung', in *CHC*, vol. 3, p.445.

30 Tu Fu, 'Song of P'eng-ya', in Watson, *The Columbia Book of Chinese Poetry*, p.223.

31 Chou, *Reconsidering Tu Fu*, pp.20, 27.

CHAPTER 10: RECONFIGURING THE EMPIRE, 755–1005

1 Backus, *The Nanchao Kingdom*, p.124.

2 Michael T. Dalby, 'Court politics in T'ang times', in *CHC*, vol. 3, p.610.

3 Quoted in C. A. Peterson, 'Court and province in mid- and late T'ang', in *CHC*, vol. 3, p.504.

4 Quoted in Hartman, *Han Yü*, p.143.

5 Peterson, 'Court and province', p.505.

6 *Jiu Tangshu* (Old Tang History), 129/ 3611, quoted in Hartman, *Han Yü*, pp.126–7.

7 Reischauer, *Ennin's Travels in T'ang China*, pp.218ff.

8 Peterson, 'Court and province', p.498.

9 Robert M. Somers, 'The end of the T'ang', in *CHC*, vol. 3, p.687.

10 Wang Gungwu, *The Structure of Power in North China*, p.208.

11 Ouyang Xiu, *Historical Records of the Five Dynasties*, pp.264, 280.

12 Blunden and Elvin, *Cultural Atlas of China*, p.90.

13 Ouyang Xiu, *Historical Records of the Five Dynasties*, p.63.

14 Herbert Franke and Denis Twitchett, 'Introduction', in *CHC*, vol. 6, p.26.

15 Adshead, *T'ang China*, p.18.

16 Needham, *Science and Civilization in China*, vol. 7, pt ii, 'General conclusions and reflections', p.188.

17 Ouyang Xiu, *Historical Records of the Five Dynasties*, pp.438–43.

18 Mote, *Imperial China*, p.980.

19 Anne Birrell, 'Women in literature', in Mair, *The Columbia History of Chinese Literature*, p.202.

20 Latham, *The Travels of Marco Polo*, pp.147–8.

21 Ouyang Xiu, *Historical Records of the Five Dynasties*, pp.21–2.

22 Denis Twitchett and Klaus-Peter Tietze, 'The Liao', in *CHC*, vol. 6, p.70.

23 Ouyang Xiu, *Historical Records of the Five Dynasties*, p.115.

24 Twitchett and Tietse, 'The Liao', p.110.

CHAPTER 11: CAVING IN, 1005–1235

1 Mote, *Imperial China*, p.329.

2 Quoted in Dunnell, *The Great State of White and High*, pp.110–11.

3 Quoted in ibid., pp.109–10.

4 Quoted in Hopkirk, *Foreign Devils on the Silk Road*, pp.200–202.

5 Ruth W. Dunnell, 'The Hsi Hsia', in *CHC*, vol. 6, p.181.

6 Ibid., p.181.

7 Ibid., p.187.

8 Ouyang Xiu, 'Essay on fundamentals', in de Bary and Bloom, *Sources of Chinese Tradition*, vol. 1, 'From earliest times to 1600', pp.594–5.

9 Ouyang Xiu, 'On parties', in de Bary and Bloom, *Sources of Chinese Tradition*, vol. 1, p.596.

10 Mote, *Imperial China*, p.137.

11 Sima Guang, 'A petition to do away with the most harmful of the new laws', in de Bary and Bloom, *Sources of Chinese Tradition*, vol. 1, pp.625–6.

12 Liu, *Reform in Sung China*, p.89.

13 Sima Guang, quoted in E. G. Pulleyblank, 'Chinese historical criticism: Liu Chih-chi and Ssu-ma Kuang', in Beasley and Pulleyblank, *Historians of China and Japan*, pp.153–4.

14 Tao Jing-shen, 'Public schools in the Chin Dynasty', in H. C. Cleveland and S. H. West (eds), *China under Jurchen Rule*, p.53.

15 Fairbank and Goldman, *China: A New History*, p.88.

16 Mote, *Imperial China*, p.165.

17 Raymond Dawson, *Imperial China*, p.152.

18 Lu You, 'The Merchant's Joy', in Watson, *The Columbia Book of Chinese Poetry*, pp.321–2.

19 Che Ruoshui, quoted in Patricia Ebrey, 'Women, marriage and the family', in Ropp, *Heritage of China*, p.217.

20 Hansen, *The Open Empire*, p.287.

21 Xu Ji, quoted in Ebrey, 'Woman, marriage and the family', p.216.

22 Lu You, 'Border Mountain Moon', in Watson, *The Columbia Book of Chinese Poetry*, p.318.

23 Mote, *Imperial China*, p.206.

24 Herbert Franke, 'The Chin Dynasty', in *CHC*, vol. 6, p.234.

25 Ibid., p.239.

26 Ibid., pp.247–8.

CHAPTER 12: BY LAND AND SEA, 1235–1405

1 Vainker, *Chinese Pottery and Porcelain*, p.88.

2 Polo, *The Book of Ser Marco Polo*, vol. 2, p.235.

3 Clunas, *Empire of Great Brightness*, p.15.

4 Polo, *The Book of Ser Marco Polo*, vol. 2, p.264.

5 Needham et al., *Science and Civilization in China*, vol. 4, pt 2, p.419.

6 Mote, *Imperial China*, pp.302–5.

7 Adshead, *T'ang China*, p.41.

8 Tu Wei-ming, 'The Confucian tradition', in Ropp, *Heritage of China*, p.131.

9 *Zhuzi quanshou*, in de Bary and Bloom, *Sources of Chinese Tradition*, vol. 1, pp.701–702.

10 Tu Wei-ming, 'The Confucian Tradition', p.131.

11 Hiyasuki Miyakawa, 'The Confucianization of South China', in Wright, *The Confucian Persuasion*, p.42.

12 Mote, *Imperial China*, p.345.

13 Polo, *The Book of Ser Marco Polo*, vol. 2, p.145.

14 Morgan, *The Mongols*, p.71.

15 Thomas Allsen, 'The rise of the Mongolian empire', in *CHC*, vol. 6, p.380.

16 Backus, *The Nanchao Kingdom*, p.263.

17 Herbert Franke, 'Tibetans in Yuan China', in Langlois, *China under Mongol Rule*, p.301.

18 Quoted by John D. Langlois, 'Introduction', in ibid., pp.3–4.

19 Needham et al., *Science and Civilization in China*, vol. 4, pt 2, pp.423–4.

20 Latham, *The Travels of Marco Polo*, p.203.

21 David M. Farquhar, 'Structure and function in the Yuan imperial government', in Langlois, *China under Mongol Rule*, pp.50–53.

22 Morris Rossabi, 'The reign of Khubilai Khan', in *CHC*, vol. 6, p.478.

23 Dardess, *Conquerors and Confucians*, pp.103–104.

24 Rossabi, *Khubilai Khan: His Life and Times*, p.212.

25 Dawson, *The Mongol Mission*, p.xxxiv.

26 David N. Keightley, 'Early civilization in China: reflections on how it became Chinese', in Ropp, *Heritage of China*, pp.32–3.

27 Edward L. Dreyer, 'Military origins of Ming China', in *CHC*, vol. 7, pt 1, pp.82–8.

28 Quoted in Mote, *Imperial China*, pp.559–60.

29 Dreyer, *Early Ming China*, p.155.

CHAPTER 13: THE RITES OF MING, 1405–1620

1 Wilkinson, *Chinese History: A Manual*, p.182.

2 Dreyer, *Zheng He*, p.9.

3 Ma Huan, quoted in Keay, *The Spice Route*, p.135.

4 Tsai, *Perpetual Happiness*, pp.70–71.

5 Hok-lam Chan, 'The Chien-wen, Yung-lo, Hung-hsi and Hsüan-te reigns, 1399–1435', in *CHC*, vol. 7, p.261.

6 Ibid., p.261.

7 Quoted in Dreyer, *Zheng He*, pp.187, 195.

8 Wang Gungwu, 'Ming foreign relations: Southeast Asia', in *CHC*, vol. 7, p.322.

9 Waldron, *The Great Wall of China*, p.79.

10 Frederick W. Mote, 'The T'u-mu incident of 1449', in Kierman and Fairbank, *Chinese Ways in Warfare*, p.254.

11 Denis Twitchett and Tileman Grimm, 'The Chen-t'ung, Ching-t'ai, and T'ien-shun reigns, 1436–1464', in *CHC*, vol. 7, p.339.

12 Galeote Pereira, in Boxer, *South China in the Sixteenth Century*, pp.14–15.

13 Charles O. Hucker, 'Ming government', in *CHC*, vol. 8, p.29.

14 Willard Peterson, 'Confucian learning in late Ming thought', in *CHC*, vol. 8, p.715.

15 Hucker, 'Ming government', p.30.

16 Fisher, *The Chosen One*, pp.53–4.

17 Ibid., p.176.

18 Hucker, 'Ming government', p.47.

19 *Wang Yangming quanshu*, in de Bary and Bloom, *Sources of Chinese Tradition*, vol. 1, p.846.

20 Fisher, *The Chosen One*, p.62.

21 Clunas, *Empire of Great Brightness*, p.5; and Mote, *Imperial China*, p.668.

22 Tsai, *Perpetual Happiness*, p.85.

23 Pereira, in Boxer, *South China in the Sixteenth Century*, pp.4–9.

24 Clunas, *Empire of Great Brightness*, p.14.

CHAPTER 14: THE MANCHU CONQUEST, 1620–1760

1 Jonathan D. Spence and John E. Wills, 'Preface', in Spence and Wills, *From Ming to Ch'ing*, p.xi.

2 Ricci, *China in the Sixteenth Century*, pp.306–7, 317.

3 Ibid., pp.343–4.

4 William Atwell, 'Ming China and the emerging world economy, *c.* 1470–1650', in *CHC*, vol. 8, p.383.

5 Spence and Wills, *From Ming to Ch'ing*, p.42.

6 Crossley, *The Manchus*, p.31.

7 Ibid., p.70.

8 Wakeman, *The Great Enterprise*, vol. 1, p.561.

9 *Qing Shilu*, vol. 14, quoted in Cheng et al., *The Search for Modern China*, p.33.

10 Lynn Struve, 'The Southern Ming, 1644–1662', in *CHC*, vol. 7, pt 1, pp.662–3.

11 Wang Xiuchu, 'The massacre of Yangzhou', in Struve, *Voices from the Ming-Qing Cataclysm*, p.33.

12 Matteo Ricci, quoted in Spence, *The Memory Palace of Matteo Ricci*, p.45.

13 Nicola di Cosmo, 'Did guns matter? Firearms and the Qing formation', in Struve, *The Qing Formation*, pp.131–3.

14 Yu Dayou, quoted in Huang, *1587*, pp.169–70.

15 Ibid., pp.179–80.

16 Liu Ruzhong, 'Manning the Wall: Qi Jiguang', in Claire Roberts and Geremie R. Barmé (eds), *The Great Wall of China*, pp.182–7.

17 Lovell, *The Great Wall*, p.265.

18 Di Cosmo, 'Did guns matter?', p.152.

19 Willard Peterson, 'Learning from heaven: the introduction of Christianity and other Western ideas into late Ming China', in *CHC*, vol. 8, pt 2, p.838.

20 Cheng et al., *The Search for Modern China*, pp.133–4; Waldron, *The Great Wall of China*, p.208.

21 Clements, *Pirate King*, pp.160–61.

22 Ibid., p.214.

23 Cheng et al., *The Search forModern China*, p.92.

24 Rossabi, *China and Inner Asia*, p.131.

25 Perdue, *China Marches West*, pp.184, 283–5.

26 Ibid., pp.291–2.

27 Joseph Fletcher, 'Ch'ing Inner Asia', in *CHC*, vol. 10, p.59.

28 Crossley, *A Translucent Mirror*, p.330.

29 Rawski, *The Last Emperors*, pp.254–6.

CHAPTER 15: DEATH THROES OF EMPIRE, 1760–1880

1 Macartney, *An Embassy to China*, pp.65–70.

2 Ibid., pp. 252–4.

3 Jonathan D. Spence, in ibid., p.254.

4 Ibid., p.165.

5 Ibid., pp.162–5.

6 'Kangxi's Valedictory Edict, 1717', in Cheng et al., *The Search for Modern China*, p.63.

7 Madeleine Zelin, 'The Yung-cheng reign', in *CHC*, vol. 9, pt 1, p.209.

8 William T. Rowe, 'Socal stabilityand social change', in *CHC*, vol. 9, pt 1, p.480.

9 Hiromi Kinoshita, in Rawski and Rawson, *China: The Three Emperors*, p.408.

10 Jonathan D. Spence, in Cheng et al., *The Search for Modern China*, pp.10-101.

11 Keay, *The Honourable Company*, pp.348–9.

12 Frederic Wakeman, 'The Canton trade and the Opium War', in *CHC*, vol. 10, pt 1, p.172.

13 Naquin and Rawski, *Chinese Society in the Eighteenth Century*, p.233.

14 Wakeman, 'The Canton trade', p.182.

15 Translation in Waley, *The Opium War*, pp.28–31.

16 Liu, *The Clash of Empires*, p.31.

17 Joseph Fletcher, 'The heyday of the Ch'ing order in Mongolia, Sinkiang and Tibet', in *CHC*, vol. 10, pt 1, pp.360, 373–82.

18 'Lord Palmerston's declaration of war', in Cheng et al., *The Search for Modern China*, pp.123–7.

19 Wakeman, *Strangers at the Gate*, p.21.

20 Teng, *The Taiping Rebellion*, pp.1–3, 224.

21 Spence, *God's Chinese Son*, p.93.

22 Wang Fuzhi, quoted in Crossley, *A Translucent Mirror*, p.248.

23 Wakeman, *Strangers at the Gate*, p.130.

24 Teng, *The Taiping Rebellion*, p.187.

25 Ibid., pp.213, 229.

26 Rutherford Alcock, quoted in ibid., pp.244–5.

27 Joseph Fletcher, 'Sino-Russia relations 1800–1862', in *CHC*, vol. 10, pt 1, p.347.

CHAPTER 16: REPUBLICANS AND NATIONALISTS, 1880–1950

1 Cheng et al., *The Search for Modern China*, p.239.

2 Ibid., p.153.

3 Wilkinson, *Chinese History: A Manual*, p.452.

4 Ting-Yee Kuo, 'Self-strengthening: the pursuit of Western technology', in *CHC*, vol. 10, pt I, p.515.

5 Rossabi, *China and Inner Asia*, p.189.

6 W. A. P. Martin, *Cycle of Cathay*, p.234, quoted in Liu, *The Clash of Empires*, p.122.

7 Jacques Bainville, *The French Republic 1870–1935*, p.93, quoted in Hibbert, *The Dragon Wakes*, p.316.

8 Hall, *A History of South-East Asia*, p.704.

9 Cheng et al., *The Search for Modern China*, p.222.

10 'Zhang Zhidong on the Central Government, 1898', in ibid., p.182.

11 Robert Hart, quoted in Preston, *Besieged in Peking*, p.232.

12 D. Varé, *The Last Empress*, pp.259–61, quoted in ibid., p.236.

13 Fairbank, *The Great Chinese Revolution*, pp.151–2.
14 Spence, *The Gate of Heavenly Peace*, pp.105–6.
15 Rossabi, *China and Inner Asia*, p.246.
16 Jasbir Singh, *Himalayan Triangle*, p.62.
17 Macmillan, *Peacemakers*, pp.331–2.
18 Ibid., p.337.
19 Spence, *The Gate of Heavenly Peace*, p.122.
20 Quoted in ibid., p.135.
21 Cheng et al., *The Search for Modern China*, p.352.
22 Keay, *Last Post*, pp.74–84.
23 Chang and Halliday, *Mao*, pp.134ff.
24 Fairbank, *The Great Chinese Revolution*, p.233.
25 Cheng et al., *The Search for Modern China*, p.423.
26 Ibid., p.339.

EPILOGUE

1 Richard Madsen, 'The countryside under communism', in *CHC*, vol. 15, pt 2, p.642.
2 Macfarquhar and Schoenhals, *Mao's Last Revolution*, p.68.
3 Ibid., p.9.
4 Stuart R. Schram, 'Mao-tsetung's thought from 1949 to 1976', in *CHC*, vol. 15, pt 2, p.89.
5 John Gittings, *The Changing Face of China*, p.290.
6 Schram, 'Mao-tsetung's thought from 1949 to 1976', p.91.

BIBLIOGRAPHY

Adshead, S. A. M., *T'ang China: The Rise of the East in World History*, Palgrave Macmillan, Basingstoke, 2004

Backus, Charles R., *The Nan-Chao Kingdom and Frontier Policy in Southwest China during the Sui and T'ang Periods*, PhD thesis, Princeton, NJ, 1978

Backus, Charles, *The Nanchao Kingdom and Tang China's South West Frontier*, Cambridge University Press, 1981

Balazs, Etienne, *Chinese Civilisation and Bureaucracy, Variations on a Theme*, trans. H. M. Wright, Yale University Press, New Haven, CT, and London, 1964

Ban Gu (Pan Ku), *The History of the Former Han Dynasty*, trans. Homer H. Dubs, 3 vols, Baltimore, MD, 1955

Barfield, Thomas, *The Perilous Frontier: Nomadic Empires and China 221 BC–1757 AD*, Blackwell, Oxford, 1996

Beasley, W. G. and E. G. Pulleyblank, *Historians of China and Japan*, Oxford University Press, London, 1961

Beckwith, Christopher, *The Tibetan Empire in Central Asia*, Princeton, NJ, 1987

Beckwith, Christopher I., *The Tibetan Empire in Central Asia: A History of the Struggle for Great Power among Tibetans, Turks, Arabs and Chinese during the Early Middle Ages*, Princeton University Press, Princeton, NJ, rev. edn, 1995

Benn, Charles, *Daily Life in Traditional China: The Tang Dynasty*, Westport, CT, 2002

Bentley, Jerry H., *Old World Encounters: Cross-cultural Contacts and Exchanges in Pre-modern Times*, Oxford University Press, Oxford, 1993

Bergere, Marie-Claire, *Sun Yat-sen*, trans. Janet Lloyd, Stanford University Press, Stanford, CT, 1988

Bielenstein, Hans, *The Bureaucracy of Han Times*, Cambridge University Press, Cambridge, 1980

Bingham, Woodbridge, *The Founding of the T'ang Dynasty: The Fall of Sui and the Rise of T'ang*, Waverly, Baltimore, MD, 1941

Birrell, A. M., *Chinese Mythology: An Introduction*, Johns Hopkins University, 1993

Blunden, Caroline and Mark Elvin, *Cultural Atlas of China*, Phaidon, Oxford, 1983

Bodde, Derk, *China's First Unifier: A study of the Qin dynasty as seen in the life of Li-Ssu 280–208 BC*, E. J. Brill, Leiden, 1938

Bol, Peter K., *'This Culture of Ours': Intellectual Transitions in T'ang and Sung China*, Stanford University Press, Stanford, CT, 1992

Boxer, C. R. (ed.), *South China in the Sixteenth Century, being the narratives of Galeote Pereira, Fr Gaspar da Cruz and Fr Martin da Rada*, Hakluyt Society, London, 1953

Boyle, John A., *The Successors of Genghis Khan*, Columbia University Press, New York, 1977

Brockley, Liam Matthew, *Journey to the East: The Jesuit Mission to China 1579–1724*, Harvard University Press, Cambridge, MA, 2007

Cambridge History of China (CHC), general eds Denis Twitchett and John K. Fairbank, 15 vols (vols 2, 4, 5, 12 unpublished in 2008), Cambridge University Press, Cambridge, 1978–

1. *The Ch'in and Han Empires, 221 BC–220 AD*, ed. Denis Twitchett and Michael Loewe, 1986
3. *Sui and T'ang China, 589–906*, pt 1, ed. Denis Twitchett, 1979
6. *Alien Regimes and Border States, 907–1368*, ed. Herbert Franke and Denis Twitchett, 1994
7. *The Ming Dynasty, 1368–1644*, pt 1, ed. Frederick W. Mote and Denis Twitchett, 1987
8. *The Ming Dynasty, 1368–1644*, pt 2, ed. Frederick W. Mote and Denis Twitchett, 1998
9. *The Ch'ing Empire to 1800*, ed. Willard J. Peterson, 2002
10. *Late Ch'ing, 1800–1911*, pt 1, ed. John K. Fairbank, 1978
11. *Late Ch'ing, 1800–1911*, pt 2, ed. Denis Twitchett and Kwang-Ching Liu, 1980
13. *Republican China 1912–1949*, pt 2, ed. John K. Fairbank and Albert Feuerwerker, 1986
14. *The People's Republic*, pt 1: *The Emergence of Revolutionary China 1949–1965*, ed. Roderick Macfarquhar and John K. Fairbank, 1987
15. *The People's Republic*, pt 2: *Revolutions within the Chinese Revolution 1966–82*, ed. Roderick Macfarquhar, 1991

Cambridge History of Ancient China (CHAC): *From the Origins of Civilisation to 221 BC*, ed. Michael Loewe and Edward L. Shaughnessy, Cambridge University Press, Cambridge, 1999

Cambridge History of Early Inner Asia (CHEIA), ed. Denis Sinor, Cambridge University Press, Cambridge, 1990

Chaffee, John W., *The Thorny Gates of Learning in Sung China, a Social History of the Examinations*, Cambridge University Press, 1985

Chan, Albert, *Glory and Decline of the Ming Dynasty*, University of Oklahoma, Norman, 1982

Chang, Hsin-pao, *Commissioner Lin and the Opium War*, Harvard University Press, Cambridge, MA, 1954

Chang, K. C., *Early Chinese Civilisation: Anthropological Perspectives*, Harvard University Press, Cambridge, MA, 1976

Chang, K. C., *Shang Civilisation*, Yale University Press, 1980

Chavanne, Edouard, *Les Memoires historiques de Se-ma Tsien*, vol. 2, Paris, 1895 (pp. 316–20 for Hsiang Yu)

Ch'en, Kenneth, *Buddhism in China: A Historical Survey*, Princeton, NJ, 1964

Cheng, Pei-kai, Michael Lestz and Jonathan D. Spence (eds), *The Search for Modern China: A Documentary Collection*, Norton, New York, 1999

Chou, Eva Shan, *Reconsidering Tu Fu: Literary Greatness and Cultural Context*, Cambridge University Press, Cambridge, 1995

Cleaves, Francis W., *Secret History of the Mongols*, Harvard University Press, Cambridge, MA, 1982

Clements, Jonathan, *Pirate King: Coxinga and the Fall of the Ming Dynasty*, Sutton, London, 2006

Clunas, Craig, *Superfluous Things: Material Culture and Social Status in Early Modern China*, University of Hawaii Press, Honolulu, 2004

Clunas, Craig, *Empire of Great Brightness: Visual and Material Cultures of Ming China, 1368–1644*, Reaktion Books, London, 2007

Coble, Parks M., *Facing Japan: Chinese Politics and Japanese Imperialism, 1931–7*, Harvard University Press, Cambridge, MA, 1991

Confucius, *The Analects*, trans. D. C. Lau, Chinese University Press, Hong Kong, 1992

Cook, Constance and John S. Major (eds), *Defining Chu: Image and Reality in Ancient China*, University of Hawaii Press, Honolulu, 1999

Creel, Herlee G., *The Origins of Statecraft in China*, vol. 1: 'The Western Chou Empire', University of Chicago Press, London, 1970

Crossley, Pamela K., *The Manchus*, Blackwell, Oxford, 1997

Crossley, Pamela Kyle, *A Translucent Mirror: History and Identity in Qing Imperial Ideology*, University of California Press, Berkeley, 1999

Crump, J. (trans.), *Chan-kuo-t'se*, Oxford, 1970/University of Michigan, 1996.

Curwen, C. A., *Taiping Rebel: The Despotism of Li Hsien-chong*, Cambridge University Press, 1977

Dani, A. M. and V. M. Masson (eds), *History of Civilisations of Central Asia*, UNESCO, Paris, 1992

Dardess, John, *Conquerors and Confucians: Aspects of Political Change in Late Yuan China*, Columbia University Press, New York, 1973

Dardess, John W., *Confucianism and Autocracy: Professional Elites in the Founding of the Ming dynasty*, University of California Press, Berkeley, 1983

Dardess, John W., *Blood and History in China: The Donglin Faction and Its Repression, 1620–27*, University of Hawaii Press, Honolulu, 2002

Davis, Richard L., *Court and Family in Sung China*, Duke University Press, Chapel Hill, NC, 1986

Dawson, Christopher (ed.), *The Mongol Mission: Narratives and Letters of the Franciscan Missionaries in Mongolia and China in the Thirteeenth and Fourteenth Centuries*, Sheed & Ward, London, 1955

Dawson, Raymond, *Imperial China*, Hutchinson, London, 1972

De Bary, W. T., *The Unfolding of Neo-Confucianism*, Columbia University Press, New York, 1975

De Bary, W. T. and Irene Bloom (eds), *Sources of Chinese Tradition*, 2 vols, Columbia University Press, NY, 1999

De Crespigny, Rafe, *The Last of the Han* (chs 58–68 of *Tzu-chih t'ung-chien* by Sima Guang), Australian National University, Canberra, 1969

De Crespigny, Rafe, *Northern Frontier: The Politics and Strategy of the Late Han Empire*, Australian National University, Canberra, 1984

Di Cosmo, Nicola, *Ancient China and Its Enemies: The Rise of Nomadic Power in East Asian History*, Cambridge University Press, Cambridge, 2002

Dien, Albert (ed.), *State and Society in Early Medieval China*, Stanford University Press, Stanford, CT, 1990

Dreyer, Edmund L., *Early Ming China: A Political History 1355–1435*, Stanford University Press, Stanford, CT, 1982

Dreyer, Edmund L., *Zheng He: China and the Oceans in the Early Ming Dynasty, 1405–1433*, Pearson Longman, New York, 2007

Dunnell, Ruth W., *The Great State of White and High: Buddhism and State Formation in Eleventh-century Xia*, University of Hawaii Press, Honolulu, 1999

Ebrey, Patricia Buckley (ed.), *Chinese Civilisation and Society*, Free Press, New York, 1981

Ebrey, Patricia Buckley, *The Cambridge Illustrated History of China*, Cambridge University Press, Cambridge, 1996

Ebrey, Patricia Buckley, *China: A Cultural, Social and Political History*, Houghton Mifflin, Boston, MA, 2006

Ebrey, Patricia Buckley et al., *Modern East Asia: From 1600, a Cultural, Social and Political History*, Houghton Mifflin, Boston, MA, 2006

Endicott-West, Elizabeth, *Mongolian Rule in China*, Harvard University Press, Cambridge, MA, 1989

Fairbank, John King (ed.), *The Chinese World Order: Traditional China's Foreign Relations*, Harvard University Press, Cambridge, MA, 1968

Fairbank, John King, *The Great Chinese Revolution: 1800–1985*, Harper & Row, New York, 1986

Fairbank, John King and Merle Goldman, *China: A New History*, Belknap, Harvard, Cambridge, MA, 1998

Fang, Achilles (trans.), *The Chronicle of the Three Kingdoms*, Cambridge, MA, 1952/65

Fay, Peter Ward, *The Opium War 1840–1842*, University of North Carolina Press, Chapel Hill, 1975

Fenby, Jonathan, *The Penguin History of Modern China*, Allen Lane, London, 2008

Fisher, Carney T., *The Chosen One: Succession and Adoption in the Court of Ming Shizong*, Allen & Unwin, Sydney, 1990

Fitzgerald, C. P., *China: A Short Cultural History*, Cresset Press, London, 1935

Fitzgerald, C. P., *The Empress Wu*, University of British Columbia Press, 1970

Garside, Roger, *Coming Alive: China after Mao*, Deutsch, London, 1981

Gernet, Jacques, *Daily Life in China on the Eve of the Mongol Invasion*, Allen & Unwin, London, 1962

Gernet, Jacques, *Ancient China: From the Beginnings to the Empire*, trans. Raymond Rudorff, Faber and Faber, London, 1968

Gernet, Jacques, *A History of Chinese Civilization (Le Monde chinois)*, trans. J. R. Foster, Cambridge University Press, Cambridge, 1982

Gernet, Jacques, *Buddhism in Chinese Society: An Economic History from the Fifth to the Tenth Centuries*, Columbia University Press, New York, 1995

Gittings, John, *The Changing Face of China*, Oxford University Press, Oxford, 2005

Gladney, Dru C., *Dislocating China: Muslims, Minorities and the Subaltern Subjects*, Hurst & Co., London, 2004

Goodman, Howard L., *T'sao P'i Transcendent*, Scripta Serica, Seattle, WA, 1998

Goodrich, Chauncey S., *Biography of Su Ch'o*, University of California Press, Berkeley, 1953

Graff, David A., *Medieval Chinese Warfare 300–900*, Routledge, London, 2000

Grousset, Rene, *The Empire of the Steppes: A History of Central Asia*, trans. Naomi Watford, Rutgers, NJ, 1970

Hall, D. G. E., *A History of South-East Asia*, 4th edn, Macmillan, London, 1981

Hammond, Kenneth J. (ed.), *The Human Tradition in Pre-modern China*, SR Books, Wilmington, 2002

Hansen, Valerie, *The Open Empire: A History of China to 1600*, Norton, London, 2000

Hardy, Grant, *Worlds of Bronze and Bamboo: Sima Qian's Conquest of History*, Columbia University Press, New York, 1999

Hardy, Grant and A. B. Kinney, *The Establishment of the Han Empire and Imperial China*, Greenwood, Westport, CT, 2005

Hartman, Charles, *Han Yü and the T'ang Search for Unity*, Princeton University Press, Princeton, NJ, 1986

Hibbert, Christopher, *The Dragon Wakes: China and the West 1795–1911*, Longman, London, 1970

Hok-lam Chan, *Legitimation in Imperial China: Discussions under the Jurchen-Chin Dynasty (1150–1234)*, University of Washington, Seattle, 1984

Holcombe, Charles, *In the Shadow of the Han: Thought and Society at the*

Beginning of the Southern Dynasties, University of Hawaii Press, Honolulu, 1994

Hopkirk, Peter, *Foreign Devils on the Silk Road: The Search for the Lost Cities and Treasures of Chinese Central Asia*, John Murray, London, 1980

Huang, Ray, *1587, a Year of No Significance: The Ming Dynasty in Decline*, Yale University Press, New Haven, CT, 1981

Hucker, Charles O., *The Ming Dynasty: Its Origins and Evolving Institutions*, University of Michigan, Ann Arbor, 1978

Hui, Victoria Tin-bor, *War and State Formation in Ancient China and Early Modern Europe*, Cambridge University Press, Cambridge, 2005

Hulsewe, A. F. P., *China in Central Asia: The Early Stage 135–123 BC*, E. J. Brill, Leiden, 1979

Hymes, Robert P. and Conrad Shirokauer, *Ordering the World: Approaches to State and Society in Sung Dynasty China*, University of California Press, Berkeley, 1993

Jagchid, Sechin and V. J. Symons, *Peace, War and Trade along the Great Wall: Nomadic–Chinese Interaction through Two Millennia*, Indiana University Press, Bloomington, 1989

Jasbir Singh, Amar Kaur, *Himalayan Triangle: A historical survey of British India's relations with Tibet, Sikkim and Bhutan 1765–1950*, British Library, London, 1988

Jenner, W. J. F., *Memories of Loyang: Yang Hsuan-chi and the Lost Capital (493–534)*, Clarendon, Oxford, 1981

Jenner, W. J. F., *The Tyranny of History: The Roots of China's Crisis*, Allen Lane, London, 1992

Johnston, Alastair Iain, *Cultural Realism: Strategic Culture and Grand Strategy in Chinese History*, Princeton University Press, Princeton, NJ, 1995

Jung Chang and Jon Halliday, *Mao: The Unknown Story*, Jonathan Cape, London, 2005

Kahn, Paul, *The Secret History of the Mongols . . . based on Cleaves*, North Point Press, San Francisco, CA, 1984

Keay, John, *The Honourable Company: A History of the English East India Company*, HarperCollins, London, 1991

Keay, John, *Last Post: The End of Empire in the Far East*, John Murray, London, 1997

Keay, John, *The Spice Route: A History*, John Murray, London, 2005

Keightley, David N., *Sources of Shang History: The Oracle-bone Inscriptions of Bronze Age China*, University of California Press, Berkeley, 1978

Keightley, David N. (ed.), *The Origins of Chinese Civilization*, University of California Press, London, 1983

Keightley, David N., *The Ancestral Landscape: Time, Space and Community in Late Shang China c. 1200–1045 BC*, University of California Press, Berkeley, 2000

Khazanov, A. M., *Nomads and the Outside World*, trans. Julia Crookenden, Cambridge University Press, Cambridge, 1984

Kierman, Frank A. and John K. Fairbank (eds), *Chinese Ways in Warfare*, Harvard University Press, Cambridge, MA, 1974

Kirkland, Russell, *Taoism: The Enduring Tradition*, Routledge, London, 2004

Kracke, E. A., *Civil Service in Early Sung China, 960–1067*, Harvard University Press, Cambridge, MA, 1953

Langlois, John D. (ed.), *China under Mongol Rule*, Princeton University Press, Princeton, NJ, 1981

Latham, Ronald (trans. and intro.), *The Travels of Marco Polo*, Penguin, London, 1958

Lattimore, Owen, *Inner Asian Frontiers of China*, Oxford University Press, London, 1940

Levathes, Louise, *When China Ruled the Seas: The Treasure Fleet of the Dragon Throne, 1405–33*, Simon & Schuster, New York, 1984

Lewis, Mark, *Sanctioned Violence in Ancient China*, Albany, NY, 1990

Li Chi (Ji), *Anyang*, University of Washington Press, Seattle, 1977

Li Yu-ning (ed.), *The Politics of Historiography: The First Emperor of China*, IAS, New York, 1975

Liu, James T. C., *Reform in Sung China: Wang An-shih and His New Policies*, Harvard University Press, Cambridge, MA, 1959

Liu, James T. C., *Ou-yang Hsiu, an Eleventh Century Neo-Confucianist*, Stanford University Press, Stanford, CT, 1967

Liu, James T. C. and Peter Golas, *Change in Sung China: Innovation or Renovation*, Heath, Lexington, NY, 1969

Liu, Lydia H., *The Clash of Empires: The Invention of China in Modern World Making*, Harvard University Press, Cambridge, MA, 2004

Liu Xinru, *Ancient India and Ancient China: Trade and Religious Exchanges AD 1–600*, Oxford University Press, New Delhi, 1988

Liu Xinru, *Silk and Religion: An Exploration of Material Life and the Thoughts of People*, Oxford University Press, New Delhi, 1996

Loewe, Michael, *Imperial China: The Historical Background to the Modern Age*, Allen & Unwin, London, 1966

Loewe, Michael, *Crisis and Conflict in Han China 104 BC TO 9 AD*, Allen & Unwin, London, 1974

Loewe, Michael, *The Pride That Was China*, Sidgwick & Jackson, London, 1990

Lovell, Julia, *The Great Wall: China against the World*, Atlantic, London, 2006

Luce, G. S. T. (trans.), *Manshui, 'Book of the Southern Barbarians'*, Cornell University Press, 1961

Luo Guanzhong (attrib.), *Three Kingdoms, a Historical Novel*, trans. and ed. Moss Roberts, University of California Press, Berkeley, 1991

Ma, Laurence J. C., *Commercial Development and Urban Change in Sung China (960–1279)*, University of Michigan, Ann Arbor, 1971

Macartney, Lord George, *An Embassy to China: Being the Journal Kept by Lord Macartney during his Embassy to the Emperor Ch'ien-lung 1793–4*, ed. J. L. Cranmer-Byng, Folio Society, London, 2004

Macfarquhar, Roderick and Michael Schoenhals, *Mao's Last Revolution*, Harvard University Press, Cambridge, MA, 2006

Macmillan, Margaret, *Peacemakers: The Paris Conference of 1919 and Its Attempt to End War*, John Murrray, London, 2001

Mair, Victor H. (ed.), *The Bronze Age: Early Iron Age Peoples of Eastern Central Asia*, Washington, DC, 1998

Mair, Victor H. (ed.), *The Columbia History of Chinese Literature*, Columbia University Press, New York, 2001

Mair, Victor H. et al. (eds), *The Hawaii Reader in Traditional Chinese Culture*, University of Hawaii Press, Honolulu, 2003

Mallory, J. P. and Victor H. Mair, *The Tarim Mummies: Ancient China and the Mystery of the Earliest Peoples from the West*, Thames and Hudson, London, 2000

Man, John, *Genghis Khan: Life, Death and Resurrection*, Bantam, London, 2004

Martin, Desmond H., *The Rise of Chingis Khan and His Conquest of North China*, Baltimore, MD, 1950/Octagon, New York, 1970

McMullen, David, *State and Scholars in T'ang China*, Cambridge University Press, Cambridge, 1988

Mole, Gabriella, *The Tu-yu-hun from Northern Wei to the Time of the Five Dynasties*, IMEO, Rome, 1970

Morgan, David O., *The Mongols*, Blackwell, Oxford, 1986

Mote, F. W., *Imperial China, 900–1800*, Harvard University Press, Cambridge, MA, 1999

Naquin, Susan and Evelyn S. Rawski, *Chinese Society in the Eighteenth Century*, Yale University Press, London, 1987

National Museum of Chinese History, *A Journey into China's Antiquity*, 2 vols, Morning Glory, Beijing, 1997/98

Needham, Joseph et al., *Science and Civilization in China*, many vols, Cambridge University Press, Cambridge, 1954; see especially vol. 4, pt 2, 1965; vol. 4, pt 3, 1971

Nivison, David S. and A. Wright, *Confucianism in Action*, Stanford University Press, Stanford, CT, 1959

Ouyang Xiu, *Historical Records of the Five Dynasties*, trans. and ed. Richard L. Davis, Columbia University Press, New York, 2004

Owen, Stephen, *The Great Age of Chinese Poetry, the High T'ang*, Yale University Press, New Haven, CT, 1981

Paludan, Ann, *Chronicle of the Chinese Emperors: The Reign-by-Reign Record of the Rulers of Imperial China*, Thames & Hudson, London, 1998

Pan Yihong, *Son of Heaven and Heavenly Qaghan: Sui-Tang China and Its Neighbours*, Western Washington University Press, Bellingham, 1997

Pearce, Scott et al. (eds), *Culture and Power in the Reconstitution of the Chinese Realm 200–500*, Harvard University Press, Cambridge, MA, 2001

Pears, C. J., *Soldiers of the Dragon: Chinese Armies 1500 BC–AD 1840*, Osprey, London, 2006

Perdue, Peter C., *China Marches West: The Qing Conquest of Central Asia*, Harvard University Press, Cambridge, MA, 2005

Perry, Elizabeth J., *Rebels and Revolutionaries in North China, 1845–1945*, Stanford University Press, Stanford, CT, 1980

Perry, J. C. and Bardwell L. Smith (eds), *Essays on T'ang Society*, London, 1976

Pirazzoli-t'Serstevens, Michele, *The Han Civilisation of China*, Phaidon, Oxford, 1982

Polo, Marco, *The Book of Ser Marco Polo, the Venetian, concerning the Kingdoms and Marvels of the East*, trans. and ed. Henry Yule, 3rd edn, 2 vols, John Murray, London, 1921

Portal, Jane (ed.), *The First Emperor: China's Terracotta Army*, British Museum, London, 2007

Preston, Diana, *Besieged in Peking: The Story of the 1900 Boxer Rising*, Constable, London, 1999

Pulleyblank, E., *The Background to the Rebellion of An Lushan*, London, 1955

Ratchnevsky, Paul, *Ghenghis Khan: His Life and Legacy*, Blackwell, Oxford, 1991

Rawski, Evelyn S., *The Last Emperors: A Social History of Qing Imperial Institutions*, University of California Press, Berkeley, 1998

Rawski, Evelyn S. and Jessica Rawson (eds), *China: The Three Emperors 1662–1795*, Royal Academy of Arts, London, 2005

Rawson, Jessica, *Chinese Bronzes: Art and Ritual*, British Museum, London, 1987

Rawson, Jessica, *Mysteries of Ancient China: New Discoveries from the Early Dynasties*, British Museum, London, 1996

Reilly, Thomas H., *The Taiping Heavenly Kingdom: Rebellion and the Blasphemy of Empire*, University of Washington, Seattle, 2004

Reischauer, Edwin O. (trans.), *Ennin's Diary, the Record of a Pilgrimage to China in Search of the Law*, Ronald Press, New York, 1955

Reischauer, Edwin O., *Ennin's Travels in T'ang China*, Ronald Press, New York, 1965

Ricci, Matthew, *China in the Sixteenth Century: The Journals of Matthew Ricci: 1583–1610*, trans. Louis J. Gallagher, Random House, New York, 1953

Robinson, David, *Bandits, Eunuchs and the Son of Heaven: Rebellion and the Economy of Violence in Mid-Ming China*, University of Hawaii Press, Honolulu, 2001

Rodzinski, Witold, *The Walled Kingdom: A History of China from 2000 BC to the Present*, Fontana, London, 1985

Ropp, Paul S. (ed.), *Heritage of China: Contemporary Perspectives on Chinese Civilization*, University of California Press, Berkeley, 1990

Rossabi, Morris, *China and Inner Asia from 1368 to the Present Day*, Thames and Hudson, London, 1975

Rossabi, Morris, *China among Equals: The Middle Kingdom and Its Neighbours*, University of California Press, Berkeley, 1983

Rossabi, Morris, *Khubilai Khan: His Life and Times*, University of California Press, Berkeley, 1988

Rossabi, Morris, *Voyager from Xanadu: Rabban Sauma and the First Journey from China to the West*, Kodansha, New York, 1992

Sage, Steven R., *Ancient Sichuan and the Unification of China*, State University of New York, Albany, 1992

Sampson, Geoffrey, *Writing Systems: A Linguistic Introduction*, Cambridge University Press, Cambridge, 1988

Schafer, Edward H., *The Golden Peaches of Samarkand: A Study of Tang Exotics*, University of California Press, Berkeley, 1963

Schafer, Edward H., *Shore of Pearls*, University of California Press, Berkeley, 1970

Schoenbauer, Susan, *Victorian Travellers and the Opening of China*, Ohio University Press, 1999

Seaman, Gary and Daniel Marks (eds), *Rulers from the Steppe: State Formation on the Eurasian Periphery*, Ethographics Press, Los Angeles, CA, 1991

Seidel, Anna and Holmes Welch (eds), *Facets of Taoism*, Yale University Press, New Haven, CT, 1979

Serruys, Henry (ed.), *The Mongols and Ming China: Customs and History*, Variorum, London, 1987

Sima Qian, *see* Watson

Smith, Richard, *Chinese Maps: All Under Heaven*, Oxford University Press, Hong Kong, 1996

Spence J. D., *The China Helpers: Western Advisers to China 1620–1960*, Bodley Head, London, 1969

Spence, J. D., *Emperor of China: Self Portrait of Kangxi*, Knopf, New York, 1974

Spence, J. D., *The Chan's Great Continent: China in Western Minds*, Penguin, London, 1999

Spence, Jonathan D. *The Search for Modern China*, 2nd ed, Norton, New York, 1999

Spence, J. D. and J. E. Wills (eds), *From Ming to Ch'ing: Conquest, Region and Continuity in Seventeenth-Century China*, Yale University Press, New Haven, CT, 1979

Spence, Jonathan D., *The Gate of Heavenly Peace: The Chinese and Their Revolution 1895–1980*, Faber and Faber, London, 1982

Spence, Jonathan D., *The Memory Palace of Matteo Ricci*, Faber and Faber, London, 1984

Spence, Jonathan D., *God's Chinese Son: The Taiping Heavenly Kingdom of Hong Xiuquan*, HarperCollins, London, 1996

Struve, Lynn A., *Voices from the Ming-Qing Cataclysm: China in Tigers' Jaws*, Yale University Press, New Haven, CT, 1993

Struve, Lynn A. (ed.), *The Qing Formation in World-Historical Time*, Harvard University Press, Cambridge, MA, 2004

Swann, Nancy Lee (trans. and ed.), *Food and Money in Ancient China: The Earliest Economic History of China to AD 25*, Princeton University Press, Princeton, NJ, 1950

Tao Jingshen, *The Jurchen in Twelfth-Century China: A Study of Sinicisation*, University of Arizona Press, Tucson, 1976

Tao Jingshen, *Two Sons of Heaven: Studies in Sung–Liao Relations*, University of Arizona Press, Tucson, 1988

Teng, S. Y., *The Taiping Rebellion and the Western Powers*, Oxford University Press, London, 1971

Tillman, Hoyt C. and Stephen H. West (eds), *China under Jurchen Rule: Essays on Chin Intellectual and Cultural History*, State University of New York Press, Albany, 1995

Tsai, Shih-shan Henry, *The Eunuchs of the Ming Dynasty*, State University of New York Press, Albany, 1996

Tsai, Shih-shan Henry, *Perpetual Happiness: The Ming Emperor Yongle*, University of Washington, Seattle, 2001

Twitchett, D. C., *Financial Administration under the T'ang Dynasty*, Cambridge University Press, Cambridge, 1963

Twitchett, Denis, *The Writing of Official History under the T'ang*, Cambridge University Press, Cambridge, 1992

Vainker, Shelagh, *Chinese Pottery and Porcelain*, British Museum, London, 1991

Wakeman, Frederic, *Strangers at the Gate: Social Disorder in South China, 1839–1961*, University of California Press, Berkeley, 1966

Wakeman, Frederic, *The Great Enterprise: The Manchu Reconstruction of Imperial Order in Seventeenth-Century China*, vol. 1, University of California Press, Berkeley, 1985

Waldron, Arthur, *The Great Wall of China: From History to Myth*, Cambridge University Press, Cambridge, 1990

Waley, Arthur, *Three Ways of Thought in Ancient China*, Allen & Unwin, London, 1939

Waley, Arthur, *The Opium War through Chinese Eyes*, Allen & Unwin, London, 1958

Waley, Arthur, *Ballads and Stories from Tun-huang: An Anthology*, Allen & Unwin, London, 1960

Waley-Cohen, Joanna, *The Sextants of Beijing: Global Currents in Chinese History*, Norton, New York, 1999

Wang Gungwu, *The Structure of Power in North China during the Five Dynasties*, Stanford University Press, Stanford, CT, 1963

Watson, Burton, *Ssu-ma Chi'en: Grand Historian of China*, Columbia University Press, New York, 1958

Watson, Burton (trans.), *Records of the Grand Historian of China Translated from the Shih Chi of Ssu-ma Ch'ien*, 2 vols, Columbia University Press, New York, 1961

Watson, Burton (trans. and ed.), *The Columbia Book of Chinese Poetry: From Early Times to the Thirteeenth Century*, Columbia University Press, New York, 1984

Watson, Burton, *The Tso-chuan: Selections from China's Oldest Narrative History*, Columbia University Press, New York, 1989

Wechsler, Howard J., *Mirror to the Son of Heaven: Wei Cheng at the Court of T'ang T'ai-tsung*, Yale University Press, New Haven and London, 1974

Welch, Holmes and Anna Seidel, *Facets of Taoism: Essays in Chinese Religion*, Yale University Press, New Haven, CT, 1979

Wilkinson, Endymion, *Chinese History: A Manual*, Harvard University Press, Cambridge, MA, 2000

Wittfogel, Karl, *Oriental Despotism: A Comparative Study of Total Power*, Yale University Press, New Haven, CT, 1957

Wood, Frances, *Did Marco Polo Go to China?*, Secker and Warburg, London, 1995

Wood, Frances, *The Silk Road*, Folio Society, London, 2002

Wriggins, Sally Hovey, *Xuanzang: A Buddhist Pilgrim on the Silk Road*, Westview, Oxford, 1996

Wright, Arthur F., *Buddhism in Chinese History*, Stanford University Press, Stanford, CT, 1959

Wright, Arthur F. (ed.), *The Confucian Persuasion*, Stanford University Press, Stanford, CT, 1960

Wright, Arthur F., *Perspectives on the T'ang*, Yale University Press, New Haven, CT, 1970

Wright, Arthur F., *The Sui Dynasty*, New York, 1978

Wright, Arthur F. and Robert M. Somers (eds), *Studies in Chinese Buddhism*, New Haven, CT, 1990

Wu Cheng'en, *The Monkey and the Monk* (abridgement of *The Journey to the West*), trans. and ed. Anthony C. Yu, University of Chicago Press, Chicago, IL, 2006

Xiong, Victor C., *Emperor Yang of the Sui Dynasty: His Life, Times and Legacy*, State University of New York Press, Albany, 2006

Yu, Ying-shi'h, *Trade and Expansion in Han China: A Study in the Structure of Sino-Barbarian Economic Relations*, University of California Press, Berkeley, 1967

Zurcher, Erik, *The Buddhist Conquest of China: The Spread and Adaptation of Buddhism in Early Medieval China*, 2 vols, E. J. Brill, Leiden, 1959

INDEX

NB Emperors will be found under the names of their dynasties.

JOHN KEAY

India: A History

Older, richer and more distinctive than almost any other, India's culture is a vibrant confluence of continuity and diversity. The peoples of the Indian subcontinent, while sharing a common history and culture, are not now, and never have been, a single unitary state. This authorative account accommodates Pakistan and Bangladesh, as well as other embryonic nation states like the Sikh Punjab, Muslim Kashmir and Assam. It readdresses the colonial era in the overall context of Indian history, and the legacy of the 1947 partition, from the standpoint of today.

From one of our finest writers on India and the Far East, this fascinating, single-volume history combines narrative pace and skill with social, economic and cultural analysis, to cover five millennia of the sub-continent's history.

'A delight... one of the best general studies of the subcontinent'

Sunday Times

'Ambitious, colourful and fascinating'

The Times

JOHN KEAY
Mad About the Mekong
Exploration and Empire in South-East Asia

From its delta in Vietnam up through Cambodia, Laos, Thailand, Myanmar and China and Tibet, the wild Mekong River has fascinated travellers for centuries. But for many years it has been a no-go stretch – until ten years ago it boasted not a single bridge, let alone a city: it flowed through a succession of cataracts and rapids buried in inaccessible gorges and impenetrable forest.

John Keay's dramatic modern-day journey up the river retraces the historic voyage of the pioneering Mekong Exploration Commission which set out to map this formidable terrain in the nineteenth century. Recounting the little-known tale of their epic journey, John Keay gives us both a brilliant account of the expedition's triumphs and disasters, and a sense of its legacy – the creation of an empire that followed in its wake.

'Impeccable . . . Keay has painted quite brilliantly a portrait of the river and those intrepid Europeans who first ventured onto it'   *Sunday Times*

'A breathtaking account of one of the greatest ever feats of exploration . . . A terrific story'   *Literary Review*

'Keay anthropomorphises the Mekong with terrific verve and imagination throughout this delightful book'   *Sunday Telegraph*